BIN LADEN

BIN
The Man Who

YOSSEF BODANSKY

LADEN

Declared War on America

FORUM

An Imprint of Prima Publishing

To the memory of
Avraham Tchernikhov
(1899–1988)

My grandfather, whose nurturing,
encouragement, and love molded and tempered me.

The opinions expressed in this book are solely those of the author and do not necessarily
reflect the views of the members of the congressional Task Force on Terrorism and Unconventional Warfare, the U.S. Congress, or any other branch of the U.S. government.

FORUM is an imprint of Prima Publishing, 3875 Atherton Road, Rocklin, California, 95765.

PRIMA PUBLISHING and colophon are registered trademarks of Prima Communications, Inc.

Library of Congress Cataloging-in-Publication Data
Bodansky, Yossef.
    Bin Laden : the man who declared war on America / Yossef Bodansky.
      p.   cm.
    ISBN 0-7615-1968-8
    1. Bin Laden, Usamah. 1957–   . 2. Terrorists—Saudi Arabia Biography. 3. Muslims—
Saudi Arabia Biography. 4. Terrorism—Religious aspects—Islam. 5. Jihad. I. Title.
HV6430.B55B63   1999
953.8.05'3'092—dc21
[B]   99-30318
                                                                                      CIP

99 00 01 02 03 AA 10 9 8 7 6 5 4 3 2 1
Printed in the United States of America

How to Order
Single copies may be ordered from Prima Publishing, P.O. Box 1260BK, Rocklin, CA
95677; telephone (916) 632-4400. Quantity discounts are also available. On your let-
terhead, include information concerning the intended use of the books and the number of books you wish to purchase.

Visit us online at www.primalife.com

Contents

Foreword

YOSSEF BODANSKY, director of the House Task Force on Terrorism and Unconventional Warfare, has done it again. He has proved that he is not only a wordsmith but also a meticulous researcher and superb political analyst. Using these skills in a private capacity, he has set forth reasonable and prudent information never before published that explains recent events such as the bombings in Kenya and Tanzania, including a well-documented sequence of events leading up to the attacks. The results are informative, for Bodansky explains the vast global conspiracy that uses terrorism as a strategic weapon that has resulted in the tragic deaths of Americans and the wounding of many innocents.

Contemporary terrorism has become a direct threat to all Americans as it casts its ominous shadow worldwide. Bodansky proves that "Fortress America" is a concept relegated to history books, for today Islamist terrorism penetrates America's geographic shield, bringing us within target range of terrorist activities. Focusing on this salient thought, Bodansky points out the fallacy of assuming that the United States is immune to terror attacks.

Understanding and reacting to the information presented here is the responsibility of all Americans, because indifference is not an acceptable option, nor a heritage we would wish to pass on to future generations. This book should provide the stimulus to all Americans to join in with their elected representatives in preparing for the major threats currently posed to the United States and its friends. There is no better armament than accurate knowledge, factual information, and elected representatives who are sensitive and responsive to the needs of their constituents and all Americans. If there is one important message that this book conveys, it is that a campaign by radical, militant Islam threatens our way of life.

Bodansky explains the subtleties that define the relationships between the extremist elements in the Muslim world, their leaders, and the more visible figures, such as Osama bin Laden. We learn not only that bin Laden is responsible for a number of bombings but also that he is part of a dynamic, political intrigue, involving the heads of state of many countries. Bin Laden's history is presented, as is the evolution of his hatred for Jews and

"Crusaders"—whom he holds responsible for debasing Saudi Arabia with "corrupting Western influences."

A tour of the many countries entangled in international terrorism is embarked upon with Bodansky as our tour guide, saying in effect, "Join with me and we will learn together." By understanding the view of the West held by Islamists, we learn about the religious and psychological justifications used by fanatics to destroy innocent civilians.

The tour begins with an overview of bin Laden's youth and his development into a wealthy ideologue whose sole purpose is to bring glory to Islam by destroying its perceived enemies. Bodansky carefully explains why the royal family of Saudi Arabia initially supported bin Laden in his efforts to purge Islam of tainting influences in such remote places as Afghanistan. A split between the Saudi rulers and bin Laden occurred, however, after the Saudis allowed the United States to remain in the country after the Gulf War. This was the catalyst for bin Laden's continued confrontation with the House of al-Saud. Bodansky reveals that the complicated involvement of other terrorism-sponsoring countries was a necessary ingredient in bin Laden's rise to a paramount role as a spiritual and military leader of his terrorist forces.

Bodansky highlights how fundamentalist Islam—as manifested in the Iranian Revolution—shaped bin Laden as the supreme ideologue whose militant identity was forged during the war in Afghanistan. Later we learn of the rise to power of Hassan al-Turabi, the spiritual leader of Sudan and a bin Laden sponsor. During this period a dramatic combination of Sunni militancy with Iranian terrorist techniques helped bring radical Islam, along with terrorist networks, into Africa.

Additional details of Islamist networks in the Horn of Africa and East Africa reveal how terrorist-sponsoring nations made inevitable the armed clash with American forces in Somalia. As bin Laden rose to power along with other terror chiefs such as Ayman al-Zawahiri, the key terrorism-sponsoring states—Iran, Sudan, and Pakistan—collaborated to form terrorist networks worldwide. This dangerous collaboration between Sunni and Shiite terrorists bodes ill for the entire world. Detailed analysis of the attempted assassination of Hosni Mubarak, president of Egypt, is provided by Bodansky, along with details never before revealed about those responsible for the bombing of the U.S. barracks known as Khobar Towers and the downing of TWA800.

Successful, the terrorist groups continued their ways and expanded their efforts from the Balkans to the Philippines—with the continued support of Tehran, Khartoum, and Islamabad. Expanding on their role, these groups set their sights on a worldwide jihad—holy war—rationalized away by religious decrees, called fatwas, issued by bin Laden. Bodansky explains why the terrorists feel they were betrayed by the United States, resulting in attempts at revenge. By placing these details in a coherent, easy-to-understand analysis and review, Bodansky brings insight and understanding to the many events that preceded and initiated the twin bombings of the U.S. Embassies in Kenya and Tanzania.

Bin Laden's narrative is geographically comprehensive and includes the latest developments in the bin Laden saga and the rise of Islamist terrorism, ranging from the acquisition of weapons of mass destruction to growing involvement in today's hot spots in the world—mainly Albania and Kosovo as well as Kashmir. Bodansky also addresses the latest developments in international terrorism such as the relationship between bin Laden and Saddam Hussein.

This clear presentation of factual information allows the reader to join with Bodansky in analyzing and predicting what may well lie ahead for the West. The information rests at your fingertips, making you a participant in understanding and analyzing the Islamist doctrines and preparing for a possible global conflict.

I know of no finer expert at unraveling and explaining the behind-the-scenes maneuvering of international terrorism than Yossef Bodansky. For almost ten years he has been the director of the Task Force on Terrorism and Unconventional Warfare—of which I was a member while in Congress. His reports were prescient in anticipating terrorist activities and threats against America and its allies. The Task Force has been an independent voice in alerting the U.S. government to these threats. During this period, it has exposed numerous state-sponsored, terrorist operations, including the counterfeiting of U.S. $100 bills by Iran and Syria. The Task Force was the first to expose and warn against the rise of Islamist militancy and the presence of Arab terrorists in the Balkans—first in Bosnia and presently in Albania and Kosovo. Similarly, last February the Task Force issued a report detailing the collaboration between Iraq, Sudan, and Libya in the production of weapons of mass destruction. Half a year after dismissing this report, the Clinton administration emphasized the same Sudanese-Iraqi cooperation as a reason for the cruise missile attack on Khartoum.

In this book Bodansky breaks new ground in the study of international terrorism. This is why it is vital that all Americans read *Bin Laden: The Man Who Declared War on America*. Only by learning about our adversaries and educating our citizens can America remain safe and protect its freedoms.

—*Congresswoman (ret.) Helen Delich Bentley*
U.S. House of Representatives 1985–1995

Introduction: The Inevitable Struggle

ON AUGUST 20, 1998, a somber President Clinton told the nation that the United States had just launched cruise missiles against terrorist objectives in both Afghanistan and Sudan in retaliation for the recent bombing of U.S. embassies in Kenya and Tanzania. "Our target was terror," the president declared. "Our mission was clear: to strike at the network of radical groups affiliated with and funded by Osama bin Laden, perhaps the preeminent organizer and financier of international terrorism in the world today." Three days later Secretary of Defense William Cohen said the United States would not regret the death of Osama bin Laden if he were killed in a future U.S. action against terrorist networks.

The bombings of the U.S. embassies in Kenya and Tanzania on August 7, 1998, were neither the first nor the most lethal Islamist terrorist strikes aimed at America and Americans. Yet never before had the United States—the world's only superpower—singled out a terrorist leader as a declared enemy. To earn this distinction, Osama bin Laden did more than just participate in terrorist operations. To date, bin Laden is the only terrorist leader to have formally declared a jihad—holy war—against the United States. And he has done so numerous times since 1996, reinforcing his original call to arms with additional and more specific decrees as his theological and command authority has grown.

This declaration of holy war is not an empty gesture. Bin Laden hates the United States passionately and considers it his principal enemy. He accuses the United States—the locus of Westernization and modernity—of

---

Note that in this book I do not use the term *Islamist* to refer either to someone who might be labeled "Muslim" because of inherited religious beliefs and culture or to aspects of Islam, such as Islamic belief or the Islamic state. The term *Islamist* denotes the overwhelming prevalence of the political aspect—particularly radicalism, extremism, and militancy—as pursued and perpetrated under the banner of Islam as interpreted by the practitioners. While commonly used in professional literature, the term *Islamist* is not often used by American journalists and other writers, who prefer such terms as *Islamic intellectual, Islamic fundamentalist,* or *Islamic militant.* Such usage, however, blurs the distinction between the majority of Muslims and a minority comprising extremist terrorists.

being the source of all crises and trouble afflicting the Muslim world. Bin Laden is convinced that the U.S. presence in the Muslim world, particularly in his home country of Saudi Arabia, prevents the establishment of real Islamic governments and the realization of the Islamic revivalism to which he and other Islamists aspire. Since a frontal assault is out of the question, the United States must be terrorized into withdrawing from the Muslim world.

Bin Laden is not a man to be ignored, for he is at the core of Islamist international terrorism. He is not an evil "Lone Ranger" but rather a principal player in a tangled and sinister web of terrorism-sponsoring states, intelligence chieftains, and master terrorists. Together they wield tremendous power throughout the Muslim world and wreak havoc and devastation upon their foes. In order to understand Osama bin Laden, one must comprehend the world in which he operates. Bin Laden has always been—and still is—part of a bigger system, a team player and a loyal comrade at arms. The terrorist operations in several parts of the world now attributed to bin Laden were actually state-sponsored operations perpetrated by dedicated groups of Islamists. Bin Laden's own role in this network has increased, and his stature has risen tremendously. Thus, the Osama bin Laden of the late 1990s has evolved in response to key events and associations that shaped his life and molded his worldview. Ultimately, however, bin Laden, his colleagues, and the states sponsoring them are all key components of the dominant megatrend in the Muslim world—the rise and spread of radical militant Islamism. They are all theologically motivated and driven, killing and dying in pursuit of an Islamist jihad against the rest of the world. To comprehend Islamist terrorism, one must address its theological-ideological roots.

Radical militant Islamism—the driving force behind and the ideology justifying international terrorism—emerged from Islam's conflict with Westernization and modernity. The antagonism between Islamic and Western civilizations has festered for several centuries. Iranian scholar and diplomat Fereydoun Hoveyda argues that Islamic civilization has been impeded since the twelfth century as a result of major crises and confrontations with Christendom. During the eleventh century the Muslim world suffered a series of major defeats: The Crusaders occupied the Levant and the Holy Land and established Christian states in areas claimed by Islam, while in the Iberian Peninsula a Christian coalition slowly but decisively began the campaign to evict the Muslims from Spain and Portugal. Meanwhile a myriad of bitter succession crises and violent struggles not only prevented the Muslims from resisting these onslaughts but also fractured and weakened the existing Islamic regimes.

The result of these setbacks was a backlash. Ruthless military commanders emerged to lead the armies of the believers to reclaim the lands of

Islam. Most famous were Saladin, the Kurd who defeated the Crusaders in 1187 to 1192, and Abdul Mumin from Morocco, who defeated the Christian armies in Spain in 1146 to 1163 and again in 1195. But as these and other military leaders rose to power, the once glorious Islamic culture and civilization crumbled. Having consolidated power by the strength of their swords, the new conquerors-turned-rulers had to prove their uniqueness— their "Islamness." They revived religious extremism as the source of their legitimacy while accusing their enlightened and sophisticated predecessors of causing the Muslim world's earlier defeats.

And so the Muslim world was swept with what Hoveyda calls an "anti-intellectual rage" that was encouraged by leaders with a lust for absolute power and an inability to cope with the achievements of their predecessors. The new elite sought and found simplistic tenets to legitimize their hold on power, and nobody dared challenge them. "The Koran contains all the truth required in order to guide the believer in this world and open for him the gates of Paradise," argued the new religious elite—a principle still guiding today's Islamists. By the time this anti-intellectual movement was well established in the twelfth century, the Muslim world had committed what Hoveyda calls "civilizational suicide": incited and excited by the lure of brute force, the community of believers willingly agreed to abandon and deny its own cultural and scientific achievements and commit itself to a process of self-destruction that still unfolds.

Thus the Muslim world has been in paralysis since religious extremism rose in the twelfth century. Aspiring to power, new generations of extremist and militant forces have repeatedly demonstrated their supremacy by ordering the destruction of cultural treasures of previous generations. For example, in 1192 the ulema—the religious leadership—in Cordova, Spain, publicly burned the books of the main scientific-medical library, including a rare study of astronomy, because these books were a "horrible calamity" to Islam. And in 1979, following the Islamic revolution in Iran, Ayatollah Khomeini issued an order ensuring the Islamization of the higher-education system. Student committees, composed of hard-core Islamist activists, complied by evicting leftist activists, both students and faculty, from the campuses and then supervised the Islamic "correctness" of both the material taught in classes and the research conducted by the surviving faculty. Finally the government closed the universities between 1980 and 1983 to complete a proper Islamic approach, that is, the elimination of all departments and courses the mullahs considered un-Islamic as well as the banishment and at times arrest and execution of all the related faculty.

Mysticism, militancy, and the quest for perpetual jihad have become the rallying cry of the latest generation of Muslim militant leaders. *Jihad,* which literally means "striving," refers to a holy war undertaken to further the rule of Islam over contested lands, particularly Muslim lands occupied by non-Muslims (any land ever conquered by Islam is considered its forever) and lands with a significant Muslim population controlled by non-Muslims. These leaders have elected to demonstrate their Islamic credentials with extremist interpretations of Islamic law. The extremists have amputated Muslim civilization from its future and condemned it to an eternal isolation.

The crisis in the Muslim world intensified as isolation turned to subjugation when the West penetrated the Hub of Islam—the area between Morocco and India, where Muslims not only constitute the overwhelming majority of the population but also determine the sociopolitical and civilizational way of life. The process began with Napoleon's arrival in Egypt in 1789. Then came the Russian wars with Turkey and the conquest of Central Asia in the nineteenth century, followed by the Turkish Empire's collapse and occupation by Britain in World War I and the ensuing artificial redrawing of the Middle East's map by the imperialist powers. The experience has been a trauma from which the Muslim world, particularly the Hub of Islam, has yet to emerge.

Historically Muslims have identified themselves through two frames of reference: in contemporary Western terminology the *supranational* and *subnational*. Both frameworks of self-identification are different from the primary framework used in the modern world—that of the nation-state. The supranational identity is the self-identification of all Muslims with a single entity—the Muslim Nation—which is expressed through pan-Islamism. The rise of political awareness in the Muslim world led to the emergence of subidentities, such as pan-Turkism and pan-Arabism, that are still all-embracing. The subnational identity refers to the blood relation(s)—clans, tribes, extended families, and the like—that have dominated the everyday life of Muslims throughout their history. In the aftermath of World War I and the Russian Revolution, the Western powers not only carved up the Muslim world into new statelike entities that had nothing to do with the character and aspirations of the indigenous population but also imposed new and alien ruling elites—whether royal families propped up by the Western colonial powers or Communist elites propped up by the Soviets—on the population. In the aftermath of World War II the various Muslim states experimented with ideologies and legitimization strategies borrowed from East and West, all of which led to the establishment of oppressive military dictatorships that abused their countries and oppressed their peoples in the name of the quest for glory, modernization, and military might.

The Islamist leaders were fully aware of the disparity in power between their nascent movements and the groups arrayed against them, ranging from the Arab military dictatorships to the enemies of the Arabs, such as Israel and the Western states. As a result leading Islamist theorists sought alternative methods for waging jihad from a position of apparent inferiority. In October 1968 Sheikh Muhammad Abu-Zahra of the Cairo al-Azhar University defined the essence of jihad under contemporary conditions: "Jihad is not confined to the summoning of troops and the establishment of huge forces. It takes various forms. From all the territories of Islam there should arise a group of people reinforced with faith, well equipped with means and methods; and then let them set out to attack the usurpers, harassing them incessantly until their abode is one of everlasting torment. . . . Jihad will never end. . . . It will last to the Day of Judgment." This definition of a perpetual jihad against superior forces constitutes a central tenet of contemporary Islamist terrorism—one that has been increasingly adopted as the Muslim world struggles to confront the growing Western influence in its midst.

This crisis reached its first boiling point in the mid-1970s, when the Muslim world, empowered by new petrodollar wealth, was exposed to Western civilization as never before—through graduate studies in the West, leisure travel, and satellite TV, still in its infancy. The shock was immense. Leading Islamist intellectuals, who had experienced life in the United States as graduate students, concluded that the personal liberties and materialism they had experienced in the West constituted a mortal threat to traditional Islamic society, which is regimented and bound by strict codes of behavior. Islam stipulates that the Sharia—the law governing mankind—is of divine origin and is to be interpreted only by the learned and the pious who rule the believers as spiritual leaders and guides. In contrast, the essence of Western democracy lies in the citizenry, who elect a few of their own to legislate for them and govern them in accordance with humanly enacted laws. The Islamists are convinced that this deviation of Western society (particularly American society, where the separation between church and state is so strongly enforced) from the Islamic divine order of authority is the root cause of its social malaise.

The Islamists' criticism of the American way of life has been scathing. Followers of the Ayatollah Khomeini in Iran view the United States as a land preoccupied with the adulation and worship of money, and Majid Anaraki, an Iranian who lived for several years in southern California, described the United States as "a collection of casinos, supermarkets, and whore-houses linked together by endless highways passing through nowhere," all dominated and motivated by the lust for money. "Those people in the West will put their own mothers on auction for profit," explained U.S.-educated Behzad Nabavi, then Iran's minister of heavy industries. Khomeini himself pointed out that the Western preoccupation with the quest for money makes "prostitution a community's way of life."

The Islamists were determined to ensure that this malaise that had already "destroyed" Christendom did not penetrate and similarly corrupt and destroy the Muslim world. All means, including the use of violence and terrorism, were justified to prevent such corruption. But the Islamists could not separate their world—the Hub of Islam—from the West. The development of their oil resources required Western technology, and so did their medical system. Muslims drove cars made in the West, used phones installed by Western contractors, and ate imported food while watching imported TVs. Meanwhile their leaders protected their dictatorial regimes using weapons purchased abroad. This stark contradiction first burst into the open as a strategic-political development in Khomeini's Islamic Revolution in Iran. In his book *Among the Believers*, V. S. Naipaul succinctly elucidated Khomeini's quandary: "Interpreter of God's will, leader of the faithful, he expressed all the confusion of his people and made it appear like glory, like the familiar faith: the confusion of a people of high medieval culture awakening to oil and money, a sense of power and violation, and a knowledge of a great new encircling civilization. That civilization couldn't be mastered. It was to be rejected; at the same time it was to be depended on." Other contemporary Islamist luminaries whose writings constitute the theological foundations of today's terrorists saw in this spread of "Westoxication" a mortal threat to the very existence of Islam. "The world as it is today is how others [that is, non-Muslims] shaped it," the leading Iraqi Shiite scholar Ayatollah Muhammad Baqir al-Sadr explained. "We have two choices: either to accept it with submission, which means letting Islam die, or to destroy it, so that we can construct the world as Islam requires."

The Muslim world has found itself at a historical crossroads. Its encounter with Western civilization seems to have failed despite the unprecedented wealth accumulated by the elite. Attempts to consolidate modern regimes brought about widespread repression and impoverishment of the masses, creating popular tension for which the state system has no solutions and that further modernization can only exacerbate. And the Islamist intellectuals—popularly called "fundamentalists"—could not transform their alluring theories into practical solutions. "In Islam, and especially the Islam of the fundamentalists, precedent is all. The principles of the Prophet—as divined from the Koran and the approved traditions—are for all time. They can be extended to cover all disciplines," Naipaul elucidates. "It is what the new, educated fundamentalists say. And it is at once sound faith, and part of their rage against the civilization that encircles them and which they as a community despair of mastering." And so, starting in the late 1970s, Islamist thinkers could see no way out of the crisis of Islam except for an all-out confrontation with the West that would be incited once an excuse legitimizing the outbreak of violence was provided. "We are at war. And our battle has only just begun. Our first victory will be one tract of land somewhere in the world that is under the complete rule of Islam," declared Abdul-Qadir as-Sufi ad-Darqawi, one of the greatest thinkers and philosophers of contemporary Islamism. "Islam is moving across the earth," he added. "Nothing can stop [its] spreading in Europe and America."

Fully aware of the might and accelerating spread of Western power, the Islamists sought an indirect form of confrontation with the West. They defined a mode of total war in which the Muslim world's inferiority in technology and military power would not affect the outcome of the jihad. This strategy was formulated by Pakistani brigadier S. K. Malik in his 1979 book *The Quranic Concept of War*. According to Malik, the Koranic way of war is "infinitely supreme [to] and [more] effective" than any other form of warfare because "in Islam a war is fought for the cause of Allah" and therefore all means and forms are justified and righteous. Terrorism, Malik argued, is the quintessence of the Islamic strategy for war: "Terror struck into the hearts of the enemies is not only a means, it is the end in itself. Once a condition of terror into the opponent's heart is obtained hardly anything is left to be achieved. It is the point where the means and the end meet and merge. Terror is not a means of imposing decision upon the enemy; it is the decision we wish to impose upon him."

For a while, it seemed that triumph was at hand. The Muslim world celebrated the consolidation of Islamist regimes in Iran and Sudan—celebrated, that is, Shiite Iran's ability to sustain Khomeini's regime despite eight years of debilitating war with Iraq and near total international isolation and Sunni Sudan's transformation of the 1989 military coup into Islamist rule through installation of Hassan al-Turabi as the country's spiritual leader. The Muslim world also celebrated the triumph of the mostly grassroots Islamist forces in Afghanistan over the Soviet Union, the collapse of the Soviet Union, and the emergence of six new Muslim states in Central Asia. And then in 1991 came the Gulf War, and the West once again demonstrated its immense technological-military supremacy. Moreover, the Saudi royal family—the custodians of Islam's holy shrines in Mecca and Medina—had to invite American and other Western forces to defend Saudi Arabia and defeat a sister Arab-Muslim state, Iraq. It was a humiliation that still haunts the Muslim world.

But again Islamist leaders saw an alternative to a fateful confrontation with the West over the spirit of Islam. In late 1991 Ahmad Khomeini, the Ayatollah's son (who died suddenly just as he was assuming the mantle as his father's successor), emphasized the fatefulness of the inevitable struggle with the United States: "We should realize that the world is hostile toward us only for [our commitment to] Islam. After the fall of Marxism, Islam replaced it, and as long as Islam exists, U.S. hostility exists, and as long as U.S. hostility exists, the struggle exists." He warned that Islam's campaigns should spread beyond the immediate challenges in the Middle East "because the struggle against Israel is a war against the U.S. and Europe with no short end."

Today this crisis is escalating because of the widening gap between the West and the Muslim world and the intensifying exposure of the Muslim world to Western civilization through electronic media—from satellite TV to the Internet. The Islamists consider this exposure an onslaught against their way of life, a constant and flagrant reminder of backward Islam's failures in science and technology. "The challenge posed by militant Islamic fundamentalism to the West is not solely 'military.' What it primarily contests is the Western democratic and secular ideology. It wants to appropriate Western technology without embracing its ethos. In short, the battle waged against the Great and lesser Satan(s) possesses an important sociocultural dimension," Hoveyda explains. "In the view of militant Islamic fundamentalists, the danger to Islam represented by the West is compounded by the policies of the present Muslim leaders who have strayed from the 'true' principles of their religion and are squandering the resources of their nations in cahoots with the infidels. These leaders and their supporters have 'confiscated' political power. Therefore, the only way open to the true servants of Allah is to seize power and reestablish the rule of the Sharia. Hence the resort to violence and the increasing use of terrorism and other means by Islamic fundamentalists in most Muslim countries."

This struggle for the soul of government in the Muslim world is at the core of the Islamists' confrontation with their own governments and society. Professor Johannes J. G. Jansen, a Dutch expert on Islamism, considers this struggle between the Islamists and the modern state the primary cause of Islamist violence, terrorism, and subversion within Muslim lands: "Many Muslims have narrowed Islam down to the demand for the introduction of the application of Islamic law. It is both political and religious at the same time, and it is the dual nature of this demand that gives Islamic fundamentalism its distinctive character. Muslims who have thus reduced Islam to the single demand for the implementation of Islamic law often accuse their fellow-Muslims of the crime of apostasy from Islam. In their eyes, anyone who neglects to apply (any of) the traditional prescripts of Islam is not only a lax Muslim but an apostate. In Islamic law apostasy is a capital crime, and thus the demand for the application of Islam and Islamic law becomes a political as well as a religious demand, which is frequently supported by terrorism and death threats."

But this struggle, violent and ugly as it may be, does not resolve the central issue confronting the Islamists. They are convinced that it is only the West, as was so clearly demonstrated during the Gulf War, that saves and sustains subservient Muslim regimes while punishing those that stand up to the West. And the radical Islamists are convinced that for as long as the West, specifically the United States, has access to, let alone a presence in, the Hub of Islam, it will be impossible to establish genuine Islamic governments and at once resolve all the problems presently afflicting the Muslim world. Islamist leaders may differ on the fine details of what constitutes a genuine Islamic state, but they all agree that the United States and Western civilization must first be evicted from their midst.

For the hard-core Islamists, the lesson of the Gulf War—that the West can coerce and defeat—is counterbalanced by the legacy of Afghanistan, where the Soviet Union was ostensibly defeated, and that of Somalia, where the United States was driven out by Islamist forces. And since the Muslim world lacks the military and scientific-technological abilities to confront the West head-on, the only way the West can be confronted is through international terrorism. These trends are leading to what Professor Samuel P. Huntington, Harvard professor and former director of security planning for the National Security Council, calls the clash of civilizations. "A global war involving the core states of the world's major civilizations is highly improbable but not impossible. Such a war, we have suggested, could come about from the escalation of a fault line war between groups from different civilizations, most likely involving Muslims on one side and non-Muslims on the other. Escalation is made more likely if aspiring Muslim core states compete to provide assistance to their embattled coreligionists," Huntington writes. More likely to happen is what Professor Mark Jurgensmeyer, dean of the School of Hawaiian, Asian, and Pacific Studies at the University of Hawaii, calls "a new Cold War between the religious Third World and the secular West." Either way, if left unchecked, Islamist terrorism will become the escalatory catalyst for this eruption of violence in both the heart of the West and throughout the Hub of Islam. "Militant Islamic fundamentalism is essentially a political movement, not [just] a religious one. Although it may pose a threat to the West in general and to the United States in particular, it will certainly be lethal to the Muslim world," Hoveyda laments. Meanwhile the Islamists' growing hostility toward the West—fueled by the seemingly unstoppable spread of Westernization through the electronic media—motivates the terrorists, such as bin Laden, to commit more horrendous, more spectacular strikes if only to demonstrate the viability of radical Islam and its rage. Their individual struggles are the essence of the Islamist movement against Westernization.

The story of Osama bin Laden is not just that of an impressive leader and an irreconcilable foe—it is also the story of the events he was part of and the overall dynamics and circumstances within which he strives. It is the story of dedicated zealots driven by hatred unacceptable and incomprehensible to a Westerner. They are ready to personally endure deprivations and death to force the Muslim world back onto the right path as they see it—even if this drive reverses the march of history in the process. And in the pursuit of their righteous goals, they are ready to punish the U.S.-led West for constituting an insurmountable challenge, for standing in their way by the mere existence of its values and affluence.

Osama bin Laden continues to top the U.S. government's list of terrorism and security threats, as CIA director George Tenet stressed in testimony on February 2, 1999, to the Senate. Director Tenet stated, "First, there is not the slightest doubt that Osama bin Laden, his worldwide allies, and his sympathizers are planning further attacks against us. Despite progress against his networks, bin Laden's organization has contacts virtually worldwide, including in the United States—and he has stated unequivocally that all Americans are targets." The CIA anticipates bombing attempts with conventional explosives and possibly kidnappings and assassinations by bin Laden's organization. Recently the CIA has noted activity similar to that prior to the African embassy bombings and fears that attacks could occur at any time, potentially involving chemical or biological weapons. According to Director Tenet, "Bin Laden's organization is just one of about a dozen terrorist groups that have expressed an interest in or have sought chemical, biological, radiological, and nuclear (CBRN) agents. Bin Laden, for example, has called the acquisition of these weapons a 'religious duty' and noted that 'how we use them is up to us.'"

Who is this Osama bin Laden—the only individual terrorist to elicit a major strike from the strongest power on earth, the United States? Is he just a crazy Saudi billionaire who gave up a life of splendor in order to live in a remote cave in Afghanistan and plot terrorist strikes against the United States while living with the constant threat of death?

A Note on Terms and Spelling

ANY BOOK DEALING with the Muslim world is bound to be full of strange names and terms. This one is no different. Moreover, there are several codes of transliteration for both Arabic and Persian—from the academically precise to what is commonly used in the media. To make the book as reader-friendly as possible, I opted to use the popular spelling of names as they appear in most newspapers and magazines. For example, although the proper transliteration of the name would be *Ussamah bin Ladin*, I go along with the commonly used *Osama bin Laden*. Similarly, instead of the proper *Umar Abd-al-Rahman*, I use the familiar *Omar Abdul Rahman*, and instead of *Tsaddam Hussayn*, *Saddam Hussein*.

Whenever possible I translated terms, albeit losing precision, and left in the original language only commonly known terms such as *jihad* or organizational names such as *al-Jamaah al-Islamiyah*. For non-translated terms I also used the common transliterations—for example, *jihad* rather than *gihad*. This should help the reader to relate the story told here to unfolding world events.

A Note on Sources and Methods

I'VE BEEN STUDYING terrorism and subversion, particularly throughout the Hub of Islam, for more than a quarter of a century now. Over such a period, one has not only the opportunity to absorb an extensive amount of material through reading and personal discussions but also the time to reflect.

Osama bin Laden's name first came to my attention around 1981. An Afghan mujahid mentioned him, and I opened a file. Bin Laden was described as a dedicated and very serious young man. Admittedly, as far as the group that would become the Arab "Afghans" was concerned, at the time I paid more attention to the collection of Egyptians and Palestinians and less to the rich youngsters from the Arabian Peninsula. They were "good guys"—seriously committed to a cause we also supported wholeheartedly. They were not "terrorists." Still, bin Laden attracted my attention more than did his compatriots. His relationship with Sheikh Azzam, the Palestinian patron of the Arab volunteers in Afghanistan, was intriguing. Among my interlocutors at the time—Pakistanis in and out of government service, Afghan mujahideen, and Arabs—everybody knew of him and had something to say about him, usually good. The file got thicker and thicker.

Sometime in the mid-1980s I was in London, meeting with an Arab Islamist friend. At that time he was still an active "Afghan." He was in London seeking medical treatment for a combat wound. We talked about his Afghanistan, and Osama bin Laden's name came up. "He is a unique man," my friend said. "You can see it in his eyes. He's doing Allah's work like nobody else. A true mujahid." And after a brief pause he added: "Pay close attention to him. If he's not martyred soon, he'll get far. He'll be a great leader of the jihad because he fears nobody but Allah." My friend was a great mujahid, older than most and grown wise by an illustrious and very special career. In 1980, after the Soviet invasion of Afghanistan, he had to join the jihad. His combat record was even more impressive than his earlier career. So I took notes on what he told me, and I've been paying very close attention to Osama bin Laden ever since.

Bin Laden: The Man Who Declared War on America is largely based on extensive indigenous source material I obtained from the Islamists,

"Afghans," and terrorist organizations. Additional primary original source material comes from the Arab Middle East, southwest Asia, and other parts of the Muslim world. I have had extensive interviews and communications with numerous officials, mujahideen, terrorists, commanders, émigrés, defectors, and otherwise involved individuals from all sides of these events. These sources supplement the large quantities of open sources—primarily regional media—that by themselves provide a wealth of data and documentation. This open-source material includes wire-service reports by local and international news agencies; articles from local newspapers, periodicals, and newsletters; articles from newspapers, periodicals, and newsletters of the Arab émigré community in Western Europe; articles from newspapers, periodicals, newsletters, and academic journals in the United States, Europe, Russia, and other countries; transcripts of broadcasts by the local electronic media (mostly translated by the U.S. government's FBIS); and huge quantities of material retrieved through the Internet. For background information I consulted a unique collection of primary sources—plus original publications, documents, and reports—developed over a quarter of a century of intensive research.

This dry definition of sources does not do justice to the human element involved. For over a quarter of a century numerous people have made tremendous contributions to my knowledge and understanding in two major ways.

First, many hundreds, if not thousands, of people from all over the world talked to me, communicated in other ways, and sent stuff from obscure places—sometimes even at a risk to life and liberty. Special thanks to those who patiently told me fascinating things as well as answered what must have been countless dumb and overly detailed questions. Thanks to those who sought, acquired, and delivered piles of documents and other material in "funny" languages and illegible scripts. Many of these individuals live and operate "on the other side." They have communicated and provided material at great risk to themselves and their families because they really care about their own countries and peoples. Others, usually members of "the other camp," have communicated because they want to make sure we understand what they stand for and believe in. Theirs was not an easy task either.

Second, it is not enough to have a wide variety of periodicals, newspapers, bulletins, newsletters, communiqués, and other written material pour in from the region. Quality varies from the absurd to the excellent, and so do reliability and pertinence. These sources are all important, for in their wide diversity and variety they constitute an accurate reflection of the colorful and vibrant civilization Osama bin Laden has emerged from. But these nuances are not easy to detect and comprehend. I thank those "native speakers" who patiently translated and explained the multiple layers of meanings and innuendo in the flowery, rich, and fascinating languages of the Muslim East. Thanks to all the translators and readers who worked with me over the years, teaching me how to "read" the material even when I thought I knew the language.

Despite the diversity and multitude of the sources used and the frequent use of published material, precise source noting is inadvisable in this kind of writing because the safety and survival of the human sources is most important. As a rule, the moment a critical work is published, hostile counterintelligence and security organs launch relentless efforts to discover and silence the human sources still in their midst. Whenever such an individual is exposed, that individual—along with his or her family—is usually punished with torture and death to deter others. Using "anonymous sources" or "officials" as specific entries in an otherwise academic-style list of sources is not sufficient to protect most human sources, particularly those providing access to highly sensitive inside information. The distinction via detailed source notes of what material was acquired from human sources expedites the ability of the hostile counterintelligence and security organs to narrow the scope of the search, better identify the institutions from where the leaks came, and ultimately hunt down the human sources. It has been the author's experience, both as the director of the congressional Task Force on Terrorism and Unconventional Warfare and as an author, that when confronted with a monolithic text in which the specific sources have been blurred, the hostile counterintelligence and security organs find it virtually impossible to narrow their searches and stifle the human sources.

We owe it to these brave individuals who, at great risk to themselves and their loved ones, provide crucial and distinct information to make every conceivable effort to protect them. The omission of precise source notes is the least one can do.

Significant Abbreviations and Organizations

AIM	Armed Islamic Movement (also known as the International Legion of Islam)
CDLR	Committee for the Defense of Legitimate Rights (a London-based Saudi Islamist organization)
DRA	Democratic Republic of Afghanistan
IALHP	Islamic Army for the Liberation of the Holy Places
IAPC	Islamic Arab Peoples' Conference (became PAIC)
IMB	International Muslim Brotherhood
IRGC	Islamic Revolutionary Guards Corps (sometimes called by the Persian name Pasdaran)
ISI	Interservice Intelligence (Pakistani intelligence)
PAIC	Popular Arab and Islamic Conference (originally called IAPC)
PDRY	People's Democratic Republic of Yemen (South Yemen)
PIO	Popular International Organization
PRC	People's Republic of China
UCK	Kosovo Liberation Army (also known as KLA)
VEVAK	Persian acronym for Iranian intelligence
YAR	Yemen Arab Republic (North Yemen)

Egyptian Muslim Brotherhood

Islamic Change Movement—the Jihad Wing in Arabian Peninsula (sometimes referred to only as Islamic Change Movement)

World Islamic Front for Jihad against Jews and Crusaders

1

The Radicalization of an Engineer

NOW IN HIS MID-FORTIES, a university graduate with computer skills, Osama bin Laden lives with his four wives and some fifteen children in a small cave in eastern Afghanistan. They have no running water and only a rudimentary heating system against the extreme cold of winter. Bin Laden is always on guard against assassins, commando raids, and air strikes. Had he followed the path chosen for him by his father, bin Laden could have been a respected building contractor in Saudi Arabia and a billionaire in his own right. Instead he freely elected to abandon the life of affluence and commit himself to waging a jihad under extremely harsh conditions.

Osama bin Laden is not the only Islamist who has abandoned a good career and comfortable lifestyle in order to wage a jihad. Dr. Ayman al-Zawahiri—bin Laden's right-hand man—now in his late forties, could have been one of Egypt's leading pediatricians but gave up a promising career and affluence to fight the Egyptian government. He then refused political asylum in Western Europe (with a generous stipend) and ended up living in eastern Afghanistan not far from bin Laden.

Although bin Laden and Zawahiri are the most notorious Islamist terrorists, there are hundreds like them. These dedicated commanders in turn lead thousands of terrorists in a relentless and uncompromising holy war against the United States and the West as a whole. The bombings of the U.S. embassies in Kenya and Tanzania in 1998 were the latest but by far not the last shots in this rapidly escalating war of terrorism. What makes these individuals—the leaders and symbols of the new Islamist upsurge—commit themselves to this kind of war?

The rise of the new radical Islamist elite is a recent phenomenon in the developing world. These leaders, from the affluent and privileged segment of society, are highly educated and relatively Westernized. They are not the underprivileged, impoverished, and embittered isolates who usually constitute the pool that breeds terrorists and radicals. These Islamist terrorist leaders are different from the typical European middle-class revolutionaries and terrorists—from the anarchists of the nineteenth century to the Communist revolutionaries of the late twentieth century—because the Islamists have become popular leaders of the underprivileged masses, while the European terrorists remained isolated from a generally hostile population. Only Ernesto "Che" Guevara—the Argentinian doctor turned revolutionary fighter of the early 1960s—came close to being the kind of populist leader these Islamists are.

To understand these Islamist leaders—particularly Osama bin Laden—one needs to understand their break with their past, their motivation, the fire in their veins, and the depth of their hatred of the United States and what it stands for.

OSAMA BIN LADEN, Ayman al-Zawahiri, and their compatriots, mostly Saudis and Egyptians, are the product of the tumultuous 1970s and 1980s. Their entire lives, from their early years up until the time they rejected a luxurious lifestyle and embraced radicalism and militancy, were strongly influenced by key events unfolding in the Middle East—most importantly, the Arab prosperity and identity crisis that accompanied the oil boom in the 1970s, the triumph of revolutionary Islam in Iran, and the rallying cry of the jihad in Afghanistan in the 1980s.

Osama bin Muhammad bin Laden was born in the city of Riyadh, Saudi Arabia, probably in 1957. At the time his father, Muhammad bin Laden, was a small-time builder and contractor who had arrived from Yemen in search of employment. Osama was one of numerous siblings—his father had more than fifty children from several wives. Muhammad bin Laden was conscientious about education and advancement in life and tried to provide his children with proper schooling. During the 1960s the family moved to the Hijaz, western Saudi Arabia, and ultimately settled in Al-Medina Al-Munawwara. Osama received most of his formal education in the schools of Medina and later Jedda, Saudi Arabia's main commercial port on the Red Sea.

The oil boom of the 1970s changed Muhammad bin Laden's fortunes. The development boom in the Hijaz brought him in direct contact with the Saudi elite, and he soon developed a special relationship with the uppermost echelons of the House of al-Saud as both a superior builder and the provider of discreet services, such as the laundering of payments to "causes." His contacts at the top enabled Muhammad bin Laden to expand his business into one of the biggest construction companies in the entire Middle East—the Bin Laden Corporation. The special status of the bin Laden company was established when the House of al-Saud contracted with it to refurbish and rebuild the two holy mosques in Mecca and Medina. During the 1970s, the bin Laden company was involved in the construction of roads, buildings, mosques, airports, and the entire infrastructure of many of the Arab countries of the Persian Gulf.

Osama was destined to follow in his father's footsteps. He went to high school in Jedda and then studied management and economics at King Abdul Aziz University in Jedda, one of Saudi Arabia's best schools. His father promised him he would be put in charge of his own company, which would enjoy the bin Ladens' direct access to the Court to gain extremely profitable contracts.

Osama bin Laden started the 1970s as did many other sons of the affluent and well-connected—breaking the strict Muslim lifestyle in Saudi Arabia with sojourns in cosmopolitan Beirut. While in high school and college Osama visited Beirut often, frequenting flashy nightclubs, casinos, and bars. He was a drinker and womanizer, which often got him into bar brawls.

Ultimately, however, Osama bin Laden was not an ordinary Saudi youth having a good time in Beirut. In 1973 Muhammad bin Laden was deeply affected spiritually when he rebuilt and refurbished the two holy mosques, and these changes gradually affected Osama. Even while he was still taking brief trips to Beirut, he began showing interest in Islam. He started reading Islamic literature and soon began his interaction with local Islamists. In 1975 the outbreak of the Lebanese civil war prevented further visits to Beirut. The Saudi Islamists claimed that the agony of the Lebanese was a punishment from God for their sins and destructive influence on young Muslims. Osama bin Laden was strongly influenced by these arguments.

The drastic personal change in Osama bin Laden's life in the mid-1970s reflects the turmoil of the Arab Middle East, specifically Saudi Arabia, during the 1970s.

What began as a period of Arab self-respect and great expectations—derived from the self-perceived restoration of "Arab honor" in the 1973 Yom Kippur War (the coordinated Egyptian-Syrian surprise attack against Israel that ended with an inconclusive Israeli military victory) and then the great affluence and influence resulting from the oil boom that followed the embargo of 1973–1974 (which the oil-producing states of the Arabian Peninsula declared in order to force the West into adopting anti-Israeli policies)—quickly turned into an era of acute crisis and trauma due to the Arab world's inability to cope with the consequences of its actions. The sudden increase in wealth of the ruling elite and the upper and educated strata and exposure to the West led to confusion and a largely unresolved identity crisis resulting in radicalism and eruptions of violence. Improved media access and availability throughout the region brought home crises in other parts of the world. Because of its conservative Islamic character and sudden wealth and influence, Saudi Arabia was uniquely influenced by these dynamics.

In Jedda, Osama bin Laden was constantly exposed to the often contradictory trends influencing Saudi society at the time. As Saudi Arabia's main port city on the Red Sea coast, Jedda was exposed to Western influence more than most other Saudi cities were. Sailors and experts came to Jedda, while the increasingly rich local elite, including the bin Laden family, visited the West. Coming from generally conservative and isolated Saudi Arabia, these visitors were shocked by their encounter with the West—by the personal freedoms and affluence of the average citizen, by the promiscuity, and by the alcohol and drug use of Western youth. Many young Saudis could not resist experimenting with the forbidden. When they returned to Saudi Arabia, they brought with them the sense of individualism and personal freedoms they encountered in the West.

The wealth and worldly character of Jedda also transformed it into a shelter for Islamist intellectuals persecuted throughout the Muslim world. Several universities, primarily King Abdul Aziz University in Jedda, which bin Laden attended from 1974 to 1978, became a hub of vibrant Islamist intellectual activity; the best experts and preachers were sheltered in the universities and mosques, providing an opportunity to study and share their knowledge. They addressed the growing doubts of the Saudi youth. Their message to the confused was simple and unequivocal—only an absolute and unconditional return to the fold of conservative Islamism could protect the Muslim world from the inherent dangers and sins of the West.

In March 1975, in the midst of the oil boom and the Islamic intellectual backlash against it, Saudi Arabia's King Faisal was assassinated. The assassin, Prince Faisal ibn Musaid, was the king's deranged nephew. He was also thoroughly Westernized and had visited the United States and Western Europe frequently. Both Islamists and Court insiders expressed apprehension that exposure to Western ways had caused Faisal ibn Musaid to go insane. Although the succession process worked and the kingdom suffered no ensuing crisis, the seed of doubt and discontent was sown. The assassination was a turning point for Saudi Arabia. For both the Saudi establishment and the conscientious elite, the assassination of the beloved king served as proof that the Islamists' warning against the sinful and perilous influence of the

West had been on target. The shock of the assassination brought home the real and communal ramifications of the Westernization of the country's educated and affluent youth, creating a grassroots backlash and sending many of these youth, including bin Laden, back into the fold of Islamism.

In the mid-1970s unfolding events in Egypt—the undisputed leader of the Arab world and politics—were also having a major impact on the Saudi educated elite. Jedda was the key entry port for printed material arriving from Egypt, and many of the Islamist intellectuals operating in the city's universities and mosques were Egyptian. They maintained close contacts with their colleagues still in Egypt and advocated their views, exposing the students of Jedda's universities, including bin Laden, to their works and opinions. Already attuned to and tilting toward Islamism, bin Laden was influenced by these Egyptian studies and the events that prompted them.

In the mid-1970s Egyptian president Anwar Sadat courted the Americans to gain political and economic assistance in working out a series of interim agreements with Israel. In the process of courting the United States, Sadat's image changed from that of a traditional village leader to that of a thoroughly Westernized world leader. The personality cult that Sadat developed domestically only alienated the educated elite, whose knowledge of and firsthand experience with the West caused them to fear its adverse impact on the traditional values of Muslim society.

The Islamist fundamentalist movement in Egypt was rejuvenated in the mid-1970s by young activists with Western—mainly secular and technical—educations who gave up their attempt to define their communal place in a world dominated by the West and its values. Intellectually active and curious, they produced high-quality literature that was widely circulated among the young Arab elite. In 1975 Egyptian writer and engineer Wail Uthman, one of the early influential ideologues of the most militant branch of the Islamist movement, published *The Party of God in Struggle with the Party of Satan*. This book divided the world into two social entities—the Party of God and the Party of Satan—and urged believers to fight to restore the rule of the former. In the preface to the second edition of his book, Uthman emphasized that in writing about the unbelievers, the members of the Party of Satan, he was actually referring to Sadat's regime. "Many thought I meant the Communist party when I wrote the Devil's party," he admitted. But although according to Uthman the Communists are an "essential support" of the Party of Satan, to him they are not the source of evil. "The Party of Satan is that group of people who pretend to believe in Islam but in reality are Islam's first enemies," Uthman wrote. He considered exposure to Western everyday life the source of the mounting crisis of Islam and saw no solution but Islamic militancy.

The Arab world was jolted in 1977 when Sadat visited Jerusalem and began the process that would lead to signing a peace agreement with Israel. Sadat's recognition of Israel was the first overt breaking of the "taboo" the Jewish state constitutes—the widest common denominator in the Arab world other than Islam. In his 1996 book *Secret Channels,* Egyptian journalist and commentator Mohamed Heikal stressed that the Arab world is motivated by "a blend of fury and revulsion" toward Israel that the present "peace process" has yet to breach. The combination of a dread of Westernization and the breaking of the "taboo" pushed many Arabs to extremes. The grassroots rejection of the president-turned-pharaoh mobilized scores of youth throughout all of Egyptian society—from the affluent and educated to the poor villagers and slum dwellers, from members of the security services to outcasts in the desert—to seek Islamist solutions to the profound crises afflicting Egypt.

Soon Islamist youth in Egypt and elsewhere had forceful proof of the righteousness of their cause. On February 1, 1979, Ayatollah Ruhollah Khomeini returned to Iran, overthrew the shah, and established the Islamic Republic. Throughout the Muslim world the masses celebrated the success of Khomeini's Islamic Revolution as the triumph of Islam over the United States and the West. The Islamic Revolution became a source of pride and envy to all Muslims, as well as living proof that local rulers could be overthrown by Islamist forces. The impact of Iran was strong in Egypt because Sadat invited the deposed shah to take shelter there, a flagrant affront to the sentiments of most of the population.

The radical Shiite movement was the force behind the Iranian Revolution, and its development in Iran, Lebanon, and Iraq was almost simultaneous to and paralleled the evolution of Sunni revivalism in Egypt. By the late 1970s the philosophy of the revolutionary Shiite thinkers, as expressed in their writings, was very similar to that of the radical Sunni standard-bearers. Their approach to the diagnosis and cure of contemporary problems and their emphasis on the singular importance of confrontation and struggle were virtually identical. Saudi Arabia, in the middle, was exposed to the mounting Islamist fervor.

Saudi Arabia was the first of the traditionalist conservative states to erupt in Islamist violence. On November 20, 1979, the Grand Mosque in Mecca was seized by a well-organized group of 1,300 to 1,500 men under the leadership of Juhayman ibn-Muhammad ibn-Sayf al-Utaibi. A former captain in the White Guards (National Guard), he now declared himself a "mahdi" (messiah). In addition to the Saudis the group's core included well-trained mujahideen (Islamic holy warriors) from Egypt, Kuwait, Sudan, Iraq, North Yemen (the YAR), and South Yemen (the PDRY).

Egyptian and Soviet sources estimated the total number of rebels to be 3,500. Although the assault was in the name of the return to the purity of Islam, most of the 500 leading attackers had been trained and equipped in Libya and especially South Yemen by instructors from East Germany, Cuba, and the PFLP (Popular Front for the Liberation of Palestine). These attackers included Communists in command positions who demonstrated excellent organizational and tactical skills. Furthermore, fifty-nine of the participating Yemenis had been trained in Iran and received weapons via the Iranian Embassy in Sana.

During the preparations for the assault Juhayman's men had recruited several members of the elite White Guards and received active support in the smuggling of weapons and equipment into Saudi Arabia and the mosque itself. A White Guards colonel was among the senior instigators of the plot and organized the smuggling of the automatic weapons, provisions, and supplies into the mosque. The bulk of the weapons used had been brought from South Yemen over a lengthy period. The rebels also smuggled in huge quantities of food and drinking water to supply themselves and their supporters for a long siege.

On November 20, after a brief firefight to secure control of the Qaaba (the center of the Grand Mosque complex, containing the holiest shrine of Islam), Juhayman addressed the crowd of trapped pilgrims and asked for their support. Sermons and discussions of corruption, wastefulness, and the pro-Western stance of the Saudi royal family quickly gained the rebels widespread support among the worshipers. Before long most of the 6,000 pilgrims taken hostage asked to be issued arms so that they could join the revolt. Juhayman's sermons gained sympathy even among the leftist and quasi-Marxist students. News of Juhayman's sermons incited militant mobs throughout Saudi Arabia to storm local mosques and government posts. Latent subversive elements came to life as almost simultaneously with the seizure of the Qaaba a series of bombs exploded in places sensitive to the royal family in Mecca, Medina, Jeddah, and Riyadh. Among these targets were palaces, personal and official offices, and businesses.

Initially the White Guards reacted chaotically to the attack and suffered a humiliating defeat. Moreover, growing discontent in the ranks of the Saudi elite units led the royal family to fear that even they might rebel. The Saudi security forces settled for a siege of the mosque that lasted about two weeks. In the end the rebellion was only subdued by a special detachment of French paramilitary special forces, antiterrorist experts who used stun grenades and chemical weapons.

The uprising in Mecca shook the world of accepted norms in Saudi Arabia. The grievances raised by Juhayman echoed throughout Saudi Arabia, being whispered about in closed meetings. In intellectual circles his arguments made people stop and think about Islam and the society they were living in. A thinking and well-read individual, Osama bin Laden was influenced by the social issues Juhayman raised. But although the crisis of November 1979 reinforced bin Laden's conviction that only an Islamic government could shield Saudi Arabia and the rest of the Muslim world from the evils of encroaching Westernization, he remained a loyal subject of King Fahd and the House of al-Saud.

———

OSAMA BIN LADEN'S WORLD, like that of most Muslims worldwide, was jolted in the last days of 1979, when the Soviet Union invaded Afghanistan. In the late 1970s Afghanistan—a desolate and backward landlocked country—was ruled by a Soviet-sponsored Communist government being challenged by Pakistani-sponsored Islamist subversion. With the Communist regime increasingly unstable, the Soviet armed forces marched into Afghanistan, occupied the country's strategic infrastructure, assassinated the president, and replaced him with a docile Soviet puppet. They also began a systematic campaign to suppress the Islamist subversion.

The Soviet invasion was the first time since World War II that non-Muslim forces had occupied a Muslim country—and these were anti-Islamic Communists to boot. Little wonder that the Soviet invasion of Afghanistan in the last days of 1979 shocked the entire Muslim world to its core. The occupation of a Muslim state by Communist forces insulted the most basic sensitivities of Islam. But however immense the shock and however great the condemnation by the Arab states, little was actually done.

Immediately after the Soviet invasion, outrage ran throughout the Muslim world. An extraordinary meeting of foreign ministers from thirty-five Islamic states convened in Islamabad on January 27, 1980. Those assembled strongly condemned "the Soviet military aggression against the Afghan people" and called for the "immediate and unconditional withdrawal" of all Soviet troops from Afghanistan. They also urged that no Muslim country recognize the Democratic Republic of Afghanistan (DRA)—the Soviet-installed government in the capital, Kabul—or negotiate with Kabul.

The Soviet Union moved quickly to blunt the Islamic militant movement, pointing to the disunity of the Arab world and challenging its right to speak for the entire Muslim population. The Soviet Union countered by claiming that it was the genuine supporter of Islam. "Showing respect for the religious feelings of the masses, the USSR holds out the hand of solidarity and friendship to all Muslims who are struggling against imperialist forces and exploitation for the right to control their own destiny, for freedom, independence, and economic and social progress," wrote A. Vasiliev, a pseudonym used by the Kremlin to signal an authoritative message delivered by a senior official. The Soviets also warned the Muslim world against "the imperialist threat" now being concealed "behind the concern for Islam" and reminded the Arabs of its long-standing support during their military confrontations with Israel and the West. Moscow urged the Muslim world to examine its intervention in Afghanistan accordingly.

Even if Arab governments were not convinced by the Soviet propaganda, they were disinclined to confront the Soviet Union, mostly because of military realities. Soviet forces were poised on the Afghan border, overlooking the Persian Gulf and an Iran in turmoil. Prince Turki al-Faisal, the head of Saudi intelligence, observed in early 1980 that the ultimate Soviet objective was "our oil. . . . At this moment we do not expect an invasion, but we do expect the Soviets to use their power to maneuver themselves into a position to make arrangements for a guaranteed oil supply." Rhetoric notwithstanding, Riyadh's interest in Afghanistan was strategic—the sanctity of Saudi Arabia's oil fields. Although the concern for Islamic solidarity expressed by the Saudis was genuine, it was not their primary concern. This distinction is important in understanding the role bin Laden would soon play in the escalating war in Afghanistan.

If the Arab world entertained any hopes after the Soviets invaded Afghanistan that the United States would save it in case of further Soviet encroachment, these hopes were soon dispelled. The United States' aborted rescue attempt in Iran on the night of April 24 to 25, 1980, demonstrated Arab vulnerability. In November 1979, after the Iranian revolution, a group of Iran's unofficial intelligence service, with the support of the country's elite and the KGB, had seized the U.S. Embassy and taken sixty-three Americans hostage, demanding U.S. disengagement and withdrawal from the region and the return of frozen funds for the hostages' release. Elite U.S. forces attempted to rescue the American hostages, held by Iranian militants in the U.S. Embassy in Tehran. The mission failed due to a shortage of helicopters and a collision between a tanker aircraft and a helicopter during preparations for withdrawal. The specter of the burned hulks of U.S. aircraft and helicopters, the bodies of a few American servicemen, and the hastily abandoned helicopters provided by a jubilant Iranian TV brought home the American humiliation. For the Arab rulers in the shadow of Afghanistan, this demonstrated America's military incompetence and proved that Washington could not be relied on to save these regimes from the growing Soviet threat. The Soviets capitalized on the failed show of force, emphasizing that the U.S. rescue operation was actually intended "to return

Iran to the zone of American influence." This opinion was shared by leaders in Persian Gulf capitals.

In the spring of 1980 fear and caution became the main characteristics
of Arab policy toward the Soviet Union and the Afghan question. Arab governments could not ignore the fact that the Soviet military presence in Afghanistan cut in half the distance that Soviet forces, aircraft, and missiles
would need to travel to reach the Persian Gulf. "The Soviet shadow over this
area looms so large that many Muslim regimes cannot find the courage to
challenge it; the more savagely the Russians deal with the Afghan resistance,
the greater the dread which they strike into the heart of other Muslim countries," observed Professor Richard Pipes, director of East European and Soviet Affairs for the National Security Council during the first years of the
Reagan administration. Changes in the Muslims' position were visible in
the follow-up conference of Islamic states in May 1980. The denunciation of
the Soviet Union that emerged was somewhat milder than it had been four
months earlier. More important, the demand not to recognize or deal with
the government in Kabul was removed from the resolution.

Osama bin Laden was one of the first Arabs to go to Afghanistan after
the Soviet invasion. "I was enraged and went there at once," he said to an
Arab journalist. In retrospect, bin Laden now considers the Soviet invasion
of Afghanistan a turning point in his life. "The Soviet Union invaded Afghanistan, and the mujahideen put out an international plea for help," he
explained to another interviewer. He was inspired by the plight of Muslims
"in a medieval society besieged by a twentieth-century superpower. . . . In
our religion, there is a special place in the hereafter for those who participate in jihad," he added. "One day in Afghanistan was like one thousand
days of praying in an ordinary mosque."

Within a few days after the Soviet invasion bin Laden, who was genuinely and selflessly committed to the cause of all-Islamic solidarity, went
to Pakistan to assist the Afghan mujahideen. On arrival bin Laden was appalled by the chaos in Pakistan and the lack of Arab unity and devoted
himself to political and organizational work, establishing a recruitment
drive that over the next few years would funnel thousands of Arab fighters
from the Gulf States to the Afghan resistance. At first he personally covered
the travel costs of these volunteers to Pakistan and Afghanistan, but more
important, he set up the main camps to train them. In early 1980 bin Laden
established Ma'sadat Al-Ansar, then the main base for Arab mujahideen in
Afghanistan.

Bin Laden's early Afghan years brought him into contact with Sheikh
AbdAllah Yussuf Azzam, who was key in establishing what is today the International Legion of Islam—the highly proficient and dedicated hard core

of international Islamist terrorism. Azzam was born in a small village near Jenin, Samaria, in 1941. His pious family sent him to get religious schooling from an early age. After receiving most of his early education in Jordan, he entered Sharia College of Damascus University, where he obtained a B.A. degree in Sharia (Islamic law) in 1966. After the 1967 Six Days War, during which Israel captured Azzam's hometown, Azzam escaped to Jordan and joined the jihad against Israel. He found his calling not on the battlefield but in education and incitement. Toward this end he was sent to Egypt, where he received a master's degree in Sharia from the prestigious al-Azhar University. In 1970 he began teaching at Amman University but returned in 1971 to al-Azhar on scholarship and in 1973 obtained a Ph.D. in principles of Islamic jurisprudence. During his stay in Cairo Azzam was drawn into the ranks of the Egyptian militant Islamists. He built many personal contacts that would have a great impact on his work in Afghanistan a decade later.

In the mid-1970s Azzam broke with the Palestinian armed struggle against Israel because it was driven by national revolutionary ideology instead of being an Islamist jihad. Azzam went to Saudi Arabia to teach at King Abdul Aziz University in Jeddah, a hub of Islamist scholarship that had a strong influence on Saudi youth. Osama bin Laden was studying at the university at the time, and there is evidence that he attended one of Azzam's lectures. In Jeddah, Azzam formulated his doctrine of the centrality of the jihad to the liberation of the Muslim world from the stifling embrace of Westernization. "Jihad and the rifle alone: no negotiations, no conferences, and no dialogues," he told his students.

In 1979, with the declaration of the Afghan jihad, Azzam left the university and went to practice what he had been preaching, becoming one of the first Arabs to join the Afghan jihad. But the Pakistani and Afghan leaders in the jihad urged him to resume teaching rather than take part in battle. Azzam was first appointed as a lecturer at the International Islamic University in Islamabad, the capital of Pakistan, but he decided to move to Peshawar, closer to the Afghanistan border, and devote all his time and energy to the jihad in Afghanistan.

In Peshawar, Sheikh Azzam founded the Bait-ul-Ansar, which received and trained the first Islamist volunteers pouring into Pakistan to participate in the Afghan jihad. Bait-ul-Ansar also provided specialized services for the Afghan jihad and the mujahideen. In this context bin Laden was integrated into the Islamist international system and became one of Azzam's closest disciples.

Bin Laden had money, knowledge, and enthusiasm and implemented Azzam's ideas. Azzam and bin Laden established the Maktab al-Khidamat—

the Mujahideen Services Bureau—which bin Laden soon transformed into an international network that sought out Islamists with special knowledge, from medical doctors and engineers to terrorists and drug smugglers, and recruited them for service in Afghanistan. By the late 1980s bin Laden would have branches and recruitment centers in fifty countries, including the United States, Egypt, Saudi Arabia, and some Western European countries. While handling the arrival and deployment of numerous Arabs, bin Laden noticed that they needed training and conditioning before they confronted the harsh conditions in Afghanistan. So Azzam and bin Laden next established Masadat Al-Ansar—the central base and home-away-from-home for the Arab mujahideen in both Afghanistan and Pakistan. In the course of these activities bin Laden made contacts with numerous Islamist leaders and mujahideen from every corner of the world—relations that now prove invaluable in his jihad against the United States.

Appalled by the mujahideen's vulnerability to Soviet and DRA artillery, bin Laden brought heavy engineering equipment from Saudi Arabia. He first rushed some of the family's bulldozers to Afghanistan to expedite the construction of roads and facilities for the mujahideen in eastern Afghanistan. Soon afterward he organized the delivery of diversified heavy equipment from numerous Saudi and other Gulf Arab companies, using the equipment to dig trenches and shelters for the mujahideen. The Soviets, fully aware of the importance of these fortifications, launched numerous helicopter gunship strikes against bin Laden's bulldozers. Many times he continued working under fire, oblivious to the danger. With military help pouring in, bin Laden trained Afghans, Pakistanis, and fellow Arabs to use the heavy engineering equipment. He then embarked on an ambitious program to build a fortified infrastructure for the mujahideen in eastern Afghanistan, building with his crews roads, tunnels, hospitals, and storage depots.

By 1980 the United States was pressuring Arab governments to take a more active role in the Afghanistan crisis. President Sadat agreed to help the fledgling Afghan resistance with weapons. Publicly Sadat claimed to provide Egyptian military assistance "because they are our Muslim brothers and in trouble." This enabled the Islamists to agitate the population in the name of Afghanistan and also to find a safe haven outside Egypt for some of their people, especially those linked to the assassination of Sadat in October 1981. Egyptian journalist and commentator Mohamed Heikal observed that since "Afghanistan was to be helped in the name of Islamic solidarity, that was playing into the hands of the unofficial Muslim groups, which were in a much better position to exploit it." Indeed, in early 1980 a few Egyptian Islamists, some of them former officers in the Egyptian army, began arriving in Afghanistan to share their military knowledge with the mujahideen. Many of the first Egyptians to arrive were led by Ahmad Shawqi al-Islambuli, currently one of bin Laden's senior terrorist commanders and the brother of Khalid al-Islambuli, Sadat's assassin. They were fugitives from purges in Egypt, and they soon established a cohesive Arab revolutionary and terrorist movement that still constitutes the hard core of bin Laden's key commanders and most trusted troops. Meanwhile, in 1983 Islambuli organized a network in Karachi for smuggling people and weapons to and from Egypt that is still functioning. But ultimately, from 1980 to 1982, the Arab world was mute on the issue of Afghanistan.

In the early 1980s Osama bin Laden returned home to organize financial support for the mujahideen and for the recruitment and transport of volunteers. Toward this end he utilized the contacts his family had with the uppermost echelons in Riyadh. He soon established contacts with Prince Salman, the king's brother; Prince Turki; the chief of intelligence; and other key officials.

Although bin Laden was urging all-out support for the Afghan jihad, Riyadh had other priorities and plans for the well-connected young militant. At the time the idea of a strategic encirclement and pincer movement by pro-Soviet forces in the Arabian Peninsula terrified the Saudis. They were most alarmed by the growing Soviet, East German, and Cuban military presence in South Yemen—then officially a Communist state, the PDRY—and the Horn of Africa just across the Red Sea. While Saudi Arabia was officially conducting a policy of appeasement and economic inducement toward the PDRY, Riyadh had other ideas in mind.

Saudi intelligence sponsored a clandestine Islamist insurgency in the PDRY, ostensibly under the banner of Tariq al-Fadli, the last sultan of Aden and a militant Islamist. Osama bin Laden was asked to form "volunteer" mujahideen units to bolster the ranks of the Adeni anti-Communist insurgents. This endeavor was fully funded by Riyadh and blessed by the highest authorities in the Saudi Court. Bin Laden established strike forces from a mixture of Islamist volunteers planning to go to Afghanistan and Saudi White Guards special forces that were seconded (formally put on leave). Bin Laden was so involved in the PDRY struggle that he even participated in several raids and clashes with the South Yemeni security forces. But despite the enthusiasm the Yemeni anti-Communist jihad never really took off. With no tangible success in sight, Riyadh pulled the plug. By now, however, bin Laden had already established close personal relations with Tariq al-Fadli, who was then deported to Sana; he and other Yemeni Islamist commanders bin Laden met and helped in the early 1980s would help him in the 1990s.

Osama bin Laden's enthusiasm, commitment, and efficiency in running the Yemeni endeavor were not lost on the Saudi Court. After the conclusion of the special operations against the PDRY, Riyadh sought to consummate the special relations with the young bin Laden through binding and most lucrative financial arrangements. In the early 1980s the Saudi Court decided to expand the two holy mosques. The project would have gone to one of Muhammad bin Laden's companies, but to honor Osama, King Fahd personally offered him the contract for expanding the Prophet's Mosque in Medina. He was told that this deal alone would net him a profit of $90 million. In an audience with King Fahd, Osama bin Laden refused the offer and instead argued passionately for greater commitment to and support for the jihad in Afghanistan. King Fahd, Crown Prince Abdallah, and Prince Turki, already convinced of the strategic importance of the situation in Afghanistan for Saudi Arabia, were strongly influenced by bin Laden's conviction and promised to help the Afghan "cause." In the end Osama did not lose much financially, for the contract went to his father. Osama later told confidants in Afghanistan that his wealth increased and his business grew with the amount of money he spent on the jihad.

Despite the efforts of the Afghan mujahideen, the impact of Afghanistan on the Muslim world grew only in the mid-1980s, when media exposure increased and organized transportation, originated by Osama bin Laden, was institutionalized. Until then even the Arab Islamists, preoccupied with the struggle against their own governments, seemed indifferent. But in 1985 hundreds of Arabs, predominantly Islamists, began joining the ranks of the Afghan mujahideen. In the early 1980s some 3,000 to 3,500 Arabs were in Afghanistan; by the mid-1980s there were some 16,000 to 20,000 associated with Hizb-i Islami (Party of Islam) alone. Arab Islamist organizations also sent some of their commanders to Afghanistan to study the jihad. In the mujahideen camps they received the kind of advanced Islamic education forbidden in many Arab states as subversive or seditious.

These foreign volunteers were easily absorbed into the Muslim environment in Pakistan because of the all-Islamic ideological character of the Afghan resistance. In the mid-1980s the Iranian analyst Amir Taheri elucidated the nature of the resistance: "The Afghan resistance movement has not confined itself to a minimum program of securing the nation's independence and territorial integrity, but openly advocates the creation of an Islamic society. It is in the name of Allah, and not of nationalism in the Western meaning of the term, that Soviet troops are gunned down in the mountains of Afghanistan. In some of the liberated zones the resistance movement has already brought into existence its ideal Islamic society. Here, women have been pushed back into the veil, polygamy has been legalized, girls are kept out of school, and the mullahs and mawlavis [religious leaders] exercise their tyrannical power in all spheres of life." All of these social values and objectives were identical to the aspirations of the arriving Arabs, especially those from the Muslim Brotherhood—the original and still the most religiously authoritative Sunni Islamist organization—and the various jihadist organizations.

By the mid-1980s Afghanistan had become a magnet for militant Islamists from all over the world. In the early 1980s it hadn't taken long for Egyptian and other Arab Islamist groups to begin using Peshawar as a center for their headquarters in exile. As a result of their growing cooperation, they established an "international jihad organization" using Pakistan and Afghanistan as their springboard for operations back home. For example, one of the first jihad movement bureaus was opened in 1984 by Dr. Ayman al-Zawahiri for the Islamic jihad movement of Abbud al-Zumur, a lieutenant-colonel in Egyptian military intelligence and a senior clandestine military commander of the Islamic jihad who was arrested on the eve of Sadat's assassination. Zawahiri escaped from Egypt in the mid-1980s, during the anti-Islamist purges launched by President Mubarak, who took over after Sadat was killed. Zawahiri is presently bin Laden's closest companion and the senior military commander of his "movement." Members of this first generation of foreign volunteers in Afghanistan, all of whom are fiercely loyal to bin Laden, now constitute the leadership and high command of the Islamist terrorist movement. The Egyptian contingent of the international mujahideen would reach singular importance in the early 1990s as a leading element of the terrorist surge into the West.

———————

STARTING IN THE EARLY 1980S, the situation had changed in both Pakistan and Afghanistan. Soon after the invasion, the Soviets seized the military initiative, and they did not lose it until their withdrawal in 1989. The resistance could not prevent the Soviet forces from doing whatever they wanted in Afghanistan. Professor Burhanuddin Rabbani, then leader of Jamiat-i-Islami Afghanistan, one of the major resistance organizations, admitted in 1982 that "the Soviets feel comfortable in Afghanistan." The Zia-ul-Haq government had determined that the situation in Afghanistan constituted a threat to Pakistan's vital interests and committed itself to actively supporting the Afghan jihad. As a result the elaborate and well-oiled machine of the ISI (Pakistani intelligence), which had been sponsoring terrorism since the 1970s—mainly against India—would now be used to support the Afghan mujahideen.

By the mid-1980s Islamabad already had proof of the strategic value of subversion from its long experience sponsoring Sikh terrorism and subversion against India. In 1985 and 1986, as the quantity and quality of weapons provided by the ISI improved, Sikh terrorism and subversion in the Punjab and throughout India showed increased militarization and radicalization. Among the novelties of the revived terrorist campaign were sophisticated bomb-making techniques identical to those being used by the Afghan mujahideen. The escalation in Sikh terrorism was attributed to the better training that Sikh terrorists of the Dal Khals separatist movement were receiving in the Afghan mujahideen camps. In spring 1985 Sikh "trainees" were killed in a Soviet raid on an Afghan resistance training camp in Paktia, in eastern Afghanistan, and documents of the Dal Khals were seized there.

The training camps, however, did not belong to the Afghan mujahideen—they were the ISI's own installations. Starting in the early 1980s, Islamabad decided to capitalize on the growing support—political, military, and financial—Pakistan was now receiving from the West to promote the Afghan jihad and thereby bolster its own strategic requirements. The ISI capitalized on the rapidly expanding and lavishly financed training and support system for the Afghan mujahideen as a cover for expanded sponsorship of and support for other insurgent groups dedicated to subversive activities in India.

It became imperative for Islamabad to establish tight control over the various subversive and terrorist entities the ISI was going to run throughout South Asia, from Afghanistan to India, as indigenous mujahideen forces. The ISI developed commanders and leaders it could control and empowered them in their respective movements. The ISI had initially perfected this process of manipulation and creation of a national mujahideen organization in the early 1970s with the Hizb-i Islami of Gulbaddin Hekmatiyar, a ruthless Afghan thug who had contacts with both the ISI and Soviet intelligence. In the 1980s Islamabad paraded Hizb-i Islami as the spearhead of the Afghan jihad to ensure that it received the most foreign aid, both weapons and funds. Islamabad had no illusions about the self-serving cynical game it was playing—President Zia-ul-Haq himself acknowledged that "it is Pakistan who made [Gulbaddin Hekmatiyar] an Afghan leader."

The same approach was used to transform the nationalist insurgency in Kashmir, India, into an ISI-dominated Islamist force. Hashim Qureshi, the founder of the nationalist JKLF (Jammu Kashmir Liberation Front), recently recalled how "in 1984 ISI generals and brigadiers approached me with the offer: 'get us young people for training from the Valley so that they could fight India on return.'" When he refused, Qureshi explained, his struggle was taken over by the ISI, who installed Amanullah Khan. "It is tragic that so-called nationalist Amanullah Khan and some of his supporters started the present struggle in Kashmir in league with the ISI. A man with common intelligence can understand that any movement started in a Muslim majority area with the help of Pakistani military intelligence will eventually mean religious struggle." Qureshi stressed that by 1993 "Amanullah proved that he was an agent of the ISI," having sacrificed the nationalist liberation struggle in Kashmir on the altar of Islamist politics. Qureshi himself had to flee Pakistan and seek political asylum in Western Europe.

All this time the Afghan jihad was gaining support in Washington, and more money was being appropriated for covert and not-so-covert support for the Afghan mujahideen. The United States was convinced that it was supporting a genuine national liberation struggle, albeit with a strong Islamic foundation, and Islamabad went to great lengths to ensure that the United States did not discover firsthand the kind of mujahideen the American taxpayers were sponsoring. Toward this end the CIA was isolated by the ISI from the training infrastructure it financed. Brigadier Mohammad Yousaf, then head of the ISI Afghan Bureau, stressed that General Akhtar Abdul Rahman Khan, chief of the ISI from 1980 to 1987, "faced many problems with the Americans and the CIA." Akhtar adamantly refused American requests to train the mujahideen or even have direct access to them. "Akhtar never allowed Americans to become directly involved in the Jihad," Yousaf recalled. Akhtar and the ISI high command strongly insisted on "keeping Americans out" of the entire training and supply system they were sponsoring.

Brigadier Yousaf emphasized that the ISI was the sole provider of training in Pakistan and Afghanistan and that "no American or Chinese instructor was ever involved in giving training on any kind of weapon or equipment to the mujahideen. . . . This was a deliberate, carefully considered policy that we steadfastly refused to change despite mounting pressure from the CIA, and later from the U.S. Defense Department, to allow them to take over." Brigadier Yousaf pointed out that "from the start," the ISI leadership "successfully resisted" all American efforts to be directly involved in the support for the Afghan mujahideen. Enjoying massive support from the highest levels of government in Islamabad, the ISI was even able to unilaterally impose limitations and other restrictions on visits by CIA and other U.S. officials to mujahideen training camps although the U.S. government was financing them through the CIA. "General Akhtar was initially adamant that no visitor should be allowed into any camp; however, the clamor from the CIA and the U.S. was so persistent that eventually he conceded that CIA officials could be admitted," Brigadier Yousaf recalled. But these were well-orchestrated visits in which the ISI was able to conceal much from its American allies and benefactors.

Islamabad's critical need to conceal the U.S.-financed training infrastructure from the American government resulted from far more than the disagreement between the ISI and Washington over the fact that the prime recipients of military assistance were Islamic militant groups. The ISI adamantly opposed supporting Afghan resistance organizations associated with the predominantly tribal-traditional Pushtun population, who were essentially pro-Western. Instead the ISI insisted on diverting some 70 percent of the foreign aid to the Islamist parties—particularly Hizb-i Islami—who were inherently and virulently anti-American. From Washington's perspective, the support for the Afghan jihad was so important as to warrant "ignoring" the ISI's use, or abuse, of the U.S.-funded training infrastructure for other "causes"—from Arab Islamists to regional groups serving Pakistan's own interests.

The main reason the ISI decided to keep the CIA out of the camps was the extent of the training and support non-Afghan "volunteers" and others were getting in these camps. Most numerous were the thousands of Islamist trainees from Indian Kashmir and to a lesser extent the Sikhs from the Punjab. In addition, thousands of Islamists from all over the Arab and Muslim world were routinely trained in the camps originally designed for the training of Afghan mujahideen. In the mid-1980s some 16,000 to 20,000 Arab mujahideen had already trained with Hizb-i Islami alone. Since then the Pakistani ISI had been training an average of 100 Arab mujahideen a month. They received military training in Peshawar, and after their return from Afghanistan, they attended advanced training in special camps in Sudan and Yemen.

The reason Pakistan and the ISI began training Arab Islamist terrorists also had to do with unfolding regional dynamics. Zia-ul-Haq's Islamabad was preoccupied with the regional posture of Pakistan—a small, overpopulated country squeezed between Soviet-occupied Afghanistan and India. Islamabad sought to gain as much economic and military support as well as strategic protection as it could from the United States and the conservative Arab states. Islamabad calculated, and not without grounds, that the Saudis would be the most effective advocates for American military assistance in Secretary of Defense Casper Weinberger's Pentagon and the Reagan administration as a whole. The ISI also needed its Saudi counterparts to endorse Gulbaddin Hekmatiyar as the most genuine and successful mujahideen leader so that most of the U.S.-funded support could go to his Hizb-i Islami despite its virulent anti-American policies. In return for delivering Washington, the Saudis were most interested in supporting the Islamist jihad in Afghanistan. Riyadh was also interested in the dispatch of Saudi Islamists to Afghanistan and Pakistan so that they could be kept away from Saudi Arabia itself and was willing to pay handsomely for the services rendered by the ISI.

———————

BY THE MID-1980S bin Laden saw that his real calling lay on the jihad battlefield, where he gained a reputation as a courageous and resourceful commander.

In 1986 he participated in the battle of Jalalabad in the ranks of the Arab mujahideen unit. That year he was also a part of a small Arab force that held in Jaji against repeated assaults by a much larger DRA force supported by Soviet firepower. In 1987 bin Laden fought in an attack on the Soviet-DRA dispositions in Shaban in the Paktia Province. A mixed mujahideen force of Arabs and Afghans with bin Laden in a command position penetrated the enemy's dispositions. Vicious hand-to-hand fighting erupted, and the mujahideen suffered heavy casualties before they had to withdraw. Bin Laden still carries a Kalashnikov (a Soviet-made assault rifle) he claims to have captured from a dead Russian general in Shaban. "He became even more fearless after Paktia," a former friend told the Associated Press; he expected to fight until the end "and die in glory."

Mujahideen who served with bin Laden described him as fearless and oblivious to danger. "He was a hero to us because he was always on the front line, always moving ahead of everyone else," recalled Hamza Muhammad, a Palestinian volunteer in Afghanistan who now manages one of bin Laden's construction projects in Sudan. "He not only gave his money, but he also gave himself. He came down from his palace to live with the Afghan peasants and the Arab fighters. He cooked with them, ate with them, dug trenches with them. That was bin Laden's way."

From 1984 to 1988 bin Laden frequently accompanied Azzam on his trips into Afghanistan, where Azzam delivered fiery sermons to the mujahideen. Azzam's message was straightforward, and the essence of his message can be found in bin Laden's current call for a global jihad. Azzam said that the jihad in Afghanistan was an all-Islamic cause that concerned all Muslims around the world. All Muslims must fulfill their obligation of jihad both in global causes—such as Afghanistan—and in the defense of their oppressed Muslim brothers and sisters by fighting the un-Islamic regimes (meaning Muslim leaders who rule secular states) of their homelands. Both types of jihad were components of a greater drive—namely, establishing Allah's rule on earth. Islamists call the unified pan-Islamic state that rules the entire Hub of Islam, and ultimately the entire Muslim world, the Khilafah (Caliphate). To accomplish the noble mission of restoring the Khilafah, the Muslim world must focus on jihad, the armed struggle to establish Allah's rule. Azzam stressed that jihad must be carried out until the Khilafah is established wherever Muslims dwell so that "the light of Islam may shine on the whole world." Sheikh Azzam constantly reiterated his basic conviction that "Jihad must not be abandoned until Allah alone is worshiped. Jihad continues until Allah's word is raised high. Jihad until all the oppressed peoples are freed. Jihad to protect our dignity and restore our occupied lands. Jihad is the way of everlasting glory."

Throughout the 1980s Osama bin Laden maintained close relations with the Saudi ruling elite and particularly Saudi intelligence. He further developed his relationship with Prince Turki. Like his father, Osama became a conduit for the quiet flow of Saudi funds to deniable causes, this time, to the mujahideen in Afghanistan. Bin Laden personally handled the politically sensitive funding of the Islamist groups considered hostile to the House of al-Saud and other conservative regimes in Arabia. The cynically pragmatic Riyadh government was happy to see these Islamists operating in distant Afghanistan, and thus away from their homeland. Paying for their keep in distant Afghanistan was a cheap price for stability.

Also during the 1980s, the center Azzam and bin Laden established in Peshawar for channeling and directing the Arab volunteers to the Islamist resistance organizations continued to operate. Within a few years this center started organizing groups of volunteers who would be of use back in their home countries. For example, some of the 3,000 Algerians who fought in Afghanistan established their own "Algerian Legion," which fought under the command of Ahmad Shah Massud. Azzam was instrumental in cementing the Massud-Algerian mujahideen relations and brought to Massud the leading Algerian commander, known as Hajj Bunua. After Azzam's assassination, his children were sent to live with Massud for protection. During the early 1990s these Algerian "Afghans" spearheaded the exceptionally vicious and violent Islamist subversion in Algeria.

Azzam devoted much time and attention to the Islamists' cause in the United States, identifying a potential nucleus of educated believers capable of providing high-quality human resources for the jihad. Most important in this respect was Azzam's influence over the American volunteers in Peshawar. He spent much time with them to instill the spirit of jihad. Many of these volunteers were convinced of the importance of this "opportunity" to fulfill the sacred duty of jihad. For example, Abu Mahmud Hammoody, now living in Chicago, was so influenced by Azzam that he spent the next eight years fighting in several jihad causes from Afghanistan to Bosnia. "Sheikh AbdAllah knew when and where he had to implement his political and religious beliefs," explained Hammoody. After returning to the United States, many of Azzam's committed followers would establish cadres of "Afghans."

In the mid-1980s the presence of Arabs in Afghanistan, primarily Algerians, Libyans, Syrians, and Palestinians, increased to such a degree that the influence of the Arab Islamists became apparent even at the highest echelons of the mujahideen leadership. Because all of the leaders of the Palestine Liberation Organization (PLO) had been affiliated with the Muslim Brotherhood in their youth, the PLO was one of the first Palestinian organizations to recognize the emerging power and significance of radical Islamist terrorism. Yassir Arafat began using Islamic terminology in his speeches. In his October 15, 1985, speech in Khartoum, he said: "The Arab revolution is alive in the Arab conscience in spite of imperialist and Zionist conspiracies. . . . The holy war and the armed struggle will escalate. . . . I tell Reagan and his agents in our Arab world that the will of the Arab nation is from the will of Allah. Therefore, the Arab nations will be victorious."

Khalil al-Wazir, then Arafat's military chief, who is better known as Abu-Jihad, was one of the first to recognize Islamist terrorism as the wave of the future. He had al-Fatah (Arafat's own branch of the PLO) "adopt" the various branches of Islamic jihad in Israel, Jordan, and Lebanon. For example, the investigation of the May 1986 riots at al-Yarmuq University in Irbid, Jordan, determined that Khalil al-Wazir played a prominent role in organizing a secret alliance between the Jordanian branch of the Muslim Brotherhood and the local secret Communist party known as the Marxist Cells. He also provided the Jordanian Islamists with funds and arranged for joint terrorist training in PLO camps outside Jordan.

In 1986 the PLO started to send the most promising radicalized youth to advance training in mujahideen camps in Pakistan, where all the Islamist parties provided special training facilities. The Palestinians joined members of such organizations as the Egyptian Takfir wa-al-Hijra—Sadat's assassins—and the Syrian and Lebanese Muslim Brothers. Prompted by Abu-Jihad, the Muslim Brotherhood in Jordan also encouraged its members to go fight in Afghanistan.

Although the Arab mujahideen—especially Egyptians, Palestinians, and Jordanians—were provided with intensive training by ISI-sponsored camps, not all of them were sent to fight inside Afghanistan. Many would disappear soon after completing their training and subsequent practice period, groomed to become the elite cadres of Islamic international terrorism. These foreign volunteers received specialized training in such areas as the use of shoulder-fired SAMs and sabotage, especially the use of sophisticated remote-control detonators and advanced plastic explosives. They also underwent extensive Islamist indoctrination that made them devout and overcommitted. The role of such Palestinian trainees in the PLO–Islamic Jihad system was exposed with the arrest of a member of Islamic Jihad in

Israel in early August 1987. He was planning to set off a sophisticated car bomb in the middle of Jerusalem or Tel Aviv.

The Iranians were quick to react to the rise of pan-Islamist sentiments in Pakistan. In early December 1985 Ayatollah Ibrahim Amini, vice chairman of the Council of Experts of Iran, stated that Iran was "happy with the efforts being made in Pakistan to establish an Islamic system." Emphasizing the significance of the Iranian experience, and especially its pan-Islamic character, Amini encouraged the Pakistanis to follow a similar path. He underscored that "it is essential when setting up an Islamic system to avoid minor differences. One should act on the established tenets of Islam and on the question of prayers and fasting instead of quarrel over minor differences. . . . If we were to remain entangled in Shiite-Sunni differences, there would be no unity among Muslims." Amini was implying that Iran supported the Jamaat-i-Islami (Pakistan's main Islamist political party, with whose ideology Zia-ul-Haq identified) approach to the Islamization of Pakistan and added that since it was Iran's "religious and constitutional duty to go to the aid of all Muslim countries," Tehran would help the appropriate elements in Pakistan to accomplish its Islamization. With that, the road was opened for the massive flow of Iranian aid, initially through Gulbaddin Hekmatiyar's Jundullah terrorist organization. Jundullah was established as an offshoot of the ISI-sponsored Hizb-i Islami, which would interact with the Iranians without implicating Islamabad.

In Afghanistan and Pakistan the Islamist resistance organizations were clearly espousing the global message of their foreign "volunteers." In his commitment to achieving a utopian Muslim state, Gulbaddin Hekmatiyar appealed to the conservative Arab world, declaring that Hizb-i Islami "will not have achieved its goal with the fall of the Kabul regime. Even with a full Soviet withdrawal, Hizb-i Islami will continue the jihad until an Islamic state is established." Gulbaddin Hekmatiyar led Hizb-i Islami according to the tenets of the Muslim Brotherhood, which believed that in such a struggle, the fight against the apostates in house takes precedence over the fight against a foreign enemy. For jihad to be successful and the Islamic Revolution to be realized, the ranks of the mujahideen ought first to be purified from apostates and lackeys of imperialism. His zealous pursuit of this utopian idea brought Gulbaddin Hekmatiyar's Hizb-i Islami to fighting the other resistance groups, to betraying their leaders and weapons to the Soviets, and to reaching regional cease-fire compromises with the DRA authorities. In his pursuit of an extremist, ideal, long-range solution, Gulbaddin Hekmatiyar was susceptible to reaching "temporary" compromises with the infidels, contributing to the containment and ultimate suppression of the genuine Afghan resistance. The Soviets manipulated and exploited Gulbaddin Hekmatiyar's Hizb-i Islami primarily through the numerous agents in his own military council, which included representatives not only from the Muslim Brotherhood but also from Libya, Iran, and the PLO. In the mid-1980s Gulbaddin Hekmatiyar was known to have visited Libya and Iran and was rumored to have visited the PDRY. For as long as Hizb-i Islami continued to suppress the nationalist and ethnically based mujahideen organizations in Afghanistan, Gulbaddin Hekmatiyar continued to receive the bulk of the Pakistani, Saudi, and American support despite his involvement in fratricidal fighting.

A corresponding ideological development in Indian Kashmir started in about 1984. The prevailing popular sentiment in Indian Kashmir had suddenly become "Islam is in danger," and that sentiment, rather than nationalism, began motivating the Kashmiri youth. By then the ISI's vast training infrastructure, ostensibly for the Afghan resistance, was bringing together numerous regional groups while instilling a sense of camaraderie and mutual solidarity as well as loyalty to Pakistan. It was not long before Afghan terrorists were smuggled into India with the purpose of organizing local terrorist forces. The first Afghans were captured in Kashmir in early 1984.

By the late 1980s the ISI program had initiated a full-fledged subversion in the Kashmir Valley. With the war in Afghanistan slowing down, the vast network of training camps for Afghan mujahideen all over Pakistan was being transformed by the ISI into a center for Islamist terrorism throughout South Asia as well as a melting pot for the Sunni jihad. Initially the emphasis was on using the Afghan support infrastructure in Pakistan to sponsor the Kashmiri militants. During the main escalation of Islamist violence in Indian Kashmir in mid-1988, Pakistan provided assistance in the training and arming of Kashmiri terrorists and offered sanctuary to Kashmiri insurgents across the border. At times the ISI's assistance to the Kashmiri Islamists was funneled through Gulbaddin Hekmatiyar's Hizb-i Islami, thus providing Islamabad with deniability. Ten years later, in the late 1990s, Afghans and Pakistanis constituted the majority of high-quality militants killed and captured by the Indian security forces in Kashmir.

Throughout the 1980s the availability of weapons, primarily from supplies to the Afghan resistance, turned Karachi into a center for Islamic international terrorism involving Palestinians and "a large number of people from Bangladesh, India, Nepal, Afghanistan, Burma, Thailand, Sri Lanka, the Philippines, and Africa who live in Karachi as 'Muslims,'" lamented Dr. Yasin Rizvi, a leading Pakistani journalist. All of them provided an excellent manpower pool for audacious sabotage and terrorist operations.

Because the ISI training infrastructure had also provided training to other Islamist terrorists, mainly Arab, this joint training and in many cases fighting in Afghanistan created bonds between the various Islamists that evolved into close cooperation between their organizations. Middle Eastern militant organizations have actively supported the Kashmiri Islamists since the late 1980s. For example, two Pakistan-sponsored Kashmiri organizations—the Hizb-ul Mujahideen and the armed branch of the Ikhwan al-Muslimeen—receive support and expertise from "brethren from Palestine" in their fight against India. These forms of cooperation and mutual assistance in the Islamist insurgency and terrorism campaign in Kashmir are important in view of the continued evolution and internationalization of the terrorist training infrastructure in Pakistan.

On August 17, 1988, Pakistani president Zia-ul-Haq, along with U.S. ambassador Arnold Raphel, the U.S. military attaché, ISI chief General Akhtar Abdul Rahman, and twenty-eight others were killed when the C-130B Hercules they had just taken off in suddenly crashed. Widely considered one of the most effective strategic covert operations conducted by the Soviet Union, this "crash" also drastically changed the world of international Islamist terrorism.

Benazir Bhutto, who became the prime minister of Pakistan in 1989, had a profoundly different perception of the role and utility of Islamist terrorism. Convinced that Pakistan's destiny lay in strategic alliances with such countries as Syria, Iran, the People's Republic of China (PRC), and North Korea, Benazir Bhutto's Islamabad reexamined all aspects of Pakistan's involvement in Afghanistan, and the world of state-sponsored terrorism became an instrument of crucial significance for Pakistan's policy. Islamabad now committed to furthering Islamism in the heart of Asia, seeing it as the sole ideology capable of containing and reversing the breakup of Pakistan along ethno-national lines. Consequently, the ISI's support for and sponsorship of sisterly Islamist terrorist movements throughout the Arab world became a cornerstone of Pakistan's national security policies. Because the targeted conservative Arab regimes, such as the regime in Saudi Arabia, enjoyed special relations with the United States, Islamabad recognized the growing specter of confrontation with the United States over strategic posture in the region. Still Islamabad shifted to active support for militant Islamism.

This change was immediately apparent in the ISI's relations with the Arab Islamist terrorist organizations. General Hamid Gul, the new chief of the ISI, introduced the new policies. In the fall of 1988 the ISI instructed all Pakistani legations to issue "special tourist" visas to any Islamist aspiring to fight in the Afghan jihad. These "visas" were provided, frequently along with paid airline tickets, to volunteers who lacked proper travel documents as well as to those who gave false names and were wanted by their governments for terrorism and subversion. At that time the Soviet Union was already implementing the international agreement on the withdrawal of Soviet forces from Afghanistan under conditions of cease-fire. The overt Soviet withdrawal was completed on February 15, 1989. While the ISI was actively courting and recruiting foreign Islamists, the Afghan jihad was actually dwindling.

Between 16,000 and 20,000 Islamist militants from twenty countries arrived in Pakistan during the late 1980s. Most of them were Arab Islamists, but many were from such diverse places as the Philippines and Malaysia, and there was as well a trickle of Bosnian Muslims and Kosovo Albanians from then Yugoslavia. Virtually all of these were Islamists committed to the liberation of their own countries and the establishment of Islamist regimes there. Unlike the volunteers of the early to mid-1980s, these newcomers had no real interest in helping the liberation of Afghanistan. They came to be trained, and the ISI was happy to oblige.

This new attitude amounted to a profound change in Pakistan's Afghanistan policy. The turning point was the major offensive on Jalalabad in March 1989, just a month after the Soviet withdrawal. Convinced by Pakistan that a major military effort by the mujahideen would result in the collapse of the DRA's hold over Kabul, the United States and Saudi Arabia provided massive help for this final push. Instead of coordinating a sophisticated campaign befitting the light irregular forces of the Afghan mujahideen, the ISI pushed the Afghan resistance to a major attack on the DRA's fortified defenses and large artillery forces in Jalalabad. Islamabad knew that such a frontal assault could only result in massive carnage of the attackers, who were not tightly controlled by Pakistan. As a result the Afghan resistance that had endured almost a decade of fighting the Soviet-DRA forces was so decimated, it could no longer constitute a viable fighting force. The road was open for Islamabad to organize and field its own "mujahideen" force, now known as the Taliban.

Osama bin Laden and many of his Arab mujahideen friends participated in the battle for Jalalabad. He witnessed and experienced the massive and essentially needless slaughter of dedicated mujahideen. Returning from Jalalabad to Peshawar, the Arab mujahideen shared their anger and sense of betrayal with Sheikh Azzam.

An infuriated Azzam began speaking up. His primary message was to urge the rejuvenation of the spirit of jihad. He reminded his listeners of their commitment to the all-Muslim causes that began with the liberation of Afghanistan. As they were deliberating the meaning of the mujahideen's failure to march on Kabul despite the Soviet withdrawal, Azzam, bin Laden, and other Islamist leaders concluded that they were victims of a U.S.

conspiracy implemented through the Pakistanis. The United States, they reasoned, was committed to the defeat of the Islamist jihad in Afghanistan and anywhere else because the ascent of Islam was endangering its power and affluence.

Azzam's most potent message was his call for the revival of the old spirit of the Afghan jihad, which envisioned a defiant struggle based on utopian theological guidelines, a message now contradictory to the ISI's priority of maintaining control in handling the Afghan, Kashmiri, and all other mujahideen-cum-terrorists. Azzam's stature in Peshawar made him a dangerous threat.

On November 24, 1989, a sophisticated and powerful bomb activated by remote control exploded underneath Azzam's car in a narrow street in Peshawar. Azzam, two of his sons, and a companion were killed on the spot. To date, nobody has claimed responsibility for the assassination. At the time there were persistent reports among the Peshawar rumor mills that the assassination was the work of a Hizb-i Islami special detachment usually controlled by the ISI, but no proof was provided.

Sheikh Azzam had been silenced, but his message would live on through his loyal disciples. One of the closest was Osama bin Laden.

———————

BY THE LATE 1980S the world of international terrorism was changing. The camps of the Afghan resistance in Pakistan actually became the center of radical Islamist terrorism, with Sunni Islamists constituting the majority of the fighters. Traditionalist radical Islam was rising throughout the Muslim world as a popular reaction of the believers to the pressures of the modern world and especially relations with the West. The building frustration of the Muslim masses led to the emergence of a dedicated militant vanguard with an unprecedented commitment to the cause of reviving traditionalist Islam. In their religious zeal, these believers became so devoted to their cause that they disregarded their own lives, the extent of carnage they inflicted on their victims, and the overall consequences of their actions.

The emergence of a new generation of Islamist terrorists from the mujahideen camps in Afghanistan and Pakistan coincided with the decline of the other major terrorist movements in the Muslim world. In the 1980s radical Arab terrorism was slowly collapsing. Although the refugee camps and the slums of the Middle East were still a source of radicalized youth, the Palestinian progressive revolutionary movement—its terrorist organizations—had failed to cultivate and mold a younger generation of commanders and leaders to take over from the old masters. These men were growing old and incapacitated, and leaders were being assassinated by both friends and foes. The failure of the Palestinian Revolution and the absence of a new generation of charismatic leaders meant that radicalized and frustrated youth were diverted from the socialist-nationalist movements into the fold of traditionalist radical Islam. In the ranks of traditionalist Islam the believers were finding young charismatic leaders, divine guidance, and self-assurance of high rewards in eternity. The suffering and frustration of this world were presented as trials on the road to martyrdom and paradise, so that the more the believer suffered and sacrificed, the better his eternal reward. The radicalized youth were joining the banner of Islamism in unprecedented numbers, and radical Islamist terrorism became the wave of the future.

In the quest for Islamist violence the camps of the Islamist Afghan resistance in Pakistan became to Sunni Islamist terrorism what Lebanon had been for radical leftist terrorism. Pakistan became a place of pilgrimage for aspiring Islamist radicals. Islamist terrorists had always considered semi-autonomy—a sort of a state-within-a state—as the ideal circumstance for their training and center of operations. The most devout and radicalized were challenging the concept of an Islamic state under contemporary conditions; during the 1980s all the Sunni states were considered apostate entities and thus enemies. The Afghan community was conducting a jihad in pursuit of a utopian Islamic entity and so was closest to a true Islamic community that could harbor and support radical militant Islam. This autonomy also had some practical benefits, such as reduced dependence on governments and their intelligence services and a feeling of accomplishment and independence. By the late 1980s the Afghan camps in Pakistan had already turned into the center of Islamist terrorism, the melting pot of the Sunni jihad. As the center of gravity of Islamist terrorism shifted to "holy terror," the significance of the Pakistani Afghan infrastructure increased.

For Osama bin Laden the carnage in Jalalabad and the assassination of Azzam constituted a grim ending to an otherwise exhilarating decade. Having experienced and contributed to the emergence of a genuine all-Islamist jihad, he now witnessed its demise in the hands of cynical politicians. But the events of 1989 could not erase his conviction, reinforced by Azzam's preaching, in the importance of all-Islamic causes and the pursuit of jihad both against the enemies of Islam and for the liberation of Muslims. Still, with the withdrawal of the Soviet forces, his mission in Afghanistan seemed completed and bin Laden decided to return to Saudi Arabia.

2

Crisis and Rebirth

IN 1989 OSAMA BIN LADEN returned to Saudi Arabia a hero. He was a wiser man, hardened by experience. His political and social views, however, were more radical. Many of the Arab "Afghans" and indigenous Afghans he had helped in Afghanistan viewed him as a leader. The Saudi government considered him a positive role model, proof of its contribution to the immensely popular Afghan jihad.

The praise and media attention made bin Laden a sought-after celebrity. He spoke at countless mosques and private gatherings. Some of his fiery speeches were recorded; well over a quarter of a million official cassettes were sold and countless illegal—and later, underground—copies were also made and distributed.

Bin Laden described Islam's great triumphs against the infidel superpower, arguing that the Afghan jihad demonstrated that nothing and nobody could stop the Muslim Nation once it was committed to the righteous practice of Islam. The House of al-Saud, which defines its right to power and the legitimacy of that power through its role as the custodian of the two holy shrines of Islam, was pleased with the message. Claiming that it was striving to establish a just Islamic way of life, Riyadh capitalized on the Islamist message to enhance its own posture. Riyadh's pleasure with Osama was manifested financially as the bin Laden businesses received numerous government and private contracts.

Meanwhile Osama bin Laden tried to readjust after a decade of jihad. He resumed working for the Jeddah branch of the family's construction firm, moved his own family to a modest apartment, and attempted to personally practice the Islamic way of life he advocated. For a while, he seemed to have settled down.

Then on August 2, 1990, Iraq invaded Kuwait. Although Saddam Hussein promised in a series of messages to King Fahd and other leading princes that he had no intention of invading Saudi Arabia, there was panic in Riyadh. The kingdom was defenseless and exposed to an Iraqi onslaught. The flow of Kuwaiti refugees into Saudi Arabia, led by the emir and his household, only exacerbated the hysteria in Riyadh.

Osama bin Laden immediately went to Riyadh and offered his help to the government. He met with Prince Sultan, the Saudi minister of defense, and presented him with a detailed ten-page plan for the self-defense of the kingdom. He argued that the heavy engineering equipment then available to the large construction companies like his family's could be mobilized to quickly build fortifications to defend Saudi Arabia. He also suggested bolstering Saudi forces with a hard core of combat-hardened Saudi "Afghans," whom he was willing to recruit. He repeated this last offer to Prince Turki, the chief of intelligence, adding that the Saudi "Afghans" could also be used as the core of a popular jihad in Kuwait.

He argued passionately in Riyadh that if the Muslim Nation could evict the Soviet Union from Afghanistan, it certainly could defeat Saddam Hussein and that as Muslims, the individual Iraqi soldiers would not resist a jihadist force. Bin Laden also warned Riyadh against inviting or permitting "infidel" forces into the sacred land of Saudi Arabia because such an invitation would contradict the teachings of Islam and would have a profound impact on the sensitivities of most Saudis—and Muslims as a whole. At this stage of the crisis, Osama bin Laden intervened as a concerned but fiercely loyal citizen.

While for Americans and their Western allies the Gulf War was waged over control of the Persian Gulf's oil reserves and the freedom of Kuwait, for the Muslim world the war was fought over the future of political Islam. Through the occupation of Kuwait and the overthrow of its royal family, Saddam Hussein sought to secure the dominance of his brand of nationalist Arabism over that of conservative regimes like Saudi Arabia's. For the House of al-Saud, the key to long-term victory lay not only in defeating Iraq but also in ensuring its Islamic legitimacy. But bin Laden warned that in accepting foreign—non-Muslim—forces, Saudi Arabia would hurt its long-standing Islamic legitimacy. Fully aware of the Islamist zeal and commitment he had encountered in Afghanistan, bin Laden knew, and warned Riyadh, that the militant Islamists would not overlook what they considered Riyadh's transgressions of the sacred principles of Islam. He argued that the House of al-Saud should prioritize and concentrate on securing their long-term Islamic legitimacy even when facing an immediate threat from Iraq.

But Osama bin Laden was ignored. King Fahd and his coterie panicked at the sight of the Iraqi forces streaming into Kuwait. Riyadh opened the gates for the flow of U.S.-led coalition forces that in early 1991 defeated Iraq in the Gulf War. United States forces have stayed in Saudi Arabia ever since.

Osama bin Laden was not the only member of the Saudi elite who strenuously objected to inviting U.S. forces. In early August 1990 King Fahd asked the ulema—the country's senior religious leaders—to endorse the deployment of U.S. forces. "All the senior ulema were categorically against the idea," a Saudi official said in a study by exiled Saudi scholar Nawaf Obaid. "It was only after long discussions with the King that Grand Mufti Sheikh Abdul-Aziz Bin Baz reluctantly gave his endorsement to the idea on condition that solid proof be presented as to the [Iraqi] threat." Meanwhile the Saudi high command insisted they were unable to protect the kingdom against an Iraqi thrust. After Defense Secretary Dick Cheney promised that U.S. troops would not stay in Saudi Arabia "a minute longer than they were needed," the king persuaded a meeting of 350 ulema at Mecca to reluctantly agree to the temporary presence of U.S. forces—just until the crisis was over. Word of this conflict between the Saudi Court and the ulema spread like wildfire throughout the Islamist circles of Saudi Arabia.

Rejected by Riyadh but emboldened by growing popular support, Osama bin Laden found a place in the tidal wave of anti-Americanism swelling through the Islamist communities all over the Muslim world. Still in Saudi Arabia, bin Laden adopted a middle way. On the one hand, he condemned Iraq for invading Kuwait and urged its eviction by force. At the same time he harshly criticized the presence of U.S. and other foreign forces in Saudi Arabia as a sacrilegious act. His call for action concentrated on such civic deeds as the boycott of U.S. goods. "When we buy American goods, we are accomplices in the murder of Palestinians," he argued in one recorded speech. "American companies make millions in the Arab world with which they pay taxes to their government. The United States uses that money to send $3 billion a year to Israel, which it uses to kill Palestinians." But bin Laden did not attack the House of al-Saud in these speeches.

In not challenging the House of al-Saud, bin Laden separated himself from the vast majority of Islamists at the time. Most of the Islamist leaders, including such veterans of Afghanistan as Sheikh Tamimi, rallied to the support of Saddam Hussein. They argued that confronting the United States—the archenemy of Islam—was of higher priority than protecting Kuwait. By siding with the United States and inviting foreign armies to the sacred lands of Arabia, these Islamists argued, the House of al-Saud effectively abdicated its legitimate rights as custodians of the holy shrines. Among the most eloquent and authoritative advocates of this position were many colleagues and allies of bin Laden from his Afghanistan days. But Osama bin Laden remained a loyal subject of the Saudi Crown. He was convinced that the House of al-Saud, whose uppermost echelons he personally knew, could still restore its Islamic legitimacy by evicting the Americans and other foreign forces. He was still willing to consider the possibility that Riyadh had succumbed to immense U.S. pressure and had panicked and willing to believe that once convinced of its safety, Riyadh would return to the righteous Islamic path. As this was a viable option, and also because the king was the custodian of the holy shrines, Osama bin Laden remained a loyal subject to his king.

Incapable of confronting any criticism, Riyadh did not bother to distinguish between bin Laden's position and that of other Islamists. All that mattered to the House of al-Saud was bin Laden's immense popularity, which made him a threat, and so official Riyadh put tremendous pressure on Osama bin Laden to halt his criticism. Saudi officials first warned bin Laden that his lucrative contracts would be canceled and, when this threat did not work, that all his property would be expropriated by Riyadh. They then threatened his extended family—his father, brothers, in-laws, and other relatives—in order to silence him. Saudi officials again threatened to sever the family's unique ties with the Court and push the entire family business into bankruptcy. At the same time, however, Saudi intelligence continued to maintain contacts with Osama bin Laden to make sure he did not cross over to the anti-Saudi subversive movement and to ask favors from him, mainly to reach out to segments in the vast network of "Afghans" and like-minded Islamists all over the world on their behalf. Riyadh knew that if bin Laden joined the Islamist movement, it would be given a tremendous boost at the grassroots level because of his immense popularity, a supposition that was eventually proved right.

Once the Gulf War ended and Saudi Arabia decided to permit the permanent stationing of foreign forces on Saudi soil, official Riyadh no longer had any use for Osama bin Laden. Committed to the retention of forces from the United States and Western Europe on its soil, Riyadh knew there could be no compromise with him. From the beginning of the crisis, bin Laden had warned that Riyadh would have to choose between short-term "security" and long-term Islamic legitimacy. The House of al-Saud had opted for the former, knowing full well that this would alienate the Islamists, including Osama bin Laden. The pressure that had been put on him turned to outright hostility. With Riyadh's belligerence mounting and fearing for the well-being of his extended family, Osama bin Laden and his family went into exile in the new haven of revivalist Islamism—Hassan al-Turabi's Sudan.

WHEN OSAMA BIN LADEN arrived in Sudan, Hassan Abdallah al-Turabi was already the country's spiritual leader. He had risen to that position in the aftermath of the June 30, 1989, military coup that brought General Omar al-Bashir to power. A devout Muslim, Bashir has been trying to impose an Islamist regime on Sudan, although his efforts have been undermined by a bitter civil war in the south, a collapsing economy, and public discontent. With Bashir's support, Turabi, one of the greatest luminaries of Islamist thought, has emerged as the ideologue and guide of the Sudanese regime.

Hassan Abdallah al-Turabi was born in February 1932 in Kassala, eastern Sudan, to a religiously active and pious family. His father, although a merchant, was a scholar of Islam. He was also a modernist, and the family had a history of anti-imperialist activism while the country was under British rule. His father's dualism, moving between Islamism and Westernized modernity, determined Hassan al-Turabi's education and ultimate outlook. He received a secular formal education in a series of English-language schools in western and central Sudan and was educated by his father in the Koran, based on the teachings at al-Azhar University in Cairo. His father also taught him and led him to love classic Arab culture and traditional Arab poetry. Turabi then attended British-run Gordon College in Khartoum and graduated in 1955 with a law degree. From 1951 on, he was a clandestine member of the Khartoum branch of the Egyptian Muslim Brotherhood. A natural leader, he quickly became the head of the university's Islamic Liberation Movement, an activist offshoot of the Muslim Brotherhood.

Turabi's piety and immersion in Islamism did not close his mind to Western culture. Unlike many of his peers throughout the Middle East, he did not fear exposure to and interaction with the West. When he won a scholarship to the University of London in 1955, he traveled to the United Kingdom, and in 1957 he earned a master's degree in law. Then in 1959 he won a scholarship to the Sorbonne, where he completed his doctorate in 1964. Turabi is fluent in both English and French and well versed in Western culture. During his stay in Europe he traveled throughout Europe and the United States, and he still travels extensively.

Back in Sudan in the mid-1960s, Turabi returned to Islamist politics. He established the Islamic Charter Front (ICF), a coalition of Islamist individuals and groups he would use interchangeably with the Muslim Brotherhood to further his political causes and public campaigns. The ICF was the first example of his propensity to advance major issues by building wide coalitions that are unified by basic objectives and common denominators. In the coming decades Turabi would move back and forth between two situations: Sometimes he would be in a position of power in government, and sometimes he would assume the posture of a righteous opposition figure untarnished by association with military dictatorships. During this period he wrote and published numerous political and religious works. He maintained a high profile and gained great fame in Islamist intellectual circles as a leading authority on political Islam, the relations between Islamic revivalism, and the modern state. In the 1980s he was preoccupied with the reconciliation between the Sharia, Islam's traditional law and the legal-legislative demands of the modern state.

It was natural that General Bashir invited Turabi to help formulate the running of an Islamist military dictatorship. Turabi rose to the challenge, turning Sudan into the world's center of Sunni Islamist revivalism. Whatever doubts Turabi might have felt about adopting a confrontational attitude toward the West dissipated in the aftermath of the Gulf War.

The period between 1991 and 1993—Osama bin Laden's formative years in Sudan—was critical for the Sunni Islamist movement. The Muslim world was slowly recovering from the shock of what is known in the West as the Gulf War. For the Muslim world, it was a traumatic experience in which the sacred all-Muslim unity was so shattered that Arab-Muslim states joined ranks with the hated West to fight and defeat another Arab-Muslim state. Not surprisingly, the Islamists call this period *al-Azma*—"the Crisis"—a calamity for Islam and its believers second only to *al-Naqba*— "the Holocaust"—the establishment of the state of Israel. The Islamists argued that it was clearly demonstrated during the Crisis that regimes as hated and corrupt as Saudi Arabia's and Kuwait's survived only because of the West's commitment to saving its own puppets by all means, including the massive use of force. The only viable strategy for the vanguard of believers was to take on the West, and especially the United States, in order to assert their divine right to establish Islamist societies and governments throughout the Hub of Islam.

Turabi has been instrumental in translating this doctrine into action. Since fall 1991, and more so since spring 1992, there has been a fundamental, if not historic, evolution in Islamist terrorism, subversion, and violence. This evolution has led to an unprecedented escalation in the Islamist jihad against the Judeo-Christian world order. The Islamists envision the climax of this struggle to be an apocalyptic spate of violence throughout the West. At the core of this new phenomenon was the integration of Sunni terrorist networks into the new Islamist International, the umbrella organization of the various "jihadist" organizations that operate within the theological framework of the International Muslim Brotherhood (IMB). Controlled and sponsored by Iran and run via Sudan under the leadership of Sheikh Turabi, the Islamist International is the realization of Ayatollah Khomeini's original vision of an ecumenical all-Islamic revolution that does not distinguish between Sunnis and Shiites.

The Shiites, who constitute about 15 percent of the world's Muslims, separated from the Sunni majority in the late seventh century in the aftermath of a bitter struggle over the succession of Prophet Muhammad. There are profound differences between Shiites and Sunnis concerning the propagation of revolutionary Islam toward the establishment of the caliphate in the modern era. The Sunni doctrine, first defined by Egyptian Sayyid Muhammad Qutb in the 1950s, stipulates that since the nation-state is an inescapable reality, Islamist movements should first establish Islamic governments in individual countries and then unite the countries into a single caliphate. The Shiite doctrine, which evolved in the mid-1940s, argues that since the nation-state is an un-Islamic entity, it is not a valid consideration for the propagation of Islam. Legitimate Islamist leaders, such as Khomeini, have the right and obligation to actively support all Islamist revolutions and to strike out against their enemies—mainly the United States—in the name of Islamic solidarity. This determination is behind the Iranian sponsorship of and support for numerous Islamist terrorist and subversive organizations.

Addressing the question of the Islamist revolution in the modern era, Turabi argued that the various subversive movements in the Middle East were no longer facing local governments but rather regimes that were puppets of and propped up by the United States. In their effort to topple these regimes and establish Islamic states in their stead, the Islamists were actually confronting the United States. And so it became legitimate to strike out all over the world by means of international terrorism to compel the United States and the West to abandon their puppets in the Middle East. Given the duality of the threat—the American presence and influence—the various national Islamist movements should combine their efforts against their common enemy. This principle cleared the way for the emergence of alliances of Sunni terrorist groups and organizations operating throughout the world in the pursuit of all-Islamist causes.

In the early 1990s this doctrinal evolution was more than theoretical contemplation; it was being implemented through the Islamist International. The terrorist and militant arm of the new Islamist International is the Armed Islamic Movement (AIM). Popularly known as the "International Legion of Islam," AIM spearheads the new international terrorism wave. The leading terrorists are commonly known as "Afghans." Most of them trained with the mujahideen in Pakistan, and some also fought in Afghanistan. Since the early 1990s the Islamist Legion has been sending its mujahideen all over Asia, Africa, Europe, and the United States to support, further, incite, and facilitate what the leadership considers Islamic liberation struggles. Affiliated Islamist groups and organizations are at present active all over the world, in essence wherever Muslims live. The Islamists have bases and support facilities in Sudan, Iran, Afghanistan, and Pakistan, where they receive advanced military, terrorist, clandestine, and subversion training from an international cadre of expert trainers. The Islamist terrorists deploy to their destination via Tehran, Khartoum, and Islamabad.

During his formative years in Sudan, Osama bin Laden made major contributions to the rise of this new Islamist International and particularly AIM. At this phase he was a major facilitator of events—not yet the theological and ideological authority that he is today.

———

GENERAL BASHIR'S RISE to power in a military coup in June 1989 was by far not just another Middle Eastern military coup but a major strategic event. Bashir's determination to impose an Islamist regime in Sudan—an impoverished, underdeveloped state immersed in a fratricidal civil war—resulted in a drastic change in the strategic posture of East Africa.

Soon after he seized power, Bashir invited Turabi for consultations on Sudan's role in furthering the spread of the Islamist revolution. Following these discussions, Turabi notified the leadership of the International Muslim Brotherhood that it had a firm hold in Sudan. The IMB leaders met in London in early August 1989 and decided to transform Sudan into a base and safe haven for Islamist movements in the Arab world, Africa, and Asia. Bashir's Khartoum and the IMB reached an agreement in which Sudan would become a "springboard to Arab and African countries" in return for substantial financial assistance. Toward this end an IMB leadership board of nineteen members was established in Khartoum under Turabi at the London meeting.

Striving to acquire an Islamist character, Sudan had shifted allies and benefactors. But the ensuing transformation of Sudan from a Libyan-Iraqi ally into an Iranian fiefdom was not simply a change in hegemony. Because of the character of both the military regime in Khartoum and the Sudanese Islamist movement, it was a profound process with far-reaching ideological ramifications for the entire Muslim world. By the early 1990s Sudan was ready to become an active outpost for the dissemination of a Khomeini-style Islamist revolution.

Sudan's profound shift toward Iran occurred in the early spring of 1991, in the wake of the Gulf Crisis and particularly because of Saddam Hussein's failure to conduct the genuine jihad he had promised to wage. Turabi stepped into the vacuum at the top of the Islamist militant movement, declaring the creation of "a universal framework for the Islamic movement." The Islamic Arab Peoples' Conference (IAPC), one of Turabi's grandiose but effective coalitions, was established in Khartoum from April 25 to 28, 1991, with Turabi as the permanent leader. As would subsequently often be true for milestone events, the key decisions were made in a closed meeting at Turabi's home in Manshiyah, Khartoum, on the eve of the conference. The actual conference was a congress of terrorist organizations and popular Islamist movements from fifty-five countries. It was the first serious attempt to coordinate a Sunni Islamist assault against both the conservatives of the Muslim world and the West in revenge for the war with Iraq.

The conference in Khartoum also established the first real Sunni Islamist revolutionary international, called the Popular International Organization (PIO). Turabi stressed in his address that the PIO's objective "is to work out a global action plan in order to challenge and defy the tyrannical West, because Allah can no longer remain in our world, in the face of the absolute materialistic power." The PIO established in Khartoum a permanent council comprising fifty members, each of whom represented one of the fifty countries where Islamic liberation struggles were taking place.

Tehran was duly impressed with the zeal and commitment displayed during the Islamic Arab Peoples' Conference and offered Turabi professional help to expedite the spread of the Islamist revolution. Most important was the Iranian assistance in establishing a headquarters for the PIO. Toward this end, Colonel al-Fatih Urwah of Sudanese intelligence traveled to Tehran within days after the conference. Returning to Khartoum, he brought back advanced communications systems, including electronic jamming equipment, donated by Tehran so that the PIO could facilitate secure communications with the numerous Islamist movements. Clandestine techniques and communication codes were also implemented in Khartoum by newly arrived experts from Iran and the HizbAllah and by Egyptians who had defected from the Mukhabarat (the Egyptian intelligence service).

With the help of Iranian experts and veteran Arab terrorists, including "Afghans," Sudan began upgrading the training provided in local camps to include preparations for spectacular operations. Most important were the preparations made for long-term terrorist operations in Western Europe, starting in summer 1991. The two most important training sites were the al-Shambat and al-Mazraah camps, where terrorists from Tunisia, Algeria, France, and Belgium received advanced training. The subjects taught in these camps included small arms, self-defense, explosives, ambushes, manufacture of explosives from local materials, topography, and use of night-vision equipment. Specialized training for Egyptian and other Islamist terrorists was developed by Abbud al-Zumur, an Egyptian former military intelligence officer then in jail in Egypt for his role in the assassination of Sadat, who continued to lead a branch of Islamic jihad and delivered his instructions via Pakistan. In one set of instructions smuggled from an Egyptian jail and distributed via Pakistan, Zumur addressed professional criteria for running international terrorist operations. To enable the terrorists to operate in Westernized society, Zumur's instructions stressed professional clandestine functioning, including having the members "wear ordinary clothes like jeans, shave their beards, and hang out in cafés." The training included elaborate instructions in counterintelligence and clandestine techniques.

Tehran was also generous in its overt recognition of Turabi and the new international organizations he had just created. On October 18, 1991, Iran convened the International Conference in Support of the Islamic Revolution of the People of Palestine, with more than 400 delegates from forty-five to sixty countries attending. The PIO attended the conference as an important member of the Islamic revolutionary movement, and several PIO-affiliated leaders, including Turabi, were seated in prominent positions during the proceedings. The PIO's terrorist and subversive groups were accepted into the Tehran-led and -sponsored system of international terrorism without challenging Turabi's supreme leadership from a religious point of view. Shiite Iran thus endorsed the uniquely Sunni character of the PIO, which impressed Turabi and his aides. Further coordination and cooperation with Iran were promised. Immediately after the conference Iranian intelligence dispatched three delegations of experts to numerous Asian, Arab, and African countries to follow up on the financial, political, and economic decisions adopted at the conference and expedite the escalation of the Islamist struggle.

Despite the Iranian hospitality, Turabi and his aides were shocked by the wide professional gap between the terrorist organizations controlled by Iran and Syria and their own PIO. As zealous and committed as they were, the Sunni Islamists had no real knowledge of such crucial aspects of international terrorism as organizing clandestine work, building secure cells, fighting the state's security forces, organizing operations, building sophisticated bombs, or organizing assassinations. They also lacked knowledge about operating outside of their country, especially in the West. Immediately after returning from Tehran on October 23, Turabi convened a forty-member ad-hoc council for a critical strategy-formulation session. He acknowledged that the Islamist drive had so far failed to deliver the anticipated results. At the same time, before the turmoil in the Middle East subsided, the need to escalate Islamist struggles would be even more urgent, especially in countries such as Egypt. Turabi assured the council that "there was no going back on the policy of giving assistance to the soldiers of Muhammad in Egypt, and that Islam is coming eventually, no matter what." The support already given to the mujahideen in Egypt, one of Turabi's priority projects since 1990, would be increased. Turabi's concluding remarks emphasized the importance of the relations with Iran to Sudan's security and the Islamist revolutionary movement worldwide.

Turabi then started work to improve the leadership, command, and control elements of the Islamist movement. In late 1991 he established a supreme council for the PIO and the IMB in Khartoum. Some 350 Islamist functionaries, professionals, and leaders from several countries who were residing in Khartoum were identified and invited to undertake specialized training so that they could contribute to the Islamists' worldwide struggle. Osama bin Laden was one of those invited to contribute skills and expertise to Turabi's PIO, and over the next few years bin Laden would make crucial contributions to the expansion of the Islamist terrorist movement. Turabi took note of bin Laden and drew him closer, sharing with bin Laden his thoughts about the role and future of the Islamist trend and contributing to bin Laden's intellectual development.

By late 1991 Iran had moved boldly and consolidated a strategic alliance with Sudan. Both countries already enjoyed very good relations and close cooperation on such issues as defense and support for Islamist terrorism. However, once Turabi defined the theological compromise between Qutubism (the doctrines of the Sunni Egyptian Sayyid Muhammad Qutb, 1906–66) and Khomeinism (the teachings of the Shiite Iranian Ayatollah Khomeini, 1902–89) on the role of Islam as the supreme force in the modern world and applied the compromise to the Islamist revolutionary process, the road was open for a close and genuine alliance. The final consolidation of this strategic alliance, which made Sudan Iran's fiefdom, was completed in mid-December during a visit to Khartoum by a 157-member Iranian delegation led by Iranian president Ali Akbar Hashemi-Rafsanjani and including the foreign minister, minister of defense, chief of intelligence, chief of the Islamic Revolutionary Guards Corps (IRGC), minister of construction jihad, minister of commerce, and head of the budget office. They signed several agreements to cooperate in the areas of defense and terrorism and an economic agreement specifying that Iran would provide oil, food, and diversified economic assistance. Taken together, these agreements would expedite the transformation of Sudan into an Iranian puppet. In early 1992 Sudan emerged as a strategic outpost and key part of the infrastructure for Iran's export of the Islamic Revolution throughout the Near East and Africa. Khartoum was committed to its role in Tehran's grand design.

Given the still wide qualitative gap between the Iranian-sponsored terrorist movement and Sudan's fledgling counterpart, Tehran resolved to examine how well the October conference resolutions were being implemented and to review the preparations for the Islamist jihad. In early February 1992 Tehran convened an international conference attended by eighty senior participants from twenty terrorist organizations. The terrorist conference was held under the guise of commemorating the Ten Days of Dawn—the victory of the Iranian Revolution. The terrorist leaders met with senior officials of Iranian intelligence, security services, the IRGC, Islamic propaganda organizations, the Shahid foundation (a government-run foundation that finances Islamist quasi-legal activities such as humanitarian and social infrastructure for militant organizations), and the Imam's foundation (then Khomeini's own source of funding of special and important projects such as terrorist and subversive activities directed at the heart of the West). Together they formulated a combined joint doctrine for the future of jihad and decided on the means for its implementation. The terrorist leaders agreed on ways to reorganize and improve their organizations and methods for enhancing their capabilities, steps that would be taken immediately with full and generous Iranian financing.

Meanwhile the Iranian buildup in and supply of weapons to Sudan continued to grow. By spring 1992 the Iranian expertise and know-how were being felt. Turabi and his deputy Ali Uthman Taha made secret visits to Tehran, the last in early February, and asked for increased assistance. Tehran agreed to provide training for the Sudanese intelligence in military and interrogation techniques. Iran also agreed to provide Sudan with comprehensive military assistance, from expert advice to weapons, for its continued war against the rebels in the south. In late February the IRGC took over Kabar prison in Khartoum and converted it to its central headquarters in Sudan—a clear indication of Tehran's long-term intentions. In mid-March, General Muhsin Rezai, commander in chief of the IRGC, led a senior military delegation on a secret visit to Sudan. He inspected and approved the Iranian and Sudanese military preparations for the offensive in southern Sudan and discussed Sudan's requirements for weapons, training, and logistics support for forthcoming operations. He also visited terrorist training camps where Islamists were receiving high-level training from IRGC experts. On his return to Tehran, Rezai delivered a positive report, and Tehran further increased its direct involvement in and massive support for both Khartoum and the Islamist terrorist movement.

A new "Islamist International" emerged in 1992, unifying and better coordinating the various Sunni militant Islamist movements from West Africa to the Far East than had its earlier incarnation. Such militant movements were now spreading rapidly throughout the Muslim and non-Muslim world. The Islamist International was the dominant force in and spearhead of the Islamist proselytization movement that was actively involved in numerous armed clashes and subversive activities all over the world. The new organization was an outgrowth and expansion of the already extensive military-political networks of the Muslim Brotherhood. The PIO acted as the supreme coordinating body for the numerous militant Islamist organizations supported by Tehran and Khartoum. Turabi also maintained senior and trusted aides in key positions overseas to ensure the global character of the Islamist movement. By mid-1992 Osama bin Laden was already an up-and-coming member of Turabi's inner circle.

OSAMA BIN LADEN had arrived in Khartoum in 1991, determined to settle into quiet Muslim life and start a new business career. He surveyed both the local economic scene and opportunities overseas, particularly in Pakistan, Afghanistan, and East Africa, and looked into entering the lucrative world of financing import-export deals. In the process he established working relations with several banks and international financial institutions. But his quest for a quiet life did not last long.

The Muslim world was shocked on July 5, 1991, when officials of the Bank of England closed down the Bank of Credit and Commerce International (BCCI), triggering a worldwide financial scandal. Run by Pakistanis and largely financed by rich Gulf Arabs, the BCCI was notorious for providing "special services" in support of worthy causes—from laundering money for terrorists, Muslim intelligence services, and mujahideen; to clandestinely funding deals for conventional weapons, weapons of mass destruction, and other sensitive strategic technologies; to shipping around and laundering huge sums embezzled by corrupt leaders throughout the developing world. During the 1980s it was the primary venue for the transfer and laundering of the CIA's covert aid to the Afghan mujahideen. Riyadh, Islamabad, and other capitals also used the BCCI's unique way of doing business for their own covert operations. Not surprisingly, the Afghan resistance and other Islamist organizations also used the BCCI. In the process of sponsoring these Islamist "causes," the BCCI's management not only did not keep any books but also took care of its own pockets on and off the books. The bank had become a hollow entity with a lot of unaccounted for and dirty money moving around the world but no real fiscal solvency. And so once a serious audit took place, it became clear that it had to be closed down before it collapsed and pulled down other banks with it. In July 1991 not only had the terrorists lost their money, but it was also quite likely that the legions of accountants, regulators, lawyers, and no doubt intelligence operatives assembled throughout the West to investigate the BCCI would retrieve the Islamists' financial secrets while going through the BCCI's innermost records.

And so, in the midst of preparations for the new worldwide Islamist surge, the principal instrument for safely funding these activities was no more. Khartoum urgently needed an expert to salvage whatever was possible and rebuild a global financial system for both the PIO and AIM. By then Osama bin Laden was the most qualified individual in Khartoum to untangle this financial mess. In late summer 1991 Turabi approached bin Laden and asked for his help.

The collapse of the BCCI and the shock waves that were still reverberating throughout the Muslim world could not have come at a worse time. Turabi had always known the importance of a reliable financial system to support and sustain Islamist activities. By the time Bashir took power, Sudan was already becoming a key center for the financing of the Islamist movements throughout the region, especially North Africa. By the late 1980s, under Turabi's supervision, the IMB had gained control and influence over several major Islamic financial institutions operating in the West, such as the Islamic Holding Company, the Jordanian Islamic Bank, the Dubai Islamic Bank, and the Faysal Islamic Bank. In early 1991 the IMB saw in the establishment of the Taqwa Bank in Algeria the beginning of what an Egyptian official called the "establishing of a world bank for fundamentalists" aimed at competing with Western financial institutions. While these activities were taking place and these banks were being conditioned to support clandestine activities, Khartoum was relying heavily on the BCCI for ongoing financial activities.

But in summer 1991 the BCCI collapsed in the middle of the IMB's effort to complete these programs. In addition, the agreements that had been negotiated between Sudan and Iran included financial issues—the funding and subsidizing of various Islamist movements. New venues for the covert holding and transfer of these funds had to be found before Iran started shipping the money. Osama bin Laden readily volunteered the use of his own international accounts and companies as venues and fronts for the Islamist funds.

So in late 1991, when Tehran transferred $30 million to Turabi to assist in financing the IMB-controlled banking system, the initial scheme perfected by bin Laden was ready. Since security services all over the world were paying close attention to Iranian banks and regulating their activities, these banks could not be used for clandestine purposes. Instead the web of accounts bin Laden established in Sudanese banks controlled by the IMB was being used for clandestine transfers of funds. These banking networks were soon capable of supporting other clandestine money transfers. For example, on the eve of the elections in Algeria, rich Iranians and Islamists from the Gulf sheikhdoms deposited $12 million in the Faysal Islamic Bank branch in Khartoum. From there the money was smuggled to Algeria to assist the Islamic Salvation Front (FIS). An additional $20 million was transferred to Sudan in early 1992 and then from Khartoum to support the Islamist movement, mainly the FIS, in Algeria. In mid-1992 Iran gave Sudan an additional $30 million to expedite terrorist training. However, most of these funds—provided in hard currency—were transferred to bank accounts in London controlled by Turabi to finance international terrorist operations. Khartoum covered all expenses of the terrorist training in Sudan from the national budget.

But these were quick fixes. Bin Laden and Turabi knew that a more intricate system was needed. Also, Gulbaddin Hekmatiyar was getting ready to ship drugs from Afghanistan to the West and divert profits from this drug trade to support the fledgling terrorist networks. Another system of money laundering was required for this.

Bin Laden adopted a twin-track approach. Initially he established a series of accounts and holdings in various Middle Eastern, African, and European banks, using his own money and that of wealthy supporters of Turabi. That money was used mainly as collateral against other transactions, although some relatively legitimate expenses were covered from these accounts. For example, a 1993 acquisition of food and medical supplies for veteran "Afghans" in Sudan and elsewhere was paid for with a $2 million check drawn on one of bin Laden's personal accounts in the Faysal Islamic Bank. Bin Laden claims he personally handed this check to Turabi.

But the large-volume money transfers and laundering required a more extensive solution. Toward this end, bin Laden and a few Sudanese rich merchants loyal to Turabi capitalized the Shamal (North) Islamic Bank in Khartoum. Bin Laden claimed he put as much as $50 million toward the bank's capital, although it is not known whose money that was. This deal is indicative of the character of bin Laden's financial activities in Sudan. In return for arranging the bank deal, the government gave bin Laden ownership of one million acres of land in Kordofan and western Sudan, which bin Laden uses for agriculture and to raise cattle. But no money changed hands, and nothing went on the books. Material retrieved by the Egyptian security authorities in 1995 gives one example of the magnitude of the sums of money involved. In the early 1990s—most likely 1993 or 1994—Turabi decided on "the establishment of a special fund to finance Islamic jihad in Islamic and African countries within the Islamic Arab People's Congress," a fund that would be used by networks of Egyptian "Afghans." "Some $100 million has been placed in this fund," an Islamist leader told his Egyptian interrogators. A special committee chaired by Ibrahim al-Sanusi, an aide of Turabi, was established to oversee this fund—apparently one of numerous such funds—and run a bureau specifically instituted to provide for the Egyptian "Afghans."

But this was only the beginning. By the mid-1990s, relying on family connections and benefactors from his days in Afghanistan, Osama bin Laden completed the organization of a comprehensive and in essence detection-proof financial system in support of the high-quality terrorist networks his closest friend, Ayman al-Zawahiri, was organizing in Europe. The financing of Zawahiri's terrorist system is organized through a totally independent entity known as the "Brotherhood Group." Its core is a group of 134 extremely rich Arabs in the Persian Gulf States. The objective of this financial system is to conceal the money trail so that it will be impossible for Western security authorities to connect the terrorists with the sponsoring states. The key members of the Brotherhood Group have a well-known and established financial presence in the West—sixty-five of them have major companies and businesses in the United States. All of these financial entities and institutions are used by the new terrorist system as cover, fronts, means of financial support, and means of internal communications. This network also facilitates the legal presence in the United States of senior supervisory operatives and terrorists by giving them permanent positions and arranging for business visas. Some eighty members provide comparable services in Western Europe.

The entire financial system organized by bin Laden seems to be functioning quite effectively and efficiently. The most important proof is that virtually no terrorist money has been seized throughout the West. Numerous and highly elaborate Islamist networks sustain themselves in the heart of the West—in expensive cities like Geneva, London, and Chicago—without visible means of income. One Islamist network after another springs into action, using large amounts of cash without any traceable origin. And since these funds make it to their intended users without any tracing or tracking, let alone impounding, bin Laden's financial system must be working well.

Working on material extracted from a senior terrorist commander, Egyptian authorities uncovered evidence in May 1993 that "business interests" connected to bin Laden helped funnel money to Egyptian Islamists so that they could buy unspecified equipment, printing presses, and weapons. The Egyptians could only point to a single large transaction and could not control the flow of cash. In 1994 the Egyptian security services calculated that "the annual amount of funding is estimated at one-half billion Egyptian pounds. The money is for buying weapons and explosives, paying the salaries of executors of terrorist operations, and aiding the families of those in prison and others. This continued flow of money is behind the continuation of terrorist operations in the recent period." Despite the capture of a few foreign-origin checks, the Egyptian security authorities could neither trace the origin of the funds nor stop the flow. And Egypt is not the only country unable to solve the problem. The repeated failure of security authorities in several countries to trace checks and cash found in the possession of terrorists back to their source testifies to the complexity of the problem.

Meanwhile Osama bin Laden organized yet another, completely separate, financial system to push funds to Islamist terrorists, particularly those operating in the West under quasi-legal status. This system was first built on the existing al-Qaida (Islamic Salvation) Foundation, a charity organization bin Laden set up for Azzam back in the mid-1980s. While the foundation was originally organized to ship funds to support the jihad in Afghanistan and Pakistan, in its reincarnation it shipped funds to help Islamic centers and charities throughout the world, particularly in areas such as Bosnia and Albania-Kosovo, where mujahideen operate. As was the case with the clandestine funding system, this quasi-legal system also quickly evolved into a multitude of seemingly unrelated charities and multilayered organizations that interacted and moved people and funds back and forth as security authorities in the West struggled to untangle the web.

One of the most thorough studies of Islamist charities was conducted in Croatia in fall 1993. The study concluded that in the former Yugoslavia, and especially in Bosnia-Herzegovina, a major component of the Iranian-sponsored Islamist terrorist infrastructure was concealed in the ranks of various Islamist charities. These organizations were operating from Zagreb, Croatia, in cooperation and coordination with the local representatives of Iranian intelligence and the HizbAllah. Mohammad Javad Asayesh, then a senior Iranian diplomat in the embassy in Zagreb, was responsible for overseeing intelligence and terrorism operations in the Balkans and Europe under the cover of humanitarian activities. The vast majority of funds for these "charities" was coordinated via either the Mostazafin Foundation, a front for Iranian intelligence, or a host of Saudi and Gulf sheikhdom foundations that through Osama bin Laden answered to Hassan al-Turabi. Altogether between 4,000 and 6,000 Islamist terrorists were operating in Bosnia-Herzegovina at the time under the cover of about two dozen "charities" and "humanitarian projects." The situation has not changed much since then.

These "charities" and "humanitarian projects" do far more than just provide cover and shelter to Islamist terrorists. These institutions do provide comprehensive, lavish social and humanitarian services—they run schools, nurseries, hospitals and clinics, farms and machine shops; they distribute clothes and assist in running a wide variety of community projects. All of these activities are conducted in the context of Islamist fervor and with the goal of educating those who receive help. Taken together, the Islamists provide sustenance, both spiritual and socioeconomic, to communities in distress. In most cases, they are the only ones doing it—operating where neither the local authorities nor Western humanitarian organizations reach. They gain widespread, genuine support and commitment, and these communities rally to contribute their share to the Islamist jihad—from sheltering and supporting terrorist networks to encouraging local youth to join the jihadist forces. With destitution and misery growing throughout the developing world, the Islamists' "hearts and minds" campaigns are proving extremely successful in building solid and resilient popular bases.

In a 1996 interview bin Laden alluded to the extent of his financial-humanitarian activities. "To put it simply, the bin Laden Establishment's aid covers thirteen countries, including Albania, Malaysia, Pakistan, the Netherlands, Britain, Romania, Russia, Turkey, Lebanon, Iraq, and some Gulf countries, which there is no need to mention," he explained. "With a vicious smile on his lips," the Egyptian interviewer notes, bin Laden added that "this aid comes in particular from the Human Concern International Society, which was founded in Afghanistan in 1982." The smile was no doubt due to the audacious claim that the impoverished and destitute Afghanistan was the source of the aid, when in fact the money was clandestinely laundered from supporters in Saudi Arabia and Gulf sheikhdoms. The offshoots of these humanitarian organizations are currently funded by several financiers from the Gulf States and should not be considered bin Laden's entities. Still, bin Laden said, he was very interested in charity work. He could reveal that "the society's main office is in Stockholm and it has branches around the world, including the al-Musa'adah (Aid) Society in Britain, the al-Najdah (Rescue) Society in Berlin, the Islamic Support Society in Italy, the Muwaffaq Society in Zagreb, and Bayt al-Ansar in Peshawar." All of these institutions are "clean."

Bin Laden proved invaluable to Turabi even beyond the help he provided in finding financing for the Islamist cause. In fall 1991 Khartoum turned to bin Laden for assistance in yet another major undertaking. One of the first principal issues to have surfaced in the early strategic negotiations with the Iranians was the poor shape, if not virtual nonexistence, of the Sudanese strategic infrastructure—roads, bridges, airports, military facilities, and the like. Tehran stressed its interest in operating off a viable military infrastructure in Sudan, and Khartoum promised to deliver. However, the Sudanese had no idea how to address a project of this magnitude. Again they approached bin Laden, with his past experience as a major construction contractor, and asked for his help.

Bin Laden established the Al-Hijrah for Construction and Development, Ltd., especially to build the Tahaddi ("defiance") strategic road linking Khartoum with Port Sudan, on the Red Sea coast, as well as a modern international airport near Port Sudan that would be capable of handling combat and reconnaissance aircraft. He used Al-Hijrah to import some $15 million worth of trucks and tractors from Germany. Turabi saw to it that the Sudanese government exempted bin Laden from customs duty on these trucks and tractors.

By spring 1993 the infrastructure construction had expanded to such a degree that bin Laden institutionalized a control system under Abu-al-Hasan, his closest Sudanese friend for over a decade now. Some seventeen men work for the "financial and accounting department" in Khartoum that manages the projects bin Laden oversees. To run the field operations bin Laden recruited numerous Afghans and Arab "Afghans" he had trained and worked with in Afghanistan. In May 1993 he brought between 300 and 480 of them from Pakistan to Sudan to take over all managerial and supervisory positions.

This inflow of skill boosted bin Laden's ability to implement Sudan's strategic development program. By early 1994 he was responsible for the construction and management of at least three major terrorist training camps in northern Sudan, with Sudanese and Iranian intelligence providing the training. By 1996, while still in Sudan, he had built and equipped twenty-three mujahideen training camps. Bin Laden also carried out a number of major construction projects, the most important of which was the al-Rusayris Dam, the largest in Sudan. He also worked on expanding the just completed key strategic highway, the 310-mile al-Tahaddi ("defiance") military road linking Khartoum with Shendi and Atbarah to the north all the way down to Malakal, and from there to both Waw in southwestern Sudan and Juba in southern Sudan. The only viable axis for the transportation of reinforcements and weapons from central Sudan, this highway is Khartoum's sole instrument for holding the south against the escalating rebellion. Bin Laden also managed the construction of the al-Rahad and Kiananah canals and numerous airports and military installations.

Taken together, these construction projects revolutionized Sudan's strategic posture. Had they been managed in an ordinary fashion, they would have cost billions of dollars that Sudan does not have and could not have paid bin Laden or anybody else. Nor is there any evidence of Iranian funding, even though Tehran is a primary benefactor of this infrastructure. Even if bin Laden had touched the money he is rumored to have inherited, he could not have funded these projects. But he likely did not, since all of these construction projects were national security undertakings for Sudan, conducted under military conditions as far as pay and support of the workforce were concerned. Bin Laden managed them in his expert capacity. The companies he "established," such as Al-Hijrah for Construction and Development, were nothing but fronts designed to launder the import of heavy equipment and other goods the Sudanese military would not have been able to purchase in the West. The widely circulated reports about huge sums of money being paid and/or still owed to bin Laden are a combination of disinformation and rumors.

The contributions Osama bin Laden had made since the early 1990s—organizing the Islamists' international financial system and building Sudan's strategic military system for the benefit of Iran—earned him the full trust of Turabi and the Islamist elite. In addition, during this period bin Laden insisted on doing all of this hard work out of the limelight and without any public recognition or honor. He was invited repeatedly but did not attend the annual Arab Islamic Popular Conferences, even though attendance at these conferences is a status symbol in the Islamist world, and bin Laden is reported to have made several million-dollar contributions to the conferences. By 1993 Osama bin Laden had worked his way into the inner circle of the leadership of the international Islamist movement. And this was only the beginning.

IN THE EARLY 1990S the Islamist terrorist training system in Pakistan-Afghanistan, Sudan, and Iran continued to expand and improve.

The Pakistani-Afghan terrorist infrastructure for the international Islamist movement increased in importance in early 1991 in the aftermath of the international pressure and consequent sanctions on Libya because of Muammar al-Qaddafi's support for international terrorism. At the time two Libyan intelligence operatives were indicted by the United States for their role in the midair explosion of PanAm103 in December 1989. Strict international sanctions have been imposed on Libya until the two are extradited to stand trial and so, although fully committed to the escalation of the terrorist struggle, Tripoli decided to take precautions beyond the heralded expulsion of terrorists. Libyan intelligence began transferring some of its training installations into other countries, including Sudan and Pakistan-Afghanistan, where active training of Islamist terrorists was already taking place. Most important was the Libyan upgrading of the terrorist infrastructure in the camps of the Afghan resistance both in Pakistan and just across the border inside Afghanistan because, as Qaddafi pointed out in December 1991, "Afghanistan is open to anyone who wants to train."

By 1991, as the fighting in Afghanistan was grinding to a near halt, the Islamist mujahideen were shifting more and more attention to the training of thousands of brethren from all over the Muslim world. In early 1991 some 2,000 to 3,000 volunteers were in the Khowst area alone. At that time the Khowst area, in eastern Afghanistan near the Pakistani border, was fast becoming a center for the training of mujahideen from all over the Muslim world. (The United States would launch cruise missiles against some of these camps in August 1998 in retaliation for the embassy bombings in Nairobi and Dar-es-Salaam.) The organized transfer of training installations to several camps in Pakistan-Afghanistan began that summer as terrorist teams began arriving from Libya or via other countries. For example, thirty to thirty-five Libyan expert terrorist trainers arrived in Peshawar in November 1991 with the declared objective "to train national liberation forces" in mujahideen camps, mainly those of Gulbaddin Hekmatiyar and Abdul-Rassul Sayyaf, another Islamist mujahideen leader. By March 1992, now in a Sayyaf camp in the Kana area, Nangarhar Province, these Libyans had become devout Islamists and joined the Muslim Brotherhood. Some of them would soon play a key role in an operation run by Osama bin Laden in Yemen on the eve of the U.S. deployment to Somalia.

Under Turabi, the Armed Islamic Movement played a major role in the consolidated emergence of a genuine international terrorist training and deployment system. For example, back in spring 1991, eighteen Kashmiri Islamists had been accepted for six months of highly specialized terrorist training in Sudan. Their progress was personally supervised by Turabi and Mustafa Uthman. In view of the success of this program, Turabi then visited Pakistan and Afghanistan in September 1991 to coordinate additional terrorist support and exchange activities. Jamaat-i-Islami (Pakistan), Hizb-i Islami, Jamiat-i-Islami (Afghanistan), and Hizb-ul Mujahideen (Kashmir) became members of the Turabi-led Popular International Organization (PIO). In this capacity, these organizations now provided assistance to and closely cooperated with Islamists from Egypt, the HizbAllah from Lebanon, the Islamic Salvation Front (FIS) from Algeria, and the National Islamic Front (NIF) from Sudan. It was not long before PIO members began exchanging experts and cooperating in joint support and training activities. Turabi also worked to expand the international relations and mutual cooperation of the terrorist infrastructure in Sudan. In late November 1991 he consolidated arrangements for the exchange and dispatch of trainees to Islamist—mainly Muslim Brotherhood—sites in Peshawar.

Meanwhile the ISI's vast and highly experienced terrorist support infrastructure, tempered by years of assistance to such regional armed struggles as those of the Afghans, Kashmiris, and Sikhs, was expanding its operations to include support for and sponsorship of global Islamist terrorism. By 1992, under the ISI's sponsorship, AIM was supporting and training Islamist terrorists and fighters for jihads throughout the world from centers in Afghanistan and Pakistan. These terrorists—popularly known as the "Afghans"—have become the quality core of struggles throughout the world. In Algeria, for example, key commanders of subversive, terrorist, and irregular fighting groups had all participated in the war in Afghanistan. Egyptian "Afghans" were also very active in the rapidly escalating Islamist uprising in Egypt, where they were responsible for key assassinations and other special operations. The "Afghans" were the spearhead and core of the new International Islamist Legion that was now sending its "Afghan" veterans—all of them commanders and key experts—all over the Muslim world to support, expedite, incite, and facilitate what they consider Islamist liberation struggles.

During the 1980s, all these "Afghans" passed through and enjoyed the services of the institutions established and run by Azzam and bin Laden. In the early 1990s, as the Afghan war was winding down, many of these "Afghans" continued to receive support from the "humanitarian organizations" established, run, and funded by bin Laden and his allies. But their relationship went beyond the providing and receiving of aid. After the assassination of Azzam, the veteran "Afghans" increasingly looked to bin Laden as an arbiter between their original and often competing organizations and movements. He was considered thoroughly committed to the all-Islamist cause and devoid of any personal aspirations and so unlikely to take sides in any dispute or misunderstanding. With time, bin Laden was recognized as a guide and leader of these "Afghans." But from 1991 to 1992 bin Laden did not wield command authority on operational matters.

The advanced training and indoctrination received by the Egyptian "Afghans" in Pakistan in 1992 and the expertise they acquired testify to the quality of training and preparations received by other "Afghan" Islamists as well. This training and indoctrination include the development of a battle culture centered on the total commitment to Islamic jihad and martyrdom in the service of God and Islam, which has become both a principle of their struggle and an ideological mind-set; the use of automatic weapons, including weapons that are easy to carry, disguise, and conceal; construction and use of sophisticated offensive and defensive bombs that would inflict the highest number of casualties on the other side and the development of skills among the "Afghans" who had to learn how to build and assemble these devices; advanced techniques and tactics of street and house-to-house guerrilla warfare, including psychological preparations for these challenging forms of struggle and warfare; and the conviction of the fighters that their goal is to topple one regime and install another based on Islamist tenets and that the only means available for that end is fighting, guerrilla warfare, and the use of arms.

The "Afghans" were thus the primary strategic product of the ISI's training system and the battlefields of Afghanistan. In the early 1990s these "Afghans" already constituted the heart of the Islamist militant opposition in several Arab countries, notably Algeria, Egypt, Tunisia, and Jordan. These "Afghans" were, in the words of an Arab observer, "the military arm of a number of Islamic movements and operations in certain Arab and Muslim countries." They became an integral part of "an extremist Islamic revolutionary movement" aided and supported by Iranian intelligence and Turabi's institutions. By using their military knowledge and experience, these "Afghans" facilitated the marked escalation of Islamist violence and terrorism throughout the Middle East. "The 'Afghans' attack, sow violence, and assassinate such 'state symbols' as government officials, policemen, security agents, and the military in Algeria and Egypt. They detonate bombs and strike state institutions and buildings," observed an Arab official. The "Afghans" were also being used as a command core around which local Islamist terrorist organizations were built.

The "Afghans" of the Armed Islamic Movement were now coordinated and supported through an international center in Peshawar that in summer 1992 included Egyptians, Afghans, Pakistanis, Sudanese, Algerians, and Saudis. As a result of the growing cooperation between the various Islamist movements, they had established an "International Jihad Organization" using Pakistan and Afghanistan as their springboard to the rest of the world. "Everything is planned inside these bureaus in Peshawar: military operations in Egypt, preparations to establish an international al-Jihad organization, and the issue of secret documents to be sent to Egypt," noted an Egyptian expert. "The attempts to establish an international al-Jihad organization have not stopped. Ayman al-Zawahiri has made many efforts in this direction. Last year [1991] he and [then his deputy] Fuad Talat Qassim conducted extensive negotiations with representatives of al-Jihad organizations in Syria, Palestine, Algeria, Libya, and Tunisia. Representatives of Gulbaddin Hekmatiyar's Hizb-i Islami also attended these talks in Peshawar." The Jihad Movement Bureau originally opened in the mid-

1980s by Zawahiri for the Islamic Jihad Movement of Abbud al-Zumur of Egypt was now in charge of foreign liaison, weapon supplies, and financial assistance for numerous Jihad organizations operating all over the world.

While this network of "Afghan" terrorists was being established, Tehran was making special efforts to align the leading Sunni organizations with the Tehran-led terrorist establishment. A major breakthrough took place in July 1992, when Zawahiri arrived in Tehran after mediation by Turabi. Tehran agreed to provide advanced training in Iran, mainly in Mashhad (in eastern Iran, near the Afghan border), for about 800 Egyptian "Afghans" then in Pakistan and Afghanistan. Iran also offered transportation to Sudan and training there by HizbAllah and Pasdaran (IRGC) experts, as well as financing and provision of weapons for implementing the Islamists' plans to escalate their jihad in Egypt. The only condition Tehran imposed was that the Egyptian Islamic Jihad join the Arab Liberation Battalions under the command of the IRGC intelligence. In late summer 1992, at Tehran's invitation, Ahmad Shawqi al-Islambuli traveled to the Bekáa Valley, Lebanon, to inspect the local HizbAllah facilities and discuss ways they would assist in training Egyptian mujahideen already in Sudan. These Egyptian Islamists would constitute the first Egyptian Liberation Battalion. In addition to the Egyptians sent to Iran, some 500 terrorists were sent to Sudan, where they joined a HizbAllah-run training program. By fall 1992 the main Egyptian Islamist groups were being integrated into the Iranian-HizbAllah terrorist system. It was not accidental that the Egyptian Islamic Jihad began issuing its communiqués from Tehran in December 1992. Before long these relationships would prove their worth in battle in the streets of Mogadishu, Somalia.

In 1992 the AIM and its International Legion/Brigade of Islam were supporting, training, and supplying Islamist terrorists and mujahideen throughout the world directly from their centers in Afghanistan and Pakistan. The several thousand Arabs who had fought in Afghanistan, initially in the ranks of Gulbaddin Hekmatiyar's Hizb-i Islami, constituted the core of these "Afghan" forces. In the early 1990s they were joined by locally raised and trained terrorists. The "Afghans" included citizens of Algeria, Egypt, Sudan, Yemen, Tunisia, Jordan, Morocco, Lebanon, Saudi Arabia, and other Arab states, as well as several Palestinians. In summer 1992 some 12,000 Arab "Afghans" were organized in and belonged to militant Islamist groups. Many brought their personal weapons and other "contributions" from their Afghan brethren back to their native countries. These "Afghans"—not only Arabs, but also large numbers of Iranians, Indonesians, Malaysians, Indians, and Pakistanis—were consolidating a network of "graduates" ready to apprentice others.

Although these "Afghans" were organized through AIM and supervised and assisted from a center in Peshawar, they constituted a unique phenomenon in the Islamist subversion and terrorism arena. The "Afghans" did not form a unified or formalized organization. "Be they Algerian, Egyptian, Tunisian, or of some other nationality, what they have in common is their use of violence, arms, and explosives in their attempt to realize their objectives and achieve their targets. They form underground organizations, manipulated pawns perhaps, in their quest for undermining stability in certain Arab countries," observed an Arab expert. The "Afghans" saw themselves, both as individuals and as components of the new International Legion/Brigade of Islam, as the spearhead of the Islamist revolution. By mid-1993 the core of this new Islamist force—the "Afghan Arab Mujahideen"—included 800 Egyptians, 700 Algerians, 400 Tunisians, 370 Iraqis, 300 Yemenis, 200 Libyans, 150 Sudanese, 100 Persian Gulf Arabs, and 70 Europeans. Most of them were deployed in Iran, Sudan, and Yemen—countries that constituted their primary forward bases. The role of AIM was to send its veteran "Afghans," commanders and key experts, all over Asia, Africa, and Europe to participate in Islamist liberation struggles. An expression of the real leadership of AIM, the "Afghans" deployed to their objectives via Tehran, Khartoum, and Karachi.

The seemingly loose organizational affiliation of the "Afghans" was misleading. Although they operated as individuals and in very small groups, they actually constituted a global unifying factor because they brought the organizations and movements they had joined into the Islamist fold. In 1992 the Khartoum-based Popular International Organization was already exercising a strong hand over the myriad of groups and movements. The PIO's tight control was evident in the alignment of the propaganda lines, motivating themes, and "Call" themes—the key educational, propaganda, and incitement themes used in Friday sermons and other Islamist religious-educational material—used by all the members all over the world. All the organizations were committed to solidarity with other Islamist causes. The growing movement of "religious professionals," clandestine organizers, and terrorist expert "Afghans" throughout the alliance's states also ensured continued contacts and mutual commitments. These "Afghans" exercised significant influence in initiating the rise of the spirit of martyrdom, the willingness to die for the Islamist revolution or cause, which tremendously increased the daring and audacity of the "Afghans" and the local terrorist organizations they were assisting. Another expression of the centralized control was the emergence of identical social, medical, and educational services and charities organized around the mosque in order to win over and control the local Muslim population. This dual approach, armed struggle and social services, was one of Khomeini's principles, dating back to the 1950s, and is currently widely used by the Hizb-Allah in Lebanon.

By mid-1992 AIM's International Legion/Brigade of Islam—its high-quality cadre of "Afghans"—was getting ready to implement Turabi's global vision of spreading the Islamist revolution throughout the world as well as bringing the jihad to the heartland of its avowed enemies—the United States, Western Europe, and Israel. And while the command structure of AIM's "Afghans" was still fledgling and at times fragile, the logistical and financial system was solid and largely unified. The efficiency of the support system, a system organized and largely run by Osama bin Laden, earned him recognition from "Afghan" commanders. Combined with his already unique relationship with and strong position among the "Afghans," bin Laden's leadership position in the international terrorist movement was becoming more pronounced. A loyal team player, bin Laden avoided assuming an overt position or taking a title. Instead he concentrated on supporting Turabi's quest for the spread of the Islamist movement by facilitating the support and financial mechanism. As a result bin Laden earned the respect and support of Turabi and other senior luminaries of the international Islamist movement.

THE FURTHERING AND EXPORT of the Islamist revolution into sub-Saharan Africa has long been a high priority shared by Tehran and Khartoum. With Turabi personally committed to the spread of Islam in Africa, African operation has become a major priority of Islamist Sudan, particularly since early 1992. Dr. Mustafa Uthman Ismail, the secretary general of the Khartoum-based International People's Friendship Council, declared that "Sudan has become the strongman of Africa, and is a helping hand to its neighbors and friends." In essence, Khartoum adopted and committed itself to the implementation of Iran's strategic programs. "Turabi has turned into a paid caretaker for the policy exporting the Iranian revolution, proposing himself as a 'grand ayatollah' and weaving new allegiances for the Sudanese state on the basis of a broad fundamentalist current with its own bases, camps, resources, and funding," noted a conservative Arab expert. In fall 1992 Turabi ordered the escalation of the campaign to destabilize East Africa as part of his desire "to realize his dream of becoming supreme Imam of a fundamentalist Islamic empire." Soon afterward new cadres and expert terrorists were sent from Sudan to several countries in East Africa, and the training and preparation of terrorists from these countries in Sudan expanded.

At first Turabi sought to capitalize on existing Iranian assets. Since late 1991 Tehran and Sudan have worked together to provide support for the Shiite elements gaining strength in Tanzania, Kenya, Uganda, Burundi, and Zaire. They have also coordinated their involvement in arms and other forms of international trade throughout Africa as a form of transferring financial assistance, placing people, and establishing stockpiles of weapons and explosives. Osama bin Laden oversaw the Sudanese end of this surge into Africa, establishing business entities and a financial presence in numerous countries in East Africa. An important role in these operations was also played by the Islamic Call Front under Muhammad al-Sharief from Tripoli, Lebanon, who maintained a senior representative in Khartoum. While Tehran gave Turabi access to and even virtual control over some of the Sunni communities, it kept the Shiite networks under direct Iranian control. For example, in Kenya the Islamic Party, supported by Sudan and Iran, emerged as a major power in Mombasa, Kenya's main port. Separately Tehran was penetrating the economic elite made up of members of the Oromo tribe, who provided multifaceted support to the Islamist subversive forces throughout the country.

The intensification of the Iranian-Sudanese drive into Africa was immediately felt. By February and March 1992 there was a marked escalation of riots in Kenya and Uganda, with Muslim organizations exploiting socioeconomic malaise to destabilize the local governments. These riots had a direct adversarial impact on the national stability and political process in both countries. Meanwhile Turabi promised to expand the work of the International Muslim Brotherhood and the jihad organizations in sub-Saharan Africa in order to spread militant Islamism and establish loyal governments.

In summer 1992 the Islamist drive into Africa became a cornerstone of Sudan's strategic posture. Turabi's penetration attempts were part of a plan coordinated with Tehran to export the Islamic Revolution. Somalia, Uganda, Tanzania, Chad, and Kenya were the theaters of major escalation. The Islamists were waging a silent war with the local governments, using clandestine means and seemingly harmless venues, such as educational and humanitarian entities. To support the intensified drive into Africa, Sudan also established a dedicated network of camps under the tight control of a small group of Turabi's Sudanese loyalists. Turabi's inner circle for African operations comprised nine men, who were each entrusted with a series of specific priorities and missions in the countries of the Islamic belt. They ran the Islamist networks and the elaborate commercial fronts as well as humanitarian, charity, and public relations façades established by bin

Laden. The countries in which they operated at highest priority were Uganda, Kenya, Tanzania, and Chad.

By now the Iranian-Sudanese grand design focused on Tanzania as a launching place for the second stage of the Islamist drive into Africa, and special attention was paid to the Zanzibar separatist movement. It was now financed through Iranian and Islamist fronts concealed as German-based international businesses. Zanzibar, one of East Africa's main ports, was considered ideal as a center for transshipment of people, goods, and weapons throughout Africa and the Third World as a whole.

At the same time Sudan's anticipation of a major escalation in the fighting in the Horn of Africa and East Africa led Khartoum to organize and begin training local "armed forces" capable of engaging military forces. The main facilities of these semi-organized forces were in a camp in Sudan's central province under the command of Colonel Suleiman Muhammad Suleiman, a member of Sudan's Ruling Council. In the early 1990s the militia force allocated for East Africa included six companies and three battalions manned by 3,000 troops from Yemen, Egypt, Algeria, Somalia, and Kenya. They were trained by IRGC experts from Iran and military officers from Pakistan. In fall 1992 a company from this camp participated in the fighting in Somalia alongside the forces of General Muhammad Farrah Aidid against Ali Mahdi Muhammad's forces. One of the main projects of Ibrahim Ahmad Omar was the Sudanese support for an 800-man Ugandan militia, mainly of the Aringa tribe, under the command of Jumah Aris, that was being trained and based in Juba and used for cross-border raids into northern Uganda.

Before long these forces—and the entire Sudan-based command, training, and support infrastructure—would be committed to Islamism's most demanding campaign to date: challenging the United States over its presence in the Horn of Africa and ultimately evicting it from this strategically crucial area. In the struggle for the Horn of Africa the Islamist international system was put to the test for the first time—and it succeeded. The Islamists proved they could conduct strategically important operations.

Although bin Laden played only a supporting role, albeit a vital one, in the struggle against the U.S. forces in Somalia, the whole experience would be crucial for his further development and that of his colleagues and life-long friends. For in Mogadishu, a desolate city in a collapsed country, the Islamists set a precedent—that the United States can be terrorized into abandoning a Muslim land.

3

Triumph over the Paper Tiger

IN LATE 1992 televised coverage of the famine in Somalia subjected viewers in the United States and the West as a whole to a profusion of images of starving and dying children. Pictured against scenes of destitution and misery, exasperated Western relief workers pleaded with the viewers to provide massive relief for the suffering. In fact, the famine was more an intentional human-made crisis than the result of a natural disaster—the drought. The famine had not only caused massive casualties among the civilian population but had also brought the social order in Somalia to a total collapse.

The catastrophe was caused by tribal wars for independence and self-determination and exacerbated by a power struggle between conflicting groups. In the power struggle among key leaders of the main Somalian factions, famine was their weapon of choice for determining the character of the civilian population in their fiefdoms. These leaders intentionally denied food to the segments of population they wanted destroyed and fed only those groups whose allegiance they sought. This convoluted and fratricidal warfare took place within the context of a radical Islamist surge throughout the whole region

The events unfolding in the Horn of Africa in the early 1990s, primarily the confrontation with and ultimate eviction of the U.S.-led U.N. military forces in Somalia, could have foreshadowed the potential power of Islamist subversion and terrorism as sponsored by Iran and Sudan. These events showed an Islamist camp overcoming profound conflicts, such as those between Sunni and Shiite Muslims and between Iran and Iraq, in order to mobilize all available resources in confronting the United States over an area of great geostrategic importance—the Horn of Africa and southern access to the Red Sea. Toward this end the Islamists, the sponsoring states, and their underlings established a strategic command-and-control system, trained and moved thousands of fighters between South Asia and Africa, clandestinely moved large sums of money for the support of covert operations, and ultimately successfully engaged the mighty United States. The Islamists consider Somalia a turning point, but for the West it sets a precedent that should not be ignored.

Osama bin Laden considers the Islamists' confrontation with the U.S.-U.N. forces in Somalia a turning point not only in the rise of the Islamist militant system but also in his own personal road to the top. It was during the preparations for the Islamist struggle in Somalia that bin Laden participated in high-level leadership activities. His own contribution to the Islamist effort, although in a supporting role, was significant.

THE STRATEGICALLY CRUCIAL Horn of Africa—Ethiopia (including now independent Eritrea), Somalia, and Djibouti—has been the playground of superpowers and regional powers for centuries. Located at the eastern tip of Africa, just southwest of the Arabian Peninsula, the Horn of Africa has a uniquely important geostrategic position. Its long coastline overlooks the southern stretch of the Red Sea in Eritrea and the approaches to and from the Red Sea into the Indian Ocean from Somalia. From bases on the Somalian coastline, it is possible to stop the sea traffic between Europe (and the United States) and East Asia by blocking the approaches to the Red Sea, which leads to the Suez Canal in the north. The sources of the Blue Nile, Egypt's lifeline, are in the mountains of Ethiopia. Dominance over the Horn of Africa yields great influence not only over world commerce and maritime transportation but also over stability in Egypt and so the Middle East. As a rule, strategic power struggles over the area—whether fought in the name of colonial aspirations or Cold War ideologies—ended up exploiting the sharp divide between the Christians of inland Ethiopia, whose church is one of the oldest still active, and the Muslims of the coastal areas. The traditional ethnic and religious rivalries and enmities that had endured for centuries exploded with renewed intensity in the early 1990s. Under Hassan al-Turabi's guidance, the Islamist leadership capitalized on this indigenous upsurge in order to further the Islamists' strategic interests—to humiliate the United States and evict it from the region.

The overthrow of President Mengistu Haile Mariam's Dergue regime in Addis Ababa, Ethiopia, in late May 1991 was an outcome of the rebels' advance and U.S. mediation but was even more a manifestation of profound dynamics overtaking the Horn of Africa that are still the primary cause of instability and chaos in that region. Analysis of regional developments in the early 1990s reveals that these events preceded an important process rapidly developing all over sub-Saharan Africa—the collapse of the state system and the redefinition of boundaries based on ethnic and tribal quests for self-identity. Local populations throughout most of sub-Saharan Africa still aspire to this.

Although the lengthy revolutionary struggles throughout the Horn of Africa since the 1970s had been fought against ruthless dictatorial regimes in both Addis Ababa and Mogadishu, the capital of Somalia, the ideological motivations of the groups challenging these regimes were largely ethnocentric. The manpower of any one of these organizations or fronts was dominated by a specific nationality, and each nationality's individual goals determined its priorities. National/ethnic goals were the real driving force behind these movements. All these revolutionary forces had endured and prevailed after decades of armed struggle, maintaining the trust and support of the population through times of unprecedented hardship, including several cycles of lethal famine. Such endurance reveals the genuine popular devotion to the leadership of these revolutionary movements and the true ideologies they stood for in the early 1990s. This grassroots alignment of the people throughout the region, including Somalia, would prove a critical factor in the intensification of the crisis and the subsequent consolidation of the anti–United States coalition.

The situation in the Horn of Africa was further complicated by the fact that although virtually all of these liberation movements were ethnocentric separatist movements, they also espoused to some extent a Marxist revolutionary ideology. This ideology, a legacy from well-wishing Western European intellectuals of the 1960s rather than an expression of popular sentiment, had resulted from a pragmatic desire to placate Cuba, initially the main supporter of all of these movements, and later pro-Soviet radical Arab regimes, such as Libya and Algeria, which also provided weapons, training, and funds. But the Westernized political leaders of these movements, especially those who ran the public awareness campaigns in Western Europe for more than a decade, were prisoners of their own policies, continuing to hold to their progressive "Westernized" ideologies even though their followers were ethnocentric and traditionalist. This contradiction between genuine popular sentiment for the furthering of ethnocentric sentiments and the all-embracing revolutionary ideologies of the political leadership was beginning to emerge as a point of contention just as the victorious rebels were trying to establish their governments. At the time of crisis, when all-out popular support was crucial, leaders had to take into consideration the prevalence of the ethnocentric sentiments in reaching alliances and taking sides.

Another external factor that would become a catalyst for explosion was the Arabs' declared objective of making the Red Sea into an Arab lake. Toward that end, Somalia was recognized as part of the Arab League and subsidized by Saudi Arabia. Similarly the Arabs encouraged and supported the Muslim Eritreans' separation from largely Christian Ethiopia. With militant pan-Arab sentiments on the rise throughout the Middle East, the collapse of the Dergue regime in Ethiopia meant that an Arab lake might become a political reality. The unbridgeable gap between Islam and Christianity served as a focus for Islamic Eritrea's struggle for self-determination and independence from Addis Ababa. In Somalia the well-financed Somali Islamic Unity Party had already launched a propaganda campaign to unify all Muslim peoples along the littoral of the Horn of Africa—namely, Somalia, Djibouti, and Eritrea. Several conservative Arab regimes led by Saudi Arabia were pouring money into this and similar Muslim unity programs.

Meanwhile, because of the position it took in mediating the Ethiopian crisis, the United States emerged as the guardian of the established order in the post–Cold War world and the guarantor of existing borders. The United States had been the driving force behind the London conference of early 1991 that brought together Dergue and various Ethiopian and Eritrean liberation organizations. The agreement facilitated the resignation and exile of President Mengistu in May 1991 and the relatively orderly entry of a coalition of Ethiopian rebel organizations led by Meles Zenawi to Addis Ababa. This agreement also ensured the unity and territorial integrity of Ethiopia despite the aspirations of several separatist movements, most of which were Muslim dominated. (Ultimately the United States would stand aside when Eritrea unilaterally declared its independence in May 1993.) As a result, Islamist separatist and revolutionary leaders were convinced that Africa was on a collision course with the United States, especially in the wake of the Gulf Crisis. Before long the United States found itself fighting radical Islam in the Horn of Africa.

SINCE 1990 the main revolutionary forces in Somalia, like all such regional forces, had been ethnically based. Most important were the United Somali Congress (USC), which derived from the Hawiye clan in central Somalia, and the Somali National Movement (SNM), derived from the Isaaq clan in Somaliland, the former British colony that is the northern arm of Somalia along the Gulf of Aden. (Somalia looks like an inverted L, with one arm consisting of the former British colony and the other, along the

Indian Ocean coast, consisting of the former Italian colony.) Smaller groups included the Somali Patriotic Movement (SPM), which originated with the Ogadeni and to a lesser degree the Kismayu (of Kenya) clans; the Somali Salvation Liberation Front (SSLF), which started with the Majerteen clan, traditionally oppressed by the Hawiye, and evolved into the movement of all oppressed miniclans inside central Somalia; the Somali Democratic Alliance (SDA), originating with the Gedabursi clan; and the Somali Democratic Movement (SDM), which started with the Rahanwein clan. The Gedabursi and Rahanwein clans are both located in the north.

These movements were divided into two distinct groups: the northern, Somaliland, movements—the SNM and its challengers—and the central, Somalia, movements—the USC and its challengers. The natural habitation zones of the two groups roughly overlapped the ex-British and ex-Italian colonies that had been united by the British in 1960 to form independent Somalia. In essence the warfare had always been a rebellion against a centralized Somalian identity and a struggle for self-determination by the main clans.

By late 1992 the primary fighting in the Mogadishu area and the central coastal area was between extended families and subclans that rallied behind key leaders based on personal loyalties. The main protagonists were General Muhammad Farrah Aidid, the USC chairman, who was supported by his own Habar Gidir subclan and a loose alliance of smaller extended families (together called the Somali National Alliance, or SNA), and Ali Mahdi Muhammad, the so-called interim president of Somalia, and his Abgal subclan and a loose alliance of smaller extended families and subclans. Muhammad rose to power in December 1990 as one of the leaders of the USC, but by early 1991 a major rift erupted between the Muhammad-led and the Aidid-led factions of the USC. Formally the crisis was over Aidid's effort to increase cooperation with the SNM, thereby retaining the unity of Somalia at the expense of the USC's monopoly of power in Mogadishu. By September 1991 the crisis had evolved into a bitter struggle for power between the Muhammad-led and the Aidid-led clans, resulting in the breakup of the USC. Aidid's contacts with the SNM would prove crucial in the fighting of 1993, when bin Laden would organize part of the support system for the anti-American forces in Somaliland.

By 1992 the most notorious and cruel fighters for Aidid were the members of the Habar Gidir subclan of the Hawiye clan from Galcaio, about 370 miles north of Mogadishu. Members of a subclan historically known for its banditry, the Habar Gidir forces were lured into Mogadishu by promises of plunder and rape. Meanwhile, because of the clannish character of the revolt against General Muhammad Siyad Barre (who had ruled for twenty-one years) in summer and fall 1991, the clans and subclans who had provided most of the city's services, including police, escaped, fearing the advancing Hawiye. This population movement deprived the Mogadishu area of any semblance of resistance or civility.

Aidid blamed the United Nations and the West for supporting Muhammad, insisting that all the humanitarian aid was brought into Somalia in order to consolidate Muhammad's power and that his own fierce struggle for the food was a liberation struggle. Muhammad stated that only he had the right to distribute the food and humanitarian aid, to determine who was truly needy and where the aid was needed first. When the United Nations refused Muhammad's demand to dominate the distribution of humanitarian aid, his forces shelled the Mogadishu harbor and attacked distribution facilities. Muhammad attributed the attacks to frustrated "uncontrolled elements" in his force, but in principle he was determined to prevent others from eating if he could not control the food.

Besieged by images of starving children and haunted by the media, Washington decided in November 1992 to deploy a large military force to Somalia on a humanitarian mission—to ensure, by force if necessary, the delivery of food to the starving innocent. But this deployment, noble intentions notwithstanding, would disrupt the intricate and vicious struggles for power and riches in Somalia. The warlords would not accept this development for long.

Muhammad claimed that the anticipated deployment of U.S. forces meant recognition of his right to power. In response, on November 2, 1992, Aidid threatened any foreign deployment with "unprecedented bloodshed," a threat he would live up to in fall 1993, when he provided the cover and troops for the Islamist clashes with the U.S.-U.N. forces. The USC issued a more moderate communiqué on November 27, 1992, announcing that Aidid "considers the deployment of armed troops in Somalia damaging for our sovereignty and for our territorial integrity." But on December 1, facing the inevitable, each of the two warlords welcomed the deployment of U.S. forces on condition that the United Nations and United States recognized him as the legitimate political power in the country. Aidid and Muhammad both considered the role of the U.S. forces to be to "help the transitional government [theirs, of course] to deliver food supplies." Both leaders also insisted that the U.S. forces should fight the "gunmen preventing food from reaching the starving" but actually expected the U.S. forces to fight their respective rivals.

Muhammad Farrah Aidid took more credible steps to effect and capitalize on the distribution of aid. In early November he organized and chaired a major meeting of the "elders and wise men" and other pillars of the traditional society to gain their support in the SNA, which meant the loyalty of the various miniforces. With that accomplished, Aidid's forces immediately stormed and by November 10 successfully seized control of about fifteen main road junctions and the local roadblocks from "free-lancer" bands.

On November 30 and December 1, Aidid visited Kismayu, a key sea-port, airport, and road juncture in the south, and established an alliance with the Somali Liberation Army, which had bases in Kenya. He also nomi-nated Ahmed Omar Jays, the chairman of the SPM (whose forces now oc-cupied the Kismayu airport and surrounding area), to be deputy chairman of the SNA, covering the USC's flanks into the Ogaden desert. Aidid reached an agreement with Muhammad Nur Aliow, the leader of the SDM in the north, whose forces could block any advance from Somaliland. In this summit Aidid described to the commanders "their obligations in areas under their control and told them to be wary of elements bent on harming the unity of the Somalian people." On the other side, Ali Mahdi Muham-mad met with representatives of Ethiopia and Eritrea to establish a cooper-ative effort against Aidid's forces.

While civil war raged, the Islamists increased their presence in Somalia through numerous charitable organizations formally affiliated with Saudi Arabia and the Persian Gulf States. As foreign intervention became immi-nent, the Islamists launched a campaign against foreign aid. For example, the Islamic World Association and the World Muslim Relief Organization declared that "only Muslim organizations have been doing [true] humane work in Somalia." One of the leaders of an Islamist charity organization accused the West of exploiting the humanitarian aid in order to implement "a suspicious plan aimed at partitioning Somalia to European countries and of implementing the partition plan by fanning the flames of dissen-sion among Somali factions fighting for government control." The posi-tion of these Islamic organizations was important in view of the financial and political power behind them. The Islamic World Association and the World Muslim Relief Organization were part of the wide network of or-ganizations answering to the Saudi fundamentalist Islamic proselytization movement, comprising both Riyadh-supported and underground Islamist elements. This network of organizations included several fronts organized by Osama bin Laden that answered to Turabi and furthered the interests of militant Islamism.

By the early 1990s a well-established financial network existed in Soma-lia. The Saudi government and the very rich supporters of the Saudi funda-mentalist Islamic proselytization movement had financed Siyad Barre and his regime after he broke off relations with the Soviet Union in 1978 until his downfall in mid-1991. The money was transferred and handled by a Somalian middleman named Mohammad Sheikh Osman. In the summer of 1991, however, Osman suddenly changed sides and became a member of Aidid's USC central committee. He brought with him the continued financial and political support of the Islamists. This switch would significantly expedite bin Laden's manipulation and ultimate takeover of the Islamist financial system in Somalia. Bin Laden would soon capitalize on Osman's network as the Somali end of his own financial network for the funding and sustaining of the anti-U.S. operations in Somalia.

───────

THE ESCALATION AND DETERIORATION of the situation in Somalia was not accidental but an essential component in the Iranian-Sudanese struggle to consolidate and expand the Islamist stronghold in eastern Africa.

While Somalians were starving, additional National Islamic Front training camps for fighters from Ethiopia, Somalia, Eritrea, Kenya, and Uganda were opened and expanded in Sudan under the direction of Dr. Ali al-Haj, one of Turabi's closest friends and confidants. Once again Osama bin Laden's managerial, logistical, and construction skills transformed Turabi's desires into working training camps. In fall 1992 Turabi ordered the escalation of the campaign to destabilize the whole of East Africa. Soon afterward additional cadres and expert terrorists were sent from Sudan to their home countries in East Africa. The pace of the deployment of these terrorists accelerated after November 1992, once the U.S. intervention was announced.

The Somalian terrorists were provided with equipment and weapons for the militias they would train and lead. Some of these militias operated within the ranks of the main Somalian parties, while others were completely independent, answering only to Khartoum. Most terrorists traveled via Eritrea, but a few of the most important operatives were clandestinely landed from the sea in southern Somalia and Kenya. Tehran, which controlled and sponsored these Somalian terrorists via Sudan, planned on using them against the U.S. forces the same way the HizbAllah had been used by Syria and Iran against the U.S. peacekeepers in Beirut in the early 1980s.

The expansion of East African terrorist activities in Sudan coincided with a marked escalation in Islamist violence and terrorism in Egypt. In late November, Cairo blamed Iran for supporting the rise of Islamist violence that was threatening the stability of the country. Most terrorists arrived from base camps in Sudan. Cairo emphasized that the escalation of subversion in Egypt was a part of Tehran's drive to become a regional superpower and warned of "Iran's ability to break Arab and Islamic ranks" as well as "the dangers that Iran posed to pan-Arab security and the strategic and vital interests of the Arab nation." These attacks on Egypt were only a component of Tehran's surge to regional hegemony, made possible by its growing hold over Sudan.

In mid-November 1992 Iran intensified its building of major facilities in Port Sudan, including radio stations and command, control, and communications facilities—indications of long-term commitments. The fast and relatively efficient completion of these installations was a result of bin Laden's takeover of the construction projects. By now Tehran and Khartoum had signed a twenty-five-year lease on Port Sudan. Iran also built military facilities in Suakin in eastern Sudan. These bases constituted Iran's main forward military bases for regional operations, and Iranian forces also enjoyed virtually unrestricted access to all of Sudan's airports and seaports, primarily Jubayat and Trinkitat. These ports had already become Tehran's naval base in the Red Sea in December 1991.

By late 1992 the United States was committing military forces into an area that was in the midst of a vicious and escalating tribal and religious power struggle. The protagonists consolidated their power on the bodies of their people. The famine was their most effective instrument for influencing the tribal and ethnic character of the population they controlled, a weapon of choice in physically eliminating the tribes, clans, and subclans they opposed.

The Somalian chaos thrived and still thrives in the context of the Islamist militant surge for hegemony in the strategically crucial areas of the Red Sea and the Horn of Africa. The strongest forces in the region—Iran and Sudan—had long been fierce enemies of the United States and considered the mere presence of the United States a grave threat to their paramount strategic aspirations. In addition all the local parties would have liked and therefore did their utmost to manipulate the American forces into doing their killing for them while legitimizing their own hold on power. Good intentions notwithstanding, the United States found itself mired in a vicious quagmire in the Horn of Africa.

———————

U.S. MARINES LANDED on the beaches of Somalia in early December 1992 under the glare of cameras—an army of American electronic media representatives was awaiting them. For the first days the mission of the marines in Somalia went peacefully and without any major clash with local forces. But the marines had not yet made contact with the country's Islamist forces.

The initial impression of relative tranquility was deceiving. For more than a year Iran and Sudan had been engaged in a fierce campaign to consolidate their control over the Red Sea and the Horn of Africa. Somalia, a Muslim country stretching along the all-important littoral of the Horn of Africa, attracted the attention of Khartoum and Tehran. The chaos in Somalia, fractured along tribal lines and immersed in a fierce struggle for self-determination and power, made segments of the population and their power-hungry leaders amenable to close cooperation with and susceptible to manipulation and exploitation by Turabi's people in Khartoum. Islamism was spreading in the ranks of the various tribal militia in Somalia, and by fall 1992 the armed Islamist movements in Somalia were growing fast.

By now Khartoum and Tehran had in place a well-organized leadership and high command system ready to spring into action. Turabi was personally close to some of the local Islamist leaders and supervised many regional activities. The IRGC deputy commander, General Rahim Safavi, and Turabi's deputy, Ali Uthman Taha, were directly in charge of the operations in Somalia itself.

After the summer of 1992 most experienced terrorist trainees were sent to the Iranian-controlled camps in Sudan. George Logokwa, the Sudanese labor minister who defected in Egypt in August 1992, described the situation in these camps at the time of his defection: "They receive tough training in all types of combat, violence, and assassinations—to be sent, from time to time, to some neighboring countries to explore the situation, carry out limited and swift operations, and await the major plan devised by the [National Islamic] Front to send its members to the countries chosen as targets for intensive activity." In the camps Khartoum intensified the training of armed units, each manned by fighters from a specific East African state and each prepared to engage conventional military forces.

As with all Islamist terrorist and subversive forces, in order for the center—Khartoum and Tehran—to implement its grand designs, it needed influence over the local strongmen. The key regional allies that Khartoum and Tehran were able to cultivate demonstrated the extent of Turabi's influence.

Turabi was very close to Abdul-Rahman Ahmad Ahmad Ali Tour, the leader of Somaliland, who proclaimed the Sharia the law of the land and consequently enjoyed Sudanese-Iranian assistance. In central Somalia, the most active and loyal adherent to Turabi was General Muhammad Abshir, the former chief of police in Mogadishu, who determined the pro-Sudanese stand of the Somali Salvation Democratic Front (SSDF), now run by Abdullahhi Yussuf. "Volunteers" from Sudan, Egypt, and Pakistan-Afghanistan joined the SSDF forces in 1992. In addition, General Aidid was already receiving material and logistical aid from Turabi's Sudan as part of a fledgling military cooperation between Sudan and Aidid. In mid-1992 a company from Colonel Suleiman Muhammad Suleiman's training facilities in central Sudan deployed to Mogadishu and subsequently participated in the fighting against Ali Mahdi Muhammad's forces. The main purpose of this deployment was to test the Sudanese ability to deploy, maintain, and control forces in Somalia.

In Ethiopia the combination of Iranian money and Sudanese pressure and subversion transformed the Oromo Liberation Front, a nationalist liberation front consisting of the largest nationality of southern Ethiopia and northern Kenya, into the Islamic Front for the Liberation of Oromo. This transformation had a direct impact on the situation in Somalia—in 1993 some of the supply lines that bin Laden organized would run through the Oromo-controlled areas. In Djibouti, Turabi's strongest supporter was the uncle of Ismail Omar Guelle, the nation's chief of security. Weapons and funds would be channeled via Djibouti.

The recruiting and running of these networks of influence required that a lot of money quietly change hands. Although Turabi himself and a few key Sudanese aides built the contacts and established loyalties, it was up to Osama bin Laden to get the money safely to its destination. In mid-1992, when Khartoum and Tehran began markedly expanding and accelerating their operations in East Africa, the support networks they had in place could not handle the new volume of activities. But bin Laden and his team were able to quickly establish the required financial networks, using existing businesses and bank accounts throughout Europe and East Africa. At first he used his own array of financial interests in the region. When these were not sufficient to cope with the volume and diversity of the clandestine flow of funds, he tapped into comparable assets of like-minded Saudi and Gulf Arab businessmen he had known for a long time and trusted. In some cases, bin Laden and his friends even established front companies and bogus bank accounts in East Africa to expedite the clandestine flow of funds.

Meanwhile some of the local terrorist and irregular forces were also coming under the influence of Sudan and Iran. Since early 1992 Turabi had overseen the establishment of numerous jihad organizations of highly trusted Islamists from Eritrea and Somalia. Turabi created the Somali Islamic Union Party (SIUP), an umbrella of a few Islamist organizations with clan or tribal loyalties, as the main vehicle for Iranian-Sudanese operations, including the insertion of expert terrorists. In Somalia the SIUP continued to be influenced by the guidance and inclinations of Turabi. Muhammad Uthman, the SIUP's nominal leader, issued political communiqués in London but was not involved in actual activities in Somalia. The SIUP conducted initial military operations in June 1992, launching an attack in the Bosaso area in the north that proved indecisive. On-site activities were consolidated on August 15, 1992, by a major Iranian-Sudanese delegation that arrived in Marka for a major conference with local SIUP commanders on their future operational plans. The two senior officers in charge of Somalian operations, Rahim Safavi and Ali Uthman Taha, personally led the delegation, indicating its importance to both Tehran and Khartoum. The visiting experts determined what kind of assistance in training and equipment the SIUP required in order to become a potent military force and, on returning to Khartoum, ordered the quick implementation of their recommendations.

By fall 1992 the Islamist armed forces in Somalia were visibly growing and improving, with centers of operations in Mogadishu, Marka, and Bosaso. Iran, via Sudan, was the primary source of weapons and funds for these movements. The SIUP had a solid presence in Bosaso in the north and Marka and Jamaame in the south. Moreover, Sudanese loyalists were holding Laas Qoray, overlooking the Gulf of Aden, which is an ideal site for an antishipping base. Additional training camps for Islamists were established in Somaliland and in Ogaden, across the border in Ethiopia. Again bin Laden played a supporting but crucial role in this endeavor. Once Khartoum decided for operational reasons to establish base camps and storage sites in the Ogaden, on Ethiopian soil, bin Laden arranged for the establishment of "legitimate" international companies. These companies then launched agricultural development projects in the area, and these projects provided the cover for the transfer of funds into Ethiopia. Bin Laden then oversaw the quick transfer of "clean" funds from these projects to purchase numerous farms, built the required facilities, and paid the running expenses. This infrastructure would soon prove crucial for the Islamist surge into Somalia.

In fall 1992, once the media campaign in the West for a military-humanitarian intervention in Somalia began having an impact on political circles, Sudanese-Iranian activities escalated markedly. Turabi's and Tehran's protégés were immersed in a feverish attempt to align bases, disciples, and followers in the context of the famine. The most important preparations were virtually completed on the eve of the arrival of the first U.S. Marines. In Mogadishu, for example, a new Islamist organization "emerged" and joined the clannish street fighting alongside the forces of General Aidid. Aidid's cooperation was ensured by the flow of additional material and logistical aid from Turabi. However, these Islamist forces "disappeared" just in time, days and hours before the marines hit the beaches.

The Islamists' decision to fight the U.S. forces was determined by the Iranian-Sudanese strategy. The tenets of this strategy were clearly outlined in the Islamist analysis of the U.S. intervention. Islamists throughout the Middle East elucidated the perception of threat and the expediency of action as perceived by Khartoum and Tehran.

The Egyptian analysis, later emphasized by the Muslim Brotherhood, set the tone. It argued that the dispatch of U.S. forces to Somalia was part of a U.S.-Israeli conspiracy to prevent Arab and/or Muslim control over the Red Sea and the Horn of Africa. Palestinian Islamists were apprehensive that the forces amassed by the United States under the excuse of supporting Somalia were "a prelude to a U.S. military strike" against Sudan. The United States was "annoyed by Sudan's successes in the Horn of Africa, especially Sudan's increasing influence in Ethiopia, Eritrea, and the influence it has on the Kenyan opposition, which is expected to win the next elections." Even semiofficial Cairo conceded that "Sudan's turn [may] come after Somalia."

Writing in the authoritative Islamist newspaper *al-Quds al-Arabi*, Dr. Hatim al-Husseini, an Islamist commentator and analyst, provided the most coherent Islamist analysis of the situation. He concluded that only an all-Islamic drastic action aimed at Arab and/or Muslim pro-Western regimes and the foreign forces could prevent another catastrophe:

> This U.S. military intervention, on the pretext of humanitarian aid for the hungry, will consolidate the U.S. military presence in a new strategic region and strengthen the U.S. military presence in the Arabian Peninsula and the Gulf. The direct cause of this U.S. military intervention is the Arab and Islamic failure to solve the problems of the Arab and Islamic nations.
>
> It is the return of Western imperialism against a background of Arab and Islamic differences and backwardness. It is a new Western direct military control of important and sensitive areas in the heart of the Islamic Nation. It is a new proof of the Arab and Islamic governments' failure to solve the Islamic Nation's problems through joint unified actions.

Expressing Tehran's view of the situation, HizbAllah warned that the real objective of the U.S. intervention in Somalia was Sudan. The United States could not tolerate the existence of a Sudanese policy based on the Sharia that challenged and confronted U.S. interests. "The [U.S.] return to the Horn of Africa is intended to confront the Islamic revival that shines from the Horn of Africa. This is not the first intervention and will not be the last. Washington must throw its weight and military strength against every Islamic or national awakening in any area that seeks to achieve independence and end subservient policies. This will be a common phenomenon by the end of this century and into the next." HizbAllah concluded that only a resolute action could reverse this trend and ensure the progress of the Islamist revolution in the entire region.

In the first days of the U.S. intervention the military and organizational capabilities of the Islamists, especially the SIUP, were not tested because their leaders had avoided exposure. This inaction, observed an Arab official in private, "must be viewed as part of al-Turabi's strategy aimed at building an Islamic belt around Sudan. Al-Turabi believes that such a belt would protect the experiment of making the country Islamic and turning it into a base for the Islamic movement in the Arab and African regions. The SIUP has counterparts in Kenya, Djibouti, and other African countries. The common denominator is that they are almost wholly guided by al-Turabi's instructions." Major intensification of the Islamist drive was taking place in Somalia, Uganda, Tanzania, Chad, and Kenya.

At the same time both Sudan and Iran not only "explicitly opposed the U.S. intervention in Somalia" but were apprehensive about the strategic ramifications of the presence of U.S. forces in the Horn of Africa. On November 28, 1992, the moment the United States declared its intention to deploy to Somalia, a large Iranian delegation led by Ayatollah Mohammad Yazdi and including some thirty members of the intelligence, security, and military services, economics experts, and diplomats rushed to Khartoum for urgent consultations on their joint reaction. As a result of Yazdi's visit, a new "protocol for security cooperation" between Iran and Sudan was signed in Tehran by the two intelligence services. The primary objective of the new agreement was to expedite Tehran's support for the Sudanese security agencies in sponsoring terrorism against and subversion of both domestic opposition and "other Arab regimes" in the region. Sudanese teams were already being trained by the IRGC intelligence in Mashhad and Qom.

Tehran and Khartoum decided on a combination of activating existing contingency plans and adopting some new drastic measures. A special committee headed by Ali Uthman Taha and including Sudanese and Iranian senior officials was put in charge of planning Somalian operations. The mission given to the Taha committee was "to turn Somalia into a trap and quagmire for the U.S. forces through a guerrilla war against them." The committee decided not to do anything before the situation in Somalia was closely studied. "The committee will follow developments in the American military intervention in Somalia and draft plans to resist it" through local organizations and the SIUP.

The Taha committee's decisions were immediately reflected by the reluctance of the SIUP and other Islamist forces to confront or resist the U.S. forces. "It is no secret that in its monitoring of the American action in Somalia, SIUP will not proceed out of Somalia's interests alone, but also from what the party considers to be the interest of Islamic internationalism, which al-Turabi seeks to establish through several frameworks he derived to attract Islamic trends worldwide. The SIUP military action against the American presence in Somalia will be linked with developments in regional sensitivities connected with the international forces' scope of action in the region," explained a well-connected Lebanese analyst.

Tehran and Khartoum anticipated a major escalation against the U.S. and other Western forces. For these highly specialized and risky operations, Tehran authorized through Yazdi the establishment of the Somali Revolutionary Guard (SRG), to be manned by Iranian Pasdaran and Lebanese HizbAllah experts already based in Sudan. The SRG was put under the command of Ali Manshawi, an Iranian intelligence officer.

The Islamist forces also increased their preparations inside Somalia for the armed struggle against the Western forces. These preparations ranged from agitating the population to specific military buildup. "Hostility toward a U.N. presence is manifested in Friday sermons in Somalia's mosques," noted an on-site observer. Trained militants and fighters gathered in the SIUP's camps in northern Somalia and the Ogaden. The flow of weapons from Pakistan, Iran, and Sudan—all channeled through Sudan—to these forces intensified markedly after late November 1992.

A coherent strategy for the Islamist struggle for Somalia was emerging. The Islamist sponsoring states decided that Somali Islamists (mainly the SIUP, with active support from the SRG and other terrorists) would capitalize on the growing politicization of the U.S. presence—such as involvement in "deal making" with warlords and tribes and/or clans—"to promote fighting the U.S. presence to drive the American forces out before the United States achieves its [real] objectives." The SIUP considered the real U.S. objectives to be (1) controlling the new oil grid in Sudan, Somalia, Eritrea, and Yemen, which was the ultimate reason for and hidden agenda behind the "humanitarian" arrival of the marines; (2) setting up a pro-American government in Mogadishu; and (3) advancing from Somalia into southern Sudan, which would then become "a region to wear out the Islamic question" the same way that Iraqi Kurdistan was already being used to wear out Saddam Hussein. The Taha committee would order the escalation of the fighting in Somalia and especially activation of the elite terrorist forces only when it perceived the American actions to be threatening the strategic interests of Tehran and Khartoum.

Despite the decision not to engage the U.S. forces in Somalia, the Islamist leadership could not afford to let the beginning of a U.S. presence in the Horn of Africa go unnoticed. It was imperative to strike—even if symbolically—at an indirect facet of this buildup just to gain attention. It was decided to hit the recently established U.S. support installations in Aden, South Yemen, because they both supported preparations for the Somalian intervention and were in Asia, across the Red Sea from Africa. With the primary Iranian-Sudanese networks preoccupied with preparations for the anticipated major confrontation in Mogadishu, someone else would need to oversee this effort. Osama bin Laden, with his comprehensive contacts in both Yemen and Afghanistan-Pakistan, was ideal for the job.

Operating under tremendous time pressure, bin Laden decided to capitalize on old and proven contacts to expedite the strike. The main strike force would be drawn from the ranks of Yemenite "Afghans." The original plan called for bombing a couple of hotels in Aden used by U.S. military personnel and facilities in the sea and at airports. To ensure the plan's completion despite all the difficulties and challenges, bin Laden convinced Sheikh Tariq al-Fadli to leave his London exile and personally take charge of the operation. Fadli was covertly inserted into Yemen in mid-November. To save time the large sums of money required for the scheme were transferred via accounts related to bin Laden's businesses in Yemen.

In early December the strike force was taking shape under the cover of the Yemeni Islamic Jihad organization. The main terrorists were drawn from the ranks of some 500 highly trained Yemeni "Afghans" under the direct command of Sheikh Tariq al-Fadli. Their main base was in the Saadah area. Because of the time constraints bin Laden and Fadli decided to use Islamic Jihad hit squads already in place in Aden to assassinate local politicians. For the planned operation against the Americans, these squads would be augmented with expert bomb makers and additional equipment.

Toward this end a special training facility was hastily organized in the Saadah area, in northern Yemen, some 50 miles south of the Saudi border. At least one Libyan expert bomb maker was brought in from Afghanistan-Pakistan. Additional expert terrorists, as well as the equipment and weapons needed for the operation, were smuggled from Sudan across the Red Sea to an isolated coast near al-Khawkhah, on the northern coast of Yemen. One of the Libyan "Afghans" established his "school" in a safe house near Saadah. His role was to train several Yemenite "Afghans" as bomb makers and bombers and supervise the construction of the bombs. The Libyan left Yemen and vanished the day before the Aden attack.

On December 29 the Islamist terrorists detonated bombs in the Aden Hotel and Golden Moor Hotel in Aden, killing three and wounding five. In addition, a strike team carrying RPG-7 rocket launchers was caught near the fences of the Aden airport getting ready to launch at U.S. Air Force transport planes, including a C-5 Galaxy, parked nearby.

The haste of implementing these quick operations resulted in numerous security lapses. On December 31 Egyptian intelligence, which was called in by the Yemeni government to help in the investigation, already had proof that "the leader of the terrorist groups that are trying to spoil security and stability in Yemen is a person named Osama bin Laden." On January 8, 1993, Sheikh Tariq al-Fadli and his followers surrendered to Yemeni authorities, their mission accomplished.

Sheikh Abdul Majid Zandani, another friend of bin Laden's and follower of Turabi, delivered the political message. In permitting the presence of U.S. troops, the Yemeni government was implementing "practices and initiatives that undermine Islam." No wonder there was an indigenous groundswell leading to terrorism, he argued. Pointing out that the mere presence of U.S. forces in Aden was causing terrorism and putting public safety at risk, Zandani asked, "Why can't the Americans go directly to Mogadishu?" This statement underscored, although indirectly, the real message of this terrorist operation.

Back in Khartoum, despite the failure of the strike on the Aden airport, Turabi and the Islamist elite were satisfied, for the Islamist rage over the U.S. activities in the Horn of Africa had been clearly expressed. Osama bin Laden was highly praised for having pulled off such a complicated operation on such short notice. His willingness to use and risk his personal assets was duly noted. He would play an even greater role in the forthcoming confrontation in Somalia.

THE MAJOR ESCALATION of the fighting in Mogadishu that took place in fall 1993 was the implementation of the long-term plan decided on by Tehran and Khartoum. This escalation was also the first manifestation of a strategic alliance between Iran, Iraq, and Sudan. In early 1993 Iraq embarked on a revitalization of its terrorist campaign under an Islamist banner, with active support from Turabi and Sudan. Baghdad was using "Afghans" who had been retrained in camps run by Iraqi intelligence and special forces near Baghdad. These Iraqi-controlled Islamist terrorists were now operating in close cooperation with the Iranian-controlled Islamist international terrorist system.

In early December 1992 Yazdi, Turabi, and Bashir decided that in February 1993 they would conduct a major and thorough reexamination of the situation in the entire region even if no major crisis had erupted. These consultations would take place during a conference of nineteen Islamist movements "linked with the Islamic Revolution in Iran" that would be convened in Khartoum by Turabi. The Khartoum conference would examine the prudence of initiating a major escalation in the Horn of Africa and its impact on such related issues as the Islamist subversion of Egypt, stability in the Persian Gulf, and the long-planned revival of Islamist international terrorism in Western Europe and the United States. The conference would also examine the influence that the anticipated developments in the Horn of Africa would have on the overall posture of the Tehran-led Islamic bloc and the various contingency plans then being studied in Tehran, from terrorism against Israel to the possibility of launching a Middle East war. But on instructions from the leaders in Tehran and Khartoum, implementation of the first phase of the plan began immediately, before this conference, so that the Islamist forces could immediately meet any challenge.

For the operations in Somalia, Tehran began to draw on never before used strategic terrorist assets—the "al-Quds Forces." In the mid-1980s Iran had drafted and trained a large number of Afghan refugees as terrorists and saboteurs under the supervision of the IRGC. Some 1,200 additional "Afghans" in Pakistan were involved in drug smuggling to Europe and the United States, using networks affiliated with Iranian intelligence. These "Afghans" constituted the core of the al-Quds Forces—the Tehran-controlled individual cadres integrated into the Sunni international terrorist system. Many of these "Afghans" had been transferred to Sudan in preparation for their use in the anticipated Islamist struggle in the Horn of Africa. Simultaneously in late fall 1992 Pakistani and Iranian intelligence officials had made hectic efforts to purchase leftover Stinger missiles held by the mujahideen. These weapons were also shipped to Sudan for possible use in Somalia.

The IRGC continued to expand the training of Sunni Islamist terrorists in Iran. By late 1992 some 9,000 Arab "Afghans," mainly from Egypt, Jordan, Algeria, and Tunisia, were in the IRGC training camps in Mashhad and Qom. A marked increase began in the training of elite terrorists from Iran, Egypt, Algeria, Tunisia, Jordan, Israel, Saudi Arabia, and the Arab Persian Gulf States. The main training center was the Imam Ali department in Saadabad, a former palace of the Shah in northern Tehran, where the al-Quds Forces were being trained. The direct commander of the al-Quds Forces was General Ahmad Vahidi, formerly the head of the Information Department of IRGC General Command, which was responsible for "the export of the revolution"—that is, sponsorship of terrorism. In the Imam Ali department the terrorists were trained primarily as instructors and commanders who would run and expand networks in their homelands. They also received sophisticated sabotage training. The Saudis and the Persian Gulf Arabs traveled to the Imam Ali department in Iran with specially provided Syrian passports. Other Sunni terrorists from Egypt, Jordan, and the Gulf countries were trained in Qom, Tabriz, and Mashhad. Candidates from "secular" states first received theological and ideological instructions and tempering in Qom and only then were sent to military training in the

Saadabad camp near Tehran. Follow-up and refresher courses were organized in Lebanon and Sudan. The instructors were IRGC and al-Quds Forces officers.

Between late 1992 and early 1993 "Afghans" associated with these Iranian al-Quds Forces were deployed to several sites in the Horn of Africa—from Sudan to Yemen, including Somalia and the Ogaden—pending an escalation. They included an elite unit of some 500 members of Yemen's Islamic Jihad, all of them "Afghans" and all loyal to Sheikh Tariq al-Fadli. The collapse of their terrorist effort in Aden did not diminish the commitment of the bulk of this force. Because the Iranian and Sudanese planners had opted for larger, high-quality forces back in 1992, Osama bin Laden organized the transfer from Pakistan to Yemen of yet another force, a total of 3,000 Yemeni "Afghans." These "Afghans" brought with them heavy weapons and terrorist equipment, including high explosives, sophisticated remote-control bombs, booby-trapped dolls, and a few Stingers. This "Afghan" elite force established bases in the Saadah area in the al-Maraqishah Mountains, Yemen. In mid-1993, with the escalation in Mogadishu looming, bin Laden moved these "Afghans," their weapons, and their equipment from Yemen to Somalia in a quick airlift. He would later tell an Egyptian interviewer that this operation cost him $3 million of his own money.

At the same time Iranian Pasdaran and Somalian terrorists, directly controlled and sponsored by Iran, were being organized in Sudan to provide support and supplies for Sudanese Islamic Union (SIUP) units trained in the art of surprise suicide operations. In addition several hundred Arab "Afghans" earmarked for intervention in Somalia were dispatched to camps in western Sudan near the Libyan border for advanced training pending dispatch to Somalia.

These initial preparations were completed on time in the middle of February 1993 to meet the scheduled February examination of progress agreed on by Yazdi, Turabi, and Bashir back in December 1992. On February 19 Iranian terrorist experts, who had just arrived from Tehran, and members of AIM's Higher Liaison Committee convened in Khartoum to thoroughly study the situation in the Horn of Africa and Egypt and the latest developments in the posture of the New York terrorist network then operating under the spiritual guidance of Sheikh Omar Abdul Rahman. The experts were satisfied with the preparations and ordered the several outstanding terrorist contingency plans to go ahead—including the escalation of terrorism in Somalia and the World Trade Center bombing in the United States. Senior commanders of the SIUP took part in the meetings in Khartoum and were intimately involved in the decision to escalate the armed struggle against the United States.

Senior commanders serving under Muhammad Farrah Aidid also took part in some of the sessions in Khartoum and agreed wholeheartedly to implement the Iranian-Sudanese operational plan. In the aftermath of the Khartoum conference, over a period of from six to eight weeks, Aidid and his key military and intelligence aides traveled repeatedly to Iran, Yemen, Sudan, Ethiopia, and Uganda to acquaint themselves with the other components of the master plan. Aidid himself traveled clandestinely at least twice to both Sudan and Iran in order to discuss strategy and methods of "dealing with the international forces" in Somalia as well as to coordinate the modalities for the arrival of "increased aid should the situation escalate into military confrontations."

While in Khartoum in early spring 1993, Aidid also held important meetings with Iraqi intelligence officials in the Iraqi Embassy. These meetings and the subsequent arrangement with Baghdad were organized by Hassan al-Turabi as a key element in his effort to further consolidate the strategic alliance between Iran, Sudan, and Iraq, with special emphasis on saving Sudan from U.S. intervention. Baghdad promised Aidid extensive help in what an Iraqi official defined as "the framework of a comprehensive confrontation plan created to resist the United States and international forces in Somalia, and turn it into a new Vietnam." Baghdad also agreed to support Turabi in strengthening other Islamist militant groups all over the Horn of Africa.

In the spring the Mogadishu operation became so important to Baghdad that Saddam Hussein nominated his son Qusay to personally supervise the anti-American operations in Somalia and the Horn of Africa as a whole. Iraqi intelligence officials in Khartoum said Saddam Hussein was determined "to achieve a Mother of Battles victory in Somalia." Soon afterward the Iraqi Embassy in Khartoum was expanded by the arrival of several intelligence and special forces experts, including members of Saddam Hussein's own Special Security Agency. They were charged with supporting the "war scenario against the United States and international forces in Somalia." Turabi was recognized as the senior authority in this joint effort.

Several detachments of expert Islamist terrorists, including Iranian Pasdaran; Lebanese HizbAllah; Arab, mainly Egyptian, "Afghans"; and local Islamist elements—members of Sudan's National Islamic Front, the SIUP of Somalia, Kenya's Islamic Republic Organization, the Islamic Front for the Liberation of Ethiopia, and Eritrea's Islamic Jihad—were secretly deployed by June 1993. This infiltration of Somalia with yet another force of some 3,000 Islamist terrorists and extensive quantities of weapons and equipment was also a bin Laden operation. The Islamist networks in Mombasa, Kenya, received a small number of these terrorists and smuggled them into Somalia.

The bulk of this Islamist force, however, converged on the "farms" bin Laden had acquired, and there they established their rear and support facilities. From these safe havens they sent forward elements that first established training camps and storage sites in the Mogadishu area. The first "Afghans" to arrive in Somalia were expert terrorists who "specialized in gang wars, street fighting, booby-trapped cars, commando operations, and sniping operations" with the task of destabilizing Mogadishu. All this time the SIUP was receiving reinforcements and supplies in Bosaso and Laas Qoray in anticipation of the escalation. Senior SIUP commanders arrived in Marka and Mogadishu in May to prepare for the escalation, study conditions in the theater, and then return to Khartoum for further consultations.

In the early summer, once the initial preparations were completed, including deployment of terrorist experts, the Islamist detachments, operating in and out of Aidid's parts of Mogadishu, began a series of ambushes, including bombing attacks, on the U.S.-U.N. forces to test the validity of the senior officials' reading of those forces' reaction. These test runs culminated in a lethal ambush on June 5, 1993. The Western (U.S. and U.N.) version is that militiamen of General Aidid killed twenty-three to twenty-six Pakistani U.N. troops, forces contributed by Islamabad in order to placate the Clinton administration and "balance" the impact of its growing sponsorship of terrorist activities. In reality, it was the baptism by fire of the "Afghan" forces.

In Somalia this clash had an immediate and dramatic impact on the strength and cohesion of the Islamist alliance under Aidid's banner. A unified high command emerged. Even allies-turned-enemies of Aidid acknowledged that in his confrontation with the "oppressive" U.N.-U.S. troops, Aidid had consolidated and solidified a widespread alliance and popular support. The former president of Somaliland, Abdirahman Tur, called Aidid a "hero" for resisting and confronting the West, especially the Americans. Mohammad Hassan Awali, Aidid's foreign affairs adviser, stressed that as a result of the operations against the U.N.-U.S. forces, many tribes and political/military forces joined the SNA-led coalition and recognized Aidid as their supreme leader.

But far more important events were already taking place elsewhere. U.N. patrols responded with heavy fire to the continued ambushes and bombing attacks. In the aftermath of this U.S.-led U.N. reaction to the escalation of the fighting in Mogadishu, Aidid warned of a widespread escalation. "If they [U.N.-U.S. forces] attack somebody, it will be the general public they attack," he warned. On June 11, soon after subsequent clashes with the Pakistani and American forces, Aidid and several of his senior military aides left Mogadishu.

Aidid and his senior aides went to Khartoum to take part in special consultations conducted under cover of a special session of the People's Arab and Islamic Congress chaired by Turabi. The public session was dedicated to condemning "U.S. genocide" against Muslims as demonstrated in Somalia and Palestine. In closed sessions the congress decided to escalate the struggle and increase Islamist help for the Somalis, including the activation of assets. Although invited to participate in this conference, bin Laden elected to act as one of Turabi's inner circle of advisers. Ayman al-Zawahiri, a leader of Egyptian Islamic Jihad based in Pakistan-Afghanistan and now a close ally of both bin Laden and Tehran, took part in the Khartoum conference. The importance of this conference is apparent from the presence of extremely high-level Iranian intelligence officials and other Islamist terrorist experts who also discussed and approved in clandestine meetings terrorist plans for a series of spectacular July 4 bombings in New York. (This plan was narrowly averted by the FBI.)

The June Khartoum conference constituted a milestone in Iran's strategic approach to the region. With Tehran concentrating on escalating terrorism in Europe—in connection with the situation in Bosnia-Herzegovina—and especially in the United States, the Iranian senior officials gave the green light for Baghdad to assume a greater role in running the operations in Somalia. These operations remained, however, under the tight control of a joint high command controlled by Tehran and Khartoum.

The Khartoum conference also formulated the Iraqi-Sudanese-Iranian contingency plans "to confront the Americans in Somalia" with the aim of "drawing them into a land war, street battles, attack and retreat, and ambushes, as was done in Vietnam." Once U.S. forces redeployed from too hot Mogadishu into seemingly safe areas in the countryside, new Islamist forces would be introduced into action, attacking them wherever they might be. All of these operations in Somalia were part of "a plan to expand the battle to other areas of the Horn of Africa, and to a broad, armed, mass mobilization against America and the West throughout the region, in a war taking on the dimension of a grand war of vengeance between the Islamists and the United States, whose outcome would be even worse than the result of the Vietnam War."

The Sudanese propaganda machine began disseminating the logic for the forthcoming clash in Somalia. Sudan's minister of state for presidential affairs explained the logic of Sudan's intervention in Somalia. If the United States succeeded in Somalia, it would turn on Islamist Sudan. But because of the Islamist intervention in Somalia, the United States "has achieved no success likely to encourage a similar operation in Sudan." In Khartoum newspapers and other media blasted the U.N. operations, insisting that the

United States had sent the Pakistanis to their death intentionally so that Washington would have an excuse to intervene and return in full force. Khartoum also argued that the singling out of Aidid by the United Nations—the Pakistanis operated near Aidid's radio station when they were ambushed—constituted proof that the United Nations was carrying out Washington's anti-Islamist policy. Sudan's foreign minister warned the United States that "if they decided to interfere in Sudan, they would be met with resistance and a declaration of Jihad."

From June 13 to 15 the United States conducted several air strikes. Despite the damage to facilities, Somali militia put up a stiff resistance. They fought the U.S. ground troops and escorting Cobra gunships that attempted to capture Aidid's house.

Meanwhile, immediately after the conclusion of the Khartoum conference, several of the key terrorist experts traveled clandestinely to Somalia, even into Mogadishu, to personally inspect the situation and assess whether changes should be made because of the escalation. The senior on-site Islamist commanders who would take charge of the forthcoming escalation participated in these trips. For example, Zawahiri visited Somaliland as part of a clandestine Islamist delegation of experts sent to set up a new logistical system that would sustain the projected flow of "Afghans" and massive quantities of weapons and ammunition for the anticipated escalation in assistance for Aidid. The predominantly Egyptian "Afghan" force—which also included Saudi, Afghan, and Algerian "Afghans"—would operate under the banner of the Vanguard of Islamic Conquest, with Zawahiri as the senior on-site commander. In Khartoum, Osama bin Laden was organizing yet another set of lines of communications and logistical support systems. In fact, he was leading an immense effort to move thousands of people clandestinely from Sudan to Somalia through third countries, Ethiopia and Eritrea. Many of these moves would take place under extremely inhospitable desert conditions. Toward this end bin Laden arranged for trucks and fuel; food and water; weapons, ammunition, and explosives; and medical kits. The forces on the move had to be provided with lodging, resupply points, means of communication, and reception points. Bin Laden also arranged for a great deal of money to be transferred to both Ethiopia and Eritrea so that locally available items and services could be purchased.

By now the Islamist infrastructure was beginning to consolidate. The main Islamist terrorist bases were south of Mogadishu and in Kismayu, Bardheere, Marka (where the SIUP was centered), and Galcaio (Aidid's backup headquarters and storage site for heavy weapons, tanks, artillery, and the like). Iranian IRGC intelligence established a separate logistical center in Bosaso to insert clandestinely antitank and antiaircraft weapons, including SA-7s. Some 900 of Iran's own Pasdaran and HizbAllah fighters, organized as the SRG, deployed in Somalia for spectacular operations. In addition, about 1,200 members of Iraq's elite strike forces—al-Saiqah Commando—deployed to Somalia. Both forces prepared to participate in the all-out attack on the U.S. forces. The Islamist experts had already trained, organized, and equipped some 15,000 Somalis in these camps and were ready to lead them into combat against the Americans.

The U.S. attack in Mogadishu on July 12, 1993, was interpreted by the senior commanders in Khartoum as the beginning of the long-anticipated escalation. Immediately a meeting of thirty senior commanders, including foreigners and members of the Habar Gidir tribe, was convened by Aidid to decide on implementing the escalation plan formulated in Khartoum. They ordered activation of the contingent in Bosaso, with operatives from Sudan, Iraq, Iran, Lebanon, and the Horn of Africa. High-level consultations also took place between Sudan and Iran on the situation in Somalia and what to do about it.

Fighting, including attacks on civilian aid workers, escalated during early July not just in Mogadishu but also all over central Somalia. This escalation reflected Aidid's widening alliances. On July 12 the SNA issued a communiqué vowing that it would "continue to fight until the last United Nations soldier departs." Special vengeance would be taken against the American troops because they continued "to carry out their own genocide and massacre of the Somali people." Leaflets in English and Somali were spread all over Mogadishu, warning the citizens to be aware of an imminent attack on U.S. forces. Aidid's followers were urged to strike at the Americans in order to "avenge their dead." In another manifesto Aidid urged Somalis to take on the superior U.N.-U.S. forces despite the odds and "sacrifice themselves for freedom" while fighting "what goes against their dignity." Aidid's forces fired at the U.S. Embassy and attacked other U.N. positions all over Mogadishu while Aidid supporters continued mass rallies and demonstrations. Sporadic attacks continued until the end of July 1993.

The new self-confidence was clearly expressed in Aidid's propaganda during the second half of July. A senior aide, Mohamad Salad Mahmud Habib, argued that the U.N. pursued a "policy of neo-colonialism [that] comes under the guise of humanitarian assistance and ensuring peace. These eventually lead to direct interference in the internal affairs of a country while pursuing the policies of divide and conquer, creating confrontations, inciting people against each other, and selling and splitting them into tribes, clans, subclans, right down to family levels." Aidid's radio repeatedly reported that the U.S.-led U.N. forces were intentionally destroying mosques and other historical Islamic sites. Farah Ali Mohammad Duur-gube, a noted writer, declared that "Somali fighters have agreed to defend their country, the dignity of their people and their religion, and to make the neo-colonialists taste hell on earth. God willing, in the hereafter they will also be cast into hell even worse than that [in Mogadishu]. Let us kill them all, right to the last of these demoralized colonialists."

Aidid's high-profile propaganda, which attracted U.S. and U.N. attention, was actually a cover for the arrival of new participants in the Mogadishu urban war. The new Islamist force, called the Vanguard of the Somali Islamic Salvation, was a "Somalization" of Iran's Egyptian-led "Afghans." On August 3, 1993, in the first communiqué broadcast on their own radio station and in leaflets, the Vanguard urged Somalis to escalate their jihad against the "satanic" U.S. forces. Somalis must "launch a Holy War against the satanic troops of the United States. . . . Every Muslim is obliged to take part in this war." The very same day Aidid's radio station stressed the Iranian propaganda line that the United States was the organizer of global terrorism aimed primarily at Muslim and Third World countries. An aide to Aidid elaborated, explaining that an important part of U.S. colonialism was also the spread of higher education among the literate in order to brainwash them into assuming pro-U.S. and anti-Islamic positions.

During early August 1993 Aidid's forces and those of his allies were making last-minute preparations for a major escalation of the fighting in southern Mogadishu. The Islamists anticipated that "a decisive battle will inevitably occur between General Aidid and the international, and particularly the American, forces." Highly trained Islamist units from the Habar Gidir tribe were first introduced into combat against the Americans. Under the name Somali Islamic Salvation Movement (SISM), they claimed responsibility for the August 11 blast, achieved by a HizbAllah-style remote-controlled bomb, that killed four American soldiers. "SISM has so far carried out several operations aimed at eliminating Yankees and their puppets, and managed to kill four devils of the U.S. Yankees," their communiqué read. The SISM explained that it was also waging an "Islamic struggle against the infidels and pagans" in order to "restore Islamic law" in Somalia. Arab observers noted that "General Aidid's calls for Jihad have come to be transmitted from the communications media of this relatively organized Islamic group that is thought to have financial resources reaching it from outside the borders." This flow of funds, the importance of which was stressed by the Arab observers, was organized and run by Osama bin Laden. Operating in the shadows, he continued to facilitate Islamist activities with a sustained and efficient support system, a contribution crucial to the Islamist war effort. Also in early August one of Aidid's envoys visited

Libya to arrange for additional financial and military assistance to implement the planned escalation of the fighting against the U.S.-U.N. forces.

The full gravity of the mid-August escalation was best expressed in Khartoum. After consultations with Tehran, General Bashir erroneously concluded that a U.S. military intervention against Sudan could be expected in late December or early January. Turabi and Ali Uthman consulted on how to best prepare for such an eventuality, emphasizing prevention or preemption of this U.S. military intervention. Reflecting the mood in Khartoum, Brigadier Abdul-Rahim Muhammad Hussein affirmed that Sudan was "on the road of Jihad and bearing arms to defend faith and the homeland." Tehran was confident that despite threats, Khartoum remained determined to continue its "struggle" with the United States. Mustafa Uthman, one of Turabi's aides, urged the establishment of an Iranian-Sudanese "common strategy" against the United States to prevent collapse of the Islamic stand in the region.

In Mogadishu, Aidid's radio stated that the crisis was "deepening day by day" and anticipated an inevitable explosion. Aidid also declared all U.N. forces to be legitimate targets in the struggle against the United States because the United Nations was serving U.S. interests and its troops were taking part in "the genocide and destruction [peddled] by the United States of America." The propaganda theme now repeated all over Mogadishu was that the United States was planning "to massacre innocent Somalis . . . to attain its colonialist objectives." Fighting in Mogadishu was just part of a major offensive aimed at subverting the Somalis and inciting civil war. Aidid accused the United States of masterminding a campaign of massacres and terrorism and urged Islamic solidarity with the plight of the Somalis. Aidid's radio predicted an imminent escalation in the attacks on civilian quarters of Mogadishu.

As before, anticipation of the escalation was not without foundation. In early September 1993, on orders from Khartoum, the Islamist elite forces, under the banner of the Somali Islamic Union Party (SIUP), engaged the American forces. Although they had been preparing for combat even before the arrival of U.S. forces back in early December 1992, the SIUP forces had not intervened in the fighting until this point and had let Aidid conduct most of the fighting. On September 3 the Somali Islamic Union announced in Tehran that it had launched a series of attacks on U.N. positions in the Mogadishu area. On September 5 Aidid's forces joined the battle and ambushed the Nigerian contingent, part of the U.N. forces, killing seven soldiers. It took a massive intervention of U.S. troops and heavy fire support to relieve the hard-pressed Nigerians.

Khartoum was now confident that the time was ripe for the next escalatory phase. On September 10 the true escalation in the Islamist confrontation with U.S. forces started. The assault began with a series of diversionary attacks by the Islamist Habar Gidir tribal forces on Somalis considered friendly to the United Nations. The U.S.-U.N. forces intervened as expected and fell into an Islamist trap. What appeared to be an intra-Somali clash suddenly turned into an organized ambush and attack on the U.N.-U.S. forces. The U.S. forces retaliated and escalated the conflict. Over the next day the U.S. forces attacked sites of Aidid's SNA forces even though they had played only a minor role in the earlier clashes. Aidid interpreted the attack, and not without reason, as an intentional U.S. effort to affect the balance of power in Mogadishu. He ordered his followers to take part in massive street demonstrations and to launch mortar shells on U.N.-U.S. facilities.

The inevitable result was the eruption on September 13, 1993, of fierce fighting between U.S. forces and Aidid's, with Cobra gunship attacks on Aidid's key sites, including a hospital also used as headquarters and a storage facility. Aidid's people claimed that American forces killed numerous civilians in their attacks and vowed revenge. A cycle of violence began. On September 15 Aidid and the Islamists launched a daylight mortar attack on the U.N. headquarters, and in retaliation the U.S. forces fired mortar shells at the site of Aidid's headquarters. Aidid's supporters, mainly women and children, stoned U.N. patrols in the streets of Mogadishu. The U.N. soldiers opened fire on the crowd to break away, further exacerbating the crisis. The repeated claims of Somalian officials, all supporters of Ali Mahdi Muhammad, and Arabs that "General Aidid is the one responsible for this confrontation" increased the confusion.

The United States embarked on an intentional confrontation with Aidid. After U.S. Rangers captured Osman Hassan Ali (Ato), Aidid's close friend and right-hand man, Aidid ordered retaliatory escalation to deter future raids on his people. Islamist expert terrorists and SNA forces started ambushing American helicopters. On September 26 a Somalian ambush shot down a U.S. UH-60 Blackhawk over Mogadishu. In the United States the televised specter of the jubilant Somalian mob dragging the defiled bodies of American servicemen through the streets of Mogadishu—and the wreckage of the U.S. helicopters—brought home the extent of the debacle. For the Islamists the clash served as a boost to further escalate the confrontation with the United States.

In late September, Khartoum interpreted the marked escalation in the fighting in Mogadishu as a turning point in the Somalian Islamist struggle that, if pursued correctly, would ultimately lead to U.S. losses and withdrawal from Somalia. Tehran ridiculed the United States' accusations of Iranian relations (a "tactical alliance") with Aidid as a mere excuse for the U.S. inability to confront, let alone prevail over, the Islamist trend in Somalia. Isse Mohamed Siad, Aidid's foreign affairs adviser, lamented the change in the character of the U.N. role in Mogadishu. "They [U.N.-U.S.] came to help the Somali people, but their operational method has become one of destruction, bombardment, and arrests with no recourse to law—but rather to the use of force and the barrel of the gun."

In fall 1993 there was no longer any doubt that the escalation of the fighting in Somalia was a result of the long-term plan decided on by Tehran and Khartoum to use the "Islamic International," all the Islamic forces, in a major operation intended to transform Mogadishu into a "second Kabul" or a "second Beirut" for the Americans. By late September the Islamists considered the United States to be entrapped in the Mogadishu quagmire, ripe for a painful humiliation. Expressing the Islamists' strategy, Aidid instructed his troops to "be ready, in concert with our friends and allies, to get rid of the Western occupiers of our country" and "send American and Pakistani soldiers back home in coffins."

Somalian rhetoric and Western propaganda notwithstanding, the escalation in Mogadishu was the first major operation conducted under the general command established the preceding summer in Khartoum for the Islamic International. Hassan al-Turabi was now functioning as the senior leader, with Ayman al-Zawahiri, Abdallah Jaweed (an Afghan Islamist), and Qamar al-Din Dharban (an Algerian) serving under him and directly responsible for the military activities. Osama bin Laden was responsible for the logistical support. In fall 1993 Zawahiri was already in Somalia, operating as the on-site commander in charge and field coordinator. He was working along with his senior "Afghan" commanders and Aidid's senior military aides.

The entire Islamist operational plan was based on the sustained availability of large quantities of ammunition and supplies, which was bin Laden's responsibility. To ensure surprise and avoid preemptive strikes by U.N. forces, these supplies had to be pushed forward from the storage sites in Somaliland to Mogadishu at the last minute. Bin Laden tackled this challenge successfully, presaging future Islamist operational successes.

The most important field commander Zawahiri brought with him to Somalia was Ali al-Rashidi, also known as Abu-Ubaydah al-Banshiri or Abu-Ubaydah al-Banjashiri. An Egyptian confidant of al-Zawahiri for many years, in the 1970s al-Rashidi was a clandestine member of Islamic Jihad in the ranks of the Egyptian police. He was arrested in 1981 in the sweeps following Sadat's assassination, and by 1986 he had spent a total of three years in prison in periodic detention. In 1986 he successfully escaped to Afghanistan, where he first fought with Ahmad Shah Massud's forces in the Panjshir Valley and later joined bin Laden's forces. He and bin Laden became close friends. According to Egyptian sources, "al-Rashidi was

Osama bin Laden's right arm" and supervised the base camps set up by bin Laden in Afghanistan to train Arab mujahideen. Al-Rashidi was also instrumental in cementing the ties between bin Laden and the Egyptian Islamist leaders, including Zawahiri. With the fighting in Afghanistan dwindling down, al-Rashidi began traveling to other jihad fronts as organizer of elite forces based on "Afghans." In that capacity he participated in Islamist jihad operations in Eritrea, Ogaden, Burma, Kashmir, Tajikstan, Chechnya, Bosnia, and Libya. In fall 1993 Zawahiri put him in command of one of his elite units in Mogadishu.

While Aidid's forces would have an increasingly high profile in the escalation in Mogadishu, the real high-quality military assistance was provided to the elite Islamist forces of the SIUP and was earmarked for carrying out the spectacular guerrilla attacks on the U.N.-U.S. forces. In addition the Islamist forces in Somalia, both Arab "Afghans" and Somalian Islamists, were receiving an intense flow of last-minute reinforcements and supplies of high-quality weapons. For the main infiltration of experts and sophisticated equipment, Abdallah Jaweed and Osama bin Laden recruited several ex-DRA Afghan military pilots, all veterans of the massive resupply efforts into besieged DRA garrisons, to fly small transport planes into isolated airfields in Somalia at night. Heavier equipment was smuggled nightly into Somaliland by bin Laden's flotilla of small fishing boats operating out of neighboring countries, mainly Yemen and Kenya. From these points of entry the weapons and people were smuggled by small nomadic caravans into safe houses in the Mogadishu area. A major outcome of this resupply surge was the establishment of a well-organized clandestine headquarters in Mogadishu from which a few Somalian, Afghan, and Algerian experts in urban guerrilla warfare would run the imminent escalation.

The vastly improved capabilities of the Islamist-supported Somalis were clearly demonstrated on the afternoon of October 3, 1993. The U.N.-U.S. forces learned about the presence of two of Aidid's senior foreign policy advisers, Osman Salah and Muhammad Hassan Awali, at the Olympic Hotel. A hasty heliborne assault of fewer than 100 American troops was organized and swiftly captured the two, as well as twenty-two other Aidid supporters, on-site. What seemed a highly successful raid suddenly turned into a major clash. As the U.S. troops prepared for their departure by helicopter, they fell into a well-organized ambush by more than a thousand Somalis. Two UH-60s were shot down, and a third crash-landed at the Mogadishu airport. The American troops established a defensive perimeter around the crash site but were then surrounded and subjected to a sustained fire attack for some eleven hours until they were relieved by a U.S.-U.N. rescue force. In the firefight eighteen American troops were killed, seventy-eight were wounded, and one helicopter pilot was captured. He would be released ten days later. At least 700 Somalis, both fighters and civilians, were injured in the fighting, and some 300 of them were killed. The next day Mogadishu celebrated a great victory, dragging the bodies of American servicemen through the streets.

Numerous Middle Eastern sources insisted that the Mogadishu fighting of late September and especially early October 1993 was a key phase in Islamist-dominated escalation. They attributed the sudden improvement in the performance of the Somali forces to the fact that Iranian-trained Somalis and Arab "Afghans," as well as troops of the Iraqi Saiqah Commando, were directly involved in the Mogadishu fighting, particularly that of October 3, 1993. Many other reports confirm the Islamist analysis.

All the sources agree that the October 3 operation was the first major endeavor by Zawahiri and his expert staff in the Mogadishu area. Additional Iranian senior advisers were on-site, operating under the cover of journalists, with Aidid and his military commanders. The Iranians' presence was also clearly reflected in repeated interviews with Aidid on Radio Tehran and in Iranian magazines.

The intelligence tip received by the U.S. forces in Mogadishu about the presence of Aidid's people at the Olympic Hotel was only a trap set for the Americans. The two SNA officials, although personally close to Aidid, were responsible for contacts and negotiations with the U.S.-U.N. that were dormant at the time, and so the two were expendable. Also, the Americans could be counted on not to kill their prisoners and to release them in due course.

The ensuing ambush was conducted by a hard-core Islamist force under the overall command of al-Rashidi and led by Arab "Afghans" and the Iraqis. The main strike force consisted of SIUP troops trained by Iranians and Iraqis. Under the command of al-Rashidi, the Arab "Afghans"—including Algerian and Egyptian fighters—played a major role in organizing and running the ambush and siege of the U.S. ground troops. Arab mujahideen fought at the front. The Iraqis organized the heavy weapons, mainly the dual-use 23mm guns and RPG-7s, which were used primarily against the U.S. helicopters. The Iraqis were also instrumental in running the external perimeter, blocking repeated U.S.-U.N. attempts to relieve the besieged force in the defensive perimeter. The Arab "Afghans" were in command of some of the Somalian blocking forces as well. Reports conflict as to the extent of Iraqi participation in the actual fighting. A few Saiqah Commando troops were definitely present, giving instructions to SIUP fighters. It is not clear whether Iraqis actually pulled triggers. The Arab "Afghans" took an active part in the fighting, leading from the front while demonstrating their immense personal bravery. Aidid's people, both militiamen and civilians, were introduced in huge numbers in time to create the enraged mob and join the onslaught, as well as take casualties and the blame.

There were strong indications of the growing Iranian and Islamist influence over Aidid and the entire SNA. On the eve of the main clash Tehran endorsed Aidid's claim, stated in a long interview with the Iranian paper *Resalat,* that the clashes with the U.S. forces were a spontaneous popular reaction to attacks on civilians by American forces. Aidid stressed that the SNA was not involved in these fights because it had already been disarmed by the U.S.-U.N. forces.

The main rally held in Mogadishu in the aftermath of the October 3 clash with the U.S. forces was Islamist. Sheikh Abdul-Razzaq Yussuf Adan led the crowd in reciting verses from the Koran. The main speaker was Sheikh Hassan Mahmud Salad, who spoke on the evil influence of the "United States and its infidel surrogates [who] were attempting to change the Somali people's culture and sacred religion that God endowed them with." Both Adan and Salad stressed that "the Somali people are Muslim and therefore want the introduction of the Sharia in the country." The entire session was broadcast by Aidid's radio.

Once the impact of the October 3 fighting became clear, the Islamists came up with a coherent position. Abdi Haji Gobdon, a spokesman for the SNA, declared that peace and stability could return to Mogadishu, and Somalia, only after the U.S.-U.N. forces had left the country. He urged the U.S.-U.N. forces not to abuse the goodwill of the Somalis, who recognized the humanitarian help they had received, by trying to interfere in Somalia's domestic issues. He warned the U.S.-U.N. forces not to engage in a popular war they could not possibly win even if they tried to occupy all of Somalia. "What is honorable is that they go," Gobdon stated. "They will not win the war. They came to help us. Let them leave and let the Somalis settle their political differences. There will be peace."

Tehran endorsed this position because by now, with additional U.S. forces being rushed to swell their besieged compounds, the Islamists' initial objectives had already been reached: "After eleven months of military presence and after confrontation with black independence-seeking forces, the world superpower has suffered heavy blows and damages." According to Tehran, Washington should have realized by now that "the existing hopelessness of the situation" in Mogadishu could only be aggravated by the resolve of the "guerrilla forces and the Muslim masses." Tehran concluded, "Deployment of political solutions after eleven months of military presence can only mean withdrawal. As a result, America is trapped in a desert where it can neither continue its actions nor revise earlier decisions." As planned by Tehran and Khartoum, the Americans were already entrapped in a new Vietnam-type quagmire.

As of October 10, Aidid and the Islamists had embarked on a twin-track approach to the Somalian crisis. They reiterated their desire to maintain a cease-fire and take part in a political process while insisting that their basic demands of a prompt U.S.-U.N. withdrawal and preservation of the Islamic character of Somalia be met to avert the resumption of fighting. Simultaneously the flow of Islamist reinforcements and resupplies into Somalia and the Mogadishu area that had been organized by bin Laden continued. The Islamists made it clear that the Mogadishu cease-fire and the fighting were merely instruments aimed at ensuring that Islamist interests were realized.

On October 17 came early indications of an impending crisis in Mogadishu that could lead to the resumption of fighting. The Islamists reacted sharply to news of the imminent visit to Mogadishu of U.N. secretary general Boutros Boutros-Ghali. The Islamists considered Boutros-Ghali, an Egyptian Copt, an implacable enemy and saw his involvement in the diplomatic process in Somalia as proof of the United Nations' commitment to impose a solution favorable to the United States. (Copts are Egypt's original Christian population, whose unique church dates centuries before the Arab-Muslim invasion of Egypt. Because of their refusal to accept Islam, the Copts are both hated and despised by the Islamists.) To reinforce the point, Aidid sent his followers to a massive demonstration in Mogadishu, where more than 1,000 of his people shouted, "Down with Boutros-Ghali! Down with UNOSOM [the acronym for the U.N. force in Somalia]!" "Boutros-Ghali has bombed us and murdered us—we don't want him here!" an Aidid aide repeatedly screamed through a loudspeaker to the cheering crowd in the streets.

IN LATE OCTOBER 1993 it became clear that Tehran and its allies, emboldened by the great success of their earlier clashes with the U.S. forces, were getting ready for another marked escalation in the fighting in Mogadishu. Tehran and Khartoum hoped that this escalation, if implemented, would bring about a speedy and shameful withdrawal of the U.S.-U.N. forces from Somalia, much like that in Beirut a decade earlier. The comparison with Beirut was not just symbolic. Tehran now deployed to Mogadishu highly specialized HizbAllah detachments.

The overall plan for escalation was prepared in Tehran with the help of commanders of several Islamist terrorist movements, most notably the

Lebanese HizbAllah and selected Arab "Afghans." The new operational plan anticipated a marked escalation in the popular fighting in Mogadishu as a cover and facilitator for high-quality terrorist strikes by HizbAllah squads. Somali fighters had already been specifically prepared in training camps in central and northern Somalia. They were organized in recently established composite units made up of Somalis led by highly professional Iranian Pasdaran, Lebanese, HizbAllah, and Arab "Afghan" terrorists. These new commanders had been smuggled into Somalia in small detachments via Kenya, Ethiopia, Eritrea, and Djibouti, with active assistance from the Organization of Islamic Republics in Kenya, the Islamic Front for Ethiopia, and the Eritrean Islamic Jihad. This separate and delicate transfer of key terrorists was also managed by bin Laden.

Once chaos and street fighting returned to Mogadishu, the Islamist contingency plan stipulated, the elite terrorists would go into action, kidnapping Americans (civilians and soldiers) and then beginning suicide bombing attacks on several U.S.-U.N. facilities. HizbAllah suicide terrorist squads already in Mogadishu to hunt the U.S. forces would conduct the lethal suicide-bombing attacks against U.S. objectives. The senior HizbAllah commander on-site was Hajj Riyadh Asakir from Beirut. He was a veteran of the suicide bombings in Beirut in the early 1980s, including the bombing of the marine barracks. In Mogadishu, Asakir answered directly to Muhsin Rezai, then commander of the Islamic Revolutionary Guards Corps in Tehran. To increase the likelihood of success, the HizbAllah also maintained in Mogadishu two main force groupings completely separated from each other. One HizbAllah force arrived via Ethiopia and the other via Kenya. Each force relied on a completely independent support system— made up of Somalis, Iranians, and Arab "Afghans"—and supply lines drawn via Ethiopia and Kenya, respectively. Tehran was convinced that these HizbAllah suicide strikes, if carried out, would have the same impact on Washington that the Beirut strikes of the early 1980s had had.

As it turned out, there was no need to activate the HizbAllah cells in Mogadishu. Shocked by the heavy casualties suffered in early October, Washington decided to withdraw from Somalia and severely curtailed the activities of the U.S. forces in Mogadishu. By March 1, 1994, the bulk of the U.S. forces were out of Somalia. The Islamists, including Aidid, were in control. Tehran and Khartoum had proved their point and demonstrated their ability to conduct strategic operations.

In fall 1994 the intense dynamics of the Horn of Africa was gradually giving way to a somewhat regulated chaos. From the ashes of the Horn of Africa rose several dangerous precedents. It was now clear that even when a distinct national group in Africa had decided to reach self-determination through secession, it still had to rely on colonial-era boundaries. The most striking example was Eritrea, which seceded from Ethiopia after a thirty-year guerrilla war and a referendum that demonstrated overwhelming popular support. Eritrea was legitimized not from a redrawing of colonial boundaries but from a return to them. Another group aspiring to follow the example set by Eritrea is Somaliland, which declared itself independent in 1991.

While central and southern Somalia has already sunk back into lawlessness and rampant violence worse than that before the U.S.-U.N. intervention, in Somaliland the self-declared government has established a working, albeit fragile, administration and peace. Like Eritrea, Somaliland had a separate colonial history, having merged with Somalia only in 1960. But the West has adamantly refused to recognize Somaliland's independence.

In several interviews and statements, Osama bin Laden has said that he considers his experience in Somalia a milestone in his evolution. Somalia was the first time he was involved in a major undertaking at the leadership level, exposed to the complexities of decision making and policy formulation. He established working relations with the intelligence services of Iran and Iraq that would prove useful in his rise to the top. Although he did not actually take part in the fighting in Mogadishu, his contribution to the Islamist effort and ultimate victory was major and decisive. Bin Laden still defines the fighting in Mogadishu as one of his major triumphs against the United States.

The achievement against the United States in Somalia convinced him that it would be possible to ultimately evict the United States from Saudi Arabia and the Persian Gulf States as well. In March 1997 he stressed this point to Robert Fisk of the *Independent:* "We believe that God used our holy war in Afghanistan to destroy the Russian army and the Soviet Union . . . and now we ask God to use us one more time to do the same to America to make it a shadow of itself." Bin Laden was convinced not only that Somalia was the answer to the Islamists' prayers but also that the legacy of the fighting in Mogadishu indicated the character of future confrontations with the United States. "We also believe that our battle against America is much simpler than the war against the Soviet Union, because some of our mujahideen who fought here in Afghanistan also participated in operations against the Americans in Somalia—and they were surprised at the collapse of American morale. This convinced us that the Americans are a paper tiger," bin Laden concluded.

Operational lessons from the conflict had more immediate ramifications. Khartoum and Tehran were now convinced of the effectiveness of their vast networks throughout East Africa. They were also cognizant of their ability to deliver painful political and strategic strikes against the United States even in such remote parts of the world as the Horn of Africa. Turabi and the Iranian and Sudanese senior officers were deeply impressed by the performance of the key Arab "Afghan" commanders, particularly Zawahiri and bin Laden. The personal relations established during this crisis would endure and prove highly useful in future confrontations with the United States. As for the three key "Afghans"—al-Zawahiri, bin Laden, and al-Rashidi—they forged a friendship and a team that had worked well together and soon would again.

4

Emir bin Laden

IN 1994 BIN LADEN emerged from the shadows when he assumed responsibility for several programs that required his hands-on involvement overseas. In these trips he proved himself a capable manager and organizer of complex programs, most of which still function. Using the private business jets of allies from the Gulf States and/or their European-registered companies, bin Laden was able to travel with little or no forewarning. After the cancellation of his Saudi passport in April 1994, he traveled with a Sudanese diplomatic passport under an alias. Bin Laden never tried to conceal his true identity when dealing with Islamists abroad, despite growing threats from local and Western security services. The real importance of bin Laden's activities in 1994 is their relation to the surge of the Islamist international terrorist movement in the aftermath of its triumph in Somalia.

AT THE END OF 1993 the Islamists were celebrating a great victory. They had evicted the Great Satan—the United States—from the Horn of Africa and now took up the standard for the developing world's anti-imperialist struggle. For Osama bin Laden and his comrades in arms, the next year or so would be a crucial time of reorganizing and building up their forces. The Islamists, who had emerged on the world scene as a major anti-American and anti-Westernization force, now had to regroup and prepare for the next round of confrontation. At the top of the list, they needed to lay the foundations for a worldwide infrastructure. Working mainly in Sudan, bin Laden was instrumental in adapting the organization of the Islamist movement for use by the sponsoring states, including the funding, logistics, and training, as those states became more directly involved and the primary actors in this drama.

In the aftermath of the Islamist triumph in Somalia, several states and organizations that had been either partially active, on the fringes of, or even completely inactive in the Islamist movements wanted to become active participants. Pakistan's ascent in the Islamist terrorist system is particularly important in a strategic context. Pakistan's growing involvement resulted in both the escalation of the war by proxy in Kashmir and the rise of the Taliban in Afghanistan, two movements that still provide shelter to and closely cooperate with bin Laden

The Islamists' surge coincided with Benazir Bhutto's return to power in Islamabad. Behind a facade of pro-Western and pro-democracy rhetoric, she initiated a program designed to make Pakistan a central member of both the Iranian-led Islamic bloc and the Trans-Asian axis, an anti–U.S. radical alliance dominated by the People's Republic of China and stretching from the Mediterranean to Northeast Asia. Toward this end Pakistan intensified its strategic cooperation with such countries as Iran and North Korea. Islamabad emerged from these alliances with distinct roles. Pakistan would serve as a center for military development and production for the Islamic bloc, including nuclear weapons production technologies, as well as a financial center for hard currency obtained through the drug trade. Pakistan would also acquire, both legally and illegally, sophisticated Western technologies and industrial systems, including spare parts for U.S.-made weapons. Islamabad and its allies were convinced that Bhutto's rise to power, especially in view of her pro-democracy rhetoric, would relax the Western guard so that at least for a while Pakistan would be able to acquire the necessary items before a tight embargo was reimposed.

Pakistan's growing role in this anti–U.S. buildup was one of Bhutto's personal priorities. Immediately after her return to power in fall 1993 she embarked on a series of political moves that would formulate the new grand strategy for a post–Cold War and post–Gulf Crisis Pakistan. The most important elements were stronger strategic agreements with Iran and North Korea, which were completed during Bhutto's visits to Tehran and Pyongyang. These visits, along with a visit to Beijing, Islamabad's closest ally, served to reinforce Pakistan's emerging grand strategy: active integration into the Islamic bloc and the Trans-Asian axis. Despite her rhetoric, Bhutto seemed genuinely convinced that the future of Pakistan lay with the Iranian-led Islamic bloc and its activist anti-U.S. posture. By the end of 1993, after her round of visits to Beijing, Pyongyang, and Tehran, Bhutto clearly demonstrated her determination to implement these policies and realize this strategic posture as soon as possible. Markedly increasing Pakistan's participation in the Islamist international terrorist system was an integral part of Bhutto's new strategy.

In mid-December 1993 Turabi organized another Popular Arab and Islamic Conference (PAIC) in Khartoum to discuss the next phase of the Islamist struggle against the West. (Turabi renamed the IAPC the PAIC to include all Muslims, not just Arabs.) Pakistani input was the most important aspect of this conference. Islamabad left no doubt that Pakistan saw itself as an active and loyal member of the Islamic bloc led by Iran. Pakistani officials in Khartoum stressed Islamabad's conviction that Islamist politics were the wave of the future and that Islamabad was determined to be an active participant. Islamabad committed itself to the pursuit of these Islamist strategies not because of Bhutto's ideological convictions—she is a populist leftist—but from pragmatic considerations about Pakistan's best interest in view of the megatrends in the Hub of Islam, China's changing strategic posture, and Pakistan's own growing domestic problems.

The new government in Islamabad wanted to ensure that its policies were understood by the Islamists. To accomplish this, Bhutto sent an adviser to the conference who held private meetings with Turabi and other Islamist leaders. He assured them that the Pakistan People's Party (PPP)—Bhutto's political party—would not attack Islamism or abolish Islamic law and of Islamabad's commitment to their common cause, including the pursuit of anti-Indian jihad in Kashmir as an inalienable tenet of the polity of Pakistan. He also stated that Pakistan was committed to finding "Islamic solutions" for Afghanistan and the various conflicts in Central Asia and that Bhutto would support any solution mediated by Turabi, now referred to by the honorific title of sheikh.

The PAIC conference focused on the role of Pakistan within the framework of AIM (the Armed Islamic Movement), in particular Pakistan's future active support for Islamist armed struggles and national liberation—that is, international terrorism. The official Pakistani delegation was led by two other Bhutto confidants, General Mirza Aslam Beg, the former chief of staff of the Pakistani armed forces and a close ally of Iran, and General Hamid Gul, the former chief of the ISI (Pakistani intelligence) who had encouraged the flow of foreign mujahideen to Pakistan and Afghanistan in the late 1980s. Both were dedicated Islamists who repeatedly declared their conviction that Pakistan's future lay with Iran and the Islamic bloc. Their participation in the Khartoum conference and leading role in the formulation of Pakistan's relations with the PAIC and the Islamist world were proof that Bhutto's Islamabad would continue to pursue Islamist policies.

Turabi hailed Pakistan's commitment to "safeguard the rights of Muslim people" in Kashmir and Pakistan's support for their struggle for national liberation. He applauded Pakistan's decision to maintain its nuclear potential despite international pressure, especially from the United States, and promised continuing support from the entire Muslim world for Pakistan's endeavor to continue and expand its nuclear program.

The Pakistani delegation assured the PAIC leadership that Islamabad would not surrender to Western pressure to reduce its support for the Arab "Afghans" and international terrorist activities. The Pakistani delegates stressed that Pakistan might have to pretend to suppress the Arab Islamists or to curb the infrastructure for international terrorism so that access to sophisticated technologies could be secured despite mounting Western pressure. But this would be only for show, and genuine support for militant Islamist causes would actually expand.

———

IN LATE 1993 the ISI began strenuous efforts to carry out the promises made in Khartoum. During 1994 the ISI, together with VEVAK (Iranian intelligence), completed a major upgrade and expansion of the terrorist infrastructure in Afghanistan, in particular the installations for the training of Arabs and other foreigners who would become a new generation of "Afghans." ISI instructors were most active in four camps where foreign "Afghans" were taught advanced weapons-handling techniques and tactics, sophisticated bomb and booby-trap making, and ways to carry out martyrdom (suicide) operations.

One such upgrade was the transformation of the mujahideen training infrastructure in the area between Zhawar and Khowst in eastern Afghanistan. During the 1980s this training complex was run by the ISI ostensibly for Jalaludin Hakkani, a veteran Afghan mujahideen commander. But by 1994 Hakkani maintained only a guard force of about 200 fighters for the local ammunition dumps of the Afghan mujahideen, whereas close to 100 Pakistani and more than 30 Arab instructors were training about 400 to 500 mujahideen from all over the Muslim world. The instructor-student ratio ensured extensive hands-on training. The complex was run in a professional manner, with all candidates subjected to thorough medical, military skill, and psychological testing and a security check by veteran ISI experts before acceptance. Courses ran between four months and two years, depending on the subject.

The composition of the student body reflected the priorities of the Islamist leadership. In 1994–95 trainees included 350 Tajiks (100 of them from Tajikistan and the rest from northeastern Afghanistan), about 100 Chechen troops, 3 groups from Bosnia-Herzegovina, 2 groups of Palestinians, 1 group from the Philippines, a Moldavian group, and 2 Ukrainian groups (mainly Crimean Tatars). The students were divided into study teams of from twelve to fourteen trainees, depending on expertise and country of origin. For security reasons communication between members of different groups or teams was strictly prohibited. Special night-only courses were also conducted when the identity and activities of the trainees had to remain secret. This training system would endure and expand. In August 1998 some of these installations were the target of the U.S. cruise missile strike against bin Laden.

Other key training centers for "Afghans" were expanded during 1994. At Chahar-Siyab, a stronghold of the Hizb-i Islami, led by Gulbaddin Hekmatiyar, the ISI also ran a major training center for more than 200 Arab "Afghans" earmarked for spectacular operations in the West and pro-Western states in the Middle East. Other ISI-run camps were in other parts of Afghanistan.

During 1994 and 1995 most logistical and overall (intelligence, financial) assistance for the Islamist organizations was channeled through ISI-sponsored Pakistani organizations such as the Harakat ul-Ansar and Markaz al-Dawat al-Arshad. In early 1995 the Harakat ul-Ansar officials in Pakistan gloated that their mujahideen were fighting in Kashmir, the Philippines, Bosnia-Herzegovina, and Tajikistan and throughout the Middle East. A 1995 recruitment document from Markaz al-Dawat al-Arshad stressed that "mujahideen from the deserts of Arab [countries] have reached Bosnia through the corridors [of jihad] of Afghanistan. [The] Western world is shaken." The main forces of Markaz al-Dawat al-Arshad in Pakistan were fighting in Kashmir as well as organizing training and support for mujahideen from the "Arab World, Kashmir, Bosnia, Philippines, Eritrea, Somalia, Africa [sic], America [the United States], and Europe" in key bases in Pakistan and Afghanistan. Markaz al-Dawat al-Arshad commanders emphasized that some of these mujahideen were already operating in the United States, Western Europe, Bosnia-Herzegovina, and Chechnya.

Meanwhile Pakistan began implementing its audacious grand strategic plans. Since the early 1990s, in the aftermath of the collapse of the Soviet Union and the Gulf War, the PRC has been organizing and leading the Trans-Asian axis—an anti-U.S. bloc stretching from the eastern shores of the Mediterranean, through South and Central Asia to the shores of the Pacific Ocean. In this alignment, because of its Islamic character and unique strategic relations with China, Islamabad emerged as the linchpin bringing together the Tehran-led Muslim bloc and Beijing. In order to consolidate Islamabad's regional posture, the ISI embarked on a series of audacious operations aimed to ensure Pakistani access to the region's key transportation choke points. The drastic change in Islamabad's direct involvement with Afghanistan, and consequently with the vast Islamist terrorist system there, was the outcome of this thorough reassessment of Pakistan's grand strategic objectives.

By the early 1990s Islamabad's quest for control of Afghanistan's road system had become one of the ISI's biggest covert operations, perhaps second only to its sponsorship of subversion and terrorism in Kashmir. The ISI embarked on an ambitious program to control the Kushka-Herat-Qandahar-Quetta highway. Stretching from former Soviet Central Asia through western and southern Afghanistan, this road feeds into the road system of southern Pakistan and continues on to Pakistan's main port in Karachi. It is the only strategic artery in fairly good shape that can be rebuilt to carry massive convoys with relative ease. A system of pipelines along this road to transfer oil and gas from Central Asia and northern Afghanistan would be the key to Pakistan's future economic development.

Islamabad was determined to control this strategically crucial artery, at almost any cost. Pakistan started to repair the most damaged road sectors inside Afghanistan, beginning work with tribal contractors who had long-established contacts with the ISI.

To ensure Pakistan's actual control over this vital road, the ISI began giving local leaders and chieftains weapons and money and providing outlets for the drugs they grew in the Helmand Valley in southwestern Afghanistan. Unending fratricidal clashes resulted over money, guns, and influence throughout southern Afghanistan, and by 1994 the ISI found most of the good commanders dead and only the bottom of the barrel left to negotiate with. Deals were struck with aspiring warlords and drug dealers who pretended to be mujahideen commanders. These newly empowered leaders turned on the population and abused their special relations with Pakistan, still Afghanistan's sole gateway to Western goods. In mid-1994 this program started to fall apart as greedy warlords in southern Afghanistan began raiding the very same convoys they were supposed to protect.

Within a few months the situation exploded, and a new force emerged on the scene—the zealot Islamist Taliban, who still control most of Afghanistan and provide shelter to bin Laden despite intense American pressure. Mulawi Mohammed Omar, from Qandahar, the recognized leader of the Taliban, is a veteran Pushtun mujahideen commander turned religious student. The story of his rise to a leadership position is illustrative of the sociopolitical motivation of the Taliban movement as a whole.

According to legend, in fall 1994 the prophet Muhammad came to Mulawi Mohammed Omar in a dream and told him to cleanse his tribe of a sinful, oppressive warlord, an ISI-installed "local commander" notorious for rapes and pillaging. After receiving permission from his mullah, Mulawi Mohammed Omar organized a force of fifty comrades, all former mujahideen who had served under him in the 1980s, and assassinated the warlord, delivering "people's justice."

Mulawi Mohammed Omar established a local religious leadership to administer the distribution of the warlord's confiscated property to the poor and needy of the Qandahar area. He took the warlord's weapons and accepted repentant fighters into a fledgling religious movement under his command. The new command would be known as the Taliban—students of religious schools—in honor of the origin of their leaders.

In fact, the Taliban resulted from the calculated organization and activation of Islamist Pushtun forces sponsored jointly by Tehran and Islamabad. The populist myth is correct in that the hard core of the Taliban were Pushtun religious students and young Islamist clergy. Many of them were veterans of the war in Afghanistan, and all were graduates of training camps and higher schools in Iran and Pakistan. Nationalist and Islamist, they were eager to rebel against the corrupt ISI-installed warlords and crime bosses. Until they began receiving support from the ISI, however, they were unable to do anything. Former Pakistani interior minister Nasirullah Babar acknowledged in fall 1998 that the Taliban were organized under his guidance in 1994. "Taliban were also given military training when I was interior minister in 1994," he said. Once empowered, they initially established themselves in the Qandahar area, where the destruction of the long-established tribal royalist leadership left a void to be filled. The Taliban's first success—the seizure of Qandahar in November 1994—was considered the beginning of their campaign.

Both Tehran and Islamabad now accepted the reality of the collapse of the Afghan state. In late fall 1994 both governments concluded that it was imperative for their respective intelligence services to consolidate a certain degree of control over the regional ethnopolitical dynamics to preserve the power position of their governments. Southern Afghanistan would be the first stage. After the Taliban's initial success in stabilizing Qandahar in mid-November and relying on the unquestionable popular support they enjoyed, Islamabad was ready to capitalize on the Taliban to expand Pakistan's hold over the Pushtun-populated parts of Afghanistan. The surge into Afghanistan, including the creation and empowerment of the Taliban, has been a sacred mission supported by all governments in Islamabad—including Bhutto's—and implemented by the ISI.

In mid-December 1994 the Taliban proved to the ISI that they were fully aware of Islamabad's strategic interests and regional priorities. By then, the Taliban were moving westward into the Helmand Valley, killing the drug lords associated with both Hekmatiyar and the ISI. The "spark" was lit when, in order to compel the ISI to do something about the Taliban, a local Hekmatiyar commander blocked and hijacked a Pakistani thirty-truck convoy on its way to Central Asia. But the ISI hinted to the Qandahar elders that the warlord was fair game, and immediately a force of 2,500 Taliban materialized in Qandahar. In fact, these were Afghan forces being held by the ISI in Pakistan and eastern Afghanistan to conduct deniable operations in both Afghanistan and Kashmir. Well equipped and well led, this Taliban force took on the Hekmatiyar warlord and freed the convoy. The Taliban did not extract any booty from the convoy and even retrieved loot from local villages and returned it to the convoy.

In late 1994 and early 1995 the ISI began providing massive assistance to the Taliban, including new Kalashnikov assault rifles, large quantities of ammunition, training, logistics, and other forms of combat support. In a meeting in Islamabad in December 1994, Hekmatiyar complained to the ISI chief about the ISI's growing assistance to the Taliban. At the same time the ISI was closely monitoring the increasing flow of Pakistani-Pushtun volunteers joining the Taliban. The Taliban's emerging political-religious leadership was made up of protégés of the Pakistani—and increasingly regional—Islamist political organization Jamiat-i-Ulema-Islam, under the leadership of Maulana Fazlur Rahman. By mid-1995 the Jamiat-i-Ulema-Islam was becoming an umbrella organization for a dozen smaller Islamist organizations, including some of the most violent in Pakistan.

By mid-December between 3,000 and 4,000 religious students had moved from madrassas (religious schools) in western Pakistan across the border to join the Taliban. By early January 1995 the movement had become a flood. Most Taliban came from Sunni madrassas in Pakistani Baluchistan, particularly from the Afghan refugee camps established in the mid-1980s by the ISI to alter the demographic character of Baluchistan. Baluchistan is a fiercely independent province of Pakistan whose unique population, the Baluchi tribes, have repeatedly rebelled against the central government. By February 1995 the Taliban forces were some 25,000 strong, predominantly Pushtuns but including over a thousand Tajiks and Uzbeks. These troops were recruited by Pakistan to add military skills and expertise to the Taliban "army."

By early 1995 the Taliban forces were deployed at the gates of Kabul. In late February they pushed Hekmatiyar from his stronghold in Maidan Shahr, nineteen miles south of Kabul, and closed on Chahar-Siyab, Hizb-i Islami's main point for shelling Kabul. Gulbaddin Hekmatiyar and a few close aides had to flee Chahar-Siyab, leaving behind their entire arsenal and stockpiles. A series of subsequent setbacks in the fighting in the Kabul area with the forces of the Afghan government and the beginning of a dramatic rift with Tehran, including the assassination of Iran's favorite Afghan Shiite mujahideen commander, did not change the overall strategic posture of the Taliban. By mid-1995 the Taliban had virtually secured control for Pakistan of the sole non-Iranian route between the Indian Ocean and Central Asia.

Afghanistan was then ready to support a serious expansion and improvement of the support system for terrorists—the establishment of the Imarat, run by Osama bin Laden. This role defined bin Laden as a prominent leader in the world of conservative-traditionalist Islam.

IMMERSED AS HE WAS in sustaining the Islamist operations in the Horn of Africa, Afghanistan-Pakistan, and elsewhere, bin Laden could not disengage himself from the growing sociopolitical upheaval in Saudi Arabia.

King Fahd's health had rapidly deteriorated, but no concrete succession plan had been implemented, engulfing Saudi Arabia in a bitter, self-devouring succession crisis between key factions of the House of al-Saud. The conspicuous corruption and insatiable greed of the leading princes resulted in the emergence of a grassroots opposition guided and driven by charismatic young Islamist preachers and activists who urged Saudi Arabia to return to what they described as "genuine Islamic ways." Riyadh reacted harshly to this essentially Islamist opposition movement by mass arrests without trials, economic deprivation, and overall suppression, although the movement posed no real threat to the regime.

This state of affairs in and around Saudi Arabia was a turning point for Osama bin Laden. In 1993–94, he began to doubt the legitimacy of the House of al-Saud. Once convinced that there was no legitimacy to honor, bin Laden, the Islamist who provided unique services for Saudi intelligence and stood by the Saudi Court during the Gulf Crisis, became a fierce and uncompromising enemy. The evolution of bin Laden's political awareness toward Riyadh had practical implications. He began considering ways to bolster the Saudi Islamist movements, both in withstanding the increasingly harsh crackdowns by the Saudi security forces and training and preparing militant forces—Islamist terrorists—who would serve as the vanguard of an Islamist uprising in Saudi Arabia. The latter task would prove demanding and take a long time to accomplish.

In 1994 foundations were laid for the still unfolding Islamist terrorist campaign against the United States and its allies. Hassan al-Turabi and the Islamist international movement recognized the worth and effectiveness of senior "Afghans," most notably Zawahiri and bin Laden, and gave them great responsibility and authority. A new command structure was built with bin Laden and Zawahiri in central positions. Islamist international terrorism—as distinct from popular revolts, such as those in Egypt and Algeria, and wars by proxy, those in Kashmir and Israel—centered on Europe. There the new generation of "Afghan" commanders proved their élan.

Both bin Laden and Zawahiri played a major role in the Islamists' war in the Balkans, in Bosnia-Herzegovina and Kosovo, following through on their experience and expertise. From Khartoum and London, Osama bin Laden expanded the network of "humanitarian" entities in the Balkans, including comprehensive support bases in Western Europe and the Middle East, into a thick web encompassing many ostensibly separate organizations. Together these organizations constitute a resilient and redundant infrastructure that sustains thousands of Islamist terrorists throughout the Balkans. The closing of any individual organization, the arrest and/or expulsion of any Islamist, has no tangible impact on the viability of this terrorist support system as a whole. The system established and run by bin Laden is also flexible, with organizations vanishing and new ones popping up frequently and a large number of the Islamist terrorists constantly moving their affiliations from one entity to another, complicating the efforts of Western security authorities to track them down. Bin Laden also organized the clandestine financial system that sustains the war effort and Islamist operations in the Balkans. During this formative period and despite the personal risks involved, bin Laden made at least one clandestine trip to the Balkans, including Bosnia and Albania, to supervise firsthand the consolidation of the Islamist support system.

Ayman al-Zawahiri organized a multilayered forward and on-site command-and-control system for running the mujahideen's contribution to the Bosnian Muslims' war effort and for conducting spectacular terrorist operations against the United Nations forces, and later U.S.-led NATO forces, when they stood in the way of the Bosnian Muslim drive for victory. Ultimately the Islamists' participation in the still unfolding Bosnian-Muslim and Kosovo-Albanian war efforts has been a joint effort of states and key organizations. No single individual can claim responsibility for the consolidation of militant Islam in the Balkans, but Zawahiri was of singular importance in organizing multiple tiers of command posts—the off-site posts in such places as Italy and Bulgaria and the on-site posts in Croatia, Bosnia-Herzegovina, and Albania. Zawahiri also organized several cells of high-quality terrorists throughout the Balkans, with bin Laden taking care of their sustenance.

Bin Laden and Zawahiri were involved in other major projects in Western Europe. In November 1993 Zawahiri began work on a forward headquarters for spectacular terrorist strikes in the United States. At the center of this offensive is a major terrorist headquarters in Geneva, Switzerland, established in late 1993 and activated in early 1994; its sole purpose is to oversee the conduct of spectacular terrorist operations in the United States. The Islamist leadership decided that this new headquarters was necessary when the FBI investigated the New York–based networks of Omar Abdul Rahman; the Islamists feared the investigation would lead to a crackdown on the other Islamist terrorist networks then dormant in the United States. Tehran decided to establish a backup headquarters outside the United States that could take over operations if the terrorists were apprehended or had to leave the country.

To be able to operate in Western Europe, Zawahiri radically changed his image by shaving his beard and donning Western attire. The primary objective of the Zawahiri European networks is to insert high-quality experts into the United States to oversee and conduct lethal terrorist operations under emergency circumstances. In the late 1990s, following the deaths of Zawahiri's deputy and his spiritual leader, the Geneva headquarters was reorganized, but it still functions.

Osama bin Laden embarked on establishing a network to disseminate propaganda and educational material throughout the West, particularly to the various Muslim communities the Islamists most wanted to influence. He worked on acquiring material and developing translation procedures as well as setting up a global distribution system, both electronic and paper driven. In 1994 bin Laden employed the fax and the computer, the Internet and e-mail, in the service of Islamist revivalism.

Bin Laden accomplished this undertaking at a personal risk. Although he was wanted by the Saudi government, he traveled to the United Kingdom using his own Saudi passport. Because of the close relations between London and Riyadh, bin Laden risked arrest and extradition to Saudi Arabia, where he would have been tortured and probably beheaded. In England he settled in the London suburb of Wembley. There he purchased property and established a group called the Advisory and Reformation Committee, which took over management of and support for various Islamist luminaries in exile throughout Europe and support for their minuscule organizations and fronts. Initially bin Laden's most important outlet was the Liberation Party, run by Sheikh Omar Bakri. Over the next few years more exiled militant Islamists would gravitate to London and establish their own minuscule organizations; together they would constitute a reliable source of data on the Islamists' activities and provide "explanations" to the intellectual elite throughout the Muslim world. The established terrorist entities could deny any connection to acts of violence, while the London-based individuals, who obviously had done nothing, could provide "explanations." Many of the most important communiqués and decrees issued in 1996 and 1998 on the key terrorist attacks in Saudi Arabia and East Africa were disseminated through this London-based system, and Sheikh Bakri would emerge as one of the most authoritative voices clarifying bin Laden's activities.

On April 7, 1994, the Saudi government stripped Osama bin Laden of his citizenship because "he committed acts that adversely affected the brotherly relations between the Kingdom of Saudi Arabia and some other countries." A few months later bin Laden had to return to his refuge in Khartoum because the Saudis were demanding his expulsion and extradition from England. By the time bin Laden left London, he had consolidated a comprehensive system of entities with a solid—though clandestine—source of funding. This London-based data-dissemination system still works efficiently.

———

WITH THESE PREPARATIONS for the next phase of terrorism in advanced stages, the Iranian-Sudanese Islamist leadership decided to thoroughly study its posture and reexamine future plans. This was to be a prolonged process to accurately reflect the magnitude and complexity of the challenges facing radical Islam. Between October 1994 and April 1995 senior officials of Iran, Sudan, and key Islamist terrorist organizations conducted an unusually large number of conferences and meetings, mostly in the Middle East. At such conferences and meetings the most important decisions about future terrorist campaigns and specific operations are made, and these gatherings are also the main venue for the secure distribution of instructions and authorization of specific operations. The sheer quantity and diversity of these gatherings reflected the intensity of the preparations then taking place throughout the Islamist international terrorist system.

The first major meeting was held in October 1994 in the Firozi Palace in Tehran. The key participants were the representative of Ayatollah Ali Khamenei (Iran's spiritual leader and Khomeini's successor), Ali Fallahian (then Iran's minister of intelligence), Muhsin Rezai (chief of the IRGC), Muhsin Rafiq-Dust (chief of the Foundation for the Oppressed, Iran's main instrument for clandestine financing), Imad Mughaniyah (chief of the Iranian-controlled HizbAllah Special Operations Forces), Sheikh Bikahi (in charge of HizbAllah's foreign operations), and senior representatives of Palestinian Islamic Jihad and the Egyptian al-Jamaah al-Islamiyah. The Egyptian delegate arrived from the United States.

Khamenei's representative surveyed the situation in the world, stressing the increase in American anti-terrorism activities worldwide. He informed the conference that Tehran had resolved to "retaliate directly in a way similar to the World Trade Center operation." This was not an empty threat. Possible future terrorist operations in the United States were studied, and some specific operations were discussed in detail.

Later that month Iranian intelligence organized a summit meeting in the Imarat Quarter in Khartoum of all the leaders involved in the Islamist subversion of Saudi Arabia and the Gulf States. The summit was co-chaired by Sheikh Hassan al-Turabi and Ayatollah Ahmad Jannati. Participants included senior representatives of Iranian intelligence, a representative of Ali Akbar Mohtashemi, the HizbAllah, Saudi Islamists—including Osama bin Laden—and leaders of the Muslim Brotherhood in the Persian Gulf States.

The participants closely reviewed the situation in the Arabian Peninsula and the status of their forces, primarily the Iranian-sponsored forces, both Shiite and Sunni "Afghan." They concluded that they would soon be ready to confront the Gulf regimes, primarily the House of al-Saud. The participants at this summit meeting decided to begin activating clandestine networks throughout the Arabian Peninsula and begin preparations for a wave of terrorism and subversion to be launched in spring or summer 1995. Special emphasis would be put on exploiting indigenous social factors and tensions in order to justify extremist and Islamist activities. Foreigners would be intentionally targeted in order to disrupt the relations between the Gulf States and the West, particularly the United States.

The summit decided that a final go-ahead for the launching of this campaign would be given only after the advance preparations had been deemed successful; an examination of these preparations was scheduled for spring 1995. Specifically the summit decided to conduct two key evaluation sessions—one in Khartoum, to be chaired by Turabi, to study the preparations for the campaign, and one in Mecca, to be chaired by Jannati, to study the situation inside Saudi Arabia.

Following these fall 1994 conferences, the Sudanese sent high-level emissaries to the United Kingdom and the United States to notify the local Islamist leaders of the resolutions and to instruct them about future plans and their respective role in them.

The terrorist elite met again in November 1994, this time at a remote villa in Larnaca, Cyprus. They discussed the next phase of operations in the United States based on material brought back by the emissaries. Among the participants were key intelligence officials from Iran, Sudan, and Syria, as well as senior commanders from various Islamist organizations—the Islamic Action Front (Jordan), the Popular Front for the Liberation of Palestine–General Command, HAMAS (the Palestinian Islamist terrorist organization operating in Israel and the territories), HizbAllah, Jordanian

"Afghans" from Pakistan, and the Islamic Liberation Party (Jordan). The terrorist leaders examined the potential operations and authorized activation of the final phase of the campaign.

The Larnaca conference decided on a twin-track approach to the future terrorist offensive in the United States—the creation of "an environment of terror" and a series of "spectacular operations." Iranian sources also described a coherent and comprehensive strategy that combined both high-quality spectacular operations against government-related objectives throughout the United States and a myriad of low-level harassment operations both in the United States and against Americans all over the world. The latter would be a concentrated effort to terrorize the people of the United States through a sustained campaign of "small" operations, essentially a kind of violent psychological warfare. The key to the success of this campaign would lie in the aggregate impact on the American people, which in turn would build popular pressure on the U.S. government to change policies in order to stop it. The Larnaca conference also discussed a wide range of terrorism options against Israel, Jordan, and other Arab states involved in the Mideast peace process.

Many highly professional working sessions followed all over the world, from Geneva to Tripoli, Lebanon, in which senior intelligence officers of the key terrorism-sponsoring states met and consulted with the on-site senior commanders and spiritual guides. They studied firsthand and in great detail the status of specific networks—the ability of local Muslim communities to withstand the aftermath of major strikes. These officers also examined the potential political and economic ramifications of spectacular strikes for the sponsoring states.

In early January 1995 high-level internal consultations were conducted in Tehran to discuss the outcome of all the conferences, gatherings, and on-site sessions held since fall 1994, which would serve as the basis for a thorough reexamination of the international terrorism strategy then being formulated in Iran. These consultations specifically concentrated on operations in the United States, Latin America, and Asia. It was also decided to launch a series of regular and suicide operations against U.S. targets throughout the Middle East, from blowing up U.S. embassies and other commercial buildings with car bombs to assassinating American diplomats. Tehran then issued specific instructions for the forthcoming operations, which would serve as the guidelines for the Islamist terrorist activities to begin at the latest in spring 1995. Because of their great importance and sensitivity, these directives and instructions were sent to the various cells and networks all over the world by trusted messengers.

These resolutions were crucial for the formulation of the long-term terrorist strategy. As a rule it takes more than a year to translate doctrinal decisions of the kind reached at this 1995 meeting into initial operational
capacity—that is, to consider specific operations that meet the guidelines. It
then takes close to a year to plan and prepare particular operations, train
and prepare the terrorists, build a support system for them, and so forth.
The decisions of the January 1995 consultations in Tehran led to the launching of an elaborate effort to case, study, and plan for attacks on diversified
U.S. targets, including embassies, that is only now being implemented.

In early 1995 Ayman al-Zawahiri made an audacious, extremely important clandestine visit to the United States to establish firsthand the strength
and reliability of the local networks and Islamist communities and confirm
the suitability of various objectives for spectacular strikes already identified
and recommended by the U.S.-based networks. Using one of his European
forged passports, Zawahiri established a forward base of operations in
Santa Clara near San Francisco, California. Ali A. Mohamed, whose real
name is Ali Abu-al-Saud Mustafa, and Khalid al-Sayyid Ali Abu-al-Dahab,
two Egyptian-American devotees of bin Laden who were the senior jihadist
operatives in the United States, facilitated Zawahiri's tour. Mohamed/
Mustafa supervised Zawahiri's secret trip and also provided cover for the
visit into and out of the United States, a forged passport, and related travel
documents Zawahiri used to get a visa to enter the United States. Dahab
provided cover for Zawahiri while he was in the United States. When the
possibility of a protracted terrorism campaign was addressed, Dahab even
organized residency for Zawahiri in California. Mohamed/Mustafa and
Dahab took turns traveling with Zawahiri all over the United States to inspect possible targets and meet local Islamists who were supporting local
terrorist networks and locally collecting and laundering funds for operational use in the United States. Zawahiri returned to Europe convinced that
the United States could become a fertile ground for a series of spectacular
terrorist operations—both acknowledged and deniable strikes—provided
they were properly planned and professionally executed.

The two Egyptian-Americans who assisted Zawahiri were typical of the
high-quality assets the Islamists could rely on in the United States. Ali A.
Mohamed, who was born in 1952, graduated from the Cairo military acad-
emy but in 1984 was eased from the Egyptian army with the rank of major
because of his Islamist leanings. He then offered his services to the CIA but
after a brief stint in West Germany was identified as a likely double agent
whose true loyalties were with the Islamists. Nevertheless, Mohamed/
Mustafa entered the United States in 1985, married an American woman,

and joined the U.S. Army, serving as a supply sergeant with the Special Forces and the Green Berets. He was later involved in raising the awareness of the Special Forces about Islamist issues. In 1988 he took a lengthy leave of absence and went to fight in Afghanistan, where he met with Zawahiri and the Arab "Afghan" leadership.

Mohamed/Mustafa left the army in November 1989 to devote all his time to the Islamist cause. He provided military training for young Islamists in both California and New York/New Jersey to prepare them for the jihad in Afghanistan, and some of these young men became members in Omar Abdul Rahman's New York terror network. In 1990 Mohamed/Mustafa embarked on a series of trips to the Middle East. In Afghanistan, applying his U.S. Army experience, he taught would-be terrorists to use weapons and explosives, guerrilla warfare tactics, and remote-controlled bomb and booby-trap techniques. Mohamed/Mustafa then helped select the most qualified graduates for dispatch to Egypt and the United States. In 1991 he went to Sudan to work closely with bin Laden, devising for him a system for protection against U.S. special and covert operations ranging from electronic and sensory protection of facilities used by bin Laden to the training and organizing of his bodyguards. In 1993 he was part of al-Rashidi's staff, contributing his experience to the fight against the U.S. forces. On bin Laden's instructions he also traveled extensively throughout Africa, between Kenya, Tanzania, Nigeria, Uganda, and Guinea, to monitor U.S. targets and installations. In late 1993 and early 1994 he entered the U.S. Embassy in Nairobi to survey its structure and defenses. All this time he was also consolidating the Islamist base in northern California. In fall 1998 Mohamed/Mustafa was arrested and indicted in connection with the embassy bombing in East Africa.

Khalid al-Sayyid Ali Abu-al-Dahab arrived in the United States in 1986, instructed to establish himself with a clear cover. Toward this end he settled in Santa Clara, married an American woman, and obtained citizenship. He was activated by Mohamed/Mustafa in the late 1980s and sent for two months of training in Afghanistan, where the Islamist leadership impressed on him the importance of support operations in the United States. Over the next few years Dahab maintained a comprehensive communication system connecting Islamist commanders operating clandestinely in the Arab world and the terrorist high command and between Islamist operatives in Pakistan, Yemen, Sudan, Austria, Britain, Qatar, the United Arab Emirates, Bahrain, Albania, and Canada. He also oversaw the clandestine transfer of funds and data via California and purchased and clandestinely delivered to their destination some of the satellite telephones now used by bin Laden, Zawahiri, and other terrorist leaders. Dahab received forged and real passports of various nationalities from Mohamed/Mustafa and shipped them to Zawahiri so that terrorist commanders could travel safely throughout the West. In the late 1980s Dahab began traveling to Egypt with instructions and funds for locally based terrorist leaders. He was arrested on October 29, 1998, while trying to escape Egypt for the United States.

By early 1995 it was impossible for the rest of the world to ignore these intensive activities, and the governments that would be threatened began to take note. Arab governments became increasingly apprehensive about the growing Islamist threat in Pakistan and Afghanistan. In February, Prince Turki bin Faisal, head of the Saudi secret and intelligence services, embarked on a series of drastic, desperate measures aimed at reducing the "Afghan" threat.

On instructions from King Fahd, Prince Turki traveled to Islamabad in early March for high-level consultations with Bhutto. The main subject was the nature of cooperation in areas of intelligence and terrorism between Pakistan and Iran. Prince Turki told Bhutto that Riyadh was extremely apprehensive about the Saudi "Afghans" operating in and out of Pakistan and Afghanistan. Turki stressed that Islamabad was the key to the entire Islamist infrastructure because the "Afghan" camps in Afghanistan were still under the control of the ISI. Most worrisome was the organization of operational units for the revival of jihad overseas under the banner of the Harakat ul-Ansar, which had—and still has—headquarters and schools all over Pakistan and a host of military camps in Afghanistan. Harakat ul-Ansar enjoyed and still enjoys close cooperation with the ISI, at minimum in connection with operations in Indian Kashmir and with the Afghan government.

Prince Turki offered Bhutto a deal. In addition to generous financial assistance, Riyadh would use its power and influence in Washington to lobby for Pakistani interests if the ISI contained the Saudi "Afghans"; the Saudis would work for repeal of the Pressler Amendment (which imposed stiff sanctions on Pakistan, including the cessation of all military assistance and deliveries, because of its reckless military nuclear program), would seek economic and technical assistance for Pakistan, and would oversee a public-relations blitz about Islamabad's crackdown on militant Islamists. Aware of the crucial importance of Pakistani-Iranian relations for Islamabad and the importance of the "Afghan" movement for both Islamabad and Tehran, Prince Turki asked Bhutto just for assurances that the ISI would limit the ability of Saudi "Afghans" to travel to the Middle East. Bhutto promised to cooperate with Riyadh, and Riyadh provided tremendous support during Bhutto's visit to Washington in early April 1995 and in subsequent negotiations on Capitol Hill. A personal emissary from Prince Turki went to Islamabad several times to consult with senior ISI officials on the promotion of Pakistan's image in the United States by, among other methods, publicizing its commitment to fighting Islamist terrorism and drug smuggling.

From the very beginning, however, Islamabad had no intention of honoring the Saudi requests. As far as the ISI was concerned, the entire effort was aimed at changing Pakistan's image rather than containing the spread of Pakistani-sponsored Islamist terrorism. Just how much for show these arrangements had been was revealed in early April 1995, on the eve of Bhutto's trip to the United States. Under cover of another PAIC conference in Khartoum, secret consultations to coordinate terrorist activities took place between high-level intelligence officials from the key terrorist-sponsoring states and terrorist leaders.

In late March and early April 1995 Osama bin Laden attended these meetings in Khartoum. The most important meetings, held in Turabi's headquarters, were organized by Mustafa Ismail Uthman, who runs the Sudanese terrorist training camps. The key participants were Osama bin Laden, Imad Mughaniyah, Fathi Shkaki (chief of Palestinian Islamic Jihad), Mussa Abu Marzuk and Muhammad Nizzal (both key HAMAS commanders), Adrian Saadedine (of the International Muslim Brotherhood), Sheikh Abdul-Majid al-Zandani (the Yemenite Islamist leader), Mustafa Hamza (a senior Egyptian "Afghan" commander) and two other representatives of Egypt's Islamic Jihad, two representatives from the Ennadha's consultative council (from Tunisia), representatives from Qazi Hussein Ahmad's Islamic Jihad of Pakistan, and military representatives from Algeria's main Islamist terrorist organizations—the AIS and the GIA.

The main subject of discussion was establishing a new series of offices and headquarters all over the world so that the international Islamist movement could better cope with forthcoming challenges. Zawahiri had proved the need to establish and expand these forward offices in the Balkans operations. The meeting participants decided on the following main offices and areas of responsibility: Sanaa, to support operations in the Arabian Peninsula; Khartoum, to support operations in Egypt, Libya, Chad, Uganda, Kenya, and Cameroon; Mogadishu, to support the Islamist forces in Somalia, Ethiopia, Djibouti, and Eritrea; Rome, for the coordination of and support for Islamist operations in North Africa; Karachi, to support operations in Pakistan, Kashmir, Afghanistan, and Albania-Kosovo; and Tehran, to support operations in Central Asia, India, and Bosnia.

In addition, two major centers would be expanded in the West, the existence of which had been made possible by bin Laden's work. The London office would be responsible for propaganda and research work, including promotion of academic and strategic research. The New York office, in Brooklyn, would be responsible for financial activities concealed as charitable work and fund-raising for humanitarian causes. The U.S.-based networks reached such magnitude that Congress passed the Anti-Terrorism Act of 1996, giving law enforcement agencies greater leverage in addressing this threat. Bin Laden had established a web of international financial entities and a myriad of bank accounts through which money, collected either as ostensible charitable contributions or clandestinely provided by the terrorism-sponsoring states, could be moved around, mixed, and laundered. Bin Laden, with his intimate knowledge of and direct involvement in international business in the computer age, solved the Islamists' problems in the clandestine movement and laundering of the huge sums of money required for supporting terrorism and subversion worldwide. He was charged with supervising and running these centers from his offices in Khartoum and given additional monies to work with. The Iranian delegate, Muhammad Said Naamani, promised $120 million to cover the expenses of these new centers.

The situation in Pakistan required special attention from the Islamists. The ISI representative explained Islamabad's political difficulties with the United States and the lucrative Saudi offer, arguing that it was imperative for Islamabad to create an area of deniability between Bhutto's government and its support for Islamist terrorism. The ISI representative urged that further modification of the terrorism-sponsorship system be made to help Islamabad.

In return for the Islamists' cooperation with Bhutto's policies, Islamabad agreed to expand the use of Karachi as a center for the clandestine financing of the international Islamist movement. To be managed by Osama bin Laden, the new financial system would be based on a wide network of non-Arab international businesses and companies to conceal the flow of cash to the various terrorist networks in the West. Toward this end and with the endorsement of official Islamabad, the Karachi center linked up with numerous Pakistani landowners, financial companies, and business-people close to the narcotics circles to utilize their international financial relations and contacts. The Karachi financial center also expanded its activities, initially to the United Kingdom, South Africa, and Mauritius, making use of the local Pakistani diaspora. Not knowing about bin Laden's prospective role in the Karachi center, Prince Turki assured Islamabad that once the center was up and running, Riyadh would tolerate the use of Saudi financial institutions and international companies for comparable "humanitarian" operations, even in the United States. When Riyadh was later informed of bin Laden's role in the Karachi center, Prince Turki ignored the information and continued to allow the use of Saudi financial institutions. By now Riyadh was so concerned with the revival of Islamist terrorism and subversion in Saudi Arabia that it was ready to do almost anything to ensure that these Islamists operated outside Saudi Arabia. For Riyadh, tacitly

assisting Islamist terrorism in third countries by transferring and laundering funds at the time seemed a cheap price for quiet at home.

In early May 1995, at the height of the Hajj, the annual pilgrimage to
Mecca, the top Iranian Hajj official, Mohammad Mohammadi Reyshahri,
who was formerly minister of intelligence, and Ayatollah Ahmad Jannati, a
prominent official in the terrorism support establishment, held a series of
meetings in Mecca with senior officials of the HizbAllah, Islamic Jihad,
and militant Islamist movements from all over the world to discuss methods
to "confront U.S. conspiracies against Islam."

OVER THE LONG RUN and at the strategic level, the theological decrees—fatwas—generated from the uppermost Islamist leadership of Khartoum in the aftermath of the PAIC conference were of great importance.
Issued by Turabi and the highest authorities of AIM in summer 1995, these
texts were intended to be used as the precedent-setting legal-religious texts
for legislating relations between Muslims and non-Muslims in areas where
the infidels were not willing to be simply subdued by the Muslim forces and
in areas contested by mujahideen forces. Palestine, Bosnia, and Kashmir
were listed explicitly as areas where the principles outlined by these fatwas
and decrees were most applicable.

One of the key legislative texts distributed by Khartoum was a fatwa
originally issued by the Islamic Religious Conference held in Al-Obaeid,
Sudan, on April 27, 1993. This fatwa decreed relations between Muslims
and non-Muslims in areas claimed by the Muslim forces.

The April 1993 fatwa did not clearly distinguish between Muslims seeking coexistence with non-Muslims and secular state authorities and non-
Muslims resisting the imposition of a Muslim state. But paragraph 1 stated
their fate specifically: "Therefore the rebels who are Muslims and are fighting against the [Muslim] state are hereby declared apostates from Islam, and
the non-Muslims are hereby declared Kaffirs [infidels] who have been standing up against the efforts of preaching, proselytization, and spreading Islam
into Africa. However, Islam has justified the fighting and the killing of both
categories without any hesitation whatsoever with the following Koranic evidence," which is stated in the fatwa text in great detail.

As for those Muslims who were not eager to kill in the name of the jihad,
the fatwa stipulated in paragraph 6 that "those Muslims who . . . try to question or doubt the Islamic justifiability of jihad are hereby classified as 'hypocrites,' who are no longer Muslims, and also 'apostates' from the religion of
Islam; and that they will be condemned permanently to the fire of Hell."

The April 1993 fatwa was a lengthy legal document stipulating in great detail, while citing evidence and substantiations from the Koran, that there was no viable and legal alternative to a bloody jihad. This fatwa was clearly organized and written as a universal Islamist legal document determining the essence of relations between Muslims and their neighbors in mixed societies and states without Muslim governments. The authors of this fatwa pointed to southern Sudan as the peculiar case that made them pass a sweeping and principled judgment applicable to all similar cases. At that time the rebellion of the black Christian and Animist population against the oppressive Islamicization campaign carried out by the Arab-Muslim government was escalating, with the rebels establishing control over a sizable area in southern Sudan. A part of Sudan, Khartoum considered this area a Muslim land occupied by non-Muslims. The leadership in Khartoum was not wrong, from their legal point of view, in selecting this fatwa as a guideline for the Islamist jihad strategy in such places as Kashmir, Palestine, and Bosnia.

Another background document issued by the highest Islamist legal and ideological authorities sought to clarify Khartoum's position on the escalation of the armed struggle in areas contested by the Islamists, from non-Arab Muslim-dominated Asia to the Middle East and even Europe. This text defined the crucial importance of the armed struggle in the context of relations between Muslims and the modern Western state.

The key document issued in late August 1995 by the Islamist authorities was a judgment decree issued by Sayyid Muhammad Qutb, a leading Egyptian Islamist thinker executed in 1965. Qutb was especially renowned for his milestone judgment decrees on the relationship between the believer and the modern secular state, both in the Muslim world and in the West. Critical was Qutb's identification of the modern state as "Jahiliyyah"—barbarity—against which Muslims are obliged to fight. The use of the term *Jahiliyyah* in this judgment decree could apply to all key theaters where the Islamists were sponsoring terrorism and subversion.

In late August 1995 the Islamist leadership in Khartoum renewed Qutb's call to arms against the Jahiliyyah, particularly in the modern states where large Muslim communities lived under non-Muslim regimes. Qutb's judgment decree, which the AIM leadership now declared to be both valid and timely, left little doubt what had to be done: "It is not the function of Islam to compromise with the concepts of Jahiliyyah which are current in the world or to coexist in the same land together with a jahili system. This was not the case when it first appeared in the world, nor will it be today or in the future. Jahiliyyah, to whatever period it belongs, is Jahiliyyah; that is, deviation from the worship of One Allah and the way of life prescribed by Allah." Qutb decreed and AIM concurred that there could be no coexistence between Muslims and jahili authorities or a jahili system: "Islam cannot accept any mixing with Jahiliyyah. Either Islam will remain, or Jahiliyyah; no half-half situation is possible." Qutb saw no alternative to an all-out armed struggle— a jihad—to free the believers from servitude to the Jahiliyyah. As a theologically driven organization, AIM had the right and obligation to participate in the worldwide struggle against Jahiliyyah. "The foremost duty of Islam is to depose Jahiliyyah from the leadership of man," Qutb decreed, and Turabi concurred.

ONE THEATER WHERE the Islamists encourage a local Muslim minority to challenge the rule of a Christian majority and an elected government is the Philippines. Since the early 1990s the Islamists had been concentrating on transforming the essentially socioeconomic revolt of the predominantly Muslim southern islands against the predominantly Christian northern islands into a Muslim revolt against Christian rule. Bin Laden became involved in the escalation of Islamist terrorism in the Philippines as part of this struggle. During 1994 bin Laden began to accumulate experience in supervising terrorist operations, and the first major network he was involved with in a supportive capacity produced a series of spectacular strikes in the Philippines and ultimately the United States.

To establish the required support system, bin Laden traveled to the Philippines in winter 1993. He presented himself as a wealthy Saudi investor eager to help fellow Muslims in the country's southern islands. Several government officials met with him to expedite his purchase of property and arrange the appropriate bank accounts. Later on, when bin Laden could no longer travel freely, support of the network was handed over to his brother-in-law, Mohammed J. A. Khalifah. Funds were now transferred by courier. In December 1994 Khalifah was detained in San Francisco on immigration charges and deported. His presence in the United States was significant given the network's ultimate plans. In summer 1998 Khalifah vehemently denied that he had been financing the Abu Sayyaf group, the most militant Islamist terrorist organization in the Philippines.

Starting in early 1994, several cells of expert terrorists, mainly Arab "Afghans," arrived in the Philippines and established operational cells all over the country, mostly in large cities. Among the senior commanders of this effort was Ramzi Ahmad Youssuf, who in early 1993 oversaw the bombing of the World Trade Center in New York. Their objective was to prepare for spectacular operations in East Asia and serve as a base for launching operations in the United States.

At first the network attempted a hasty operation—to assassinate President Clinton during his 1994 visit to Manila. But the network failed to collect the necessary intelligence to breach the president's security cordon, and the operation was aborted.

The key operations planned for East Asia were to assassinate the Pope during his visit to the area and to blow up two U.S. airliners simultaneously. The network also planned to assist the local Islamist terrorist leader, Abu Sayyaf, in the conduct of sophisticated operations in order to intensify his struggle against the government in Manila as well as enhance his power position vis-à-vis the other Islamist organizations in the southern islands.

On December 11, 1994, the network exploded a bomb on a Philippine Airlines (PAL) Boeing 747 flight from Cebu to Narita, Tokyo. Traveling with fake Italian documents, Youssuf personally planted the bomb onboard before disembarking safely at a stopover in Manila. The bomb exploded above Okinawa, but the aircraft was not destroyed because it was too low and the bomb was too small. This bomb was a test run for a major operation prepared by Youssuf's associate Said Akhman, who planned to arrange the simultaneous midair explosion of two United Airlines Boeing 747s as they were approaching Hong Kong from different directions. This plan was not carried out because the network collapsed.

The Abu Sayyaf organization in Manila claimed responsibility for the December 1994 bomb. The organization insisted that it was responsible despite initial doubts because the organization seemed to lack this kind of sophistication and skill and by late 1994 had no record of terrorist activities in Manila. When the plot to assassinate the Pope was exposed in early January 1995, the Abu Sayyaf organization again took responsibility for the threat and claimed that the operation was planned by its "Manila force" in the name of "the Islamic liberation struggle against the Manila government and the Catholic Church."

The attempt on the Pope's life was averted in early January 1995 when a Manila-based cell of expert terrorists, including Youssuf, had an operational accident. An attempt to mix explosives went wrong; the mixture began emitting toxic fumes, and the terrorists escaped from their safe apartment. There police found evidence of a wider plot for operations in the Philippines and the United States. A few of the terrorists were arrested in Manila, including Said Akhman, who was later extradited to the United States, while others, including Youssuf, fled to Thailand. Youssuf then traveled to Pakistan. The U.S. government confronted Islamabad with precise information about Youssuf's hiding place—an apartment complex sponsored by a bin Laden–related company—after a tip from a neighbor. Islamabad had no alternative but to cooperate or be put on the U.S. terrorism list and face stiff sanctions as stipulated by law. All of Youssuf's comrades and other Islamist terrorists dwelling in the complex, however, had been safely evacuated by the ISI before the U.S.-Pakistani law enforcement detachment raided the place and captured Youssuf, who was extradited to the United States. In late March 1995 the Filipino police broke another Islamist terrorist cell, consisting primarily of Arab "Afghans," this time in the Caloocan suburb of Manila. Among these "Afghans" were followers of Sheikh Omar Abdul Rahman, who were plotting ways to avenge his arrest and humiliation in the World Trade Center bombing case.

When it collapsed, the Ramzi Youssuf cell was in the advanced stages of planning and preparing a series of spectacular terrorist operations against U.S. targets. A plan to strike CIA headquarters in Langley, Virginia, with a light aircraft loaded with powerful explosives was the most ambitious. Said Akhman was one of the candidates to be the suicide pilot in this operation. Another plan the network was working on envisaged blowing up eleven American airliners simultaneously as they were approaching U.S. airports.

Although the Philippine networks collapsed before they could carry out any major operation, their fall was accidental and not caused by a breach of security, successful infiltration, or discovery by hostile intelligence agencies. For his part Osama bin Laden proved his ability to establish a comprehensive and resilient support and finance system, which survived the subsequent Filipino and American investigations. The U.S. authorities could not even charge Khalifah when they had him.

In early 1995 bin Laden put the Philippine operations behind him and began preparing for a marked escalation of direct confrontation with the Islamists' Mideast archenemies—Saudi Arabia and Egypt. In these operations he would play even more important roles as in 1995 an escalating, relentless jihad was launched against the U.S. presence in the Hub of Islam. Emboldened and better organized, the Islamists would take on the key allies and protégés of the United States in the Muslim world. Through this series of audacious terrorist operations a coherent doctrine emerged for the Islamists' fateful struggle against the United States. Bin Laden, a loyal and committed team player, continued to climb in the ranks of the Islamist International, proving himself once again a stalwart mujahid.

5

Inciting the Revolution

IN 1995 THE ISLAMISTS showed their hand to friends and foes alike with a series of audacious operations that constituted the dramatic beginning of a continuing, relentless campaign against the governments of Egypt and Saudi Arabia. The Islamists also delivered a pointed reminder to Pakistan of the expediency of Pakistan's continued, wholehearted support of Islamist terrorism. The spectacular operations of 1995 had a direct impact on the policies of three key governments in the Hub of Islam: Cairo, Riyadh, and Islamabad. The Islamists' gambit constituted terrorism par excellence—brief acts of extreme violence that affected government policies at the highest levels. During this series of operations in 1995 Osama bin Laden consolidated his place as a prominent radical Islamist leader.

As 1995 began, Osama bin Laden was operating in Khartoum as a member of Turabi's high command controlling the Armed Islamist Movement. He had become one of Turabi's coterie of confidants, and his advice and opinion were sought in making decisions. As one of Turabi's inner circle bin Laden played a part in formulating the strategic campaign against the main U.S. allies in the Arab world—Egypt and Saudi Arabia. It was during this time, while in Turabi's shadow, that bin Laden became fully established at the center of power in the Islamist international terrorist movement.

Other key players were also rising in the ranks of Islamist terrorism. The most important were Ayman al-Zawahiri and the Egyptian senior terrorist commanders under him. The spectacular terrorist operations they commanded consolidated this Egyptian team as the most effective terrorist command cell of the Islamist movement. Zawahiri worked closely with the support system run by bin Laden, from the training camps in Sudan to logistical and financial support overseas, and in the process the two grew even closer. In late 1998 Zawahiri and the Egyptian command cell operated under bin Laden as bin Laden's primary terrorist commanders.

———————

THE ISLAMIST DECISION to launch a strategic campaign against Egypt and Saudi Arabia—to which bin Laden was a vital contributor—was reached because events unfolding in Saudi Arabia in 1994 convinced the Islamist leadership that the country was vulnerable to an Islamist surge. The Islamists also knew that unless Egypt were otherwise preoccupied, it would intervene to ensure the stability of Saudi Arabia or any other conservative Arab regime challenged by Islamist subversion and terrorism.

The escalation of terrorism in Saudi Arabia was a direct result of the relatively nonviolent crisis that had been developing inside Saudi Arabia. This internal crisis over succession and legitimacy reached a turning point when the Islamists declared the launch of an armed struggle. As part of a movement driven by ideology and theology, the Islamists felt compelled to elucidate their reasons for undertaking drastic acts even before they acted. The crisis began with the arrest in mid-September 1994 of Sheikh Salman bin Fahd al-Udah, a charismatic Islamist preacher. Sheikh Udah was one of the young, populist leaders who rose to prominence from the grassroots of Bedouin society by reaching out to the average Saudi and gaining his trust and support.

This younger generation of populist Islamists grew up on the legacy of bin Laden's generation, the heroic young Islamists who participated in the Afghan jihad. Their movement is unstructured but strong and cohesive. At the grassroots level the leaders are eloquent, charismatic preachers who begin by building a following within the local mosques. These young preachers rely on the endorsement of the local "Afghans" or other veteran Islamists of comparable stature. The local Islamist cells gain their inspiration from clandestine Islamist texts, both printed and on cassettes, which they receive from regional and national networks; these networks also provide clandestine funding if needed. The networks are run by veteran "Afghans" and militant Islamists at the organizational level, while older preachers, who have usually become popular beyond their first mosque, provide Islamist guidance. By 1994 these Saudi "Afghans" and like-minded Islamist militants, including veterans of other Arab/Palestinian terrorist organizations, had established a loose network of terrorist and militant cells for their own security against the ever present threat of the Saudi secret police and in preparation for the jihad they hoped to one day launch against the House of al-Saud and the American forces bolstering it. This largely amorphous structure looked up to senior leaders as a source of inspiration and support.

Osama bin Laden was such a leader of the grassroots Islamist movement in Saudi Arabia. A mujahideen leader with an unparalleled record in Afghanistan, his exploits were known to all. He was a charismatic and eloquent speaker whose speeches, both written and recorded, were widely circulated by the Islamist underground throughout Saudi Arabia. The heavy personal price he paid for pursuing what he was convinced to be a just Islamist policy—loss of riches and ultimately exile—added to his stature. From his exile in Sudan, bin Laden did not abandon the Saudi Islamists. He arranged and sustained much of the support system for the Islamist movement from Sudan, the Gulf States, and, more recently, London. Although he acted from genuine benevolence, his efforts kept his name at the forefront as a leader and source of inspiration for the ranks of Saudi Islamists. The more they looked up to him, the more committed he became to them.

The arrest of grassroots leader Sheikh Udah led to the first initiative taken by the Saudi Islamist system. A few days after Udah's arrest came the first threat of violence against the House of al-Saud—the release of the first overt communiqué of an Islamist terrorist organization inside Saudi Arabia. An organization calling itself the Brigades/Battalions of Faith issued an ultimatum to the Saudi authorities to release Sheikh Udah within five days or the organization would begin a campaign of terrorism against Saudis and Americans. The communiqué concluded that "all the Arabian Peninsula is an open theater for our Jihad operations." The Brigades/Battalions of Faith never carried out their threats. Their ultimatum was carefully phrased so that it didn't suggest that Sheikh Udah or the Islamist leadership were actually involved in or even endorsed the call for armed struggle, leaving a convenient gap of deniability between the Islamist leadership and the Saudi mujahideen.

But Sheikh Udah himself authorized and legitimized an armed jihad. Although still in prison, in early 1995 he began smuggling out taped sermons calling for an intensification of the Islamist protests against the rulers of the House of al-Saud. On April 9–10, 1995, the followers of Sheikh Udah issued the text of a taped lecture recently smuggled from jail. The lecture, titled "Death Workmanship," covered the whole logic of the relationship between Islamist and Western civilization and amounted to a declaration of an armed jihad against the House of al-Saud. It provided justification for perpetual confrontation.

Sheikh Udah argued that the prevailing conditions throughout the Muslim Nation, primarily in Saudi Arabia, necessitated resumption of a comprehensive armed struggle: "The world today is pushing Muslims and compelling them . . . to Death Workmanship, the profession of Death, and is making of them strong fighters." Sheikh Udah warned that the Muslim Nation was suffering "from political underdevelopment, economic dependence, and military weakness" so that it could not "race and compete in the big theater of life." Although the present plight of the Muslim Nation might seem irreversible, "this religion proved its eternity and historical extension and its survival. Many nations attacked it, but these nations went and Islam stayed." Nevertheless, it was imperative for the believers to strive to reverse the trend and save the Muslim Nation. Udah emphasized that conventional spiritual methods, such as widespread teaching of Islam and knowledge of its laws, "will not be enough" to resolve the current crisis. Nor would the adoption of Western ways—"importing technology, manufacturing and graduating experts and specialists"—be enough to reverse the trend. Sheikh Udah acknowledged that the work of preachers and teachers like himself "may contribute, but it will not do what is required; even the efforts of guides and preachers, however great it is, it can only affect a small piece of the [Muslim] Nation."

Sheikh Udah stressed that only an intense jihad could cleanse and rejuvenate the Muslim Nation so that it could prevail in the modern world: "It is death that gives life, yes it is Jihad in the sake of Allah, the obliged fate [of] this Nation. Otherwise it is extinction. If the [Muslim] Nation abandoned Jihad and ignored it, then Allah [would] hit it and punish it by making it low among the nations; [as] the Prophet, peace and blessings be upon him, said: 'If you abandon Jihad, and become satisfied with growing plants, then Allah will direct at you being low among the nations, and you will not be able to come out of it until you return to your religion and declare Jihad in the sake of Allah.'"

Sheikh Udah warned that the rejection of jihad in its original meaning—an uncompromising armed struggle—in favor of interpretations of modernity—namely, other forms of nonviolent activities—was also dangerous to the very survival of Islam: "The abolishing of Jihad in the sake of Allah and its rejection and the refusal to believe in it as part of our Islamic creed is an apostasy from Islam, and makes the person outside the people of Islam. [This is] because Allah the Almighty has ordered us to do Jihad clearly in the Koran without any ambiguity, and it was mentioned in the noble authenticated Hadith, and Islam can never be established and sustained without Jihad."

"Death Workmanship" amounted to a fatwa, that is, a religious decree, ordering the launch of jihad against the Saudi royal family. Sheikh Udah decreed that any rejection of jihad in favor of another form of resistance was apostasy, a capital offense according to Muslim law, which left the believer with no alternative but to fight—anybody who considered himself Muslim had to commit himself to the waging of jihad. Thousands of illegal audio-cassettes and text copies of Sheikh Udah's lecture were distributed clandes-tinely throughout Saudi Arabia, and Saudi opposition organizations in the West were flooded with requests from individuals in Saudi Arabia for copies of the lecture.

Although Sheikh Udah did not specifically mention the House of al-Saud or the United States as the primary objectives of the jihad, his follow-ers filled in the blanks. "Death Workmanship" was distributed in the United States with the comment: "Sheikh Salman al-Udah is still in prison with hundreds of other scholars in the Arabian Peninsula. He was jailed by the cowardly oppressive regime of Al-Saud family [at] what some believe [was] the urging of the U.S. government."

Soon after the publication of Sheikh Udah's fatwa, other Islamist circles began to act on it, mostly by preparing their supporters for the transforma-tion of the Islamist resistance in Saudi Arabia. A key change took place in the position of the London-based Committee for the Defense of Legitimate Rights (CDLR). In the early 1990s the CDLR was a "modernistic" Islamist movement making a concentrated effort to create an image of a "moderate" Islamist movement in the West. The CDLR stressed its commitment to non-violent populist opposition to the Saudi government. Committee activists organized a host of sit-ins and other forms of public protest in Saudi Arabia and Western capitals to appeal to the Western media and embarrass the Saudi government by demonstrating Riyadh's inability to deal with or even conceal widespread opposition to its regime. At the time the CDLR was the primary group speaking for the Saudi Islamists in the West.

Immediately following the release of Sheikh Udah's lecture, the CDLR changed its policy line, stressing that such popular protests were no longer sufficient to cause the overthrow of the government in Riyadh. These popu-lar activities would be conducted in support of a struggle carried out by a small core of activists who were willing to sacrifice everything, including their lives, for the Islamist cause. In its mid-April 1995 communiqué the CDLR stressed the need for an all-sacrificing elite—mujahideen—at the forefront of the struggle against the Saudi regime:

> No one can doubt the unity and agreement of the Nation in support of the legitimate leaders and that the reform process has the sympathy of all levels of society. This, however, was not the real test. The test in ques-tion was regarding "who is prepared to sacrifice." Those hundreds of thousands, or perhaps millions, of supporters and sympathizers are unable to present any real opposition unless they are led at the forefront by a committed group of people who are readily prepared to sacrifice their

all for the cause. Indeed, sacrifices such as detention, torture, and even death must be prepared for and accepted. Unless this leading group is solidly steadfast, then the rest of the support will collapse. The leading group does not necessarily need to be large, as it was a small group that Allah gave victory to in the story of David and Goliath.

To ensure its audience understood that this general statement was an endorsement of Sheikh Udah's call for jihad, the CDLR used the protests in Sheikh Udah's stronghold in Buraydah, Saudi Arabia, after his arrest in September 1994 as an example of able leadership and sacrifice. The CDLR explained that the loyal and devoted followers of Sheikh Udah, who were the most likely to implement his call for the jihad, already constituted part of the committed group of people required to bring about success: "The method the Government adopts now is of no real significance because the main obstacle has been overcome and the leading group has been formed. If tyranny and oppression were in any way effective, or served any purpose, this would have been evident after the first Buraydah uprising."

On April 10, 1995, an Islamist organization calling itself the Islamic Change Movement—the Jihad Wing in Arabian Peninsula warned of impending armed attacks against American and British forces throughout the Arabian Peninsula and against the House of al-Saud. The communiqué gave the Western forces until June 28, 1995, to evacuate the Arabian Peninsula. If they did not, starting on that date the U.S. and British forces would become a legitimate target for the jihad. The communiqué accused the Saudi royal family of turning against Islam in the service of the "Crusade forces," as demonstrated in their purges and persecution of notable Islamic preachers and teachers. The communiqué of the Islamic Change Movement was issued in support of the jailed Islamist leaders.

Sheikh Udah's "Death Workmanship," the CDLR's endorsement, and the communiqué from the Islamic Change Movement reflected the decision by the Saudi Islamist leadership to begin jihad as the only viable approach for overthrowing the Saudi regime. This was not an idle threat. For several years a large cadre of Saudi Islamists, from 15,000 to 25,000 fighters strong and spearheaded by over 5,000 Saudi "Afghans," had been being trained, prepared, and equipped in camps in Iran, Sudan, Yemen, and Pakistan-Afghanistan. A large Islamist underground network inside Saudi Arabia claimed to be ready to support these Saudi mujahideen.

———————

BUT THE SAUDI ISLAMISTS had to postpone their plans. By late June 1995 the entire Islamist elite was preoccupied with a far more important operation against Turabi's other archenemy, Egypt, although for security reasons the Saudi Islamists did not know about this operation. An underground movement constantly under the threat of exposure, arrests, torture, and betrayal would not be informed about a key operation planned by another terrorist group. The Saudis were merely notified by Khartoum and Tehran to wait for the go-ahead, and because of the tight discipline of the state-sponsored terrorist system, the Saudi Islamists obeyed the order.

The attempt on President Hosni Mubarak's life in Addis Ababa, Ethiopia, on June 26, 1995, was a milestone in the evolution of the Islamist struggle for control over the Arab world and the Hub of Islam. Operations of such magnitude, even if ultimately claimed by or attributed to obscure terrorist organizations, are actually instruments of state policy and are carried out on behalf of the highest echelons of the terrorism-sponsoring states. The assassination attempt, a strategic gambit sponsored by Sudan and Iran, had regional and long-term effects. Although President Mubarak survived and the Islamist popular uprising envisaged by the conspirators failed to materialize in Egypt, the mere attempt gave a major boost to the Islamist surge throughout the region.

This audacious operation was initiated for two reasons: (1) to rejuvenate Islamist armed struggles in the Middle East, in particular on the Arabian Peninsula, with the collapse or neutralization of Egypt seen as a prerequisite to any tangible success, and (2) to squelch the emerging schism in the Egyptian Islamist leadership—honor and turf battles among exiled leaders—before it spread to the ranks inside Egypt.

Both the Egyptian Islamists and their sponsoring states were determined to kill Mubarak, whose regime is a constant reminder of the Islamists' failure to overthrow a U.S.-supported government. Following the 1981 assassination of his predecessor, Anwar Sadat, by Islamist terrorists, Mubarak not only stabilized the government but launched a violent crackdown on Egypt's Islamists. Under his leadership Egypt retained its peace agreement with Israel and was the leading force in consolidating the Arab communities in support of the U.S.-led coalition against Iraq during the Gulf War. Mubarak has repeatedly reiterated his determination to support any conservative Arab government against Islamist challenges, even if it requires the use of Egyptian expeditionary forces. Mubarak epitomizes a Western-supported Arab leader, and the Islamists believed his assassination would shatter the entire concept of such a thing. Given the prevailing dynamics in the Islamist Middle East, a harsh reaction from Cairo after even a failed Islamist operation could still serve the Islamists' purposes. The Egyptian Islamists would be united in their response to success or in a sense of martyrdom from retribution by state security organs. Meanwhile, the

Islamist leadership reasoned, Cairo would be too preoccupied with the ramifications of the terrorist operations, whether successful or not, to protect the conservative regimes on the Arabian Peninsula.

The Addis Ababa operation was the outcome of lengthy deliberations at the highest levels of the sponsoring states and the Islamist terrorist movement. Osama bin Laden was part of these deliberations. Although the operation was claimed by the al-Jamaah al-Islamiyah—Sheikh Omar Abdul Rahman's organization—in the name of Egyptian domestic issues, the operation was actually an international undertaking.

This time it was Turabi's Sudan, rather than Iran, that moved to the forefront of the assault on pro-Western regimes, especially Egypt. Sudan had been directly involved in the overall expansion of the Islamist armed struggle throughout Egypt. Sudanese officials, including Hassan al-Turabi, had maintained tight control over covert Islamist operations at both strategic and operational levels.

Starting in fall 1994, Tehran, Khartoum, and the AIM leadership had repeatedly authorized the formulation of plans to assassinate Mubarak. For example, Islamist networks in Italy and Bosnia-Herzegovina were activated for Mubarak's planned November 1994 visit to Italy to attempt his assassination. Islamist networks in Italy were already under close scrutiny by Western security forces, however, and the plot was exposed and neutralized. Next, one of the best Islamist networks in Egypt itself was activated and, in effect, sacrificed on orders from Khartoum to kill Mubarak and incite an Islamist popular uprising. This network lived up to expectations as in the first three weeks of January 1995 its members launched three determined attempts to kill Mubarak. But by then the core of the network was exhausted and its key operatives on the run. Fearing that revelation of such relentless efforts to kill the president would damage the stability of the regime, Cairo decided to conceal them. Meanwhile the key leaders of the terrorist group fled safely to Sudan, traveling via other Arab countries. Other Islamist networks in Egypt that had nothing to do with the assassination attempts were hurt by the ruthless dragnet operations of Egyptian security forces.

With the arrival of these Egyptian terrorists in Khartoum, senior intelligence officials working with AIM, in particular Iranian counterintelligence experts, demanded a thorough after-action analysis of both the advisability of further assassination attempts and the peculiarities of the January operations. This thorough intelligence study concluded that in principle, when the overall dynamics in the Middle East and especially the course of the Islamist struggle in early 1995 were taken into account, the assassination of President Mubarak was imperative.

But the analysts left two major issues unresolved pending subsequent studies. The first issue was the ability of the Islamist network throughout Egypt to withstand the massive retribution that any future attempt on Mubarak's life, even if it failed, would inevitably cause. The second issue was the belief of Iranian intelligence experts that some of the Islamist networks in Egypt had been penetrated by the security services, so that any future plans were bound to be betrayed. The Iranian experts recommended using only networks of the highest quality for any future operation of strategic importance. This precluded operations inside Egypt because locally based support networks could no longer be fully trusted.

After evaluating these conclusions, Turabi decided to raise the issues with the prominent leaders of the Egyptian Islamist jihad forces before any strategy was formulated. In March 1995 Turabi convened an emergency conference in Khartoum with the three leading Egyptian commanders: Dr. Ayman al-Zawahiri, the Geneva-based leader of the al-Jihad organization then in charge of a special headquarters for key operations in the United States and on the American continent as a whole; Mustafa Hamzah, a Khartoum-based senior commander of al-Jamaah al-Islamiyah, who was responsible for the training and preparation of Islamist cadres for operations inside Egypt; and Rifai Ahmad Taha, a Peshawar-based senior commander of al-Jamaah al-Islamiyah who was responsible for the training and preparation of Islamist cadres in camps in both Pakistan and Afghanistan.

Despite the tension among these commanders, all three showed up for Turabi's emergency meeting. Opening the meeting, Turabi stated that the only issue on the table was the Islamist revolution in Egypt. All future operations, such as the subversion of Saudi Arabia, should be examined against the criterion of the impact they might have on the revolution in Egypt. All outstanding disputes among Egyptian commanders would also have to be eliminated before their schism affected the networks inside Egypt. Turabi believed that the modus operandi of the Islamist networks had to change drastically to reverse the effect of recent clashes with the security services, which had paralyzed the movement in parts of Egypt.

Turabi and the three Egyptian commanders concluded that a long-term Islamist revolutionary strategy would be determined by the three commanders present. The Egyptians were also told to prepare a comprehensive proposal stating their needs in terms of weapons and money for the next stage of the Islamist armed struggle and to have it ready for the forthcoming PAIC assembly, scheduled to open in Khartoum in late March 1995.

At Turabi's meeting with the three commanders the question of a major operation to assassinate President Mubarak using high-quality assets from all over the world was first brought up. The Egyptian commanders agreed that if the assassination resulted in a large-scale popular Islamist uprising in Egypt and the operation bolstered other Islamist operations throughout the Middle East, it would be worth the extraordinary effort and risk entailed. Although Turabi endorsed these conclusions, the Egyptian commanders could not decide on the operation themselves—the ultimate decision was up to the sponsoring states.

Considering the magnitude of the required investment in operatives and funds, Turabi decided to raise the issue at the PAIC conference in Khartoum at the end of March 1995. The Friendship Hall sessions resulted in the formulation of a strategy for an Islamist revolutionary and terrorist surge around the world. Turabi brought with him Osama bin Laden and Mustafa Ismail Uthman of Sudanese intelligence. Mohammad Said Naamani of Iranian intelligence, an expert on Algeria and North Africa, represented Tehran. The other leaders and commanders consulted were Imad Mughniyah and Naim Qassim (HizbAllah), Fathi Shkaki (Palestinian Islamic Jihad), Mussa Abu Marzuk and Muhammad Nezzal (HAMAS), Adrian Saad-ad-Din (International Muslim Brotherhood), Abdul-Majid al-Zandani (Yemen), and a few North African Islamists.

The participants in the Friendship Hall sessions discussed all aspects of a possible assassination of Mubarak outside of Egypt. After lengthy deliberations they gave their blessing to an all-out effort to kill Mubarak and incite a widespread, popular Islamist uprising in Egypt in which the entire international Islamist movement would participate. They stressed that the Cairo regime would be toppled in the aftermath of a lengthy fight by highly trained mujahideen and not by popular violence. Once Cairo started fighting for its life, it would be unable to react to the subversion of Saudi Arabia and the other Persian Gulf States. Hence the overthrow of the Saudi regime necessitated the collapse or at least the neutralization of Egypt.

Initial plans for the operation were made during April in consultations between the Egyptian commanders and numerous experts. Mustafa Hamzah was nominated as the senior commander in charge of the Egyptian uprising. He would personally supervise preparation of cadres and logistical support in Sudan and arrange to smuggle them into Egypt. But no decision was made on who would be the senior commander of the assassination operation.

From the very beginning Turabi preferred Zawahiri as the supreme commander even though the Egyptian doctor was preoccupied with preparations for a new wave of terrorist operations in the United States. A strong personal trust had grown up between Turabi and Zawahiri in Somalia in fall 1993, when Zawahiri, as senior on-site commander, oversaw the lethal clashes with the U.S. forces. The Islamists did not have many leaders with capabilities comparable to Zawahiri's. In addition, his excellent headquarters in Geneva, with auxiliary installations throughout Western Europe and Bosnia-Herzegovina, was considered secure from hostile penetration. Zawahiri had good contacts with other Islamist networks, in particular numerous Arab "Afghans." Because diverting Zawahiri's attention to Mubarak would adversely affect the highly important operations in the United States, Turabi decided to examine the issue in one-on-one consultations with the Egyptian.

In the last week of May, Turabi traveled to Paris, allegedly for medical treatment. From there he made a brief secret visit to Geneva to meet with Zawahiri. After lengthy discussions both agreed that Zawahiri had to command the operation to assassinate Mubarak. The two decided that the assassination attempt would take place in Addis Ababa in late June during the African summit. In order to stress the importance of the operation, Turabi met with Zawahiri's closest aides and promised to provide them with all the assistance they needed in their endeavor. Zawahiri moved quickly to begin preparations. He would run the operation under the banner of the Vanguard of Conquest Organization, the cover name for the organization he used in Somalia, which would identify him to the Egyptian government.

In the last days of May, Zawahiri convened a summit of terrorist experts in Ferney-Voltaire, a small village on the French-Swiss border. The site was selected so that the conspirators could flee to France on the spot if anything went wrong. The list of participants reflected the importance and magnitude of the undertaking. The meeting was chaired by Zawahiri and Mustafa Hamzah. Hamzah arrived in Geneva for this summit using a Sudanese passport with a false name. Zawahiri's deputy—Fuad Talat Qassim, then based in Copenhagen—sent his operations commander. The Peshawar-based Ahmad Shawqi al-Islambuli also sent a senior representative. The son of Said Ramadan, spiritual leader of Zawahiri's terrorist campaign, then living in Germany but acting as the imam of a small mosque in Switzerland, attended. Ramadan's mosque was being used as a center for clandestine communications for Egyptian and North African Islamist groups. Subsequent sessions also included senior representatives of Arab "Afghan" networks and commanders in Western Europe, mostly Algerians, and other senior commanders from Afghanistan, Pakistan, and Europe.

In their first meeting the Egyptian terrorist commanders decided on the basic tactics to be employed in Addis Ababa and on the assets to be used for this all-important operation. They decided that a team of highly professional "Afghans," including senior officers (either still serving or recently retired) from numerous countries, would form a special planning cell under Islambuli and his representative then present in Switzerland.

In the second set of meetings, which included members of other groups as well, the participants determined the role and contributions of all other networks and their regional assets. Zawahiri expressed concern that his preoccupation with the assassination attempt could delay the launching of the terrorist campaign in the West, especially the United States. He asked the Algerian "Afghan" commanders to consider expediting their own plans for operations in Europe to ensure an overall continuity of Islamist terrorist strikes. The Algerians must have agreed, as was demonstrated by the bombing of the Paris Métro on July 26, 1995. Hamzah returned immediately to Sudan to select operatives and refine the training program for the Egyptian strike. Two weeks later he reported that the system was essentially ready. Meanwhile Islambuli's planning teams in Peshawar and Khartoum worked out a detailed, sophisticated operational plan.

Once the initial preparations were completed, Zawahiri made an all-important inspection visit to Sudan and Ethiopia between June 12 and 19, 1995. Zawahiri and Hamzah studied in great detail the preparations for both the Addis Ababa operation and the Islamist uprising in Egypt. The sense of unity that the attempt on Mubarak's life brought to the Islamists in Egypt soon became apparent. Colonel Muhammad Makkawi, who had broken away from the Vanguards of Conquest in August 1993 over disagreements with Zawahiri concerning strategy for the Islamist revolution in Egypt, now met with Zawahiri and Hamzah, swore allegiance, and put the networks of his al-Jihad Movement at Hamzah's disposal.

Using forged documents and with help from Turabi's loyalists in the ranks of the Ethiopian Islamic Jihad, Zawahiri made a brief, clandestine visit to Addis Ababa to see the sites of the planned attacks with his own eyes. He then returned to Khartoum to go over the fine details of the operational plan. Satisfied, Zawahiri met with the terrorists training for the operation. He delivered a fiery speech, stressing the importance of the operation and of martyrdom. He dwelt on the need for professionalism for the operation to succeed.

Zawahiri returned to Switzerland, convinced that the operation would succeed. For final approval he called his closest Egyptian friends, Mustafa Hamzah and Fuad Talat Qassim, to meet in Geneva on June 23. The three repeatedly went over all the details of the operations, carefully studying all the good and bad possible ramifications, and then decided to issue the final go-ahead to their networks in both Addis Ababa and southern Egypt. By this point there was no turning back. The success of the operation now depended greatly on the quality of the operatives.

To increase the likelihood of success, Hamzah and the other organizers of the hit teams had selected the operatives from the ranks of highly trained fighters already vetted by Iranian intelligence. In summer 1995 all the candidates were being trained by Iranian Revolutionary Guard experts in camps of al-Quds Forces north of Khartoum. The organizers decided to tap the assets of the IRGC's internationalist Islamist battalion because Iranian intelligence had repeatedly checked their reliability. To further enhance the success of the operation, the teams were selected and organized from troops of special forces units comprising Egyptian, Sudanese, Algerian, and Ethiopian "Afghans." In this way, it would be more difficult for Western intelligence services to penetrate their ranks or guess the intended objective of their operation as they began deploying abroad.

The operational plan called for the possible use of a suicide bomber. The candidate selected was an Arab who had just graduated from a suicide school in Afghanistan run under the banner of the Vanguards of Conquest. This individual had originally volunteered for an operation connected with the Palestinian cause. While on hold in Sudan, he was being trained by Palestinian Islamic Jihad specialists under the close supervision of Iranian experts. Only a week or so before the operation the candidate was primed to participate in the assassination attempt on Mubarak.

Meanwhile, in mid-June, Hamzah oversaw the selection of the operatives for the strike-force teams. By this time Islambuli's operational plan had been adopted in principle, and the selection of operatives and their specific training programs had been organized accordingly. Once selected for the operation, the terrorists were moved to another camp near the village of Kango, some forty miles south of Khartoum. It was there that the final, specific training of the assassination squads took place and the participants were provided with details of their assignments.

The operational plan was based on the coordinated work of three separate teams. The first team would be a diversionary force. Using small arms, it would attack Mubarak's convoy from the roofs of buildings overlooking the road from the airport to the convention center. It was assumed that once under fire, the entire convoy would slow down for a moment, perhaps even stop. Taking advantage of this confusion, the second team would approach the center of the convoy and blast the president's car with RPG rockets, completely destroying it. If they could not hit the president's car, the second team was ordered to blast instead any official Egyptian vehicle it could. Excellent sources in the Egyptian security forces, including Mubarak's bodyguards, had provided material for the third team's assignment. The planners had been told that in case of emergency, Mubarak's driver was instructed to "storm the roadblocks and proceed at full speed regardless of the cost." The third team would be ready to intervene in case the first two teams failed and Mubarak's driver was able to move the car forward. Islambuli's planners assumed that once safely out of the fiery gauntlet, Mubarak's driver would inevitably relax a bit and perhaps even slow down. At this stage a massive car bomb driven by a martyr-to-be would close in on the presidential car and either ram it or blow himself up near it. Either way, Islambuli's bomb experts assured him that no car in the world, no matter how well armored, would be able to survive an explosion at such close proximity.

Just how committed Turabi and the Egyptian Islamist leadership were to assassinating Mubarak could be seen from the preliminary actions they took. By late April, in the aftermath of the initial planning in Sudan but a month before a commitment had been reached in Geneva in late May, the Islamists had already started preparing a support and intelligence system in Addis Ababa.

At first a small team made up of Sudanese intelligence officers and members of the Ethiopian Islamic Jihad, including highly experienced "Afghans," inspected possibilities for the main on-site base. In late April they rented the villa that would become the forward headquarters and weapons cache for the operation.

In May, as the training and planning were becoming specific, on-site preparations in Addis Ababa accelerated. A team of ten operatives was dispatched from Khartoum to Addis Ababa. Their first task, completed in the second half of May, was to survey the possible strike site and identify possible deployment positions. They drew detailed maps of the entire area. With the cooperation of Ethiopian Islamists, the Sudanese were able to activate sources within the Ethiopian security command. These Ethiopian officers provided the team with detailed advance information on the summit schedule as well as on the movements of and security procedures for all the leaders expected to attend.

In early June, with the operation now approved for implementation, the ten-operative network in Addis Ababa shifted its priorities to arranging for the smuggling of weapons and explosives into their villa. The Sudanese operatives also worked with the Ethiopian security officers to facilitate the safe deployment of the three armed teams to their assault positions and to secure cover for their escape and exfiltration on completion of the operation. The contacts cemented with the Ethiopian security officers proved highly advantageous, for the attackers would have exact and timely intelligence about Mubarak's arrival and route.

In mid-June, at the time of Zawahiri's visit to Sudan and Ethiopia, the final phases of the preparations were launched. The Sudanese activated a vast network of Ethiopian Islamists to do the groundwork—smuggling the weapons and explosives to Ethiopia; leasing the vehicles to be used in the operation, including the car bomb; leasing numerous apartments and houses to be used as living quarters for the operatives; and filling them with food and other supplies. After Zawahiri's visit, with these preparations completed, Sudanese intelligence evacuated some thirty Ethiopian Islamists from Addis Ababa to Khartoum. These individuals knew too much about the impending operation, and the Sudanese did not want to risk the ramifications of the capture and interrogation of any one of them.

The weapons delivered at this time left no doubt about the direct involvement of the Sudanese government in the operation. Virtually all the weapons seized with the terrorists in Addis Ababa belonged to the Sudanese army. The serial numbers on the seized RPG-7s confirmed that these were part of a Sudanese arms deal with China. The Russian-made small arms seized in Addis Ababa were identical to and from the same general production series as comparable weapons found by the Egyptian army on the Sudanese border—weapons that had been provided to Egyptian Islamists in training camps in Sudan.

In mid-June, Turabi personally took over the job of overseeing the operation in Addis Ababa. A senior Sudanese intelligence officer identified as Siraj Muhammad Hussein, also known as Muhammad Siraj, arrived in Addis Ababa and assumed operational command over the actual execution of the operation. Colonel Abdul-Aziz Jafar, an officer in Sudanese intelligence who defected to Egypt, identified Siraj as Major Muhammad Siraj-al-Din of Sudanese intelligence. According to an Egyptian security source, Muhammad Siraj is the same intelligence officer who, as the Sudanese consul working under a pseudonym in New York in 1993, actively participated in the World Trade Center bombing and the July 4 conspiracy to blow up the United Nations building.

It did not take long for Siraj to establish himself as the overall coordinator of the Islamist operation in Addis Ababa. He personally handled the acquisition and dissemination of intelligence information to ensure maximum secrecy. He oversaw the arrangements for renting the villa used as the main cache and for securing an alternative residence to shelter the perpetrators pending their exfiltration back to Khartoum. It was only around June 20, after Siraj was satisfied with the security and safety of the advance preparations, that the actual infiltration of the perpetrators began.

To reduce the risk of early exposure, the operatives received their weapons, including the road-blocking truck and car bomb, from a separate network of Sudanese intelligence on the eve of the strike. This network was run by Sheikh Darwish, a Sudanese national who was personally loyal to Turabi and who had carried out numerous special missions for him between Khartoum and Addis Ababa. The fact that Sheikh Darwish was personally involved in handling the weapons for the operation demonstrated just how important the operation was to Turabi himself. In late June, Darwish delivered two big suitcases full of small arms, RPG launchers, shells, ammunition, and explosives. The first team would carry the weapons on their bodies while the second team brought along travel bags so that they wouldn't have to expose their RPGs until the very last minute. This decision would soon prove to be a fatal error.

The day of the attack, June 26, 1995, began perfectly. Siraj, who was constantly fed with up-to-the-minute data about Mubarak's planned schedule by Ethiopian security officers, started to deploy his people. Throughout the assassination attempt intelligence on Mubarak's arrival and route was both exact and timely; Siraj must have had very secure and efficient communications with both his Ethiopian sources and the assault teams.

What ultimately spoiled the operation were delays and confusion in the ranks of Mubarak's entourage. President Mubarak was supposed to arrive at the airport just before 8:30 A.M. and immediately leave for the summit center, a little over half a mile away. As planned, Ethiopian and Egyptian security forces deployed along the route shortly after 8:15 A.M. Mubarak's plane arrived on time, but his entourage was unable to organize his convoy in a timely fashion. With Mubarak's convoy delayed, the bored Ethiopian policemen started wandering around. To avoid looking suspicious, the second assault team had to put their RPGs back in their travel bags and slightly withdraw from their firing positions.

Meanwhile Mubarak was getting impatient. Around 8:55 A.M. he suddenly ordered whatever elements of the convoy were available to immediately start heading for the summit center. Although the Ethiopian security officers were able to alert Siraj and his people on time, parts of the assault team were no longer in place.

As Mubarak's convoy sped by, the first team opened up with small-arms fire as planned, but the blue Toyota truck that was supposed to block the road in front of the convoy didn't move quickly enough. The vehicle blocking or slowing down Mubarak's convoy had been a last-minute addition to the terrorists' plan to slow down the convoy as it sped along this segment of the road. Because the members of the second assault team had been told to keep their RPGs inside their bags for security reasons, the team were now unable to unpack, take out, and fire their weapons on such short notice.

The third team with the car bomb and the martyr-driver was in place. But here the short delay of the blue Toyota truck proved decisive. The first team had been concentrating its fire on the main limousine—Ethiopia's official car—where Mubarak was supposed to be. But Mubarak was actually traveling in a special Mercedes, supposedly not just bulletproof but also able to withstand RPG rockets, that he had brought with him from Cairo.

Into this confusion entered the blue Toyota truck. After the slight delay, the driver could no longer position himself in front of Mubarak's convoy to block the road. Instead, with the convoy's cars speeding just ahead of him, he almost slammed into the Ethiopian limousine.

With cars braking in all directions to avoid a crash, still under a hail of small-arms fire, Mubarak's driver decided he could not break through the mess. Instead he drastically deviated from the security plans. He turned the Mercedes 180 degrees and sped immediately back to the airport. This split-second decision saved Mubarak's life, for around 300 feet down the road from the ambush site, the car bomb was waiting.

Disappointed as they were, the principals of the operation immediately activated their exfiltration plan. Siraj and the operatives who knew the organizational and intelligence aspects of the operation disappeared within hours, making their way safely to Khartoum. The surviving operatives were left behind as bait for the security forces and so that they would not overload the exfiltration system. Some of them would soon die in gun battles with Ethiopian police and Egyptian commandos operating clandestinely in Addis Ababa.

But the excellence of the planning and preparations for the operation became apparent to everyone. As part of the plan Mustafa Hamzah had organized a series of bombings and other types of armed operations throughout Egypt to create the impression of a widespread popular uprising and to induce a general state of panic throughout Egypt in the wake of the shocking news of Mubarak's assassination. Toward this end, Turabi had provided Hamzah with forward bases in Sudan with training camps and military instructors, as well as the weapons and explosives required for their operations. The operational plan called for the advance deployment of large numbers of teams of highly trained Egyptian operatives. Once given the green light, in the predawn hours of June 26, they would infiltrate Egypt, advance along specific routes, and link up with just activated networks of supporters in virtually all the cities and towns in Egypt. Together they were to launch an unprecedented wave of terrorism and violence.

Late on the morning of June 26, when news of the failed assassination attempt reached Khartoum, Turabi and Hamzah decided to call off the operation. Despite the now heightened alert inside Egypt, the Islamist command center in Khartoum was able to call back the vast majority of the teams that had already infiltrated Egypt even before they had been noticed by the Egyptian security authorities and well before they clashed with them. The Islamist command center was also able to alert its vast support networks all over Egypt to go back underground before the Egyptian dragnet was activated. As a result the majority of these Egyptian Islamist forces, both in Sudan and in Egypt, survived to strike another day.

The Egyptian Islamist leadership took a few days to assess what to do next. Finally on July 4 responsibility for the attempt on Mubarak's life was claimed by al-Jamaah al-Islamiyah—Sheikh Omar Abdul Rahman's organization. The communiqué claimed that the operation was carried out by the Talat Yassin commando in honor of an Islamist commander killed by Egyptian police in 1994.

In its communiqué al-Jamaah al-Islamiyah explained that the assassination attempt was part of its relentless, escalating struggle to destroy the secular regime and establish an Islamic government in Egypt. The assassination was designed to "save the Egyptian people [who] presently [live] under conditions of plight and poverty. . . . Our Jihad will not cease for as long as Allah's Sharia is not implemented in Egypt." Al-Jamaah al-Islamiyah reminded the world that it had been involved in the assassination of Anwar Sadat in 1981 and stressed that it would kill any Egyptian leader deviating from the right way, particularly Mubarak. "Al-Jamaah, which was honored with executing the promise of God against al-Sadat for his heresy and betrayal of Islam, had to execute the punishment of God on the Un-Mubarak because he has taken the same path." ("Un-Mubarak" is a pun on the president's name; it means the "un-blessed.") Al-Jamaah al-Islamiyah also urged members of the army, the security forces, and all others who were cooperating with "the dictator and his aggressive methods against Islam and Muslims as a whole to repent their sins in front of Allah, and reject all the cursed actions of the dictator." The only way to truly achieve repentance was to join the Islamist uprising, which, the communiqué stressed, would continue. The operation "proved that al-Jamaah can strike painful blows to the enemies of Allah no matter how long it takes."

Like the attempt on Mubarak's life, major terrorist operations are conducted by agencies of states in pursuit of the long-term, strategic interests of the controlling and sponsoring states. The names and profiles of the organizations issuing the communiqués and claims are an integral component of the state-sponsorship mechanism. These named entities serve a specific function—they state the identity and essence of the interests involved in the operation, and they outline the logic and objectives behind these operations without the sponsoring states assuming formal responsibility.

Given the marked escalation of international terrorism and the higher stakes involved, the importance of the front groups speaking for the sponsoring states—in particular Iran and the global Islamic Revolution it is running—is increasingly central to international terrorism. But despite the evolution in the role of the terrorist organizations, actual control over the operations remains under the sponsoring states.

———————

ON THE FACE OF IT, the assassination attempt on President Mubarak was clearly a failure because he survived and the amount of evidence unearthed was sufficient to implicate the sponsoring states. But a closer look at the operation and its aftermath suggests that both the sponsoring states and the Islamist movements extracted some gains from the attempt.

The grand design of Tehran and Khartoum reveals much about the ramifications of this operation. The Islamist leadership was convinced that the Middle East was increasingly vulnerable to Islamist subversion. They felt that escalation of the political Islamization process—from violent subversion of the population to a full-fledged political and military challenge to the regimes—was now possible in many countries.

The Islamists had correctly read the dominant regional trends from three major developments: (1) Islamism is the sole growing, developing, and truly popular populist ideology in the Middle East. It has already replaced nationalism and other Westernized ideologies. Most people genuinely believe that "Islam is the solution," even though ideas vary about what this "Islam" is. (2) The pro-Western conservative regimes are near collapse, more from self-destruction than anything else, especially in Saudi Arabia. (3) The Westernization of the Middle East—consolidated under the heading of the so-called Arab-Israeli peace process—is at a historic turning point. The peace process itself has already proved a failure because the key demands of Israel and the Arabs cannot be reconciled, and the dominant historic trend in the region is adamant opposition to the mere existence of Israel, let alone peace with it.

Both Tehran and Khartoum were convinced that they could bring about the collapse of the conservative regimes of the Arabian Peninsula and take over the holy shrines rather quickly. The only impediment was Mubarak's Egypt—a pro-Western nation, it was likely to protect the Saudi regime. The Islamists could only take over the Arabian Peninsula if Cairo were so preoccupied with a domestic crisis that it could not come to the assistance of the conservative regimes on the Arabian Peninsula.

But Egypt itself was on the verge of a popular Islamist uprising. The population had increasingly demonstrated a genuine desire for an Islamic regime of some sort. The Islamists intensified their penetration and takeover of society through what Egypt-born British journalist and Middle

East expert Adel Darwish calls "Islamization by stealth"—a gradual domination of society while conditioning the population to an Islamic regime. The Egyptian population, who had lost faith in the ability of Mubarak's Cairo to resolve its economic plight and reverse the overall deterioration of the sociopolitical situation in the nation, was ready for imposition of Sharia as a cure-all panacea.

This was not merely a theoretical development. Egyptian state institutions, most notably the court system, have increasingly and rigidly applied the Sharia instead of the civil law, even in cases where only Westernized and secular matters are involved. For example, in mid-July 1995 a Cairo court ruled that an Egyptian couple must divorce against their will because the works of the husband—Nasr Abu Zeid, a professor of Arabic literature—amounted to apostasy and so he could no longer be married to a Muslim woman. The higher courts and other state authorities adamantly refused to challenge the court's Sharia-based decision.

At the same time the Islamist leadership, both the Egyptian Islamist leaders and their sponsors, were fully aware that the Mubarak regime would fight for survival. Achieving Islamization of the public at large was a far cry from acquiring the subversive and military capabilities needed to successfully take on a regime determined to defend itself by massive use of force. The Islamist leaders needed to instigate a major clash to paralyze if not neutralize Cairo on the eve of any Islamist assault on the Arabian Peninsula. The assassination attempt on President Mubarak would have served such a purpose.

Bin Laden, as part of Turabi's inner circle and someone devoted to achieving an Islamist state in Saudi Arabia, played an integral part in formulating the plot against Mubarak. Bin Laden is still committed to the spread of the Islamist revolution throughout the hub of Islam, including Egypt, and knows that paralyzing Cairo would expedite the Islamist plan to impose an Islamist government on Riyadh.

Preferably, from the Islamist perspective, Mubarak would have been killed, expediting the Islamist popular uprising throughout Egypt and the entire region. But his survival and the subsequent implication of Sudan in the assassination plot still served a strategic purpose in the Middle East. By fall 1995 President Mubarak was leading Egypt toward a confrontation with Sudan, and at the same time he was preoccupied with a domestic cleanup. As a result Egypt was less likely to commit major military forces to save Riyadh, where the status quo was rapidly deteriorating.

Saudi Islamists did not take long to capitalize on the chaos created by the Addis Ababa operation. While the Islamist leadership was focused on the Addis Ababa operation, Osama bin Laden was patiently orchestrating his first, however belated, confrontation with the House of al-Saud.

ON NOVEMBER 13, 1995, dozens of Americans were eating lunch in the snack bar at the Military Cooperation Program building in Riyadh, a military training center run by the United States for the Saudi National Guard. At 11:40 A.M. a car bomb exploded in the parking lot in front of the three-story building. This blast blew off one side of the building, destroyed more than forty-five cars, and shattered windows more than a mile away. Within a few minutes a secondary antipersonnel bomb exploded in the parking lot, inflicting additional casualties among the people rushing to help those injured in the first explosion.

This car bombing in the middle of Riyadh was much more than a spectacular terrorist strike. This operation demonstrated the activation of a comprehensive, vibrant Islamist subversive infrastructure inside Saudi Arabia. The core of the Saudi Islamist armed movement consisted of expert cadres meticulously organized and now tightly controlled by Tehran and Khartoum. The network that struck in Riyadh epitomized the Saudi Sunni Islamist underground—a combination of Saudis from grassroots movements, cadres consisting primarily of Saudi "Afghans," and Islamist supporters at the heart of the Saudi security establishment. The Saudi Islamist underground had evolved when the younger ulema gave up on the corrupt, collapsing House of al-Saud, and the explosions in Riyadh showed that the Saudi Islamist leadership, as well as the exceptionally well informed Islamist leadership in Tehran and Khartoum, had already concluded that an Islamist jihad might hasten the demise of the doomed House of al-Saud.

The anticipated regionwide escalation of Islamist violence began in fall 1995. As early as late October Islamist violence had escalated in Egypt, in particular as renewed attacks on police stations, trains, and tourist buses. As anticipated, Cairo was preoccupied with a new cycle of crackdowns on the increasingly effective, popular Islamist forces. By early November, Egypt was again on the verge of a popular Islamist uprising.

Both Tehran and Khartoum remained convinced that they could bring about the collapse of the conservative regimes of the Arabian Peninsula and take over the holy shrines fairly quickly. Their assumption that the only way the Islamists could take over the Arabian Peninsula was if Cairo were so preoccupied with a domestic crisis that it could not afford to come to the assistance of the conservative regimes remained valid. In early November the experts and leaders in Tehran and Khartoum concluded that the road was open to carrying out the Saudi part of the grand design.

The Islamist forces in Saudi Arabia were activated and received the green light in early November. The Islamist network operating in the Riyadh area consisted of a local support infrastructure and a small group of expert terrorists, most of whom were Saudi "Afghans." The local network was bolstered on the eve of the operation by a few expert terrorists who arrived separately from Europe and Asia. Arab Islamist sources stressed that the heart of both the support network and the perpetrators was made up of "Saudi nationals."

Islamist sources, as well as Saudi and opposition sources, are unanimous that the expert terrorists in command and at the center of the Riyadh operation were "disgruntled young Saudis trained in Afghanistan." Saudi Islamist opposition sources specified that Saudi expert bomb makers "trained by the CIA and Pakistan's military intelligence" were now providing expertise to the "Afghan" networks in the Middle East and Bosnia. The main concentrations of Saudi "Afghans" active in international Islamist terrorism were in Afghanistan, Pakistan, and Sudan.

Pakistani and Afghan sources in Peshawar also divided the network into a Saudi-based infrastructure and a quality core made up of "Afghans." The Saudi-based cadres were motivated by home-grown considerations. These Pakistani and Afghan sources stressed, however, that Saudi foreign policy, rather than oppression by the House of al-Saud, was the primary reason for the confrontation. "The Saudi monarchy continues to play the murky game of inter-Arab politics with the unspoken and effective shield of American military support. At home, critics of the monarchy have shown some resilience despite ruthless repressive measures," explained a knowledgeable Pakistani. The international Islamist character at the center of the Riyadh operation was stressed by all Pakistani and Afghan sources. "There are reasons to believe that these critics, mostly wedded to Islamic revivalism, have their contacts with similar movements across the Islamic world," the Pakistani explained. He identified the key perpetrators as Saudi "Islamic radicals" frustrated by the fact that King Fahd "has sought, time and again, to impart an Islamic gloss to the unrepresentative character of his rule."

THE TWO BOMBS that exploded on November 13 caused six fatalities, five of them Americans, and wounded more than sixty, more than half of them Americans, some critically. The main bomb, which had been installed in a white van, was constructed of between 200 and 225 pounds of high explosives, most likely the highly effective Czech-made plastic high explosive SEMTEX. The Mitsubishi 81 was professionally "cleaned," with all serial and identification numbers thoroughly erased, even from the chassis. The bomb was activated by a sophisticated timing device with a possible remote-control backup system. The secondary antipersonnel bomb was also expertly constructed, placed, and timed to cause maximum casualties despite its small size. The bomb combination was quite sophisticated and required expertise to build and install.

The timing of the explosion proved that the operation was specifically anti-American. At this hour the Americans usually went to lunch in the snack bar at the forward part of the building while the Saudis and other Muslims were in the nearby mosque for noon prayers. The timing showed inside knowledge and lengthy monitoring of the site. The double-bomb arrangement of the operation also reflected expert preparations.

Saudi sources quietly acknowledged that "whatever quarter hatched and planned the explosion, it chose its target very carefully and displayed extraordinary professionalism in implementation. The danger lies not only in the explosion and its victims—and they are U.S. military experts— but also in the acquisition of advanced detonation technologies and the use of all kinds of advanced camouflage and security infiltration methods to reach the target." Another well-informed Saudi source in London explained that "those who carried out the explosion have a very advanced security and political sense. They chose a U.S. target in the heart of Riyadh city in order to attract the biggest amount possible of world media attention and to cause a huge political furor." He pointed out that the strike served as "a clear message to the Americans to the effect that the regime is not in control and [is] unstable."

Even the House of al-Saud could not ignore or conceal an explosion of such magnitude in the heart of Riyadh. It was impossible to deny the terrorist aspect of the explosion and the security implications. The government-owned newspaper *al-Yawm* acknowledged that the bombing was "a desperate attempt to destabilize the security of this country." In the United Arab Emirates the newspaper *al-Fajr* warned that the explosion in Riyadh indicated an expression of "ill-intentions being hatched for the region."

Still, Riyadh insisted that the act of terrorism was aimed at a third party and not the Saudi regime. The daily *al-Riyadh* stressed the point. "Terrorism takes place where it is most unlikely," because "terrorism sometimes takes place in one territory as a kind of vexation or the settling of accounts with another territory." But Prince Nayif bin Abdul-Aziz, the interior minister, acknowledged to the newspaper *al-Jazirah* that the explosions were part of "this dangerous epidemic."

Riyadh refused to confront the root causes for the emergence of Islamist terrorism on its soil. The highly authoritative *al-Hayah*, a mouthpiece of Prince Sultan and the Saudi defense establishment, stated: "No one believes that the blast has internal connotations, but it is true that the perpetrators have taken advantage of the atmosphere of security to carry it out. . . . The act is 'alien,' which simply means that it is foreign-made and serves a foreign purpose, regional to be precise." Having examined possible motives of Iraq, Iran, and Israel to strike in Riyadh, *al-Hayah* concluded that the Saudi government could have done nothing to warrant such an act of terrorism. "That is why it is difficult to detect any genuine purpose in the Riyadh blast, except for those hostile and resentful elements whose interests reside in sabotage for sabotage's sake."

A closer examination of the Riyadh terrorist operation, however, leaves little doubt that it was the beginning of the long-advocated Islamist jihad against the House of al-Saud. The target selected—a U.S. military installation used to support the hated Royal Guard (known in the West as the National Guard)—fit to perfection the recent and still-building ultimatum campaign. The target matched the declared ultimatums so completely that even without any communiqué, the public would undoubtedly have associated the bombing with the Islamist opposition. The April 10 communiqué from the Islamic Change Movement had stated that the Royal [National] Guard and military police forces, as well as other forces that protected the regime, would be a target of operations. In July another communiqué clarified that although active preparations had been made since April, reaching the June 28 deadline did not mean that the operations would be carried out immediately. The actual launch of operations depended on the judgment of the Islamic Change Movement, and the deadline set for the foreign forces was an ultimatum, after which these forces would have become a legitimate target. Some of the logic in this communiqué, and particularly the reference to the American/Western forces as "Crusader forces"—that is, Christian occupiers of Muslim states ultimately to be defeated—would be repeated in the various decrees and fatwas bin Laden issued in the coming years.

In addition the style of the bombing—a major car bomb combined with a smaller antipersonnel bomb and the types of high explosives and fuses used—was identical to that taught in the Islamist elite terrorist training camps in Pakistan and Sudan. In these camps bin Laden's small cadre of Saudi "Afghans" had been taught the art of sophisticated bomb making and techniques of bomb placement in order to launch a wave of spectacular terrorist operations starting in the summer of 1995.

These operational preparations, peaking in early spring 1995, closely coincided with the strategic and political activities at the highest levels of the international Islamist movement, activities in which bin Laden played a major role. As a member of Turabi's inner circle, bin Laden took part in the primary decision making and policy formulation process. He was also responsible for the "public policy" aspect, helping to define the key messages of the operations and formulate the communiqués issued. Some of the key phrases that would characterize bin Laden's "declarations of war" in 1996–98 first appeared in the 1995 communiqués.

In spring 1995 bin Laden and the Saudi Islamist leadership concurred with Turabi's recommendations, based on thorough research done by Iranian intelligence and Arab experts operating in Khartoum, to escalate their struggle against the House of al-Saud into an armed jihad. Toward this end Iranian intelligence launched an audacious program of surveillance of a host of U.S.-related potential targets all over Saudi Arabia that would continue for at least the next eighteen to twenty-four months. Both the Riyadh building and the Khobar Towers, which were attacked in summer 1996, were included in this effort. Soon afterward Sheikh Udah smuggled from jail his lecture "Death Workmanship," which sanctified the calls for an armed jihad against the House of al-Saud and was endorsed by the CDLR. The ensuing communiqué from the Islamic Change Movement reflected the decision by the Saudi Islamist leadership to begin the armed jihad as the only viable instrument to overthrow the Saudi regime. This was not an idle threat.

Final preparations for the November 13 operation had been so intense that there were leaks. Ranking Saudi officials later conceded that the authorities in Riyadh had been warned about an imminent terrorist action for nearly a week before the explosion. A week before the blast the Islamic Change Movement sent warning faxes to the U.S. and British embassies in Riyadh and other institutions. The Saudi and Western security authorities, however, did not take these warnings seriously. Riyadh placed the Saudi security forces on a low-level alert primarily as a pro forma response.

Highly knowledgeable Saudis in the Middle East and Western Europe speculated that Prince Salman bin Abdul-Aziz let the terrorist operation take place so that he could capitalize on it for his own personal gain. The governor of Riyadh and aspirant successor to King Fahd, Prince Salman planned to use the growing Islamist threat, the dread of the entire House of al-Saud, and his reputed ability to suppress Islamism as his ticket to power, acceptability, and ultimately the throne. According to both Saudi Islamist leaders and Arab insiders, in the fall of 1994 Prince Salman had already obtained "a personal mandate" from King Fahd "to administer the country's affairs," namely, internal security and stability.

Prince Salman was known to have maintained contacts with Islamists as recently as fall 1995. The CDLR's Muhammad al-Massari insisted that

Prince Salman "is more intelligent and more open than the others [in the House of al-Saud]. But he is also the most hypocritical: His overtures [to the Islamists] are only apparent and he aims really only to stay in the saddle." Many Saudis spread the rumor that Prince Salman had allowed the explosion to happen to increase the fear of Islamist violence among the uppermost echelons in the House of al-Saud and thus his own power as the key to their suppression.

Those at the highest levels of the House of al-Saud were working feverishly to suppress a real investigation into the bombing because it would expose a colossal failure of Saudi intelligence. The main issue was the secret Saudi-Pakistani deal reached by Prince Turki back in March 1995. By fall 1995 Riyadh had begun to realize that the ISI had been taking Saudi money and Islamabad had been building on Saudi influence in Washington while Saudi "Afghans" were being trained and supported in Pakistan, Afghanistan, Sudan, and Iran for operations in Saudi Arabia. The car bomb that exploded on November 13, 1995, shocked the entire Saudi establishment, causing more damage to the innermost corridors of power in the Saudi government than to the buildings in Riyadh.

The various organizations' claims of responsibility that followed the November 13 explosions served mainly to clarify and substantiate their position in the beginning of the Islamist jihad in Saudi Arabia.

The first claim was issued by a previously unknown organization, the Tigers of the Gulf. This was a bogus name for a nonexistent organization used to disassociate any legitimate Islamist organization from the bombing. The claim was important only because it had been issued by phone from inside Saudi Arabia, proving the existence of locally active Islamist cells. "The attacks will continue until the departure of the last American soldier" from Saudi Arabia, the caller said in two successive calls from Saudi Arabia. The Tigers' use of the standard Islamist phraseology identified them as components of the larger Islamist umbrella.

Only after the viability of a communicating network inside Saudi Arabia had been established did the primary front organization responsible for the operation, the Islamic Change Movement, issue its own statement through regular Islamist channels. The primary objective of this communiqué was to legitimize the Islamic Change Movement as a component of AIM while confirming its ability to live up to warnings and ultimatums.

In its communiqué the Islamic Change Movement repeated the Tigers' position that it was opposed to Saudi Arabia's "total surrender to the USA and its Western allies" and its commitment to "exert all available means to evict these forces." The communiqué repeated all the well-established objectives of the Islamist movement—its intention to overthrow the House of al-Saud, have the "invaders" leave the country, and make the nation regain its pride and dignity. To ensure that the objective of the bombing was not lost, the communiqué also vented rage at the Saudi leaders because they had become "infidel agents" who had "opened the land of the Two Holy Shrines and the peninsula of the Arabs to invading colonialist, Crusader forces." The communiqué stressed that the Islamic Change Movement would continue to target foreign troops, the Saudi royal family, and the Saudi security forces.

The CDLR's endorsement of both the Islamic Change Movement and the bombing in Riyadh was critical. The London-based CDLR is the largest and best-organized Saudi Islamic opposition group, and it enjoys access to the Saudi elite at home and in the West. "We found that the group, The Movement for Islamic Change, is a legitimate group and might be behind the blast," declared Said al-Faqih, the CDLR's London director.

The international- and state-sponsored aspect of the Riyadh operation was not neglected either. The Armed Islamic Movement, especially its Pakistan-based Islamist "Afghan" forces, moved to take credit for the Riyadh operation only after the Saudi entities had had ample time to advocate their justification.

The Armed Islamic Movement claimed credit on the next day by disseminating through AIM-affiliated venues a communiqué in the name of a previously unknown group calling itself The Militant Partisans of God Organization. The AIM communiqué also stressed that the Riyadh operation was "the first of our jihad operations." However, AIM stressed the universal and anti-American character of its jihad. The communiqué first demanded that "the U.S. occupying forces leave the territory of the Arabian Peninsula and the Gulf States, and that His Eminence Dr. Omar Abdul Rahman, Dr. Musa Abu-Marzuq, and Ramzi Youssuf and his comrades be released from U.S. jails immediately." (Abdul Rahman and Youssuf were in jail for their role in the bombing of the World Trade Center, and Marzuk was held as a HAMAS commander pending an extradition request by Israel. The request was later withdrawn because of the "peace process.") The AIM communiqué agreed with the demands of previous groups, urging that the "Saudi authorities lift all the restrictions imposed on Muslim ulema and preachers, immediately release all detainees from Saudi jails, and apply all the rules of the Islamic Sharia."

The AIM communiqué included an ultimatum, warning that "if these just demands are not met, the Militant Partisans of God Organization will declare its pledge to die for Allah's cause, targeting US interests on the territory of the Arabian peninsula and the Gulf States," a warning that would be realized in the 1996 bombing of the Khobar Towers. The communiqué went beyond previous ones and warned of an escalation of its anti-American war beyond the region. The Militant Partisans of God concluded with this warning: "O Americans, our blessed operations will not be halted until all our demands are met, otherwise you are imposing on yourselves a relentless war . . . a real war that makes you know your real worth . . . a war to break your false arrogance."

The CDLR stressed that the explosion in Riyadh was the beginning of an armed struggle devised to overthrow the regime. The CDLR's Muhammad al-Massari predicted that "there will be more acts similar to this incident because the [al-Saud] regime is known for its enmity toward its citizens." He pointed out that the bombing was carried out by "disgruntled young people who oppose the Saudi leadership," including "some trained in military tactics in Afghanistan or elsewhere." Al-Massari suggested that the Islamists decided to act when they did "because all important and vocal reformers and activists and preachers have been detained since September 1994 without any end in sight." At the same time he noted that although Americans were the intended victims of the attack, the ultimate target was the House of al-Saud. Al-Massari stressed that "the question is to whom the war declaration is directed and that's to the Saudi regime."

A well-informed Saudi source in London explained that the audacity of the Riyadh operation was also "designed to draw attention to the fact that the arrival in Saudi Arabia of the technology of booby-trapped cars is a serious turning point which could have repercussions." He stressed that this did not mean that future operations would be car bombs: "oil installations could become potential targets in the future to ensure the largest possible amount of world publicity."

The most important legacy of the November 13 explosions in Riyadh was that Osama bin Laden and the Saudi Islamists, along with Iran, Sudan, and other states sponsoring them, finally crossed the line to launch their armed jihad inside Saudi Arabia. There could be no turning back. The growing popularity of the Islamists in virtually all segments of society, from the widespread popular following of Sheikh Udah to the attention paid to the CDLR in the higher strata of society, would put pressure on the militant Islamists to continue to escalate their armed struggle and terrorism until they overthrew the House of al-Saud.

Shortly after the explosion there were reports of an escalation in the terrorism campaign inside Saudi Arabia. According to highly reliable Egyptian sources, at least two major sabotage operations were narrowly averted around November 20–25. One car bomb was defused near the Defense Ministry building, and another car bomb was defused at the parking lot of the Petromin Oil Company. These bombs were similar to but not identical to the November 13 bomb, suggesting that there was more than one highly trained bomb maker in Riyadh and that these bomb makers had graduated from the same training program. In the first week of December, Western diplomatic and commercial entities were warned again of impending strikes. This time the United States and other embassies issued formal warnings. With the Saudi investigation of the November 13 bombing largely at a dead end, more Islamist terrorist strikes could be expected.

With active support and sponsorship from Tehran and Khartoum, the Islamist forces, of impressive size and capabilities, were ready for such an escalation. Ultimately, however, the primary threat of these Islamist forces was that they were providing the coup de grace in the rapidly accelerating self-destruction of the House of al-Saud.

WITH THE RIYADH succession crisis still in full swing and the initial shock of the November 13 bombing not yet over, the Egyptian "Afghans" settled scores and delivered a warning. On the morning of November 19, 1995, at 9:50 A.M. a small car, apparently a taxi, crashed through the gates of the Egyptian Embassy in Islamabad, Pakistan. Soon afterward there was a small explosion in a forward reception area where a crowd of visa seekers and other individuals waiting to do business in the embassy had gathered. According to some reports, this explosion was caused by a hand grenade tossed from the small car. According to the Islamic Jihad, a martyr-operative left the passenger seat and carried a briefcase full of explosives through the gates of the Egyptian Embassy and into the visa section, where he blew himself up. Pakistani interior minister Nasirullah Babar added that the small bomb was actually carried into the embassy "by individuals known to the embassy who were allowed into the premises because the blast occurred inside the compound." The objective of the smaller explosion was to divert attention and cause the crowd to move in the direction of the embassy's main entrances, where they would be hit by another explosion.

Exploiting the commotion and confusion caused by the smaller explosion, a double-cabin pickup van—a blue Mazda—surged through the broken gates. It was loaded with high explosives, likely around 900 pounds' worth. The van accelerated until it got inside the yard, slammed into the front of the main building, and exploded. The explosion created a crater twenty feet wide and ten feet deep, killing an additional nineteen, including the van's driver, and wounding more than sixty.

Soon afterward the main Egyptian Islamist organizations—al-Jamaah al-Islamiyah, al-Jihad al-Islami, and the International Justice Group—claimed responsibility for the attack.

The first communiqué issued by al-Jamaah al-Islamiyah was a general statement of opposition to the Mubarak government, designed to stress the overall responsibility of the Islamist organizations affiliated with AIM. A few days later, as the main reason for the operation was clarified, al-Jamaah al-Islamiyah withdrew its claim for the blast. Officially the disclaimer was issued because the organization "does not believe in suicide operations."

The second communiqué, issued by the Islamic Jihad, highlighted the operational responsibility. "The Jihad group claims responsibility for the event. The squad of the martyr Issam al-Qamari and the martyr Ibrahim Salamah are responsible." Islamic Jihad later clarified that the two names referred to the suicide bombers who actually perpetrated the explosions in Islamabad. This initial brief announcement by Islamic Jihad was designed primarily to establish the organization as the main outlet for authoritative clarifications about the motives behind the terrorist strike.

Another communiqué, issued by the International Justice Group, pointed to continuity with the assassination of President Sadat. "The squad of the martyr Khalid Islambouli carried out today's operation," it said. The International Justice Group was a cover name used by the Iranian-trained security and intelligence operatives of Ayman al-Zawahiri. On November 15 in Geneva they assassinated Alaa al-Din Nazmi, Egypt's number-two diplomat in Switzerland—actually an intelligence officer who was investigating near Zawahiri's lair. The bomb communiqué reiterated that the International Justice Group would continue to pursue "all those involved in actions against the sons of the Islamic movement."

Like the assassination attempt on President Mubarak, the Islamabad bombing operation was conducted under the tight control of and financed by the higher Islamist headquarters in Western Europe—Ayman al-Zawahiri in Geneva and his new second-in-command, Yassir Tawfiq Sirri in London. There can be no doubt that the explosions at the Egyptian Embassy were carried out by Egyptian Islamists as part of their rapidly escalating struggle against the Mubarak government. But the choice of Islamabad was more than one of obvious expediency. The Egyptian Islamists did have a solid network of headquarters and training bases in Pakistan, in particular in the Peshawar area and just across the border in Afghanistan. In addition, many senior Egyptian terrorists were in the camps of the Kashmiri mujahideen, as well as in facilities of the International Islamist organizations, such as Harakat ul-Ansar, and their key headquarters, mainly in the Karachi area. In principle, it would not have been difficult for the Egyptians to carry out the Islamabad operation from any of these facilities.

But the Islamists were guests in Pakistan—hosted and sponsored by the local intelligence service. Initially it did not make sense that they struck out at the capital of a state that had been so hospitable to them and supportive of their cause. The facilities and camps of the Egyptians, just like those of all other international Islamist groups, were tightly controlled and supervised by Pakistani intelligence, the ISI. Very little could escape the notice of the ISI. The senior Egyptian commanders, many in Peshawar, Islamabad, and Karachi for more than a decade now, had always had very close relations with the senior echelons of the ISI. It did seem unreasonable for the Egyptians to risk this relationship for a single bomb. And in fact, they did not risk it. The relationship of the Egyptians with the ISI dictated the selection of Islamabad as the site for a spectacular act of terrorism.

Because of the ISI's close relations with and tight control over the Islamists, it was virtually impossible for the Islamists to plan much less carry out such an operation without the ISI's knowledge. With Pakistan under international pressure to close down the Islamist terrorist infrastructure, the Egyptian Islamists would not have made the lives of their friends and benefactors in the ISI, who fought for their survival and sought permission for them to remain in Pakistan, more difficult by embarrassing them. The explosion in Islamabad served to confirm at least tacit support from individuals within the ISI. So although the Egyptian Islamists had many good reasons to strike at Egypt, it was the interests of the ISI—based on the internal power struggles in Pakistan—that determined Pakistan and not a third country as the site for the bombings.

The roots of the explosion in Islamabad can be found in the "legend of the coup" against Benazir Bhutto. According to the official version, an Islamist military coup was narrowly averted in late September 1995. On September 26 a routine customs check of an official car in Kohat, on the Afghan border, caught Brigadier Mustansir Billah and a colonel in civilian clothes trying to drive a car full of AK-type assault rifles and RPGs into Pakistan. When stopped, Billah tried to call another colonel in Lahore to confirm that the weapons shipment was authorized official business. The officers were all arrested anyway. The investigation led to Major General Zaheer ul-Islam Abbasi, a former senior ISI officer recently nominated commander of the Infantry Training Center in Rawalpindi. According to the official version, these two generals, along with Colonels Kiyalu, Zahid, and Amjad, were planning a coup for September 30. Using the weapons Billah was trying to smuggle, these senior officers would have tried to eliminate the high command and declare an Islamist state. More than thirty officers were arrested in connection with the alleged coup attempt.

In reality the "coup" was a setup, a purge of current or former ISI elements who had actively sponsored terrorism against the United States. Both Billah and Abbasi had cooperated with and supervised Harakat ul-Ansar, Hizb-ul-Mujahideen, and other Islamist terrorist organizations. They were deeply and directly involved in Kashmiri operations. If they had wanted to, they could have acquired all the weapons they needed from stockpiles of the Kashmiri terrorists on Pakistani soil rather than trying to smuggle them in from Afghanistan. Billah was arrested delivering weapons from the Taliban to be used in deniable international operations. All the weapons and explosives in Billah's possession could be traced to U.S.-financed supplies from the war in Afghanistan or to Soviet supplies to the DRA and not to purchases of the Pakistani government. If any of these items had been captured in the course of a terrorist operation, the Afghans would have been blamed, not Pakistan.

In early September, Islamabad had concluded that as a result of the interrogation of Ramzi Ahmad Youssuf in the United States and Fuad Talat Qassim in Cairo, Washington was likely to learn how extensively these individuals, in particular the senior ISI officers, were involved in Islamist terrorism. In fall 1995 the United States was conducting investigations in Pakistan of Islamist subversive activities. In late September and early October Pakistani politicians made repeated queries to the government about what they called the "obtrusive presence" of FBI agents in Pakistan and especially their "interference in local affairs" in Islamabad.

To maintain deniability for Bhutto, the ISI officials most likely to be implicated had to be sacrificed. Since Bhutto had insisted repeatedly, even while at the White House in April 1995, that Pakistan was not involved in sponsoring terrorism, the purge could not be related to the "discovery" of, say, "rogue elements" in ISI who were involved in international terrorism. Hence the arrest of the purged officers for plotting a coup.

Soon the real motives behind the purge surfaced. Already in early November authoritative sources in Pakistan reported that the plot had been masterminded by the Intelligence Bureau (IB) on Bhutto's orders "to use this drama to create a 'congenial' atmosphere in the United States prior to Prime Minister Benazir Bhutto's [second] visit to that country." It was reported that the "IB succeeded in staging this drama" at the expense of the army and the ISI, two institutions Bhutto hated and mistrusted. Evidence was presented to support this argument. For example, a Pushtun driver was discovered and punished by a tribal Jirgah (a council that acts as a court) after he admitted that in early September he had been involved in shipping weapons to and from the Taliban on behalf of Billah and the ISI. He acknowledged that he had coordinated the shipments he was to undertake, including the one intercepted on September 26, with the local authorities as official business.

The upper echelons of the ISI were reported to be "fuming." They pointed to the previous purge carried out by Bhutto in May 1993 as a precedent. Then it had been the unceremonious "retirement" of ISI chief Lieutenant General Javed Nassir and the transfer or retirement of several senior officers because of U.S. pressure. At that time Washington demanded their removal because of Nassir's active involvement in sponsoring Islamist international terrorism in and out of Pakistan, including the advance preparations that had been conducted in Peshawar for the February 1993 bombing of the World Trade Center in New York. Pakistani sources connected to the ISI stressed that the September 1995 purge was little more than a continuation of the May 1993 purge. The ISI-affiliated sources also insisted that the current purge, just like that of 1993, was carried out on behalf of Washington.

Another reason for the growing agitation and fury in the ranks of the ISI and military high command was that the hypocrisy of the purge instigated by Bhutto was fully exposed. Pakistan's continued commitment to sponsoring Islamist terrorism had been formally reaffirmed in the November 8 agreement with Iran reached during Bhutto's visit to Tehran. In the aftermath of the visit Islamabad emphasized the importance of "the close brotherly relations existing between the two fraternal countries." The agreement included two elements of key importance for the ISI. First, it ensured Iranian noninterference with the ISI's Taliban operations in western Afghanistan. This understanding was immediately manifested in the launch of an all-out Taliban offensive on Kabul, which necessitated the transfer of forces from western Afghanistan, where they had been used to block Afghan forces crossing over from Iranian territory. Second, the agreement stipulated an increase in VEVAK (Iranian intelligence) involvement in, and support for, the jihad in Kashmir, greatly assisting the ISI. The flow of comprehensive, diverse assistance from Iran that would manifest itself in spring 1996 was about to begin. The agreement also provided for high-level reaffirmation of and support for the close cooperation between the ISI and VEVAK in Central Asia, the Caucasus, the Middle East, and Bosnia-Herzegovina.

Citing the recent agreement with Tehran, Bhutto's Islamabad resumed a more defiant and anti-American line. For example, on instructions from Bhutto, the Pakistani foreign ministry announced that it would not brief the U.S. Embassy on the visit to Tehran. The statement emphasized that Pakistan "will not provide them [the Americans] any information."

As tension built with the United States, the ISI and the military high command felt there was no longer any reason to placate Washington. They renewed their demand that the "coup" be put to rest and the purged officers released. Some of the arrested officers originally involved in Kashmiri operations were released and restored to their positions. On instructions from the highest levels in Islamabad, the ISI began active preparations to escalate the Kashmiri jihad, with the anticipated Iranian assistance, as well as to expand their own sponsorship of and support for a host of Islamist terrorist operations worldwide.

This commitment to the Islamist jihad did not resolve the "coup" issue. Not only did Bhutto refuse to discuss the "coup" issue with the high command, but Bhutto loyalists, in particular Defense Minister Aftab Shab Mirani, began a second wave of "coup revelations" in mid-November. This time it was reported that the plotters—now only thirteen officers—were actually planning to assassinate Bhutto, President Leghari, and other notables as well as the entire high command. Bhutto loyalists began talking in Islamabad about civilian courts and capital punishment for the "plotters."

At the same time Islamist senior ISI and military officers provided high-level Islamist leaders in Pakistan with "conclusive evidence" that the arrests were the result of a U.S.-instigated plot. "America's CIA provided the Benazir Government with a list of Islamist officers in the Pakistan Army four months ago. The arrests of the Pakistan Army officers [are] part of a U.S. conspiracy," explained a highly placed Islamist official. According to several Pakistani sources connected to the ISI and the army, in mid-November numerous Islamist-leaning senior officers were genuinely convinced that the CIA had provided the "incriminating" evidence against their arrested colleagues and that Bhutto had ordered their arrest to please Washington. By late November high-level politicians would openly repeat these allegations. For example, Sahibzada Fazal Karim of the Jamiat-ul-Ulema-e-Pakistan (Niazi Group) stated, "I can say with full confidence that the arrests of the officers [are] a part of the same American conspiracy under which the CIA provided a list of Islamist officers in the Pakistan Army."

According to Pakistani sources connected to the ISI, it was at this stage, in mid-November 1995, that senior elements within ISI decided it was imperative to demonstrate to Benazir Bhutto who was boss. They resolved to shock her and hint about "possibilities" without being implicated in coup plotting or conspiracy or even being accused of a political challenge. The best solution was to have friendly Arabs go after a target of their own interest and choosing, but in the heart of Islamabad. They believed their signal would be understood.

Circumstantial evidence supports advance ISI complicity. On the eve of the attack many Arab "Afghans" had been warned and moved from the Peshawar area, where they were dwelling in ISI-supported compounds, across the border into Afghanistan. They were now out of reach of a possible Pakistani dragnet, although in the aftermath of the bombing Pakistani authorities made only symbolic arrests of thirteen Egyptian scholars leaving Pakistan after religious conventions. Interior Minister Babar acknowledged that these Egyptians were "being questioned at the airports and will be allowed to leave after 'screening.'" The only one held in the case was suspected of assisting in the transfer of funds to the terrorists. By late November, Egyptian intelligence confirmed that the key terrorists involved in the Egyptian Embassy bombing had safely escaped to Afghanistan, where they were under the protection of Gulbaddin Hekmatiyar's Hizb-i Islami in the Samar Kheyl area near Jalalabad.

Meanwhile, the ISI used its Arab allies to ensure that the Islamists' grievances against the overall policies of Bhutto were aired. On November 21 the Islamic Jihad released a major communiqué via Cairo clarifying that Bhutto's Islamabad was as much a target of their wrath as Mubarak's Cairo. The communiqué stressed that the operation was "a clear message to the secular Pakistani government that, by its agreement with the Egyptian government, which is fighting Islam in Egypt . . . and by supporting India over Kashmir, it will reap only failure. The Pakistani government should not think it is handing over weak and powerless individuals. These innocent people, despite their weakness, possess what America and all governments subservient to it do not possess—faith in Almighty Allah and love of death for His sake." The communiqué bitterly criticized the betrayal of Islamists—Arabs, Afghans, and Pakistanis—by Islamabad after they had saved Pakistan from a Soviet invasion and ensured its Islamic character: "Their reward from the secular Pakistani government was ingratitude and extradition to their governments, so now they languish under torture, oppression, and maltreatment." The Islamic Jihad concluded with a vow to continue to escalate the armed struggle against all enemies of the Islamist movement worldwide.

By late November 1995 Pakistani Islamists sensed a growing vulnerability in the Bhutto government and began raising the level of attacks. Nawaz Sharif claimed that Benazir Bhutto was "trying to convert Pakistan into a socialist state," warning that "the Islam-loving people of the country would not let her fulfill her nefarious designs." These threats were more than just verbal attacks. Pakistani security officials reported to Bhutto that "the impression is very widespread among the general public that their country is being turned into an American colony." They also warned Bhutto that among wide segments of the mid- and upper-level officers and officials there was a growing apprehension about the "reported sell-out of our security and commercial interests" to the United States. These sentiments were already so widespread as to be considered cause for security concerns. There were growing signs of closer collaboration between Pakistani Islamists and their Arab "Afghan" colleagues in preparation for toppling the Bhutto government in an "Islamic Revolution." Some of these preparations were shielded and supported by senior and mid-rank officers and officials, particularly in the security and defense apparatus, who were convinced that the Islamist wave was "on the march in Pakistan."

The explosion at the Egyptian Embassy in Islamabad was more than another stage in the escalation of the relentless Islamist jihad against the Mubarak government—a comprehensive campaign sponsored and guided by Tehran and Khartoum. The reverberations of the blast were felt through the corridors of power in Bhutto's Islamabad, delivering a delicate "message" from the ISI and military high command. The aggregate impact of the continuation of the Islamist terrorist surge and the crackdown of Islamists within the Pakistani establishment and throughout the country would further erode both Bhutto's already tenuous hold on power and Islamabad's efforts to avoid sinking into Islamist radicalism. As for the ISI, they did not forget their Egyptian "Afghan" allies and the crucial services they provided. By early 1996 the ISI's comprehensive support for Islamist terrorism would reach new heights.

The attempt on the life of President Mubarak in Addis Ababa in summer 1995 was the first major operation conducted by the Sunni Islamist terrorists on their own. Through this endeavor, followed by the strikes in Riyadh and Islamabad, the "Afghans" and their leaders came of age as a strategic force. Both bin Laden and Zawahiri now played central roles as senior commanders in a series of strategic operations of immense significance for Turabi and the entire Islamist movement. As events in 1996 would soon demonstrate, the strikes of November 1995—both in Riyadh and Islamabad—were just the beginning of the escalating Islamist jihad. Bin Laden's performance and dedication were duly noted by Tehran, and in early 1996 Tehran would recognize bin Laden's importance as a key leader and theological guide for the "Afghans" and other Sunni Islamist radicals. This recognition would pave the way for a new series of devastatingly effective spectacular terrorist operations later that year.

6

The Committee of Three

ON THE NIGHT of June 25, 1996, two men drove a tanker truck into the Saudi compound that surrounded the American sector at the al-Khobar military establishment near Dhahran. Earlier the truck had tried to get into the foreigners' compound, where U.S. soldiers lived, but was rebuffed because of the late hour. The men parked the truck against the external barrier some 80 to 100 feet from Building 31. They got out of the cab and drove away in a waiting white Chevrolet Caprice, a common car in Saudi Arabia. Three to four minutes later the truck exploded.

The enormous explosion killed dozens, including nineteen American servicemen, and wounded hundreds, many of whom were badly burned and blinded. The entire front of the nearby high-rise building collapsed, and buildings up to a quarter of a mile away sustained minor structural damage and broken glass windows.

The Dhahran bomb was a sophisticated directional charge constructed with 5,000 pounds of military-class high explosives reinforced by tanks of incendiary material that created a secondary blast and also shock and heat waves. The bomb was constructed by expert bomb makers who not only knew how to shape the explosives and incendiary materials to achieve maximum effect but also were able to perfectly place and install a very sophisticated electronic fuse system. The bomb was installed in an ordinary Mercedes Benz tanker truck that had been stolen a few days beforehand.

DURING THE FIRST MONTHS of 1996 Osama bin Laden and Ayman al-Zawahiri were involved in a host of logistical and organizational activities

151

that would later prove of immense strategic and political importance. In Iran the prudent and sophisticated Islamist leaders were absorbing the lessons of the 1995 operations. In the early months of 1996 Tehran started laying the foundations for the next phase in the terroristic jihad, establishment of the HizbAllah International, with bin Laden in a senior position. The significance of this organization for the prevailing terrorist threat was demonstrated in its first strikes: the bombing of the U.S. barracks in Khobar, Saudi Arabia; the downing of TWA800; and the assassination of a U.S. intelligence officer in Cairo. The Iranians now clearly acknowledged not only the importance of the "Afghans" and the other Sunni Islamist radicals but also the distinction of their chosen leaders—specifically, bin Laden and Zawahiri.

International terrorism, like any other human endeavor requiring personal sacrifice, is driven by theological zeal and/or nationalist fervor. Leaders decide to bomb a certain place, logistical masters get the explosives into place, and the expert bomb makers design and build the bomb. But ultimately, in human terms, the few individuals on the spot face the greatest challenge. They risk life and limb, they risk capture and most likely torture and execution, and, in the case of suicidal operations, they face death without flinching. The individual perpetrator-terrorist can overcome these challenges only through psychological tempering and immense conviction in the righteousness of the acts to be performed. That others consider the terrorist act evil is irrelevant, for the martyr-to-be driving the bomb-loaded vehicle is convinced that he is doing God's work.

At the beginning of the 1990s, as the terrorist campaign picked up speed, its leaders paid little attention to this human element. At the root of the problem lay the simple reality that Iran was Shiite, whereas the bulk of the Islamist terrorists were Sunni—in other words, Khomeini's incitement was not enough to inspire and energize these Sunni terrorists. They looked for inspiration from their own Sunni Islamist world beliefs. And although the abstract and intellectual issues concerning the use of force had been resolved by Turabi and contemporary Sunni intellectuals in the early 1990s, bringing Sunni radicalism and militancy closer to the Khomeinist Shiite doctrine, communication of these important theoretical-theological developments to the rank-and-file terrorists was slow and incomplete. As the campaign of Islamist terrorism picked up momentum and a growing number of terrorists were committed to action, the issue of how a high command dominated by Shiite Iranians could inspire and energize the Sunni expert terrorists could no longer be ignored by the high command and leading ideologists.

The question of Shiite-Sunni inspiration and cooperation came up just as the international community was paying closer attention to Iran as a leading terrorist state. Events in the 1990s led to the West's "rediscovery" of Iran: First came the widespread fear of Iraqi-sponsored terrorism during the Gulf War, followed by spectacular terrorist strikes, such as the World Trade Center bombing and the assassination in Western Europe of "enemies of the Revolution," traced to Tehran. The aggregate impact of these events was an increase in Western awareness of and willingness to fight terrorism, whether sponsored by Iran, Iraq, or any other nation or group. Although Tehran was able to carry out a few spectacular operations during this period, most notably the two bombs in Buenos Aires in 1992 and 1994 and the World Trade Center bombing in 1993, Tehran was aware of the urgent need to thoroughly reexamine the modalities of its terrorism sponsorship. After Iran addressed these two issues—the growing prominence and importance of the Sunni Islamists, mainly the "Afghans," and the need to reduce the profile of its direct operations—Islamist international terrorism took a jump in quality the West is only beginning to face.

During 1995, while Iran and other nations sponsored the series of spectacular terrorist strikes throughout the Middle East, the Iranians thoroughly studied the role of intelligence and the organization of intelligence services required for contemporary operations. They also fully investigated the question of the human element, in particular theological motivation, as it pertained to the new generation of terrorists. Senior Iranian officers and officials conducted lengthy discussions, sometimes spanning several days, with the leaders of the Islamist jihadist trends to better understand their beliefs, motivations, emotions, and fears. The results were implemented in the first half of 1996 in the most profound change in Iranian intelligence since Khomeini's Islamic Revolution. The establishment of the HizbAllah International reflected this new direction in state-sponsored international terrorism.

Central to the April 1996 reorganization of the Iranian intelligence system was the establishment of the Supreme Council for Intelligence Affairs directly under President Ali Akbar Hashemi-Rafsanjani. The two main areas allocated funds and assets were internal security and the export of the Islamic Revolution—that is, foreign intelligence and terrorism sponsorship. The major expansion of the system for the export of the Islamic Revolution included the destabilization of the West as a primary challenge.

A critical aspect of this reform was that Dr. Mahdi Chamran Savehi, who was nominated chief of the organization External Intelligence, took over the entire system of international terrorism, including the al-Quds Forces. Over the last decade Chamran has been in charge of Tehran's primary venue of confrontation with the Great Satan, the United States. His selection as chief demonstrates how crucial the whole issue of international terrorism was for Tehran.

Dr. Mahdi Chamran Savehi, who was born around 1940, is one of the key intellectuals serving the Islamic Revolution. The brother of Mostafa Chamran Savehi, father of the Islamic Revolutionary Guards, who was killed in 1982, Mahdi Chamran has impeccable revolutionary credentials. He was a physics student in California in the late 1950s. In 1965, still in California, the Chamran brothers established a guerrilla organization, Red Shiism, to prepare Iranian fighters for the revolutionary struggle. In 1968 the Chamran brothers established the Muslim Students' Association of America, which attracted a large number of members, including future leaders of the Khomeini revolution.

When Mostafa moved to Lebanon in 1971 to join a Palestinian terrorist organization, Mahdi remained in the United States and assumed command of the organization. Since 1968 he had served as an active Islamist terrorist and intelligence operative for radical Palestinians and their Soviet sponsors. In the meantime he received a Ph.D. in nuclear physics.

Mahdi Chamran returned to Iran soon after the revolution and joined the IRGC high command. In the late 1980s he was assigned primary responsibility for formulating contingency plans for the Arabian Peninsula and the Persian Gulf, including the confrontation with the United States in 1986–88, when the U.S. Navy destroyed Iranian oil installations in the Persian Gulf with the excuse that the United States was protecting Arab oil exports. In reality the United States provided tremendous assistance— military, moral, and financial—to the Iraqi war effort, a situation not lost on Tehran. Mahdi was made the senior official in charge of planning in the Iranian General Command Headquarters. He was also involved with various programs in electronic intelligence and advanced military production, which put him in touch with the Soviets and acquainted him with their military technology. Until 1996 Mahdi Chamran remained a senior official of the General Command Headquarters in the planning branch, drawing war plans, and concentrated on the integration of nuclear weapons into Iran's contingency plans, especially those concerning the struggle against the United States for dominance of the Persian Gulf and the Arabian Peninsula. In summer 1993 he surfaced with a high position in Iranian intelligence, with responsibility over illegal technology acquisition for strategic programs such as military nuclear projects; he also had responsibility for weapons development and production.

By mid-1995 Chamran had become increasingly involved in Iran's subversive and terrorist operations. Key HizbAllah leaders from Lebanon met him during their working visits to Iran, in particular to coordinate training and operational preparations. In retrospect, these meetings were held to help Chamran prepare for his next major assignment—his April 1996 nomination as chief of External Intelligence. Since mid-1996 Chamran has maintained a public profile. His official title is head of the general staff of the Armed Forces' Office for Cultural Affairs. He has a higher political and media profile, which may indicate a growing interest in a public political office.

If in late 1995 Tehran needed any reminder of the importance of the Sunni Islamists and especially the up-and-coming "Afghan" leaders, the crisis in Bosnia-Herzegovina over implementation of the U.S.-sponsored Dayton Accords or retention of the Muslim character of Bosnia's government provided one. The Dayton Accords was the U.S.-inspired and -imposed agreement aimed at ending the fighting in Bosnia-Herzegovina and establishing a unified, ostensibly multinational state shielded by the presence of U.S.-led NATO peace enforcement units. The timid reaction of the Clinton administration to the eruption in early April of the "Iran-Bosnia scandal," when the Clinton White House looked the other way as Iran shipped weapons and fighters to the Muslim forces in Bosnia in violation of U.N. sanctions, emboldened Tehran. Washington's reluctance to confront both Tehran and Sarajevo over the remaining Iranian intelligence and military personnel in Bosnia-Herzegovina convinced Tehran that the Clinton administration would not retaliate firmly to a major terrorist strike. This Iranian assessment was confirmed in early June when Washington used numerous international venues to entice Tehran into entering "a full and frank dialogue" with the Clinton administration. Tehran interpreted this initiative as a demonstration of America's weakness and lack of resolve.

By now the Islamist elite forces established by bin Laden and Zawahiri in Bosnia-Herzegovina in 1994 were fully organized and well deployed. The terrorist forces were concealed as elite units of the Bosnian army or as members of Islamist "humanitarian work" and "charity" organizations. One of the principal terrorist forces ready to strike at American forces in Bosnia-Herzegovina was made up of bin Laden's Saudi "Afghans." Because these veteran "Afghans" had served with Osama bin Laden in Afghanistan, he felt particularly responsible for their well-being. Bin Laden directed resources to them and ensured that they were assigned some of the most difficult and lethal missions in the Bosnian jihad so that they had the best chances for heroism and martyrdom.

Back in late 1995, once it had become clear that I-FOR, enforcing the implementation of the Dayton Accords, was to be deployed to Bosnia-Herzegovina, Ayman al-Zawahiri moved his headquarters to a Sofia suburb and started using the name Muhammad Hassan Ali. Soon after he activated a rear senior headquarters for anti-West/anti-U.S. operations in the Balkans. Bulgaria became the key headquarters for deniable operations so as not to embarrass Sarajevo. In mid-November 1995 some twenty to twenty-five senior Islamist commanders met in Sofia to discuss the new wave of operations in the aftermath of Fuad Talat Qassim's August arrest in Zagreb and extradition to Cairo, where he was tortured and probably executed. They also discussed the inevitable deployment of I-FOR to Bosnia-Herzegovina. On November 20, 1995, these Islamists "announced" the emergence of their center in Bulgaria, sending a gunman to open fire on the Egyptian Embassy—a reminder to the Egyptian government not to look too closely at the Islamists' activities in Sofia.

In early 1996, confident in his ability to maintain secure, solid lines of communication to the Islamist terrorist forces in Bosnia-Herzegovina, Zawahiri ordered the deployment of key experts capable of planning, overseeing, and leading major terrorist strikes against such objectives as U.S./I-FOR facilities. The arrival of forty Egyptian terrorists was the first major forward deployment for this purpose. Additional Iranian and other Islamist expert terrorists continued to arrive in Bosnia-Herzegovina in April 1996 in anticipation of a possible resumption of war when Muslim Bosnians threatened to reclaim Serb-held lands.

Tehran could not ignore the fact that the terrorist elements ready to strike and deter the United States on its behalf were Sunni "Afghans." Committed and dedicated as these terrorists were, they were also fiercely loyal to their own spiritual leaders and commanders. Through this devotion they were integrated into the international Islamist terrorist movement. With the role of the Sunni Islamists so central, it became imperative for Tehran to demonstrate to the devout and overcommitted Sunnis that their spiritual authorities and direct leaders, the people who told them to kill and die, were indeed respected. Tehran resolved to promote the rising stars of Sunni Islamist terrorism—the charismatic commanders, especially those with extensive experience in Afghanistan, Kashmir, Bosnia, and the Middle East, such as Zawahiri and bin Laden—to key and distinct leadership positions in the international Islamist movement that Tehran sponsored. Tehran was adamant about avoiding any schism and mistrust just as the new strategy of spectacular terrorism was being formulated.

It took a few months for the Iranians to complete the modification of their intelligence system and bring it into operational status. In early June the highest authorities in Tehran were confident of their capabilities. Tehran made a major decision to markedly escalate the Islamist armed struggle—spectacular terrorism—all over the world under the banner of a rejuvenated HizbAllah. In his Friday sermon on June 7, 1996, Iran's spiritual leader, Ayatollah Ali Khamenei, declared that the HizbAllah must reach "all continents and all countries."

In early June Tehran resolved to transform the HizbAllah into "the vanguard of the revolution" in the Muslim world. Toward this end Tehran organized an important terrorist summit whose primary objective would be setting up an international coordination committee to oversee the anticipated escalation. Ayatollah Ahmad Jannati, known to be close to Ayatollah Khamenei and very active in terrorism-related issues, emerged as the official spokesman for the new HizbAllah International. The HizbAllah International was established during a terrorist summit held in Tehran on June 21–23, 1996, organized jointly by the Supreme Council for Intelligence Affairs and IRGC high command. Tehran invited a large number of senior leaders of Iranian-sponsored terrorist organizations to discuss the establishment of a joint working committee—the HizbAllah International—that would come under the jurisdiction of the IRGC and Chamran's External Intelligence. Tehran was determined to ensure global cooperation, and the conference was attended by delegates from terrorist organizations throughout the Middle East, Africa, Europe, and North America. After lengthy discussions and deliberations the participants at the summit issued a joint communiqué in which they agreed to set up a coordinating committee to better unify their actions and attacks.

Most important were the senior commanders who attended and agreed to integrate their forces into the new HizbAllah International framework. They included Ramadan Shallah (head of the Palestinian Islamic Jihad); Ahmad Salah, also known as Salim (Egyptian Islamic Jihad); Imad Mughaniyah (Lebanese HizbAllah's Special Operations Command); Muhammad Ali Ahmad (a representative of Osama bin Laden); Ahmad Jibril (head of the PFLP-GC, or Popular Front for the Liberation of Palestine—General Command); Imad al-Alami and Mustafa al-Liddawi (HAMAS); Abdallah Ocalan (head of the Kurdish People Party, the terrorist organization fighting against Turkey); an envoy of Turkey's Islamic Party, Refah; and a representative of George Habbash (Popular Front for the Liberation of Palestine). Leaders of the Islamic Change Movement also participated in the conferences as part of a small group of key organizations, including the Palestinian Islamic Jihad and HAMAS, that were identified as operating under Tehran's "inspiration." In other words, Iran gives these organizations the highest level of trust even though the groups are Sunni. Leaders of other Arab Islamist organizations with close ties to Tehran also attended the summit.

The summit participants agreed on the unification of their financial system and the unification and standardization of the training of HizbAllah supporters in more than thirty countries to establish interoperability of both individual terrorists and strike forces. That way a force from any country would be able to deploy at the last minute to any part of the world, operating and interacting effectively with the local Islamist forces. This flexibility would increase the surprise factor. Supervision of the new training system would be conducted through al-Quds Forces and Iranian intelligence, and there would be a marked expansion of the high-quality, expert training provided through al-Quds Forces to foreign operatives and terrorists all over the world.

A vital step was the establishment of the Committee of Three directly under Mahdi Chamran for the "coordination, planning, and attacks" by the new HizbAllah International. The committee members were Imad Mughaniyah, Ahmad Salah (Salim), and Osama bin Laden. Two of these three—bin Laden and Salah—are Sunnis. Their nomination to such high positions served as clear proof that Tehran recognized the centrality and importance of the Sunni Islamists. But Tehran did not relinquish control. The summit resolved that the Committee of Three would meet every month to go over operational proposals from the various Islamist terrorist organizations, decide on the most appropriate ones, and submit these to Chamran for Iran's approval. Special emphasis would be put on "operations designed to destabilize the [Persian] Gulf area and to weaken the countries of the region."

The first operational decision of the new Committee of Three was to recommend the execution of three terrorist operations, all of them already in the last phases of preparation. These operations represented the personal priorities of the three principals of the committee: First, the bombing of the U.S. barracks in al-Khobar, Dhahran, for Osama bin Laden; second, the fatal stabbing of a U.S. female diplomat for Ahmad Salah (Salim); and third, the downing of TWA800 for Imad Mughaniyah. The ideological justification of these operations reveals the overall logic of the perpetrators. All the related communiqués stressed the regional justifications for the operations in the context of the ongoing escalatory dynamics of the global anti-U.S. jihad.

The importance of the emergence of the HizbAllah International was its doctrinal and command roles. Virtually all major and spectacular terrorist strikes are state sponsored, and they are not hasty undertakings. The key perpetrators of these terrorist strikes are dedicated and disciplined operatives, completely under the control of the intelligence services of the terrorism-sponsoring states.

Although formally conducted under the leadership of the HizbAllah International, these three operations had actually been in preparation since at least mid-1995. Their implementation and execution were conducted, however, as the responsibility of the leadership of the HizbAllah International, specifically the Committee of Three. The new mechanism for decision making concerning worldwide spectacular terrorist strikes introduced under the banner of the HizbAllah International had already given the go-ahead order for the execution of these strikes. Enabling the Committee of Three to formally authorize the carrying out of major operations—even if the technical and operational aspects of the strikes themselves had been prepared well in advance—proved Tehran's commitment to the new era of cooperation with the Sunni terrorist elite.

THE KHOBAR TOWERS BOMBING near Dhahran was a highly professional operation, reflecting meticulous preparation. Lengthy collection of intelligence and on-site observations led to the selection of primary (inside) and fallback (perimeter) sites for the placement of the tanker bomb. The availability of a getaway car and ready concealment for the perpetrators also showed the professionalism of the network. The mere accumulation of such large quantities of military-grade high explosives and incendiary materials, the availability of sophisticated fuses, and the actual design and construction of the bomb itself all pointed to a highly sophisticated, expert network. All these preparations were completed in great secrecy by a security-conscious network. Not even a general warning was given about the operation, despite the spreading tentacles of the Saudi police state, with its numerous, overlapping, competing internal security organs, and the ruthless dragnets against real and suspected Islamists that had taken place since fall 1995.

As is true of the overall convoluted policies and political developments in Saudi Arabia, the circumstances that led to the Dhahran bombing were dominated by the drive to consolidate tangible power in the post-Fahd era. The spasmodic and dramatic eruptions in this complicated process, such as spectacular terrorist strikes, were the outcome of the symbiotic relationship between the two main currents in the Saudi power structure: (1) the internal succession and power struggle within the House of al-Saud and (2) the escalating indigenous, widely popular Islamist quest for an Islamic revolution in Saudi Arabia and the establishment of an Islamist government. Although in essence indigenous, all the key players sought and profited from a web of foreign sponsors and supporters. Because of the high strategic stakes involved, the key foreign sponsors, in particular Iran and its allies, assumed dominant roles in manipulating the indigenous developments in Saudi Arabia.

The series of developments leading to the June 25 explosion in Dhahran were all phases in the intensifying struggle for the shape of a post-Fahd

Saudi Arabia. The two players who acted as the primary catalysts for this escalatory process were Osama bin Laden and Ayatollah Khamenei of Iran. Although the power-struggle machinations within the House of al-Saud had created conditions conducive to a spectacular terrorist strike, the actual perpetrators came from the ranks of Saudi Islamist "Afghan" and "Balkan" networks, sponsored and sustained by Osama bin Laden but tightly controlled by Tehran through Iranian and allied intelligence services. The Saudi Islamists, their sponsors and allies, could not and would not have carried out the operation without specific and explicit orders from Tehran, orders that were ultimately determined on the basis of Iran's own strategic interests.

The immediate crisis began with the debilitation of King Fahd in late 1995. The nomination of Prince Abdallah, the crown prince, as acting ruler of Saudi Arabia exposed deep mistrust in his leadership throughout vast segments of the House of al-Saud. In late February 1996 King Fahd formally resumed power, not only refusing to abdicate and go into exile but also insisting on holding on to power even though his lucidity was limited at best. The already uncertain position of Prince Abdallah as heir apparent deteriorated further, and the succession struggle intensified with growing anticipation of King Fahd's death.

Three distinct factions within the House of al-Saud were fighting for the Saudi throne in 1995–96: (1) the increasingly isolated Prince Abdallah; (2) the younger-generation Sudairis led by Prince Bandar and enjoying the support of his father, Prince Sultan, a full brother of the king; and (3) the Salman-Nayif group, led by two other full brothers of King Fahd, who offered Prince Salman as a compromise king instead of the other two candidates. The Sudairis are the seven children King Ibn Saud had with his beloved wife Hassa al-Sudairi. The sons, King Fahd and his six full brothers, are very close to one another.

In December 1995, once the gravity of King Fahd's debilitation had been ascertained, the king's Sudairi brothers—Sultan, Salman, and Nayif— tried to form a coalition to bolster their joint position. With Prince Abdallah, only a half brother of King Fahd, formally in power, the Sudairis decided to join forces in a conspiracy to undermine the prospects of Crown Prince Abdallah's faction. By early 1996 the efforts to thwart the Abdallah faction had markedly intensified, but the gap between the two Sudairi factions continued to grow.

The first shot in this campaign had been fired when, exploiting a visit by Prince Abdallah to the Gulf Summit in Muscat in December 1995, Prince Sultan, the defense minister, summoned members of the Supreme Council of the ulema and demanded their support for what Islamist sources call "a peaceful coup leading to his [Sultan's] proclamation as heir apparent." The issue of Islamist terrorism as a factor in the succession struggle was first brought up in this context. Prince Sultan also asked the ulema to support his effort to dismiss Prince Abdallah from the position of head of the National Guard because the November 1995 bombing in Riyadh, an inside job, proved Prince Abdallah's inability to ensure the loyalty of the Guards.

This was an audacious if not desperate move by Prince Sultan. Prince Abdallah is a devout Islamist and a staunch supporter of the ulema's political power. He is also a staunch supporter of pan-Arab and pan-Islamic causes, including worldwide jihads, and moreover is anti-Western and mistrustful of the United States. The Abdallah faction is convinced that the United States is conspiring to empower Prince Bandar bin Sultan, the Saudi ambassador to Washington, because of his close relations with official Washington. The official ulema is therefore a natural ally of Prince Abdallah. Members of the ulema not only refused to support Prince Sultan, citing his close ties to the United States as the reason for his unsuitability for the throne, but also reported the conspiracy to Prince Abdallah.

In fact, the Abdallah faction felt shamed by the November 1995 Islamist terrorist attack against the National Guard in Riyadh and was increasingly worried by Salman-Nayif's widely publicized struggle against Islamic terrorism and the political gains that resulted. In February 1996, with King Fahd refusing to abdicate and leave the country, Prince Abdallah needed to find a drastic solution to the growing threat to his power and posture from the Sudairi brothers.

Salvation came from Damascus. Prince Abdallah has unique and close relations with Damascus, in particular the Assad clan, the family of Syria's president, Hafiz al-Assad. In early spring 1996 some members of Prince Abdallah's inner circle developed a plan to bring about the downfall of the Sudairis. Syrian intelligence would run a series of low-level anti-American "terrorist operations" that would be attributed to an assortment of Islamist organizations. The conspirators concluded that such a wave of terrorism would shame the Sudairis because they are responsible for internal security (Nayif) and defense relations with the U.S. (Sultan) and reduce American support to the point that they would no longer be eligible for the Saudi throne. Meanwhile Prince Abdallah's own Royal Guard would "solve" these "terrorist crimes" and destroy the Islamist networks—all provided by the Syrians—further enhancing Abdallah's popularity and posture. After consulting with his closest military and intelligence aides, President Hafiz al-Assad authorized the beginning of these operations in February 1996.

There was little benevolence in President Assad's support for the anti-Riyadh terrorism. Beyond repeated and profound conflicts with King

Fahd's Riyadh over relations with Tehran and Baghdad and the extent of Iranian influence in the Persian Gulf, Damascus was receiving special aid from Prince Abdallah. Beginning in the early 1990s, Abdallah had arranged for the tacit transfer of a few billion American dollars from the Saudi treasury for construction of a huge chemical warfare plant at Aleppo, in northern Syria; acquisition of ballistic missiles from North Korea and the People's Republic of China; and construction of a vast system of underground tunnels to ensure the safety of these surface-to-surface missiles and their chemical warheads. In early 1996, still the acting king, Abdallah promised President Assad to increase Saudi support for the Syrian strategic effort by orchestrating formal Saudi pressure on the Clinton administration to prevent Israel from bombing the Aleppo facilities and the Syrian missile bases and increase Saudi financial assistance to the Syrian strategic buildup.

Preparations for the Syrian special operations began immediately. Syrian experts recommended that emphasis be put on striking U.S. military facilities under the Islamist banner because it would be killing two birds with one shot. The Salman-Nayif faction, whose leaders are responsible for internal security and claim to have suppressed Islamist militancy in the aftermath of the 1995 Riyadh bombing, would be shamed by the fact that there was Islamist terrorism in Saudi Arabia, and the standing of the Sultan faction in both Riyadh and Washington would be badly hurt. Initial preparations had begun by early spring 1996, a joint effort by Syrian and Iranian intelligence. The Syrians had to rely on the excellent Iranian terrorist assets in the Bekáa Valley in Lebanon as well as on their superb networks in Saudi Arabia. It is not clear whether Damascus bothered to inform Prince Abdallah about the close cooperation with the Iranians, whom he both hates and fears. The Syrians and Iranians began running initial operations inside Saudi Arabia, however, ranging from investigation and selection of possible sites to doing what was necessary to bring in terrorists and explosives.

In the meantime, by early 1996, the violence in Karachi, Pakistan, had reached the level of rebellion, and Islamabad was apprehensive that it might spread and escalate to the point of overthrowing the Bhutto administration. For several years Islamabad had blamed the MQM—Muhajir Qaumi Movement, the organization of the Muslim emigrants from India who arrived in Pakistan in 1947–50—for the violence. In January 1996 the ISI learned that MQM leaders had arrived in Mecca to perform the Umra, a minor pilgrimage to Mecca that does not take place during the formal Hajj season, and asked for asylum on the basis of the Bedouin sacred code of hospitality. The Pakistani interior minister, Nasirullah Babar, immediately traveled to Riyadh to meet with his Saudi counterpart, Prince Nayif. Islamabad offered to trade the MQM leaders for a Saudi Islamist leader, Hassan al-Saray, who had been involved in the November 1995 Riyadh bombing and sought refuge in Pakistan. The deal was completed in the first days of February. After torture by both the ISI and Saudi intelligence, Hassan al-Saray betrayed a few of his supporters in the Riyadh area, including the four Saudis arrested and beheaded for the Riyadh bombing. The interrogation exposed the trail by which the Islamists smuggled explosives and terrorists from Syria via Jordan.

In trying to expedite the flow of terrorists and explosives to the Saudi Islamists, Syrian intelligence found it difficult to rely solely on assets and operatives from Saudi Arabia and other Persian Gulf States. By now, however, Syrian and Iranian intelligence were also markedly intensifying their "Palestinian" operations in and via Jordan against both King Hussein and Israel. Back in the spring of 1995 Syrian and Iranian intelligence had established the joint Jihadist Consultative Council for the entire Palestinian Islamist terrorist movement as well as other Palestinian terrorist organizations sponsored by Tehran and Damascus to ensure sophisticated operations and efficient use of existing assets. By late 1995 these "Palestinian" networks were running large-scale operations so effectively that in early 1996 Damascus and Tehran decided to rely on them to bolster the logistical support for the fledgling operations in Saudi Arabia.

But in March 1996 Jordanian security forces began cracking down on these Syrian operations. Before long the Jordanians learned about the use of their territory for the transfer of terrorists and explosives into Saudi Arabia. From material extracted from al-Saray and other Islamists and data provided by Jordan, the Saudi security forces were able to intercept a Saudi car with more than 84 pounds of various types of high explosives at a Saudi-Jordanian border-crossing point. The car was traveling from the Bekáa, Lebanon, via Syria and Jordan.

In late April 1996 Princes Sultan, Salman, and Nayif decided to use these incidents to bolster their power posture through a heightened scare about Islamist terrorism and subversion. On April 20 Prince Nayif called an unprecedented press conference and warned that additional sabotage attempts could not be ruled out. "We are within the circle of terrorism. We are part of this world and we are being targeted. We cannot rule out the possibility of other attacks," he said. "But we are alert and our eyes are open to confront any attempt." He also stressed that all suspects in both the November 1995 bombing in Riyadh and the seizure of explosives at the Jordanian border were Saudis, excluding the possibility of external involvement in terrorism in Saudi Arabia.

A few days later Prince Nayif announced the arrest of the four young Saudi conspirators ostensibly responsible for the Riyadh bombing. That evening Saudi TV aired their confessions. (They claimed that Yemen provided the explosives, despite evidence to the contrary from Hassan al-Saray.) One of them "confessed" to having met Osama bin Laden and to being one of "his men." This mention, whether correct or not, served to boost the power of the Salman-Nayif faction. Prince Salman had been maintaining clandestine contacts with bin Laden on behalf of Riyadh to channel Saudi support for Islamist jihads worldwide. Riyadh's approach was cynical and pragmatic—better to keep Saudi militant Islamists and "Afghans" engaged in faraway jihads, even at Riyadh's expense, than have them return home and agitate the Saudi population. In Riyadh, Prince Salman used these contacts as a proof of his ability to negotiate the cessation of Islamist subversion with bin Laden.

In late April 1996 the Sultan faction was alarmed by the surge in the popularity and power posture of the Salman-Nayif faction within the House of al-Saud. Using King Fahd's name, Prince Sultan approached the Sudanese president, General Bashir, then in Mecca for the Hajj, and offered Sudan a supply of oil at low prices, a large sum of hard currency, and support in Washington to fight accusations of terrorism sponsorship in return for the expulsion of bin Laden. The deal seemed to have been completed in early May, but Khartoum and bin Laden actually cheated the Saudis. Meanwhile Saudi media affiliated with the Sultan faction, including the main United Kingdom–based Arab periodicals, hailed bin Laden's "eviction" from Sudan as a major achievement of Saudi diplomacy and a crucial contribution to Saudi internal security.

By April 1996 the Sultan faction had embarked on a bold initiative to ensure its hold on power. In the aftermath of his confrontation with the ulema and because of the widespread popular hostility toward the older generation of the House of al-Saud, Prince Sultan virtually gave up his claim to the throne and began concentrating on ensuring that his son, Prince Bandar bin Sultan, would become the next Saudi king. Prince Sultan invited all the senior and junior members of the Sudairi faction to an urgent session in Riyadh to discuss the transfer of power to the younger generation. Sultan warned the younger princes that unless they formed a solid united front behind him, they would all lose their power and perks. Prince Sultan informed the gathering that Prince Abdallah would soon be coming to power and would surely reduce the Sudairis' power. Given his own advanced age, however, Abdallah's reign would be transitional, and the real challenge facing the Sudairi clan was seizing and maintaining power for the younger generation of princes. Prince Sultan virtually demanded support for a next-generation leadership to be formed around Prince Bandar.

Prince Sultan succeeded in gaining King Fahd's support for this maneuver. Soon afterward Prince Bandar bin Sultan and Prince Muhammad bin Fahd, the king's son, struck a deal on joint control of the second-generation princes. The secret agreement was blessed by both fathers—King Fahd and Prince Sultan. Prince Bandar started to endear himself to increasingly incapacitated King Fahd to obtain concessions in the bitter power struggle and a royal guarantee of a high-ranking position in the imminent Abdallah Court, from which Prince Bandar should be able to ultimately seize the throne. With Prince Sultan, Bandar's father, all but secured as the new crown prince to Abdallah's throne, Prince Bandar's position was basically secure. In May the Sultan faction was virtually able to guarantee Bandar's position as the top prince in the second generation of the Sudairis at the expense of Princes Saud al-Faisal, the Saudi foreign minister, and Turki bin Faisal, the Saudi director of intelligence, both sons of Prince Faisal bin Abdul-Aziz, the former king. But later that month Princes Bandar and Muhammad were compelled to accelerate their plans because of the rise in power of the Salman-Nayif faction.

Israeli elections took place in late May 1996, and the rise to power of the security-conscious Likud-led bloc shocked the Arab world. On behalf of King Fahd, Prince Abdallah immediately called for a minisummit with President Mubarak of Egypt and President Assad of Syria. During this summit in Damascus, Prince Abdallah had several quiet meetings with President Assad to discuss the situation in Saudi Arabia. They decided that the resumption of their recently stalled effort to launch a wave of ostensibly Islamist terrorism was urgently needed. Given the inner tensions in Saudi Arabia, even symbolic terrorist strikes would cause mayhem in the country. Abdallah and Assad wanted to ensure that the widespread anger would be directed at the Americans and their "lackeys"—the Sultan faction. With the Salman-Nayif faction equally discredited by the mere threat of terrorism, Prince Abdallah's National Guard would "save" Saudi Arabia, and Abdallah's own hold over power would be undisputed.

In Damascus, Prince Abdallah expressed a genuine sense of urgency. By mid-June feuds within the House of al-Saud had reached what Saudi opposition sources called "a boiling point." In Riyadh military units were placed on alert—a first. The crisis was instigated by a new wild card, Princes Mishaal bin Abdul-Aziz and Talal bin Abdul-Aziz, both about seventy years old, who claimed seniority over the Sudairis because they are the sons of king Abdul-Aziz and demanded the title of crown prince. Prince Sultan, confident that he had already secured the post for himself or his son Bandar, ordered military units in both Riyadh and Jiddah to be put on alert to frighten the newly established Abdul-Aziz faction.

Although this sudden crisis only further fractured the anti-Abdallah forces, it alarmed Abdallah and his Syrian allies. By ordering a military alert, Sultan demonstrated new resolve to struggle for his faction's power. It became imperative to strike swiftly, to decisively demolish the impression of power and authority the Sultan faction had just established. In early June Prince Abdallah urged Assad to expedite the implementation of their joint designs for a wave of low-level anti-American terrorism in Saudi Arabia.

On June 25, 1996, as if on cue, the tanker bomb exploded in Dhahran, killing nineteen Americans. There is no evidence to suggest Prince Abdallah or any other member of his faction expected such a spectacular and lethal strike. The Abdallah faction was looking for low-level harassment, not a major terrorist strike that only emboldened the Islamist opposition. Apparently Tehran, approached by Damascus to assist in this endeavor, had decided to capitalize on these unique circumstances and deliver a master strike of its own choosing. In so doing, Tehran delivered an unambiguous signal to everybody in Riyadh: Iran is a major regional force in its own right and can cause tremendous problems if its interests are not taken into account.

The launching of the real terrorist campaign was not a hasty undertaking, however. It had been under way since the early 1990s, long before Abdallah asked Syria for help. The main training center for the terrorist elite operating in Arabia remained the Imam Ali department in Saadabad, Iran, and a clandestine IRGC/VEVAK camp some 60 miles south of Tehran. Special emphasis was put on the preparation of clandestine cadres to operate in the Arabian Peninsula in order to destabilize governments and lead Islamic revolutions. To ensure their cover, the Saudi and other Persian Gulf Arabs attending the Imam Ali department traveled to and from Iran through third countries and then Syria. On these trips they used Syrian passports provided by Iranian and Syrian intelligence at their first stop, usually Western Europe, but increasingly also the Far East. Since 1994 these elite terrorist cadres had been organized into what Tehran called "The Gulf Battalion" of al-Quds Forces—Iran's international force for the spread of the Islamic Revolution.

At the same time the Islamist infrastructure and networks inside Saudi Arabia were being expanded and consolidated. Indicative of the strength of the local Islamist infrastructure was the use of Saudi Arabia in 1995 by cadres of al-Quds Forces and HizbAllah Bahrain as a site for safe meetings between their operatives in Bahrain, the Bahraini senior commanders (then based in Iran and Syria), and Iranian intelligence officers supervising and guiding the preparations and conduct of the Shiite subversion. In late June 1996, after the Bahraini crackdown on the main network of the HizbAllah Bahrain, Tehran decided to demonstrate that Islamist terrorist networks were still operating in Bahrain. VEVAK and HizbAllah Bahrain arranged for a small car bomb to be detonated next to Le Vendome hotel, in the al-Qudaybiyah district of Manama. This operation was actually organized by a Saudi-based Shiite network that constructed the bomb in eastern Saudi Arabia and drove it, in a car with legitimate Saudi Arabian license plates, across the border into Manama.

This was a highly important operation, not because of the magnitude of the bomb, which was small enough to make the operation in essence symbolic, but because it was accomplished at the very same time that the last-minute preparations for the Dhahran bomb were taking place in eastern Saudi Arabia. The concurrent conduct of two operations reflects the redundancy and resilience of the Iranian-controlled terrorist infrastructure in Saudi Arabia and Tehran's confidence in its ability to run several operations simultaneously without fear of security breaches. Not surprisingly, by early 1996 the Tehran-sponsored terrorist infrastructure in Saudi Arabia was eager and ready to go into action.

Ultimately the Dhahran bomb was the first move in a sustained, escalatory campaign aimed at overthrowing or at least thoroughly destabilizing the House of al-Saud. Although controlled and run by Shiite Iran, this campaign was organized around Saudi Sunni cadres to give "legitimacy" to the claim of a popular uprising.

The Dhahran operation had three main elements: First, the operation demanded advanced reconnaissance, planning, and organization of support infrastructure in the Dhahran area. This element was provided largely by local networks, which were augmented for brief periods by experts. These experts were also responsible for operational security. Most experts arrived from either the Bekáa, via Syria and Jordan, or Pakistan, directly and via third countries. Multiple targets were examined at this stage. One target was initially selected, but other operations were likely also prepared at the time and are probably still ready for implementation. Second, the operation required delivery of supplies, mainly explosives, from the stockpiles of Syrian and Iranian intelligence in the Bekáa and near Damascus. This logistical effort was a buildup of the system already serving the Islamist terrorists in Jordan and Israel. Despite setbacks in March 1996 this venue was still being used for the smuggling of goods and low-level terrorists who completed basic training in HizbAllah camps in the Bekáa. Third, key expert terrorists, mostly Saudi Shiites and Iranians, arrived in Dhahran toward the end of the preparations from bases in Iran, Afghanistan-Pakistan, and Bosnia-Herzegovina, traveling via third countries to Saudi Arabia or to Gulf States from which they were smuggled across the border. These senior experts took over the actual preparations for the bombing, including the construction of the tanker bomb.

Osama bin Laden was involved in key aspects of the Dhahran operation because of his prominence, knowledge, and expertise. His continued involvement in the dynamics of the Saudi Islamist opposition gave him a good understanding of their strong points and weaknesses. He comprehends the inner dynamics of the power struggles in Riyadh that the Islamists were determined to affect. Bin Laden also has a wide following in the ranks of the Saudi "Afghans" and other terrorists operating throughout the world—terrorists who would be recruited to participate in the operation. Bin Laden remained a loyal team player throughout this phase, contributing much to a state-sponsored operation.

For security reasons initial organization of the support system in northeast Saudi Arabia, including the Dhahran area, was based on local Sunni assets, even though the majority of the population in the area is Shiite and largely friendly to Iran. The support system began operating in late summer 1995, after a few leading Saudi Islamists, including devotees of bin Laden, convened in Beirut with Bahraini and Kuwaiti Islamists, HizbAllah commanders, and Iranian and Syrian intelligence officials. Among the issues discussed were the modalities for the forthcoming expansion of the Islamist terrorist networks in northeastern Saudi Arabia.

Abdul Wahab Khairi, a Saudi Islamist originally from the Dhahran area who participated in the Beirut meeting, was selected to begin establishing networks from the ranks of his own extended family and Islamist acquaintances. With Iranian schooling on the organization of terrorist cells and capitalizing on the widespread hostility to the House of al-Saud, Khairi had no problem laying the foundation for a solid, redundant support system. A special effort was made to include Saudi "Afghans" and "Balkans," primarily those who had served with bin Laden and were thought to be loyal to him, as the militant core of these networks. But these veterans of internationalist jihad were not fit for command or leadership positions in clandestine networks, so the networks were amateurish and somewhat vulnerable to the ruthless dragnets run by the Saudi security services. For clandestine preparations to succeed, it was imperative to introduce professionalism.

Khairi's apprehension about the security and efficiency of the local networks, aggravated by the leadership's worries about possible implications from the material the Saudi security authorities were extracting from Hassan al-Saray, prompted a decision that the highest commanders take a closer look at the state of affairs in northeastern Saudi Arabia and the Gulf States. A few senior commanders, including bin Laden himself (who by now was traveling at great risk because of the Saudi hunt for him), arrived in Qatar in mid-January 1996 for brief consultations with the on-site commanders. They surveyed the status of the ongoing preparations and discussed several possibilities and potential contingency plans. They decided that although conditions in the theater lent themselves to a spectacular operation, a marked improvement in the professional skills of the local networks was direly needed.

Consequently dozens of Saudi Sunni Islamist youth were recruited in early 1996 in northeastern Saudi Arabia and sent to the Bekáa for four to six weeks of study in terrorism and clandestine activity in HizbAllah camps, mainly Janta, Anjar, and Baalbek. A few Saudi recruits attended crash courses in field intelligence and operational security in safe houses of Syrian intelligence in the greater Damascus area. All the graduates were then smuggled back to Saudi Arabia, mainly via Syria and Jordan, and assigned to provide professional guidance for the expanding networks.

In early 1996 arrival of the first graduates from Syria had directly improved the preparations for an attack. Guards at the al-Khobar compound had recorded incidents of professional surveillance over several months prior to the bombing. Individuals conducted observations of the al-Khobar compound by driving slowly around the perimeter or using binoculars for lengthy observation from afar. At least one truck tried the strength of the fence by ramming it, and two weeks before the bombing a tanker truck similar to the truck that carried the bomb was seen trying to enter the compound and then driving around. These incidents represent only a fraction of the observation and reconnaissance actually carried out in the months leading to the bombing. Similar incidents were recorded throughout Saudi Arabia, suggesting comparable preparation for strikes against other objectives. The United States, convinced that terrorism did not exist in Saudi Arabia, did nothing in response.

The final phase in the preparations for the bombing in Dhahran began in late April 1996. Iranian intelligence officials who had visited Saudi Arabia during the Hajj season returned to Tehran in late April, convinced of the fragility of the regime and encouraged by the commitment, resolve, and skills of the Saudi Islamists. Exploiting the chaos and huge crowds in Mecca, VEVAK operatives had the opportunity to meet with Saudi Islamists and gain a firsthand impression of their capabilities. Back in Tehran, Ayatollah Ahmad Jannati strongly recommended a marked escalation in the Islamist assault on the House of al-Saud. Ayatollah Khamenei and President Hashemi-Rafsanjani agreed.

Two types of expert terrorists arrived in Saudi Arabia in spring 1996 for brief sojourns. The first round of expert terrorists, mostly Saudi HizbAllah (Shiites), Sunni "Afghans," "Balkans," and Iranian operatives, began arriving in Dhahran in early May 1996. Originating from bases in Iran, Afghanistan-Pakistan, and Bosnia-Herzegovina, they traveled to Saudi

Arabia or to Gulf States. Some of the Iranians were then smuggled across the Saudi border. The terrorist experts arrived in small numbers, two or three operatives at a time. They inspected the site of the intended operation and the sites of a few alternate fallback objectives to ensure that the contingency plans agreed on in Tehran fit the field conditions. Some experts inspected the stored explosives and other materials to ensure their operability. Other experts, mainly Saudis, checked the reliability and commitment of the local Islamist networks.

The second round of expert terrorists began arriving in Dhahran in early June. These terrorists were predominantly Shiites; the Saudis and Gulf Arabs among them had been recruited a few years before while studying in Iran and had since been trained under the supervision of Brigadier Ahmad Sherifi of IRGC intelligence. For obvious security reasons these teams stayed out of touch with the local networks except for a few of Iran's own agents in place. These senior experts now took over the actual preparations for the bombing, including construction of the tanker bomb.

One of the visiting expert terrorists who was captured and is still imprisoned by the Saudi security authorities testifies to the importance of these initial inspection visits. Mahmud Abdul Aziz, also known as Abu Abdul Aziz, was the organizer and commander of the mujahideen forces in Bosnia-Herzegovina in 1992. By then Mahmud Abdul Aziz was a veteran of six years of fighting in Afghanistan under Ahmad Shah Massud, the legendary mujahideen commander from the Panjshir Valley in northeastern Afghanistan, and had fought for "the sacred cause" in the Philippines and Kashmir; he had also conducted clandestine operations in Africa for Sudan's Hassan al-Turabi. In the mid-1990s Mahmud Abdul Aziz devoted most of his time to the Kashmiri jihad and to organizing Islamist clandestine networks in the United States. He was in Saudi Arabia ostensibly to perform the Umra. But the Saudis had learned from Hassan al-Saray about the role of Mahmud Abdul Aziz in the organization of militant Islamist networks and promptly arrested him, violating the sanctity of the Umra and Mecca. Mahmud Abdul Aziz is still in detention in a Saudi Arabian prison. That a leader as senior as Mahmud Abdul Aziz risked a trip to Saudi Arabia testifies to the importance assigned to the Islamist struggle against Riyadh.

By spring 1996 the logistic push through Jordan was picking up pace. Given the magnitude of the push and the intensity of the concurrent support for the Palestinian Islamists, it was inevitable that both operations would eventually mix as well as share resources, such as high explosives, from the same basic stockpiles. Despite the effectiveness of the Jordanian and Israeli intelligence services, the supply effort of the Saudi Islamist networks proved quite resilient. Additional evidence of the flow of explosives and terrorist systems between the HizbAllah camps in the Bekáa and Saudi Arabia came in spring 1996, when the Jordanian authorities captured equipment used to assemble suicide bombs on its way to Saudi Arabia. Exactly the same kind of equipment had been used to assemble the suicide bomb detonated in Tel Aviv's Dizengoff Center on March 4, 1996. The periodic loss of shipments of weapons or explosives was of little strategic importance. The Syrians and the Iranians had huge stockpiles and, because they had begun to push supplies well in advance, could easily replace captured shipments without any impact on overall operational schedules.

The capture of people while traveling through Jordan was another matter. As a rule, the Saudis returning from the Bekáa camps traveled clean, with proper documents and without anything such as printed material, weapons, or explosives that might indicate they had just been to a terrorist training base. They had no intelligence knowledge other than the identity of some of their cell comrades. Some were captured carrying Islamist literature, however, while others could not resist stopping on the way to consult with Saudi guides or "assist" their Palestinian brothers. It was during such a meeting that the Jordanians arrested Sheikh Abu Muhammad Isam al-Maqdisi, a leading Palestinian Islamist spiritual guide. Al-Maqdisi is the author of several inflammatory books and leaflets that declare that the leaders of Arab states, in particular the Saudi government and body of senior ulema, are unbelievers. These public writings stop short of inciting violence. Al-Maqdisi's arrest provided the first authoritative glance into the ideological motivation for the terrorism campaign launched by the Saudi Islamist movement.

By June the bulk of the components of the bomb—high explosives, incendiary materials, and sophisticated fuses—were already in Saudi Arabia. The explosives and incendiaries were smuggled from Syria via Jordan. Various bomb-making tools of the types used during training in the Bekáa were also transported via the same route. The sophisticated electronic equipment and fuses were smuggled from Western Europe disguised as computer parts. Some of the main shipments, including the fuses, were actually addressed to the Saudi National Guard, where Islamist sympathizers hid them.

By mid-June the professional, thorough observation and reconnaissance of the al-Khobar area was completed. A few weeks before the local support network had stolen a Caprice, which was later used as the getaway car and abandoned in Dammam, six miles from Dhahran. The Mercedes-Benz tanker truck to be used for the bomb was stolen from a construction company only a few days before the bombing, which means that the sophisticated bomb was constructed on-site just before the operation—in other words, expert bomb makers were on hand on the eve of the bombing. The bomb was a sophisticated directional charge reinforced by tanks of fuel oil mixed with incendiary materials to create the secondary blast and shock and heat waves. The bomb's oil and incendiary materials were installed so that they would evaporate and explode only a few fractions of a second after the high explosives. Consequently the duration of the pressure wave increased to the point that human organs could not tolerate the pressure. This specific mixture was aimed to kill people and not just destroy huge buildings. This kind of bomb is characteristic of the Iranians and their protégés.

The fuses and detonators used in the Dhahran bomb were identical to those used in high-quality HizbAllah operations in Lebanon and the ones taught in the terrorist training camps in the Bekáa. The bomb must have been constructed and the fuses placed through the small hole at the top of the tanker. It is impossible to, say, remove a wall of the tanker, build the bomb, and then weld the wall back, as smugglers often do when carrying goods to be sold. The heat generated by the welding would have blown up the bomb.

The expert terrorists left Dhahran safely soon after completing the preparations, most likely just before the operation. They left the Saudi operatives—a small cell of HizbAllah members thoroughly trained in numerous camps in Iran and the Bekáa—to carry out the operation. These experts were so important to Tehran that their travel and presence remained completely clandestine, concealed even from the Syrians.

TWO MAJOR CLAIMS of responsibility were made soon after the explosion. The claims cited the names of previously unknown and in essence bogus organizations. The claims were genuine, however, in that the organizations' names correctly represented the two major institutions participating in this spectacular operation.

The first claim was made by a caller to the London Arabic newspaper *al-Arab*. He claimed the attack in the name of a Saudi group calling itself The Legions of the Martyr Abdallah al-Huzayfi. "The [Legions] threatened to undertake further actions against foreign military units without exception unless the Saudi government yields to the group's demands," *al-Arab* reported. The caller added that the Legions of the Martyr Abdallah al-Huzayfi vowed to carry out similar attacks unless Riyadh expelled all U.S. and other foreign troops "occupying the holy Saudi land." The message was a quintessential Islamist demand.

Abdallah al-Huzayfi had been executed by the Saudis the year before despite having been sentenced earlier to twenty years in prison for murdering a policeman by throwing acid in his face. Huzayfi claimed the policeman had tortured him and members of his family. Riyadh claimed that Huzayfi and several of his followers were arrested for conspiracies against the regime and that arms caches were found in their quarters. At first Huzayfi and his followers received jail terms, but then Huzayfi was beheaded without any forewarning and became a martyr. Huzayfi was made a martyr and a hero by supporters of Sheikh Udah as a symbol of an individual sacrificing life and liberty to fight the evils of Saudi oppression. The use of Huzayfi's name signaled that the perpetrators were followers of the Islamist line and Sheikh Udah. The language used in the communiqué was identical to that in other Islamist writings, in particular communiqués by supporters of Sheikh Udah. The communiqué emphasized the grassroots background of the perpetrators. By going back to Huzayfi, the perpetrators stressed the element of continued struggle as opposed to simple revenge for the beheading of the four Islamists, which was claimed for the Riyadh bombing.

The second claim was made in Dhubai by a group calling itself Hizb-Allah al-Khalij, that is, HizbAllah—the Gulf. "In the name of Allah the merciful . . . HizbAllah—the Gulf declares its total responsibility for the Saudi explosion. . . . We threaten to carry out more attacks," the caller said.

The mere use of the term *HizbAllah* was important. Not only had it previously been associated with Iranian-backed groups but also since early June, Tehran had been stressing HizbAllah's growing importance as the standard-bearer for the Islamic Revolution throughout the world, especially as the struggle expanded and escalated. Starting in late June, Tehran began reorganizing the HizbAllah International with bin Laden as one of the Committee of Three, responsible for interfacing with various Islamist terrorist forces all over the world, channeling support and expertise and approving, on consultation with Tehran, key spectacular operations. The use of the name HizbAllah in taking responsibility for the Dhahran bombing not only confirmed Iran's responsibility but also confirmed that the operation was the first in the new jihad, which had been decided on in the Tehran terrorist summit of June 21–23, 1996.

A few days after the bombing, threatening letters were faxed to the private numbers of several senior Saudi officials. Recipients included King Fahd's private secretary, Prince Turki; the head of Saudi intelligence; and Interior Minister Prince Nayif. The faxes warned that additional civilian targets would be bombed unless a number of Islamist leaders and some 200 of their disciples were released. The importance of these faxed letters lay not in their content but in the mere fact that they existed. The private fax numbers were for exclusive use by the uppermost members of the House of al-Saud—they were not even known to, let alone used by, senior officials and other functionaries. By gaining access to these numbers the perpetrators demonstrated the extent of their reach into the heart of the House of al-Saud, showing that theirs was an inside job.

As the dust was settling in Dhahran the long-term ramifications of the strike were emerging. "This latest terrorist incident marks a new beginning for Saudi Arabia on a road of turmoil and an uncertain future," warned a Westernized opposition group. "This new era of fundamentalist terrorism in the heartland of Islam can trace part of its roots to . . . the decay and corruption of al-Saud family." Ultimately the rise of Islamist violence as the sole expression of despair within the kingdom is the greatest threat not just to Saudi Arabia but to the entire Middle East: "Fundamentalism is the most important threat the Middle East will face for years to come. Keeping a despotic regime like the one concocted by the Sudairi Seven will perpetuate trouble in the region."

The common denominator expressed by the various Islamist analysts was their expectation of a marked escalation and expansion of Islamist terrorism against both the United States and the House of al-Saud. They considered the Dhahran bomb to be a long overdue first eruption in the radicalization of a major sociopolitical development in Saudi Arabia.

Beyond the anticipated righteous condemnations of terrorism and denials of any Iranian involvement, Tehran's reaction to the Dhahran bombing was both interesting and sophisticated. Tehran was convinced that the Dhahran bombing had been the first shot in an Islamic Revolution in the Arabian Peninsula, the importance of which would be second only to Khomeini's revolution. Tehran expected that "in the next few years, a second Middle East explosion [the first was Iran's Islamic Revolution] will take place in Saudi Arabia."

While it saw the ultimate establishment of an Islamic republic in Saudi Arabia as inevitable, Tehran warned of the horrendous ramifications of the imminent eruption in an effort to get U.S. troops out of the Arabian Peninsula. Such a violent uprising might spread throughout the region, Tehran argued, and there was no substitute for defusing the regional crisis by having the American forces leave. Tehran warned that "such acts [of terrorism] will continue as long as the American forces are present in this part of the world, particularly in Saudi Arabia." The crisis had already reached such proportions that half measures would no longer be sufficient: "The only solution to the problem is . . . unconditional withdrawal of the American forces from Saudi Arabia."

Tehran stressed, however, that the root cause of the crisis was the corrupt and un-Islamic policies of the House of al-Saud: "Once more a bomb blast in Saudi Arabia has drawn world public attention, and experts have come to the conclusion that apparently there is no full stop to such acts if drastic changes are not brought about in the attitude of the Riyadh kingdom." The Iranian analysts considered the Dhahran bombing the beginning of a long wave of terrorism intended to rid Arabia of the House of al-Saud.

Tehran argued that opposition to the presence of U.S. forces created a backlash within the host societies: "The presence of American forces in countries with strong traditional and religious social structures has provoked the sensitivities of . . . people who see this presence as an obstacle to their own cultural identity and national independence." But in the case of Saudi Arabia the situation was far more complex because the mere presence of the American forces was considered the primary guarantor for the survival of the House of al-Saud. The United States was considered the primary impediment to realizing the genuine aspirations for an Islamic state, and these circumstances were behind the growing hostility to the United States. Tehran stated that "the strong and unabated opposition to a foreign presence in the Arab desert remains the main force for religious and political groups working inside and outside of the country [Saudi Arabia]."

The Iranian analysis of the popular support for the Dhahran bomb and other anti-U.S. terrorism highlighted the possibility of an inside job. Iranian experts concluded that "the powerful explosion targeting U.S. bases in Saudi Arabia has not been possible without the cooperation of some Saudi military and security groups." These analysts did not rule out "the possibility of the Saudi servicemen's information cooperation in this and earlier operations." This possibility, Tehran explained, should serve as an indication of just how thorough and widespread support was for the Islamist movement and how strong anti-U.S. and anti-al-Saud sentiments were.

But if these sentiments had been latent for a long time, Iranian experts stressed, it was the mujahideen factor that served as the catalyst awakening the entire Saudi society: "Of significance is the return of hundreds of Saudi youth who took part in the jihad in Afghanistan and returned home after the mujahideen takeover in Kabul in 1992. These youth, who devoted their life to the new era of Islamization in the Muslim world, refused to accept the Western-oriented foreign relations of the ruling regime. The sense of failure and frustration of the youth, coupled with the already tense situation among religious as well as academic circles in universities and religious centers, posed a formidable and serious challenge to the political establishment." Short of a mention by name, this was the warmest endorsement official Tehran could openly give Osama bin Laden and his "Afghans."

It was Riyadh's refusal to confront the just demands of the young Islamists, Tehran added, that ignited the current crisis: "The failure of the ruling regime to address the main demands of the opposition groups, particularly to widen the scope of their political participation and break the level of close relations between Riyadh and Western capitals, prompted the opposition to take a tough and militant stance against the presence of foreign troops on their land." The latter action was imperative because the U.S. and foreign forces constituted the key to the House of al-Saud's ability to survive and stay in power. Given Tehran's confidence about the buoyancy and bright future of the Islamic Revolution in Saudi Arabia, a marked escalation of the Islamist jihad against the House of al-Saud and their Western guardians was all but certain.

EMBOLDENED BY THEIR early success and the prospects of imminent spectacular strikes, Tehran and its allies were determined to intensify their campaign of international terrorism under the banner of the HizbAllah International. Their primary objective was to better utilize existing assets and to acquire and develop new capabilities. Soon after the conclusion of the June Tehran summit came a clandestine working terrorists' summit in Pakistan.

This operational summit took place in the central northwest border area between Pakistan and Afghanistan between July 10 and 15. The participants met in a huge tent at the edges of the biggest training camp for Arab "Afghans," close to the Pakistani border town of Konli. The key leaders of militant Islam, including Osama bin Laden, gathered under heavy guard of both Arab "Afghans" and Pakistani intelligence. The primary objective of this working summit was to improve coordination between the various "Afghan" and "Balkan" groups and their Iranian and Pakistani patrons. The summit clearly established the prominent role of bin Laden and his close military lieutenants as a distinct entity at the uppermost echelons of the Islamist international terrorist movement.

Formal deliberations took place during at least a couple of nightly sessions. Many informal discussions and consultations between groups and individuals occurred in the days between. Key participants included Osama bin Laden; Ayman al-Zawahiri; Abdul Rasul Sayyaf, a senior official of Iranian Intelligence responsible for the intelligence support for al-Quds Forces; and Ahmad Vahidi, the commander of al-Quds Forces. Other participants included senior Iranian and Pakistani intelligence officers; representatives of Egyptian and Persian Gulf Islamists, including leading commanders in exile or training in London, Tehran, and Beirut; senior commanders of Hizb-i Islami (Gulbaddin Hekmatiyar's group); HAMAS; HizbAllah; Algerian groups; and numerous delegates from Tehran and Khartoum.

The Islamist trend, the gathered leaders and commanders believed, was under fierce attack from the U.S.-led West. This onslaught was expected to intensify in retaliation for the already unfolding Islamist offensive. An Islamist leader from Western Europe explained that "there is a ferocious offensive being readied against Islam under the slogan of an international war against terrorism." He stressed that "there is a need for an Islamic effort to counter the ferocious attack being mounted against Islam behind the smokescreen of combating terror. For this Islamic effort to get off the ground, the Muslims, wherever they are, will have to join hands and set their minor interpretive differences aside in the interest of the larger cause; namely, facing war with war and force with force so that the arrogant [United States] may get to learn that Islam has teeth and muscle and that there are Muslims who are prepared to sacrifice their lives for their faith."

Another commander concurred, adding that "there is an imperative need for an integrated plan to deal a fatal blow to the international forces of arrogance." A United Kingdom–based commander from a Persian Gulf State stressed that given the immense strategic importance of the Persian Gulf to the United States and its allies, the only way to compel the West to withdraw was to inflict so much pain on these countries that their governments would find it impossible to tolerate the public outcry and be compelled to withdraw to stop the Islamist terrorism at home.

Rasul Sayyaf stated that "the time to settle accounts has arrived." The senior representative of Iranian intelligence declared that "attack is the best means of defense." He urged a combined offensive, both in the Muslim world, in particular the Persian Gulf and the Arabian Peninsula, and in the heart of the West. He repeated Iran's commitment to the cause and reiterated Tehran's willingness to provide the Islamists with all possible aid.

The conference resolved "to use force to confront all foreign forces stationed on Islamic land." One Arab observer with direct knowledge of the conference considered the resolution to be "a virtual declaration of relentless war" on the U.S.-led West. The Islamist leaders agreed to form a planning committee; a financing, supply, and mobilization committee; and a higher military committee to oversee the implementation of their joint operational plan. The military group would operate under the Committee of Three established in Tehran and would be made up of key veterans of the Afghan jihad—Arab "Afghans"—as well as an Iranian and a Pakistani. All resolved to embark jointly on "the road toward confronting the arrogant international offensive against Islam." Although there was no specific outcome from the discussions in Konli, Zawahiri and Vahidi agreed on additional sessions to be held soon in Tehran on launching joint operations and spectacular strikes in order to evict the United States from Muslim lands.

ALTHOUGH THE OFFICIAL INVESTIGATION of the mid-air explosion of TWA flight 800 in the evening hours of July 17, 1996, has so far failed to determine the actual cause of the aircraft's explosion, ample evidence points to a terrorist bombing. Because the aircraft exploded and burned over the Atlantic Ocean, off the Long Island coast, it is virtually impossible to recover conclusive forensic evidence. The official investigation concluded only that the explosion of fuel vapors in the central fuel tank doomed the jumbo jet. Still left unresolved, however, is the crucial question: What caused the fuel tank to explode?

The time line of the last minutes of TWA800 provides the key. The time line can be established on the basis of three separate components: (1) the aircraft's black box, which recorded all voice and electronic activity in the cockpit; (2) the aircraft's transponder, which broadcast the aircraft's identification when prompted by ground radar; and (3) the ground radar's detection of echoes, the returns from any large object. As a rule there is complete correlation to the second between the timing of these three components. Any discrepancy between them is a good indicator that something went wrong.

In the case of TWA800 all the black box recorders "died" suddenly with a brief sound that was virtually identical to the sound heard during the last fraction of a second on PanAm103. Pan American flight 103, also a Boeing 747, exploded in midair on December 21, 1988, over Lockerbie, Scotland, killing all 259 onboard and an additional 11 on the ground. Because the aircraft exploded above land, a massive on-foot search by British security forces yielded microscopic pieces of evidence, which established beyond a shadow of a doubt that a bomb had brought down the plane. Incidentally, as originally planned, PanAm103 should have blown up above water as well. But the plane was delayed for about an hour on the runway in London, so that when the timer activated the bomb, the plane was still over land. The TWA800 aircraft's transponder also "died" at the very same second. This indicates an instantaneous, complete loss of electrical power throughout the aircraft—the kind of catastrophic event usually attributed to a bomb blast. The radar echoes, however, tell a different story. The radar continued to track a large object—the entire plane or most of it—for about half a minute. TWA800's echo vanished from the screen a few seconds before eyewitnesses on the ground reported seeing twin fireballs. This means that the bulk of the aircraft remained intact for half a minute after the catastrophic failure of its electrical systems. The most logical explanation for this seeming discrepancy is that first a small bomb exploded, cutting the electricity and affecting the central fuel tank, and then, half a minute later, the tank exploded.

This chronology is also supported by the dispersion of the debris on the bottom of the ocean. The remnants of the cockpit were concentrated in a separate "field" closer to the beach than the twin "fields" where the bulk of the aircraft debris was located. This dispersion means that the cockpit and forward area of the plane separated from the rest of the aircraft several seconds before the fatal twin explosion of the fuel tank. The timing of this initial separation corresponds to the "death" of the aircraft's electrical systems. This sequence of events is virtually identical to that of PanAm103. In TWA800 the twin explosion of the central fuel tank followed the initial explosion that silenced the "echo."

When these dynamics are compared with bomb techniques known to terrorists and used in schools and training camps, an even more coherent explanation of the downing of TWA800 emerges. A small, twin-charge bomb was placed against the middle of the forward wall of the central fuel tank. The bomb was inserted and attached in place, in either the dry storage area or the wheel well. The twin charges were a blast charge made of powerful plastic explosives (SEMTEX-H class) and an incendiary device. The direction of the explosion was toward the tail of the aircraft.

Once activated, the first charge blew a gaping hole in the fuel tank and then created a shock wave that continued toward the tail of the aircraft. As with the PanAm103 bomb, the bloating and squeezing effect on the aircraft's rear structure magnified the strength of the countershock wave. As a result a stronger set of shock waves rushed forward, reinforced by the continued reaction of the aircraft's fuselage. By the time this shock wave reached the forward tip of the aircraft, it was so strong that it tore away the cockpit area. This explains why the cockpit section fell down first.

Meanwhile two things were happening simultaneously inside the central fuel tank: (1) Because of the movement of the shock waves back and forth along the aircraft, the fuel droplets inside the central tank were moving in a way that created a congestion of the fuel droplets with twin foci. (2) The secondary, incendiary, charge was swooped into the fuel tank and then exploded. Because of the distribution of the droplets this explosion instigated two fuel-air explosions, each of them in the general direction of the nearest wing root. These explosions, which destroyed the aircraft, were seen by witnesses on the ground.

The circumstances of the downing of TWA800 make it virtually impossible to acquire conclusive forensic data or any other absolute proof of the reasons for the explosion. The main area around the explosion, forward sections of the fuel tank, evaporated. Most of the missing parts and all the missing bodies are from the area covered by rows 17 to 28—just above the fuel tank—in particular right-side rows 24 and 25. There are still unexplained fist-sized holes in the back of the seats in row 23. These holes may point to the core of the secondary—incendiary—explosion that sent tiny shrapnel pieces upward. Nitrates, a main component of bombs, are damaged by fire and seawater—and in TWA800 both were present. Hence the likelihood of finding microscopic residue is minuscule.

The radical Islamists, some with established track records, quickly claimed responsibility for downing TWA800. The sequence of early warnings and communiqués claiming responsibility, in the context of the overall Islamist dynamics in the Arab world, is critical in understanding the reasons for the downing of TWA800. Through such publications the perpetrators and their sponsoring states explain the logic and context of the terrorist strikes.

Several claims, including an unspecific warning, were made about TWA800. All of them were in the name of Islamist terrorist organizations and groups. To date, however, the sophisticated bomb technology of minute size had been limited to state-sponsored terrorists, and so the validity of any of these claims must be examined in the context of known relationships with terrorism-sponsoring states. Such spectacular terrorist strikes are always launched in the context of long-term strategies and national interests.

Two events on the eve of the downing of TWA800 on July 17, 1996, merit attention. The first was an editorial in the London-based Islamist paper *al-Quds al-Arabi* that outlined the logic for escalating the armed/ terrorist struggle against the United States. The editorial in *al-Quds al-Arabi* identified the recent fatal stabbing of a U.S. female diplomat in Cairo and the Dhahran bombing as the beginning of a major Islamist campaign against the United States. The authors explained that "there is a wave of hatred toward the Americans on the Arab scene" and that the recent terrorist strikes were the result: "Some people choose to express this hatred in such a bloody manner." Given U.S. policies, these attacks should be considered the beginning of a larger terrorist campaign: "Thus we would not be surprised if such attacks on the Americans continue on a large scale in the future."

The *al-Quds al-Arabi* editorial blamed the United States for the eruption of Islamist violence: "If those who killed the Americans in Saudi Arabia and Cairo belong to the Islamic extremist camp, it was Washington, its policies, and its allies in the region that created this phenomenon and supplied it with the fuel needed for its expansion in the region as a whole." The editorial concludes with a specific warning that "what has happened in Cairo, Riyadh, and Khobar is only the beginning." Not only is *al-Quds al-Arabi* a highly respected Islamist newspaper, but the editor, Abdul-Bari Atwan, is also personally close to Osama bin Laden.

The second event was a fax sent to *al-Hayah* in London and delivered to *al-Safir* in Beirut. *Al-Hayah*, the most important Arabic-language newspaper, is owned by and close to Prince Khalid bin Sultan of Saudi Arabia. Sending a fax to *al-Hayah* meant issuing a direct challenge to the uppermost echelons of the House of al-Saud, in particular the Sultan faction, perceived to be Washington's favorite.

The July 17 warning was signed by the Islamic Change Movement—the Jihad Wing in Arabian Peninsula. This warning came only one day after the Movement had suddenly taken credit for the Dhahran bombing in addition to credit for the November 1995 Riyadh bombing. Dated July 16, the communiqué from the Islamic Change Movement was first released in Beirut quietly, without any explanation. The communiqué gained attention in the West only after it reached *al-Hayah*. This document laid the foundations for the downing of TWA800, introducing the logic of sharp escalations and expansion of terrorist strikes.

The July 16 communiqué began with a restatement of the Movement's reasons for conducting terrorism in Saudi Arabia. The Movement's support for Sheikh Udah was clearly stated: "The blasphemous al-Saud regime continues its injustice by detaining preachers and reformers, combating Islam and Muslims, and allowing invading enemy crusaders to control the land of the two Holy Shrines and the Arabian peninsula." The United States should have understood from the Riyadh bombing the extent of the Islamists' hostility and resolve to evict the Americans: "Instead, their Defense Secretary has come to threaten the mujahideen that he will fight them if necessary." The Islamic Change Movement stressed that instead of drawing the right conclusions and withdrawing from the Arabian Peninsula, Washington only aggravated the situation by issuing threats it could not implement. It was imperative for the Islamists to raise the ante: "The [mujahideen's] reply was harsh and suitable to the challenge of the invaders' secretary, the insolent William Perry. Once again the Islamic Change Movement has proven that it has long and capable arms by targeting the pilots' complex in Khobar."

On July 16 the Islamic Change Movement declared that it was confronting the president of the United States rather than Defense Secretary Perry. In light of the ideological "logic" elucidated on July 16, the warning fax the Movement issued on July 17 was very authoritative. The warning stated that given the United States' reluctance to withdraw its forces and increased threats from the U.S. government, dramatic escalation was needed in the anti-U.S. struggle: "The mujahideen will give their harshest reply to the threats of the foolish U.S. President. Everybody will be surprised by the magnitude of the reply, the date and time of which will be determined by the mujahideen. The invaders must be prepared to leave, either dead or alive. Their time is at the morning-dawn. Is not the morning-dawn near?" When TWA800 exploded, it was early morning in the United Kingdom.

The next day, July 18, the Islamic Change Movement issued a follow-up communiqué, this time in Beirut via well-established Islamist terrorist channels. The communiqué repeated the diatribes against the continued U.S. presence in Saudi Arabia and its protection of the House of al-Saud. The communiqué stated specifically that although the Islamists' objective was to evict the United States from the Arabian Peninsula, their jihad would amount to "destroying their [the Americans'] interests anywhere in the world." The communiqué concluded with a statement of responsibility for the downing of TWA800 and a warning of further escalation: "We carried out our promise with the plane attack of yesterday. You will hear of the fourth event very soon." A fourth event was indeed planned, but it was eventually thwarted.

The use of the Islamic Change Movement as the vehicle for the warning was significant. Since early April 1995 the Islamic Change Movement had proved a highly reliable organ for joint messages of the Tehran-sponsored Islamist organizations dealing with the Arabian Peninsula and Persian Gulf and the Saudi militant Islamist movement associated with both Sheikh Udah and Osama bin Laden. Given the recent activation of the HizbAllah International in Tehran and the rise in prominence of Osama bin Laden, the use of an organ with proven authority and associations served to ensure that the importance and legitimacy of both the warning and the communiqué were not lost on the Arab world. Leaders of the Islamic Change Movement participated in the late June terrorist conferences in Tehran. Further developments in Tehran underscored Iran's preoccupation with the Arabian Peninsula and the Persian Gulf as the primary objective of its terrorist surge.

ON JULY 19 the Friday prayer sermon was delivered by Ayatollah Mohammad Emami-Kashani, spokesman for the Guardian Council. Second only to Iran's spiritual leader, the Guardian Council comprises six of the most senior theologians and six of the most senior Islamic jurists in Iran, whose task is to review and affirm the Islamic correctness of any law and policy of the Islamic Republic of Iran. The sermon was devoted to security issues and a veiled threat to the Gulf States to either be "friends with Iran" and enjoy regional security and stability or face the inherent dangers of making peace with Israel and relying on the United States. Ayatollah Emami-Kashani warned that "the world of Islam, Islamic countries, and Islamic governments must pay attention to the cry of Iran, of the Islamic Republic, which says: We are friends with all of you. Let all of us safeguard the region, let all of us make the region a safe and secure place; let us make the Islamic world a safe place."

On July 20 a follow-up conference of the HizbAllah International opened in Tehran. The primary objective of this terrorist summit was to plan a new wave of attacks on U.S. targets around the world. Again leaders of the Islamic Change Movement participated in this terrorist conference as part of the small, distinct group of most trusted organizations. At the Tehran conference the Islamic Change Movement was singled out for recent "achievements."

In Tehran the Iranians and the three-man leadership committee celebrated their recent achievements as having demonstrated the intensity of the struggle against the United States. But the self-congratulatory messages were general in their phrasing. Nor did any participant take credit for any specific operation. This kind of vagueness was characteristic of all previous Iranian and Iranian-influenced phrasing of responsibility for specific acts of Islamist terrorism. The participants vowed to further escalate their struggle, in particular to evict the United States from the Arabian Peninsula and the Persian Gulf, along the same lines of the warning and communiqué issued by the Islamic Change Movement.

The Islamist leadership left no doubt as to the strategy it had adopted. Again an editorial in the London-based *al-Quds al-Arabi* served to outline the logic in the already unfolding escalation in Islamist terrorism, specifically in and against the United States. Without mentioning TWA800 by name, the editorial stressed that "the terrorism issue . . . has reached the United States, which has always been immune from terrorist operations" because of its distance from the Middle East and lack of colonial legacy. This situation had already changed drastically. *Al-Quds al-Arabi* explained that "U.S. domestic and foreign policies have removed this immunity, and we had the bombing of the New York World Trade Center, the Oklahoma bombing, and recently the explosive charge which spoiled the Atlanta Olympics." Furthermore, Washington should expect Islamist terrorism to strike American objectives all over the world because "U.S. foreign policies . . . helped provide solid excuses for some groups which believe in using violence to target U.S. bases in Riyadh, Dhahran, and, earlier, Beirut."

The *al-Quds al-Arabi* editorial declared that the new antiterrorism measures declared by the United States and its allies would not be able to reverse the surge of Islamist terrorism. "The Paris conference will make security decisions to confront political issues, but it will not succeed in putting an end to terrorism," the editorial concluded. The theme that Western antiterrorism measures themselves become the motive for additional waves of preventive and retaliatory Islamist terrorism had also been stressed by the participants in the Konli summit as the justification for the forthcoming escalation.

With the Islamists' track record of authoritatively explaining their strategic decisions about escalation and of issuing credible warnings of and communiqués assuming responsibility for terrorist acts, the emerging trend in state-sponsored Islamist terrorism had to be taken very seriously. As these events were unfolding, Osama bin Laden was also busy consolidating a new support infrastructure for spectacular Islamist terrorism—the new Imarat in Afghanistan. By now bin Laden's established prominence was apparent in the overall Islamist dynamics. He was a member of the Committee of Three; he played a distinct role in the Konli summit, where important doctrinal issues were decided; and *al-Quds al-Arabi,* edited by a confidant of bin Laden's, was emerging as a noteworthy venue for the dissemination of the Islamists' material.

Again the convergence of seemingly unrelated events brought about yet another milestone in the rise of Islamist international terrorism. This time the events were bin Laden's relocation of his main base from Sudan to Afghanistan and the establishment by Pakistan of the Taliban's rule over that country. Those conditions facilitated the emergence of bin Laden's Imarat and as a consequence a new era in the anti-U.S. Islamist jihad.

7

Declaration of War

WHILE THE WORLD focused its attention on the series of spectacular terrorist operations, the most significant terrorist event of 1996, the consolidation of Osama bin Laden's Imarat in Afghanistan, was quietly accomplished
in the shadows. In the summer of 1996 bin Laden settled down in the
Taliban's Afghanistan and established a system of camps and training sites.
The aspect of territorial rule in the Imarat system established bin Laden as a
leader—an emir—even though he lacks formal religious education. Religiously motivated to the extreme, Islamists usually rally around charismatic
religious leaders for guidance and motivation. Such leaders have included
Sheikh Omar Abdul Rahman, of World Trade Center fame; Sheikh Abd-
Allah Yussuf Azzam, bin Laden's mentor in Afghanistan; and Ayatollah
Ruhollah Khomeini, who inspired Iran and ignited a global Islamist movement. Historically only a few men lacking formal Islamic education have
been recognized as leaders, mostly on the basis of their piety, knowledge,
and unequaled contribution to the progress of Islamic and Islamist causes
through military means—the jihad. One of these men was Saladin, who defeated the Crusaders and liberated Jerusalem. Bin Laden's emergence as an
emir amounts to recognition by the Islamist leadership that he is a unique
leader and an important mujahid. He was now called Sheikh bin Laden, a
title of honor among Muslims. Later that year, after his recognition as a senior leader at the Tehran conferences, bin Laden began to express his positions and opinions. His ideology centers on the declaration of relentless and
uncompromising war on the United States until it abandons first the Arabian Peninsula and then the whole Muslim world.

In August 1996 bin Laden issued his first lengthy and detailed bayan (a doctrinal manifesto, or policy statement), which constituted his first formal "declaration of war." Because of bin Laden's unique posture—he became an emir because of his qualities as a mujahid and a commander—the importance of the decree cannot be underestimated. In essence, this bayan justifies and explains bin Laden's new role in the Islamist hierarchy. The fact that no previous terrorist leader of any ideology dared to confront the United States so directly testifies to bin Laden's resolve and dedication.

The emergence of bin Laden's terrorist empire in Afghanistan was made possible by two key developments: his relocation to Afghanistan and the establishment of the Taliban's rule over that country.

In mid-May 1996 Sudan's General Bashir succumbed to Saudi pressure and financial incentives, ordering the expulsion of Osama bin Laden and his numerous followers. Bin Laden had been a driving force behind and an inspiration for the Islamist forces striving to overthrow the House of al-Saud and establish an Islamist state in its place. With the succession crisis in Riyadh worsening, the House of al-Saud sought to reduce pressure by silencing its chief and most eloquent foe—Osama bin Laden. Riyadh exploited Sudan's economic plight by trying to trade bin Laden's expulsion for lavish economic support, including nearly free oil. Actually, the expulsion was a long while coming, because a dispute had been building between bin Laden and the Sudanese government, especially Bashir and Turabi, ever since the fall of 1995. Bin Laden objected to the use of Islamist assets, especially the Arab "Afghans," in the Sudanese civil war when they could have been used in strikes against the West. In early 1996 bin Laden threatened to withdraw his financial assets from Sudan, even though such a withdrawal would have ruined the economy. With the Saudi pressure and economy-saving inducements, Turabi, Bashir, and bin Laden worked out arrangements for his organized departure from Sudan.

Bin Laden's departure was not the hasty expulsion Bashir and Turabi sought to portray. Bin Laden's plane flew out of Khartoum Airport and immediately landed in Wadi Saydna Airport, a few miles away. He was then moved by Sudanese intelligence to a secret location in Darfur Province in western Sudan, where there is a vast terrorist-training infrastructure. There bin Laden and his aides organized his forces and assets to be transferred to Pakistan and then on to Afghanistan over a period of a few weeks. Their arrival in Afghanistan in May 1996 upgraded the capabilities of an already impressive terrorist system.

By 1996 the Islamist terrorist infrastructure in Afghanistan had been consolidated with the assistance of Pakistani intelligence, the ISI. In spring 1995 the Armed Islamic Movement had started transferring some of its key training camps for Sunnis to Afghanistan. The most important of these were the training camps for martyrdom operations used for recruits from numerous Arab, Islamic, and even European countries. The key training camps for sophisticated and spectacular terrorist activities—including martyrdom operations—using sophisticated explosives such as C-4 and SEMTEX were in Paktia and Chahar-Asiab in eastern Afghanistan and run by Gulbaddin Hekmatiyar's Hizb-i Islami.

The importance of these assets was clearly shown by Pakistan's efforts to save them as Afghanistan slid into a ruthless fratricidal civil war. By fall 1995 it had become increasingly difficult for Islamabad to conceal and deny the extent of the ISI's sponsorship of international and regional terrorism. A senior Arab official and a supporter of Benazir Bhutto tried to reconcile her declared pro-Western inclination with the growing support provided by the ISI to the "Afghans" and other Islamist terrorists. Despite Bhutto's desire "to please the Americans" by joining the struggle against Islamist terrorism, the Arab official explained, "she was thwarted by domestic difficulties and by a political-military-economic trend opposed to surrendering the Arab 'Afghans.' This trend encompassed military intelligence, civilian political parties, and the drug merchants' lobby. All of these groups were—and still are—anxious to protect these Arab fundamentalists, including those wanted for crimes in their own countries."

The strongest supporters of the Arab "Afghans" and of Islamabad's continued sponsorship of their operations was the Pakistani defense establishment. Islamabad, the senior Arab official explained, "uses groups of 'Afghans' in the war that is being waged against India in Kashmir. They are also used in the factionalist war in Afghanistan. Because of all this, the official Pakistani campaigns to expel Arab 'Afghans' lost their effectiveness." The Arab "Afghans" had always been able to remain in Pakistan, although they had to stay away from the center of Islamabad.

In principle, militant Islamists, including known terrorists, had little to worry about in Pakistan-Afghanistan: "Despite the fact that the Americans demanded that Benazir Bhutto take action to purge the security agencies, and she did, she was unable to carry out a serious counter-terrorism campaign and, at least, get rid of the 'Afghans' who were known to be extremists and who were wanted for crimes in their countries," the Arab official stated. He saw no breakthrough in the future: "Pakistan—with Afghanistan—continues to form the largest stronghold for . . . Arab terrorists," who continued to operate under "the protection of Pakistani security agencies."

Predictably, during the Taliban offensive on Kabul, the Pakistani ISI took over these specialized training camps. The ISI moved many of the Arab "Afghans"—from Egypt, Algeria, and Sudan—to special training centers it was running in Lahore, Pakistan. There the terrorists' skills and expertise were further upgraded after a few months of intensive training. The Arab "Afghans" were then regrouped and sent back to Afghanistan with the help of Qazi Hussein Ahmad, the leader of the Pakistani Islamic Group. Consequently in spring 1996 a solid, well-organized base emerged for the "Afghans" and "Balkans" in Afghanistan. This infrastructure was ready for the arrival of Osama bin Laden and his assets.

On arriving in Afghanistan, bin Laden established his headquarters in an encampment in Nangarhar Province with Sheikh Younis Khalis, a veteran leader of Hizb-i Islami (not Hekmatiyar's) during the war in Afghanistan and whose mujahideen forces bin Laden helped in the 1980s. The Arabs had already set up three semiautonomous Imarat in the Kunar, Wakhan, and Paktia provinces. The Arab "Afghans" and "Balkans" had training centers, hiding places, logistics coordination units, and command and communication centers for their fighting elements in Egypt, Saudi Arabia, Algeria, India, Tajikistan, Azerbaijan, and some other Arab states. Extremely important in the terrorist effort were the fortified villages used by the Arabs. These power centers included power generators, satellite telephone and television equipment, workshops for printing secret bulletins, and huge quantities of modern weapons, ranging from weapons supplied to the Afghan mujahideen during the 1980s to recently acquired, more modern systems delivered via Pakistan. Moreover, the Imarat in Afghanistan served as long-term rear-area bases for Islamist terrorists; they deployed from them to augment and run high-quality operations in the Middle East, India (not just Kashmir), and, increasingly, Western Europe.

This vast, comprehensive terrorist infrastructure could not have been sustained without extensive support from the ISI. The patronage of Qazi Hussein Ahmad ensured active support for the Islamist terrorists from his followers throughout the Pakistani defense establishment. Ahmad Wali Massud, the pre-Taliban Afghan government spokesman in Kabul, complained that these "Arab 'Afghans' are ensconced in fortified villages previously loyal to Hizb-i Islami. They continue to maintain Pakistan's approval and support." The "Afghans" and "Balkans" enjoy freedom of travel through Pakistan, and all their international movements as well as the flow of goods, services, and international communications are conducted via Pakistan.

In spring 1996 several Arab expert terrorists were using the Imarat in Afghanistan as their home base to support jihads in the Arab world, including their homelands. For example, Mustafa Hamzah, alias Abu-Hazim, operates safely from a base in the Kunar Imarah, Afghanistan. In summer 1995 Hamzah played a major role in organizing a popular Islamist uprising in Egypt to exploit the shock of the planned assassination of President

Mubarak in Addis Ababa. The entire operation was planned and organized in Khartoum. Following the failure of the assassination bid, Turabi asked Hamzah to move his staff and headquarters to Pakistan and Afghanistan.

The Taliban's victory in Afghanistan elevated the status and posture of the foreign "Afghans," not just the Arabs, to a new height. The Taliban have a profound theological and historical commitment to the "Afghans" for their contribution to the anti-Soviet jihad. The Taliban's perception of a global, boundary-free Islam is also largely identical to that of the Islamists. The extent of the Taliban's genuine commitment to the "Afghans" was clearly expressed in one of their first encounters with bin Laden in Jalalabad. According to the account of Islamist writer Abu Abdul Aziz al-Afghani, the Taliban's deputations passed by bin Laden and saluted him with honor and dignity. One of the senior Taliban commanders then said to bin Laden: "O Sheikh! Our lands are not the lands of the Afghans, but it is the lands of Allah; and our Jihad was not the Jihad of the Afghan, but it is the Jihad of [all] the Muslims. Your martyrs that are in every region of Afghanistan, their graves testify to that. You are between your families and kinsmen, and we bless the soil that you walk upon." It is this profound Islamic commitment that secures bin Laden's shelter in Afghanistan despite inducements and threats from the United States and other nations.

If the members of the Taliban were enthusiastic about sheltering bin Laden, their masters, the prudent but audacious ISI commanders, wanted to make sure they were not running into a major conflict with the Saudi leadership. In April 1997 the ISI approached Prince Turki bin-Faisal, the chief of Saudi intelligence, and queried him about bin Laden. After repeated accusations of bin Laden's involvement in the strikes in Saudi Arabia, the ISI even had a loyal Taliban force put bin Laden under a loose house arrest in Qandahar pending a possible extradition to Saudi Arabia. Within a few days the Saudi ambassador to Islamabad delivered a formal reply that read: "Mr. bin Laden has committed no crime in Saudi Arabia. The Kingdom has never called for his arrest." To date, Riyadh has neither recanted this message nor issued an alternate message, even in the dozens of meetings Prince Turki has had with the Taliban leadership and the ISI's high command.

Once safe in Afghanistan and with his stature as a leader recognized both locally through the Imarat and internationally, as demonstrated in the new HizbAllah International, bin Laden began publicly expressing his opinions concerning the future of the Islamist struggle in Saudi Arabia. In early July 1996 Robert Fisk of the British newspaper *Independent* was one of the first to interview Osama bin Laden in Nangarhar Province, Afghanistan.

Bin Laden considered the recent bombings in Saudi Arabia "the beginning of war between Muslims and the United States." Bin Laden's objective was the establishment of a "true" Islamic state under the Sharia. The realization of this objective would require confrontation with the United States because Saudi Arabia had been turned into "an American colony." Asked if he was declaring war on the West, he replied, "It is not a declaration of war—it's a real description of the situation. This doesn't mean declaring war against the West and Western people—but against the American regime which is against every Muslim."

Bin Laden told Fisk that the Dhahran bombing was a mere demonstration of the depth of hatred for the United States. "Not long ago, I gave advice to the Americans to withdraw their troops from Saudi Arabia," he said. "Now let us give some advice to the governments of Britain and France to take their troops out—because what happened in Riyadh and Khobar showed that the people who did this have a deep understanding in choosing their targets. They hit their main enemy, which is the Americans. They killed no secondary enemies, nor their brothers in the army or the police of Saudi Arabia. . . . I give this advice to the government of Britain."

The United States could not have had such power in Saudi Arabia without the collusion of the House of al-Saud, bin Laden explained. It allowed the United States "to Westernize Saudi Arabia and drain the economy." Bin Laden stressed that the hatred of the United States went beyond its support for the House of al-Saud and reflected the Muslims' anguish with U.S. policies. "The explosion in Khobar," he said, "did not come as a direct reaction to the American occupation but as a result of American behavior against Muslims, its support of Jews in Palestine, and of the massacres of Muslims in Palestine and Lebanon—of Sabra and Chatila and Qana—and of the Sharm el-Sheikh ('anti-terrorist') conference."

Bin Laden considered the arrest of Sheikh Udah and his supporters a turning point in Islamist relations with the House of al-Saud. "After it insulted and jailed the ulema 18 months ago, the Saudi regime lost its legitimacy," he stated. Since then the House of al-Saud had committed numerous other "mistakes": "At the same time, the financial crisis happened inside the kingdom and now all the people there suffer from this. Saudi merchants found that their contracts were broken. The government owes them 340 billion Saudi riyals, which is a very big amount; it represents 90 percent of the national income inside the kingdom. Prices are going up and people have to pay more for electricity, water, and fuel. Saudi farmers have not received money and those who get grants now receive them on government loans from banks. Education is deteriorating and people have to take their children from government schools and put them in private education, which is very expensive."

According to bin Laden, the average Saudi blamed the United States for these crises. "The Saudi people have remembered now what the ulema told them and they realize America is the main reason for their problems." Bin Laden added that "the ordinary man knows that his country is the largest oil producer in the world, yet at the same time he is suffering from taxes and bad services. Now the people understand the speeches of the ulema in the mosques—that our country has become an American colony. They act decisively with every action to kick the Americans out of Saudi Arabia. What happened in Riyadh and Khobar . . . is clear evidence of the huge anger of Saudi people against America. The Saudis now know their real enemy is America."

"There was a dark quality to bin Laden's calculations," Fisk observed. According to bin Laden, elucidating in one sentence the logic of spectacular terrorism, "If one kilogram of TNT exploded in a country in which nobody had heard an explosion in a hundred years, surely the exploding of 2,500 kilos of TNT at Khobar is evidence of the people's resistance to American occupation."

Still, bin Laden stressed that the confrontation with the United States was based on more than resistance to the presence of American troops in Saudi Arabia. "We as Muslims have a strong feeling that binds us together," he explained. "We feel for our brothers in Palestine and Lebanon. The explosion at Khobar did not come as a direct result of American occupation but as a result of American behavior against Muslims. . . . When 60 Jews are killed inside Palestine (in suicide bombings earlier this year), all the world gathers within seven days to criticize this action, while the deaths of 600,000 Iraqi children (after U.N. sanctions were placed on Iraq) did not receive the same reaction. Killing those Iraqi children is a crusade against Islam. We as Muslims do not like the Iraqi regime but we think that the Iraqi people and their children are our brothers and we care about their future."

As far as bin Laden was concerned, there could be no escape from an imminent confrontation between the Saudi Islamists and the United States. "Our trusted leaders, the ulema, have given us a fatwa that we must drive out the Americans. The solution to this crisis is the withdrawal of American troops. . . . Their military presence is an insult for the Saudi people." Bin Laden added that this struggle would be the beginning of a wider confrontation that in turn would spread throughout the Muslim world. "I believe that sooner or later the Americans will leave Saudi Arabia and that the war declared by America against the Saudi people means war against all Muslims everywhere. Resistance against America will spread in many, many places in Muslim countries."

Bin Laden's bayan, a twelve-page document titled "The Declaration of War," made lucid, coherent arguments for his stand against the United States. As in all important Islamist documents, bin Laden cites the Koran to substantiate key points and conclusions. His bayan is clearly the work of an erudite scholar. Making a substantive argument why the presence of U.S. forces in the Arabian Peninsula is detrimental to the growth of Islam, the bayan issues a final warning for all American troops to withdraw from Saudi Arabia before force can be used against them by the local Islamists. The bayan reminds Americans that the Islamist youth had already defeated the Soviet Union in Afghanistan.

A comprehensive analysis of the bayan by Islamist scholars stressed its significance in the context of bin Laden's own personal experience, in particular his break with Riyadh despite his efforts to be a loyal subject. "Sheikh Osama has been a symbol of generosity in terms of himself and his possessions," the scholars said. "Nobody can entertain any doubt or argue about Sheikh Osama's contribution to the Jihad in Afghanistan. Despite his military prowess and the large number of trained followers he had under his command, Sheikh Osama refrained and made his followers refrain from confronting the regime [in Saudi Arabia]—or for that matter the Americans either—during the Gulf crisis because of factors and conditions that pertained to that period of time." It was the House of al-Saud that earned the wrath of the Islamists by choosing the Americans over the Saudi Islamists. The bayan left open the question of addressing Riyadh if the Americans were evicted from Arabia.

The analysts stressed that because of bin Laden's background and record his warning should be taken very seriously. "At the level of the plan which Sheikh Osama has pursued and become renowned for, namely, the message of Islam and the banner of Jihad, Sheikh Osama felt that Islam has found itself in a state of war with the United States. . . . So a man like Sheikh Osama, who sees all this happening in the world, in his own country, and finally within his own soul, cannot be expected—with his long record in the Jihad and his renowned piety and asceticism despite all the worldly goods God has bestowed on him—to be pushed in that direction [allowing the destruction of Islam]. Indeed, those who were fully familiar with Sheikh Osama's personality and conditions were surprised at his delay in taking this attitude and his failure to take this attitude long before."

Addressing the bayan, Islamist sources emphasized that bin Laden and the Islamist forces were ready for and capable of implementing bin Laden's call to arms. They noted that "military action in the form of guerrilla action does not require a huge cadre equal to that of the armies and security establishments. It would be possible for it to achieve its objective with limited numbers of people—particularly against such a target as the Americans. . . . All the indications are that there are enough cadres, formations, and logistical preparations for the realization of the minimum degree of the objectives that are defined in the statement in question." These Islamist sources further noted that "all the indications at our disposal suggest that Sheikh Osama and his followers will begin to strike." And these sources have advice for the United States: "So if the mujahideen begin to actually move against the Americans, then it is better for the Americans, in order to save themselves from humiliation, to move out before they have to move out in defeat as happened to them in Somalia and Lebanon. Incidentally, anything that takes place in this direction will only have the force of a policy leading to further incidents and the militarization of the youth to join this current, as has happened following the explosions at Riyadh and al-Khobar. We have pointed this out on more than one occasion."

Bin Laden himself addressed the distinction between Saudi and Western policies. "The external policy of the Saud regime toward Islamic issues is a policy which is tied to the [British and U.S. policies]," he explained. "It is well known that the policies of these two countries bear the greatest enmity toward the Islamic world." Thus the Saudi mujahideen attacked U.S. objectives in Saudi Arabia as a signal to both Riyadh and Washington: "There were important effects to the two explosions in Riyadh on both the internal and external aspects. Most important among these is the awareness of the people [of Saudi Arabia] to the significance of the American occupation of the country of the two sacred mosques, and that the original decrees of the regime are a reflection of the wishes of the American occupiers. So the people became aware that their main problems were caused by the American occupiers and their puppets in the Saudi regime, whether this was from the religious aspect or from other aspects in their everyday lives."

Bin Laden also addressed the effect of previous terrorist operations on both Riyadh and Washington. He stated that "these operations have embarrassed both sides and have led to the exchange of accusations between them. . . . In addition to this is the behavior of the Americans with crudeness and arrogance with the Saudi army and their general behavior with citizens, and the privileges which the Americans enjoy in distinction from the Saudi forces." Taken together, the aggregate impact of these terrorist strikes was to embolden the Saudi grassroots opposition to the U.S. presence. Most important, he argued, the bombings had reminded the House of al-Saud of its vulnerability and "paved the way for the raising of the voices of opposition against the American occupation from within the ruling family and the armed forces; in fact we can say that the remaining Gulf countries have been affected to the same degree, and that the voices of opposition to the American occupation have begun to be heard at the level of the ruling families and the governments of the Cooperative Council of Gulf countries."

Bin Laden stressed that ultimately the jihad being waged in Saudi Arabia was only a small component of an urgently needed global jihad to confront the U.S.-led "international campaign against Islam." Bin Laden underscored the magnitude of the threat: "What bears no doubt in this fierce Judeo-Christian campaign against the Muslim world, the likes of which has never been seen before, is that the Muslims must prepare all the possible might to repel the enemy on the military, economic, missionary, and all other areas. It is crucial for us to be patient and to cooperate in righteousness and piety and to raise awareness to the fact that the highest priority, after faith, is to repel the incursive enemy which corrupts the religion and the world, and nothing deserves a higher priority after faith, as the scholars have declared, for this cause, it is crucial to overlook many of the issues of bickering in order to unite our ranks so that we can repel the greater Kufr [apostate]."

Bin Laden's bayan was published just as the HizbAllah International was holding a summit in Mogadishu. Fearing international repercussions for the earlier conferences in Tehran, where the 1996 strikes at Khobar Towers and Cairo and the downing of TWA flight 800 had been decided on, the Iranians insisted that the conference convene in Mogadishu for deniability purposes. It is not clear whether bin Laden attended or sent a trusted emissary. The conference was dominated by "Afghan" senior commanders from numerous Arab countries, mainly Persian Gulf States. The conference was also attended by senior officers of al-Quds Forces, from both Tehran and Khartoum forward headquarters—the command facilities from where actual terrorist and intelligence operations are controlled. Also attending was the senior representative of Iranian intelligence in Khartoum, who was in charge of Iranian operations in Africa, and the senior officer coordinating Iranian cooperation with the various Islamist terrorist organizations and radical movements. An emissary of the Islamist leadership in London also attended.

The conference examined various aspects of "the need to seriously escalate the war against the U.S. presence in the [Persian] Gulf with operations similar to those that took place in Riyadh and Khobar." Several specific contingency plans were studied. The leaders of the "Afghan" organizations from the Gulf States urged the launching of a wide-scale terrorism campaign against all aspects of the American presence in the region. They were willing to commit all their forces to this campaign, including commando brigades with special units that had received training in underwater operations at several camps in Iran, Sudan, and Lebanon. The prudent Iranians urged caution in view of the anti-terrorism alert existing in most of the Persian Gulf States. Instead the Iranians suggested that the Islamists concentrate on planning and preparing for a few spectacular anti-American operations both on the Arabian Peninsula and in faraway theaters, where the readiness might be lower. The resolutions adopted also included instructions on specialized training to be provided to expert terrorists in the camps in Afghanistan.

In late 1996 the Taliban not only permitted Osama bin Laden to keep his camps in the Jalalabad area but even extended the Taliban's protection to these installations and traffic between them and Pakistan. Bin Laden himself established staunch relations with the Taliban leadership in both Jalalabad and Kabul. The Taliban informed Islamabad that they welcomed the continued presence and operations of the more than 400 Arab "Afghans" now based in Taliban-held Afghanistan. Moreover, the Taliban asked the ISI for access to and use of some of the terrorist training facilities, in particular near Khowst, in eastern Afghanistan, for their own elite forces. Despite pleas from Saudi Arabia, the Taliban assured the ISI that they had already ruled out the possibility of extraditing the Arabs to their countries. As of early October, the Taliban was actively recruiting Arab "Afghans" in Afghanistan and Pakistan to serve as military experts in its special forces.

With the Taliban running eastern Afghanistan, the ISI accomplished yet another improvement of the terrorist training system. In mid-November 1996 the ISI asked the Taliban to ostensibly close down the training camps run by Hizb-ul Mujahideen, a group affiliated with Pakistan's Jamaat-i-Islami. This move helped both Islamabad's public relations campaign in the West and its struggle against the growing power of the Islamists at home. This was a deceptive exercise, however, because the ISI then ordered the Taliban to hand these camps over to the Harakat ul-Ansar, supposedly in order to help the Kashmiri jihad. By late November the ISI transferred control over the Khowst area infrastructure to the Harakat ul-Ansar, which the ISI in turn tightly controlled. The Harakat ul-Ansar had a good track record of running ISI-sponsored terrorist operations not only in Kashmir but also all over the world, in particular in Burma, Tajikistan, Bosnia, Chechnya, the United States, and Canada. The change in immediate control over the Khowst training infrastructure was accomplished to ensure that the ISI had better control over terrorist training. The staff was upgraded to include several mujahideen described by a Pakistani official as being "battle-inoculated, [having] fought in Afghanistan, Kashmir, Tajikistan and Chechnya." This staff consisted of about 300 mujahideen, mostly

Pakistanis and Kashmiris, as well as Afghans and Arab "Afghans." They were now running both a forty-day basic training program in small and heavy arms and basic guerrilla warfare tactics, and a lengthy advanced-training program that varied in length from several months to a couple of years. In August 1998 the United States would launch cruise missiles against these training camps.

The ISI's training bases in eastern Afghanistan and movement to and from support bases in Pakistan continued to operate without any interruption. Osama bin Laden's activities during this time were of great importance in consolidating a comprehensive support infrastructure for the next rounds of terrorist operations. In early October 1996, on his way back from the terrorism summit in Khartoum, bin Laden stopped in Tehran for consultations. While there, he met with several terrorist leaders, including Sabri al-Bana (Abu-Nidal), to discuss the escalation of the terrorist offensive throughout the Middle East. Bin Laden and Abu-Nidal considered the use of al-Bana's assets throughout the Persian Gulf to carry out spectacular terrorist strikes, including assassinations, sabotage, and bombings. They also discussed using several commercial and financial fronts, originally established in the 1980s with the help of the ISI and Bank of Credit and Commerce International for Abu-Nidal, in support of the new wave of Islamist terrorism. Although Abu-Nidal was sponsored and shielded by Tehran, he still demanded a lot of money for contributing to the jihad.

Another major issue addressed by bin Laden and his entourage while in Tehran was solidifying the unity between the various Egyptian terrorist organizations. Iranian intelligence minister Ali Fallahian chaired a high-level meeting with representatives from the Iranian Interior Ministry, Islamic Guidance Ministry, and Foreign Ministry, as well as representatives from the two main Egyptian organizations and bin Laden's representative. Among the Egyptian "Afghans" attending were Zawahiri's Tehran-based aide, Kamal Ujayzah, and Mustafa Hamzah, who arrived from Afghanistan. The Iranians discussed specific long-term operational plans and explained to the Egyptians that the extent of Tehran's support—from funding to highly specialized training—depended on the extent of their unity. The Egyptian "Afghans" agreed to form a unified command for operational purposes. Bin Laden would supervise the implementation of these resolutions.

Bin Laden's visit to Tehran was significant in the planning of the new wave of Islamist international terrorism that the ISI would support and benefit from. Bin Laden, with his high position in the Tehran-dominated HizbAllah International, was determined to ensure continued Iranian support for his terrorist infrastructure and forces in Afghanistan. This became a touchy subject because of the growing rifts between Tehran and Kabul.

Nevertheless, clearly expressing Tehran's true priorities, the Iranians did not urge bin Laden to abandon his safe havens in Afghanistan and assured him of their continued support, albeit now via Pakistan.

As a result bin Laden became a kind of go-between for both Tehran and Islamabad on issues concerning regional activities and the support for a myriad of Islamist movements. The frequency of bin Laden's trips to Tehran continued to grow. In late January 1997 bin Laden participated in a meeting in Tehran along with senior officials of VEVAK and an Afghan delegation headed by Ahmad Shah Massud's lieutenants. This was an intriguing assembly since bin Laden still enjoyed the hospitality and protection of the Taliban, while Ahmad Shah Massud was and still is one of the Taliban's most determined and effective foes. His hold on the rugged area of northeastern Afghanistan prevents the Taliban from consolidating their control over the entire country.

The primary objective of this summit was to establish the mechanism for the organization and preparation of a new generation of "clean" Islamists, in particular Arabs from the Persian Gulf States; a new support and intelligence system; and other related activities. In view of the growing attention Western intelligence services were paying to the existing Islamist system of international terrorism, the high command of Iranian intelligence and HizbAllah International had decided to establish a second-generation system, whose operatives and terrorists would be completely unknown to the West and so more likely to succeed in infiltrating and operating in enemy states.

Osama bin Laden emerged as the chief of these preparatory activities. The new system is multilayered. Initial and basic training for large numbers of potential terrorists is provided in the training camps in eastern Afghanistan. The more promising mujahideen are then transferred to advanced training in Iran, mainly at Mashhad. The Mashhad center also oversees training activities in a series of new camps for Arab "Afghans" in southwestern Afghanistan near the Iranian border. After the Tehran summit, bin Laden established a new headquarters in Mashhad, and he can move there if conditions in Afghanistan become intolerable. He also acquired a house in Qom, the heart of Iranian Islamism, in an area where a new school of higher religious learning and indoctrination for Sunni Islamists is being established.

In early February 1997 the new training system was already operational. In eastern Afghanistan bin Laden and the Taliban were running the Badr I and Badr II camps in Khasteh near Khowst. Khasteh is near the Pakistani border, and the ISI remains actively involved in the training program. The two Badr camps use a new all-weather road, built in 1996, which links Khasteh with Miranshahr in Pakistan. There are about 600 foreign volunteers in the Badr I and II camps, many of them Arabs and the rest mainly from Pakistan, Indian Kashmir, the Philippines, and, increasingly, Central Asia and the Caucasus. In southwestern Afghanistan bin Laden and the Taliban oversee three clusters of training camps in the districts of Shindand, Wahran, and Farah. There are about 1,000 Arab "Afghans" in these new camps.

An early 1997 report from Egyptian intelligence about the growing Islamist subversive threat noted that "Osama bin Laden is working behind closed doors preparing a new group of Arab 'Afghans' under the cover of the Afghan Taliban Movement, with the aim of creating fundamentalist organizations in a number of Arab and Islamic countries." The report stressed the international character of this effort in the Islamist subversion of Egypt. "The heart of this conspicuous activity [against Egypt] runs through Afghanistan, Iran, and Sudan, but centers in the mountainous area of Khorassan in Afghanistan, home to training camps of the new wave of Arab 'Afghans.'" Comparable training programs were being run for potential mujahideen from other Muslim countries as well. The ultimate objective of this effort, Cairo warned, was to "prepare a second generation of Arab 'Afghans' charged with installing fundamentalist regimes in several Arab and Islamic countries."

In addition, bin Laden maintained a few fortified bases and headquarters in the mountains of Khorassan that included a major headquarters hidden in deep caves. According to a recent Arab visitor, Abdul-Bari Atwan, editor of al-Quds al-Arabi, "the 'eagles' nest' or the Arab Afghans' base" was in caves, 8,200 feet up in snow-covered mountains, with numerous armed guards. "The base enjoys good protection," Atwan reported. "There are antiaircraft guns, tanks; armored vehicles take control of the road, and there are checkpoints for the mujahideen everywhere. There are also rocket launchers and I am told that there are Stinger missiles to confront any air raids." Despite its isolation bin Laden's base had good, modern communications with the rest of the world. Atwan said that "the base has a small generator, computers, modern reception equipment, a huge data base on computer disks, and other information kept in the traditional way. There are also press cuttings from all Arab and foreign newspapers. The sheikh [bin Laden] receives press reports from London and the [Persian] Gulf daily."

Atwan was highly impressed by the quality of bin Laden's key aides and commanders. "The mujahideen around the man belong to most Arab states, and are of different ages, but most of them are young. They hold high scientific degrees: doctors, engineers, teachers. They left their families and jobs and joined the Afghan Jihad. There is an open front, and there are always volunteers seeking martyrdom. The Arab mujahideen respect their leader although he does not show any firmness or leading gestures. They all told me that they are ready to die in his defense and that they would take revenge against any quarter that harms him." Many mujahideen told Atwan that each and every one of them "was ready to face the bullets at any time in defense of the man." Atwan had no doubt they meant every word.

In mid-February 1997 a very self-confident and assertive Osama bin Laden discussed the anticipated escalation of the jihad, in particular against the U.S. presence in the Arabian Peninsula and the Persian Gulf. "The prophet has said that the people of the peninsula are duty bound to expel the unbelievers from their country when they come from abroad with their men and weapons in number and power that exceeds that of the people of the area," bin Laden explained. The United States should have realized by now that the previous terrorist strikes in Saudi Arabia were only the beginning of a fierce jihad. Bin Laden stressed that "the bombings of Riyadh and al-Khobar were a clear indication for the crusading forces to correct this grave mistake and for them to depart before it is too late, and before the battle begins in earnest. People will treat the Americans as they were treated by them. They will not only hit American military but also demand the expulsion of civilians."

For bin Laden, the jihad on the Arabian Peninsula was just a component of a global struggle between the U.S.-led West and the Muslim world: "Moreover, I emphasize that this war will not only be between the two people of the sacred mosques and the Americans, but it will be between the Islamic world and the Americans and their allies, because this war is a new crusade led by America against the Islamic nations." Bin Laden used the eviction of the American and U.N. forces from Somalia as a precedent for their ultimate fate in Saudi Arabia. He claimed that his Islamist forces played a major role in the Mogadishu fighting against the United States and promised to repeat this feat in Arabia.

Osama bin Laden issued a call to arms in mid-February 1997: "I confirm that all the youth and the whole nation should concentrate their efforts on the Americans and the Zionists because they are the head of the spear that has been pointed at the nation and delivered into the nation's heart, and that every effort concentrated on the Americans and the Zionists will bring good, direct, and positive results. Therefore, if someone can kill an American soldier, it is better than wasting his energy on other matters."

This was the first in a series of messages urging the escalation of the jihad. In early March 1997 bin Laden increased his threats. He announced the escalation of the armed struggle against U.S. forces in the Persian Gulf area and Israeli forces wherever they were. He stated that the U.S. refusal to withdraw from the Middle East and the reaffirmation of U.S. support for

Israel kept bolstering anti-American Islamist militancy. "After American foolishness, we are expecting an intensification of resistance against the American occupation of Saudi holy places and the Zionist occupation of the land of Palestine," bin Laden said in a statement released in London.

Despite pressure from key Arab countries such as Saudi Arabia and Egypt for his extradition, Osama bin Laden remained well protected by the Taliban and their Pakistani masters. In early March Kabul formally announced its support and protection (in religious terms) for Osama bin Laden. "He is my guest," Taliban information minister Amir Khan Muttaqi said. Muttaqi acknowledged that bin Laden was living near Jalalabad, in the Tora Boora military base of Nangarhar Province. With bin Laden were fifty of his assistants, and forty of them had their families with them; also with him were numerous bodyguards and his own family members. At Tora Boora bin Laden established a forward base in a stone building, protected by lookout posts and even a few tanks, as well as ground- and air-defense facilities. This Tora Boora Arab base was used as a point of contact with the Pakistani authorities and the flow of Arab and other Muslim visitors who continued arriving and departing via Pakistan.

While bin Laden established himself in Afghanistan, Islamist forces in the Persian Gulf area and the Balkans continued to increase. Back in July 1996, at the terrorist summit in Konli, Pakistan, bin Laden and Zawahiri had resolved to strike at the U.S. forces in Muslim lands. In early 1997 Osama bin Laden completed the construction of training camps and support installations in Albania. The camps in Albania provided the Islamists with a regional safe haven, allowing the conduct of sustained operations even if the Sarajevo authorities turned their backs on their Islamist allies, and also supported the planned escalation of Islamist terrorism and subversion in Kosovo. Well over a hundred expert terrorists, mainly Arabs, were sent from Pakistan and Sudan to the Albanian camps. The remaining terrorists were already operating inside Bosnia-Herzegovina, using a host of Islamic charitable and religious organizations as their cover—at this time the activities of Islamist charitable and humanitarian organizations in central Bosnia and Albania markedly increased. The extent of this intense activity indicated that the Islamist high command was seriously considering the resumption of international terrorism.

———

BIN LADEN'S ASCENT was not taking place in a vacuum. Moreover, his ostensible expulsion from Sudan did not mean that Khartoum had given up on the leadership of Sunni Islam. With the immediate operational considerations shifting to Tehran—the establishment of the HizbAllah International and the running of the first series of operations—Hassan al-Turabi could return to his preoccupation with his favorite calling: the contemplation of grand doctrines for Islam. Turabi spent much of late 1996 and early 1997 formulating the next phase in the rise and expansion of the Islamist trend. His vision was grand and all-encompassing—searching for and defining the modalities for the contemporary relations of Islam with the rest of the increasingly Westernized world and the path of Islam toward its inevitable, ultimate triumph. Much of his vision was elucidated in a series of discussions Turabi had with the French author Alain Chevalerias. Transcripts of these discussions were collected in a book fittingly titled *Islam— the Future of the World*.

Turabi elaborated on his vision of where the modern Muslim world was heading in the confusing era of post–Cold War modernity. For the Arab world, Turabi noted, the key challenge was the accelerating decline of pan-Arabism as a political doctrine. In every area politicized pan-Arabism had entered an era of regression. This was an inevitable by-product of the decline of the Arab state in the Muslim era. Many of the ardent supporters of pan-Arabism were currently looking for ties of a different kind to unify the Arabs and revitalize their self-respect. Growing numbers of them had already entered a profound discourse with the Islamist parties in an effort to find common language and objectives. Consequently, Turabi argued, many of these formally pan-Arab entities had evolved to such a degree that it was difficult to distinguish if they now held a pan-Arab or a pan-Islamic position.

Obviously all of these entities, whether pan-Arab or pan-Islamic, had continued to adamantly refuse any foreign rule. Nationalistic rhetoric notwithstanding, this was in essence an Islamic principle. Turabi stressed that as such this principle exceeded the confines of the Arab world to include the entire Muslim world. Beyond their Arabness, a term stronger than simply "Arab identity," all these peoples needed to unite—the Arabs, the Turks, the Iranians, and the like. This was a widely recognized reality, for Islamism constituted the sole expanding positive and promising ideology. Turabi noted the rapidly growing number of thinking people—including diehard Marxists and thoroughly Westernized intellectuals—who were discovering, returning to, and adapting Islamism. Turabi emphasized that the present-day dynamics in the Muslim world should be examined and studied with this perspective.

Turabi twisted and turned on the issue of the rights and obligations of the Islamist movements in their quest to establish Islamist rule in Muslim states. In essence, he explained, there was no justification for a violent rebellion that caused casualties among the civilian population even if the government were far from being Islamic or even legitimate. The need to abstain from inflicting hardship and casualties on the innocent would override the urgency of enforcing the Sharia. Islamist parties had to struggle relentlessly and forcefully to establish Islamic rule through peaceful means. However, the Islamists also needed to protect themselves and ensure their ability to act freely and propagate their doctrines and teachings. For example, if the government in an ostensibly Muslim state actively suppressed the Islamists, the Islamists had a right to rebel and even use force, for such a government was apostate—suppressing political Islam and the propagation of Islamism. Without mentioning any specific government by name, Turabi elucidated as a theoretical legal option the case being made by the Egyptian militant Islamists against the Mubarak government.

But this principle, Turabi stressed, did not apply to Muslim states under foreign occupation, whether the state was an actual colony or a multiethnic state where a distinct minority was deprived by the rest of the population and government from realizing their just aspirations of control. Examples were Bosnia-Herzegovina and Israel. In these cases the population was obliged to wage armed jihad until they realized their aspirations. Turabi even endorsed the HAMAS campaign for the destruction of Israel.

Finally, for Turabi the most important category in studying the causes for Islamist uprising and violence were those ostensibly Muslim governments under such strong influence from foreign powers that they had lost their Islamic character and legitimacy. Turabi singled out Saudi Arabia as a state that had sold its soul to the Americans. He sharply criticized Riyadh's decision to invite and permit foreign forces on its soil before exhausting other possibilities of defense, such as with Muslim forces, Muslim states, and Islamic ways. In effect, Turabi repeated bin Laden's core argument against Riyadh. Furthermore, Turabi emphasized, if one could understand the panic at the height of the Gulf Crisis that prompted Riyadh's permission to U.S. forces to deploy to Arabia, there could be no excuse or justification for their remaining on the sacred soil of the land of the two holy shrines.

While he stopped short of endorsing the terrorist strikes against Americans in Saudi Arabia, Turabi stated that he could understand and empathize with the perpetrators, particularly given the unique importance of Saudi Arabia to all Muslims. However, Turabi noted that he knew the Saudi rulers and believed that they were inherently Muslim. He was convinced that given the right conditions, they would strive to implement Islam. Some members of the House of al-Saud might even be exemplary Muslim rulers and worthy guardians of the holy shrines. Hence there was no reason for a violent revolt against the House of al-Saud. The principal problem lay in the overwhelming American presence in Saudi Arabia, a presence that oppressed and stifled the ability of the House of al-Saud to establish the genuine Muslim rule it truly aspired to. The Americans would do whatever it took to retain their control over the oil treasures of Arabia. And, Turabi said, given the American track record of near-genocidal warfare—as demonstrated in Vietnam and Somalia—no wonder Riyadh was apprehensive about challenging its influence.

Moreover, the problem of American hegemonic expansion was getting worse because in their desire to compete with as well as overwhelm the British and the French, the Americans were penetrating and attempting to take over the traditional spheres of influence of the Europeans. For example, Turabi pointed out, the United States was presently wresting Kenya from the British sphere of influence. This was a most worrisome development.

And it was here, in evicting the Americans from Muslim lands, that the Islamists could play a role. Again Turabi stopped short of endorsing or encouraging terrorism or violence. Later on, in relation to HAMAS and its bombing campaign against civilians in Israel, he did endorse and justify such strikes. At times, he noted, it was most expedient "to terrorize" one's implacable enemies. Turabi could understand the use of bombs against civilians under such circumstances. But for terrorism to be acceptable from the Islamic point of view, the Islamists had to simultaneously offer their enemies a positive alternative and a viable way out of the violence—just as God created both heaven and hell.

In the end Turabi skirted an outright call for or endorsement of an Islamist terrorist campaign against the Americans to evict them from Arabia and create an opportunity for the House of al-Saud to prove whether it could establish an Islamic government on its own. He merely theorized that this was the right Muslim way to address the burning problem of America's defiling presence in Arabia. There are sinister implications to this doctrinal formulation because Turabi in effect expanded the theater of war against the United States to include everywhere in the world Americans were, especially places where the Americans' quest for additional influence, hegemony, and control was endangering the interests of Muslims—say, Bosnia-Herzegovina or Kenya. Turabi had no doubt that these campaigns were destined to be triumphant, for Islam was, after all, the future of the world.

In these discussions Turabi was formulating abstract theories and providing answers to hypothetical questions. Or so he pretended. It would take only a few months, however, for the essence of Turabi's contemplations to emerge. In the summer of 1997 the Islamists would discover what practical measures Turabi envisioned to realize his noble ideas. By then the key terrorism-sponsoring states—Iran, Sudan, and Pakistan—had embarked on both thorough preparations for the next wave of international terrorism and the formulation of the doctrinal logic and justification for them. The role of bin Laden and his followers would grow throughout this period to the point where he was permitted, in early 1998, to issue key doctrinal and religious edicts defining the further escalation of the Islamist jihad.

New Allies in the War

8

AT THE END of June 1997 Sudan's spiritual leader, Hassan al-Turabi, convened a secret meeting of Sunni terrorist leaders at his home in al-Manshiyah, Khartoum. The participants included the leaders of Sudan's intelligence and terrorism apparatus; Ayman al-Zawahiri, a close confidant of Osama bin Laden's; two senior commanders of the Algerian "Afghans" (one from France, one from Bosnia/Italy); and commanders of jihad forces from several countries in the Horn of Africa and East Africa.

The participants at the meeting resolved to reverse the sorry state of the Islamist movement by launching an invigorated assault on the West and its allied regimes in the Muslim world. In his opening statement Turabi warned that the Islamist jihad had sunk to such a low due to "the disgraceful condition of the mujahideen because of their splintering, disputes, and inability to consider their risks." If this process were not reversed, the Islamist trend would suffer setbacks it could not withstand. What really concerned Turabi was Sudan's loss of leadership and prominence in Sunni Islamic terrorism as the increasingly dynamic alliance of Iran and bin Laden's Afghanistan-based "Afghans" took over. Turabi considered this state of affairs detrimental to the very existence of Islamist Sudan.

The resolutions that came out of the meeting reflected Turabi's anxieties and priorities, but within the context of the greater Islamist strategy formulated in Tehran. The participants agreed to rejuvenate the PAIC from its present state of "lethargy." They decided to concentrate on practical and operational issues, convening a conference in secret once every three months. The participants would be drawn from the ranks of those wholly committed to "exporting the Islamic revolution" and "to Jihad." Recognizing bin Laden's growing posture and prominence, the meeting participants resolved to invigorate Khartoum's relations with the Arab "Afghans" and "intensify contacts with them, so that they will join with their brothers in the Jihad in Khartoum, provided that the [Sudanese] government furnishes the required travel documents for their departure from their areas in complete secrecy." All in attendance agreed with Turabi's analysis of the growing threat to Islamist Sudan and the urgent need to address the challenge through jihadist operations—that is, international terrorism.

Initial implementation of the resolutions began almost immediately. By August significant preparations were already evident in the Islamist camps in Sudan when Osama bin Laden arrived for an inspection tour. After reviewing the operational plans, he committed his forces and assets currently in Afghanistan and Pakistan to the forthcoming terrorist offensive. A special camp for the Arab "Afghan" expert terrorists was built on bin Laden's plantation in al-Damazin, Sudan. Abdul-Majid al-Zandani, who was then running operations into the Hijaz in western Saudi Arabia, also arrived from Yemen to confer with bin Laden and Turabi. The three leaders resolved to launch a "true war of Jihad" against Israel, Egypt, and Saudi Arabia and also a war to protect Sudan against what they believed to be U.S.-inspired conspiracies and assaults now centered in East Africa. To better prepare for concurrent terrorist strikes at the heart of the West, several Arab "Bosnian" agents and terrorists were pulled out of their posts in Western Europe and brought to Khartoum for consultation, training, and preparation.

But the Islamists had other priorities that overshadowed Turabi's anxieties about Sudan. In summer 1997 the Islamists had committed themselves to launching spectacular operations during the 1998 Soccer World Cup in France. Toward this end, in early September Zawahiri "vanished" for nearly a month in Western Europe. While there he traveled all over the continent, using at least six passports. His tour led to the reactivation of dormant terrorist networks and the restoration of contacts between Islamist networks and cells in Spain, Italy, France, and Belgium and the command center in London. In London, Zawahiri met at least three senior terrorist commanders: Adil Abdul-Majid (also known as Abdul-Bari), Yassir Tawfiq al-Sari (Abu-Ammar), and Mustafa Kamil (Abu-Hamzah). Zawahiri also went to Italy, where he dealt with the local chief of Iranian intelligence, Mahmud Nurani, a veteran of the Iranian terrorist system who had served in Beirut in the early and mid-1980s, operating under Ali Akbar Mohtashemi, a former HizbAllah supervisor. Nurani had been directly involved in establishing and running the HizbAllah. In Italy, Nurani is the chief supervisor of intelligence and terrorism operations for Italy and the Balkans, mainly Bosnia-Herzegovina and Albania-Kosovo.

In mid-September 1997 the highest echelons of the Iranian leadership met to discuss the new course of the anti-American struggle. The participants included both veteran and new officials, such as Iran's spiritual leader Ayatollah Ali Khamenei. Also present were newly elected president Mohammad Khatami, who has a reputation in the West as a relative moderate despite his commitment to Iran's sponsorship of terrorism and acquiring weapons of mass destruction, and the previous president, Ali Akbar Hashemi-Rafsanjani, who is heavily involved in terrorist-related issues. This was the first major conference attended by Iran's new minister of intelligence, the assertive and efficient Qorban Ali Dari Najafabadi. Other key participants in this conference were General Rahim Safavi, the commander in chief of the IRGC; General Mohsen Rezai, former commander in chief of IRGC, now responsible for reorganizing the Iranian security services and their networks; Intelligence Minister Qorban Ali Najaf-Abadi; former intelligence minister Ali Falahian (not confirmed); former intelligence minister Mohammad Mohammadi Rayshahri, who is at present Khamenei's special adviser on intelligence affairs; Hossein Sheikh-ol-Islam, Iran's former deputy foreign minister and once again director of the Office of Liberation Movements; Ali Akbar Mohtashemi; General Diya Sayfi, the commander of the IRGC forces in Lebanon; and members of the Supreme National Security Council and senior IRGC and intelligence officials.

In their meeting the Iranian leaders determined that if they were going to change the strategic map of the Middle East, they needed to capitalize on the despair and anger sweeping the Arab world over Israel and the United States. The conference decided to send "warlike and terrorist" messages that would shock the world. The conference approved with slight modifications "a confrontation plan prepared several months ago" and ordered the Supreme Council for National Security to press ahead with the implementation of "plans to export the [Islamic] Revolution by force" using Iranian-controlled terrorist forces—specifically networks of the HizbAllah and Arab "Afghans" already in the West. According to a high-level Iranian source, "There was unanimity among Iranian leaders that an important part of the Islamic Revolution's assets and Iran's power lay in Tehran's ability to terrorize its enemies and in possessing the means to pose a threat to security and stability in the [Persian] Gulf, the Middle East, and the [entire] world."

The conference's formulation of guidelines for the terrorist campaign was not a manifestation of arbitrary zeal but a prudent conclusion that terrorism was the most expedient method for furthering Iran's strategic objectives. The high-level Iranian source explained that Tehran resolved "to send the message to all concerned that Iran was capable of imposing its revolution and spreading terror to the territory of whoever calls into question its status as a key regional player." With its economy in shambles and internal discontent and problems on the rise, Tehran acknowledged that "Iran's prowess lies mainly in its capacity to mount terror and [its] possession of the means to pose a threat to the [Persian] Gulf and world stability and security." Within this pragmatic definition of Iran's national strategic objectives, it was the issue of ensuring Iran's posture as a "key regional power" that put East Africa on the short list of terrorist objectives. Tehran determined that it was in Iran's self-interest to address Sudan's strategic aspirations. The coincidence of Sudan's and Iran's interests would contribute directly to the spectacular terrorist operations of August 1998—the bombing of the U.S. embassies in Nairobi, Kenya, and Dar-es-Salaam, Tanzania.

On September 20–23, 1997, Iranian intelligence organized a major summit of terrorist leaders from all over the world under the cover of commemorating the anniversary of the outbreak of the Iran-Iraq War. Again the list of participants was impressive: Imad Mughaniyah and Abdul-Hadi Hammadi, both leaders of HizbAllah Special Operations; Ayman al-Zawahiri and another Egyptian "Afghan" commander who arrived from London; Ahmad Jibril, chief of the Popular Front for the Liberation of Palestine—General Command (PFLP-GC); Osama Abu-Hamdan and Imad al-Alami of the HAMAS; Ramadan al-Shalah, chief of Palestinian Islamic Jihad; and three commanders representing branches of HizbAllah in the Persian Gulf States.

Participants at the terrorist summit examined the Islamists' ability to markedly escalate the struggle against the U.S.-led West. Several senior Iranian officials addressed the summit and ordered the terrorist leaders "to be ready to launch an unprecedented international terrorist campaign." For example, Mohsen Rezai warned that the U.S.-led campaign to undermine Iran "would orphan the Mujahideen and destroy their dreams [for an Islamist Nation] unless we declare a Jihad everywhere." According to Iranian and Arab sources, the summit adopted a contingency plan focusing on the United States, Israel, and Turkey. At the top of the terrorists' tasks were "the launching of attacks against diplomatic missions and commercial legations and the assassination of representatives of the three countries." (Among other reasons, Turkey became a target in 1997 when the democratically elected Islamist government was forced out by the military.) This Tehran conference, one of the most important terrorist summits in recent years, focused on the "immediacy" of "embarking on a worldwide and unprecedented campaign of terror."

To meet the operational and organizational deficiencies identified by some of the attending terrorist commanders, Tehran arranged for advanced training in camps in Iran and the Bekáa. Key to the effort would be the specialized training sessions conducted under the command of Ahmad Abrari (from the IRGC's central training unit) for HizbAllah and Arab "Afghans/ Bosnians" from the West (mainly Europe) at al-Imam al-Muntazar Seminary, also in the Bekáa.

In late September 1997 the Iranian leadership met again to discuss the course of the forthcoming terrorism offensive in light of the resolutions and findings of the just concluded international terrorist summit. They also received an updated report on the status of Islamist terrorist networks in Western Europe and elsewhere.

In early October major preparations began in Afghanistan and Pakistan for an escalation of Islamist terrorism throughout the world. Several key events took place.

First, veteran, highly trained Arab "Afghans" were pulled out of Kashmir and other regional fronts and brought to training camps in Pakistan (mainly in the Lahore area, where the ISI prepares people for operations in the West) and Afghanistan (mainly the Khowst and Qandahar areas) for advanced training and preparation "to activate their operations against Arab and Islamic targets in the Middle East." Meanwhile new cadres—Kashmiri (Indian and Pakistani), Afghan, Pakistani, Indian-Muslim, and Arab—were prepared to launch "a genuine Intifadah" throughout India. (The reason for the Islamist sponsoring states' change of strategy in the armed struggle in Kashmir and India as a whole was Islamabad's apprehension that its sponsorship of terrorism in Kashmir would be increasingly exposed. The proposed "Intifadah" would be made to look like an indigenous grassroots development.)

Second, Osama bin Laden held a war council in Qandahar with senior Islamist commanders from all over the world to discuss forthcoming operations to undermine the U.S. presence and influence in the Middle East. Ayman al-Zawahiri participated in this conference after traveling back clandestinely from Western Europe. Conference participants resolved to concentrate on hitting American objectives wherever they could be found. Emphasis would be put on striking objectives whose destruction would severely interfere with the U.S. ability to implement its policies and strategies. Recognizing the centrality of Egyptian "Afghans," Zawahiri was put in charge of operations aimed at bringing down the Mubarak government.

Finally, Nurani was assigned responsibility for a group from the Middle East who would arrive clandestinely in Italy later in the winter of 1997–98 via the small Albanian port of Sendein, north of Durres, and/or Bosnia-Herzegovina. He would then bring them into Western Europe, using the

Algerian and Tunisian "Afghan" networks in Milan, Bologna, and other Italian cities.

In late October 1997 the Iranian leaders held a final session to study the preparations for escalation throughout the international terrorist system. Representatives of between twenty and thirty terrorist organizations, fronts, and entities, predominantly Islamist but also non-Muslim, gathered in Tehran for a secret conference sponsored by the Intelligence Ministry. Among the participants were HAMAS, the Palestinian Jihad, al-Jamaah al-Islamiyah and related Egyptian organizations, the Supreme Council for Islamic Revolution in Iraq, the Kurdistan Workers Party, the Algerian Armed Islamic Group, and Moroccan Islamists. Also present at the meeting were non-Islamic extremist organizations such as the Armenian Secret Army, the Greek 17 November Movement, and several representatives from Latin America.

A meeting for select Islamist leaders was held in Qum immediately after the Tehran conference concluded. In that meeting Iranian officials tried to estimate how well certain Muslim communities could withstand the retribution that would result from the anticipated wave of terrorism. The Tehran summit also decided to use non-Iranian Islamist organs as the mouthpieces for the new campaign to give it a pan-Islamic character.

Later that month the Vanguard of Conquest and the Jihad Group, both under the command of Ayman al-Zawahiri, issued a major communiqué that declared the forthcoming terroristic jihad. "The Islamic Jihad against America's world dominance, the international influence of the Jews, and the U.S. occupation of Muslim lands will continue," the communiqué declared. "The United States realizes that its real enemy, as it has declared many times, is Islamic extremism, by which it means the Islamic Jihad, the Jihad of the entire Muslim Nation against the world dominance of America, the international influence of the Jews, and the U.S. occupation of Muslim lands. The Islamic Jihad is against the theft of the Muslim Nation's riches, this disgusting robbery, the like of which has not been witnessed in history." To avert the promised wave of violence against the United States and its Middle East allies, the United States would have to leave the region and accept the establishment of Islamic governments. Otherwise the Islamists promised a relentless terrorism campaign against the United States. The communiqué concluded with a bold reaffirmation of the Islamist trend as the paramount enemy of the United States. "Yes, America's enemy is Islamic extremism, meaning the Islamic Jihad against America's preeminence . . . the Islamic Jihad which stands against Jewish expansion."

These were not idle threats. On November 17, 1997, Zawahiri's forces carried out an act of carnage in Luxor, Egypt, killing close to seventy West European tourists and wounding hundreds more. On December 6, 1997, a series of bombings and other terrorist strikes took place throughout India, presented as a commemoration of the anniversary of the December 1992 destruction of the Babri Mosque in Ayodhya by militant Hindu extremists. In Pakistan, Islamist leaders stressed that these events were the beginning of an "Intifadah."

Tehran continued to actively prepare for the new campaign of spectacular terrorism. In the second half of November 1997 Khamenei convened a meeting with Safavi and Ahmad Vahidi, the former commander of al-Quds Forces, Iran's primary terrorist forces, to discuss the establishment of a new elite terrorist force to carry out spectacular but deniable terrorist strikes against the United States and the West. The force was allocated special training facilities in Mashhad. The first combat team of sixty terrorists was recruited from both "clean" and "Afghan" Muslims in Chechnya, Holland, Belgium, Germany, and France. They were smuggled to Iran via Pakistan and Afghanistan and trained as five strike teams of twelve terrorists each. Tehran planned for the first missions to be carried out in Argentina and France. On December 2 Khamenei and the leadership received an updated report on the preparations for these operations and approved the implementation of certain specific operational plans, including the two operations against Argentina and France. The new terrorist force was formally named "The Heroes of the Islamic Jihad." Tehran also ordered the launch of a doctrinal campaign to prepare and mobilize the Muslim Nation. The Argentinean operation was aborted soon afterward when the terrorist team proved unprepared for the operation. The French operation—striking at the Soccer World Championship—was aborted in 1998 when the support headquarters was discovered in Belgium.

Islamist leaders stressed that the events unfolding in fall 1997 were only the beginning of a major clash with the West. In early December Zawahiri's Jihad group determined that a fateful confrontation between the United States and militant Islam, in which the Jihad intended to "offer martyrs," was both inevitable and imminent. "A conflict between the Muslim Nation and the United States is unavoidable; in fact we have no other option but to confront atheism and its ringleader, the United States, which is confronting us everywhere. With God's help, we know the United States well," the Jihad bulletin noted; "we also know its weaknesses." The bulletin stressed that "the most vulnerable spot of the United States and Israel is to send them the bodies of their sons." Therefore, the Jihad declared, "we should throw in their faces the flesh of their sons, minced and grilled. The United States must pay the price; it must pay dearly." Zawahiri's Jihad had no doubt about the ultimate objective of the forthcoming confrontation: "The Americans themselves admitted half of the truth when they said that the United

States' first enemy is Islamic extremism, but they hid the other half, namely that the United States' destruction will . . . be at the hands of Muslims."

———————

AT THE TIME that the terrorist warnings of late 1997 were being issued, Zawahiri, bin Laden, and the highest echelons of the leadership of Islamist international terrorism were preoccupied with one of the most significant yet least understood or known dramas of Islamist terrorism: an apparent secret deal between the Islamist terrorists and the Clinton administration that drove Egypt into de facto cooperation with the Islamist terrorism-sponsoring states against the United States.

This incident determined Egypt's position vis-à-vis U.S. policies in the Middle East and also the reaction of both major and minor players in the Middle East to the U.S. handling of the Iraqi crisis of February 1998, when the Clinton administration attempted to build support for the use of force against Iraq in response to Baghdad's refusal to cooperate with U.N. monitors. The larger regional dynamics more often than not determined each actor's attitude toward the crisis in Iraq and the Clinton administration in particular. Mubarak's Egypt effectively prevented Arab support for the use of force against Iraq.

Cairo's position throughout the crisis of early 1998 was shaped by Mubarak's reevaluation of the role and posture of the United States in the region and the Muslim world as a whole rather than merely by his reaction to the unfolding crisis with Iraq. Changes in the regional strategic relationship of forces that are still unfolding all resulted directly from what is known as "the Abu-Umar al-Amriki incident," which took place in late fall 1997.

If very senior Islamist terrorist leaders are to be believed, the Clinton administration was willing to tolerate the overthrow of the Mubarak government in Egypt and the establishment of an Islamist state in its stead as an acceptable price for reducing the terrorist threat to U.S. forces in Bosnia-Herzegovina. This trade-off was raised in discussions between Egyptian terrorist leader Ayman al-Zawahiri and an Arab American known to have been an emissary of the CIA and the U.S. government as a whole. Egypt's president, Hosni Mubarak, is convinced that the information about this meeting is accurate and has taken major steps to address the challenge.

In the first half of November 1997 Ayman al-Zawahiri met a man called Abu-Umar al-Amriki (al-Amriki means "the American") at a camp near Peshawar, on the Pakistan-Afghanistan border. High-level Islamist leaders insist that in this meeting Abu-Umar al-Amriki made al-Zawahiri an offer: The United States would not interfere with or intervene to prevent the Islamists' rise to power in Egypt if the Islamist mujahideen currently in

Bosnia-Herzegovina would refrain from attacking the U.S. forces there. Moreover, Abu-Umar al-Amriki promised a donation of $50 million (from unidentified sources) to Islamist charities in Egypt and elsewhere. This was not the first meeting between Abu-Umar al-Amriki and Zawahiri. Back in the 1980s Abu-Umar al-Amriki openly acted as an emissary for the CIA with various Arab Islamist militant and terrorist movements—including the groups affiliated with Azzam, bin Laden, and Zawahiri—then operating under the wings of the Afghan jihad. In some of their meetings in the mid-1980s, Zawahiri and Abu-Umar al-Amriki discussed the long-term fate of Egypt and Zawahiri's own role in an Islamist Egypt. In the late 1980s, in one of his meetings with Zawahiri, Abu-Umar al-Amriki suggested that Zawahiri would need "$50 million to rule Egypt." At the time Zawahiri interpreted this assertion as a hint that Washington would tolerate his rise to power if he could raise this money.

The mention of the magic figure, $50 million, by Abu-Umar al-Amriki in the November 1997 meeting was interpreted by Zawahiri and the entire Islamist leadership, including Osama bin Laden, as a reaffirmation of the discussions with the CIA in the late 1980s about Washington's willingness to tolerate an Islamist Egypt. In October 1997 the war council chaired by bin Laden had put Zawahiri in charge of the Islamist operations aimed at bringing down the Mubarak government. In November 1997 the Islamist leaders were convinced that Abu-Umar al-Amriki was speaking for the CIA—that is, the uppermost echelons of the Clinton administration.

Arab Islamist observers stress that the horrendous terrorist strike in Luxor on November 17, 1997, was actually a test of the credibility of Abu-Umar al-Amriki. The senseless slaughter of tourists was more than an affront to Mubarak's Egypt. The outright attack on Westerners, who might have been American tourists, was designed to gauge how Washington would react. The virtually deafening silence of the Clinton administration had to reassure Zawahiri and bin Laden that Abu-Umar al-Amriki had spoken with its backing, and a rejuvenated call to arms followed. On the eve of the strike in East Africa, the Islamists' belief in the validity of their "deal" with Washington would lead to a major, continuing crisis.

In fall 1997 the United States had reason to worry about Zawahiri's plans and intentions. While the Clinton administration was strenuously attempting to convince Congress and the American people of the need to keep U.S. forces in Bosnia beyond the June 1998 deadline—despite a promise explicitly made to Congress—the U.S.-sponsored government in Sarajevo was actively preparing for a military confrontation to regain control over the Republika Srpska (the Serb-controlled parts of Bosnia) by force, using weapons and training provided by the United States under the "Train and Equip" program. One of the scenarios Sarajevo contemplated in fall 1997 was the use of Islamist terrorism against the Americans to expedite the withdrawal of the U.S. forces if the Clinton administration refused to support the Bosnian Muslim military surge. The most effective and lethal Islamist terrorists in Bosnia were under Zawahiri's command.

By mid-December 1997 Cairo had learned about the Abu-Umar al-Amriki episode. Egyptian officials confirmed that they had known about him and his role as an emissary for the CIA since the 1980s. As far as President Hosni Mubarak and his immediate advisers were concerned, the evidence they had was reliable enough to act on, and a sense of urgency dominated official Cairo. Cairo knew that the Egyptian Islamists and their key sponsors, Iran and Sudan, were convinced that only massive U.S. support for President Mubarak had prevented the Islamists from establishing an Islamist state in Egypt. Official Cairo also knew that even the appearance of a withdrawal of U.S. support from Mubarak was sure to embolden the Egyptian Islamists and their sponsoring states to markedly escalate their armed struggle, and Cairo was already having troubles withstanding Islamist terrorism and subversion.

In early December 1997, days after reports of the meeting between Zawahiri and Abu-Umar al-Amriki surfaced, Egypt's government-owned newspaper *al-Jumhuriyah* published a story that began as follows: "A security source has revealed fresh information on the way foreign parties exploit terrorist elements. The information indicates the existence of mutual benefits between terrorist elements inside and outside Egypt in destabilizing the country and crippling its economy. The source said that an official of one Western security organ had a meeting with Ayman al-Zawahiri, leader of the al-Jihad Organization, at a camp in Peshawar on Pakistan's border with Afghanistan." The story then went on to recount the meetings held between Zawahiri and Abu-Umar al-Amriki, "who acted as a go-between for the CIA" back in the 1980s, during the war in Afghanistan. The story served as notice to those who knew more that official Cairo also now knew more about the subject, in particular the most recent developments.

The Egyptian media immediately began preparing the public for a drastic change in policy vis-à-vis the United States, Israel, and Sudan—the latter being the primary sponsor of Islamist terrorism against Egypt and the safe haven from which terrorists strike out into Egypt. For years Sudan's spiritual leader, Hassan al-Turabi, had been Mubarak's archnemesis.

Early in January 1998 the Egyptian media started to report CIA plots against Egypt. The opposition paper *al-Shab*, which is well connected to and identifies with the nationalist sector within the defense establishment, published a long survey of an American-Israeli conspiracy run by the CIA. The paper observed that the new U.S. ambassador to Egypt, who was Jewish, "has come to Cairo to implement U.S. plans hostile to Egypt. Meanwhile, President Bill Clinton's administration has started to carry out an organized plan to besiege Egypt on all fronts that can threaten Egypt's national security." The paper provided a long list of anti-Egyptian, as well as anti-Sudanese, political and military activities it attributed to a joint CIA-Mossad (Israel's foreign intelligence agency) conspiracy against Cairo. One item mentioned was the CIA's central role in the conspiracy to deprive Egypt of its rights to Umm-Rashrash, the southern part of Israel's Negev desert and Eilat, its port city on the Red Sea coast. This has been Egypt's official reason for a future war with Israel since August 1997 despite the existing peace treaty.

In another article *al-Shab* established the logic for the sudden improvement of relations between Cairo and Turabi's Sudan. The paper noted that Egyptian intelligence had recently acquired critical information shedding new light on crises that determined Cairo's relations with Khartoum. Cairo now knew of the "involvement of the CIA and the Mossad in planning the assassination attempt on President Mubarak in Addis Ababa" in 1995, not only in order to kill the president but also "to pin the accusation against Sudan, in an attempt to spark an immediate war between the two countries." Egyptian intelligence was also "examining the link between this attempt [on Mubarak] and the recent massacre in Luxor." The CIA and Mossad, Egyptian intelligence had discovered, "have succeeded in indirectly recruiting some Arab 'Afghans' and provided the financial and military backing needed for Mubarak's assassination attempt and the Luxor massacre." The terrorist commander of both the 1995 attempt on Mubarak's life and the 1997 carnage in Luxor was Turabi's protégé, Ayman al-Zawahiri—a point not lost on Mubarak's Cairo. Cairo realized that Zawahiri's efforts at overthrowing Mubarak were sponsored by Sudan and therefore Turabi. The key to collapsing the Islamist armed movement in Egypt would be for Cairo to befriend Sudan—then Turabi would stop funding Zawahiri.

Al-Shab explained that taken together, the evidence of the ongoing CIA-Mossad conspiracies against Egypt and their past duplicity in trying to implicate brotherly Sudan in their own crimes against Mubarak now warranted a profound reexamination of Egypt's strategic priorities. "The evidence made available to the Egyptian [intelligence] agencies [has] resulted in a strategic change in Egypt's stance vis-à-vis Sudan," *al-Shab* reported. The new policy had already caused "President Mubarak's announcement that

Sudan does not sponsor terrorism and Dr. Hassan al-Turabi's statement that he [had] nothing to do with the attempt to assassinate Mubarak," *al-Shab* explained. "In both cases, the conspiracy sought to divide the Arab and Islamic ranks. The high-level Egyptian-Sudanese contacts show that both sides are serious about exposing the role of the CIA and the Mossad in conspiring against Egypt and Sudan and containing the consequences caused by this conspiracy over the past years."

This was a dramatic, swift reorientation in the strategic outlook of a major regional power—and it went virtually unnoticed in Washington, now solely preoccupied with the elusive Iraqi weapons of mass destruction. By late January 1998 the Abu-Umar al-Amriki episode had already had a devastating impact on Mubarak's Cairo because it confirmed what President Mubarak wanted to believe—that the United States would betray Egypt if it could get what it wanted from the Islamists in the Balkans. Mubarak resolved to mend his ties with Tehran, the key to which was joining the drive to undermine the U.S. presence and influence in the Middle East, including the reversal of the Peace Process and the beginning of preparations for a possible military confrontation with Israel.

By early 1996 Mubarak had decided that the United States could not determine the shape of the Middle East. By mid-1996 the Egyptian armed forces had begun active preparations for a possible war with Israel. Mubarak raised the issue of Umm-Rashrash in spring 1997 as a casus belli for Egypt in a closed forum of his high command. In the summer, during Mubarak's brief, dramatic visit to Damascus, Egypt joined a regional military alliance led by Iran and comprising Syria, Iraq, and the PLO. A few days later Cairo leaked the Umm-Rashrash issue, using a Saudi venue associated with the Sultan faction in Riyadh—that is, Washington's closest ally within the House of al-Saud. The Egyptian leak was a clear message to both the Clinton administration and the Saudi royal family.

Previously Mubarak's plans to switch Egypt's strategic alliances had been lacking a reason for the Islamists to cease their terrorism and subversion, a source of strong pressure on Mubarak, and also a formal excuse that would enable Cairo to break its close relations with Washington. Now the Abu-Umar al-Amriki episode, which President Mubarak believed to be true, resolved both issues. Cairo now had "proof" of a U.S.-inspired conspiracy against President Mubarak, a legitimate excuse for a crisis in bilateral relations and a motive for revisiting Egypt's relations with Sudan in order to nip in the bud any design Turabi might have for empowering his protégé Zawahiri in Cairo. This episode reaffirmed Mubarak's growing conviction that Egypt's future lay with joining the Iranian-led strategic alliance and participating in any ensuing conflict with Israel. This decision would not only ensure that Egypt would continue to have a prominent role in the Arab and Muslim world but would also secure Mubarak's own survival at the helm.

The specter of a wave of Islamist terrorism led by bin Laden, Zawahiri, and their supporters against the United States and its allies, the realignment of forces in the Middle East to the detriment of U.S. strategic interests, and the growing likelihood of major crises and war in this region all emerged as the price Washington paid for its effort to prevent the violent collapse of the Dayton Accords in Bosnia-Herzegovina.

In summer 1998 leaders as diverse as bin Laden, Mubarak, al-Baz, Turabi, and Zawahiri remained convinced that Abu-Umar al-Amriki spoke for the CIA and the Clinton administration. All acted accordingly. At the climax of the crisis management for "the Abu-Umar al-Amriki incident" the United States came calling in the Iraqi crisis and expected Cairo to concentrate on meeting the Baghdad challenge. But Mubarak was more interested in dealing with Turabi and Zawahiri in the context of a challenge to his own vital interests—a challenge he was convinced had been instigated by Washington.

By early 1998, just as the crisis in Iraq was heating up, Cairo had given up on meaningful cooperation with the United States and was reaching out to the Islamists. Egypt emerged as a militant leader of the Arab world and a dominant actor in regional strategic dynamics. Tehran's effort to solidify the emerging regional military alliance with Egypt had been relentless, as the Organization of Islamic Countries (OIC) summit in Tehran in late 1997 had shown. During the summit the Iranian hosts went out of their way to demonstrate their friendship with and respect for the Egyptian delegation. Tehran accorded Egypt the honor of an Arab leader—a sharp deviation from Tehran's past hostility over Egypt's close relations with the United States, its peace with Israel, and the sanctuary President Sadat gave the Shah of Iran after his overthrow in the Islamic Revolution. The "Abu-Umar al-Amriki incident" constituted the last straw for Mubarak, who rushed to mend fences with Sudan's Turabi and, through him, Tehran. For Turabi and Tehran these signs of improved relations between Egypt and Sudan would serve as a major factor in the decision to launch the attack on the U.S. embassies in Kenya and Tanzania.

STARTING IN EARLY 1998, other major maneuvers were taking place throughout the Islamist Middle East, all aimed at strengthening the coalition against Israel and the United States. The turning point occurred in early February 1998 with the formalization of the strategic cooperation between Iraq, Iran, Syria, and Egypt. Although strategic coordination and de facto cooperation had existed among these countries for a long time, the Iraqi crisis of early 1998 provided a legitimate reason to raise the level of these relations.

Back in mid-January, with the crisis with Iraq mounting, Tehran sent clandestine messages to all its neighbors, urging closer cooperation and co-ordination. Baghdad reacted quickly, proposing the formation of a common front against the American buildup. Baghdad also offered various concessions to entice Tehran, promising to cut support for the Iraq-based Iranian opposition group the Mujahideen ul-Khalq and expressing willingness to reexamine Iran's demand for some $100 billion in compensation for the Iran-Iraq War.

The initial overtures were followed by a visit to Tehran by Muhammad Said al-Sahhaf, Iraq's foreign minister and Saddam Hussein's secret emissary. Baghdad was ready to commit itself formally to the new relationship with Tehran, and Sahhaf and Kamal Kharrazi, the Iranian foreign minister, signed a memorandum of understanding toward this end. Ultimately Sahhaf convinced the Iranians that Baghdad was serious about the new relationship. Both countries then established the mechanism for a direct channel of communication between the chiefs of the Iraqi and Iranian intelligence services. Iran's highest leaders, Khatami and Khamenei, approved these measures.

Soon afterward senior intelligence and security officials from Iraq and Iran began meeting secretly to discuss the practical aspects of their new alliance against the American military presence. In early February, Saddam Hussein dispatched his son Qusay, who is in charge of the Iraqi intelligence system, to represent him at a major clandestine meeting with senior Iranian officials. On February 5 Qusay Hussein and Rafia Daham al-Takriti, the chief of Iraqi general intelligence, arrived in al-Shalamja on the Iraqi side of the Iran-Iraq border. There they met the Iranian intelligence minister, Qorban Ali Dari Najafabadi, and senior Iranian officials. The two delegations reached agreement on several key issues, including the joint sponsorship of international terrorism all over the world, and the Iranian and Iraqi intelligence delegations surveyed areas where they could quickly begin joint operations. Because of their recent successful cooperation in Sudan and Somalia, the two intelligence services decided to give priority to Sudanese-related operations in the near future. Both countries also agreed through their senior intelligence officials that they would escalate any American attack on Iraq into a regional war against Israel, making it impossible for any Arab or Muslim country to cooperate with the United States against Iraq.

EGYPT COULD NOT ESCAPE the widespread grassroots opposition to U.S. threats to Iraq. Cairo was rocked by demonstrations of widespread popular support for Iraq—demonstrations orchestrated by the Islamists. For example, on February 13 about 7,000 people, not just students, gathered at al-Azhar University, the bastion of militant Islam, to demand that Muslims enact jihad against the United States because of its threats to Iraq. The protest erupted in the aftermath of the afternoon prayers led by the Grand Imam of al-Azhar, Sheikh Muhammad Sayid al-Tantawi, a supporter of Mubarak's who stressed the need for unified Arab support of Iraq. "The Arab world must be united in response to American aggression against the people of Iraq. The Islamic world is one body and if a part of that body suffers, the whole body is affected," he told the crowd. The crowd yelled in response, "There is no God but Allah, and Clinton is the enemy of Allah!"

On February 17 Adil Hussein, an activist in the nationalist Labor party whose support Mubarak had sought in restoring ties with Turabi's Khartoum, delivered a fiery anti-American speech to a huge crowd. He led the crowd in cheers of "God is great, oh America. . . . God is great, oh enemy of God!" In his speech Hussein called the Americans "cowards" for "striking with missiles and planes." He vowed that the avenging jihad would reach America. "But no matter how high they fly in the air, we will bring them down to earth with Jihad. We will teach them that the Arab and Islamic Nation will not submit to their will. Can you imagine a whole nation on which these dogs have imposed starvation? They kill children, [they kill] the sick, and there is no food." The crowd erupted with calls for jihad and revenge.

The Islamists took advantage of this excitement and militancy. Dr Ayman al-Zawahiri's Islamic Jihad group issued its own bulletin, "A Word of Truth," for the Friday prayers of February 20. The Islamic Jihad praised the anti-U.S. activities at the al-Azhar Mosque as "the bastion of popular Islamic resistance in Egypt." The bulletin urged the al-Azhar ulema to "strongly confront the humiliations that its men and leaders are subjected to in the media organs which like to portray them as buffoons." Going beyond the current crisis, Islamic Jihad also demanded that the ulema insist on "the return of the Senior Ulema Council, respect for al-Azhar's views on court rulings, its right to ban publications detrimental to Islam, its financial and administrative independence from the government, and the lifting of the legal ban preventing the mosques' imams from criticizing government laws and decisions." The Islamic Jihad bulletin sought to capitalize on the Islamist activism demonstrated at the mosque to further the call for an Islamist government in Egypt.

This bulletin from al-Azhar University carried tremendous weight. Located in Cairo, the university is considered the most important and prestigious institute of higher learning in the Muslim world. Although its faculty leans toward Islamist and Muslim Brotherhood theological interpretations of Islam, al-Azhar does not confront the government in Cairo or challenge Egypt's policies. Thus the adoption of an anti-U.S. political line that Islamic Jihad could and did endorse would not have taken place without the advance approval of the Mubarak government. Still dependent on generous foreign aid from the United States, the Mubarak government increasingly uses such authoritative venues as al-Azhar University as organs for the dissemination of policies it cannot afford to express directly.

Baghdad was confident about the reluctance of both Arab governments and Arab people on the street to support the United States in the mounting crisis. "If America attacks, the doomsday will take place," the government-controlled newspaper *al-Jumhuriya* predicted on February 14, 1998.

IN EARLY FEBRUARY a new Islamist international front emerged. In Western Europe especially, Arab/Muslim émigré communities reacted to the building pressure on Iraq and to the propaganda presenting the crisis as a U.S.-led Western attack on a Muslim state that dared to stand up to Western pressure by moving from passive and legal protest to radical activism. Several local Islamist leaders launched preparations for subversive activities in support of Iraq and militant Islamist causes as a whole. For example, in Germany the Federal Public Prosecutor's Office launched an investigation of Metin Kaplan, the Cologne chief of the Association of Islamic Societies and Communities (ICCB), on suspicion of "forming a terrorist association."

As the radicalization and disquiet of the émigré communities was intensifying, the international Islamist leadership sought to legitimize the call for jihad. Of great significance was the formulation of the initial fatwa for a jihad issued in the name of the London-based al-Muhajiroun, one of the organizations supporting bin Laden and orchestrated by the Islamist headquarters in Britain. This fatwa was issued at the instigation of Khartoum and Tehran. It was intended to test the reaction in the West, as well as build overall support, without committing the sponsoring states directly in case European security forces moved swiftly against the organizations involved. The choice of London was not accidental. Back in the mid-1990s, bin Laden had been instrumental in organizing the myriad of Islamist institutions in London, and Zawahiri coordinated Islamist activities while in England back in September 1997. Now these plans were being implemented.

At the beginning of the second week of February 1998, al-Muhajiroun issued a major fatwa declaring war on the United States and the United Kingdom. "The Fatwa is Jihad against the U.S. and British governments, armies, interests, airports, and institutions, and it has been given by the most prominent scholars of Islam today because of the U.S. and British aggression against Muslims and the Muslim land of Iraq." After enumerating their grievances against London and Washington, the signatories stressed that "the only Islamic Fatwa against this explicit aggression is Jihad. Therefore the message for the U.S. and the British or any non-Muslim country is to stay away from Iraq, Palestine, Pakistan, Arabia, etc., or face a full-scale war of Jihad which will be the responsibility and the duty of every Muslim around the world to participate in." The signers then called upon "the Muslims around the world, including the Muslims in the U.S.A. and in Britain, to confront by all means whether verbally, financially, politically or militarily the U.S. and British Aggression and to do their Islamic duty in relieving the Iraqi people from the unjust sanctions." The fatwa was signed by a large number of Muslim leaders—both expatriate and British—as well as the leaders of British Muslim organizations and groups in the name of these entities.

The next milestone occurred a few days later, in the aftermath of an accidental plane crash that killed Sudanese vice president al-Zubayr Muhammad Salih and many other high officials. Osama bin Laden used the occasion to send a letter to Turabi, urging him to authorize the launching of a genuine terrorist campaign along the principles agreed on at Turabi's own urging in the summer of 1997. "This tragedy [the crash] has come at a time when the international Christian crusade is rushing madly against our country Sudan and against the heart of the Islamic world," bin Laden wrote. He stressed further that the international Christian crusade's fleets were "plowing the seas of Islam. They are besieging and blockading the peoples of the region as a whole with total disregard for pledges and charters, and are violating the sacred sites and draining all the wealth, while the al-Aqsa Mosque remains the prisoner of this Christian-Jewish alliance." (By "Christian-Jewish," bin Laden means the West in all its political, religious, ethical, and cultural aspects.) This correspondence served as the cover for the initial consultations with Turabi and Bashir on practical steps to revive terrorism.

As a result the Islamist terrorist leadership—specifically Osama bin Laden and Ayman al-Zawahiri—received the green light to proceed with the declaration of jihad and to unleash a wave of terrorism in and against the West. It was time for Tehran to step in.

At first Tehran addressed a major operational consideration: the lingering schism between the theological leaders of various Egyptian Islamist groups that needed to work closely together. Tehran summoned the key Egyptian commanders it was working with, in particular Kamal Ujayzah, Zawahiri's Tehran-based aide, and a special emissary of Rifai Ahmad Taha, chief of the Islamic Group. The Egyptians met with senior officials of Iranian intelligence, who notified them that a very lavish and comprehensive support package was ready for them once they improved their operational cooperation. The Iranians stressed that it was both counterproductive and dangerous not to have a tight, smoothly operating terrorist system in as challenging a theater as Egypt. The representatives of the Egyptian organizations concurred with the analysis and promised to embark on a gradual merger of their forces. They conditioned the next steps on theological blessings by their respective spiritual leaders. The Iranians were satisfied with the arrangements and released funds to the Egyptians. They also increased the slots allocated to Egyptian terrorists in key schools.

To make sure that this agreement was implemented, bin Laden held additional meetings with Taha and Zawahiri to discuss better cooperation. Both leaders endorsed the agreement reached in Tehran and agreed to surmount the disagreements between their organizations. Bin Laden stressed that unity was imperative so that all could focus on joint efforts to launch spectacular attacks on U.S. and Israeli targets. Zawahiri and Taha agreed to form a functional united group, although the organizations would retain their independent political-theological leaderships and organizational formats. Initially their military actions would be independent though firmly coordinated through bin Laden and a joint supreme front's high command then being formulated, of which both Zawahiri and Taha are members. These specific arrangements would apply only to their operations inside Egypt. For the international operations both Zawahiri and Taha had long committed to operating within the ranks of the Tehran-dominated networks.

In early 1998 bin Laden and his closest aides also held several meetings with senior terrorist commanders operating overseas. One of those present was Ahmad Ibrahim al-Najjar, a senior Islamic Jihad leader in Albania. (Soon after his return to Albania from Pakistan, Najjar was captured with the help of the CIA and is now in jail in Egypt.) In their meeting bin Laden urged "guerrilla warfare against Israeli and American interests not only in Arab and Muslim countries but everywhere in the world," Najjar recounted. "Bin Laden believed that the Jewish lobby pulled the ropes of politics in the United States and was behind the weakening of Muslim people and governments and that this hegemony should be broken," Najjar explained. Therefore, bin Laden argued, the Islamic Jihad, like all other Islamist terrorist organizations, must "turn its guns" on Israel and the United States instead of Egypt, Saudi Arabia, or other Arab countries. Without the eviction of the United States from the Middle East and the destruction of Israel, it would be virtually impossible for the Islamist forces to defeat the "puppet regimes" bolstered by the United States. As proof Bin Laden pointed to the sorry state of the jihad throughout the Middle East despite the heavy casualties suffered by Islamists. A unified Islamist front, bin Laden repeatedly insisted, would be able to take on the United States and Israel effectively. Najjar and the other commanders enthusiastically endorsed bin Laden's plan.

On February 15, 1998, General Safavi and a delegation of senior Iranian officials met with bin Laden, Zawahiri, and several key Islamist terrorist leaders. The Iranians presented their long-term plans for terrorist operations and outlined the roles of the Islamist terrorists in this master plan. To present a deniable cover for Iran, the meeting decided on the establishment of a new Sunni umbrella organization, later to be named the World Islamic Front for Jihad against Jews and Crusaders. The meeting participants decided on modalities for training and supporting the strike units through the IRGC. Both delegations also agreed on joining forces to increase support for the armed rebellion in Kosovo and to reinforce the Islamists' forward base in Zenica, Bosnia-Herzegovina. The delegations agreed that the Muslim-inhabited areas of the Balkans should become the main base for spreading Islamist terrorism and subversion into Europe. The participating Arab Islamist leaders were very satisfied with the meeting, fully convinced that Tehran recognized their importance as theological luminaries and not just as operatives. Both bin Laden and Zawahiri were reassured of Tehran's great respect toward and confidence in them.

February 20 saw the beginning of a new theological process: the legitimization and authorization of an all-out terrorist jihad against the West, and not just as a reaction to the ongoing crisis in Iraq. In London the Azzam Organization, the mother organization of "Afghan" and "Bosnian" mujahideen as well as Islamist terrorists within the émigré communities in the West, issued the text of a dua (a prayer-sermon instructing the believer how to answer the call of Islam) to be read in mosques worldwide during the key Friday prayer. This dua codified the role of the anti-American jihad over Iraq in the context of the escalating worldwide jihad. The Azzam Organization reminded the listeners and readers that Prophet Muhammad decreed that "indeed Dua is the weapon of the Believer."

Azzam's dua stressed the gravity of the current situation. "At this time, whilst the Muslim Ummah [nation] is engulfed in another wave of oppression, many Muslims are crying, shouting and issuing empty declarations."

According to the Sharia, Muslims could do three things—participate in the jihad, contribute in support of the jihad, or identify with and pray for the success of the jihad. All three deeds were important, for their implementation would bring the entire community together, unified in the pursuit of a sacred cause. "Allah knows best in what category Dua comes, but that is something that every Muslim can and should do. In short, we ask all the Muslims everywhere in the world, all the Mujahideen, all the righteous scholars in the prisons, all the oppressed Muslims, all weak and poor Muslims, to join us and make Dua to Allah against the invading forces."

The first part of the Azzam dua was a lengthy, detailed list of calamities that could befall the U.S.-led aerial forces in the Persian Gulf, such as air crews missing their targets on bombing runs, technical malfunctions, and special forces becoming subject to fright. Well versed in high-tech and modern warfare, the authors of this dua made sure that the believer repeated a long, precise, detailed list of the calamities to befall the Western forces arrayed against Iraq.

Then came a long list of missions and tasks to be performed by mujahideen in the context of the current crisis. This important decree tied up all the challenges and theaters of jihad into a single global struggle against a common enemy:

> O ALLAH! Inspire Muslims in important, strategic and influential positions around the world to use their skills, whether it be computer knowledge or financial ability, to RETALIATE against the enemy in every part of the World!

> O ALLAH! KUFR IS ONE NATION, so even though the MUJAHIDEEN may not be able to retaliate in Iraq, allow your MUJAHIDEEN fighters in the other parts of the World to retaliate against the KAFIR NATION!

> O ALLAH! Cause this retaliation to come in the form of attacks by HAMAS on Israel!

> O ALLAH! Cause this retaliation to come in the form of attacks by Ibn-al-Khattab and the Foreign Mujahideen in CHECHNYA against the Russians!

> O ALLAH! Cause this retaliation to come in the form of attacks by Osama bin Laden and other brave fighters from the Arabian Gulf on the FOREIGN FORCES in the GULF COUNTRIES!

> O ALLAH! Cause this retaliation to come in the form of intensified attacks on the Hindu forces in KASHMIR!

O ALLAH! Cause this retaliation to come in the form of intensified attacks on ISRAEL from Mujahideen across the borders of Jordan and Lebanon!

O ALLAH! Cause the RIGHTEOUS SCHOLARS IN THE ARABIAN GULF to rebel against the foreign policies of their Governments and speak out for the TRUTH!

O ALLAH! Cause the authorities of Muslim countries to turn a BLIND EYE on retaliatory attacks by Mujahideen on Foreign Forces on their soils!

O ALLAH! CAUSE SO MUCH DAMAGE AND DESTRUCTION AND CONFUSION TO THE INVADING FORCES THAT THEY LEARN A LESSON WHICH WILL GO DOWN IN HISTORY AND CAUSE THEM LOSSES WHICH WILL MAKE THEIR GULF WAR LOSSES LOOK LIKE NOTHING!

Given the control and influence exercised by the Azzam Organization over the myriad of mujahideen in the West, in particular "Afghans" and "Bosnians," their call for a comprehensive jihad constituted a major development.

A series of fatwas followed, by the leaders of the key groups and organizations that would actually implement this call to arms and uncompromising jihad. These fatwas outlined the objectives and analysis of militant Islamism in conjunction and accordance with the centers of Islamist leadership in Khartoum, Tehran, Islamabad, and London. The key fatwa was primarily the work of Osama bin Laden, Ayman al-Zawahiri, and Rifai Ahmad Taha (Abu-Yassir) and so was a major achievement in furthering Islamist militant unity despite the ideological differences and doctrinal disagreements between Zawahiri and Taha. The call for violence followed the dua's announcement that a single world of Kufr threatened the entire Muslim world and Islamist revivalism as a whole. Now viable, legitimate targets for the Islamists' jihad could be found anywhere on earth.

The first Islamist fatwa in this series was also issued on February 20 and set the tone and direction for the call to jihad. Professor Bernard Lewis, a leading scholar on Islam, called this fatwa "a magnificent piece of eloquent, at times even poetic, Arabic prose." In essence the fatwa announced the establishment of a "world front for Jihad against Jews and Crusaders"—now known as the World Islamic Front—and declared its commitment to "kill the Americans, civilians and military" in retaliation for any U.S. attack on Iraq or any other demonstration of hostility anywhere else in the Muslim world. The term *Crusaders* was used to stress the continuity of threats posed by foreign forces present in the Middle East, such as the U.S. forces in Saudi

Arabia, and as a reminder of the ultimate victory of the Muslim forces over the original Crusaders. The fatwa decreed that the U.S. threat was profound and all-encompassing because "U.S. aggression is affecting Muslim civilians, not just the military." The key signers were Sheikh Osama bin Muhammad bin Laden; Ayman al-Zawahiri; Rifai Ahmad Taha (Abu-Yassir); Sheikh Mir Hamzah, secretary of the Jamiat-ul-Ulema-e-Pakistan; Fazlul Rahman Khalil, leader of the Ansar Movement in Pakistan; and Sheikh Abdul Salam Muhammad, emir of the Jihad Movement in Bangladesh.

The establishment of the World Islamic Front was a major achievement for the Islamist terrorist groups sponsored by Iran, Sudan, and Pakistan. In jointly signing the fatwa, high-level Islamist sources stressed, these leaders "put their differences aside and agreed to unify the aim for which they are working" and were "in the process of drawing up mechanisms for implementing what was stated in the statement." The prominence given to Pakistani and Bangladeshi Islamist leaders was "aimed at expanding the area containing U.S. targets against which operations can be carried out and at splitting the efforts of security services in more than one state." This distinction was intended to reinforce the declaration of a comprehensive worldwide jihad in the dua of the Azzam Organization.

According to the authors of this fatwa, the world situation in early 1998 was uniquely grave because it brought to the fore a three-element U.S.-led conspiracy against both Muslims and Islam. The three elements were (1) the U.S. occupation of the Arabian Peninsula, its economic exploitation, and its use as a springboard for aggression against sisterly Iraq; (2) the continued slaughter of the Muslims of Iraq by the "the Crusader-Zionist alliance"; and (3) the furthering of the interests of "the Jews' petty state" in conspiring "to destroy Iraq, the strongest neighboring Arab state, and their endeavor to fragment all the states of the region such as Iraq, Saudi Arabia, Egypt, and Sudan into paper statelets and through their disunion and weakness to guarantee Israel's survival and the continuation of the brutal crusade occupation of the [Arabian] Peninsula."

The authors decreed: "All these crimes and sins committed by the Americans are a clear declaration of war on Allah, his Messenger, and Muslims. And ulema have throughout Islamic history unanimously agreed that the Jihad is an individual duty if the enemy destroys the Muslim countries. . . . On that basis, and in compliance with God's order, we issue the following Fatwa to all Muslims":

> The ruling to kill the Americans and their allies—civilians and military—
> is an individual duty for every Muslim who can do it in any country in
> which it is possible to do it, in order to liberate the al-Aqsa Mosque [in

Jerusalem] and the Holy Mosque [in Mecca] from their grip, and in order for their armies to move out of all the lands of Islam, defeated and unable to threaten any Muslim. . . . We—with God's help—call on every Muslim who believes in God and wishes to be rewarded to comply with God's order to kill the Americans and plunder their money wherever and whenever they find it. We also call on Muslim ulema, leaders, youths, and soldiers to launch the raid on Satan's U.S. troops and the devil's supporters allying with them, and to displace those who are behind them so that they may learn a lesson.

Also of great importance was a concurrent fatwa issued by the Tehran-sponsored "Partisans of the Sharia." This document provided the legal and theological justification for Islamist support for Saddam Hussein even though he was not an Islamist leader and has a record of fighting both Iran and Iraqi Islamists. The document, undersigned by Abu-Hamzah al-Masri, who is closely allied to Turabi and Zawahiri, addressed the Islamists' enduring hostility toward Saddam Hussein and set clear priorities for the Islamist struggle under the current circumstances. Escalating the jihad against the United States was of such importance as to justify cooperation with Iraq.

The statement from Partisans of the Sharia left no doubt about the hostility toward Saddam Hussein's Baghdad, which was described as "apostates from Islam's laws and rules." In principle, the Islamists noted, present-day Iraqi officials were "atheists and apostates who must be fought . . . and should be fought by the police and the army if they defend the regimes or if they prepare for such action; their wealth should become spoils, and they should be driven away and their wounded finished off." The fatwa stated that the Partisans of the Sharia still adhered to its original conviction that "championing this [Iraqi] people against Saddam and his government, against the Jews and Christians, and against all those who avail themselves of this Muslim people's blood, money, or honor by fear or by words or deed, is the duty that all Muslims must perform with their swords, money, words, and hearts; and from each according to his means." The prevailing circumstances in the Middle East, however, made it necessary for the Islamists to concentrate their jihad against the true enemy of and predominant threat to Islam. The Partisans of the Sharia emphasized that "the Jews and the Christians have no business there [in Iraq and Arabia] and have no legitimate, recognized mandate. Their presence poses a threat and their blood can be shed with impunity. In short, every Muslim must try in earnest to drive them away in humiliation." The Muslims should do so even if in the process they gave aid and comfort to Saddam Hussein.

On February 23 al-Zawahiri's Jihad Group issued the first of several clarification communiqués designed to better define the essence of the anti-U.S. jihad just declared. The Islamic Jihad vowed "to teach the Americans a lesson" and blamed President Clinton for "the aggression against the nation of Islam." The Iraqi people "for whom Clinton is shedding crocodile tears are the same people, hundreds of thousands of whom, the U.S. President intends to burn to punish Saddam Hussein, as he claims. Clinton has warned against the threat of chemical and biological weapons in Iraq at a time when he is stockpiling them in Israel to strike against the Muslims, establish the Greater Israel, and destroy the al-Aqsa Mosque to build Solomon's temple on its ruins. O Muslims, rise against the United States throughout the world and teach them lessons wherever you find them."

Two days later AbdAllah Mansur, secretary general of the Egyptian Jihad Group—Armed Vanguards of Conquest, issued a statement titled "A Step Forward and in the Right Direction" that urged the just established World Islamic Front for Jihad against Jews and Crusaders to expand its membership to include the other activist Islamist trends and formulate new strategies suitable for the forthcoming stages of the global jihad. "The time has come for us to move from hasty thinking based on [emotional] reactions and fighting non-enemies, and hence exhausting almost all our energies, to strategic thinking that takes account of rules of defense and the ability to adapt and develop, because without that, the outcome is a total freeze," Mansur wrote. In essence, Mansur urged diverting the main efforts of the Egyptian jihad away from confronting the Mubarak government to striking at the United States and Israel.

The statement of the Jihad Group—Armed Vanguards of Conquest also stressed that in order to carry out the proposed, most necessary jihad it was imperative to "form a higher committee that represents all colors of the fundamentalist movement wishing to join such an alliance in the Arab and Islamic Worlds, in addition to drawing up mechanisms for implementing and focusing on these aims while earnestly working to eliminate all psychological barriers among the various Jihad forces and tendencies in order to close ranks against falsehood and its party." The statement warned that given the magnitude of the challenges, "addressing problems without finding suitable solutions is liable to lead eventually to bad results."

In this context the Jihad Group—Armed Vanguards of Conquest praised the establishment of the World Islamic Front for Jihad against Jews and Crusaders as a major step in the right direction. Mansur enthusiastically endorsed the fatwa's stipulation that "killing the Americans and their allies is an individual duty for every Muslim." He also endorsed the inclusion of the Islamic Group, the Jihad Group, and the Armed Islamic Group in the new front even though there had been ideological and theological frictions between these groups in the past over the conduct of the Islamist jihad in Egypt.

On March 3 the Egyptian-based leadership of Zawahiri's Jihad Group reiterated its commitment to the armed jihad in the context of the new international alliance. The Jihad Group was convinced that "there is no point in partial solutions" for the challenges facing the Muslim world and that "Jihad is the only way" to achieve these total solutions. The mere issue of a statement titled "No Solution Except through Jihad" by the Media Office of the Jihad Group in Egypt served as a tacit reminder to the Mubarak government that debilitating, violent Islamist terrorism could be revived if Egypt joined the U.S.-led camp. Over the next few days, before the Friday prayers of March 6, high-level Egyptian Islamists received messages from Zawahiri's inner circle that the Jihad Group, as a leading component of the World Islamic Front, "will begin open activity soon." The messages also reasserted the validity of the recently issued fatwa with emphasis on the stated requirement that members of Islamist groups "kill Americans and steal their possessions anywhere."

With these clarifications by Zawahiri and his lieutenants, the exploitation of the Iraqi crisis to enhance Islamist militancy and radicalism—even though Saddam Hussein himself is neither liked nor trusted by the Islamist leaders—came full circle. Islamist leaders used the building, traumatic conflict with the West to revive the widespread, popular fear of the extent of Western influence over the Muslim world and fuel an Islamist surge. The Islamists proved very effective in capitalizing on the media blitz in the West about Iraq's sins and Saddam Hussein's fate—a discussion interpreted in the Arab world, as well as among the Muslim émigré community and intellectual elite in the West, as a demonstration of Western hostility toward Islam. By early March 1998 Saddam Hussein as an individual and his ideology were no longer of importance to most Muslims. All that counted was their impression of a massive, U.S.-dominated high-technology military force arrayed to bomb and devastate innocent Muslim civilians already emaciated by the U.S.-imposed sanctions. The immense, long-lasting impact of the crisis in Iraq on the revival of international terrorism at the heart of the West was irreversible.

Most telling was the reaction of the Arab establishment to these developments. In Iraq, in the aftermath of the emergence of a U.N.-endorsed agreement, even official Cairo expected the United States to instigate another provocation to ignite the region. A March 1 editorial in the official *al-Ahram* by Abduh Mubashir titled "Iraq and the Siege of Fire" elucidated the Mubarak government's worldview. Abduh Mubashir described a history of

U.S. hostile intervention in the Middle East since the 1970s that was designed to stifle Arab awakening and serve the West and Israel's self-interest. The current crisis with Iraq was only the latest but by no means the last stage in this process. Abduh Mubashir stressed that more crises with Iraq were sure to come whether Saddam complied with the United Nations or not because it was in the interest of the United States to hit Iraq and strike at all Arabs. "This squeezing, particularly if viewed as part of the siege of fire that surrounds the Arab world, leads us to expect a further hardline attitude from the United States and the United Nations. . . . There is a likelihood that U.S. planners might drive President Saddam to provoke a crisis, either through an action on his part or as a reaction to something else. This is not a difficult thing for those people who have long known how to lay traps for political regimes. In order to maintain the ability to direct a military strike, senior U.S. officials have announced that the military force massed in the region will stay in place," *al-Ahram* stated.

With Egypt, one of the most pro-U.S. and secular governments in the Middle East, openly endorsing the Islamist position that the United States was bent on punishing the Arab world for being Muslim and that there could be no compromise between the United States and the Muslim world, the surge of Islamist militancy and terrorism could not be stopped. With popular support building, the World Islamic Front for Jihad against Jews and Crusaders would have to strike out if only to preserve its legitimacy in the Muslim world.

In March 1998 the main question was, Where and when would the Islamist terrorists strike at a U.S. objective? By then two major trends were evolving. First, the overall development of the global Islamist international terrorist capabilities was being consolidated. The World Islamic Front for Jihad against Jews and Crusaders now provided the theological and supreme command framework on which the new operational networks of expert terrorists could be organized and ordered to strike out. This effort would start in April 1998, and it is still unfolding, setting the stage for an era of international terrorism with unprecedented lethality. Second, committed and determined to strike out as soon as it was prudent, the Islamists simultaneously expedited their preparations for a low-risk spectacular operation. East Africa emerged as the most suitable theater. The twin car bombs that shook Nairobi and Dar-es-Salaam proved the Islamists' analysis of risk to be correct.

9

The U.S. Embassy Bombings

ON AUGUST 7, 1998, two bombs exploded simultaneously outside U.S. embassies in Nairobi, Kenya, and Dar-es-Salaam, Tanzania, 450 miles apart. In Nairobi all windows within a quarter-mile splintered, the doors were blown off the embassy, people were blown out of buildings, and a seven-story building next to the embassy collapsed. In Dar-es-Salaam the bomb blew off one side of the embassy. Altogether more than 250 people died and more than 5,500 were injured, mostly Africans.

The two bombings were state-sponsored operations conducted by the Tehran-dominated, recently rejuvenated HizbAllah International, with Sudan and Pakistan also playing an active role. The elite forces of the Armed Islamist Movement, with Osama bin Laden as political leader and Ayman al-Zawahiri as military commander, were instrumental in carrying out these strikes. The bombings in East Africa are representative of contemporary Islamist terrorism, including a highly professional execution and intentionally blurred chain of responsibility that complicates Western retaliation, in particular against the sponsoring states.

In contrast to the strategic and political importance of the August 1998 operation, the bombing was operationally low risk: a contingency plan had been activated that relied on forces already in place. The specific strikes in East Africa resulted from a high-level political commitment to a spectacular strike against the West; the failure of the primary operation, an attack on the Soccer World Cup games in France; and Turabi's mounting insistence on anti-U.S. operations in East Africa to enhance the spread of Islamism and hurt countries supporting the rebels in southern Sudan.

HASSAN AL-TURABI, the spiritual leader of Sudan and preeminent guide of militant Sunni Islam, has always been committed to the spread of Islamism into sub-Saharan Africa. Since the early 1990s Iran and Sudan have been engaged in a fierce campaign to consolidate their control over the Red Sea and the Horn of Africa. The clashes with and ultimate eviction of the U.S.-led U.N. forces from Somalia in 1993 constituted the first major round in the Islamist struggle for East Africa. Despite the dramatic outcome of the Islamist jihad in Somalia—effecting the U.S. withdrawal—Khartoum and Tehran were fully cognizant that they had not made tangible gains. After all, no Islamist government was established in Mogadishu in the aftermath of the Islamists' triumph, and the fratricidal fighting between the various militias and other armed groups continued. The escalating civil war in southern Sudan served as a constant reminder of this. In addition, the foreign assistance reaching the blacks of southern Sudan via East African states added an incentive to strike out against these states and their strategic protector, the United States. Khartoum was convinced, not without logic, that if it made assistance to the rebels in southern Sudan prohibitively "expensive" to the neighboring states through terrorism, subversion, and destabilization, these governments would be reluctant to permit access to southern Sudan through their territories. Khartoum also thought that once the United States began to "suffer"—to be subjected to international terrorism—as a result of its support for the Sudanese rebels, Washington would immediately cease its support and stop encouraging neighboring countries to assist the rebels.

Reinforcement of the Islamist clandestine networks in East Africa started immediately after U.S. forces began withdrawing from Somalia. The primary objective in consolidating these key networks was to establish a long-term presence. In early 1994 Ayman al-Zawahiri started bolstering the Islamist networks. The senior on-site commander in Somalia at the time, Zawahiri considered the buildup in Kenya so important that he managed it personally, making numerous clandestine visits to both Nairobi and Mombasa. At the core of the new force in Kenya were several Jordanian "Afghans." Some of them arrived in Kenya from Pakistan and others from the Middle East. Their primary task was to establish themselves in Kenya and prepare for the absorption of other Islamists, who were most likely to arrive from Pakistan, and provide them with operational support throughout East Africa.

Muhammad Sadiq Odeh, the man arrested in Pakistan in early August 1998 for involvement in the bombing of the U.S. embassies, was one of these Jordanians deployed by Zawahiri. The Jordanian passport he used to enter Kenya carried the name Mohammed Saddiq Howaida and showed that he was born in Saudi Arabia, although he is a Jordanian-Palestinian. He entered Kenya in mid-1994 as a student. According to the Pakistani authorities, Odeh described himself as the son of Palestinian parents, born in Tabuk, Saudi Arabia. He studied in Jordan, where he joined the Palestine Liberation Organization. In 1990 the PLO sent him for training in Afghanistan. There he was influenced by militant Islamism, trained in one of bin Laden's base camps for Arab "Afghans," and joined the mujahideen in their fight against the government in Kabul. Having proven his zeal in combat, Odeh was recruited by the Zawahiri–bin Laden "organization" and trained for terrorist operations. His instructions, like those of Zawahiri's other long-term assets, were to build a life in Kenya. In October 1994 Odeh married a local Muslim girl and settled down.

The vital contribution of the East African networks to the Islamist world terror organizations was confirmed by the nomination in 1994–95 of Ali al-Rashidi, also known as Abu-Ubaydah al-Banshiri or Abu-Ubaydah al-Banjashiri, as the Kenyan-based regional senior commander. An Egyptian confidant of al-Zawahiri's, al-Rashidi commanded one of the elite units in the fighting with the U.S. forces in Mogadishu in fall 1993. Now, from his home base in Kenya, al-Rashidi's mission was to establish a complex of clandestine networks made of a mix of Egyptian, Arab, and African Islamists in several African states.

Starting early in 1994, the Islamist networks in East Africa were preoccupied with logistical tasks related to the shipment of drugs grown and produced in Afghanistan and Pakistan and to the laundering of monies for funding the rapidly expanding Islamist networks in Western Europe and the United States. The primary ports of entry used by the Islamists were and still are Zanzibar (Tanzania) and Mombasa (Kenya), from which the drugs are shipped into East and West Africa and on to the West. To handle these shipments, several key experts were sent from Sudan to bolster and solidify the clandestine Islamist networks in both port cities.

Because of its good relations with the West, Kenya was also made into a major station for the "laundering" of terrorists and operatives on their way to the United States and Western Europe. Operatives would travel clandestinely to Saudi Arabia (via Yemen), Egypt (via Sudan), or Kenya (via Somalia) and then on to Turkey and Italy; from there, they would continue to the West using a new set of travel documents. But by the mid-1990s, with the growing suppression of Islamists in Egypt and Saudi Arabia, Kenya had become the key insertion point for terrorists headed to the West. Additional expert terrorists were sent to Kenya to support the infiltration operation.

The growing importance of East Africa for the terrorist support system throughout the world increased the area's acquisition of operational capabilities for spectacular strikes. The decision to acquire and maintain terrorist operational capabilities in East Africa in addition to the region's critical support system shows the vital nature of this region to the terrorist leadership. As a rule, support networks are run by a different group of people than operational networks. Support networks require expertise in logistical support, money laundering, and smuggling. Operational networks require such skills as bomb making and assassination. To ensure security, efforts are made to separate the networks and, if possible, keep them geographically apart so that the collapse of one network will not lead to the destruction of the other.

The assassination attempt on Egyptian president Mubarak in summer 1995 in Addis Ababa demonstrated the expediency of having sophisticated, capable networks in East Africa. As a consequence in spring 1996 the Islamists began rebuilding their forward base in Somalia as part of the overall improvement of operational capabilities in East Africa. For example, bin Laden established a system of safe houses in southern Mogadishu, an area under Aidid's control. By this time the terrorist infrastructure in Kenya was also ready to absorb expert terrorists. In early summer 1996 several strike groups of Arab "Afghans" were moved from their training bases in Sudan to the Khartoum air base, situated inside the compound belonging to the army's general command. From there they were flown to Nairobi on commercial flights. Some remained in Kenya, while others moved clandestinely to southern Mogadishu.

The Islamist preparations suffered a major setback in late May 1996 when al-Rashidi died in an accident. At the time he was on his way to establish additional regional networks. Because of his immense prominence and stature in the jihad forces, he had been considered the number-two man in the jihad organization, second only to Zawahiri. It would take the organization time to recover from his death.

Khartoum tried to activate two prominent Islamists who had been in Nairobi since 1994 as substitute commanders, but they proved incapable of meeting the challenge. The first was Mustafa Mahmud Said Ahmad, an Egyptian "Afghan" born in Zaire and a graduate of al-Azhar University. Operating from a base in Kuwait, he performed several espionage tasks for the Islamists in Kuwait and Egypt. But by the mid-1990s his heart was no longer in Islamist militancy. The other commander was Wadih el Hage, an Arab American who had served as bin Laden's secretary in Khartoum since the mid-1980s. Although fiercely devoted to the cause, he also proved unsuitable because he attracted attention to himself. In August 1997 a joint force of Kenyan security services and the FBI raided el Hage's home in

Kenya and in effect "burned" him as an operative. Both were sent out of Nairobi during 1997 as new, more assertive commanders stepped in.

The new military commander in East Africa was Subhi Abdul Aziz Abu-Sittah, also known as Muhammad Atif Mustafa and by the nom de guerre Abu-Hafs al-Masri. He is an Egyptian and a veteran Arab "Afghan." Although Islamist from an early age, Abu-Hafs was not involved in subversive activities while in Egypt even though he maintained some contact with an Islamic Jihad cell. He arrived in Pakistan in the late 1980s and befriended Ali al-Rashidi, who ultimately introduced him to bin Laden and Zawahiri. Over the years Abu-Hafs became a devoted lieutenant of Zawahiri's. Abu-Hafs assisted al-Rashidi in several clandestine operations, usually being responsible for the military-terroristic aspects of the operation. In South Africa he organized and trained local Islamist networks. When al-Rashidi moved to Africa, abu-Hafs also assumed some of his supervisory roles in the training camps in Afghanistan. In 1997 Abu-Hafs emerged as the ideal candidate to step into the shoes of his late close friend. As the military commander for East African operations, Abu-Hafs shuttled between Afghanistan-Pakistan and East Africa. While Islamist operations became more high profile in the region, he mostly stayed in the shadows, avoiding direct contact with local terrorists and operatives.

All of these activities were conducted under the close scrutiny of the sponsoring states, primarily Iran. Since the establishment of the HizbAllah International in the summer of 1996, Tehran has tended to stay in the background, letting such prominent but fiercely loyal Sunni leaders as bin Laden and Zawahiri carry out the hands-on activities. Tehran formulates the terrorist strategy, sets the overall priorities, and determines and/or approves the specific targets. Through the Committee of Three, one of whom is bin Laden, the Islamist commanders now have greater latitude and autonomy in running the actual operations within the guidelines set by Tehran. But as preparations for spectacular operations approached completion in 1996, Tehran stepped in to inspect directly the status of the Islamist terrorist networks. By now Iran was in the midst of a profound strategic assessment of its regional requirements and capabilities. As a result East Africa would acquire a greater significance in Tehran's own strategic interests.

The most important firsthand examination of the situation in East Africa was conducted in September 1996 under the cover of Iranian president Ali Akbar Hashemi-Rafsanjani's visit to six East African countries—South Africa, Zimbabwe, Tanzania, Sudan, Uganda, and Kenya. A group of senior intelligence officers accompanied Hashemi-Rafsanjani and used their stay to personally investigate the situation throughout the region. In

mid-October, Hashemi-Rafsanjani explained that his visit "opened a historical opportunity for Islamic Iran to help develop and reconstruct the African
continent." He noted "the vain attempts of the U.S. to pressure African states
against broadening their relations with Iran" and concluded that "the
African states and people have evaluated the benefits of trade and economic
ties with Islamic Iran and are ready to become free of the self-interested policies of the West." To capitalize on the success of this inspection visit, Tehran
formed five expert committees to study the prospects of Iran's contribution
to Africa in five specific fields—politics, trade, economics, culture, and technical and medical services. Several steps were immediately implemented. For
example, on October 17 Iran Air started a flight to Nairobi via Dubai as the
first step in a planned extension of services to other African capitals.

In mid-November 1996 Javid Ghorban Oghli, the director general for
Africa at the Iranian Foreign Ministry, reaffirmed the centrality of East
Africa for Tehran: "Today, Africa has turned into an important and focal
point in the world. Even the Americans acknowledge that African nations
fully understand the Islamic Revolution and are sympathetic toward our
country and revolution. This has led to the consolidation of our ties with
African states. This reality of course does not fit into Washington's declared policy to isolate Iran." That Oghli was named to this position is significant, for he is Iran's former ambassador to Algeria, where he was
implicated in support for and organization of Islamist activities, including
terrorism and subversion.

Because of the lingering impact of al-Rashidi's death, the buildup of
the Islamist networks did not resume until fall 1996, and then it resumed
primarily in the relative safety of Somalia. Bin Laden made several trips to
Somalia to revive the Islamist preparations. During these trips he stayed in
southern Mogadishu, an area under the control of Hussein Aidid, the son
of the late warlord Muhammad Farah Aidid, who grew up in the United
States. In the winter of 1996–97 bin Laden also agreed to permit some of
the Arab "Afghans" to fight in the Islamic Liberation Party in the Somalian
fratricidal wars so that in exchange he could get permission to establish a
series of base camps and training facilities in Somalia. The operational
arrangements were concluded in Peshawar, Pakistan, in a meeting between
Ahmad Shawqi al-Islambuli, the Egyptian Islamist commander, and emissaries of the Islamic Liberation Party. Islambuli agreed to send a few detachments of al-Jamaah al-Islamiyah members from Afghanistan to bolster
the Liberation Party's forces in Somalia. The Islamist leaders—bin Laden,
al-Zawahiri, and al-Islambuli—agreed to these arrangements because they
believed that Somalia was a very suitable place to reorganize and forge

unity among armed Arab "Afghan" groups in preparation for the challenges ahead.

Concurrently, in the winter of 1996–97, the significance of East Africa to Iran's grand strategic calculations profoundly changed. The Iranians were improving their naval capabilities, a development of global strategic importance. The recent acquisition of naval vessels and antishipping missiles from the People's Republic of China and the arrival of the third KILO submarine (one of the most modern, quiet, lethal nonnuclear submarines in the Russian arsenal) from Russia boosted Tehran's self-confidence in its ability to conduct combat operations over a wider area. These weapons deliveries were only the first phase of a major, far more comprehensive naval expansion program, based mainly on the acquisition from China of numerous surface combatants (all combat ships that sail above water), that would take several years to complete. When the process is completed, Iran will have the most powerful navy in the Persian Gulf region.

The most critical development was Iran's attempt to acquire regional blue-water capabilities (the ability to operate in the deep sea outside its territorial waters). The Iranian navy had already proven its ability to operate over long distances. Iranian operations during joint naval exercises with the Pakistani navy throughout the Arabian Sea were impressive, as were the visits to Indonesia by Iranian naval combatants. The Iranian navy also operated from several port facilities in Sudan, where Iran maintained what amounted to several military and naval bases, and from Somalia.

In early 1997 Iran gained access to naval facilities in Mozambique. In return for diversified military aid, the Iranian navy was permitted to use port facilities in Maputo and Nacala, where the Soviets and Cubans had built military-compatible port facilities during the Cold War. The agreement between Iran and Mozambique specifically permitted Iran to use these port facilities for its submarines—to station technical support teams in Mozambique and to maintain replenishment and crew-support installations.

The true significance of all these activities becomes apparent in the context of Tehran's assertive military doctrine—to forestall, perhaps even launch, preemptive strikes against U.S. forces in case of a major escalation in the Persian Gulf region. Tehran's war plans in the Persian Gulf depend on prevention of a quick U.S. military intervention, and so it is imperative for Tehran to be able to prevent the timely arrival of U.S. naval forces. Tehran is determined to acquire military capabilities to perform this mission. Because of the disparity between the U.S. and Iranian navies, the only way the Iranians can affect an American intervention is by actually seeking out and engaging the U.S. naval forces far from the Persian Gulf.

Once ordered to do so, the U.S. Navy will be able to quickly locate and sink both the Iranian submarines and their surface combatants. The Iranian naval strategy is tailored to this imbalance of forces. Tehran's ultimate objective is to buy time for their initial activities on the Arabian Peninsula, from helping a friendly Islamist government to establish itself to launching a surprise attack in the context of a regional war. By their calculations, the mere existence of an Iranian naval threat would compel the U.S. Navy to seek them out and engage them before the United States could effectively intervene in any emergency in the Persian Gulf. Even if the Iranian Navy ultimately loses in such a confrontation—and it would undoubtedly be sunk—the mere diversion of U.S. attention and the time it would take to resolve the challenge would provide Tehran with valuable time to consolidate initial gains on the Arabian Peninsula or in the Persian Gulf.

Iran would not have to engage such major objectives as U.S. Navy carrier task forces. For example, sinking the prepositioned ships operating from Diego Garcia—a British-ruled island in the middle of the Indian Ocean where the United States and the United Kingdom maintain the forward-based military equipment crucial for quick reaction to any emergency in the Persian Gulf area—will significantly hinder any U.S. military buildup in the Middle East. A credible threat to these resupply ships would compel the U.S. Navy to divert naval assets that could be used elsewhere to escort and protect the resupply efforts.

Iran's ability to maintain submarine patrols between Mozambique and the Arabian Sea constitutes a threat because it creates a barrier between Diego Garcia and the Persian Gulf. Iran is already capable of threatening the shipping lanes along the Red Sea from its bases and facilities in Sudan and Somalia. Tehran is convinced that in case of a major war in the Persian Gulf area, this kind of naval operation can delay intervention by the United States until it is too late to save the local Arab governments.

Tehran continued to raise the ante against the United States and the Arab states of the Persian Gulf, specifically Saudi Arabia. Anticipating a new round of brinksmanship and a possible eruption in the Middle East, Tehran warned the Arab states against permitting the United States to operate against the Iranians. In early February 1997 Ayatollah Khamenei delivered explicit threats during his al-Quds Day sermon. (Al-Quds Day, originally an Iranian holiday, is the last Friday of the month of Ramadhan and is devoted to reiteration of the Muslims' commitment to the liberation of holy places under infidels' occupation.) "If any of these foreigners in the Persian Gulf makes one miscalculated move that could lead to instability, the first country that will burn will be the one that invited these foreigners here in the first place," he declared.

As for all Islamist theological milestones after the establishment of HizbAllah International, the Iranian statements were echoed by even stronger declarations from the Islamists. In this case the rejuvenation of the Arab "Afghan" forces in Somalia reverberated in bold doctrinal statements. Key to the events unfolding in East Africa was a warning issued by Islambuli's al-Jamaah al-Islamiyah in February 1997. The decree stated that U.S. interests throughout the world had become legitimate targets for the organization. The decree also urged the Islamic people "to go and besiege the U.S. embassies and ask their rulers to close them." In the Islamists' terminology, this statement translates into terrorizing the local population into pressuring their respective governments to close U.S. embassies and other facilities. The decree stresses that "the U.S. Government's policy of confronting the Islamic movement" is unchangeable and is "a continuation of repression and terrorism against Islam and its people." The only way to reverse the course is with a resolute struggle throughout the world.

Meanwhile Tehran had launched a comprehensive campaign, involving both overt and covert initiatives, to bolster the Islamist presence in Africa, with emphasis on the six states Hashemi-Rafsanjani had visited. This campaign was in full swing by early spring 1997. While encompassing the five fields addressed in fall 1996, a major new element was added in early 1997— support for Islamist terrorism and subversion as an integral component of the overall Africa policy. The sprawling training system in Sudan and the forward bases in Somalia would be modified to cope with the new challenges.

The intelligence officials who studied Hashemi-Rafsanjani's visit formulated the plan. The principles were then presented at the offices of Ayatollah Ali Khamenei, Iran's spiritual leader, who called for an even bolder and more far-reaching initiative. The revised plan was drawn up by Ali Hijazi, a senior official in Khamenei's private office. In early 1997, after a thorough study and slight modifications by intelligence experts, the plan was submitted to the Supreme Council for National Security, chaired by Hashemi-Rafsanjani, for approval and authorization of implementation.

The council approved the plan unanimously. It also appropriated a budget of $9 million specifically for intelligence operations in East Africa. Additional funds were allocated to the IRGC for the preparation of special units to assist in this endeavor. Headquarters were established to supervise and coordinate this initiative under cover of the Office for Islamic Culture and Guidance in Tehran.

The ultimate objective of this initiative could be deduced from the initial propaganda onslaught unleashed on the Muslim population in East Africa. Quotations from Hashemi-Rafsanjani's September 1996 speech to the Shiite community in Tanzania in support of Iran were now used by the

Iranian propaganda machine. The most critical message of this speech, Tehran now argued, was the reaffirmation of Iran's commitment to "helping the oppressed African Muslims to throw off the shackles of colonial exploitation." The Iranians capitalized on this message as a cover for establishing a wider, more professional network of terrorist cells throughout East Africa. Comprising a mix of Arab "Afghans" and local Muslims, this network was organized so that it could be activated at a moment's notice to launch spectacular terrorist strikes, specifically against Western targets.

In retrospect, the networks established in Tanzania were of paramount importance. Iranian counterintelligence experts noted that because of their close cooperation with Israel and the United Kingdom, the security services in Nairobi (Kenya) and Harare (Zimbabwe) would complicate Iran's ability to run the kind of clandestine intelligence operations in which it specializes. Although in Nairobi the Iranians could rely on the locally based Islamist networks organized by bin Laden and Zawahiri, the challenge of hostile counterintelligence remained strong. Conditions were very conducive to terrorist networks in Tanzania, where the government was struggling with political and economic problems. Moreover, the Islamist community of Zanzibar had long maintained close relations with the intelligence services of both Iran and Pakistan. Iranian intelligence began covert funding of various Tanzanian opposition groups, from radical Islamists to those fighting for the independence of Zanzibar. Meanwhile Tanzanian activists were recruited by the Iranians and sent for military and terrorism training in camps in Sudan and Iran. A major aspect of this undertaking was to identify "soft" Western targets throughout East Africa and quickly build terrorist networks capable of strategic operations nearby.

In early 1997 veteran intelligence operatives were nominated to key diplomatic and quasi-diplomatic positions in Iranian legations throughout East Africa. Their posting constituted an accurate reflection of Tehran's priorities.

In Tanzania the Iranian ambassador is Ali Saghaian. In his previous posting as Iran's ambassador to Argentina, he was involved in the 1994 bombing of the AMIA building—the Jewish center in Buenos Aires—that claimed the lives of 104 people and injured close to a thousand more. The cultural attaché is Mohammad-Javad Taskhiri, a veteran intelligence officer who was expelled from his previous post in Jordan for supporting the local Islamist networks. His brother, Mullah Muhammad Ali Taskhiri, heads the Organization of Islamic Culture and Communications. The representative of the Construction Jihad Organization in Tanzania, Reza Muhammad-Pour, is an IRGC colonel who served with al-Quds Forces prior to becoming a civil engineering expert.

Iran's diplomatic representation in Kenya is no different. The ambassador to Nairobi is Kazem Tabatabai, an intelligence officer who served in Baghdad. The cultural attaché is Ahmad Dargahi. He is the former director general for Europe and America in the Communications Directorate of the Organization of Islamic Culture and Communications, one of Tehran's primary organs for support of local Islamist cadres.

In spring 1997 Tehran knew it was heading toward a crisis in Africa because of the anticipated strategic confrontation with the West. It thus became imperative to reexamine both the resilience of the local Islamist networks and the overall diplomatic situation. In late May and early June 1997 Hossein Sheikh-ol-Islam, a veteran terrorist supervisor and then Iran's deputy foreign minister, led a delegation of senior intelligence officials throughout sub-Saharan Africa, meeting local Muslim leaders and surveying the conditions of the local support networks. His other objective was to get a firsthand impression of the extent of the African leaders' willingness to support the United States and stand in the way of the Iranian and Islamist strategic ascent. He accomplished the latter objective in Harare while attending the Thirty-third Summit of the Organization of African Unity as a guest. There he talked with several African leaders about African-Iranian relations. Among the leaders he met were Congo president Laurent Kabila, South African president Nelson Mandela, and Zimbabwean president Robert Mugabe. All these African leaders rose to power in the aftermath of a long, arduous national liberation struggle they characterize as anti-imperialistic (that is, with an anti-U.S. and anti-West ideology). Beginning in the early 1980s, Khomeini's Iran had provided extensive financial, military, and humanitarian assistance to these movements. The African leaders and revolutionary commanders established close relations with Tehran—relationships Tehran was now capitalizing on. The warm reception Sheikh-ol-Islam enjoyed, the interest shown in improving relations with Iran, and the overt hostility toward the United States convinced Tehran that Iran would not suffer a lingering diplomatic-economic setback in case of a major confrontation with the United States in Africa.

But not everything was going Tehran's way. Although strategic objectives were being met, unexpected setbacks occurred at the tactical operational level. In June–July 1997 Iranian counterintelligence officers and bin Laden's own security experts started to suspect that Hussein Aidid had become "a pillar for U.S. intelligence in the Horn of Africa." At first bin Laden changed his allies in Somalia. He renewed contacts with Othman Gatu, a Somali millionaire with whom the bin Laden family had long had financial relations in some Persian Gulf States—relations that had brought Gatu a lot of money. Unfortunately for Bin Laden, Gatu was a strong supporter of

Mahdi Muhammad, Aidid's nemesis since the early 1990s, when they fought over the control of Mogadishu, and even conducted the weapons trade for Muhammad's forces. Then bin Laden's shelter at Gatu's house was betrayed, and it was no longer safe for bin Laden to remain in the Mogadishu area. He returned to Sudan in summer 1997.

According to Arab sources close to bin Laden, he said that he "had information that the United States was depending on Aidid's son for any future move in the Horn of Africa" and that "U.S. intelligence agencies could help Aidid decide the situation in Mogadishu and Somalia." But in summer 1997 bin Laden believed that "the time for deciding matters has not yet come, because if matters are decided, a state would be established and this state would have responsibilities, obligations, and commitments." Instead, bin Laden argued, "Leaving things as they are will create security chaos, thereby aiding in the carrying out of certain operations and liquidations in the Horn of Africa at the hands of Aidid's sons without any accountability." So the Islamist forces disengaged from the area controlled by the Aidid forces and moved back to camps in neighboring countries—Sudan, Kenya, and the Ogaden, Ethiopia.

———————

STARTING IN SPRING 1997, the terrorism-sponsoring states and Islamist leaders had embarked on a lengthy process of ongoing deliberate, prudent strategy formulation and operational planning accompanied by theological formulations. This process was aimed at developing a worldwide campaign of terrorism to extend beyond the 1998 bombings in East Africa.

Iran began to seriously address strategic operations in Africa in June 1997. The great success of Sheikh-ol-Islam's trip to Africa convinced Tehran that low-risk spectacular operations could be conducted on short notice, primarily in East Africa. After Turabi was informed of this impression of Africa, he convened the secret meeting of the leaders of Sunni terrorism at his home in al-Manshiyah, Khartoum, and the participants resolved to reverse the current sorry state of the Islamist movement by launching an invigorated assault on the West and its allied regimes in the Muslim world.

The advisability of launching operations in East Africa was addressed at the meeting in the context of what Turabi saw as a mounting international conspiracy against Sudan. This was a topic he dwelt on for a long time. Turabi noted that there was a growing threat to the Islamist trend because of an emerging coalition of enemies of Islam "among the countries of the West, the secular Arab governments, and the collaborating African nations." The latter countries were becoming more important because the

West was adamant about securing the collapse of Islamic Sudan—the pioneering experiment in implementing Islam and a source of inspiration to Muslims worldwide. Therefore the plot hatched against Sudan was actually a plot against the entire Islamist trend. Turabi then stressed "the necessity to unite the efforts of Islamists faithful to Jihad and . . . the joining together of all efforts to defend Islam in Sudan." He declared a formal jihad against those who plotted directly against the Sudanese Islamic Party—both Sudanese opposition forces and the African states supporting them.

The conference also decided to take several concrete steps to expedite the launch of this jihad campaign. First priority was given to expansion and revitalization of the training camps for Arab "Afghans." Muslim youth from several countries would be sent to these camps so that they would be influenced by the spirit of commitment of the "Afghans." Bin Laden and Zawahiri agreed to oversee the management and funding of these camps. Most of the funds would be laundered through Europe. Confidants of Turabi were assigned key roles in the new effort. Ibrahim al-Sanusi was charged with supervising the camps on behalf of Turabi, and Ghazi Salah-al-Din was made responsible for local funds and other services. Meanwhile Nafi Ali Nafi was instructed to develop a comprehensive operational plan for the Eritrean jihad aimed at ultimately overthrowing the Afwerki government.

But the Islamist terrorist system was rattled by the ramifications of a major security breach. In mid-May 1997 Saudi security authorities arrested Sidi Tayyib, a businessman married to a relative of bin Laden. Tayyib provided the Saudi interrogators with material about bin Laden's bank accounts and businesses in Pakistan and Afghanistan and the smuggling of money from there to Islamist communities in London, Brooklyn, Jersey City (New Jersey), and Detroit. Tayyib also provided names of several individuals involved in laundering and moving money for bin Laden. Although imprecise and of varying quality, this list enabled the FBI and British intelligence to launch several investigations overseas. One of the more effective investigations took place in Nairobi, where Tayyib's information could be checked against material extracted from captured Islamists in Egypt to provide valuable leads to the local operational terrorist cells.

Also in mid-May Abdallah Mohammad Fazil, a senior member of the network who would play a central role in the bombing of the U.S. Embassy in Nairobi in August 1998, wrote a status report to bin Laden and the Islamist leadership. (Kenyan security forces recovered this report in August 1997 from the hard drive of a computer in Wadih El Hage's house in Nairobi and shared it with the FBI.) Fazil wrote that he was worried about the safety of the network because of intensified security operations. The Islamist networks in East Africa "should know that there is American-Kenyan-Egyptian intelligence activity in Nairobi aiming to identify the names and residences of the members who are associated with the Sheik [bin Laden] since America knows well that the youth who lived in Somalia and were members of the Sheik's cell are the ones who killed Americans in Somalia." Not by accident, counterintelligence activities were centered in Nairobi. "They know that since Kenya was the main gateway for those members, there must be a center in Kenya," Fazil noted. "We are really in danger."

Fazil stressed that these counterintelligence operations were triggered by the acquisition of firsthand intelligence. Analyzing the security operations in Nairobi, he concluded that "an important man with close links" to bin Laden must have "fallen into the enemy's hands." On the basis of this information, "The American forces carry [out] kidnapping operations against anyone who threatens its national security and its citizens." Fazil warned, "Cell members in East Africa are in great danger" and the "security position of the [Nairobi] cell is at 100 percent danger." This danger left the Nairobi network "no choice but to think and work hard to foil the enemy's plans which is working day and night to catch one of us or to gather more information about any of us." Fazil concluded with a warning for the entire Islamist network in East Africa. "My recommendation to my brothers in East Africa was to not be complacent regarding security matters and that they should know that now they have become America's primary target." Still, Fazil assured his superiors that the East African networks remained dedicated and committed to furthering the Islamist struggle against their enemies.

Fazil's dire assessment had an impact on the Islamist leadership. In August 1997 Turabi, bin Laden, and Abdul-Majid al-Zandani, the Yemeni Islamist leader, conferred in Khartoum and resolved to launch a "true war of Jihad" against Israel, Egypt, and Saudi Arabia as well as to protect Sudan against U.S.-inspired conspiracies and assaults. According to Turabi and Sudanese intelligence, these plots were being hatched in several East African states, in particular Uganda, Kenya, and Tanzania. Bin Laden, Zawahiri, and Zandani believed that a new strategy should be formulated for their jihadist struggle in order to rejuvenate the Islamist trend, to "return them to the forefront after their recent period of eclipse and reunite their ranks." The conferees identified only two sacred causes that could rejuvenate the Islamists: a jihad for the liberation of Palestine or a jihad to support the Islamist Sudanese state and preserve the Islamic model by challenging the United States. The Islamists were convinced that the United States was adamant about overthrowing the Turabi government. The intensifying security and counterintelligence operations in East Africa, highlighted by Fazil, served as a confirmation of the Islamists' analysis.

After examining the overall situation in the Middle East, the conferees decided to elect "Sudanese Jihad" as their rallying cry. This choice also made sense given the readily available Islamist infrastructure throughout the country. Turabi announced that Khartoum was prepared to provide all types of patronage and support. Tehran endorsed the idea, ensuring that additional cadres of the IRGC would be ready in the various training camps by the time the reinforcements of Arab "Afghans" began arriving in Sudan. Another group of Iranian military experts arrived in Khartoum to assist in the preparation and formulation of the new jihad strategy. Tehran also arranged for the timely delivery of cargos of Iranian and Chinese weapons to Port Sudan and Khartoum by sea and air.

These new measures reflected Turabi's mood. In fall 1997 he was convinced that Sudan and the Islamists faced a major conspiracy. A knowledgeable Arab source explained that "it has become clear that the American plan in Africa is aimed at establishing an American belt to succeed the Islamic belt . . . which al-Turabi is preparing [for] in cooperation with Iran. This presumes getting rid of the present Sudanese regime, along with what that means in terms of dealing a major blow to Iran and its plans 'to export the revolution' to Africa."

Initial reconnaissance of potential targets and planning for spectacular strikes began almost immediately under the overall guidance of Abu-Hafs. For example, in late October 1997 Hosni Abu Nimreh, a Palestinian originally from the West Bank, and Mustafa Mahmud Said Ahmad surveyed and took pictures of the U.S. and Israeli embassies in Nairobi. Nimreh even made general plans to destroy the U.S. Embassy with powerful bombs in an attack involving three vehicles. The Israeli embassy would be destroyed by a powerful shaped charge installed in a room at the nearby Fairview Hotel. By this time, however, Said Ahmad was having second thoughts about his future as a militant Islamist. He approached the U.S. Embassy with information about Nimreh's plans but was rejected and ignored. Ahmad left for Zaire and later moved to Tanzania, where he was arrested in the aftermath of the August bombs. There is no indication the Islamists were even aware of this security breach, much less affected by it.

East Africa, however, was not treated as a primary target in the complex, critical terrorist conferences conducted by Iran during 1997. Priority was still given to spectacular operations at the World Cup matches scheduled for France in summer 1998. During sessions devoted to organizing elite terrorist strike forces, many potential objectives were discussed, from Argentina to the Philippines, but not Africa. At this stage, East Africa was a priority of Turabi's Sudan and the Sunni Islamists. Iran recognized Africa's importance but felt no urgency to strike out.

Africa returned to the list of priority targets as a result of the crisis between the United States and Iraq. In early February 1998 Iran and Iraq
reached their agreement on cooperation in intelligence and terrorism issues.
To expedite its implementation, Tehran and Baghdad resolved to examine
operations in areas where they already cooperated successfully. Both Iran
and Iraq maintain large intelligence and special forces resources in Sudan—
assets that had already cooperated in fighting in southern Sudan and Somalia and could be used for operations in East Africa.

In spring 1998, with the unfolding of the Abu-Umar al-Amriki incident
and after consultations with both Zawahiri and bin Laden, Turabi felt certain that the "negotiations" with the United States were genuine. The ensuing initiative for a rapprochement by President Mubarak reinforced
Turabi's conviction. As these dynamics continued to evolve, Turabi became
increasingly convinced that the time was uniquely ripe for striking out in
East Africa, because there was no longer a threat from Egypt—either of a
direct Egyptian intervention or the chance that Mubarak would permit the
United States to use bases in Egypt against Sudan.

The overall principles for future spectacular Islamist terrorist opera-
tions had been determined in the meeting on February 15, 1998, when the
new Sunni umbrella organization, the World Islamic Front for Jihad against
Jews and Crusaders, was established to present a deniable cover for Iran.
The meeting participants had also decided on modalities for training and
supporting the Islamist strike units through the IRGC. Back in 1992–93
Safavi, the commander in chief of the IRGC, and Turabi's deputy Ali
Uthman Taha had been directly in charge of the operations in Somalia and
worked closely with both Zawahiri and bin Laden. In summer 1998 these
networks would conduct the bombings in East Africa.

With operations in Africa contemplated, the Islamists moved quickly to
develop alternate capabilities. In early 1998 they established a new forward
headquarters near Sana, Yemen. Bin Laden himself was reportedly sighted
in Sana at that time. The Islamist forward facilities in Sana were protected
by Abdul-Majid al-Zandani, the spiritual leader of the Islamists in Yemen.
Soon afterward Odeh was activated. At the time he was operating out of
Mombasa, running two operatives in Nairobi. The operatives were known
as Khalid Salim (from Yemen, whose real name is Mohammad Rashid
Daoud al-Owhali) and Abdallah Nacha (from Lebanon). As a cover story
Odeh claimed to be a Mombasa-based fisherman, and Owhali and Nacha
were his two subcontractors in Nairobi who sold the fish to city hotels and
restaurants. This story gave them a reason for traveling around the city and
doing reconnaissance. In early 1998 they began to seriously study potential
objectives, including the U.S. and Israeli embassies. Concurrently the core

of the Islamist network in Tanzania, then under the command of Mustafa Muhammad Fadhil, an Egyptian in his early twenties, was also activated. The initial operational plans were ready in March. The plans included a general estimate of the strength of the buildings and sketch maps of the areas surrounding the key objectives; the maps included all roads around the area that would provide easy access, effective points of bomb detonation, and escape routes. The U.S. Embassy topped the list of potential targets. Also in March an Egyptian Islamist (who has a genuine U.S. passport) arrived for a meeting with bin Laden. He traveled via Pakistan, where he had met ISI senior officers. This Egyptian was given specific management and supervision tasks in connection with the forthcoming terrorist operations. The successful completion of these initial steps prompted Tehran to reexamine the terrorism plans.

At the same time Owhali was sent to Pakistan and Afghanistan for intense training pending the possible operation in Nairobi. Owhali was trained in a number of camps in Afghanistan on such subjects as handling explosives, making bombs, hijacking, and kidnapping. He was identified as a potential recruit for martyrdom operations and groomed accordingly. Thus although Owhali was relatively junior and in essence expendable, he was permitted to attend conferences and meetings at which bin Laden spoke. For example, he was present at the press conference bin Laden held in Khowst in May 1998. Owhali was duly impressed by bin Laden's fatwas calling for a relentless jihad against the United States.

In April 1998 Khamenei ordered the Iranian minister of intelligence, Qorban Ali Dari Najafabadi, and Muhsin Rafiq-Dust, former commander of the IRGC and now in charge of Iran's Foundation of the Oppressed, a major financial instrument used for both economic and intelligence/ terrorism, to prepare for the launching of the international terrorism campaign. Najafabadi then called a clandestine meeting at the security and intelligence building in Daraj, Iran. Najafabadi instructed that all Iranian installations—the Islamic centers, Iranian embassies, the study and information centers, trade and tourism corporations, and the cultural centers of the Iranian cultural attaché offices—conduct surveys of suitable conditions for resumption of terrorism and prepare to be used as cover for any clandestine operation. Special case officers were nominated for various parts of the world, including Africa.

The Nairobi network in Kenya and the Dar-es-Salaam network in Tanzania began to coordinate their activities. Toward this end, Fadhil traveled to Kenya in April for a meeting with Odeh. They discussed the implications of the recently published fatwas as well as specific operational and organizational issues related to the anticipated operations.

In May 1998 operations in East Africa were featured as the primary fallback contingency plans to Islamist operations in Western Europe and Latin America. Fallback operations are usually kept in reserve in case the primary planned operation has to be aborted for whatever reason while there is an imperative to strike out at a certain time. Once a proposed operation is adopted as a fallback contingency plan, every effort is made to swiftly ready the forces and assets involved for a quick activation should the need arise. In spring 1998 the Islamists and their sponsoring states were committed to a "string of operations" that would demonstrate both the extent of their commitment to the jihad and the breadth of their reach throughout the world. Zawahiri assumed direct command over these activities throughout the world, an indication of their growing importance. A rough draft of a comprehensive operational plan prepared by Abu-Hafs and his team was studied by several leaders of the World Islamic Front for Jihad against Jews and Crusaders in a series of meetings held in bin Laden's encampment in Afghanistan. In addition to bin Laden and Zawahiri, the participants included Sheikh Abdallah Abu-al-Faruq; Ibrahim Fahmi Taha (from the Egyptian al-Jamaah al-Islamiyah); and senior commanders of the Egyptian al-Jihad, the Jordanian Army of Muhammad, the Kashmiri Harakat ul-Ansar, al-Muhajiroun from the United Kingdom, and the Partisans of the Sharia. The May meetings also produced a policy for claiming—although denying—all future operations. The claims, to be made by "new" entities, would be coordinated by Yasir Sirri through the London-based Islamic Information Observatory Center. Yasir Sirri now formally commands the Vanguards of Conquest, one of Zawahiri's "entities" for international operations such as Somalia. Further explanation of and justification for the planned spectacular terrorist operations would be provided by various European-based Islamist groups and organizations that could legitimately claim no contact with the perpetrators of terrorism.

With the basic operational plans ready, bin Laden and Zawahiri traveled to Khartoum for intense consultations with Turabi on the strategy and modalities for implementation. In mid-May, Turabi oversaw two concurrent events to expedite the plans for the strikes in East Africa.

First, a high-level strategy-formulating session in Khartoum was conducted, as usual at Turabi's home in al-Manshiyah, Khartoum. Because of bin Laden's growing notoriety, these meetings were conducted in great secrecy, and only the small group of Turabi's inner circle attended. On the first night Turabi, bin Laden, and Zawahiri discussed the mounting threats to Islamist Sudan and agreed on the urgent need to deter the United States from closing in by inflicting punishment—much the same logic used in Somalia in fall 1993. The next morning they were joined by Sheikh Qassim (Abdul-Majid al-Zandani's emissary) and Abu-Jafir (the HizbAllah's representative to Khartoum). Two major items were on the agenda: (1) strike operations against U.S. targets in East Africa and (2) revival of the strike operations in Latin America (operations that were canceled by Tehran back in January because the strike teams were not ready; they remained a high priority for Tehran). After two days of consultations the HizbAllah promised to provide on-site support and intelligence. Should the need arise, the HizbAllah would also deploy Palestinian operatives of Islamic Jihad and HAMAS to give the strikes anti-Israel coloration. Meanwhile a forward headquarters and logistical springboard would be established in Yemen for the African operations since Yemen provided quick, easy transportation of goods and people. On the last night Turabi, bin Laden, and Zawahiri met alone once again. They went over the entire strategy for resumption of the jihad in East Africa, including its benefits and risks. According to a knowledgeable Arab source, they decided "to execute a pre-prepared plan to escalate action against American targets in the world, especially in Africa." Other sources concur that by the time this nocturnal meeting was over, they had resolved to strike out.

Second, Turabi convened and chaired a major terrorist conference in Khartoum in mid-May. Because of security considerations bin Laden did not attend the open sessions. The participants reiterated the standing jihadist policy to rally to the defense of Islamist Sudan by repelling all foreign threats. They surveyed the progress made in expanding the training camps and in upgrading and energizing the Eritrean Jihad and the God's Army organizations in Uganda so that they could take on the Eritrean and Ugandan governments respectively. To expedite the movement of Arab "Afghans," Turabi instructed his deputy, Ibrahim al-Sanusi, to provide the commanders and other expert terrorists with Sudanese diplomatic passports. The conference then drew up a series of contingency plans and lists of operational requirements that included "a coherent plan for hitting U.S. interests in the Middle East and Africa" as a high priority. Other plans—ranging from the assassination of Sudanese opposition leaders to the training of a new Islamist army to fight the rebellion in southern Sudan—were also discussed. In quieter sessions Zawahiri and Mustafa Hamza secured the general support and commitment of various groups throughout Africa.

But in late May 1998 all Tehran's plans for a new wave of spectacular terrorism in the West came to a halt. Security authorities in Western Europe learned about the nearly completed preparations for the strike during the World Cup games. Hassan Hattab, also known as Abu-Hamza, an Algerian Armed Islamic Group operative running one of the support networks, was arrested in Belgium. Within days a support network that extended throughout Western Europe was rolled over, and most of its members were arrested. Although this crackdown failed to arrest any of the senior commanders or the expert terrorist operatives, it effectively destroyed all the preparations in Europe.

It became imperative to reexamine all other contingency plans from both security and viability points of view. Representatives of the sponsoring states and senior Islamist commanders met in late May near Peshawar, Pakistan. They surveyed the status of preparations for numerous operations and decided which of them could be implemented and when. The meeting also nominated a group of senior Islamist commanders—predominantly Egyptian "Afghans"—who would closely study and refine outstanding terrorism contingency plans pending implementation. Final approval would be given by the sponsoring states on the eve of the planned launch.

Meanwhile, to justify the presence of so many Islamist leaders in Peshawar, bin Laden and Zawahiri called a press conference to discuss their latest statements. In the press conference Osama bin Laden delivered an opening speech in which he stressed the gravity of the current threat to Islam and the justification for the jihad he was calling for:

> At present, we have got into trouble, which is very dangerous and unfortunate. By this trouble, I mean the presence of Christian forces in Arab lands. They are constantly trying to establish their full control in this region. This is the first time since the annunciation of the Holy Prophet Muhammad, peace be upon him, that our sacred places, including the Kaaba [in Mecca], the Nabavi Mosque [in Medina], and the Aqsa Mosque [in Jerusalem] are under the open and covert control of non-Muslims. It has become obligatory for Muslims throughout the entire world to start their struggle to oust the infidels from our sacred places. Mecca is the place where God sent divine revelation to the Prophet Muhammad, peace be upon him. There has never been such an unfortunate time in Kaaba as there is now. It has been surrounded on all four sides by US forces.

Bin Laden announced that numerous Muslim scholars had already "issued a Fatwa for a Jihad against these forces that have dared to occupy our sacred places. The Holy Prophet, peace be upon him, said that infidels should be ousted from the Arab lands. . . . It is very unfortunate to have Christians and Jews present in such sacred places." He noted that the Saudi scholars among them had since been arrested by Riyadh. Bin Laden emphasized that the essence of this fatwa was that "Muslims should sacrifice their lives and resources to expel the infidels from Mecca. We pray to God that he may provide courage to Muslims to rise for a Jihad. The United States is helping the infidels and the Christians and Jews have established control over one third of the Muslim nation, something which we aim to halt." He pointed to the mujahideen's triumph in Afghanistan as a proof that Islam can take on a superpower and win.

Bin Laden concluded with a milestone decree legitimizing the conduct of a global jihad irrespective of whether local forces were governments or Islamist movements. "I announce that geographical boundaries have no importance for us. We are Muslims and wish to be martyred. We have no discrimination on the basis of color and race. We support every oppressed Muslim and we pray to God to provide us with help and to enable us to help every oppressed Muslim," he declared. In a subsequent conversation with Islamists present, bin Laden used this argument to justify supporting the jihad in Kashmir against India; that is, Pakistan's war by proxy. Not only were the Muslims of Kashmir under duress, but "the alliance between India and Israel was a big threat to the Muslim world." All concerned Muslims both in Pakistan and throughout the world must unite and help "the brotherly Islamic country of Pakistan to examine the situation and give a stern reply to India one way or the other." Bin Laden singled out the Islamist support for Pakistan as a manifestation of his commitment to a worldwide jihad. "We will provide every possible help to the Mujahideen in Pakistan. Not only in Pakistan, but wherever Mujahideen are fighting against the enemies of Islam, we will help them. We will support Pakistan in its war against India."

Discussing the situation of the Islamist jihad in Saudi Arabia, bin Laden alluded to the logic behind the forthcoming strike in East Africa. Bin Laden explained that "the Jihad has already started in a practical form. In Saudi Arabia, modern arms are used against the Americans. The first incident took place in Riyadh and the second in Al-Khobar. In these bomb blasts, 19 Americans were killed and more than one hundred wounded. With every passing day, resistance to the United States is increasing and young men are being recruited against the United States. That is why the United States had to decide to reduce its forces in Saudi Arabia." However, despite these early successes there had also been setbacks, in particular one in the Mecca area. Back in March 1998, bin Laden noted, "the Saudi government confiscated a sizeable quantity of arms used by our Mujahideen, including seven rockets and Stinger missiles. The Americans were shocked to see the type and size of the arms. They wondered what would have happened if those arms had been used against them. Fear of the Mujahideen has overtaken the Americans and they are being defeated by the Mujahideen everywhere." He added that some 820 Islamists were arrested in the dragnet that followed in the Mecca area. These weapons were intended for use against American combat aircraft operating out of Saudi bases against Iraq. Bin Laden assured those attending that there were many other weapons already stockpiled in Saudi Arabia so that although this setback thwarted a single operation, it was now impossible to reverse the ascent of the jihad in Saudi Arabia.

At the same time, bin Laden conceded, security operations, such as the dragnet in Saudi Arabia, required bolder responses. "The United States is plundering our resources and wandering about our sacred places. It may do anything it wants but it can never harm us because God is with us," he declared. This did not mean the Islamists must confront their enemies head-on, where they might suffer setbacks. Bin Laden explained that just as the Islamists "have inflicted considerable damage on the United States in different places [they] will continue to do the same in the future." In this context bin Laden returned to his overall theme that the key to liberating Islamdom was the defeat of the United States and Israel. "We have focused our attention on Israel and the United States. First we want to expel them, after which a Muslim state will be established and those who are forcefully ruling the people will be given severe punishments," he said. Toward this end, bin Laden pushed for the establishment of the Islamic Front. "By the grace of God, we have established an organization named 'Islamic Front' with the help and suggestion of a lot of Jihadi organizations. The purpose of this organization is to fight against the Americans and Israelis. An important leader of this organization is Dr. Ayman al-Zawahiri. We are receiving assurances of support from many Mujahid organizations. Everything is occurring exactly according to our expectations." Bin Laden repeatedly stressed that the Islamist resurgence and organization were aimed at delivering practical results. When a reporter wondered out loud how the Front could take on the United States, bin Laden quipped that America would see his latest threats come true "in a few weeks."

Given the advanced state of the networks in East Africa, the operations planned for there were now adopted as the primary contingencies. And so an operational conference was convened in the first half of June to reexamine the specifics of the operational plans and the on-site capabilities. This conference took place in the governorate of Abyan, Yemen. Bin Laden and several senior commanders attended the meeting. In addition to thoroughly studying the operational plans, the attendees also approved the publication of an eight-page statement outlining the objectives of the World Islamic Front, explaining once again why the organization had been formed, stressing the need for urgent action, and repeating the threats to the United States and Israel. The significance of this document lies not in its contents, which are basically a lengthy repetition of past fatwas and other statements, but in its mere existence. By issuing a document of such theological importance the Islamist leaders revealed the overall importance of the conference without disclosing the crucial operational planning that actually took place in Yemen.

To address the latest doctrinal and theological developments and issue a declaratory statement, bin Laden convened an international conference in Qandahar, Afghanistan, on June 24, 1998. About 100 Islamists participated, including representatives from most Arab states and organizations; several Afghans and Pakistanis; and a few representatives from Chechnya, Bosnia, Somalia, and Yemen. A senior member of al-Muhajiroun from London also attended. Bin Laden and Zawahiri chaired the conference and delivered the key addresses. The deliberations on the future jihad continued for a day and a night straight. At the end of the formal conference, and with a few private consultations on the side, bin Laden and Zawahiri announced "a plan of action for all the members of the World Islamic Front," which was then accepted unanimously.

By now Tehran was getting ready for the forthcoming East Africa operations. During the first half of July the Iranian "diplomats" conducted a thorough independent assessment of the situation in both Kenya and Tanzania to make sure that the local networks could conduct the operations and the local communities could endure the inevitable anti-Muslim backlash. Once satisfied with the overall likelihood of success, Tehran began evacuating its senior terrorism-related "diplomats." Kazem Tabatabai, the ambassador to Kenya, was recalled to Tehran on July 15 for two months of urgent consultations. He left Nairobi on July 18. On July 25 Ahmad Dargahi, Iran's "cultural attaché," also left Nairobi for Tehran. At about the same time Mohammad-Javad Taskhiri, the Iranian "cultural attaché" in Tanzania, left Dar-es-Salaam for consultations in Tehran.

By late July all the preparations for the operations were in place. If the sponsoring states, in particular the terrorist leaders, needed any proof of U.S. duplicity and anti-Islamist venom to warrant issuing the final go-ahead, Washington seemed eager to provide it.

In mid-June the United States, along with the security authorities of several countries in the Balkans—including Albania, the former Yugoslav republic of Macedonia, and Bulgaria—launched a major operation against Egyptian Islamist networks concealed within the various locally active Islamist charities. The suspects were arrested by the local police and security forces and handed over to the American authorities, who in turn handed them over to the Egyptian authorities—where they would meet with certain torture, long imprisonment, and possibly death. Some of these "extraditions" were conducted with questionable, summary legal procedures.

The first round in this campaign was extremely offensive to Zawahiri and his colleagues. Isam Abdul-Tawwab Abdul-Alim, a veteran Egyptian terrorist, was arrested in Sofia, Bulgaria, by a team of Bulgarian and American security officials. At the time of his arrest he was living in Sofia—legally—with his Albanian wife and children, taking care of both Islamist charities and some of Zawahiri's headquarters facilities. These facilities had been dormant since the "deal" with Abu-Umar al-Amriki. According to Islamist sources, Isam Abdul-Tawwab Abdul-Alim was taken by the Bulgarians to an isolated detention site, where "he was kept for two days during which he was subjected to investigations by the Bulgarian police and American intelligence elements." He was then "repatriated to Egypt under American auspices" without any legal procedure taking place in Bulgaria. Because all Bosnian-related Islamist terrorist activities had been closed down since early 1998, after the Abu-Umar al-Amriki "deal" with the Clinton administration, the Islamist leadership was baffled and enraged by this arrest and extradition.

Then in late June the Albanian National Intelligence Agency (ShIK) arrested four Egyptian charity workers in Tirana on suspicion that they were Islamist terrorists. At the time the workers and their organization—Renaissance of the Islamic Heritage—had been legally active in Tirana for about a year. Albanian security sources readily admitted that the four were "arrested following information given to the Albanian authorities by U.S. intelligence sources." In the absence of any legal cause for holding them, two of the Egyptians were immediately released. Albanian police claimed it had recovered assault rifles and ammunition in the apartment of the other two Egyptians, Magid Mustafa and Muhammad Houda, and, because of their adamant denials, put them under house arrest pending further legal procedures. These two Egyptians were "kidnapped [on Thursday, July 2,] midday in their apartment in the center of town by four masked and armed persons who took them away in an armor-plated vehicle," Artan Bizhga, the Albanian interior ministry spokesman, lamely explained. Albanian ShIK sources later acknowledged that the two Egyptians were handed over to the U.S. authorities, who handed them over to the Egyptians.

On July 16 another Egyptian Islamist, Muhammad Hassan Mahmoud, the director of the Islamic Revival Foundation, was arrested in Tirana and sent swiftly on his way to Egypt. Official Tirana presented these arrests as the beginning of a new relationship and cooperation with the U.S. government—specifically, the CIA and the FBI. Albanian ShIK authorities stressed that "the Islamists' arrest operations in both cases have been aided by the authorities of the Federal Bureau of Investigation (FBI), which had taken permission from the Albanian authorities earlier." The handing over of the Egyptians was termed "expulsion," and Tirana justified it as being pursuant to Washington's assurances. "Albania arrested and expelled the three

Egyptian suspected terrorists in an operation in which the Albanian secret service ShIK cooperated with the CIA," a senior police official explained in mid-August. A few days later a senior official of the Interior Ministry acknowledged that he knew nothing about "the extradition of three Egyptians" because they had been "taken over by the CIA" on the basis of advance arrangements with Albanian police and the ShIK.

In early August, once the story broke and criticism was leveled at the Albanian authorities about the fuzzy legal procedures leading to the extraditions, Tirana scrambled to come up with explanations. "Through Albania, these Islamic terrorists have managed to carry out some illicit profit-making activities, from arms trafficking to money laundering," police officials reasoned. "In fact, in Albania, the Islamic terrorists have found a place where they can make more of a profit. Under the guise of religion, or as charitable humanitarian associations, they continue to live in Albania and engage in criminal economic activities to make money to finance their organizations operating in other states. This was the case with some other Islamic terrorists who were arrested and extradited from Albania to the United States by the CIA and FBI." But these Egyptians did not make it to the United States. Because they operated against the Egyptian government in Egypt, they cannot even be indicted in the United States, and so there is no legal reason for their extradition to the United States. The United States simply handed them over to the Egyptian authorities in a procedure the legality of which remains vague and unexplained.

For Zawahiri and the Islamist leadership this was a flagrant violation of the deal they were convinced they had made with Washington through the good services of Abu-Umar al-Amriki. For their part, the Islamists had curtailed the Bosnian operations planned for spring 1998, in effect compelling the Bosnian Muslims to call off the major offensive they were planning. The outbreak of major fighting in the Balkans, initiated by the forces Washington favored, supported, and equipped, would have had a calamitous effect on U.S. policies. The Islamists now expected Washington to live up to its part of the "deal."

The United States has said that it does not negotiate or "make deals" with terrorists, implying that the Abu-Umar al-Amriki incident has no foundations in reality. But back in late 1997 and again in early 1998, when prompted by the highest levels of several governments—including those of Egypt and the United Kingdom—to clarify the persistent rumors about the Abu-Umar al-Amriki "deal," the Clinton administration did not deny those rumors outright. If the Clinton administration's vague but adamant denials about the "deal" are true, the White House most likely found it expedient to keep the Abu-Umar al-Amriki issue alive at the time. With the threat of a new Bosnian war and the collapse of U.S. policy looming, someone in Washington thought it wouldn't hurt to create the impression that a deal was there and contain the Islamists, saving the Clinton administration's Balkans policy.

But for friends and foes alike, especially in the conspiracy-driven world of Middle Eastern politics, Washington's refusal to issue a denial and its capitalization on the Islamists' inaction served as solid confirmation that the "deal" had been struck. President Mubarak was convinced this was so and refused to support the U.S. stand against Iraq in February 1998. Cairo has since made every effort to scuttle U.S. diplomatic initiatives in the Middle East. President Mubarak, and most other conservative Arab leaders, are now convinced that the United States would "trade" them for expedient interests—such as the "deal" with Zawahiri—and are not inclined to support U.S. interests. Sheikh Turabi, Khamenei, bin Laden, Zawahiri, and the rest of the terrorist elite are convinced that Abu-Umar al-Amriki was negotiating for the highest officials in Washington. For them there is no better proof of the effectiveness of spectacular terrorism on Washington. In fact, they reasoned, Washington was so apprehensive about the impact of spectacular terrorism on U.S. policy that it negotiated away such a close ally as Mubarak. Future spectacular terrorist operations, and even credible threats of such were bound to compel Washington to make concessions to the Islamists. The Islamist elite could not have a better incentive for escalating their campaign of terrorism.

Meanwhile shock and rage were sweeping the Islamist terrorist leadership over the crackdown in Albania and Bulgaria, which they interpreted as a brazen breach of the "deal" they had made with Washington. Once the pattern of the U.S.-sponsored and -overseen campaign to arrest Egyptian Islamist terrorists and extradite them to Egypt was established, the Islamist leadership issued a formal warning. On August 3 Islamist Egyptian activist Yasir Tawfiq Ali al-Sirri acknowledged the arrest in Albania of the three Egyptians—Majid Mustafa, Muhammad Huda, and Muhammad Hassan Mahmoud—and announced that they were "being detained at a police station in the Lazughli area of Cairo," where they were "being subjected to measures to force them to confess on their own behalf and on behalf of the others to something they did not commit." He also alluded to the arrest in Sofia, talking about four "victims." Sirri stressed that "elements belonging to the U.S. intelligence services participated in the arrest of the four and subjected them to interrogations in order to make the process of extraditing them to Egypt easier for the Albanian authorities." The Egyptian Islamists were now holding Washington responsible for the well-being of the four—the fourth being Ahmad Ibrahim al-Najjar, a senior commander.

Sirri recalled that the U.S. intelligence services had taken "similar action in the past, about two years ago, when they arrested Islamic Group spokesman Engineer Fuad Talat Qassim—who was living as a refugee in Denmark—while he was in Croatia on his way to Bosnia, and handed him over to Egypt." Qassim was one of Zawahiri's closest personal friends, and his 1995 extradition to Egypt had been a festering wound.

Zawahiri had to react to what was perceived as a unilateral American violation of a deal he had made. On August 5 the Islamic Jihad Group formally vowed to take revenge against the United States for sending their colleagues to arrest, torture, and possible execution in Egypt. Their communiqué stated that the Egyptian Islamists were told by the Albanian authorities they had been arrested on charges of terrorism. "The accusation leveled at our three brothers was participation in a group declaring Jihad against the United States and Israel and their trade, and cooperation with the Mujahideen in Kosovo outside U.S. influence." This accusation, even if true, contradicts the semi-official Albanian announcement that the Egyptians had been arrested for "some illicit profit-making activities, from arms trafficking to money laundering." The Islamists were furious, as their communiqué made clear: "We are interested in briefly telling the Americans that their message has been received and that the response, which we hope they will read carefully, is being [prepared], because we . . . will write it in the language that they understand," the Islamic Jihad Group concluded.

Immediately after the bombings in Nairobi and Dar-es-Salaam, the Partisans of the Sharia, a Sunni Islamist organization, connected the bombings with the extradition of their Egyptian comrades. The Partisans left no doubt where they stood on the bombings in East Africa. "We bless this operation," their communiqué read. "We openly announce that we rejoice in the misfortune of the Americans, the enemies of God." The communiqué stated that Cairo should now expect similar attacks for as long as they mistreated the Islamists. The East Africa bombings had shown that the United States would not be able to help Cairo. "No doubt that the Egyptian regime is shaking with fear, waiting for its sorrowful fate . . . after the attacks in Nairobi and Dar-es-Salaam," the statement read. "They know that their backward security system cannot compare with the sophisticated American system." The statement of the Partisans of the Sharia was signed by Abu-Hamzah al-Masri [the Egyptian], a code name for Mustafa Kamil, a close colleague of Zawahiri, Turabi, and bin Laden's.

The August 7 bombings in East Africa had been long planned and prepared for, however—long before the first arrests took place in Albania and Bulgaria. Zawahiri's and Hamzah's rhetoric notwithstanding, the attacks on the U.S. embassies were not revenge for Washington's duplicity as perceived by the now enraged Islamists. Their wrath over the ongoing suppression of their brethren in the Balkans will likely be expressed someday—in yet another round of spectacular terrorist operations.

THE EXTENT of the professionalism and capabilities displayed in the August 7 bombings can be deduced not only from the terrorists' ability to conduct such operations in two countries simultaneously but also from the fact that close to a ton of military-type high explosives was used in both operations. This large quantity of explosives was shipped from Pakistan to both Dar-es-Salaam and Mombasa, and from there the high explosives were driven to safe houses. The bombs were constructed at these safe houses and then moved to the middle of the two capitals. From a security point of view as well, this was a highly professional and compartmentalized operation. All the key participants used code names and noms de guerre. Odeh later disclosed that even he, a senior operative, did not know about the involvement of certain individuals in the operation until after the bombings, when they met on the Pakistan International Airline flight from Nairobi to Karachi, Pakistan. Not surprisingly, there had been no credible advance warning of either operation.

Final planning and preparations for the operation had begun in July. The chief planner of the Kenya operation, and perhaps also the Tanzania operation, was identified by Odeh as Ali Saleh, an Egyptian "Afghan" who was a veteran member of the Islamic Jihad and a close associate of Osama bin Laden's. Odeh was in Pakistan-Afghanistan at the time and, given his intimate knowledge of Kenya and Nairobi, must have been a party to the operational planning. Once these plans were ready, in mid-July, they were subjected to an on-site independent assessment by a high-level supervisor. This supervisor was the Egyptian Islamist with the American passport who had visited bin Laden back in March. Now, about two weeks before the bombing, he visited both Nairobi and Dar-es-Salaam. In both cities he inspected numerous potential objectives, including the U.S., Israeli, and Egyptian embassies. He also met some of the local commanders in order to assess their capabilities and readiness. Apparently the supervisor was satisfied with the state of affairs, because soon afterward the final preparations began. For example, Odeh arrived in Mombasa in late July and took a bus to Nairobi, and Mohammad Rashid Daoud al-Owhali, one of the martyrs-to-be in Nairobi, traveled from Lahore, Pakistan, to Nairobi, Kenya, on July 31. Other operatives arrived in Dar-es-Salaam at about the same time.

About then another significant development took place in London. In late July, about a week before the bombing, London-based Sheikh Rifai

Ahmad Taha (Abu-Yassir) issued an "important announcement" in the context of a brief interview with the journal *al-Murabitoun,* the organ of al-Jamaah al-Islamiyah. In three laconic sentences Taha denied that he or the Islamic Group was member of the World Islamic Front for Jihad against Jews and Crusaders organized by bin Laden back in late February. The message was highlighted on the Internet home page of *al-Murabitoun.* There was no crisis or disagreement between Taha and his close friends bin Laden and Zawahiri. The reason for this statement was the urgent need to "clean" Taha so that he and *al-Murabitoun* would be able to act as "spokesmen" and "organs" for the forthcoming operations in Nairobi and Dar-es-Salaam without being implicated.

The final green light for the operation was given on August 4 or 5. Odeh and Fadhil then coordinated the last operational details by phone, making sure that their respective car bombs would detonate simultaneously. From this point on, there was no going back.

The Nairobi operation was organized around and run by two separate networks totaling about a dozen terrorists. One network comprised the experts and supervisors; the other network comprised the actual perpetrators, including the martyrs-to-be. To ensure security there was no direct contact between the two networks.

Odeh, Owhali, and Nacha provided the support for the experts' network. Over the years Odeh had built close relations with Andreas Searty, a German born in Baghdad and the general manager of the Grand Regency Hotel in Nairobi. Odeh was a major supplier of fish for the hotel. In early August advance booking under one name was arranged through Searty's office for about five Middle Eastern individuals who stayed at the hotel between August 4 and 6. They checked out on the morning of August 7 and "vanished." Most likely, Odeh did not meet them.

The other network was concentrated in rooms A107 and B102 of the Hill Top Hotel off Accra Road, Nairobi, a cheap hotel frequented by youth from the Middle East. Three terrorists—a Palestinian, an Egyptian, and a Saudi Arabian—stayed in these rooms between August 3 and 7. Odeh joined them on August 4. They assembled parts of the bomb, most likely the activation mechanism and the fuses, while in these rooms. They then took the parts in an enclosed pickup truck to an outside location for the completion of the bomb, in particular the installation of the high explosives. Janitors who cleaned these rooms could not recall seeing tools, wires, chemicals, or any unusual containers in the rooms, testifying to the professionalism of the bombers, who knew how to conceal potentially incriminating evidence. A porter, David Kioko, recalled that he carried several heavy bags for the three men when they checked out on August 6. "They were just like any other guests," he told the Associated Press. "We cleaned their rooms every day, and they never tried to stop us from entering." Abdallah Mohammad Fazil, a senior member of the network, frequently visited the Hill Top Hotel and met with the members of the network. It is not clear where the two martyrs—Owhali and another still unidentified person—stayed during this time. Possibly they stayed with Fazil.

Fazil seems to have been the coordinator and contact man between the two networks. Fazil, now in his mid-twenties, is a native of the Comoro Islands off East Africa. A pious child prodigy, he received a scholarship for advanced Islamic studies in Sudan, where he was won over by radical Islamism and, in his own words, joined "military service" for Islam. He later visited Yemen and Afghanistan as well. Fazil lived in Nairobi for some time and in 1996 falsely obtained a Kenyan identity card with the name Haroon. During 1997 he traveled repeatedly between Khartoum, Karachi, and Nairobi, always paying cash. He also seemed to have a lot of cash that he used for medical and other expenses for his parents and in-laws.

Once the March decisions were made, Fazil arrived in Kenya from the Comoros and started the initial operational preparations. One of his first steps was to rent a villa near Nairobi for May through August. At least one other terrorist, most likely Owhali, moved into the villa. The high explosives were also moved and stored there. Once the terrorists at the Hill Top hotel finished constructing the bomb mechanism and fuses, they moved their material to the villa, and it was there that the bomb was ultimately built and the martyrs-to-be acquainted with it.

In the last few days before the strike all components of the operation conducted last-minute reconnaissance and observation of the U.S. Embassy. Only one of these forays was noted by the embassy guards. According to the Nairobi *Nation*, one of the embassy's Kenyan security guards "saw three Arab-looking men filming the U.S. Embassy for about twenty minutes, four days before the bombing. He alerted [U.S. Marine] guards at the embassy, but they brushed him off." The men were Odeh, Owhali, and Nacha. According to the guard, one of the three also "filmed the embassy using a micro-video camera at close range." Fazil also conducted his own observations of the embassy in the days before the attack. On August 4 he took one or two other terrorists for an inspection of the buildings and grounds, going over the routes they would have to take on the day of the attack. A few expert terrorists sent by Zawahiri and controlled by Abu-Hafs also inspected the embassy separately to provide bin Laden and his lieutenants with an independent assessment of the situation in Nairobi and the viability of the operational plan.

On the morning of August 7, 1998, at about 10:30 A.M. (local time), the terrorists approached the U.S. Embassy building in two cars. A command vehicle—a white Mitsubishi Pajero driven by Fazil—was followed by the yellow Mazda or Mitsubishi Canter pickup with Dubai license plates on which the bomb was loaded. Owhali was sitting next to the driver, and there was a third terrorist in the cabin. He later told his interrogators he had prepared to die in the bombing. It was to be "a martyrdom operation in which [he] did not expect to survive." At first the terrorists tried to place the car bomb against the front wall of the embassy. They approached the embassy's front gate, claiming to be carrying sandwiches for the cafeteria. They were refused entry by the U.S. Marines on guard and sent to the back entrance. The terrorists backed off without incident and drove around the building. The embassy's rear entrance is in a U-shaped enclosure with the Cooperative Bank and the Ufundi building. The terrorists tried to get past the gate and into the underground parking. The third terrorist got out of the pickup and argued with the embassy's local security guards, but they refused entry. With time running out—since the explosion was scheduled to take place concurrently with the one in Dar-es-Salaam—the terrorists attempted a tactical approach similar to the attack on the Egyptian Embassy in Islamabad in late 1996. The white car surged forward and a few terrorists jumped out, throwing at least one grenade and firing small arms at the embassy's unarmed guards. That action was taken to divert the guards' attention. Meanwhile the pickup truck's driver sat calmly for about five minutes, contemplating and praying. Finally the pickup's driver fired a handgun and Owhali threw a stun grenade. The pickup truck tried to break its way into the embassy, but apparently the driver lost control for a fraction of a second. Nevertheless, right on time the bomb inside the pickup exploded. A couple of the terrorists, then firing on the Kenyan guards, were killed by the explosion. Since Owhali, who survived the explosion, does not remember if either he or the driver activated the bomb's fuses, it must have been activated by remote control. Most likely this was done by Fazil from the white command vehicle.

The bomb that completely destroyed the Ufundi building and severely damaged the U.S. Embassy building was made of nearly 1,800 pounds of military high explosives (most likely TNT, even though traces of SEMTEX-H were also found on the scene). It was expertly built, with the high explosives molded and shaped to enhance the blast effect. Captain Rhyl Jones, a British Army engineer who has extensive experience with Irish Republican Army (IRA) bombs, was one of the first to arrive on the scene of the bombing in Nairobi. He stressed the professionalism of the bomb makers, noting that most of the blast went upward but was bounced back toward the embassy by the towering wall of the Cooperative House building, whose structure withstood the shock wave. "If the Cooperative building hadn't been there, there would have been a bigger space for the blast to dissipate," he said. "Had the bombers managed to gain entrance to the underground parking garage, it would have devastated the embassy building, killing most of the people inside it." Eliud Mbuthia, former head of the Kenyan police bomb squad, observed that the bomb must have been made of moldable high explosives such as SEMTEX-H. The charge was shaped to create a high-speed, high-temperature blast wave—"leaving in its wake mass destruction caused by the huge flames ignited." Mbuthia attributed most of the deaths, injuries, and destruction to the secondary effects of the explosion. "The direct effect," he said, "forces everything away with tremendous force and creates a vacuum. As the air is returning back to its place through the sucking effect, it pushes everything else again, causing great damage." The bomb structure and blast dynamics are characteristic of Iranian-sponsored terrorists and bomb makers.

Fazil and other expert terrorists stayed in Nairobi to clean up after the operation. They were to remove all traces that would identify the perpetrators and their sponsoring states. They did a good job, except that they did not realize Owhali had survived the blast and been picked up by the Kenyan security authorities in a hospital. Fazil and his colleagues stayed in Nairobi for about a week before leaving uneventfully. Fazil arrived in Moroni, Comoros, on an Air Madagascar flight on August 14. He already had a ticket for travel from Dubai to Karachi, which he would not use. He stayed with his family until August 22. They escorted him to the airport, unlike on previous trips, and he boarded a flight to Dubai. There he vanished. Fazil is known to have had numerous passports and identification documents beyond the Kenyan national identity card and a Pakistani passport that police found in his Comoros home.

IN CONTRAST to the networks operating in Nairobi, the terrorist network in Dar-es-Salaam operated tightly and has not yet been unraveled. Iran's long-term investment in the multitude of opposition movements—from separatist to Islamist—seems to have paid off. The terrorists were capable of relying on local assets even for such major activities as converting a refrigerator truck into a car bomb. The two remaining suspects still in the hands of the Tanzanian authorities further complicate the reconstruction of the operation. The key suspect is Mustafa Mahmoud Said Ahmad, an Egyptian with passports from Yemen, Congo, and Iraq. He was arrested in Arusha near the Kenyan border. Ahmad had warned the United States about a plot to bomb the U.S. Embassy in Kenya, a highly irregular act for a would-be terrorist bomber. "Mustafa Ahmad is either the mastermind behind the [Tanzania] bombing or is a key person in the bombing conspiracy," said Ali Ameir Mohamed, the Tanzanian home affairs minister. The other suspect is Rashid Saleh Hemed, a Tanzanian from Zanzibar, who was seen at several sites surrounding the embassy. He is also known as Said Ahmed and Saleh Aben Alahales. Police discovered traces of chemicals that could have been used to make the bomb in Saleh's home and car. The operation's funds had been transferred from the Middle East to an account in Saleh's name in the Saudi-financed Greenland Bank of Tanzania.

The main operational network, however, comprised about six terrorists, all of whom are either still at large or dead. The on-site commander was Mustafa Mohammad Fadhil, who was largely unknown to both Western and local security forces. The key members were Ahmad Khalfan Ghailani, a Tanzanian of Omani origin from Zanzibar; Khalfan Khamis Mohammad, also a Tanzanian of Arab origin from Zanzibar; Fahad Mohammad Ali Msalan, a Kenyan of Arab origin from Mombasa; Sheikh Ahmad Salim Sewedan, a Kenyan of Yemeni origin from Mombasa also known as Fahad; and one "Ahmad the German," an Egyptian who would be the suicide driver of the car bomb. This cell was activated in its operational structure in early June. Soon afterward Fadhil instructed Khamis Mohammad to rent a house in Ilala, a sprawling low-income neighborhood of Dar-es-Salaam about four miles southwest of the embassy along the road to the airport. This house would serve as the bomb factory.

The operational plan was audacious—to install a massive bomb inside a refrigerator truck that would penetrate the compound just behind the water truck serving the embassy. This plan presupposed that the truck would likely be waved into the embassy compound, allowing the explosion to cause greater destruction. The bomb was installed in a specially converted refrigerator installed on a two-ton Nissan Atlas truck. For security reasons the truck was purchased from Jaba Tanzania Ltd., a local firm that specializes in secondhand vehicles.

Evidence suggests that the truck was converted at the Tommy Spades Manufacturing Co. plant near Dar-es-Salaam. The plant includes a huge repair unit that specializes in large tank trucks. The nearby Tommy Spades factory builds large metal tanks for water, gasoline, and other liquids. The facility is equipped with modern machine tools imported from Germany and Italy and welding facilities capable of converting the truck. The embassy's water truck was also in the garage for repairs shortly before the explosion, so the conspirators had an opportunity to coordinate their activities with its crew. Sewedan and Ghailani, who are still suspects at large, visited Tommy Spades Manufacturing to inspect progress on the building of a gas cylinder that was part of the bomb. At the Tommy Spades factory, investigators found canisters of acetylene gas and other chemicals identical to those recovered from the large bomb crater. Even if the bomb was built in this shop, no conclusive evidence points to the origin of the high explosives used.

The bomb itself was constructed at the house in Ilala. Khamis Mohammad had rented the house and was later joined there by Msalan. Starting in late July, eyewitnesses reported, four "Arab-looking men" regularly visited it. These men came at night, driving a white Suzuki Samurai—the one that took part in the bombing. After the bomb was built, Ghailani transferred a Chinese-made mixer used to mix the chemicals of the explosives to the house of a relative in the Ubungo neighborhood of Dar-es-Salaam.

On August 7 the tanker truck carrying water pulled up in front of the embassy gate at about 10:35 A.M. Just as the tanker was slowing down, the Nissan Atlas refrigeration truck, which had a white or beige cab with a silver-colored cargo box on top, surged forward and parked at the side of the tanker truck. The Atlas exploded four or five minutes later. "Ahmad the German," the driver of the Atlas truck, remained in the cab and was killed. The explosion killed eleven people, all Africans, and injured seventy-two others. A lingering question is why the bomb exploded before the tanker truck got closer to the embassy building, to the usual water download point. With everybody but one person in the immediate vicinity presumed dead, it is not clear what transpired in these last few minutes. Witnesses described one or more guards approaching the truck for the standard security check. Beno Msimde of Ultimate Security Company, which provides the embassy guards, said that a guard with a bomb detector determined that "dangerous material" was under the hood of the tanker and went to open it. "That did it," said Msimde. "The bomb went off, killing the guard and the driver." The top half of the driver's body hit the embassy building, still clutching the steering wheel. The traces of explosives in the embassy's water tanker might have been a ruse to distract the attention of the embassy's guards. The tanker driver, named Ndange, was a longtime employee of the embassy and is not suspected as a martyr-terrorist. Another possibility is that the terrorists, with time running out but determined to blow up the bomb on time, decided not to wait for the truck to be cleared into the embassy and just activated the bomb.

All these theories indicate that a command vehicle from which the bomb was activated must have been on the scene. According to witnesses, a white Suzuki Samurai utility vehicle approached the embassy at high speed and pulled up alongside the water truck as it was backing into the embassy's driveway. Khamis Mohammad jumped out of the vehicle and took pictures of the wreckage after the bomb exploded. The utility vehicle then vanished. No definite wreckage of the utility vehicle was discovered, and so it might have pulled off immediately. Eyewitness reports also state that four Arabs were seen driving away from the general area of the embassy just before the explosion. They were seen changing vehicles, abandoning the Suzuki Samurai they had been using near the embassy.

These Arabs could have been the command cell that activated the bomb. The mysterious Suzuki Samurai, which was later found by the police, may provide a clue to the whereabouts of the assistant driver—the "turn boy," who turns the tanker's spigot on and off. He should have been riding in the water truck when it was blown up. But his remains have not been found, and his family has adamantly refused to assist in the investigation by providing DNA samples or coming to view the clothes and shoes recovered at the site of the explosion. Possibly the turn boy, after placing a trace of explosives in the tanker truck as a distraction, escaped at the last minute in the mysterious Samurai.

The bomb itself was made from several hundred pounds of military-type high explosives, such as TNT, reinforced with tanks of combustible acetylene gas and oxygen. The gas and oxygen created the secondary blast wave that caused most of the damage to the building. As with the Nairobi bomb, the structure of the Dar-es-Salaam bomb and the dynamics of the explosion are similar to those in other bombings by Iranian-sponsored terrorists.

The remaining principals of both operations—led by Odeh and Fadhil—vacated their respective scenes on the eve of the actual bombing. At the Nairobi airport Fadhil, Odeh, and other operatives caught PIA flight 746 to Karachi. (Odeh would later say that he rushed to the airport soon after the explosion, while Nairobi was still in shock.) At the airport, Odeh recalled, he was surprised to discover operatives he had not known to be involved in this operation. They all had forged passports and travel documents that should have been enough to get on the plane in Nairobi. Nobody expected any trouble from the ISI-controlled airport authorities in Pakistan. But on his arrival in Karachi, Odeh, who was traveling under his alias Muhammad Sadiq Howaida, was picked up by the airport authorities. The other six terrorists, all carrying passports of equal quality, were permitted entry without any problem. Exasperated, Odeh told the officials he was a terrorist returning to hiding in Afghanistan. He then tried to bribe the officials at the airport, thinking they were simply corrupt. Odeh, however, was a marked man—he had been identified by the CIA, which specifically asked the ISI for his capture. Islamabad had no choice. Refusing to address such a specific request from Washington would have served as legal proof of Islamabad's sponsorship of terrorism and would have put Pakistan on the State Department's Terrorism List, which would have meant severe sanctions.

According to Pakistani officials, for the next three days Odeh "was met by an experienced team of Afghan and Arab affairs experts from the ISI that had [a] long history of dealing with Afghan and Arab Mujahideen." The wording is important—"met," not "interrogated." Islamabad's official announcement was that Odeh "calmly and proudly claimed that he had provided technical, engineering, and logistical support for the August 7 truck bombing in Nairobi." There is no evidence Odeh told the Pakistanis anything. The "confessions" later provided by the Pakistani security authorities to the United States and leaked to the American media are the ISI's reports of what Odeh said. The material is a combination of truth and self-serving disinformation, such as blaming bin Laden for the assassination of his mentor Azzam back in 1989.

After his extradition to Nairobi, Odeh refused to corroborate the Pakistani material and did not admit his involvement in the bombing to U.S. interrogators. To date, U.S. officials have not been able to independently confirm the details attributed to Odeh in the Pakistani account of the interrogation. In New York, Odeh told his first lawyer that the Pakistanis coerced him into making the statements by depriving him of food, water, and sleep for three days. That may be an excuse, even though the ISI's interrogation techniques are notorious for their "efficiency." But there seems to be a grain of truth in Odeh's statement to his lawyer about one of his interrogators, who, in the lawyer's words, seemed to have taken "pity on him." "The guy said to him, we're going to use you—these confessions—to help us with the Americans on the nuclear sanctions," the lawyer quoted Odeh as telling him. By the time Odeh, a victim of Islamabad's convoluted policies, left Pakistan for Nairobi, he knew he would not be returning.

AS FOR THE 1996 bombing in Saudi Arabia, the very first claim of responsibility came from a locally based "organization" to ensure that the local networks and supporters received recognition for their contributions. Two claims were made almost simultaneously in London. First, a claim for the African Revolutionary Front was faxed to the London offices of *al-Quds al-Arabi*. Written in broken English, the statement explained that the two attacks "aimed to take revenge against the United States, which is responsible for starving African peoples by several means; it also interferes in private African affairs." The statement also warned that unless the United States stopped interfering in African affairs, the African Front would "destroy U.S. interests in Africa." A nearly identical statement, signed by the African Revolutionary League, was faxed to the London offices of *al-Sharq al-Awsat*, a Saudi-owned paper affiliated with the Salman-Nayif faction.

The Islamists waited a day before they started issuing their claims. First, a man speaking a non-Egyptian Arabic dialect called the Cairo offices of *al-Hayah,* most likely from a Persian Gulf State. He claimed the bombings in the name of the Liberation Army of the Islamic Sanctuaries. The caller alluded to the possibility that the Liberation Army was "a kind of a military wing" of bin Laden and Zawahiri's International Front. The caller explained that the Liberation Army of the Islamic Sanctuaries comprised "Islamic holy warriors [mujahideen] from all countries of the world and who belong to all Muslim people." In deciding on the operation, the Liberation Army was inspired by several Islamist scholars and ulema from Egypt and Saudi Arabia, including "the statements of the Sheikh and Mujahid Osama bin Laden." The caller sharply criticized unspecified Arab regimes for "obstructing the implementation of Sharia laws" and imposing instead "blasphemous laws" while under the protection of the United States. The Liberation Army demanded the "withdrawal of American and Western forces from the Muslim lands in general and from the Arabian peninsula in particular." The message ended with a call on Washington to end all forms of support to Israel and to stop "the stealing of Muslim fortunes, especially oil."

The next, more elaborate, statement was sent to a television station in Dubai in the name of the Islamic Army for the Liberation of Holy Places. The communiqué included three statements discussing details of the two bombing operations and a list of demands. "The Islamic Army for the Liberation of Holy Places announces responsibility for the Nairobi bombing under the name operation Holy Kaaba," the statement read. The Nairobi bombing was carried out by "two men from Mecca." The attack in Dar-es-Salaam was code-named "operation al-Aqsa Mosque," and it was carried out by "a man from Egypt who belongs to the Abdallah Azzam battalion," named after the hero of the Arab "Afghans."

The demands issued by the Islamic Army for the Liberation of Holy Places and their justification for the operations merit attention. The Islamic Army promised to escalate its campaign of anti-U.S. terrorism until the following demands were met: (1) "The withdrawal of U.S. and Western forces from Muslim countries in general and from the Arabian Peninsula in particular, including civilians; . . . (2) the lifting of the naval blockade imposed around the Arabian Peninsula and the withdrawal of warships from Islamic waters; . . . (3) the release of ulema and young Muslims detained in the United States, Israel, and in Saudi Arabia, and first and foremost Sheikh Omar Abdul Rahman and Sheikh Salman al-Udah; . . . (4) a halt to the expropriation of Muslim riches, in particular the oil wealth of the Arabian Peninsula and of Muslim countries; . . . (5) an end to all forms of U.S.

support to Israel; . . . (6) an end to the war of eradication being waged by the United States with the aid of governments in its pay, against young Muslims under the pretext of fighting terrorism; . . . and (7) an end to the campaigns of extermination conducted by the United States against certain Muslim nations in the guise of economic sanctions."

To further justify its jihad through bombings, the Islamic Army for the Liberation of Holy Places stressed its all-Islamic character. An all-out jihad against the United States could be fully justified because of the sanctioned and perpetrated "occupation of the holy places in the Arabian Peninsula where U.S. forces are close to the Al-Aqasa Mosque [in Jerusalem]." The Islamic Army stressed the inspiration it had derived from "fatwas from contemporary Muslim theologians including Sheikh Omar Abdul Rahman . . . and statements by Sheikh Osama bin Laden." The statement concluded with a vow to continue and escalate the jihad. "The Islamic Army for the Liberation of Holy Places announces its absolute determination to chase the American forces and pronounces its resolve to strike at American interests in all places until all its objectives are met," the statement concluded.

Bin Laden, Zawahiri, and the Islamist leadership had decided prior to the East African operations that the thorough elaboration and explanation of any future terrorist strikes would be carried out by ostensibly unrelated but "understanding" entities in the West. Key to this are the various miniresearch institutions in London, a convoluted myriad of entities launched by bin Laden back in 1994–96. On August 12 Rifai Ahmad Taha clarified both the general context of the operations and the London-based Islamic Group's position. High-level Egyptian Islamist sources close to Taha explained that "the Group will support the two operations, launch an attack on [that is, vehemently criticize] the United States, and explain the reasons that prompt Islamists to be hostile toward it, but it will not mention anything that would indicate that it is linked with the two bombings." This position set the tone for the analysis and explanations by the other Islamist leaders in the West.

The first major statement was issued by Adil Abdul-Majid, who runs the International Office for Defending the Egyptian People in London and is known to be very close to Zawahiri. Denying any firsthand knowledge of the bombings, Abdul-Majid nevertheless noted bin Laden's news conference in Afghanistan in May, in which he predicted that "Jihad against the United States has started and bombings against U.S. interests will be carried out in the next few weeks." Abdul-Majid said he could surmise that the operations in Nairobi and Dar-es-Salaam confirmed that "forces, which are moving in various countries, stand behind them and that there was a very high degree of consultations before they were implemented."

An article called "American Harvest of Blood," by Abdul-Bari Atwan, the editor of *al-Quds al-Arabi,* who is close to bin Laden, analyzed the ramifications of the East Africa bombings. "The suicide attacks launched against the two U.S. embassies in Nairobi and Dar-es-Salaam last Friday were the logical results of the unjust and demeaning policies which the United States has been pursuing in the Arab region and in the Islamic world. These policies help only to encourage extremism and to promote acts of violence and terrorism and to turn U.S. embassies and interests into eternal targets. The actions perpetrated by America's enemies, who are so numerous in the Arab homeland, stem from the present state of frustration at the two-faced American policies and the joint American-Israeli objective of inflicting the maximum possible degree of harm and humiliation on the Arabs and Muslims out of all the other nations in the world."

A litany of grievances followed, going back to World War II, with the main criticism, in Atwan's opinion, aimed at the U.S. "policy of [having bolstered] all dictatorial regimes, encouraged corruption and the corrupt, prevented the democratic tide from spreading to the region, and dedicated its intelligence apparatuses to safeguarding the rotten conditions prevalent in the Arab world, whereas in other countries it has speeded up the collapse of dictatorships, exposed corrupt and corrupting regimes, sided with re- form forces, and bolstered the process of democratic change." America's insistence on imposing its own puppets on the Muslim world in order to ex- pedite exploitation of oil and other riches—and not U.S.-Israeli relations— was at the core of the Islamist eruption, Atwan emphasized. These were profound issues that would not disappear soon, and the United States would be wise to brace itself for forthcoming rounds of terrorism:

The Nairobi and Dar-es-Salaam explosions are messages to the U.S. Ad- ministration and to all the regimes attached to it, enjoying its protection, and carrying out its designs. They are a clear message written in clear let- ters and containing clear features. They contain numerous warnings: Either change the unjust and demeaning policies pursued against the Arabs or there will be more explosions. The senders of this message know Washing- ton and its security apparatuses much better than anybody else. For they fought alongside them in Afghanistan and learned their experiences and methods, and now they are making them drink from the same chalice. . . .

In conclusion, we would like to say that America's enemies, most of whom are Arabs and Muslims, are now operating with sound timing, be- cause the U.S. Administration is paralyzed and unable to make any move because of the sex scandals surrounding it on all sides. So it is quite likely that the two recent explosions are merely the harbingers of further similar explosions or different explosions in other parts of the world, which is indeed regrettable, pushing the world back into the days of the law of the jungle and heralding the death of more innocent victims.

Different in kind, but of no less importance, were the messages issued by the London-based al-Muhajiroun Movement, led by Sheikh Omar Bakri. These communiqués are important because of their populist appeal and widespread distribution. The Movement was the first to directly tie the two bombing operations to bin Laden's Islamic Front. In a subsequent statement the Movement said, "The message that was sent confirms that the U.S. interests are not safe anywhere in the world. And that the Americans will be buried under the rubble as was the case in Nairobi and Dar-es-Salaam. The U.S. Army should know that it cannot continue to murder women and children and go unpunished."

On August 7, immediately after the first announcement, the Movement came out with a message under the headline "The International Islamic Front Pledges to Continue Struggling against the Enemy of Islam." This communiqué leaves no doubt about the Movement's position: "We, al-Muhajiroun, as much as we regret the innocent deaths among the civilians who are nothing to do with the U.S. embassies, declare that we endorse and applaud today's bombing of U.S. embassies in Dar-es-Salaam, Tanzania, and Nairobi, Kenya. This is because they are the embassies of the enemy of Islam and the Muslims, and the occupiers of Muslim Land, e.g. Saudi Arabia." The communiqué then endorsed the message that these two bombings were just the beginning of a new wave of Islamist terrorism. "Al-Muhajiroun salutes the message that has been sent—American interests are not safe anywhere in the world. The Mujahideen will seek out and obliterate them into rubble as happened today. Let the cowards in the USA army know that they will not always slaughter women and children and go unaccounted. The day is approaching when the dead will not include the few civilians caught up in the power games of the infidel Americans."

The continued U.S. presence in the Arab world was the greatest affliction: "As we have previously stated, the presence of U.S. bases and military in Muslim countries will lead to many casualties and will cause instability in the whole area since their presence is contrary to Islamic law and their education is a duty upon Muslims everywhere wherever they may be." But, al-Muhajiroun stressed, the issue at hand was not a simple withdrawal of American forces but the reversal of Western influence over the Muslim world, a trend as suffocating and threatening to the Muslim world as the actual presence of Western forces:

The Muslim Ummah is in a constant state of Jihad, physical, financial and verbal against the terrorist state of America, Israel, Serbia, etc. We can envisage that this is the beginning of much more bloodshed and deaths, should the U.S. continue to occupy Muslim land and to oppress Muslims in the Gulf and elsewhere. The Muslims will never rest until their land is liberated from the occupiers and the authority to rule restored to the Muslims from the tyrant, self-appointed, puppet leaders in Muslim countries such as Mubarak of Egypt, Fahd of Arabia, Zirwal of Algeria, Qaddafi of Libya, etc. The struggle will continue against regimes in Muslim countries until al-Khilafah (the Islamic State) is re-established and the law of God dominates the world.

In the aftermath of the bombings in Nairobi and Dar-es-Salaam, Islamist sources also underscored the centrality of the Afghanistan base for the anti-American jihad while denying direct involvement in or responsibility for the bombs in East Africa. Islamist sources reiterated the importance of the World Islamic Front for Jihad against Jews and Crusaders and the fatwas issued in February 1998 over the signatures of Osama bin Laden and Ayman al-Zawahiri. They noted, however, that despite the explicit call for jihad, the recent bombings were claimed by the previously unknown Islamic Army for the Liberation of the Holy Places in a statement repeating the tenets of the fatwas. An Islamist source told *al-Hayah* that this kind of claim was issued in order to spare bin Laden, Zawahiri, and their Afghan hosts "embarrassment." With the Taliban striving for good relations with the United States, the Islamist leaders were determined to "prevent Washington from submitting an official request to the [Taliban] movement for the extradition of bin Laden, al-Zawahiri, or both if they openly claim responsibility for the two operations."

Similarly Adil Abdul-Majid, an Egyptian Islamist in London known to be close to Zawahiri, explained to *al-Hayah* the greater context of these claims. The organization that claimed responsibility for the bombs in Nairobi and Dar-es-Salaam was likely to be "the product of fatwas, statements, and assertions issued by Islamic leaders recently, among them Osama bin Laden and Jihad Group leader Dr. Ayman al-Zawahiri, who are both based in Afghanistan." Adil Abdul-Majid explained that bin Laden's presence in the Taliban's Afghanistan "does not enable him to announce any action he runs from there." Operations such as the embassy bombings had to be claimed by such entities as the Islamic Army for the Liberation of the Holy Places. Their statement confirmed that "new factors have emerged, that these must be read carefully" to realize who was really responsible for the operation. For example, Adil Abdul-Majid noted, the Islamic Army's name "points to the existence of numerous nationalities operating within its framework and proves that the circle of enmity toward the Americans has broadened and that the recent rapprochement among the Islamic movements, which resulted in the establishment of the World Islamic Front for Jihad against Jews and Crusaders, now enables any party to know beforehand of any future action even if it is not going to take part in it." He added that "the Jihad Group or bin Laden had been expected to claim responsibility for the two operations, but the announcement by the Islamic Army for the Liberation of the Holy Places, which claimed responsibility for the two blasts, confirms that a new entity capable of carrying out operations in faraway places has emerged and that there is now someone who can reactivate events without taking part in the implementation."

While these communiqués were diverting attention from the sponsoring states, Hassan al-Turabi moved quickly to exploit the initial shock effect in order to consolidate the Islamist position in East Africa. In a series of communications with close allies such as the leaders of the Oromo Liberation Front in Ethiopia and God's Army in Uganda, he argued that because the United States was preoccupied with the bombing investigation, it was unlikely to conduct activist policy in the region. Thus the time was ripe for the consolidation of a regional Islamist alliance and for seizing the initiative in determining the character of the region. Turabi launched still ongoing negotiations among thirteen Islamist organizations in the countries of East Africa and the Horn of Africa to form a consultative council under the sponsorship of his National Islamic Front.

Specific, ambitious programs have already been launched in the wake of the East African bombings. Capitalizing on contacts and relationships established by bin Laden in the early 1990s and operating out of "farms" he had established in the Ogaden, the leadership of the Oromo Liberation Front has already established a working alliance with both the Ethiopian and Somali branches of the Islamic Union, as well as the hard-core militant Dergue (communists) under the leadership of Kasa Kid, the illegitimate brother of the former Ethiopian dictator Mengistu Haile Mariam. The alliance took over the Islamic Union's military bases in southwest Somalia and established seven military bases in the Budhabu area in the border triangle between Somalia, Ethiopia, and Kenya. These bases were organized and supplies delivered using the "companies" and other financial institutions established by Osama bin Laden. Turabi envisions that these facilities will serve as a springboard for a militant Islamist surge that will dismember Ethiopia and establish independent Islamist ministates instead.

Concurrently, at the request of Khartoum, the Islamists of Uganda unleashed a series of attempted bombings of the U.S. Embassy in Kampala, Uganda, and other installations. At first only low-quality and expendable assets—those the Islamists could afford to lose to the security authorities—were used. But the expert terrorists operating through the ranks of God's Army will eventually be committed to operations. By fall 1998, even though all the Islamist terrorist efforts had failed, the Ugandan government was considering the reduction of support for the rebels in southern Sudan as a way to reduce Islamist militancy. And this is exactly what Turabi wanted.

In Afghanistan the Taliban reciprocated for the deniability provided by bin Laden and his forces by defending him and reiterating their determination not to extradite him or any other Islamist mujahid. The Taliban's spirited defense of Osama bin Laden, even after he was accused of involvement in the bombing of the two U.S. embassies in East Africa, is indicative of their doctrinal orientation. Senior Taliban leader Abdul-Hai Mutmaen stressed that bin Laden is a "guest" of the Taliban—a loaded term in Islam. "He does not have the capability or permission to conduct such deeds," Mutmaen said. "Any suggestion to the contrary is false propaganda of the enemies of Osama and Islamic Emirate of Afghanistan." According to Mutmaen, the subject of bin Laden is closed. "Osama is a guest of the Islamic Emirate. We cannot extradite him to anybody," he emphasized. Despite the Taliban's vigorous denials, Afghanistan is a hub of and safe haven for Islamist terrorists.

By mid-August the building of both the justification campaign for the terrorist strikes and the deniability front for the Taliban's Afghanistan and the other sponsoring states was disrupted by the launching of U.S. cruise missiles against a factory in Khartoum and in particular against several training camps in eastern Afghanistan. That direct attack pushed the Islamists into taking an even more extremist and uncompromising position toward the United States. In essence the American attacks led the Islamist international leadership to adopt maximalist positions in the development and formulation of policies that had been ready since spring. These doctrines are more dangerous for the West because they take into consideration the interests of several Arab states and so bring them into the fold as, at the very least, tacit supporters of anti-U.S. Islamist terrorism.

10

Humiliating the Enemy

FOR THE INTERNATIONAL Islamist movement, in particular its upper-level leadership, 1998 was a turning point. Although besieged by a growing Western presence and penetrating Westernization, made possible through satellite TV and the Internet, the Islamists surged, conducting several spectacular strikes and actively planning others. During the spring and summer of 1998 the Islamists prepared for a host of operations, from the World Cup to East Africa, and the Pakistanis were escalating their war by proxy in Kashmir. Moreover, the Islamists were considering new approaches to confronting the conservative regimes in the Arabian Peninsula. These intense activities were manifested in the plethora of theological and ideological declarations issued during the year. This doctrinal documentation placed the various activities in the context of the dominant trend sweeping the Muslim world.

By mid-March 1998 the Iraqi crisis had passed and the Islamists were once again preoccupied with overall doctrinal issues and long-term objectives. The planning and preparations for a host of spectacular operations covered not only East Africa but the entire world. In mid-March 1998 bin Laden and his colleagues sent a threatening letter to the U.S. Embassy in Islamabad. Although this letter was not of great theological significance, it served to assert the "end" of the February Iraqi crisis and the return of the Islamists to confrontation with the United States and the West over the main issue of contention—the presence of the West in the Muslim world.

Tehran also addressed the new realities of the Middle East and the Muslim world as a whole. In April 1998 Ayatollah Khamenei ordered Intelligence Minister Najafabadi and Muhsin Rafiq-Dust, chief of the Foundation of the

Oppressed, Iran's main instrument for clandestine financing, to prepare to launch the international terrorism campaign that would confront the United States and Israel rather than other Arab/Muslim regimes, meeting the new demands of Islamist revivalism. Toward this end Najafabadi convened a secret meeting at the security and intelligence building in Daraj. Among the officials attending were several senior Iranian intelligence officers. They discussed the challenges ahead and novel methods to consolidate a new, much larger, terrorist and intelligence infrastructure. To better study the matter, Najafabadi instructed all Iranian installations—the Islamic centers, Iranian embassies, study and information centers, trade and tourism corporations, and cultural centers of the Iranian cultural attaché offices—to conduct surveys of suitable conditions for resumption of terrorism and prepare for their eventual use as cover for any clandestine operation. Special case officers were nominated for various parts of the world, who would analyze the results of these surveys and recommend further improvements.

Both bin Laden's note and the Iranian intelligence conference coincided with a profound change in the alignment of forces in the Middle East—the Saudi-Iranian rapprochement. Riyadh had finally begun to confront reality. The aggregate impact of the overall dynamics in the region—in particular the growing military power of Iran, the building Islamist radicalism and militancy throughout the Arab Gulf States, the growing threats of local terrorism, and the Clinton administration's regional policies toward Iran and Islamist militancy—convinced the House of al-Saud it must reexamine its own regional posture. With the summit of the Organization of Islamic Countries (OIC) due in Tehran in December, Riyadh had to study its political options. After fall 1997 Riyadh was no longer oblivious to the dynamics throughout Islamist circles, and, with the succession crisis worsening, the House of al-Saud decided to reduce the threat by striking a deal with the real master: Tehran.

The turning point in this process took place in March 1998 with the dramatic, ten-day visit to Riyadh by former Iranian president Ayatollah ali Akbar Hashemi-Rafsanjani, who is now the chairman of Iran's Expediency Council. The declared objective of the visit was the opening of a new era in Saudi-Iranian relations, emphasizing common stands on regional and economic (oil price) policies. The driving force on the Saudi side was Crown Prince Abdallah bin Abdul-Aziz, who strove to reconcile Riyadh's need for U.S. forces to protect against Iranian and Iraqi strategic aspirations with the threat from the rapidly expanding, indigenous Islamist opposition—whose strength and popular support derived from widespread grassroots opposition to the American presence. To resolve these contradictory trends Riyadh had to reduce the need for a U.S. presence by improving relations with Tehran, enhancing internal stability.

Crown Prince Abdallah initiated the Saudi drive for rapprochement with Iran when he attended the eighth OIC Summit in Tehran in December 1997. He emerged from several meetings with Iranian leaders convinced of the sincerity of his hosts. The crown prince's visit led to a series of bilateral agreements, such as the resumption of direct scheduled flights between the two countries, the signing of a $15 million industrial cooperation deal, and the formation of a joint economic committee to formulate strategies to raise the price of oil. In early March 1998 the new relationship was formalized during the brief visit to Saudi Arabia of Iranian foreign minister Kamal Kharazi. Kharazi had an audience with King Fahd bin Abdul-Aziz—a major honor Riyadh accords only to allies and superpowers—who extended a formal invitation to President Muhammad Khatami.

The real turning point was the ten-day visit to Saudi Arabia by Hashemi-Rafsanjani. On the public side of his visit, he performed the Hajj and visited other holy shrines of Islam, including the main mosque in Medina; there the local Imam subjected Hashemi-Rafsanjani to an attack on Shiism, but he disregarded it so as not to insult his Saudi hosts. Saudi authorities fired that Imam soon afterward.

Critical were the meetings Hashemi-Rafsanjani held with King Fahd, Crown Prince Abdallah, Defense Minister Prince Sultan, Interior Minister Prince Nayif, and Prince Turki, the chief of intelligence, who is responsible for antiterrorism and security matters. Hashemi-Rafsanjani held extensive, wide-ranging talks that covered all key aspects of the Saudi-Iranian bilateral relations, "practical" cooperation in stopping the continued decline in oil prices, and regional and global issues.

Hashemi-Rafsanjani surprised his hosts with a revolutionary offer in the name of the highest authorities in Tehran: the Islamic Republic of Iran formally pledged to stop all its terrorist and subversive activities against Arab countries—in particular Saudi Arabia, the Persian Gulf sheikhdoms, Egypt, and Jordan—in return for Riyadh's joining the all-Islamic campaign to determine an Islamic future for the region. He vowed that Tehran would end its support for the regional Islamist terrorist organizations once these governments adopted "proper" Islamic policies.

Hashemi-Rafsanjani stressed that Tehran had nothing in principle against the House of al-Saud or any of the other governments at present under assault by Iranian-sponsored Islamist subversion, except for their reneging on the sacred duty of jihad. Once any of these governments resumed living up to its Islamic obligation to contribute to the liberation of al-Quds (Jerusalem)—meaning the destruction of Israel—Iran would have no reason to encourage Islamist terrorism and subversion against that government. Significantly this message was also expressed by HAMAS leader

Sheikh Yassin and his entourage during their triumphant tour throughout the Arab world. Sheikh Yassin repeatedly endorsed governments that still oppressed their own Muslim Brotherhood and other Islamist organs, most notably the Assad regime in Syria, solely because they actively contributed to the armed struggle against Israel.

To drive his point home, Hashemi-Rafsanjani not only gave the Saudis "full and formal" assurances about Iran's "determination and pledge" to stop sponsorship of terrorism against them but also delivered a letter from President Khatami affirming that Tehran had decided "to stop exporting the revolution, supporting terrorism, undermining the Middle East, or destabilizing neighboring countries" under the right circumstances. The only exceptions were the organizations fighting Israel—such as HAMAS, the Islamic Jihad, HizbAllah—all financed, equipped, and backed by Iran. The Saudis, who currently provide extensive financial and organizational help for HAMAS and other Palestinian Islamist terrorist organizations, had no problem with these exceptions.

Hashemi-Rafsanjani's discussions with the leaders of Saudi Arabia also touched on the Khobar bombing. Evading explicit acknowledgment of Tehran's involvement or responsibility, Hashemi-Rafsanjani could tell both Prince Nayif and Prince Turki that the terrorists' motive was despair over Saudi Arabia's cooperation with the United States and virtual peace with Israel—and not a challenge to the al-Sauds' hold on power. He suggested that Riyadh and Tehran study the available evidence to ensure that it was not misinterpreted in a way that would only aggravate an already delicate situation. To guarantee that no such misunderstanding happened and to show its "good will," Riyadh provided the Iranians with a copy of Saudi findings about the Khobar Towers bombing. (Saudi Arabia has adamantly refused to share this information with the United States despite several personal requests by senior officials visiting Riyadh.)

The "clarification" of the Khobar issue led to an immediate improvement in intelligence and security cooperation between Saudi Arabia and Iran. To further such cooperation, Iranian interior minister Abdollah Nuri visited Saudi Arabia in early April at the invitation of Prince Nayif. With the Khobar issue "resolved," Nuri declared in Riyadh, both governments "believe that if more rapprochement takes place between the two major countries in the region, we will be able to achieve security and peace of mind for the people of the region." He highlighted the new era of cooperation between Riyadh and Tehran in which "the two interior ministries can discuss ways to fight drugs and terrorism, security cooperation, the movement of both countries' citizens, and the exchange of information to help clarify the positions."

278 · HUMILIATING THE ENEMY

The new rapprochement was endorsed by the highest echelons in Tehran. Even Ayatollah Khamenei expressed his "satisfaction" at the state of relations between Iran and Saudi Arabia in a public speech in mid-April. He then called for the "further promotion and development" of cooperation between the two regional powers. For Tehran the primary common objective of Iran and Saudi Arabia is to further reduce mutual tensions and strive for better cooperation in the anticipated campaign to evict the "Great Satan" [the United States] from the region and destroy its "Illegitimate Offspring" [Israel] as preconditions for the Muslim liberation of al-Quds.

Riyadh reciprocated on May 24, 1998. Saudi Arabia announced the results of its investigation into the June 1996 Khobar bombing in which nineteen American servicemen were killed. The Saudi investigation, Saudi interior minister Prince Nayif told the Kuwaiti newspaper al-Rai al-Amm, conclusively proved that the Khobar bombing "was executed by Saudi hands. . . . No foreign party had any role in it." Prince Nayif added that Riyadh now rejected any implication of Iranian and Syrian involvement. Prince Nayif's interview left many issues unresolved, including such basic ones as the extent of Riyadh's knowledge of who the actual perpetrators were, let alone whether they had been arrested, tried, and, with customary Saudi justice, already summarily beheaded.

The release of these findings by Prince Nayif was extremely important, but not for setting the record straight—there is airtight evidence that Iran and Syria were the masterminds and facilitators of this terrorist strike. As a key political-strategic event, Prince Nayif's assertion that no foreign power was involved in the Khobar bombing formally absolved Iran of any involvement in terrorism against Saudi Arabia, which constitutes a major event in the consolidation of a Tehran-led all-Islamic front. Prince Nayif's statement was the latest in a series of milestone events unfolding over some six months.

Officials throughout the region explained this rapprochement among the Muslim and Arab states in terms that anticipated fateful events. Very significant was the frequent invocation by Arab leaders of the Muslim defeat of the Crusaders as a metaphor to describe the challenges currently facing the Arabs in their confrontation with Israel. For example, Yassir Arafat compared his position vis-à-vis Israel to that of the Islamic conquerors who defeated both the Jews of Arabia and the Crusaders. "We respect agreements the way that the Prophet Muhammad and Salah al-Din [Saladin] respected the agreements which they signed," Arafat explained. The truce agreements in question were signed at a time of weakness and unilaterally violated by both leaders once circumstances were ripe for defeating their enemies. Arafat used these examples to justify a possible unilateral violation of his agreements with Israel in order to revive the war against Israel whenever the Arabs were ready.

Islamist leaders were even more explicit in comparing current circumstances in the Middle East with those in the days of the Crusaders, when the entire Muslim world united behind a single (non-Arab) leader—Saladin—in order to defeat and evict the Crusaders and liberate al-Quds. In Jordan the Islamic Action Front (IAF) issued a statement in mid-May that stressed this point: "The conspiracy partners are Zionists and Crusaders, who are helped by the fact that the Arabs are divided among themselves and dominated by colonialist powers." The IAF stressed the all-Islamic character of both the historic struggles and the forthcoming one: "The causes of Jerusalem and Palestinian people never were the exclusive concerns of the Palestinians; they are the concern of the entire [Muslim] Nation. Neither Omar bin-al-Khattab nor Salah-al-Din al-Ayyubi or Qutuz hailed from Palestine. All were Muslims whose Islamic faith and responsibility toward their God prompted them to surmount all the obstacles that had blocked their path as they sought to liberate Palestine." The IAF argued that the same commitment and effort should be embarked on by the Muslim world.

Concurrently HAMAS leader Sheikh Yassin emphasized the significance of an all-Muslim front unified in order to destroy Israel, again comparing the prospects of such an alliance to the Muslims' triumph against the Crusaders under the leadership of Saladin. In striving to liberate Palestine from the Israeli occupation, Sheikh Yassin explained in mid-May, "the [Muslim] Nation can play an effective role. I have not lost confidence in this Nation. Who liberated Palestine from the Crusaders? The Arab Nation, of course, specifically Egypt and Syria when they united and formed a strong force and front that Salah al-Din used in his battle against the Crusaders. The Arab and Islamic Nation can play this role at present. However, this requires the unification of the ranks and the achievement of more freedom and justice for their people so that mercy and victory may come from Almighty God." The new Iranian initiative to suppress Islamist terrorism and subversion in the Arab world was aimed to expedite exactly this kind of all-Arab rapprochement and, possibly, unity.

It did not take long for the World Islamic Front for Jihad against Jews and Crusaders to come up with an authoritative statement, emphasizing the growing importance of the Israeli issue and, even more significantly, the unity of messages from all Islamist movements. On May 17, 1998, this group issued its statement urging all Muslims to wage "the Jihad against the Americans and the Israelis wherever they are." The statement identified the role of the Front in the Muslim world as that of "one of the trenches pooling the [Muslim] Nation's energies in order to perform the duty imposed by God, namely the Jihad against the atheists among American Christians and Israeli Jews." Special emphasis was put on supporting the Islamist struggle against Israel in a segment titled "Wounds of al-Aqsa Mosque." The Front urged greater support for "the sons of Muslim Palestine and their blessed Intifadah, through which they have renewed their rejection of capitulationist solutions." The Front was convinced that "despite the scale of the catastrophe, the glimmer of hope has become a reality and hopes are kept alive through the martyrs' blood, the pain of the sufferers, and the bullets of those fighting for the sake of God's cause." The statement portrayed the struggle against Israel in the greater context of the global jihad against the United States: "The U.S. Jews and Christians are using Israel to bring Muslims to their knees. . . . The Jewish-Crusader alliance led by the United States and Israel is now operating blatantly. . . . The United States, government and parliament, has always worked to spoil Israel and bolster its economic and military power."

Oblivious to the reality in the Middle East but following Saudi "advice" and in line with the pro-Arab tilt of its policy, the Clinton administration hailed the "moderation" of Khatami's Tehran and sought rapprochement with Iran. As a result the United States not only lifted the threat of sanctions from Europeans doing business with Iran but also made it easier for U.S. companies to use European "fronts" as well. Little wonder that even the most conservative Arab leaders no longer feared Washington's wrath as they struck deals with Tehran to reduce the Islamist threat to themselves while joining the all-Arab–all-Muslim quest to defeat the contemporary Crusaders and liberate al-Quds.

Taken together, these seemingly unrelated developments and esoteric events constituted the overt part of a profound change in the Islamist terrorist movement—among both the sponsoring states and the key perpetrators. The ramifications of these changes in Tehran's policy for bin Laden and the Islamist terrorist elite were ideologically far-reaching but in practice nil: the United States, not the local rulers, was reaffirmed as the ultimate foe and thus an object of terrorism. The Arab/Muslim rulers, including the House of al-Saud, were now defined as victims, to one extent or another, of U.S. oppression and presence. In the Islamist view once the United States and Westernization were evicted from the Hub of Islam, even these rulers would adopt Muslim ways and rejoin the Muslim Nation. This was a very slight difference between past and current perceptions of threat. This distinction, however, was not lost on official Riyadh, and once again

Prince Turki was sent to make "deals" to enhance the stability and survivability of the House of al-Saud.

———————

SAUDI ARABIA has been second only to Pakistan in the extent of its support for the Taliban. Saudi funds have been instrumental in the Taliban's rise to and hold on power. Saudi support for the Taliban has stemmed from Riyadh's determination to find an outlet—as far away from Saudi Arabia as possible—for the Islamist zeal of Saudi radicalized youth. Support for the propagation of Islamism also cleansed the collective conscience of the House of al-Saud, the declared guardians of the quintessence of conservative Islamism, for whatever infringements of Islamism's strict code of conduct they carry out in Saudi Arabia to ensure their own hold on power. The Taliban's brand of Islamic revolution, with its strong conservative Islamist connotations and desire for a greater Arabic coloration, is perfect for Riyadh. The Taliban's affinity with Saudi Arabia is also strong because the hard core of the Taliban are the Afghan refugees from the Pakistani Islamist schools whose teachers and clerics received their formal schooling and degrees from Islamist institutions in Saudi Arabia. They brought with them and instilled in their Afghan and Pakistani students a strict, conservative brand of Islamist theology and jurisprudence. And the Saudi support is also formal. "According to a high-ranking official in the [Saudi] ministry of justice, Sheikh Mohammad bin Jubier [current chairman of the Saudi Consultative Council], who has been called the 'exporter' of the Wahhabi [conservative Islamist] creed in the Muslim world, was a strong advocate of aiding the Taliban," Saudi opposition scholar Nawaf Obaid explained.

The Taliban's affinity for Saudi Islamism is also manifested in their declared support for the basic demands of Saudi Islamist opposition. For example, one of the Taliban's supreme commanders demanded "a removal of all U.S. troops from Saudi Arabia." Ominously, Obaid noted, "this is the same call made by Wahhabi fundamentalists in the Kingdom before the Riyadh and Dhahran bombings. And if Mr. bin Laden actually was behind these attacks, there is even more reason to fear Taliban-inspired terrorism." For Riyadh this ideological commitment of the Taliban warranted generous subsidies to ensure that neither the Taliban nor the Arab guests actively turned against the kingdom.

In early summer 1998 Riyadh consulted with Islamabad about ways to contain the anti-Saudi revolutionary zeal in Afghanistan. Pragmatic Islamabad connected Riyadh's trepidation over an Islamist revolt in Saudi Arabia with the ascent of the Taliban. Riyadh made the first major move in early June. Prince Turki and Mahmud Safar, the Saudi Hajj and Awqaf (religious property) minister, arrived in Qandahar, leading a delegation of intelligence and religious officials. The Saudis broached various ways to improve relations, including the possibility that the Taliban would extradite bin Laden and a group of Saudi "Afghans" in return for lavish Saudi support and U.S. recognition; joint containment of the Saudi Islamists in Afghanistan was also considered. The Taliban would hear nothing about extraditing anybody, but the delegations decided to work jointly to ensure that the Arab "Afghans" did not constitute a threat to Saudi Arabia and the other Gulf States. Just to be on the safe side, two representatives of leading Saudi families arrived at bin Laden's compound soon after with a large sum of money as a "donation" on the "understanding" that he would not conduct operations in Saudi Arabia. The two emissaries told him that the "donations" they brought also included backing from members of the House of al-Saud.

Crisis erupted barely a month later, when Salman al-Umari, the Pakistan-based Saudi chargé d'affaires for Kabul, came to Qandahar for a special meeting with a Taliban senior official. At first al-Umari complained that he had been shot at by Taliban forces near Jalalabad. The official responded that had these been the Taliban, al-Umari would already be dead. Then al-Umari demanded that the Taliban extradite bin Laden to the United States, stressing that Saudi Arabia was not interested in bin Laden. When the Taliban official queried how a Muslim emissary could suggest that a fellow Muslim be extradited to a non-Muslim state, a heated quarrel ensued. "Are you an ambassador for Saudi Arabia or the United States?" the Taliban official asked, adding, "If you are an ambassador for the United States, I am honored to be ambassador for bin Laden."

The Taliban immediately notified Islamabad of the apparent drastic changes in Riyadh's policies. An alarmed Riyadh assured Islamabad that there had been no change in Saudi policy and offered to reassure the Taliban. In the second half of July 1998 Islamabad mediated a meeting in Qandahar that led to a far-reaching deal between Saudi Arabia and the Taliban. The key participants were Prince Turki—chief of Saudi intelligence—and Taliban leaders, as well as senior ISI officers and representatives of Osama bin Laden. The agreement stipulates that bin Laden and his followers will not use the infrastructure in Afghanistan to subvert the Saudi kingdom, and the Saudis will make sure that no demands—including American—for the extradition of individuals and/or the closure of (terrorist) facilities and camps are met. Prince Turki also promised to provide oil and generous financial assistance to both the Taliban's Afghanistan and Pakistan. For Islamabad the high-level negotiations with Riyadh and the long-term promises amount to Saudi recognition of the Taliban reign over

Afghanistan. Russian sources noted that soon after this agreement was reached, large sums of money were transferred from Saudi Arabia and the United Arab Emirates to Ukraine as payment for the purchase and quick delivery of weapons for both Pakistan and the Taliban. These weapons played a crucial role in the Taliban's swift offensive in early August 1998 that consolidated their hold over all of Afghanistan.

Then on August 7 the two car bombs demolished the U.S. embassies in Nairobi and Dar-es-Salaam. As far as the Pakistanis and the Taliban are concerned, bin Laden should not be blamed for these bombings. Islamist sources stressed the centrality of the Afghanistan base for the anti-American jihad but denied any direct involvement in or responsibility for the bombs in East Africa. Although the World Islamic Front for Jihad against Jews and Crusaders and the fatwas issued in February 1998 over the signatures of bin Laden and Zawahiri were very important, they argued, and despite the explicit call for jihad in them, the bombings in East Africa had been claimed by the previously unknown Islamic Army for the Liberation of the Holy Places. The Islamist leaders were determined to "prevent Washington from submitting an official request to the [Taliban] movement for the extradition of bin Laden, Zawahiri, or both if they openly claim responsibility for the two operations." But Islamabad had no intentions of helping Washington anyway.

On August 20 the U.S. Navy launched seventy-five to eighty cruise missiles at the training-camp complexes in the Khowst area of Afghanistan. According to surveys done on the ground by Pakistanis, Afghans, and the British, thirteen of the missiles hit an area called Markaz Khalid bin Waheed, ten missiles hit an area called Markaz Amir Muavia, and five hit a base belonging to Jalaludin Hakkani. The other missiles hit nearby villages. According to eyewitness reports, "a large number of villagers" were killed not only by flying shrapnel but also by collapsing homes and shattered windows. About 1,200 members of the ISI-controlled Harakat ul-Ansar—all of them Pakistanis, Indian Kashmiris, and Afghans—were in these camps, about 200 of Hakkani's Afghan mujahideen, and "a score" of Arabs. Between them they suffered twenty-six dead and thirty-five wounded. Fourteen Afghans, eight Pakistanis, three Egyptians, and one Saudi died. (According to bin Laden, there were twenty-eight fatalities—fifteen Afghans, seven Pakistanis, two Egyptians, three Yemenis, and one Saudi.)

Little wonder that Mullah Jalaludin Hakkani, the original commander of the Khowst area, ridiculed the U.S. claim that the missile strike inflicted heavy damage. "The camps at Zhavara survived two air and ground offensives by the Red Army and couldn't be captured or destroyed despite frequent air raids and shelling. What can about 60 or 70 long-range, largely inaccurate American missiles do to a fortified place built into mountains?" he asked. According to Hakkani, the Salman Farsi camp "emerged largely unscathed"; the al-Badr camps, also known as Abu Jindal or the Arab camps, "suffered minimum damage"; and the Khalid bin Waleed and Amir Muawiyya camps "suffered some damage." The ammunition dumps, in deep caves near these camps, "were almost all intact."

Hakkani noted that five mosques were built in the camps' area and that they offered religious services not only to the mujahideen in the camps but also to the villagers living in the vicinity. Four mosques in the camps and nearby villages were destroyed and, in the words of an on-site observer, "the burned pages of 200 Korans" were strewn over the area. Militant Islamists, particularly those associated with the ISI-sponsored organizations, began circulating in Pakistan pictures of two damaged buildings, which could be easily identified as the local mosques when compared to old pictures of the camps. The Islamists also had pictures showing fragments of Korans scattered about the area. "America has desecrated our mosques and holy books," said a member of Harakat ul-Ansar. "President Bill Clinton will be hanged for this." These sentiments were shared by others. "The U.S. has invited death by attacking our mosques," said Ahmad Sarwar, a survivor from the Harakat ul-Ansar camp. "They have destroyed our holy things and turned the religious schools we had at the camps to rubble. The U.S. has lit a fire and the U.S. will itself burn in that fire." Within a couple of days Islamist propaganda throughout the Muslim world was contrasting the widespread damage, particularly to the local mosques, with the U.S. media's gloating over the precision of guided munitions during the Gulf War—the inevitable implication of this comparison being that the U.S. destruction of the mosques and the defiling of the Korans were intentional.

Immediately after the strike Taliban and Pakistani officials also disputed the U.S. claims about the camps' population. According to a Harakat ul-Ansar official, the bombed camps were "staffed by members of Pakistan's Inter-Services Intelligence—the country's foreign intelligence agency—who assisted in the training of Harakat-ul-Ansar militants for the war against Indian rule in Kashmir." "The Arabs were not there," said another Harakat militant. "That is why almost none of them died and why many of the martyrs were Pakistanis and local Afghans. This operation has done more to embarrass the Pakistani government than hurt bin Laden." Taliban leader Mullah Omar claimed he had ordered the removal of the Arab "Afghans"— Saudis, Egyptians, Sudanese, and Yemenis—to a more secure base just south of Kabul two months before the bombing. Not surprisingly, the local Islamists were vowing revenge. "America has invited its own death upon itself," declared Maulvi Fazl-ur-Rehman Khalil, head of Harakat ul-Ansar.

"If we don't get any justice from the world court we know how to get our own justice."

On the other side of the world, in an effort to justify the U.S. cruise missile strike on terrorist training facilities in the Khowst area of Afghanistan, President Clinton and several U.S. officials alluded to intelligence information that determined the timing of the strike. U.S. intelligence had learned that a major terrorist conference was to take place in the area, and the strike was timed to hit the participants, including Osama bin Laden and his close lieutenants. They all survived; they and many other terrorists being trained in these facilities were simply not there when the cruise missiles hit. There is good reason to believe that high officials in Pakistan warned the terrorist elite about the impending U.S. strike.

According to a chronology published by the *New York Times* of the White House activities leading to the August 20 strike, the president was notified on August 12 about the evidence connecting Osama bin Laden to the bombing of the U.S. embassies in Kenya and Tanzania and of the essence of the planned retaliatory missile strikes. U.S. intelligence had already proposed August 20 as the strike date based on knowledge that a high-level terrorist gathering was planned for that day. Appearing on PBS on August 21, National Security Adviser Sandy Berger noted that much of the data that prompted the U.S. strike had been accumulated by monitoring telephone conversations of bin Laden and others.

However, on August 12, when the strike plan was originally presented to the president, both U.S. intelligence and the national decision makers should have questioned the validity of the information. Starting on August 8, U.S. intelligence had learned of unusual movements at terrorist bases and camps throughout Afghanistan. There was "a [dispersal] of people away from bin Laden's bases of operation within Afghanistan in the aftermath of the explosions," a U.S. official told CNN on August 13. This information served to reinforce Washington's conviction that bin Laden was responsible for the bombing in East Africa. Pakistani security sources told *al-Hayah* that "some moves ha[d] been detected among bin Laden's Arabs between their headquarters in Qandahar and Jalalabad and their stronghold in the mountain province of Paktia." Then in the days leading to the U.S. strike, usually reliable Saudi intelligence sources throughout the Middle East and Western Europe widely and openly discussed the latest movements among bin Laden's people, stressing that Riyadh had learned about them from the ISI. Even *al-Hayah* wrote that Pakistani "sources did not rule out that there may be preparations for a large meeting of militants which bin Laden himself might attend, and hinted that the Americans may be aware of this meeting."

Concurrently evidence surfaced that the Taliban had moved bin Laden far from any potential danger. On August 13 Abdol Rahman, an Afghan citizen interrogated by Iranian intelligence in Tashkent, Uzbekistan, claimed that "Osama bin Laden toured Mazar-e Sharif, in northern Afghanistan, for an hour Wednesday [August 12] evening." Abdol Rahman claimed he had seen how bin Laden "arrived at Shadian quarter of Mazar-e Sharif in a Datsun pickup truck, escorted by a large number of Taliban militia." After the U.S. strike Dr. Saad al-Faqih, leader of the London-based Movement for Islamic Reform in Arabia (MIRA), confirmed that "a Taliban official said bin Laden was 500 km [more than 300 miles] away from the strike site."

Both the movements and the rumors that the United States knew about a terrorist meeting should have raised doubts about the reliability of the intelligence on the forthcoming terrorist summit. It does not make sense that senior commanders would convene in camps from which lowly trainees had already been evacuated for fear of American retaliation or that a "summit" would take place when the chairman—bin Laden—was far away in northern Afghanistan. Nor does it make sense that the world's most wanted terrorists would attend a "secret meeting" after it had been written about, with the observation that the United States knew about it, in *al-Hayah*—a newspaper owned by the son of the Saudi minister of defense and the brother of the Saudi ambassador to Washington. The United States should have suspected a hidden agenda behind the publicity bin Laden was suddenly getting from the Pakistanis and Saudis.

There was no apparent impact on the U.S. preparations. Indeed, Washington began delicate negotiations with Islamabad—in particular with the office of Prime Minister Nawaz Sharif and the ISI—about the arrest of Muhammad Sadiq Odeh and the material he might have divulged about the embassy bombings. This issue was very delicate, given Pakistan's sponsorship of and direct involvement in Islamist terrorism, primarily against India but also throughout Asia and the Balkans. Moreover, Pakistanis run and train terrorist forces in the same camps the United States was now planning to strike.

At first there were conflicting reports about the extent of Islamabad's foreknowledge of the U.S. strike. Initially, on the night of August 20, Pakistani officials insisted Islamabad was shocked and surprised by the news of the attack. Foreign Minister Sartaj Aziz stated that Pakistan had not been warned by the United States about the strikes. "We were not aware of anything and no facilities were provided by Pakistan," he said.

It did not take long, however, for the more complex reality to emerge. Pakistani officials noted intense direct contacts between Washington and Islamabad on the eve of the strike: (1) President Clinton and Prime Minister

Nawaz Sharif spoke on the telephone, (2) U.S. secretary of state Madeleine Albright contacted Nawaz Sharif on the eve of the attack, and (3) Punjab chief minister Shahbaz Sharif, who is Nawaz Sharif's brother and confidant, held talks in Washington with senior U.S. officials in the White House, the State Department, and other parts of government.

A reliable military source in Islamabad confirmed that "State Department officials had informed their Pakistani counterparts of their plans for a military strike" several days beforehand. Several Pakistani military and intelligence sources confirmed that President Clinton had briefed Prime Minister Nawaz Sharif about the U.S. plans by August 14. All the Pakistani sources consulted believe this was the date "the countdown for the strike" began. They stress that the United States decided to launch the strike against Afghanistan on August 18 in the wake of consultations with Islamabad. The U.S. attack, they note, was carried out "with the full knowledge of Pakistan." The *New York Times* chronology of activities in Washington identifies August 14 as the date "Clinton [met] with his foreign policy advisers to begin planning military action." On August 18, according to this chronology, "Clinton call[ed] Berger to confirm that the military actions [we]re in place."

Western diplomatic sources in Islamabad also confirmed that Shahbaz Sharif "made an unscheduled visit to Washington late last week for talks with U.S. officials." They attributed great importance to the visit because of the close relations between the Sharif brothers. They had no doubt that Washington had notified Islamabad through this and/or other channels. "Given the close relations with Washington, Pakistan would have been privy to U.S. plans," a senior Western diplomat stated.

Fazal-ur-Rehman Khalil, chairman of the ISI-sponsored Harkat-ul-Mujahideen, said on August 22 that he believed Pakistan knew beforehand about the U.S. attacks. Other sources within the Afghan-based terrorist movements concurred, noting that key ISI officials and instructors evacuated the camps in eastern Afghanistan during the week preceding the strikes.

Not only did Islamabad have advance knowledge of the impending strikes, but at the very least it warned the Taliban leadership—whom Islamabad created and is sponsoring—so that they could ensure that bin Laden, Zawahiri, and their lieutenants were not harmed in the strike. According to Arab sources, the ISI even sent a senior official to Afghanistan to personally warn bin Laden about the impending U.S. strike. After the strikes no effort was made to conceal the Pakistani warning to bin Laden himself and not just the Taliban. "Informed sources in Islamabad and Afghanistan" readily acknowledged to *al-Sharq al-Awsat,* a London-based paper affiliated with the Salman-Nayif faction in Riyadh, that "bin Laden had left the Khowst region, which was hit by U.S. missiles, two or three days before the bombing after he received 'signals' from Pakistani sources that the United States [might] fire missiles at sites which he frequents." The sources added that bin Laden was also assured by Islamabad that there would be no commando raid on him because "the United States is not willing to risk sending commandos to the region and because Pakistan would not allow the United States to use its territory as a springboard."

The widespread leak campaign by Pakistani and Saudi official and security sources about the secret meeting of terrorists to be chaired by bin Laden and Zawahiri raises doubts about whether such a meeting was ever really planned; no terrorist would even have considered attending such a well-advertised event. The "terrorist summit" did not take place at the time of the U.S. strike, no key commander was harmed, and no sensitive equipment was damaged.

Most telling, however, is the behavior of both bin Laden and Zawahiri in the hours preceding and soon after the U.S. strike. On August 20 at 9 P.M. local time—about an hour before the cruise missile strike—Zawahiri placed a call from bin Laden's satellite phone to Rahimullah Yusufzai, a friendly Pakistani journalist based in Peshawar. In English, Zawahiri spoke for bin Laden, who speaks only Arabic. At first Zawahiri read a brief statement: "Osama bin Laden calls on the Ummah to continue Jihad against Jews and Americans to liberate their holy places. In the meantime, he denies any involvement in the Nairobi and Dar-es-Salaam bombings." Then he stayed on the line for a jovial conversation that lasted about a quarter of an hour. He acknowledged he was calling from Afghanistan and that bin Laden "was somewhere in the area." Yusufzai got the impression that "bin Laden was sitting next to al-Zawahiri" during their telephone conversation. Despite the prospects of monitoring and homing in on such conversations, bin Laden and Zawahiri were clearly not bothered by the U.S. threats.

Barely forty-five minutes after Zawahiri ended his conversation with Yusufzai, on August 20 at 10 P.M. local time, the cruise missiles struck the terrorist camps in the Khowst area. Bin Laden, Zawahiri, and the terrorist elite were not there. Tehran was the first to provide a clue about their safety. On August 21 Mullah Muhammad Omar, the chief of the Taliban, explained why bin Laden was not hurt. "Osama bin Laden [had] been moved to a safe place before the U.S. strike on his bases," he told the official Iranian news agency, IRNA. The next day, August 22, the Taliban issued a formal reaction to the U.S. strike. The American strike was nothing but proof of the U.S. "enmity against Islam and the Muslim world." Reiterating their pledge never to forsake bin Laden, the Taliban emphasized that he was safe. "Before the attack, Osama [had] been transferred to a safer place and no force and no attempt can force Afghanistan to hand him over to the American government," the Taliban announced. "Osama is a guest of the Afghan people who has assured that he will not act from the territory of Afghanistan against any country."

On August 21, at around 11 P.M. local time, Zawahiri called Rahimullah Yusufzai again, using the same satellite telephone. Zawahiri confirmed that he was together with bin Laden "somewhere in Afghanistan," where they were all "safe and sound." The main purpose of Zawahiri's call was to deliver bin Laden's warning in English: "The war has just started. The Americans should wait for the answer. . . . Tell the Americans that we aren't afraid of bombardment, threats, and acts of aggression. We suffered and survived the Soviet bombings for ten years in Afghanistan and we are ready for more sacrifices," Zawahiri declared. He then reiterated bin Laden's call to all Muslims to continue their jihad against the Americans and Jews, as well as liberate Islam's holy places. "The whole Ummah must change its attitude and fight the challenges posed by America and its agents. We should strengthen bin Laden's hands in this struggle," Zawahiri stressed. As was the case on August 20, Zawahiri talked in a leisurely manner and displayed no concern about possible interception and tracing of his call.

The same day, August 21, bin Laden further clarified the issue of the terrorist conference the United States had attempted to hit. This clarification came in the form of a satellite telephone conversation between bin Laden's confidant, known only as "Abu-Haq" or "Dr. Haq," and Abdul-Bari Atwan, the editor of the London-based *al-Quds al-Arabi,* who is close to bin Laden. A conference had indeed been planned for that Friday, August 21, Abu-Haq acknowledged. (All Islamist events of significance start with the Friday midday prayers and sermon and then proceed to discussion of the issues at hand. There is no precedent for an event taking place on a Thursday.) Bin Laden, Zawahiri, and numerous senior commanders were to participate. While a gathering was to have taken place at the Zhawar Kili al-Badr training camp near Khowst, the key summit meeting would have taken place off the camp compound itself. (For security reasons, most recorded Islamist terrorist conferences in Pakistan-Afghanistan were held in isolated tents or remote buildings to ensure that the trainees and other occasional bystanders could not see the participants.)

Thus, whether or not such a terrorist summit was ever planned, bin Laden effectively exploited its use by the United States as an excuse for the strike in order to ridicule and dare Washington. Abdul-Bari Atwan quoted Abu-Haq's admission that "President Clinton was correct. There was going to be a meeting at Khowst last Friday, but it was canceled because bin Laden knew a raid was being planned by the Americans. He called it off."

Abu-Haq asked Atwan to convey bin Laden's defiance and resolve. "We will answer Bill Clinton in deeds not words. The battle has not started yet," Atwan quoted bin Laden's message. "Osama bin Laden is unhurt and the American attack failed to accomplish its aim in eliminating him," Abu-Haq also told Atwan.

It is not difficult to surmise that bin Laden, Zawahiri, and the Islamist terrorist elite were not harmed because they and the Taliban had been forewarned by Islamabad. The reason for the Pakistani breach of American trust goes beyond the Pakistani sponsorship of and commitment to Islamist terrorism. Pakistan's direct involvement in Islamist terrorism should not be belittled, however. About a quarter of the terrorist casualties were Pakistani trainees for the ISI-run proxy war against India in Kashmir. But the safety of these terrorists could not have been Pakistan's reason for betraying the U.S. strike plans to the Taliban—after all, many of them were left in the Khowst area camps and were subjected to the strike.

In fact, by the time Islamabad was formally told by Washington, through General Joseph Ralston, of the U.S. intent to strike bin Laden and the terrorist camps in Afghanistan, Islamabad had already committed itself to protecting the terrorists. As far as Islamabad and Riyadh were concerned, bin Laden and Zawahiri had not violated their part of the recent agreement concluded with Prince Turki. With Saudi support so crucial to consolidating the Pakistani control by proxy of Afghanistan, Islamabad could not afford to permit the Clinton administration to negate their July agreement with Prince Turki, who, after all, claimed to have been negotiating with Washington's concurrence. Both Islamabad and Riyadh had no doubt that if any harm were to befall bin Laden, Zawahiri, or any of the other charismatic Islamist leaders scheduled to convene in the Khowst area, an intense Islamist Intifadah and insurrection would erupt throughout the Arabian Peninsula and most of the Arab world. The Saudis wanted to prevent this prospect at all cost, especially given the prevailing tension and uncertainty in Riyadh, where King Fahd's health is in sharp decline. Islamabad had no choice but to issue the warning and provide assistance to bin Laden, Zawahiri, and their lieutenants. Therein lies the essence of Pakistan's support for the U.S. war against terrorism.

Ultimately the U.S. cruise missile strike on the training camps in Afghanistan—particularly in view of the repeated hints and allegations in the U.S. media that the Clinton administration had hoped to kill bin Laden and his lieutenants in the attack—has had a major, long-term strategic impact. Whether back in July Prince Turki had misspoken or overstated or exaggerated Prince Bandar's ability to "deliver" the Clinton administration for the Pakistanis, bin Laden, and the Taliban, for the Islamic world the fact remained that as a pious Muslim, Prince Turki had given his word, and that word could not be disputed. So it had to have been the United States that broke its promise. The strike was yet another proof of the duplicity of the Clinton administration, no different from the unilateral violation of the "deal" agreed on with Abu-Umar al-Amriki. This American shaming of all Muslims involved—the Saudis, the Pakistanis, bin Laden, Zawahiri, and the Taliban—would have to be avenged.

Formulation of the Islamists' revenge doctrine and legitimization had begun even before the first cruise missiles slammed into the Khowst area. Pakistani sources had defined the period between August 14 and 18 as when President Clinton consulted with Pakistani prime minister Nawaz Sharif about the forthcoming American retaliation. During those same days bin Laden, Zawahiri, and their allies formulated their first communiqué discussing the next phase of their anti-American jihad.

On August 17, in their first major announcement since the bombing in Nairobi and Dar-es-Salaam, the World Islamic Front for Jihad against Jews and Crusaders endorsed and praised the operations of the Islamic Army for the Liberation of the Holy Places (IALHP). Moreover, the Front's statement was delivered virtually simultaneously with three messages from the army, leaving no doubt of their connection. This communiqué is vital because it further shifted Islamist emphasis toward attacking the United States.

The August 18 message of the World Islamic Front for Jihad against Jews and Crusaders said that the East Africa bombings were only the beginning of a long campaign. Anti-American "Jihad operations," like those conducted against the embassies, would continue until "the U.S. troops withdraw from the land of the Muslims." The statement endorsed the operations of the Islamic Army for the Liberation of the Holy Places as the kind of jihad the Front was referring to without admitting any links to the perpetrators themselves. "When the formation of the [Islamic Army for the Liberation of the Holy Places] was announced through these deeply significant operations, it became clear to everyone, including the American people, that we did not lie to them when we warned them," the statement read. The Front held the entire American public responsible for the actions of the U.S. government, making everybody a legitimate target for terrorism. The statement clarified that "when the American people believed their dishonest and disgraced leadership, which has led them to destruction and ruin, they faced a succession of blows. The American people were distracted by the Jews' talk of interests and designs which threw them into the furnace of a holy war between militant Islam and the United States, the occupier and the usurper."

In its statement the World Islamic Front for Jihad against Jews and Crusaders also sought to establish continuity between earlier Islamist operations and the East Africa bombing. "These two embassies that were blown up by the [Islamic Army for the Liberation of the Holy Places] had supervised the killing of at least 13,000 Somali civilians in the treacherous aggression led by the United States against that Muslim country," the statement explained. The August 1998 operations were not motivated by revenge, however, but were just punishment for "the U.S. Government's injustice against the peoples of Islam." The statement concluded with a warning and a threat for further escalation: "The coming days will, God willing, make the United States face a dark fate similar to that which has befallen the Soviet Union. It will face successive blows from everywhere and Islamic groups will emerge and follow other groups, and all will be fighting U.S. interests which are still based on theft and pillage. Islamic armies will follow armies in the fight against the criminal U.S. forces; and tomorrow will soon come."

The statement issued by the Islamic Army for the Liberation of the Holy Places was titled "An Open Letter to the Kenyan People" and sought to apologize for the losses suffered by Kenyan civilians during the operation of the "Martyr Khalid al-Said Company" in Nairobi by stressing that "the operation targeted only the U.S. presence. . . . The objective of an Islamic army is not to strike at Kenyan citizens. All their capabilities were focused on killing and humiliating the American tyrants and plunderers," the IALHP explained. The statement emphasized that the responsibility for the civilian casualties "lies with the United States" and that the United States "must compensate the Kenyan people for bringing onto their land the consequences of war." The IALHP added that the Kenyan people should blame their own government for the casualties suffered in the blast. "It is your government that has brought death to you and ruin to your country when it allowed the Americans to use its territory to kill the neighboring Islamic peoples and besiege their economy. . . . Israel's role in the tragedies which have befallen the Muslims and which have originated from Kenya, Tanzania, and other states in North Africa [sic] is no secret to anyone. Cooperation with the Israelis while they occupy the al-Aqsa Mosque amounts to a declaration of war against all Muslims throughout the world." The statement added that the two specific U.S. embassies were selected as targets because "Kenya and Tanzania have become the biggest U.S. bases used against the Muslims."

In another statement the Islamic Army for the Liberation of the Holy Places declared that their battle with the American Crusaders and the Jews was a "battle to the death." They promised more spectacular and lethal operations. "Our method thus far in this battle has been to continue to pile up more American corpses onto their unjust government until we break the arrogance of the United States, crush its pride, and trample its dignity in the mud of defeat." The IALHP urged all Muslims "not to get near anything American in order to avoid a repeat of what happened in Nairobi and so that they are not unwittingly affected by the flames of God's Army."

Immediately after the U.S. strike, bin Laden reiterated the relevance of the Front's statement in a personal message delivered to Abdul-Bari Atwan of *al-Quds al-Arabi*. In his message bin Laden threatened President Clinton with further attacks on U.S. targets in retaliation for the raid in Afghanistan. Bin Laden warned the president that "the battle has not yet started and that the answer is what you see, not what you hear." Bin Laden's statement ridiculed the impact of the U.S. strike and the casualties inflicted because "the human losses within the ranks of the Arab 'Afghans' is a natural thing to which they have grown accustomed. They all seek martyrdom and want to meet God as soon as possible." Bin Laden also used the satellite phone call made from Afghanistan to reassure Atwan and his other friends that he, bin Laden, and his people had survived the strike. Atwan concluded that it was his impression that "bin Laden has gained popularity and become an 'Islamic symbol' in the face of U.S. arrogance in the wake of the latest attack."

Islamist leaders in London were of the unanimous opinion that "the U.S. strikes will increase the fundamentalists' determination to attack U.S. interests all over the world." Omar Bakri, leader of al-Muhajiroun, said, "The U.S. attacks on sites in Sudan and Afghanistan [are] an attack against Arabs and Muslims everywhere." Mustafa Kamil, also known as Abu-Hamzah, of the Partisans of the Sharia, emphasized the mobilizing effect of the U.S. strike: "If there were differences between the fundamentalists in Afghanistan and the fundamentalist leaderships in Europe on ways to deal with Muslim countries and regimes, the U.S. aggression against Sudan and Afghanistan has now unified the stand of all the fundamentalist trends." Yassir al-Sirri, also known as Abu-Ammar, of the al-Jamaah al-Islamiyah in Egypt, anticipated escalation of international terrorist operations: "The cooperation of the governments that have offered logistical support to the U.S. aggression will not go by in peace." The Islamists in Afghanistan "will be more alert for more strikes against them; as for the countries that have offered support, they too are not safe from retaliation." Concurrently the International Islamic Front issued a statement demanding that all U.S. embassies throughout the Muslim world be shut down, all their employees kicked out of Muslim lands, and an economic boycott imposed on the United States. The statement concluded that "this savage act will not be left unanswered."

On August 23 a confidant of Zawahiri's called *al-Hayah* in the name of both Zawahiri and bin Laden. He stressed that "although Osama bin Laden will continue with his call for Jihad against the Crusaders and the Jews, he was not involved in the Nairobi and Dar-es-Salaam operations." He also noted that "none of the Egyptian and Arab Islamists [affiliated with bin Laden and Zawahiri] in Afghanistan have been harmed by the U.S. shelling." The confidant also repeated the Taliban leaders' guarantee of protection to bin Laden and all his people. Zawahiri's confidant now expected the U.S. strikes "to cause a new escalation by the Islamists against U.S. targets." Echoing bin Laden and Zawahiri, he opined that the Clinton administration "was mad to embark on a reckless action which has only increased the Islamists' anger against the Americans. This suggests that new confrontations between the two sides in the future will take a dangerous turn."

On the night of August 26, to ensure that the gravity and seriousness of the warning message was comprehended in the West, Ayman al-Zawahiri called Rahimullah Yusufzai once again from Afghanistan. "Assalam-o-Alaikum, brother. I am all right. Brother Osama bin Laden sends his regards to you and he has a message for you," Zawahiri said. "Osama bin Laden calls on the Muslim Ummah [Nation] to continue Jihad against the Jews and Americans to liberate their Muqamat-i-Muqadassa [holy places]. Meanwhile, he denies any involvement in the Nairobi and Dar-es-Salaam bombings."

Several Islamist movements added their analyses of the implications of the U.S. strike. The August 24 bulletin of the Movement for Islamic Reform in Arabia (MIRA) is noteworthy because it reflected the sentiments of the Saudi Islamist opposition. The group considered the U.S. strikes the beginning of a major confrontation with the United States. MIRA stressed that the strike played into the hands of the Islamists. "It seems that America has started implementing, without being aware of it, parts of the program of the Jihad groups. It is perhaps one of the things pre-destined by God that Clinton's scandals increased in this period and added this factor to the timing of the American strike. Thus, the American strike is turned into another factor of increase of anger and hostility against America in the Islamic world and this is the very thing wanted by the Jihad groups."

Moreover, the political dynamics was extremely beneficial for bin Laden because of the immense publicity in the Western media. "This representation will give a strong impulse to those who are regarded as belonging to the Jihad movement, particularly the followers of bin Laden, will lift their morale and their impressions that they are a major power confronting America. For them, these wrong and hasty attacks will be regarded as evidence that America has lost its reason and does not know where to strike. The situation is not so different regarding Arab and Islamic public opinion, since people are experiencing a crisis of heroism and a crisis of readiness to make sacrifices. They are awaiting someone to satisfy their feelings of vengeance against America and [desire] to subdue it and terrorize it, just as it terrorized the Muslims and oppressed them in Palestine, Iraq, the [Arabian] peninsula, Africa, Turkey, and other places. Therefore, the sight of American officials admitting their confusion and fear of bin Laden during these strikes was tantamount to satisfying these feelings and increasing bin Laden's popularity."

The same dynamics occurred in Pakistan. Rahimullah Yusufzai noted that the strike had made bin Laden a "cult hero" throughout Pakistan, creating widespread endorsement for the jihad he advocates: "In an Islamic world desperately short of genuine heroes, Osama bin Laden has emerged as a new cult figure." He symbolized the defiance and hostility toward the United States the Muslim world aspires to. Since *Osama* means "lion" in Arabic, many speakers in mass rallies declared that "Osama the Lion had come out of his cage to devour the enemies of Islam." This popular support and adulation created an expectation among the Islamists that they had to live up to the popular sentiments: "Lastly, the U.S. attack has made bin Laden and his World Islamic Front for Jihad against Jews and Crusaders desperate to reply in kind." And there should be no doubt that the Islamists will soon satisfy their supporters.

On August 25 al-Murabitun, a London-based group affiliated with the Egyptian al-Jamaah al-Islamiyah, issued an important communiqué addressing the aftermath of the bombing. "The U.S. President made a gross mistake when he thought he could divert attention from his sexual and ethical scandal through barbaric, unjustified missile attacks against Sudan and Afghanistan." The communiqué ridiculed Washington's claim that the strike was in retaliation for bin Laden's part in the bombings in East Africa and earlier terrorist operations: "It remained only for Washington to accuse bin Laden of assassinating John Kennedy!" The communiqué then criticized U.S. support for the oppression of Islamists in Egypt and its coercion of Riyadh to keep U.S. troops despite growing public discontent. This state of affairs made the governments of Saudi Arabia and Egypt active puppets of Washington: "The Americans in turn have found their long-awaited prize, and they are using those governments to fight Islam and the Muslims under the pretense of aiding them." This dynamics is creating a dangerous situation: "The policy America is conducting is the only cause for the atmosphere of hostility that has become evident against it. And America is the party which must reconsider its racist and arrogant view toward everything Islamic." The only way to remedy the current crisis is for the United States to withdraw from the Muslim world, al-Murabitun's communiqué concludes. With this communiqué al-Murabitun joined the Islamist organizations concentrating on ending the U.S. presence in the Muslim world rather than the overthrow of the Arab governments hostile to them.

The intensity of the grassroots anger toward the United States created a demand for religious guidance on what to do next. Throughout the Muslim world is widespread conviction that the U.S. strikes on Afghanistan and Sudan must be answered by striking back, so hard that even a superpower like the United States will take notice. The Islamists capitalized on this thirst for guidance and intensity of emotions, distributing fatwas and other inciting literature. One such fatwa was written by Sheikh Omar Abdul Rahman and smuggled out of jail:

> Cut all links with their country [the United States]. Destroy them thoroughly and erase them from the face of the earth. Ruin their economies, set their companies on fire, turn their conspiracies to powder and dust. Sink their ships, bring their planes down. Slay them in air, on land, on water. And (with the command of Allah) kill them wherever you find them. Catch them and put them in prison. Lie in wait for them and kill these infidels. They will surely get great oppression from you. God will make you the means of wreaking a terrible revenge upon them, of degrading them. He will support you against them. He will cure the afflicted hearts of the faithful and take all anger out of their hearts.

Copies of this and similar fatwas can be obtained in all religious schools in Pakistan, where they are in great demand. As a consequence those who had not even heard of Abdul Rahman now read his works and admire his courage. And bin Laden and his jihadist movement offer them venues to implement their rage and hatred. At present the terrorist schools are overflowing with volunteers.

On August 29 al-Jamaah al-Islamiyah issued its own warning to the United States in response to the U.S. strikes and the continuation of the "American-Jewish conspiracy against Islam and our holy sites." Since they were ultimately aimed at covering up "the scandals of the White House," the strikes were "a crime that would not go unpunished." The Jamaah urged the Arab masses to "express their anger and to support our people in Sudan and Afghanistan by besieging U.S. embassies in Islamic countries and forcing their rulers to close them down and expel the spies inside." Furthermore, the Jamaah promised, "Islamic movements, and those embracing Jihad in particular, [would] carry out their duties in facing this arrogance and address the United States in the language it understands." Islam's might was unstoppable, for "one billion Muslims are capable of turning their bodies into bombs which are equal in force to all the weapons of extermination and mass destruction possessed by the Americans." The message of al-Jamaah al-Islamiyah left no doubt about Islamist commitment to a prolonged, lethal terrorism campaign.

In early September an emboldened Hassan al-Turabi summarized the outcome of the recent crisis. "The [American] President wanted a target, and on his list Sudan was there," he told the *Christian Science Monitor*. "He finished his battle with Iran [a reference to the rapprochement with Khatami], and now it's our turn. This is a terrorist act against Sudan, a terrorist act." But with the rejuvenation of militant Islamism throughout the Muslim world, Turabi no longer needed to worry about the survival of Islamist Sudan. "Islam now is entrenched, and no one can remove it by force anymore," he said. "If you use force, we can defend ourselves. If you come in peace, we welcome you; if you come to fight us, we can fight back. We are powerful." Turabi attributed this positive and encouraging development to the rise of bin Laden's stature, in itself partially an outcome of the U.S. strike. Bin Laden "lives in a very remote place there, but now—ho, ho!— you [Americans] raised him as the hero, the symbol of all anti-West forces in the world," Turabi noted. "All the Arab and Muslim young people, believe me, look to him as an example." The widespread hatred of the United States would "create 10,000 bin Ladens," Turabi predicted.

IN EARLY SEPTEMBER 1998 the Islamist struggle in Kosovo began escalating again. The UCK (the Kosovo Liberation Army) was bolstered by hundreds of Iranian fighters arriving via Albania. The key trainers and elite-unit fighters of the UCK include many veteran "Afghans" and "Bosnians"—Iranians, Afghans, Algerians, Saudis, Egyptians, and even Chechens who had fought in Afghanistan and/or Bosnia. These forces are now about 7,000 mujahideen strong. Most of them are loyal to bin Laden and Zawahiri, and the financial and logistical system that sustains them in Albania and into Kosovo is run by bin Laden. The London-based Islamic Observation Center (IOC) warned that "a major campaign is being waged under U.S. intelligence supervision against Islamic activists of various nationalities in Macedonia, Kosovo Province, and in Albania." Under the guidance of U.S. officials, local police forces continued raiding Islamist institutions as well as "the apartments and homes of Islamists who were active in Bosnia for a while and who left after the signing of the Dayton agreement" and continued arresting many Islamists. Some of these Islamists were swiftly "extradited" to Egypt and Saudi Arabia. The IOC also accused the United States of "setting up an intelligence center in the Albanian capital to coordinate positions with the authorities in the Balkans with the aim of hunting down and apprehending Islamists." The IOC repeated previous warnings that the suppression of Islamists in the Balkans "will not produce any good results and instead will only exacerbate the feelings of Muslims against everything American." With the Islamists yearning for excuses to strike out, the Clinton administration could not have been more accommodating.

In late 1998, despite the growing pressure from U.S. intelligence and its local allies, the Islamist terrorist networks operating in and from Albania continued to expand. Starting in late November, a new network made up of bin Laden's supporters was being established in Albania under the cover of various Muslim charity organizations. According to Fatos Klosi, the head of ShIK, the Albanian intelligence service, this network was using Albania "as a springboard for operations in Europe." Klosi said that the network is made of "Egyptians, Saudi Arabians, Algerians, Tunisians, Sudanese, and Kuwaitis" operating under the cover of several different humanitarian organizations. Klosi explained that the network's "terrorists had already infiltrated other parts of Europe from bases in Albania through traffic in illegal immigrants, who have been smuggled by speedboat across the Mediterranean to Italy in huge numbers."

The senior supervisor of these activities is engineer Muhammad al-Zawahiri, the brother of Ayman al-Zawahiri. That a relative of Ayman al-Zawahiri is running the activities in the Balkans testifies to their growing importance to both bin Laden and Zawahiri and the Islamist leadership. Muhammad al-Zawahiri is a graduate of advanced terrorist training in both Pakistan and Afghanistan, where, according to Egyptian security officials, he was "trained in the use of weapons, in drawing up plans to assassinate officials and security men, and in carrying out attacks on public establishments." Recently he moved to Albania, ostensibly to work for a relief agency in Tirana. In reality he established an organization similar to the one bin Laden formed in Pakistan in the early 1980s—receiving the Islamists arriving in the Balkans and providing them with shelter until they deploy to operational cells or units. Muhammad al-Zawahiri also travels between Afghanistan, Pakistan, Yemen, and Sudan, meeting with aides of Ayman al-Zawahiri and supervising local preparations for activities in the Balkans.

Bin Laden's Arab "Afghans" also have assumed a dominant role in training the Kosovo Liberation Army. In late November a few dozen Arab mujahideen joined UCK forces at the heart of Kosovo as part of preparations for a spring offensive. Most of these mujahideen deployed from Bosnia and are hardened combat veterans. "I interviewed one guy from Saudi Arabia who said that it was his eighth jihad," a Dutch journalist said. By mid-December these mujahideen were overseeing a major training, organizational, and logistical buildup of the UCK forces, estimated at about 1,000 trained soldiers (mostly veterans of the war in Bosnia) and a few thousand armed supporters. These mujahideen oversee the still growing flow of significant amounts of antitank rockets, antiaircraft guns, shoulder-fired Stinger antiaircraft missiles, and long-barreled sniper rifles, all smuggled in from Albania. As a consequence the UCK forces are now far better armed, better equipped, and better organized than in the seven months of fighting in the spring and summer of 1998. But the ultimate objective of these Arab mujahideen is far more sinister than helping the anti-Serb struggle of their Muslim brethren in Kosovo. According to a senior Croat security official, "there are 'indications' that they are planning to mount operations against U.S. objectives in the Balkans, particularly since most of the new Arab 'Afghan' arrivals are supporters of Osama bin Laden."

THE TIMING of the anticipated Islamist escalation is all the more significant given the recent deterioration in the health of King Fahd. The round of problems that started in early August has already exacerbated the succession crisis, and bin Laden's activities strengthen the hands of the Islamists and anti-Americans. The Saudis seek compromises such as the deals negotiated by Prince Turki to help reduce the likelihood of a challenge to al-Saud power.

The Islamists are fully aware of this dynamics. The August 24 bulletin of the Movement for Islamic Reform in Arabia (MIRA) addressed the Saudi context of the strike: "The Kingdom [of Saudi Arabia] has an ailing monarch, and a dispute [over the succession] is on the point of breaking out in the [Saud] family. Oil prices have collapsed, the situation is fragile, and America is unable to deal with all this in the midst of these dangers. If the current American administration was aware of these dangers, it would have avoided rushing into this strike and would have absorbed the problems for a limited period. But we say once more that it was predestined by God that the [U.S.] President's scandals should occur at this time so that the cards got mixed up and the administration confused, or at the very least so that haughtiness overcame study, planning, and farsightedness."

At the core of the current crisis in Riyadh is a realignment of the key forces that enhanced the power of the Abdallah faction, reinforcing their Islamist and anti-American policies. This process started in the early summer, even before King Fahd's latest medical decline. The promotion of Prince Abdallah bin Abdul-Aziz, King Fahd's youngest and most-loved son, to minister status was interpreted by insiders in Riyadh as an indication that "King Fahd had decided to step down before the end of this year."

Prince Abdallah began looking for expansion of his power base, especially for allies who would serve as a buffer against the Americans. He found a key ally in Prince Khalid al-Faisal, the son of the first wife of the late King Faisal bin Abdul-Aziz and presently the governor of Asir, near the Yemenite border. Prince Khalid has recently emerged as the mouthpiece of Prince Abdallah. To demonstrate his power over defense matters—the prerogative of the Sultan faction—Prince Khalid instigated border clashes with Yemen in late July. Prince Khalid's brother is Foreign Minister Prince Saud al-Faisal, who is considered the most prominent among the Faisal clan. One of the stories making the rounds in Riyadh is that back in 1996, when Prince Abdallah was formally in charge, the United States, realizing that Prince Sultan's posture was rapidly declining, tried to promote Prince Saud as the next crown prince to the future King Abdallah (the present crown prince). The gravitation of both prominent al-Faisal brothers toward the Abdallah faction represents a major realignment.

Then in early August, King Fahd collapsed once again while in Jedda. The situation was so grave that he was flown to Riyadh, accompanied by two of his sons and his brothers, Defense Minister Prince Sultan and Prince Salman. Prince Abdallah was also rushed to Riyadh. Officially the king received minor treatment. Then on August 12 a special medical team, led by an American surgeon (always an indication of a major complication), removed King Fahd's gallbladder. He was released from the hospital on August 17, but on August 24, in the predawn hours, he was readmitted to the hospital. Again he was reported to have received routine postsurgery treatment. Meanwhile, without any special announcement, Crown Prince Abdallah formally resumed managing the day-to-day affairs of the kingdom. If anybody in the House of al-Saud needed a reminder of the instability in Riyadh, the continued deterioration of the king's health provided it.

Rumors that the king intended to abdicate the throne revived. With anti-American sentiments sweeping the country and the rapprochement with Iran working, the posture of the Sultan faction was on the decline. Prince Saud al-Faisal made a master gambit. His sister Hayfa is married to Prince Bandar bin Sultan. With Prince Bandar visibly losing influence in the wake of King Fahd's illness, Prince Saud offered Bandar a private deal through his sister. Although Prince Saud would remain foreign minister, Prince Bandar would take active charge of the kingdom's foreign affairs. In return he would not stand in the way of the Faisal brothers. Given the climate in Riyadh, Bandar had to accept the deal. As a consequence, noted a Riyadh insider, the "al-Faisal family seems to have become reinvigorated, while their brother-in-law the ambassador [Bandar] has started to become marginalized."

With the growing popularity of bin Laden and the Islamist trend and promises by Tehran and Islamabad not to challenge the House of al-Saud's hold on power as long as they pursue an anti-American policy and embark on the eviction of U.S. forces, both the Abdallah-Faisal and Salman-Nayif factions have every incentive to adopt such a policy. The pragmatic, prudent Islamists—from the leaders in Tehran to bin Laden—know that it would be impractical to expect a sudden U.S. withdrawal. They have settled for a series of quiet guarantees from Riyadh accompanied by some visible initial moves. In the meantime the uppermost echelons in the House of al-Saud will continue to appease the Islamists through indirect actions, from funding the Taliban and other Islamist jihads to containing Washington. In mid-September 1998 Riyadh was actively formulating a new anti-American strategy that would enable it to satisfy the Islamists without arousing Washington's ire. Those in the House of al-Saud have no illusion, however, that if forced to choose between pacifying bin Laden or the Clinton administration, they would pacify, placate, and appease bin Laden.

Saudi policy was put to the test toward the end of September, when Crown Prince Abdallah made an official visit to Washington as part of a worldwide trip intended to introduce him and his policies pending King Fahd's anticipated death. According to high-level Saudi officials, on the eve of the visit the White House assured Prince Abdallah that the Clinton administration would favorably consider Abdallah's position on a host of key issues such as the Arab-Israeli conflict, the rapidly warming Saudi-Iranian relations, and even Abdallah's opposition to the presence of U.S. forces in the Persian Gulf if Saudi Arabia could "deliver" Osama bin Laden. Eager to ensure the successful outcome of the visit, Saudi officials assured their American counterparts that Prince Abdallah had already secured a promise from the Taliban leader, Mullah Omar, that bin Laden would be extradited to Saudi Arabia as a result of his responsibility for the bombing in Riyadh and the Khobar Towers. Since the victims were American, the Saudi officials added, Riyadh would then extradite bin Laden to the United States. Prince Abdallah's visit to Washington proved most successful, as the ensuing changes in U.S. Middle Eastern policy—in particular the distinctly pro-Palestinian position in the proposed negotiations with Israel and the ensuing presidential visit to Gaza—aptly demonstrate.

Riyadh's problem, of course, was that there had never been such a deal with the Taliban. Moreover, having learned about these maneuvers, Islamabad feared that as the Taliban's patrons, they would be blamed by Washington for the inevitable collapse of the deal that never existed. The legacy of the recent U.S. cruise missile strike on the ISI's own training camps in Khowst did not add to Pakistan's incentives to help the United States.

Riyadh was apprised of the situation, and a high-level delegation led by Prince Turki and Mahmud Safar was immediately dispatched to Pakistan and Afghanistan. At first the Saudis offered an incentive package. If the Taliban would extradite bin Laden to the United States, their government would be recognized by the United States and numerous other states, granted lavish foreign aid, and assume Afghanistan's seat in the United Nations and the Organization of the Islamic Countries. Riyadh also offered to mediate for both the Taliban and Islamabad in their mounting dispute with Tehran. At the time joint Taliban-Pakistani forces were advancing in northern Afghanistan, committing atrocities against the local Shiite population—Iran's protégés. Tehran reacted by mobilizing and deploying large forces on its border with Afghanistan. In fall 1998 a tense near-war situation existed.

The Taliban's response was alarming. The head of the Taliban's delegation in essence questioned Riyadh's Islamic credentials because of the Saudi suggestion that a Muslim be extradited to the United States. Instead he suggested that three delegations of senior Muslim legal scholars—from Afghanistan, Pakistan, and Saudi Arabia—meet to study both the possible guilt of bin Laden and his supporters and the validity of their claim that the presence of U.S. forces in Saudi Arabia was un-Islamic. The Taliban's position amounted to tacit support for bin Laden's interpretation of the situation in Saudi Arabia, a most dangerous situation for Riyadh in view of the large number of Arab terrorists in Afghanistan and the Taliban's sponsorship of Islamist terrorism. An exasperated Prince Turki told the Taliban they were wasting his time. At this point Salman al-Umari intervened in the conversation, accused the Taliban of being ungrateful for the Saudi assistance, and threatened them with dire consequences if they did not extradite bin Laden to the United States. The Afghans demanded that al-Umari leave the country immediately on Turki's plane. For honor's sake, they relented and gave al-Umari a few days to leave.

Two days later Riyadh announced the withdrawal of al-Umari from Kabul for security reasons and the concurrent expulsion of the Afghan chargé d'affaires from Riyadh. At the same time Riyadh embarked on massive damage control. The reason for the crisis with the Taliban, Saudi officials intimated, was "attributable to several factors, most importantly the Taliban's failure to deal in an acceptable manner with the tireless endeavors made by Saudi diplomacy to mediate in the crisis between Iran and Afghanistan." The crisis had nothing to do with bin Laden, let alone the question of his extradition. Even al-Umari was compelled to take part in the charade. Meeting Saudi journalists in Pakistan while on his way back to Saudi Arabia, he insisted that "the deteriorating situation in Kabul" was the cause of his leaving Afghanistan. He then stressed that bin Laden's extradition had never been an issue between Saudi Arabia and the Taliban. "Osama bin Laden is a Yemeni," he explained, and so not subject to Saudi jurisdiction.

In late September 1998 Mullah Muhammad Omar, the Taliban leader, seized the initiative and moved swiftly to resolve the bin Laden issue. He convened an Afghan Ulema Council meeting in Kabul to decide what to do about bin Laden. The council resolved that because bin Laden had been made an Afghan citizen and granted an Afghan passport, only an Afghan Islamic court should determine his guilt or innocence. The Taliban stressed, however, that the only issue at hand was the U.S. accusation that bin Laden was responsible for the bombings in East Africa. As for the possibility of his involvement in terrorism in and against Saudi Arabia, the Taliban offered to send a delegation of their ulema to study the evidence available to their Saudi counterparts. Specifically this would be an interaction between the religious authorities of both countries—and thus a snub to official Riyadh. Saudi Arabia began to distance itself from the bin Laden issue. Prince Nayif, the interior minister, refused to address it, stating that "Bin Laden is not a Saudi, and I speak only about Saudis." Nevertheless, the Taliban increased their pressure on Riyadh. In early October, Kabul sent a formal request that a meeting be arranged for Afghan ulema with families of Saudi casualties of the Khobar bombing so that they could request a trial pending demand for blood vengeance—a procedure the Taliban maintain in Afghanistan. Riyadh turned down this proposal as well.

Prince Abdallah arrived in Islamabad in late October for major discussions with Nawaz Sharif on a host of issues, ranging from the Pakistani nuclear program to resolving the conflict with Iran. The Saudis agreed with the Pakistanis that the bin Laden extradition issue should be brought to a quick, conclusive end. Islamabad promised to have the Taliban resolve the issue once Riyadh disengaged. There was a flurry of Saudi-inspired leaks about Riyadh's enduring interest in resolving the Riyadh and Khobar bombings. Then Mullah Mohammad Hassan, the Taliban foreign minister, stated that Riyadh had not asked the Taliban to extradite bin Laden. Saudi officials did not deny the assertion. The Taliban's position was clarified in early November by a Kashmiri confidant of Mullah Omar's. The Taliban, he explained, would not extradite bin Laden or even ask him to leave Afghanistan "as long as Mulla Muhammad Omar is alive and remains in his official post because he is the only person who has allowed Osama bin Laden and other Arab groups to officially stay in Afghanistan." The Kashmiri also noted that all other Taliban leaders were united in refusing to hand him over to any foreign country.

On October 28 the Taliban announced the convening of a special Muslim court directly under Higher Court Judge Mowlawi Nur Mohammad

Thaqib—the highest Islamic judicial authority in Afghanistan—to study whether there was any basis for the accusations leveled against bin Laden. In essence, the mandate of this court was the Islamic equivalent of an American grand jury convened to examine available evidence and, should the evidence merit, indict. In a rare move Mowlawi Thaqib appealed to non-Muslim countries, a move aimed primarily at the United States, and asked that all available evidence against bin Laden be shared with the Afghan court.

On November 5 Saudi Arabia formally extricated itself from the bin Laden issue. Saudi interior minister Prince Nayif bin Abdul-Aziz exonerated bin Laden of all involvement in the Riyadh and Khobar bombings. "It has been reported that the two explosions in Riyadh and Khobar were planned by Osama bin Laden. This is not true. But maybe there are people who adopt his ideas. That is possible," Prince Nayif explained, echoing the Islamist "logic" used in the aftermath of the East Africa bombing. Prince Nayif stated that Saudi Arabia disowned bin Laden and no longer had any interest in him. "He is no longer a Saudi citizen. He lives outside and we are not concerned with him," Nayif stressed. "He does not constitute any security problem to us and has no activity in the Kingdom. Regarding his external activity, we are not concerned because he is not a Saudi citizen and constitutes no security risk to the Kingdom."

With that, the only accusations pending against bin Laden were the American ones over the bombing in Nairobi and Dar-es-Salaam. The Islamists now shifted the burden of proof to the United States as Kabul decided to permit direct U.S. participation in the investigation of bin Laden. Using Saudi intermediaries, Mowlawi Thaqib appealed directly to the U.S. government.

He assured American officials that they would be permitted to participate in the hearings as a formal part of the prosecution, provided they submitted detailed accusations supported by evidence. He also emphasized that any trial of bin Laden, if one were to take place, would be public and open for attendance by the international media and any interested foreign officials.

It is here that the peculiarities of the U.S. legal system, coupled with official Washington's insensitivity to Muslim issues, played into the hands of the Islamists. On November 5 Osama bin Laden and his military commander Abu-Hafs were formally indicted in New York, with the U.S. authorities presenting a 238-page document to bolster the case. The Taliban immediately asked for these documents. Fearing a claim of double jeopardy by the defense in case bin Laden were ever brought to justice in the United States, Washington refused the request. But instead of explaining this legal consideration, Washington chose to ignore the Taliban while U.S. officials leaked derogatory remarks about the "kangaroo" Islamic court in Kabul. On November 19, the day before the deadline set by the Kabul Sharia court, Taliban officials again appealed to the United States to deliver "the documents proving bin Laden's involvement in two attacks against American embassies in Nairobi and Dar-es-Salaam" that Washington claimed to have.

The next day, as expected, Mowlawi Thaqib declared that in the absence of any evidence against him, bin Laden would not face charges by any party and so was free to go anywhere he wished in the Taliban-controlled areas. The Taliban immediately exploited the anticipated court's decision for political purposes. Mullah Amir Khan Mottaqi, the Taliban's acting minister of culture and information, stated Kabul's position:

> As required, the Islamic Emirate [of Afghanistan] has fulfilled its responsibility in relation to Osama bin Laden. Firstly, the Islamic Emirate announced that Osama bin Laden will not use the territory of Afghanistan against other countries, and Osama bin Laden himself accepted it. Secondly, the Islamic Emirate's body for dealing with Osama bin Laden's case passed the task to the highest judicial body to investigate the issue and collect documents. More than one month has elapsed and no document has been presented to the Supreme Court and no one has brought an action against him. The Islamic Emirate [of Afghanistan] has fulfilled its major responsibility, and on the other hand, before the Taliban victory Osama was also living in Afghanistan and when he was fighting against Russia, America was pleased but after that the issue of Osama bin Laden was raised and this is a pretext for creating difficulties for the Afghans. . . .
> On the other hand, if anyone attempts to worsen the good relations with the Islamic Emirate of Afghanistan and raises the issue of Osama again it means that they are acting against the Islamic Emirate of Afghanistan through the issues of Osama bin Laden and this is an unreasonable action.

The outcome of the Taliban's legal exercise is of great importance for future Islamist terrorism. Bin Laden's exoneration was inevitable, because it was in the interests of both Pakistan and Saudi Arabia. By ignoring the court's appeal for evidence, however, the Clinton administration aggravated the problem by shifting the propaganda line away from grappling with the American accusations, which are based on facts and evidence, to the easy, palatable claim that the United States never had any evidence against bin Laden and that its ensuing campaign, including the bombing of Khartoum and Khowst, was fueled by hatred for Islamism. The Saudi opposition group the Movement for Islamic Reform in Arabia elucidated this theme: "The Taliban has announced that it has set 20 November as a deadline for the acceptance of evidence of bin Laden's implication in any terrorist act. Therefore, it has called on the Americans and others to provide evidence so as to present it to an Islamic court, which will be open to the public. . . . Following this logic, the Taliban won the argument and the Americans were embarrassed, as they rely solely on their strength, hegemony, and threats to deprive the Taliban of recognition and incite other forces against them." Legally the road is open for revenge and retribution against the United States by the wrongly accused and maligned Islamists—retribution that will be implemented through spectacular acts of terrorism.

———————

THROUGHOUT THE MUSLIM WORLD, from the Philippines to Morocco and in numerous Muslim émigré communities from Western Europe to the United States, Islamist terrorist and subversive cells are getting ready to strike out. As of late 1998, with the confrontation escalating between the United States and the Islamist international terrorist system as represented in the person of Osama bin Laden, the terrorists have become increasingly ready with redundant and resilient networks, weapons of mass destruction, and powerful bombs, as well as zeal and readiness for martyrdom—all for what they perceive to be the noble cause of bringing the United States suffering and pain.

11

Strengthening the Arsenal

AT THE END OF 1998 Osama bin Laden is fully entrenched in the Taliban's Afghanistan. His protection is anchored in the "Pushtunwali"—the dominant code of behavior of the Pushtun tribes of Pakistan and Afghanistan—and not just what is politically or financially expedient for Afghanistan and Pakistan. Bin Laden recently married his oldest daughter to Mullah Muhammad Omar, the Taliban's leader. Bin Laden himself took a young Pushtun woman as his fourth wife. Her identity is not clear, but she is no doubt a member of an important family and related to key leaders in the area, from senior Pakistani officials to the Taliban elite. According to rumors prevailing in Peshawar and Qandahar, she may be the daughter of Mullah Omar or the niece of the governor of Pakistan's North-West Frontier Province (NWFP), known to be a friend and patron of bin Laden. Because bin Laden is now related to the Pushtun elite by blood, the surrender of him to outsiders, especially non-Muslims, is inconceivable. The ferocious Pushtuns will now defend him and fight for him because that is what their Pushtunwali code stipulates. The lure of international recognition or American foreign aid is irrelevant in the Pushtunwali framework. Under this protective umbrella bin Laden and his team prepare to escalate their jihad.

In September 1998 Islamist leaders in both Western Europe and the Hub of Islam were braced for a marked escalation in the terrorists' confrontation with the West, in particular the United States. "The bombing of the two U.S. embassies in Nairobi and Dar-es-Salaam on 7 August is merely the beginning and the harbinger to a large-scale plan that will be translated into deeds under the slogan of 'Jihad Against America,'" a knowledgeable Arab observer in Europe noted at the beginning of the month. Other highly reliable, well-informed Arab sources were convinced that "the United States, by its action in Afghanistan and Sudan, has virtually stirred up a hornet's nest." Events in the terrorist camps and hideouts seemed to reinforce these observations.

This sense of hectic preparations for a marked escalation among the Islamist terrorists did not escape the attention of the Taliban leadership. In mid-September they undertook symbolic moves to contain bin Laden's overt belligerency and reduce world hostility, especially in view of the escalating crisis with Iran, in which Taliban-Pakistani forces were committing atrocities against Shiites in northern Afghanistan. Rumors spread that bin Laden had been placed under house arrest at his Qandahar base. But Wakil Ahmed Mutawakil, a senior Taliban official, denied that any restriction had been put on bin Laden's movements inside Afghanistan, and the Taliban provided tight security around bin Laden to protect against surprise raids, assassination attempts, or kidnapping operations. The Taliban did ban his contacts with international media to avoid provoking additional clashes with the United States. "I believe the Taliban movement was extremely angry because he was in touch with the newspapers," said Abdul-Bari Atwan, the editor of al-Quds al-Arabi. "Because of that they put him under house arrest, and also to protect him from any American raids or attempts to nab him." This did not prevent bin Laden from renewing his threats against the United States and President Clinton. "He told us he was safe and well, and also that he will answer Mr. Clinton with deeds and action. The man has been attacked by the Americans, and usually when he threatens he delivers. We should take this threat as seriously as we can."

Neither the Taliban nor the ISI interfered with the consolidation and expansion of the terrorist infrastructure in and out of Afghanistan. Osama bin Laden and his close staff are believed to be in his underground cave headquarters in the mountains not far from Jalalabad, eastern Afghanistan. The cave consists of three rooms hollowed into the rock face. The key room is bin Laden's control and communications center, which includes several computers (at least two laptop computers and one desktop), fax machines, and a satellite telephone system. The headquarters is constantly fed with material from all over the world, from status reports to newspaper clippings. From this headquarters bin Laden uses a state-of-the-art communications system, purchased from the West he hates so much, to communicate with Islamist networks throughout the Middle East, Asia, Africa, Western Europe, and the United States. Most of the communications are done via e-mail. The second room contains a small arsenal for the defense of the cave, ranging from assault rifles to mortars and machine guns. The compound itself is well protected. The third room is bin Laden's private room—a large library of classic Islamic writing and three uncomfortable beds with wool blankets and thin mattresses. During the day they are pushed up against the walls.

There are a few cave-bunkers in nearby mountains for the use of his immediate staff. Key Egyptian and Saudi "Afghans" and terrorist leaders—Ayman al-Zawahiri, Taseer Abdallah, Mustafa Hamzah, and Ahmad al-Islambuli—live in the same camp with bin Laden and work with him closely. In recent years their relations have evolved into close personal bonds that make this team very efficient. A source who maintains close relations with the jihadist groups recently observed that "the two men, bin Laden and Zawahiri, had nothing but admiration for each other's roles even before they met." He explained that Zawahiri made bin Laden change his way of ideological thinking and transform himself into a profound radical Islamist. As a result bin Laden has adopted the tenets of the Egyptian jihadist movements that place the armed or terroristic jihad above propaganda and advocacy for the cause. Bin Laden recently put his weight behind Zawahiri's claim for supreme leadership of the Egyptian jihad while marginalizing both Sheikh Omar Abdul Rahman (who is in an American jail) and Abbud al-Zumur (in an Egyptian jail). Although both remain supreme ideological authorities, Zawahiri and the command cells around bin Laden are now well entrenched as the undisputed operational commanders. The current crisis provides them with a unique opportunity to prove their worth and earn their mantle—by launching spectacular terrorist operations.

Fully aware of the U.S. effort to get him, bin Laden is working to ensure that the jihad he has launched will outlive him. Toward this end he is grooming his close friend and confidant Sheikh Taseer Abdallah, also a Saudi Islamist, as a political-theological leader. The public elevation of Taseer Abdallah started at the May 26 press conference bin Laden organized in the al-Badr camp in Khowst, Afghanistan. Rahimullah Yusufzai, a Pakistani journalist who participated in this press conference, noted that "Dr. Al-Zawahiri sat to bin Laden's right while to the left was seated Sheikh Taseer Abdallah, introduced to our group of 14 Pakistani journalists as the right-hand man of bin Laden." Since then Taseer Abdallah has become more active in leadership issues. His relationship with Zawahiri, the undisputed senior military commander of bin Laden's jihad, is very good, and so there will be continuity in this respect as well.

But Bin Laden is also considering his legacy. Although he has established a command structure that would be able to function if he were killed, Osama bin Laden would like to see the name bin Laden remain among the leaders of the Islamist jihad. He is grooming his eldest son,

Muhammad, who is fourteen, as a special aide and ultimate successor. Since August, Muhammad has rarely left his father's side, traveling with him throughout Afghanistan and Pakistan as he visits training installations and hideaways. Muhammad bin Laden is being given extensive military and terrorist training, and he now carries his own Kalashnikov assault rifle. He also fulfills tasks of great personal responsibility on behalf of his father. For example, on recent visits to training camps in Afghanistan, Muhammad stood guard and mounted an all-night vigil while his father slept in a safe house. He refused to rest or be replaced even though his father had assured him that they were "among friends" who could be fully trusted. If Osama bin Laden is killed in the near future, Taseer Abdallah and Zawahiri will take over. But young Muhammad bin Laden will remain on the roster, perhaps one day assuming leadership of the Islamist jihad.

Recently Osama bin Laden has embarked on his most ambitious Afghan project yet—the reconstruction and rejuvenation of Qandahar, which was destroyed by ceaseless fighting between the mid-1970s and the rise of the Taliban in the mid 1990s. Qandahar is the Taliban's "hometown" and center of power, so that its restoration by bin Laden is of immense political importance. The rebuilding of Qandahar, the only such effort in a major Afghan city since the mid-1970s, is a huge project that includes the construction of military infrastructure for both the Taliban and bin Laden's own strategic needs as well as the reconstruction and rejuvenation of the city. Although the Qandahar project started in mid-1997 and early 1998, construction of some of the military aspects expanded and accelerated in the aftermath of the U.S. attack. When completed, Qandahar will serve as a secure bastion of power for the Taliban against both domestic and foreign enemies. This construction work is carried out under the supervision of Arab teams, some distinct in their Bedouin kaffiyah (headdresses). In early 1998 bin Laden brought back from Sudan some of the key Arab "Afghans" who had run his construction projects there, and they now manage the rebuilding of Qandahar.

The primary military projects are a series of camps around Qandahar for the defense of the city and its vital infrastructure—the airport. One such garrison site, an expansive complex of mud-walled, turreted fortresses, has already been completed on the outskirts of Qandahar. It is manned by some 3,000 Arab "Afghans" and a large unit of Taliban forces. A second such garrison site is almost complete. In fall 1998 convoys were already bringing both Arabs and Afghans troops to the completed parts of this complex at night. Teams of Pakistani and Arab surveyors, the latter distinctive with their checkered headdresses, are already at work on the site of a few more garrisons around Qandahar. Heavy earthmoving equipment has begun digging at one of these sites. Additional teams of surveyors are looking for locations for new bases that when built will constitute an exterior ring of fortifications extending right up to Pakistani Waziristan.

The key to the Taliban's hold of Qandahar is the extensive compound inside the main airport, some twenty miles from the city, which is being expanded. The fortified zone surrounding the airport is already a massive defensive perimeter, built by the Soviets during the 1980s, when it withstood all mujahideen attacks, including those involving "seconded" Pakistani units, who fought in the ranks of the mujahideen when they failed on their own. The expansion and refurbishment project run by bin Laden is impressive. The runways have already been repaved, reinforced, and extended so that they can now support the latest heavy aircraft. The main fortified complexes have all been repaired. A new complex of about 300 houses, hidden behind walls and trees, was completed in the fall of 1998. This complex is already manned and protected by large armed guards who prevent unauthorized access even to its approaches.

Bin Laden is building clandestine strategic bases for his own use, exceptionally well fortified bunkers concealed in ravines in the mountains east of Qandahar. During the Afghan war the resistance maintained several large-scale clandestine facilities there. Those in the highland of Toba, from which there is a mountain pass down to Quetta, Pakistan, successfully withstood countless bombing and commando raids by Soviet and DRA forces. In the 1970s the Soviets oversaw the construction of similar underground facilities between Qandahar and Chaman, Pakistan, for the Baluchi rebels, which also withstood numerous attacks by the Pakistani armed forces. This myriad of underground facilities, a combination of refurbished old sites and many new ones, constitutes one of the strategic cores of bin Laden's terrorist empire— his own emergency dwelling and a key site for his weapons of mass destruction. Bin Laden is already using some of these secret facilities. His convoy of twenty or so black four-wheel-drive vehicles with tinted glass emerges at night from an obscure mountain pass and often rushes to his compound in the city and/or the fortified, well-defended complex near the airport.

The reconstruction and rejuvenation of Qandahar under bin Laden's supervision is the only attempt to revive the country in the aftermath of more than two decades of fratricidal and extremely cruel war. Pakistani officials acknowledge that bin Laden took the initiative in the rejuvenation of Qandahar, which shows that he understands the importance of winning over the "hearts and minds" of the civilian population. In the Taliban's Afghanistan this is a daunting task because of the harsh Islamist rules, such as forbidding music and all other forms of entertainment, imposed by the Taliban on a traditionally free urban population.

Under the supervision of Arab and Pakistani foremen a maze of scaffolds has emerged all over Qandahar since mid-1997. The construction projects have become the largest source of employment in the Qandahar area and distinctly improved the overall standard of living in the city. The water and sewage systems were repaired by 1997, and for the first time in a decade clean drinking water became available. By fall 1998 electricity had also been restored to most of the city. Bin Laden is overseeing the construction of a new commercial center for Qandahar that is boxed between a new market complex—a monumental shopping center by European and Middle Eastern standards—adjacent to the city's traditional main bazaar area and a huge mosque and religious institution built on the site of the city's old cinema (destroyed and forbidden by the Taliban). Bin Laden is also rebuilding a section of Qandahar as the residence area for the Taliban elite. The first building in that site was his own home, a massive stone building with a tower surrounded by a tall wall on a side street just across from the Taliban's "foreign ministry" building. Next to be completed was a magnificent housing complex in the style of rich Saudi Arabians. This complex comprises several houses hidden by walls and topped with pink and green pinnacles. Above the gate is an Arabic inscription with the Koranic verse: "Remember Allah at all times." Bin Laden gave this complex to Mullah Omar as a wedding present, but only Omar's two wives and numerous children live there. To enhance his religious-mythical stature Mullah Omar lives in a nineteenth-century palace attached to Qandahar's most revered shrine, where a relic of the Prophet Muhammad's cloak is preserved. Bin Laden renovated the palace and mosque as well.

In the aftermath of the U.S. cruise missile strikes, bin Laden launched a crash program to build a new command and control center for international terrorism operations far from the Pakistani border. The new headquarters and communication center are being constructed in a natural cave system in the Pamir Mountains in Kunduz Province, near the border with Tajikistan. Special attention is paid to concealment and protection against both espionage and bombing. Pakistani experts consider it "impervious" to known forms of espionage and strike. Bin Laden's calculations in selecting this remote site are (1) the site is so close to the Tajik border, where Russian forces are stationed, that the United States would not dare to strike or bomb for fear of a Russian response; and (2) the site provides added security in a time of emergency because of the strong presence of Iranian intelligence in Tajikistan—a support system ready to provide a safe way out of Afghanistan should the need arise. At the current pace of construction and barring a major accident, this new headquarters will become operational by the first half of 2000.

———————

FROM HIS CAVE HEADQUARTERS bin Laden supervises a tangled web of financial entities, both his own and those filling the coffers of the Islamist movement. He also handles the foreign assets of the Taliban movement. There is no distinct Osama bin Laden, Inc., or even Zawahiri, Inc.; instead bin Laden maintains a tangled web of "companies," partnerships, and other-name entities that interact with one another and are ultimately concealed in another layer of bigger international financial entities so that his involvement in any of these investments cannot be discovered. The bin Laden financial system, both his own and that of the Islamist movement, comprises several interacting cores.

The first core is the Amsterdam-Anvir-Luxembourg triangle (Anvir is in Belgium). The bulk of the contributions and other transactions from the Persian Gulf States are laundered through this core. Contributions from individuals and "other entities" throughout the Arabian Peninsula are collected by two separate financial networks, one dominated by Kuwaiti and the other by Qatari businessmen. They route the money through area banks and London accounts. From there the money is transferred to a host of accounts in the triangle core and moved around into a web of Luxembourg companies (completely anonymous entities) that can use the money. The nerve center of this core is a holding company in Luxembourg, registered in the names of lawyers and businessmen from Arab and Gulf States, which has an interest in a multitude of joint companies and administers investments, real estate holdings, maritime transport, trade companies, public works projects, construction companies, contracting companies, and agricultural companies. These companies have interests in Asia, Africa, and Latin America. Whenever possible European businesspeople administer, perhaps unknowingly, the operations and interests of the Luxembourg companies that are owned by local legal firms. The diverse activities of these companies include real estate, maritime transport, lease of aircraft, import and export, and public construction works. Amsterdam is another principal financial center, where money is invested in local companies that operate in shipbuilding, maritime contracting, and maritime transport.

Another core is the Far East, with the main centers in Indonesia and Malaysia. The money gets to the Far East from the Persian Gulf, again through Qatari and Kuwaiti networks, as well as networks in Hadhramaut (Yemen) and Italy. At first the bin Laden financial activities, conducted via Islamist entities throughout the region, expanded rapidly. But even bin Laden was not immune to the economic crisis plaguing the Far East, and so he began to scale down operations, moving assets and resources to Luxembourg via Italy.

An up-and-coming venue for Islamist funds is a combination of the former Soviet states of Central Asia with Germany and Eastern Europe. Access to this seemingly unrelated group of states was made possible through bin Laden's building of relations with the Russian Mafia, in particular the branches operating in Qatar and to a lesser extent Cyprus. What started as a series of simple deals in the mid-1990s—purchasing explosives and weapons for bin Laden in Ukraine and smuggling them to Qatar and elsewhere—has since been transformed into a more comprehensive relationship. The Mafia's involvement in prostitution and drug and alcohol distribution in Muslim Qatar and the United Arab Emirates does not seem to bother the Islamists when it comes to business. The Russian Mafia now smuggles bin Laden's funds to the key areas of its operations, Central Asia and Central-Eastern Europe, where they are invested in the huge gray markets. This connection is becoming extremely important with the vast expansion of the Afghan drug trade.

In addition bin Laden maintains an interest in politically correct businesses, helping to keep Sudan, Yemen, and Afghanistan economically afloat. To do this he maintains large deposits in key local banks and invests heavily—through covers, fronts, partnerships, and so forth—in a wide variety of local companies and businesses. Much of the money used for these activities is actually that of the Islamist movement. Vital are the $500 million deposited in the Sudanese Central Bank to cover the Sudanese pound and Sudan's import ability and the $200 million deposited in the Yemeni Central Bank, as well as other deposits in the name of Sheikh Zanadani, the leader of the Yemeni Islamists. Turabi's son Issam handles bin Laden's financial assets in Sudan.

Recently, with advances in electronic banking and international transactions and with world attention increasingly focused on him, bin Laden ordered the establishment of yet another web of commercial and financial entities to further reduce the risk of exposure and seizure of his money. Based on the European banking system, the new web also rotates money through Africa and Latin America. Bin Laden's money is buried in numerous front institutions, most of which are holding companies with large shares in financial, real estate, and commercial institutions throughout the world. The new system was described as a "global network"—a highly complex, tangled, and multilayered organizational network that spreads throughout the world and in which bin Laden's name does not appear at all. The types of companies and entities into which this money is ultimately invested are identical to those of the original triangle core.

As the sums of money available from the drug trade have increased, bin Laden and the Russian Mafia have established yet another complex money-laundering operation described by an insider as "an extended and octopus-like network that uses political names in Asia and Africa in return for commissions." These funds are used to finance the Taliban movement and a host of Islamist terrorist operations. Bin Laden makes a commission on these transactions, which is laundered by the Russian Mafia in countries other than Russia and Afghanistan.

Nobody really knows how much money is involved in these transactions. The available estimates and fragmentary evidence are mind-boggling. In attempting to analyze the worth of these networks, it is virtually impossible to distinguish between Islamist funds and bin Laden's own personal funds. Since he has repeatedly devoted himself and all of his possessions to the cause of the Islamist jihad, this distinction may not really exist. The only personal funds Osama bin Laden is known to have are those earmarked for his children. Estimated at anywhere between $50 and $100 million, these funds are concealed in a multitude of private bank accounts in London, Monaco, and various Caribbean islands, all held under non-Arab names. In the early 1990s the net worth of the Islamist network was estimated at $600 million in the West alone. In addition a host of deposits and investments in Sudan, Yemen, Somalia, Afghanistan, and Pakistan totaled well over a billion dollars. Since then annual donations from the Kuwaiti Islamist establishments have been estimated at about $200 million and from the other Gulf States—Saudi Arabia, the United Arab Emirates, Qatar, Bahrain, and Oman—at about an additional $400 million. The annual income of the Taliban from the drug trade is estimated at $8 billion. Bin Laden administers and manages these funds—laundering them through the Russian Mafia—in return for a commission of between 10 and 15 percent, which provides an annual income of about a billion dollars. Bin Laden also launders operational funds on the back of the semiofficial assistance the Taliban are getting from Pakistan, Saudi Arabia, and other Gulf States.

A lot of money is being spent on a rapidly expanding web of Islamist charities and social services, including the recently maligned al-Qaidah. Bin Laden's first charity, al-Qaidah never amounted to more than a loose umbrella framework for supporting like-minded individuals and their causes. In the aftermath of the bombings in Nairobi and Dar-es-Salaam, al-Qaidah has been portrayed in the West as a cohesive terrorist organization, but it is not. These Islamist charities and social services organizations capitalize on the growing misery and destitution prevailing throughout the developing world to build popular support bases for Islamist causes. These entities entice people into the fold of militant and radical Islam by providing food and medical and educational services as well as work, religious services, and housing projects. This web of seemingly legitimate organizations is also used for sheltering Islamist terrorists and laundering operational funds. For practical reasons—so as not to run into trouble with local governments—the organizations themselves remain "legally clean." Meanwhile, the growing dependence of ever-growing segments of the population on these Islamist services, especially when local governments prove incapable of providing comparable services, has already built grassroots support for the Islamists that many governments would not dare challenge to assist the United States in its fight against terrorism.

WITH NO FINANCIAL PROBLEMS in sight, since early 1998 bin Laden has been able to devote himself to transforming the World Front for Jihad against Jews and Crusaders into a potent military-terrorist organization. Bin Laden and Zawahiri first had to overcome a number of personal and ego problems among the parties to the Islamic Front. In the spring the Islamic Front's command moved on to dealing with more pertinent issues, such as the structure of the main forces to be set up and the mechanism of coordination among the member-entities and with Tehran and the Hizb-Allah International. All the outstanding problems were resolved by early summer 1998. Bin Laden and Zawahiri personally checked all the details. In the process Zawahiri emerged as the leader behind the idea of the Islamic Front as an operational entity. His high standing among all Islamist terrorist leaders and commanders provided him with the necessary contacts to make the Islamic Front a success. Bin Laden and Zawahiri were able to actually reorganize relations among the member organizations, ensuring high levels of mutual cooperation and coordination on the organizational, logistical, and increasingly operational levels.

In the aftermath of the resounding support for the idea of the Islamic Front throughout the Muslim world, many clandestine organizations joined without adding their name to the original fatwa of February 1998. The organizations that announced their membership in the Islamic Front are Egyptian Islamic Jihad, the Egyptian Armed Group, the Pakistan Scholars Society, the Partisans Movement in Kashmir, the Jihad Movement in Bangladesh, and the Afghan military wing of the "Advice and Reform" commission, led by Osama bin Laden.

The most significant development was that of a mechanism for formulating long-term strategies and coordinating worldwide operations for all of these organizations and entities. The Islamic Front established a shura (consultative) council consisting of the highest leaders of all the participating entities. The shura is chaired by bin Laden with Zawahiri as the senior military commander. The emergence of a unified command center increased the effectiveness of the forces available to the Islamic Front. The long-established theological-ideological harmony among these organizations has now been fully translated into military cooperation. The joint cooperation with the sponsoring states—Iran, Pakistan, and Sudan—is already apparent in the growing "professionalism" of these entities, in particular at the organizational and financial levels, as they have adopted better communications and clandestine practices.

A lot of money was spent to implement these changes. Bin Laden oversaw the laundering and distribution of the funds, and his religious authority was also critical to the realization of this undertaking. But it was Zawahiri who formulated and implemented these organizational configurations on the military-terroristic level. By early summer 1998 the differences over establishing the Islamic Front as an operational entity ended. All available evidence suggests that there is widespread, voluntary compliance by all the organizations involved with the decisions that were made in Afghanistan. The command structure and responsibilities of key commanders were determined and are recognized. The new, reorganized logistical and funding system is operating. The Islamic Front has moved from the constituent and organizational phase to being fully operational. The intensifying travel of key individuals and emissaries throughout Europe and between Europe and the Middle East suggests heightened coordination of forthcoming operations. These preparations are conducted in accordance with bin Laden's decree that "Americans, be they military or civilian, will become the targets of armed attacks." He and Zawahiri asked their commanders to formulate tactics "for tracking down Americans and striking their interests" for their own areas of operations.

In fall 1998 the forces of the Islamic Front were organized in three layers. At the core were bin Laden, Zawahiri, and a nucleus of loyalists, both commanders and small groups of mujahideen. These mujahideen were deployed with bin Laden, Zawahiri, and Taseer Abdallah as their personal guards; they also make up independent cells all over the world. The second tier comprises the various organizations that make up the Islamic Front. There the operational and administrative cadres answer to their own command structure, which in turn is integrated into the global system. The fact that bin Laden does not take credit for operations but rather encourages the local entities to take credit under identifying though bogus names—such as the Islamic Army for the Liberation of the Holy Places used in East Africa—endears him to the local commanders, who do not see him and Zawahiri as a threat to their personal standing. The third tier is made up of the multiple Arabs and other "Afghans" who operate in the ranks of other groups but maintain close contacts with their former comrades. These "Afghans" and the younger generation of local followers have repeatedly proven their ideological zeal and willingness to rally to Islamist causes irrespective of organizational affiliation. The organized, directly controlled networks of bin Laden supporters are strongest in Afghanistan, Pakistan, Sudan, Yemen, Somalia, Bosnia-Herzegovina, Tajikistan, Chechnya, Albania, and numerous Gulf States. Strong cells and small terrorist networks exist throughout most of the Middle East, Western Europe, and the United States. Altogether a few thousand terrorists, supporters, and volunteers are under the command of bin Laden and Zawahiri at any given time.

According to Arab sources, U.S. intelligence briefed conservative Arab governments that the bin Laden organization—the Islamic Front—"is an informal coalition of former Afghan Mujahideen of various nationalities, including Egyptians, Jordanians, Palestinians, Lebanese, people hailing from the [Persian] Gulf, Algerians, Pakistanis, and Afghans, among other Muslims from elsewhere, including the United States itself." The American briefers noted that the bulk of bin Laden's forces "are permanently based in Sudan, Yemen, Ethiopia, and Somalia, as well as in Pakistan and Afghanistan." A new generation of mujahideen is being prepared in the numerous training camps, especially in eastern Afghanistan and Pakistan. A recent Arab visitor to Afghanistan identified in one cluster of camps some 5,000 trainees, between sixteen and twenty-five years old, who have come from virtually all corners of the world. The most promising among them are assigned to the Martyrdom (suicide) Battalions of the (Armed) Islamic International. They call themselves human bombs and are trained and molded to carry out spectacular operations worldwide in the name of all-Islamic causes. "They are there to wage a global war of Jihad and are poised to fight on all fronts wherever they are needed," the visitor observed. The next time these martyrs strike, they might be carrying weapons of mass destruction.

The entire Afghanistan-based mujahideen force under Osama bin Laden includes more than 10,000 trained fighters. In fall 1998 the status of this force was greatly enhanced with the addition of the Taliban elite. The Taliban joined bin Laden's forces after the two groups successfully defended the Kabul war front against overwhelming forces and defeated Ahmad Shah Massud's forces in Bamyan, where Arab "Afghans" spearheaded the capture of "Ho Chi Minh City"—Massud's fortified center in the Hindu Kush mountains near Bamyan, a center that had held against repeated DRA assaults in the late 1980s. At the core of bin Laden's forces are about 3,000 Arab "Afghans." In early November Egyptian intelligence estimated the number of these Arab "Afghans" at 2,830: 594 Egyptians, 410 Jordanians,

291 Yemenis, 255 Iraqis, 177 Algerians, 162 Syrians, 111 Sudanese, 63 Tunisians, 53 Moroccans, and 32 Palestinians in addition to scores from Gulf and other states. The rest of the fighters are Pakistanis, Bangladeshis, Tajiks, Uzbeks, Chechens, and members of other nationalities. They are all fiercely loyal to bin Laden as well as to pan-Islamic causes and their own national causes. A growing number of these mujahideen already show up in jihad fronts all over the world, mainly in Kosovo and Kashmir.

The spreading notoriety of bin Laden's Islamic Front and the growing solidarity with him and his message in the aftermath of the U.S. cruise missile strikes on Sudan and Afghanistan are not lost on the terrorism-sponsoring states, primarily Pakistan. These recent developments only reinforce existing relationships with bin Laden. For example, Osama bin Laden has a deal with the ISI, solidified in spring 1998, in which his people will carry out spectacular terrorist strikes at the heart of India under the banner of anti-Israel and anti-U.S. "campaigns" and "organizations" in return for Pakistani support, protection, and sponsorship. This agreement enables the ISI to strike in India while denying any involvement.

The ISI actively assists bin Laden in the expansion of an Islamist infrastructure in India. Very effective are the propaganda cassettes distributed throughout India's Muslim population. In these cassettes bin Laden and other Islamist authorities describe India, along with the United States and Israel, as the greatest enemy of Islam. Primary venues for the distribution of Islamist propaganda and incitement material are the institutions run by the Ahl-i-Hadith religious charity, which is associated with the Lashkar-i-Tuiba Islamist Kashmiri organization. Under the command of Abdul Karim Tunda, the Lashkar-i-Tuiba has already been responsible for several bombs in New Delhi. In addition bin Laden has major cells in the southern cities of Bangalore and Hyderabad that support the Kashmiri cause, mainly Harakat ul-Ansar, a Pakistan-sponsored Islamist organization that actively participates in the jihad in Kashmir and trains mujahideen for jihad fronts all over the world. The propaganda distributed by these cells also stresses the significance of other Islamist jihads all over the world. These activities are funded through some of bin Laden's charities.

The U.S. strike on the ISI's training camps in the Khowst area only provided formal justification and added motivation for the unfolding escalation. For example, Emir Bakht Zamin, the supreme commander of al-Badr Mujahideen, an ISI-sponsored Kashmiri group based in Muzaffarabad, Pakistan, stresses the all-Islamic character of his organization. "In any part of the world where Muslims are oppressed, from Algeria to Kosovo and from Palestine to Egypt and to the Kashmir, we fight our battle for justice and for equality," he recently explained. Al-Badr Mujahideen and thus the

ISI openly support the Algerian Armed Islamic Group and the Egyptian al-Jamaah al-Islamiyah, and their main camp in Pakistan harbors "an international Muslim brigade" comprising Arab volunteers. Zamin endorses and supports the jihad declared by bin Laden. He emphasizes that the recent U.S. attack, which also hit al-Badr's own training site in Afghanistan, only served to reinforce his conviction of the centrality of the anti-U.S. jihad. "Bin Laden is right to fight for the withdrawal of U.S. troops from the holy places in Saudi Arabia. Clinton is involved in a sex scandal," Zamin stated, "and so he bombs Afghanistan and Sudan in the hope of saving his job. It is the United States that is forcing us to make war."

Islamabad has no reason to refrain from capitalizing on these sentiments to escalate its war by proxy against India behind the cover of bin Laden and his Islamist jihad. In fall 1998 the combination of bin Laden's growing notoriety and the U.S. strike against the ISI's Kashmiri bases in Khowst made it logical for bin Laden to avenge the victims of Khowst by supporting their cause. The escalation of the Islamist struggle for Kashmir also appeals to the Taliban. Rashid Karimov, the head of the Asia-Pacific Department of the Institute for Strategic Studies in Moscow, noted that "the Taliban leaders, emboldened by their recent military successes in Afghanistan, are most likely contemplating expanding their horizon beyond their present frontiers." Taliban leaders have recently called for "launching a holy war for the victory of Islam in India and Central Asia." Bin Laden is a natural ally in this regional jihad. Moreover, bin Laden's near-mythical notoriety has created expectations among the Islamists of Kashmir. "Bin Laden is coming—he will purge the Indian army from Kashmir" is an opinion frequently heard among the Islamists of Kashmir.

Since September 1998 the anticipated escalation in the Pakistan-sponsored Islamist terrorism in Kashmir has been associated with bin Laden. For example, Ghulam, a Harakat ul-Ansar (now called Harkat-ul-Mujahideen) commander in Srinagar, Kashmir, who had been trained in the Badr camp in Khowst, stressed his loyalty to bin Laden. "Our 'father' bin Laden has sent brothers from Afghanistan to wage Jihad," he explained. The ISI has recently adapted existing organizational frameworks to reinforce the "new character" of the war in Kashmir. Very important is the emergence of the Taliban-i-Kashmir organization—ostensibly an Afghanistan-based Kashmiri Islamist terrorist organization whose existence warrants the growing numbers of Afghan, Pakistani, and Arab "Afghan" terrorists in the ranks of the ostensibly Kashmiri national liberation forces. These foreigners are largely Islamists fighting for a sacred cause, not the mercenaries the ISI recruited in the mid-1990s. There is already evidence of popular support for bin Laden in the ranks of the Islamist terrorists fighting in Kashmir. For example, on November 1 Indian security authorities engaged a well-armed Harkat-ul-Mujahideen detachment trying to cross over from Pakistan in the Poonch area. In the pockets of four Pakistani terrorists killed, the Indians found for the first time photographs of bin Laden along with the usual pocket Korans and a book on guerrilla warfare.

The overt involvement in the Islamist war against India of an "arch-terrorist"—the popular image of bin Laden—provides a deniability cover for the ISI that goes beyond the war by proxy in Kashmir. For Pakistan sheltering and sponsoring other Islamist strikes against U.S. and Israeli targets all over the world is not a heavy price to pay for exploiting the Islamists' zeal and commitment to further Pakistan's own strategic objectives. The arrangements between Osama bin Laden and the ISI, in which the World Islamic Front will carry out spectacular terrorist operations in India, mainly against Jewish/Israeli and American targets, on behalf of the ISI in return for sponsorship, become all the more appealing to Islamabad. This type of evolving relationship is not unique to Islamabad but is the precursor of things to come as the confrontation between the U.S.-led West and the Hub of Islam continues to escalate. International terrorism will become the strategic weapon of choice of more and more states that find themselves besieged by Westernization and a grassroots counterclash they cannot endure.

A concurrent intensification and diversification of the Islamist buildup has taken place at the heart of the West—Western Europe, the United States, and Canada—not only for the support of spectacular terrorist strikes but also to accelerate the ongoing erosion of Western society. The surge in arrests and indictments of known and suspected associates of Osama bin Laden in the United States and Western Europe in the wake of the East Africa bombings exposed the extent and diversity of his networks. In the United States, for example, a former personal secretary of bin Laden's—Lebanese-born Wadih El Hage—was discovered in Arlington, Texas, managing a tire shop, while another operative—Egyptian-born Ali Mohamed—served in the U.S. Army's elite Green Berets. Mamduh Mahmud Salim, a Sudanese troubleshooter for bin Laden, was arrested while visiting a friend in Munich, Germany, and extradited to the United States in mid-December. But most of the assets raided by the security forces all over the world were related to the support networks, such as al-Qaidah and the U.S.-based al-Kifah, which were established during the 1980s in conjunction with the Afghan jihad. Although the arrest of several suspected lieutenants of bin Laden's and the rush underground of others no doubt disrupts Islamist activities, a new generation of networks is already operating throughout the West completely outside the realm usually associated with Islamist terrorism.

The support and management echelons of the new Islamist networks operate in conjunction with organized crime. What started as active participation in the drug trade, encouraged by Iranian intelligence as an effective instrument of obtaining cash and cover in the West, has now expanded into a myriad of criminal activities, including even prostitution, an incredible development given Islam's obsession with women's modesty and its ban on all nonmarital sexual activities. The new Islamist networks locally obtain operational funds by selling drugs, laundering money, and disseminating Iranian-printed high-quality $100 bills and by providing support services and intelligence to operational terrorist teams whenever they deploy locally. The prostitution rings, which use mainly Bosnian-Muslim and North African women, are the latest development. Using modern, promiscuous women enables the Islamists to penetrate segments of high society in the West beyond the reach of Islamists or even ordinary Muslim men. Not accidentally one of the key control centers of these networks is in Anvers, Belgium—also a key center of bin Laden's clandestine financial empire.

The operations of these networks take place with extremely deep cover within the tangled web of organized crime, an environment that already goes out of its way to shield its activities from law enforcement authorities. This multiple-layered security significantly increases the likelihood that the Islamists will achieve surprise when they launch a major spectacular terrorist operation in the West. The involvement in criminal and promiscuous activities does seem to lessen the Islamist zeal and commitment of the participants. Specific fatwas from Islamist luminaries authorize these highly irregular, seemingly un-Islamic activities because they also contribute to the destruction of Western society and civilization. The Sunni Islamist fatwas are based on and derived from earlier rulings of the higher Shiite courts issued in connection with operations of HizbAllah and Iranian intelligence. The logic of these activities was elucidated in the mid-1980s in the HizbAllah's original fatwa on the distribution of drugs: "We are making these drugs for Satan—America and the Jews. If we cannot kill them with guns so we will kill them with drugs." These Sunni Islamist activities and fatwas constitute another expression of the growing influence of Tehran on the Sunni Islamist terrorist movement. But just when Western law enforcement and security authorities had begun to unravel one component of the Islamist clandestine infrastructure in the West, a more complex, sinister, and surreptitious network went into action.

———

OSAMA BIN LADEN has already completed backup plans if the Taliban renege on their promise of hospitality. Bin Laden's main problem in Afghanistan, however, is neither the threat of extradition to the United States by the Taliban nor a building conflict with the Taliban's leadership. Bin Laden maintains very close relations with the Iranian leadership and, as a member of the Committee of Three since its inception in summer 1996, in effect answers to the chief of Iranian foreign intelligence. In early September 1998 the crisis between Iran and the Taliban over the Taliban's killing in August of nine Iranian diplomats and the slaughter of over 4,000 Afghan Shiites during the fighting in northern Afghanistan almost reached the point of a war between Iran and the Taliban. Although bin Laden tried to mediate between Kabul and Tehran, the overall crisis has complicated his ability to operate just as a major escalation is about to be unleashed.

On August 31, 1998, before the crisis reached its peak, Hassan al-Turabi approached Iraqi vice president Taha Yassin Ramadan, then visiting Khartoum, and asked if bin Laden could move his headquarters and operations to Iraq. Ramadan immediately responded with a resounding yes, and bin Laden was notified within a few hours. Bin Laden has had some relations with Iraqi intelligence since 1993, when he played a role in the preparation and running of the Islamist operations in Somalia in which Iraqi special forces and Arab "Afghans" retrained by Iraqi intelligence also took part. In June 1994 bin Laden met Faruq al-Hijazi, then the director of the Iraqi Intelligence Department and at present the chief of the entire Iraqi intelligence apparatus, while he was in Khartoum. Turabi mediated the meeting, hoping they could formulate a joint strategy against the pro-Western regimes of Arabia. But the Iraqis were still apprehensive about bin Laden's Islamist zeal and close contacts to Tehran, and the contacts did not develop into practical cooperation.

Recently Baghdad's overall attitude toward militant Islamism has changed. As Iraq's crisis has mounted, Baghdad has encouraged the Islamists—a combination of Arab "Afghans" and Muslim Brotherhood offshoots—because of a series of pragmatic considerations. Saddam Hussein needs their anti-Shiite zeal to counterbalance the Shiite revivalism in the south. Their all-Islamic ideology also limits Kurdish nationalism. In the Sunni Arab parts of Iraq the Islamists have developed a comprehensive social services program to ease the suffering of the Iraqi people that has resulted from the U.N. sanctions, distributing food, medicine, clothes, and money to the growing numbers of Iraqis attending religious lessons in their mosques. These activities are financed by Osama bin Laden's charities. Starting in the mid-1990s with a few mosques at al-Fallujah, about 60 miles west of Baghdad, and Mosul, in Kurdistan, the Islamists—bearded and wearing their special outfits, which are a combination of traditional Arab gowns and camouflage militarylike uniforms—can now be seen all over

Iraq, especially in Baghdad but also in such places as al-Azamiyah on the al-Rasafah embankment, al-Fallujah, Mosul, al-Nasiriyah, and al-Ramadi. Because of their proximity to Arabia, some of the Arab "Afghans" consider their presence in Iraq more important than being in Afghanistan.

The development of the Iranian-Saudi rapprochement back in spring 1998 caused Turabi to revive his efforts to mediate between Saddam Hussein and bin Laden. Baghdad had been impressed by the anti-American zeal displayed by the Islamists during the U.S.-Iraqi crisis. Turabi was apprehensive about Tehran's promise to Riyadh to stop terrorism and subversion against Arab regimes and began looking for an alternate support system should the need arise to confront the House of al-Saud. As a consequence two of bin Laden's senior military commanders, Muhammad Abu-Islam and Abdallah Qassim, visited Baghdad between April 25 and May 1 for discussions with Iraqi intelligence. The importance of these contacts to Baghdad was shown by their meeting with Qusay Hussein, Saddam's son, who is now responsible for intelligence matters and was personally involved in both the Iraqi contribution to the Somalia operation and later the intelligence cooperation with Iran. Both sides were very satisfied with the results of the negotiations.

One of the first concrete outcomes of these contacts was Baghdad's agreement to train a new network of Saudi Islamist intelligence operatives and terrorists from among bin Laden's supporters still inside Saudi Arabia. Special clandestine cross-border passages were organized by Iraqi intelligence to enable these Saudis to make it to Iraq without passports or any other documents. The first group of Saudi Islamists crossed over in mid-June for a four-week course in the al-Nasiriyah training camp. Most were trained in intelligence—how to collect intelligence on American targets and plan and launch strikes. The other Saudis were organized into a network for smuggling weapons and explosives from Iraq into Saudi Arabia. This group has returned to Saudi Arabia and is operational, having smuggled in the first loads of weapons and explosives. Later in the summer a second group of eleven Saudi Islamists received a month of training in the most sophisticated guerrilla techniques. By then Iraqi intelligence anticipated a marked expansion in the training of Saudi Islamists, for Iraqi intelligence took over two training camps they had previously used for training the Iranian Mujahideen-ul-Khalq.

Bin Laden moved quickly to solidify the cooperation with Saddam Hussein. In mid-July, Ayman al-Zawahiri traveled to Iraq clandestinely. He met senior Iraqi officials, including Taha Yassin Ramadan, to discuss practical modalities for the establishment of bin Laden's base in Iraq, the expansion of training for his mujahideen, and a joint strategy for an anti-U.S. jihad throughout the Arab world and North Africa. Baghdad could not have been more helpful, conditioning its support on bin Laden's promise not to incite the Iraqi Muslim Brotherhood into establishing an Islamic state in Iraq; in other words not to conspire against Saddam Hussein's reign. While in Iraq, Zawahiri was also taken to visit a potential site for bin Laden's headquarters near al-Fallujah and terrorist training camps run by Iraqi intelligence. In al-Nasiriyah he saw the training provided to Saudi Islamists. In the name of Osama bin Laden, Zawahiri assumed responsibility for a training camp in the al-Nasiriyah desert established by Iraqi intelligence in about 1997 for terrorists from Saudi Arabia and the Gulf States. This largely symbolic event indicates Baghdad's recognition of bin Laden as the "local authority" in the struggle against the U.S. presence in and influence on the Arabian Peninsula.

The strategic significance of bin Laden's improving relations with Baghdad, whether he decides to move there or not, lies in Saddam Hussein's hatred of the House of al-Saud. If bin Laden decides to strike at the House of al-Saud rather than at American targets in Saudi Arabia, despite the positions taken by Tehran and Islamabad, Baghdad will surely provide him with all possible support. At present bin Laden shows no inclination to violate the strategy formulated in Tehran. The mere existence of an Iraqi-sponsored option, however, already alarms Riyadh. Meanwhile Baghdad will be only too happy to help bin Laden strike any American objective anywhere in the world, even with weapons of mass destruction.

THE ISLAMIST TERRORISTS did not arrive lightly at considerations of using weapons of mass destruction. International terrorism is in the midst of a quest for the super-spectacular terrorist strike. There is a growing urgency among the terrorism-sponsoring states to strike out at the heart of the West—especially the United States—and to be able to terrorize the Americans and their allies. The case of TWA800 served as a turning point because of Washington's determination and to a great extent ability to suppress terrorist explanations and float "mechanical failure" theories. To avoid such suppression after future strikes, terrorism-sponsoring states must raise the ante so that the West cannot ignore them. The temptation is growing to use weapons of mass destruction—chemical, biological, and radiological weapons—to ensure exposure. Recent precedents in Tokyo (use of chemical weapons) and Moscow (the Chechens' use of radioactive material) mean that the thresholds have already been crossed with impunity, increasing the self-confidence of the would-be perpetrators.

Bin Laden himself alluded to the need to escalate the level of strikes against the United States, including the use of horrific weapons, most likely weapons of mass destruction. "We saw the Riyadh and al-Khobar bombings as a sufficient signal for people of intelligence among American decision-makers to avoid the real battle between the nation of Islam and the American forces, but it seems they didn't understand the signal," bin Laden told Abdul-Bari Atwan, the editor of *al-Quds al-Arabi*. "Military people are not unaware that preparations for major operations take a certain amount of time, unlike minor operations. If we wanted small actions, the matter would have been easily carried out. But the nature of the battle calls for operations of a specific type that will make an impact on the enemy, and this, of course, calls for excellent preparation." The only conclusion to be drawn from this statement is that the next strike will be so horrific that Washington will have no option but to comprehend the message.

These are not empty threats. In recent months the Armed Islamist Movement has been actively preparing to launch spectacular terrorist strikes using weapons of mass destruction. Bin Laden has sponsored a special program in Sudan since fall 1997 that will ready Islamist terrorists for highly specialized operations. These facilities are situated around the Islamic Center in Soba, one of bin Laden's farms southwest of Khartoum. The primary objective of this training center is to prepare veteran Arab "Afghans" to serve as commanders of extremely sensitive operations and networks. The special training program is organized accordingly. The installations in Soba include facilities for studying sophisticated bomb-making techniques, communication encryption, clandestine techniques, document forgeries, network running, and so forth. Several senior officers of Iranian intelligence are among the instructors. The Center provides religious tempering for potential martyrs to strengthen their religious conviction. A unique center for the development of chemical weapons for use by Islamist terrorists is also being built within this compound.

Since early summer 1998 Islamist terrorists—both Afghans and Arab "Afghans"—under the command of Osama bin Laden and sponsored by the ISI have been actively preparing for spectacular terrorist strikes using chemical, bacteriological, and perhaps radiological weapons in a well-equipped, fortified compound concealed near Qandahar. They are being trained and the weapons prepared in special chemical- and biological-agent production laboratories purchased in the former Yugoslavia in early May 1998 and shipped via Pakistan. The first weapons factory has already been set up. Samples of agents and toxins were obtained from numerous places around the world. Viruses causing deadly diseases, such as Ebola and salmonella, were procured in Russia. Samples of botulinum biotoxin were acquired in the Czech Republic along with equipment for mass production. Samples of deadly anthrax—a favorite agent for use in biological weapons all over the world—were obtained from North Korea for relatively small sums of hard currency. Radioactive material and pesticides purchased in Ukraine have already arrived in Afghanistan. The radioactive materials are to serve as the contaminating components of radiological weapons. According to a knowledgeable source, the key weapons prepared are "toxins for poisoning water mains. Lethal gases for use against human beings. Fungi for destroying harvests."

These weapons are being developed and produced under the supervision of a few Ukrainian experts (chemists and biologists). They also train the Islamist experts who will be in charge of preparing operations and training terrorists. In early July 1998 this group included seven Saudis and one Egyptian, all of whom had studied pharmacy, medicine, and microbiology in Hungary and Romania. They were recruited by Arab "Afghans" while still in Eastern Europe so that they are completely "clean" from an intelligence point of view.

The first group of terrorist-operatives being trained in Qandahar comprises Islamists from Egypt, Pakistan, Bangladesh, and various Persian Gulf States. Their training includes the preparation of highly sophisticated explosive devices and "kits" with toxins and chemical agents. The nerve agent sarin was specifically mentioned by a source with firsthand knowledge of these preparations. In addition some of the terrorists are being trained to grow "lethal biological cultures" and turn them into weapons using substances readily available on the commercial market or in university laboratories. An example of a possible operation studied in Qandahar is poisoning a water main in a major European city with equipment that would fit into a single backpack.

The second base from which operations using weapons of mass destruction can be launched was established in Zenica, Bosnia-Herzegovina. The Islamists converted an isolated farmhouse into a "research center" for advanced weaponry. Egyptian "Afghans" loyal to Zawahiri, including human bombs, were recently dispatched to Zenica to get ready for a possible spectacular operation. One of the unique features of the Zenica base is its force of expert terrorists made up of European Muslims—both Europeans who converted to Islam and second-generation émigrés from the Muslim world. These terrorists are being actively recruited by followers of bin Laden through a program run by Sheik Omar Bakri, leader of al-Muhajiroun and the spokesman for the International Islamic Front in Europe. The program has centers in Great Britain, France, Belgium, and Italy. The recruits are sent to Afghanistan for training. Then, Bakri noted, they are encouraged to go fight in Bosnia, Albania, Kosovo, or Kashmir "against foreign armies occupying Muslim lands. This is the Jihad, and it has nothing to do with terrorism."

Islamist sources told *al-Quds al-Arabi* that the casualties of the U.S. bombing in Afghanistan included Muslim Britons, Germans, French, Canadians, Americans, Bangladeshis, Pakistanis, and Arabs. Although this claim has not been independently confirmed, it is important because it provides the European Islamists with legitimization for terrorist strikes—avenging their dead comrades.

Bin Laden and his followers are very serious about the use of chemical and biological weapons in future terrorist strikes. Already in summer 1998 senior field commanders of the Islamic Front were aware of the availability of chemical weapons and specific contingency plans for their use. This was confirmed by Ahmad Salamah Mabruk, a prominent commander of Zawahiri's Islamic Jihad, who was captured in Azerbaijan and extradited to Egypt in September 1998. Mabruk told his interrogators that bin Laden's World Islamic Front against Jews and Crusaders, of which Islamic Jihad is a member organization, "has biological and chemical weapons which it intends to use in operations against US and Israeli targets." In April 1999 Mabruk's information was independently confirmed by another Islamist commander based in Western Europe. According to this commander, "these weapons [of mass destruction] have been purchased from East European states and the former Soviet Union" since 1996. The commander stressed that these weapons are already operational and that "plans had been drawn up to distribute quantities of these weapons to elements belonging to the [Islamic] Front in several states for use when necessary against U.S. and Israeli targets in the event of the failure to carry out operations against these targets through the use of explosives and conventional weapons."

Bin Laden is reported to have spent well over $3 million since 1996 in an effort to purchase a nuclear suitcase bomb from the former Soviet Union. Most of the effort known to Western intelligence took place in Kazakhstan. Bin Laden's own Arab buyers were frequently offered and at times even purchased radioactive junk and other useless stuff. But there might be other sources for these bombs. For example, back in 1994 a Moscow-based Palestinian Islamist claimed he had purchased two such suitcase bombs with the help of the Chechen Mafia. At the time the Chechens claimed to have acquired a few such nuclear weapons. Bin Laden has very close relations with the Chechens since he contributed both "Afghan" forces and financial resources to their war against Russia. Bin Laden continues to maintain terrorist forces there and to conduct some of the Taliban's drug deals via the Chechen Mafia. Leaders in Grozny, the capital of Chechnya, are fully aware of just how decisive the assistance received via Afghanistan was for its war against the Russians. In late November 1998 Chechen president Aslan Maskhadov announced that Grozny would recognize the Taliban's regime in Kabul, which had been recognized only by Pakistan, Saudi Arabia, and the United Arab Emirates.

Once the issue of mutual diplomatic recognition was settled, Qandahar and Grozny engaged in comprehensive discussions about cooperation on a host of pariah subjects. A major issue at hand was the expansion of cooperation in the smuggling of drugs, weapons, and strategic materials. The Chechens expressed their desire to send to Afghanistan some of the leading Arab mujahideen now based in Chechnya—in particular Commander Khattab and his men, who were involved in the kidnapping for ransom of Westerners. Qandahar broached the idea of bin Laden receiving temporary asylum in Chechnya if the international pressure on Afghanistan to extradite him became unbearable.

In early December, Abdul-Wahid Ibrahim, the head of the Afghanistan and Central Asia office in the Chechen foreign ministry, arrived in Qandahar for a few days of negotiations with the Taliban leadership that led to a comprehensive agreement on cooperation. "The Chechens are indebted to the mujahideen of bin Laden and the other Arab 'Afghans' for fighting along with [them] against the Russians," Ibrahim acknowledged in Qandahar. But since Grozny needs support from the West, it cannot be identified with bin Laden. Ibrahim suggested that should the need arise, bin Laden would be granted asylum as a "guest" of radical militant Salman Raduyev, whose private army controls areas that the Chechen government's forces cannot enter. Raduyev's areas already provide a safe haven for numerous Arab "Afghans," including bin Laden's men. With this arrangement Grozny would be able to deny supporting bin Laden. A few days later Chechen deputy prime minister Yusup Soslambekov declared that Chechnya "refuses to become a swamp for terrorists" and denied that bin Laden had been offered asylum there. He did confirm part of the deal with Afghanistan, that Khattab might move there if he had to escape Chechnya.

With bin Laden's limitless financial resources and the economic crisis in the former Soviet Union nearly out of control, a sale of nuclear suitcase bombs could ultimately be arranged by the Chechen Mafia. After all, General Aleksandr Ivanovich Lebed, the former security czar of Russia, acknowledged back in 1997 that several nuclear suitcase bombs had disappeared from Russia's arsenal.

A senior Arab intelligence official asserted in early October 1998 that "Osama bin Laden has acquired tactical nuclear weapons from the Islamic republics of Central Asia established after the collapse of the Soviet Union." This overall assessment is shared by Russian intelligence and several Arab intelligence services based on recent evidence of bin Laden's quest for nuclear weapons. Although there is debate over the precise quantities of weapons

purchased, there is no longer much doubt that bin Laden has finally succeeded in his quest for nuclear suitcase bombs. Bin Laden's emissaries paid
the Chechens $30 million in cash and gave them two tons of Afghan heroin
worth about $70 million in Afghanistan and at least ten times that on the
streets of Western Europe and the United States.

Evidence of the number of nuclear weapons purchased by the
Chechens for bin Laden varies between "a few" (Russian intelligence) to
"more than twenty" (conservative Arab intelligence services). Most of the
weapons were purchased in four former Soviet states—Ukraine, Ka-
zakhstan, Turkmenistan, and Russia. These weapons are a mix of suitcase
bombs and tactical warheads/bombs. An Arab nuclear scientist, a Western-
educated expert who worked for Saddam Hussein's nuclear program before
he became Islamist, supervised the acquisition process for bin Laden and
now runs the program for him. He is assisted by five Muslim Turkoman nuclear experts and a team of engineers and technicians, all of them Central
Asian Muslims, whom they brought with them. For security reasons they
condition these weapons for operational use in two clusters of facilities—
one in the deep tunnels in the Khowst area and the other in the deep caves
in the Qandahar area.

Preparations for the possible use of these weapons are conducted separately and in great secrecy. When compared against known background material, however, the few details gleaned about bin Laden's efforts make
sense. Leaders of the Chechen Mafia are known to have approached
Ukrainian and Baltic mercenaries in Shali, Chechnya, on behalf of bin
Laden, asking for veterans of the Soviet SPETSNAZ (Special Forces)
trained in using the suitcase bombs. In 1995 the Chechens established a special detachment of about a hundred Chechens, Arab mujahideen, and mercenaries—mainly Ukrainian and Baltic former members of SPETSNAZ,
OMON (also Soviet Special Forces), and similar units—to secure the shipment of highly sensitive cargos (such as nuclear materials) and passengers
(such as Islamist leaders) between Afghanistan/Pakistan and Europe via
Shali. The Arab mujahideen in this force are veteran "Afghans" and so loyal
to bin Laden. Bin Laden has been using Shali for some of his own smuggling of people, goods, and money, and so it is logical that he would try to
recruit SPETSNAZ veterans there.

If bin Laden succeeds in finding a nuclear-qualified former SPETSNAZ
trooper, he will have overcome the greatest hurdle to carrying out a nuclear
terrorist strike in the West—specifically in the United States. According to
former GRU (Soviet military intelligence) colonel Stanislav Lunev, who defected to the United States in March 1992, GRU and SPETSNAZ teams
during the Cold War had already selected sites for potential use of these

suitcase bombs near the main cities of the United States—sites and a mode of operation that can now be taught to bin Laden's terrorists by the former SPETSNAZ personnel he has recruited. Colonel Boris Alekseyev, chief of the Russian Federation Ministry of Defense Ecological Center, noted that once authorized by a coded radio transmission from Moscow, a single SPETSNAZ trooper can prepare a suitcase bomb for explosion within half an hour. It is not inconceivable that bin Laden's nuclear experts would be able to "hot-wire" a suitcase bomb so that the coded transmission is no longer required to activate the bomb. Then only a single would-be martyr could activate it.

BY LATE AUGUST 1998, if there were any doubts about what were the intentions and plans of bin Laden and his followers, Omar Bakri, the head of al-Muhajiroun, one of the Islamist organizations in London that considers itself "the mouth, eyes, and ears of Osama bin Laden," provided the answer. According to Bakri, the World Islamic Front for Jihad against Jews and Crusaders renewed its pledge to mount "pitiless and violent" terrorist attacks against Israeli and U.S. targets. Faxes sent from Afghanistan instructed all Muslims to "take the necessary steps" to wage the jihad. According to Bakri, bin Laden claimed in one fax that "the war has begun." He noted that bin Laden sent instructions about four specific objectives: "Bring down their airliners. Prevent the safe passage of their ships. Occupy their embassies. Force the closure of their companies and banks." Subsequently Bakri reiterated that Israeli and American planes are "legitimate targets" in the Islamist jihad against the West. "American or Israeli passengers are legitimate targets, but I do not think that the question at present is whether there will be hijackings. That question is theoretical."

Over time the Islamist reaction to both the East Africa bombings and the U.S. retaliation became more sophisticated. The Islamists now argue that the reason for both the bombings of the U.S. embassies and the U.S. attacks was the overall U.S. confrontational attitude toward Islam. The August 28 analysis by Hizb-ut-Tahrir—the Liberation Party, another major U.K.-based Islamist organization—elucidated this approach.

Hizb-ut-Tahrir argued that there is no point in trying to come to terms with the United States. "America deals with the Islamic lands as if they are her own farm. She deals with the rulers of the Muslims as if they are her servants, rather her slaves. She deals with the Islamic peoples as if they are tools. She exploits them for her service." The U.S.-Saudi connection exemplified this relationship. However, the United States was pursuing this relationship not because of greed but because of its profound hostility to Islam and Muslims. "America is a true enemy to the Islamic Ummah. Her allies who share with her in the aggression against the Islamic Ummah or who support her in this aggression like the English and the French and others, are true enemies to the Islamic Ummah." Hizb-ut-Tahrir emphasized that the United States and its allies fit the Koranic definition of *devil*.

The analysis stresses that Hizb-ut-Tahrir does not endorse terrorism, just retaliation for crimes against Islam. "We do not mean that by taking America as an enemy that we bomb the embassies or attack the people. Because Islam orders us to protect the covenant of protection for whoever we gave it to. But when America hits us on our own ground and destroys our factories and homes and kills us without respecting any ties or covenants as if we are insects that have no sanctity or dignity, without any justification, in addition to her previous aggression, what would the world expect of Muslims?" The fine point of this analysis is that since the East Africa bombings were but a phase in an ongoing confrontation between the United States and the Muslim world, they were not, by Hizb-ut-Tahrir's definition, acts of terrorism.

Ultimately Hizb-ut-Tahrir is upbeat about the present state of the Muslim world. The current confrontation, it argues, has already rejuvenated the Muslims, demonstrating to them the extent of U.S. hostility. As a result the Muslim world is getting ready to struggle for the realization of an Islamist way of life. Hizb-ut-Tahrir is convinced that "a new dawn is rising over the Islamic Ummah. She has started to quest for the return of Islam as her way of life, so as to come back to her previous might and glory. Her sons have started to work for establishing the Khilafah [a global, pan-Islamic state] to restore Islam as a system for life, state, and society. Many of her sons are not distracted by the dunya [that is, the allure of the West], nor do they hate death nor fear it, rather they seek Shahada [martyrdom]." The struggle ahead would be long and challenging. The Muslim world would have to acquire weapons of mass destruction and confront the United States at the strategic level. But victory is certain, Hizb-ut-Tahrir assures the believers: "The world will not recognize you until you become a real power feared by others. And you will not become such a power unless you unite. And you will not unite unless you hold by the rope of Allah (Islam) and establish the Khilafah and implement Islam."

The union of weapons of mass destruction and international terrorism makes up the new strategic reality in the Hub of Islam. The Hub of Islam is in a transitional period of historical significance. On the one hand, the Muslim world is on the defensive against the penetration of Western values and culture now expedited through the electronic media. On the other, the

Muslim world has embarked on a strategic ascent made possible by the acquisition of nuclear weapons, ballistic missiles, and other strategic capabilities. The impact of these megatrends is further compounded by the inherent instability of the most affected parties within the Hub of Islam. Pakistan and Iran are plagued with acute, seemingly insoluble socioeconomic problems. At the same time because of their strategic developments—the acquisition of nuclear weapons and ballistic missiles—Pakistan and Iran are perceived as the leaders of the strategic ascent. Their face-off over Afghanistan only complicates matters and enhances instability. The conservative Arab governments are plagued with a crisis of legitimacy that is compounded by the succession crisis in Saudi Arabia, Iraq's economic woes and bellicosity, and Egypt's shifting of directions. As a consequence, overall, the strategic center within the Hub of Islam has shifted eastward to the non-Arabic nations of Iran and Pakistan. But with the predominance of Arabism in Islam, both countries need a major achievement to demonstrate to the Arab world their right to power and leadership. Sudan, which has historically been on the fringes of the Arab world, is striving under Turabi to assert itself as an all-Arab leader and ideological-theological guide. Rejected by the conservative Arab regimes, Sudan has been pushed into strategic alliance with the up-and-coming non-Arab forces.

The quest for hegemony over the Hub of Islam is a vital interest of Iran, Pakistan, and Sudan. All three capitals—Tehran, Islamabad, and Khartoum—know that a precondition for the realization of this aspiration is the eviction of the United States from the Muslim world, in particular the Arabian Peninsula. These sentiments are shared by growing circles of both citizens and governments throughout the Hub of Islam. For the radical Islamists, however, this is an existential prerequisite. They are determined to use every form of terrorism, from nuclear blackmail to spectacular terrorism at the heart of the West, to attain their goal. Meanwhile the onslaught of Westernization through the electronic media and the growing dependence on imported goods has created a backlash in the Muslim street that the Islamists incite and manipulate to create grassroots hostility toward the United States. In the entire Hub of Islam fertile ground exists for anti-Western terrorism to excite the people and compel governments to take notice.

The transformation of the Hub of Islam was recently explained by retired lieutenant general Asad Durrani of Pakistan. Durrani's opinion is important because while he held a senior position in the ISI during the 1980s, he closely cooperated with the CIA and was considered a close friend of the United States. His analysis of recent events speaks volumes about his transformation. "The bombing of the U.S. embassies in Kenya and Tanzania must have gladdened many a heart. Of course the happiness was marred by the tally; too many Africans and too few Americans. The U.S. response was, however, rather unsettling. Not because the chemical complex in Khartoum was 'clean' (it would have been worse if it were not, we would have lost a useful facility), or because many killed in the Afghan camps were innocent (thank God, Osama survived), but because of the 'reach' that the other side has demonstrated by these strikes." Durrani speaks for a large majority of his colleagues and compatriots throughout the Hub of Islam.

Durrani states that the Islamist trend has grown and will continue to expand because of its genuine grassroots and popular appeal. According to Durrani, governments find it an expedient way to address problems plaguing their countries. Both because of the relative weakness of governments and movements in various Muslim states and the overall commonality in the approaches of Islamist movements in addressing the challenges ahead, Islamists have a strong tendency to network—for transnational cooperation, coordination, and close ties. After all, this is the essence of the Muslim Nation, Islam's most genuine form of sociopolitical identity. Thus the West's adverse reaction to these trends is justly perceived as reflecting anti-Islamic sentiments. "The U.S. leads the way because of its global reach and interests, and has therefore become, in the eyes of the Islamists, the symbol of all that is evil. This perception about America, and by implication about the rest of the West, however, does not remain confined to a small number of activists," Durrani observes.

The relationship the United States maintains with various governments throughout the Muslim world must be examined in this context, Durrani explains. Governments find themselves pressed between the groundswell of Islamism and growing dependency on an anti-Muslim West. "In this spiraling conflict, the most acute dilemma is faced by those 'moderate' governments that are unpopular, lack legitimacy, and are on the wrong side of the Islamists at home. Their need to look for outside support to sustain their tottering regimes and the growing antipathy at home toward their external supporters, put the policymakers in a quandary." The mere existence of deniable outlets—such as sponsorship of Islamist terrorism of so-called individuals—becomes a tempting instrument for reconciling the inherent contradictions governments find themselves facing.

This dynamics, Durrani says, is bolstering popular support for otherwise unstable and illegitimate governments that dare not confront the West directly. "The Muslim masses . . . therefore have no option but to admire, applaud, and eulogize the only group that can act for effect, hurt the 'enemy,' and get counted. The enemy too does not seem to be able to do much better than resort to punitive actions and hit whatever it can. Getting across the message, it believes, was more important than getting the 'culprit.'" And so, determined to placate their own citizenry and under growing pressure from the West, more and more regimes throughout the Hub of Islam found it expedient to sponsor international Islamist terrorism.

Durrani believes that because "the term [Islamic] fundamentalism was freely interchangeable with radicalism or extremism" in Western political culture, there is no likelihood of reconciliation and understanding between the U.S.-led West and the Hub of Islam anytime soon. On the contrary, the only viable polity of the Hub of Islam will "deepen the divide, harden the positions, and broaden the base of the conflict." Durrani suggests that barring a major war between the Hub of Islam and the U.S.-led West, there can be no escape from a persistent, escalating indirect confrontation through the use of international terrorism because there is no substitute for wearing down and punishing the West. [Durrani concludes that "if the past is any guide, the course correction will only take place if one or the other side was no longer willing to bear the cost. That point of time still seems far away, and can only be expedited by some more rapid fireworks. Let us therefore wait for the next action."

This sentiment is also shared by the Islamists in Western Europe. The extent of hostility toward the West and the support for Osama bin Laden as the symbol of Islam's resurgence were demonstrated in the conference "Western Challenge and the Islamic Response," organized by Omar Bakri in London in mid-November 1998. Representatives of more than fifteen Islamist organizations, including terrorist organizations, attended. Bakri said that the conference discussed "the acts carried out by the World Islamic Front for Jihad against Jews and Crusaders to determine whether they are in accordance with Islamic law and whether we should support them or advise the Front to refrain from acts that might lead to the killing of innocent civilians." As for the bombings in Saudi Arabia, Kenya, and Tanzania, "those still remain legitimate acts," Bakri insisted, and so all the American charges against bin Laden should be dismissed. What legitimizes these acts of Islamist terrorism is that they were conducted in the context of the U.S. crimes against Islam, Bakri said. "The American troops in the Gulf region are there to fight against Islam and Muslims. Their presence is not legitimate and fighting against them is the duty of every Muslim. The American bombing of Sudan and Afghanistan, the war against Iraq, and America's blind support for the Israeli enemy—these are acts of war against God and his Prophet."

The nine-point Declaration of the Conference of Islamic Revivalist Movements adopted on November 20 was even more belligerent but stopped short of outright endorsement of terrorism and armed struggle. "The Islamic Movements agree that the U.S. government and their alliance are the greatest enemy for Islam and Muslims today. They require us to put all of our resources together in order to counter the aggression whether it be cooperation militarily, politically, or economically." The Islamic revivalist movements consider bin Laden to be the standard-bearer in this Islamist struggle and support his jihad. "The Islamic Movements endorse the struggle of Sheikh Osama bin Laden against the U.S., their alliance, and all non-Muslim forces in Muslim countries," the declaration reads. It ends with a statement of commitment to continue the struggle until the Islamist movement realizes its maximal objectives. "The Islamic Movements will continue their struggle against the corruption of man-made law [that is, Western democracy] and the distortion of Islam by the Media. We pledge to continue . . . working sincerely for the domination of the World by Islam and the Supremacy of Allah's Commands on Earth, which is inevitable," the declaration concludes.

As all-around instability and other tensions grow in the Hub of Islam, regimes face internal problems that are nearly impossible to reconcile and resolve, and tension between the United States and the Muslim world increases, Islamist international terrorism will only escalate. At present spectacular, highly lethal terrorism is the only "mode of communication" between the Hub of Islam and the United States that gets Washington's attention. With key players such as Osama bin Laden and Ayman al-Zawahiri providing a semblance of deniability to the sponsoring states, mainly because the Clinton administration uses this fig leaf for its own self-interest, the terrorism-sponsoring states have no reason to unilaterally abstain from using such effective instruments of statecraft. The Clinton administration's reluctance to confront international terrorism and Islamist militant radicalism seriously and thoroughly—that is, by going after the sponsoring states—only emboldens the perpetrators. The perpetrators of Islamist spectacular terrorism, who have a new arsenal of weapons of mass destruction at hand and have found such terrorism an effective instrument of state polity, are prepared to take the struggle to the next level.

12

The Bin Laden Plans

DURING THE LATE SPRING of 1999 the security services of the United States, the United Kingdom, and other Western European states, as well as those of Israel and India, were working fiercely to prevent Osama bin Laden's Islamist terrorists from launching any of several spectacular, horrendous strikes they were readying. What makes this struggle unique are the diversity and scope of the planned operations that Western security services know about—and not all of them are known—because if any of these operations is carried out, the magnitude of casualties and carnage will be unprecedented. The Western security services are certain that the key terrorism-sponsoring states and the terrorists themselves are ready to withstand the retaliation such strikes will entail.

The current crisis is primarily the result of two factors: (1) the marked intensification of the "Talibanization" of Pakistan, which reached a crisis and turning point in early December 1998; and (2) the impact of the U.S. bombing of Iraq in the middle of the month. While the "Talibanization" of Pakistan—the growth of radical Islamist influence on the policy of the nation—has created an overall climate conducive to the escalation of spectacular terrorism, the U.S. bombing of Iraq, as interpreted throughout the Muslim world, introduced a sense of both rage and urgency. Osama bin Laden has emerged as a key leader, not only the deniable instrument of the terrorism-sponsoring states and the willing perpetrator of the most outrageous strikes but a popular hero whose mere involvement builds grassroots support for the strikes and a willingness to endure retaliation. As a result bin Laden has come to symbolize the Islamist surge against and confrontation with the West. This posture, irrespective of the outcome for bin Laden himself or any of his key commanders, is the realization of his aspirations and manifest destiny—he cannot and will not avoid a confrontation.

———————

THE "TALIBANIZATION" of Pakistan—the transformation of the state and society into the kind of harsh ultraconservative regime run by the Taliban in Afghanistan—has been in progress since late summer 1998. Faced with insoluble social, political, and economic crises that threatened the very existence of Pakistan, Prime Minister Nawaz Sharif sought to compensate by adopting a strict version of the Sharia as the country's legal system. In late August he vowed to replace the country's British-influenced legal system with one of "complete Islamic law" based on the Koran and the Sunnah (the traditions attributed to the prophet Muhammad, on which Sunni Islam is based). "Simple changes in laws are not enough," Sharif told Parliament. "I want to implement complete Islamic laws where the Koran and the Sunnah are supreme."

By mid-September, Islamabad was arguing that Islamization offered the only chance of holding Pakistan together as it slid toward political and social collapse amid technical bankruptcy and increasing political assertiveness by the local Islamist parties. Relying on their powerful militias and allied Kashmiri terrorist organizations, the Islamist parties flexed political muscle Nawaz Sharif could no longer confront. By the end of the month the Pakistani government was hanging by a thread, and the crisis was exacerbated by economic disaster and a collapsing social order that brought the country to the verge of a civil war. The Islamist members of the army and ISI high command warned Nawaz Sharif that the only alternative to chaos was to implement "Talibanization"—the transformation of Pakistan from a formally secular pseudo-democracy into a declared extremist Islamic theocracy. Shortly afterward the National Assembly voted 151 to 16 to pass the constitutional amendment formalizing the Talibanization of Pakistan. Within days Sharif orchestrated a profound purge of the entire military and ISI high command, throwing out the Westernized elite and replacing them with Islamists who are ardent supporters of bellicosity toward India, active aid for the war by proxy in Kashmir, and assistance to the Taliban in Afghanistan and other Islamist jihads. By mid-October, Pakistan was formally an Islamist theocracy committed to the spread of militant Islam.

This transformation took place in the midst of a profound social upheaval that has had a direct impact on Pakistani grand strategy. By mid-1998 the flow of Taliban, students of the small, largely private religious schools in Pakistan, reached a volume the country could no longer endure. According to Pakistani authorities, the nearly 4,000 religious schools registered have more than 540,000 Taliban students at any given time. Many more unofficial Taliban "schools" exist, with a student body of about two million. Most of these schools—both registered and unregistered—are run by militant ulema who indoctrinate their Taliban in the obligation to fight for Islam and Islamist causes. By the time these Taliban leave school, they lack skills for jobs other than manual labor. Many remain unemployed. And so they form an ideal pool for the recruitment of terrorists for local and foreign jihads. Former interior minister Nasirullah Babar, himself a supporter of the Afghan Taliban as well as Pakistani sponsorship of Islamist and jihadist causes, considers some of these schools to be "hotbeds of terrorism" that endanger Pakistan. "The fact is that it affects the entire society. . . . You can see the result in the sectarian clashes that take place," Babar said. "There are not only Afghan Taliban but there also are Pakistani Taliban. . . . There are no frontiers in Islam," pointed out Qari Shabir Ahmed, head teacher at Markaz-Uloom-i-Islamia, one of Pakistan's leading Islamist schools. "We stress peace, but if there is a hurdle to Islam, then it is their [the students'] duty to fight." The Pakistani Taliban have no doubt of the direction their country must take. "We are struggling for Islam in Pakistan like in Afghanistan," explained one of them. "It is our duty to enforce it using any means."

The political might of the militant Islamist resurgence was clearly demonstrated in late October when about a half million supporters of Jamaat-i-Islami converged on Islamabad for a three-day rally aimed at enforcing "a true Islamic order" in Pakistan. The organizers announced that Jamaat-i-Islami Pakistan had formally invited "the hero of the Muslim world, Osama bin Laden," to attend the conference and that it also had "made extensive security arrangements in case of Osama bin Laden's visit to Pakistan and [had] formed special squads of mujahideen." Bin Laden did not attend but sent a fiery message of support. Other speakers were equally militant. "We need an Islamic revolution in Pakistan," said a participant. The first step in the thorough Islamization of Pakistan would be to combat the influence of Western culture in Pakistan, including a boycott of Western-style fast food and soft drinks. "Can't we live without Pepsi, Coke, and Fanta?" asked Qazi Hussein Ahmad, the chief of Jamaat-i-Islami. "They are now forbidden for us," he decreed. More ominously Qazi Hussein Ahmad urged a public uprising against the government if Islamization was not completed. He also urged the army high command to join the revolt because the government was "trying to barter away" Pakistan's nuclear weapons program "in deals with the United States."

Another Islamist group, Lashkar-i-Tuiba, rallied 500,000 supporters in Lahore. The Lashkar has a well-armed militia and a large ISI-sponsored force actively fighting in Indian Kashmir, and its participation in the Islamist pressure on the Sharif government indicated the ISI's endorsement and support. Another Pakistani Islamist group implicated in terrorism in Kashmir and elsewhere, Markaz-al-Daawa wal-Irshad, had a massive rally in Muridke in which violence and terrorism were advocated. Professor Hafiz Mohammad Saeed, the Markaz leader, stressed that "jihad is not terrorism; rather it is the guarantee of peace in the world. Jews and Christians are inflicting [the] worst brutalities on the Muslims. Jihad is the only solution to all the problems faced by the Muslims." Surveying the enemies of Islam, Saeed emphasized that "the White House is the source of all mischief in the world" and anticipated that "the day is not far off when the mujahideen will blow it up through their jihad." Representatives of other Islamist terrorist organizations, such as the Palestinian HAMAS, HizbAllah, the Islamic Jihad of Egypt, the Islamic Front of Jordan, and the Iraqi al-Dawa participated in these gatherings, expressing their solidarity with and support for the Islamist jihad in South Asia. Ibrahim Ghawusha, a prominent HAMAS leader from Jordan, led the delegation to Pakistan. "What we are doing in occupied Palestine [is being] done by Kashmiris in Indian-occupied Kashmir," he said. He also noted that "Islamic understanding exists between the two sides" even though at the time there was no operational coordination. The visit of the HAMAS delegation would change this situation, asserted both Palestinian and Pakistani Islamist leaders.

By late fall 1998 Pakistan was mired in a vicious cycle that caused Islamabad to be increasingly dependent on the support of and legitimization by the radical Islamist power base. The Islamists, however, constitute a largely disenfranchised, unskilled segment of the population, with no prospect of self-betterment in impoverished Pakistan. Islamabad must provide an outlet for their frustration and justification for their support by sponsoring foreign jihads—international terrorism—in which these Pakistani Taliban can participate. The Taliban taking part in remote struggles are not in Pakistan, where they would threaten the stability of the regime and be on hand to participate in an Islamist revolution against Islamabad. The mere existence of ostensibly independent terrorist leaders such as Osama bin Laden greatly simplifies Islamabad's predicament because bin Laden provides deniable venues for both Pakistani sponsorship and placement of the local Taliban.

Under these circumstances Prime Minister Sharif visited the United States in early December. Pakistan was ripe with rumors that he might strike a deal with Washington for Pakistani assistance in capturing and/or killing bin Laden in return for American recognition of Pakistan as a nuclear power; removal of American sanctions imposed because of Pakistan's involvement in drug trafficking, military-nuclear development, and sponsorship of terrorism; and the massive economic assistance Pakistan desperately needs for survival. For the Islamists an agreement on funds for embargoed F-16s—a contentious issue between Washington and Islamabad for nearly a decade—only served as a confirmation of deal making. In reality the Clinton administration did make such an offer regarding bin Laden and strongly pressured Sharif to accept it. He adamantly refused, and then the White House came up with the F-16 deal to prevent a total breakdown of relations.

Hosting Sharif, the Clinton administration should have known better than to raise false expectations. Washington cannot offer Islamabad anything that would be worth provoking a major confrontation with the Pakistani Islamists. Even if Sharif gave an order to apprehend bin Laden, his order would not be carried out by the Pakistani security services because they are riddled with, even actually controlled by, militant Islamists. For them bin Laden is a hero, not a villain. These Islamists are also the new army and ISI elite Sharif just empowered. The Pakistani security establishment knows that any cooperation with Washington will place it in a "state of war" with the local Islamist militias, the Arab "Afghans," and the Kashmiri terrorist organizations they sponsor. With the Afghan Taliban providing safe haven to these groups, they can easily destabilize Pakistan and drag it into a fratricidal civil war the Islamists are sure to win.

To sustain pressure on the Sharif government to remain pro-Islamist, the Islamists spread rumors—some loosely based on facts and some pure imagination—about a myriad of conspiracies against bin Laden in which the Pakistani security and secret services had a role. These rumors included covert attempts by Arab and Afghan mercenaries to assassinate bin Laden, with several of the attackers caught and summarily executed by the Taliban; Western Europeans caught by bin Laden's Arab bodyguards spying on behalf of the CIA; several police raids in Pakistan, mainly in Lahore and Islamabad, in an attempt to capture the visiting bin Laden; and even deployments of CIA-FBI special forces to Pakistan and Tajikistan in preparation for raids into Afghanistan. These rumors spread as intelligence activities by American, Western European, and conservative Arab services intensified, serving to confirm the most outrageous rumors. The periodic raids by the Pakistani security services against Islamist subversive organizations conspiring against Islamabad are habitually presented as parts of the campaign against "the heroic mujahid Osama bin Laden" on behalf of the hated CIA. Given Sharif's dependence on the Islamists, the immediate outcome of these rumor campaigns has been the scaling down of whatever anti-Islamist actions the ISI was really contemplating.

The relationship between Islamabad and the Islamists came to the fore soon after Sharif's return from Washington, as Islamist leaders openly made their support for Islamabad conditional on Pakistan's support for the Islamist jihad. An early December editorial in the Islamabad *al-Akhbar*, a respected Islamist paper, elucidated the Islamists' approach to their government. "[The] United States' enmity toward Pakistan [had] been exposed" during Sharif's visit to Washington, the editorial argued. The paper surveyed the tenets of the hostile U.S. policy, primarily in regard to Pakistan's nuclear weapons and the Islamic struggle for Kashmir, and concluded that "under the influence of the Jewish lobby, the U.S. is supporting India because of the alliance of Jews and Hindus and is demonstrating its enmity toward the Muslims." The Islamists believed not only that "the U.S. has adopted an opposing attitude to Pakistan" but also that "the U.S. has purposely tried to raise a new conflict in Pakistan's internal politics" to eliminate the Islamists' influence. The *al-Akhbar* editorial considers the primary indication of this American policy to be "the U.S. insistence throughout the talks that Pakistan should [pressure] the Taliban and arrange for his [Osama bin Laden's] extradition to the U.S."

The *al-Akhbar* editorial concludes with an offer of cooperation with Sharif provided he adopts the policy advocated by the Islamists. "This insulting attitude by the U.S. should spark a moment of thought for those claiming the leadership of the nation. The time has come for us to announce a war against the hypocritical policy of the U.S. This treatment of Pakistan on the occasion of the U.S. visit requires that the rulers and leaders supporting the U.S. should forget that the U.S. will do something for Pakistan. Now we will do everything on our own. But for this purpose, we will have to unite all our forces and will have to promote national thinking. And after uniting as a nation, we will have to announce war against the American imperialists and to give up the dream of friendship with the U.S." Sharif's dependence on the Islamists' support of his Islamization policy forces him to accept their advice.

Despite rumors of plans for his capture, bin Laden's visits to Pakistan continued. Since early winter the primary change in bin Laden's posture has been his emergence as a major political player in Southwest Asia. Because of his unique standing among all Islamists and his diverse, intimate relationship with all of the region's powers, bin Laden has emerged as a troubleshooter and mediator of key disputes. At present he is involved in mediating the face-off between Iran and the Taliban-Pakistan over Afghanistan. He succeeded in convincing both Tehran and Islamabad of the overriding importance of building a regional anti-U.S. strategic bloc using their respective nuclear and ballistic missiles arsenals, and he argued that any disagreement they have over Afghanistan only serves the interests of the United States. As a consequence Pakistani-Iranian strategic cooperation has resumed. Bin Laden is also negotiating with various Afghan Islamist mujahideen organizations that are opposed to the Taliban in the hopes of establishing a wide Islamist solidarity front. All of these maneuvers not only strengthen his patrons but also build his position as a leader. In mid-January bin Laden, Zawahiri, and the Islamist terrorist movement, having consolidated active support from Pakistan, were gearing up for a major escalation—the launching of a series of spectacular operations.

THE U.S. BOMBING of Iraq and the grassroots rage it engendered throughout the Muslim world did not come as a surprise to bin Laden's operational elements. In the wake of the relationship established between bin Laden and Saddam Hussein, bin Laden, Zawahiri, their lieutenants, and also Turabi and his inner circle began to pay closer attention to the situation in Baghdad, in particular the continued face-off between Saddam and the United States–United Nations. Sometime in fall 1998 Turabi concluded that the international dynamics in and around Iraq could not continue for long. Assuming, and rightly so, that the United States would not let Saddam "go free," he saw in the inevitable confrontation an opportune catalyst for the escalation of the Islamist jihad with massive grassroots support. The Muslim world's rallying behind Iraq and the Islamists in February–March 1998 served as a precedent for the populist dynamics he could expect. Turabi was determined to prepare for and properly capitalize on what he was now confident was the inevitable, imminent eruption of a crisis.

Operational preparations for the next wave of Islamist spectacular terrorism to be launched in conjunction with a U.S.-Iraqi crisis began in early October. At the core of the planned terrorist offensive are the "bin Laden plans"—a series of thoroughly delineated, validated contingency plans to be executed by networks built around key commanders. In the first half of October, in preparation for the activation of these operational plans, about fifteen of bin Laden's close senior operatives arrived in Khartoum from several countries, including Yemen, Qatar, Dubai, Jordan, and Cyprus. They traveled clandestinely, using Sudanese and Albanian travel documents they picked up at several Sudanese diplomatic legations. Most of these terrorist commanders received instructions and special briefings in Khartoum on the forthcoming operations and then returned to their countries before the end of the month.

The United States had some inkling of these and related activities concerning the Arabian Peninsula, because on October 7 all U.S. missions in

Saudi Arabia closed for a four-day thorough review of their security procedures. This unusual step was prompted by intelligence that the U.S. embassy in Riyadh was under threat of an imminent terrorist attack. The
warning specified that such an attack would be in retaliation for the U.S.
cruise missile attack on Sudan and Afghanistan in August; thus it would
most likely be a bin Laden operation. On October 14 Attorney General
Janet Reno organized a crisis management exercise at FBI headquarters to
plan for a possible terrorist attack by bin Laden against targets in Washington and New York. The four scenarios examined by the 200 participants
were an assassination attempt on the secretary of state, a car bombing, a
chemical weapons strike on a Washington Redskins football game, and the
explosion of a "device" in a federal building. But as *Time* reported, "the
war game—intended to help the agencies practice working together—
quickly melted down into interagency squabbling and finger pointing." It
was clear to all that the United States was far from ready to deal with a
spectacular terrorist strike even at a time when intelligence indicated that
bin Laden was planning strikes in Washington and/or New York.

In the second half of October, Turabi sent emissaries—small delegations of terrorist commanders and Sudanese senior officials—to Saddam
Hussein and bin Laden with handwritten letters containing both Turabi's
analysis of the strategic-political situation in the Middle East and sugges-
tions about the launching of the terrorism campaign. Turabi stressed that
the United States was extremely vulnerable to a resolute confrontation with
militant Islam. Washington's preoccupation with domestic crises made it
confused and therefore susceptible to a surprise launch of terrorist strikes,
Turabi argued. Building pressure on Washington on many fronts would
make the United States lose its orientation. The more confused and angry
the United States became, the more serious diplomatic mistakes Washington would make, both exacerbating the hostility and militancy throughout
the Muslim world and alienating local governments. Turabi estimated that
the application of pressure on the United States could start immediately so
that by the end of December—the time of Ramadan (starting December
19) and Christmas—the Islamist terrorist system would be ready to launch
the first operations in this wave. Then, according to Turabi's plan, bin
Laden's terrorists would capitalize on the first crisis between the United
States and Iraq to launch their campaign against Americans and America.

Toward the end of October, Qusay Hussein, Saddam Hussein's son,
sent a close confidant, along with Turabi's emissary, to Peshawar, where
they linked up with an ISI official and together traveled to Kabul. There
they conferred with bin Laden in a safe house provided by Mullah Omar

and discussed the implementation of their joint plans in accordance with Turabi's analysis and sense of urgency. According to a well-connected Arab source, "the meeting was extremely serious." Bin Laden and his guests "laid down the details of the biggest act of cooperation and coordination between the extremist Islamic organizations and Baghdad for confronting the United States, their common enemy." The use of chemical and biological weapons in the anticipated terrorist strikes was explicitly addressed. Bin Laden promised to activate the entire Islamist movement—in the Middle East, Africa, East Asia, Europe, and the United States—as part of the joint campaign. In addition bin Laden sought Iraqi help for expediting the construction of special bombs containing chemical and biological agents. He was promised anything Baghdad could deliver. To better understand bin Laden's needs, the group traveled to the Khowst area and visited some of the local secret hideouts, weapons' stores, and laboratories. Afterward Baghdad promised to provide bin Laden with weapons that would combine major explosions with chemical calamities. These were not empty promises. Between late November and early December, in preparation for the anticipated operations, a total of twelve Iraqi chemical weapons experts arrived in Afghanistan and began working with bin Laden's own experts.

In early November the next incident in the face-off between Iraq and the U.N. weapons inspectors took place. By then Baghdad's crisis management and intransigence were being timed according to the operational requirements for launching another wave of terrorist attacks on American targets and possibly other terrorist/subversive activities in the Middle East, such as assassination attempts on leaders and major sabotage operations. As part of these preparations, Iraqi intelligence dispatched a delegation to Pakistan and Afghanistan to further the operational coordination with bin Laden. The Iraqi team was led by an Iraqi senior intelligence official known by the nom de guerre Abu-Walid and included an Iranian-born operative—ostensibly a senior member of the Iraq-based Mujahideen ul-Khalq opposition group, which had been to Afghanistan repeatedly since August 1998, assisting the Taliban with the interrogation of captured Iranian officials and diplomats and broadcasting anti-Iranian propaganda on radio Kabul. In Pakistan the delegation was joined by a retired Pakistani senior officer close to former ISI chief Hamid Gul, who maintains contacts with the Taliban leadership on behalf of the ISI. In Qandahar, Abu-Walid and the Pakistani escort held a lengthy, frank meeting with Mullah Omar, bin Laden, and Zawahiri in which the Iraqi sought to ascertain the extent of the Islamists' commitment and resolve to assist Baghdad in its forthcoming confrontation with the United States. Within days a senior Taliban official visiting the Gulf sheikhdoms met a high-ranking Iraqi envoy who arrived clandestinely. They reached an agreement on close cooperation "in the security, military, and intelligence spheres." Local intelligence services learned about this meeting.

During the first half of November the U.S. government was warned by more than one allied government about Turabi's plans and the steps already undertaken to implement them. There were also ample indications of a buildup and mobilization of terrorist assets throughout the Arab sheikhdoms along the Persian Gulf. The U.S. embassies in Riyadh and several Gulf sheikhdoms issued warnings on November 13 about "continuing threats of attacks by leading Saudi dissident Osama bin Laden against Americans in Saudi Arabia." Not surprisingly, Arab leaders showed little appetite for supporting the proposed U.S.-led military strikes against Iraq. The Clinton administration's insistence that it had international support for the use of force was of no interest or relevance for these leaders. Nevertheless, the Clinton administration continued to pressure the United Nations to refuse to compromise with Baghdad. The confrontation with Iraq reached the point that the White House authorized a strike on November 14—only to call it off as some of the bombers were already in the air. By then the United Nations had succeeded in reaching a compromise with Iraq on a revived inspection regime.

In retrospect, the U.S.-Iraqi crisis of mid-November was the turning point in galvanizing Baghdad's resolve to strike out and sponsor an unprecedented terrorist campaign. A well-connected Arab source stated that "Saddam Hussein became convinced for the first time that Washington was seriously seeking to topple him and had decided to bring him down in any possible way. He chose to confront [the United States] with all possible means, too, particularly extremism and terrorism, since he had nothing else to lose." Convinced that he had to act urgently, Hussein held lengthy discussions with the two people he truly trusts—his sons Qusay and Uday—on how to confront the United States and spoil its designs against their family. Qusay argued, and Saddam ultimately agreed, that there was no way emaciated Iraq could deflect a determined American attempt to assassinate them and bring down the regime. The key to their survival was in deterring such a campaign in the first place through a series of devastating anti-American terrorist attacks that would persuade Washington of the futility of challenging the Hussein regime. The option of conducting such a terrorist campaign under bin Laden's "deniable" banner was irresistible.

A few days after this conversation Qusay dispatched two of his most loyal intelligence operatives—al-Jubburi and al-Shihabi—to Afghanistan.

They held a series of lengthy meetings with bin Laden, Zawahiri, Abu-Hafs, and other senior Islamist terrorist conmanders in an isolated building not far from Kabul. Al-Jubburi and al-Shihabi brought with them detailed lists of Iraq's contributions to the joint effort, including the anticipated arrival of the chemical weapons experts. They then worked out a detailed, coordinated plan for a protracted anti-American war. They decided that spectacular and martyrdom operations should be carried out throughout the world. In addition bin Laden agreed that Islamist hit teams should hunt down Iraqi opposition leaders who cooperated with the United States and the West against the Hussein regime. Bin Laden assured the Iraqis that the Islamists could now reach areas that Iraqi intelligence could not. The series of meetings concluded with an agreement to study closely and formulate details of specific operations and then meet again to decide on the first round of strikes.

At the same time the Islamist terrorist system associated with bin Laden and Zawahiri was accelerating preparations for a new wave of spectacular terrorist strikes virtually all over the world. In Afghanistan the network of recruitment centers, theological tempering sites, military training camps, and weapon stores had been markedly expanded. "The training of Islamic radicals has been fully reactivated inside Afghanistan," a Pakistani intelligence official acknowledged in mid-December. Two new camps of significance were opened in fall 1998. The first was the Tora Boora base—originally a CIA-funded ISI-run mujahideen camp near Jalalabad—rebuilt to serve as a dedicated installation for handling the flow of terrorists traveling clandestinely to and from Afghanistan via Pakistan. The second site was a new, completely isolated installation in the general area of Galrez, some thirty miles west of Kabul. There a small number of select terrorists receive special training for the most sensitive operations under complete secrecy.

Meanwhile Islamist networks throughout Europe and the Middle East had activated a large, diverse system for clandestine travel by terrorists. In fall 1998 this system shipped hundreds of new recruits and dozens of expert terrorists from North Africa, the Middle East, the Balkans, and Western Europe to and from Pakistan, Afghanistan, and to a lesser extent Yemen. This system acquired numerous genuine passports and other travel documents in Western European cities and smuggled them to Pakistan and Afghanistan for use by the terrorists deploying for operations worldwide. In addition the Islamists actively recruited hundreds of Pakistani Taliban for a "new jihad" to be launched "soon." Thousands of volunteers joined their ranks and received basic training in camps in eastern Afghanistan. Several expert terrorists were also redeployed from the forward camps of the Kashmiri terrorist organizations in the Muzaffarabad area. The flow of recruits and veteran terrorists traveling via Pakistan reached such a level that in fall 1998 Zainul Abideen—a thirty-eight-year-old Palestinian known as "the school-teacher"—established special facilities in the Peshawar area to streamline and ease the safe flow of people, funds, and goods to bin Laden's camps in Afghanistan. The ISI began shielding this buildup in early November. In a series of security sweeps it arrested several suspects from Iraq, Saudi Arabia, and Bosnia who were carrying stolen and forged travel documents and were hanging around Abideen's facilities without explanation.

As this buildup and preparation accelerated, Osama bin Laden did not remain silent about his ultimate objectives. In mid-November he was invited to attend an Islamist conference in Pakistan but decided against it when Islamabad suggested that such an affront would adversely affect Prime Minister Sharif's forthcoming visit to the United States. Instead he sent a short note to the organizers in which he elucidated once again his objectives and goals. Bin Laden brought together the various struggles facing Islam and stressed the centrality of jihad and sacrifice to their solution:

We are thankful to God who blessed us with the wealth of faith and Islam. We are pleased to express our gratitude to you and the Pakistani mujahid nation. We thank you for your efforts to support the mujahideen's struggle to expel the U.S. forces from the sacred land [of Saudi Arabia]. I do not need to tell you that this sacred struggle should continue until Bait-ul-Muqaddas [the Temple Mount in Jerusalem] and other holy places of Muslims are liberated from the occupation of non-Muslims and the Islamic Sharia is enforced on the land of God. Obviously, for the enforcement of Sharia, it is essential for all Muslims that they should establish an Islamic system on the basis of teachings of the Prophet Muhammad. At this moment, Israel and [the] United States are dominating Palestine and other holy places in such a way that mujahideen are being killed and besieged and Muslims have been economically ruined. Therefore, it is obligatory for all Muslims to continue Jihad by sacrificing their wealth and life as long as their holy places are not liberated from the subjugation of Jews and Christians. This freedom is not possible until we sacrifice all our wealth and our lives. As it is a religious obligation for every Muslim to support the mujahideen fighting for freedom of sacred places, similarly they are also obligated by their religion to support the Taliban government in Afghanistan, because by enforcing Sharia in Afghanistan, Taliban have established the system of God on God's land. They are busy in Jihad to rid the Muslims of Afghanistan from the tyranny of non-Muslims. In conclusion, I pray that God may enlighten us with the light of faith and forgive our sins and help us all the time.

For their part, the Taliban reciprocated bin Laden's endorsement and declared their support for his jihad in a major fatwa. In Qandahar in late November the Taliban convened the country's key ulema, who operate as the Ittehad Ulema-i-Afghanistan under the leadership of Maulana Abdullah Zakiri, one of Afghanistan's most distinguished and respected religious scholars. On December 1 the Ittehad Ulema-i-Afghanistan issued a fatwa that decreed "armed jihad against America by the Islamic world" was "mandatory" and "all the Muslims [are] ordered to rise against America and kill Americans." The fatwa also made it "compulsory" that "no steps for total elimination of America by force should be avoided"—clearing the way for possible use of weapons of mass destruction against the United States and/or Americans anywhere else in the world. To make sure that there was no misunderstanding, the fatwa was reinforced by an edict from the country's eminent ulema and scholars, according to which America is "an enemy of the Islamic world [that] should be eliminated." The Taliban leadership concurred with this fatwa, and the Supreme Court of Afghanistan declared that it complied with "the principles of Sharia" and therefore "its legal position" should be accepted by Afghanistan. The Court issued a legal opinion clarifying that the fatwa also "[called] upon all the Muslim states to prepare for jihad against America and forces of infidelity the world over" and ordered all Islamic governments "to demand [that]America . . . immediately withdraw its forces from the Gulf and Saudi Arabia and stop interfering in the Islamic countries." Both the fatwa and the Court's legal opinion were issued in Arabic and have since been widely distributed in Islamist circles throughout the Hub of Islam as well as émigré communities in Europe.

By early December, Osama bin Laden had already acknowledged that he was ready for the escalation of his jihad. The Taliban's fatwa clearly demonstrated that he had a solid base and safe haven to operate from. It did not take long for bin Laden and Zawahiri to demonstrate their self-confidence and assertiveness. At this time an Iraqi intelligence official held a series of meetings in the Iraqi Embassy in Islamabad with the leaders of several Pakistani militant Islamist movements and representatives of the Taliban. These meetings took place with the full knowledge and endorsement of the ISI.

In the first half of December bin Laden and Zawahiri arrived in Peshawar, Pakistan, to chair a periodic meeting of the Arab "Afghan" leaders residing in Pakistan. About a dozen people participated, including Asadallah Abdul Rahman, the son of Sheikh Omar Abdul Rahman of World Trade Center fame, who was seated next to Zawahiri, symbolizing the enduring importance of Sheikh Omar. Bin Laden's visit was not a clandestine surge into Pakistan. He was the guest of NWFP (North-West Frontier Province) senior officials, including relatives of his fourth wife, and as before during his frequent visits, Pakistani security authorities provided him with a special escort. Bin Laden's other recent visits had been kept quiet, but the Pakistani Islamists highlighted the early December visit as proof of the cooperation they enjoy with Sharif's Islamabad. As for official Islamabad, the NWFP authorities "appeared to be ignorant about the reported presence of Saudi dissident, wanted by [the] U.S.A., Osama bin Laden in Pakistan," when they were contacted by a correspondent from *Dawn*, a Pakistani newspaper.

Participants at the meeting discussed the anticipated escalation in the jihad against the United States, including specific operations in various stages of preparation. They resolved to deploy more than fifty Arab mujahideen from the Peshawar area to the training camps in Afghanistan so that they could be used in these operations. This was not an idle gathering. On December 11 the Islamists issued a communiqué in the name of Zawahiri's Islamic Group, vowing to fight the Americans "ferociously in a long and sustained battle." The communiqué defines the United States as "the biggest enemy which is seeking to uproot Islam." Alarmingly, the communiqué alluded to a role for weapons of mass destruction in the evolving confrontation with the United States. "We must demonstrate the strength of the Muslim nation by deterring those committing aggression against it, first and foremost the United States and Israel. Our Muslim nation has in its possession numerous weapons to fight the United States, Israel, and their agents." The Islamic Group emphasized that the role of spectacular terrorism was still important. They reminded all Muslims of the importance of "training in the use of arms" and that "the door to training is open." The communiqué also called for an increase in the terrorists' intelligence and support system, urging "every Muslim to consider himself a vanguard for the mujahideen everywhere by detecting the movements of the Americans, the Jews, and their agents and then informing the mujahideen of them [their movements]."

The Islamic Group communiqué stressed the growing vulnerability of the United States to Islamist terrorism: "Our Muslim nation should know that the United States—even if it pretends that it has not learned a lesson from the blows that the mujahideen have dealt it, as attested by the Americans themselves—is extremely scared and unable to stop the mujahideen. The Americans are convinced that the young men of Islam are competing to die for God's cause in pursuit of martyrdom in the jihad against the

Americans, the Jews, and their agents." There is a good reason for this fear of the Islamists' rage, the Islamic Group concluded: "Let the Americans know that we are determined to fight them ferociously in a long and sustained battle in which generations will pass the trust to one another . . . so if the remains of the Americans are scattered, and if the planes carry coffins to them containing a mixture of charred parts of their criminals, they should blame no one but themselves." The communiqué concluded with the reiteration of the warning that the Americans must "brace themselves for a ferocious, long war."

If there had been any doubt that bin Laden and the Islamist terrorist elite were behind this warning, ostensibly issued by the Egyptian Islamic Group, Islamist sources in London hurried to put the communiqué in the proper context. They noted Zawahiri's decision to break his silence "after the measures taken by the United States in the wake of the bombing of its embassies in Nairobi and Dar-es-Salaam in August." Most authoritative was the analysis of Adil Abdul-Majid, Zawahiri's friend and confidant. He stated that recent U.S. policies "prompted Islamic movements to react violently." He explained that "the Islamic movements have fundamental issues that collide with U.S. positions. Injustice; the lack of justice in the U.S. Administration's handling of the Palestinian issue; the United States' claim that it supports freedoms in the world while it continues to ignore what is happening to the Islamists in their own countries; and the involvement of U.S. intelligence in pursuing the Islamists, rounding them up, arresting them, and handing them over to their own states . . . all these increase the Islamic movements' hostility toward the United States." Abdul-Majid also hinted at bin Laden's responsibility for the communiqué, saying that the limitations imposed on bin Laden by the Taliban did not apply to Zawahiri's Egyptian organization. "As is known, the Jihad Group is Egyptian, and its main entity and weight are not in Afghanistan. Al-Zawahiri's presence there does not negate the fact that the group has elements in other places, and al-Zawahiri's case differs from bin Laden's."

THE ISLAMISTS' PREPARATIONS suddenly became urgent in mid-December when, on orders from President Clinton, the United States and the United Kingdom launched a bombing campaign against Iraq, alleging an unacceptable breakdown of the U.N. weapons inspection regime. That the bombing were launched on December 16, the very same day the U.S. House of Representatives was debating and ready to vote on the impeachment of President Clinton, did not go unnoticed. In Washington several former and current government officials openly charged that the Clinton

White House had orchestrated events so that Saddam Hussein was pro-voked into defying U.N. weapons inspectors and President Clinton could justify air strikes, diverting American public attention away from his predicament in Congress. "What Richard Butler [the chief of U.N. weapons inspections] did last week with the inspections was a set-up," former U.N. weapons inspector Scott Ritter told the *New York Post.* "You have no choice but to interpret this as 'Wag the Dog.' You have no choice."

The Islamists never had any doubt that the U.S. bombings were not a reaction to Saddam Hussein's latest confrontation with the United Nations but yet another stage in the United States' relentless confrontation with Islam. One of the first to elucidate this argument was Abdul-Bari Atwan, the editor of *al-Quds al-Arabi.* "Once again U.S. President Bill Clinton is using the Iraqi people as a 'scapegoat' to extricate himself from his own domestic crises and avoid—or postpone—Congress's decision on his im-peachment," Atwan wrote. "Clinton's survival in the White House for two more years is more important than the lives of hundreds of thousands of Iraqis and their children who will be killed by cruise missiles and bombs dropped by U.S. aircraft in all directions." Although prompted by the presi-dent's current crisis, the bombing campaign should be considered as a com-ponent of the overall policy of the United States. "This [campaign] represents U.S. arrogance in its ugliest form. It is aimed against the Arabs, and no one else, with a view to humiliating and weakening them in prepa-ration for plundering their riches and imposing the Israeli mandate on them. When the Pentagon experts talk of killing at worst 10,000 Iraqis in the early days of the attack, they talk as though these martyrs are not human beings, but rather insects." Atwan wondered what the Iraqis did to warrant such disdain and hostility from Washington and concluded that their only sin was that they were proud Arabs trying to stand up to the United States. Therefore the entire Arab world should consider the U.S. bombing as aimed at them: "It is a bloody attack aimed against the Arab nation as a whole, represented in the Iraqi people, and the responsibility for confronting it by all legitimate means lies on the shoulder of every Arab, whether he is a government official or not."

Atwan stressed that this all-Arab aspect was the reason the future de-velopment of the Iraqi crisis would not be under Washington's control. "It will definitely be a long war that will not be limited to a few missiles as has happened in the past." The primary challenge facing the United States was not the direct outcome of the actual bombing of Iraq. "The United States might solve a problem by hitting Iraq, but it will definitely create numerous other problems that will adversely affect its interests and those of the West, let alone the states of the region and their geopolitics." Atwan identified an outburst of Islamist violence and terrorism as the most significant and lasting outcome of the U.S. attack on Iraq and blamed Washington for instigating this far-reaching imbroglio. "It is U.S. terrorism that will undermine the stability of a region containing 65 percent of the world's oil reserves. It is terrorism because it does not enjoy any international authorization or any moral or legal justification. It is likely to lead to the fire of extremism being ignited in a region full of frustration, disappointment, and groups that are ready to translate this frustration into violent actions and terrorism against the United States and all the Western states." Atwan concluded by wondering, "Does Clinton's survival and remaining in power warrant all these catastrophic and destructive results?"

Throughout Pakistan the Islamists' reaction built on existing themes. Most of the Friday sermons delivered on December 19 emphasized that the U.S. bombing campaign reaffirmed American hostility toward the entire Muslim world. This theme dominated the several rallies held that afternoon. All over Pakistan marchers shouted "Death to America" and agreed with the calls to launch avenging jihads against the United States. "We consider the American attack on Iraq an attack on the entire Islamic world," Qazi Hussein Ahmad told a Jamaat-i-Islami rally in Lahore. He spoke under a banner reading, "Muslims are bleeding in Kosovo, Bosnia, Kashmir, Palestine, and Iraq. America, we are coming. Russia has lost the war and it is the turn of America." In Peshawar speakers at a rally jointly organized by Jamaat-i-Islami and Jamiat-i-Ulema-Islam spelled out the anticipated Islamist revenge. Because nobody had "struck fear into the heart of America" like Osama bin Laden, he should lead the avenging campaign, making Washington "terrified about the reaction to its Iraq attacks by militant Islamic states." The revenge would not be limited to bin Laden. "Osama is only one mujahid and America is afraid of him," one speaker noted. "America is also fearful of Iraq."

The harsh reaction to the U.S. bombing throughout the Muslim world was not limited to Islamist circles. Religious luminaries expressed the exasperation and hostility of "establishment" Islamists, strengthening the hands of militant Islamists eager to translate their rage into violence and terrorism. One of the first religious leaders to publicly "denounce the aggression against the Iraqi people" was Sheikh Muhammad Sayyid Tantawi, Grand Imam of al-Azhar University in Cairo. He declared that "the al-Azhar and the Egyptian President, Government, people, men, and women stand alongside the Iraqi people to defend them with all the means of defense, adding that we can never abandon them under any circumstances." The Egyptian government did not deny or challenge Tantawi's statement. In a major step toward legitimizing revenge against the United States by "establishment" Islamism, Tantawi decreed that "whoever of the Iraqi people is killed is a martyr because whoever defends his land, honor, and property is a martyr." And Islam stipulates that the blood of martyrs must be avenged against those who shed it—the United States. The continuation of the bombing into the beginning of the holy month of Ramadan served to further exacerbate the situation. "The Americans and the British, of course, don't care about Ramadan and the feelings of one billion Muslims," Egyptian Islamic theologian Sheikh Abdel Sabur Shahin opined. "The Americans do want to hit during Ramadan. They get pleasure out of putting down the Arabs," added Sheikh Abdel Adhim Dib, another Egyptian professor of theology.

Cairo went public on the Friday before Ramadan. In his sermon at al-Azhar Mosque, Sheikh Tantawi openly called for the mobilization of the Muslim world in support of Iraq and against the United States. "The duty of Muslims is to help, by all means, the Iraqi people face up to the unfair aggression and the humiliation they are being subjected to," he decreed. He urged Allah "to ensure the victory of the Iraqi people against the unjust." Sheikh Tantawi then led the 5,000 worshipers in reciting a special prayer for the Iraqis martyred in the air attacks. The emotionally weighted prayer triggered a passionate response that soon evolved into calls for a jihad. "Allah-hu-Akbar. Open the doors to the jihad," the worshipers chanted. "Jihad, jihad against the usurper," they added. "With our blood and souls we will redeem you, O Islam," and "Death to the enemies of Allah!" The chanting continued as the worshipers emerged from the mosque. By then somebody had begun distributing inflammatory leaflets and placards reading, "Must the Iraqi people die for Monica?" Egyptian police and security forces did not intervene in the spontaneous rally. Official Cairo signaled its endorsement of the Islamist position through the government-controlled media. For example, an editorial in the newspaper al-Gumhuriya warned that the U.S. bombing campaign would trigger "a new wave of terrorism against Washington." The blame for the widespread carnage would lie with the United States—"the mother of terrorism"—and its British "puppet," the editorial concluded.

There was widespread outrage throughout the Arab world. In Damascus heavily armed security forces stood aside as a young mob broke into the U.S. Embassy's compound and tore and burned the American flag. Marine guards had to rescue the ambassador's wife from a mob rampaging through the ambassador's residence area. In Gaza, shouting "Death to Clinton!" the mob tore down and burned the American flags that had been hanging since President Clinton's unprecedented visit only a few days before. Palestinian police participated in the riots. Similar displays of grassroots rage and violence were reported from virtually every Muslim state. Government-owned and/or -supervised media blasted the United States for its bombing of Iraq and urged revenge. A concurrent theme in the media was the assertion that since Arab governments were intimidated into passive action and lame protests by the display of massive American firepower and the resolve to bomb Arabs at will, it would take dedicated non-state Islamist forces to avenge the American crimes and restore Arab/Muslim honor. Street vendors and preachers from Morocco to the Philippines urged and expected Osama bin Laden to rescue Muslim honor by striking out against the United States and its allies.

At some of the rallies there were explicit calls for revenge and anti-American terrorism. Very important were the calls for terrorism among bin Laden's Pakistani Islamist supporters. In the Friday sermons delivered in Jamaat-i-Islami mosques and rallies, the speakers warned that the continuation of the U.S. bombing of Iraq would lead to attacks on its embassies in Muslim countries. The address of Jamaat-i-Islami's Naib Amir Liaqat Baloch to a protest demonstration at Masjid-i-Shuhada in Lahore is indicative. "Islamic movements all over the world will target U.S. embassies and make life hell for Americans if Clinton does not stop the attacks immediately," Baloch stated. The enmity between Muslims and the United States was already irreconcilable because of the inherent character of the U.S. bombing of Iraq. Baloch argued that "the U.S. acted . . . as if only the blood of American citizens was precious while that of Muslims was worthless." In reality "Clinton was shedding the blood of thousands of Muslims in Iraq who were already the victims of the U.S.-backed international food and medicine sanctions for the last eight years." The U.S. bombing was actually "an attack on the entire Muslim world." Baloch stressed that "Clinton opted to kill thousands of innocent Iraqis only to avoid his impeachment." And Baloch had "a message to the U.S. citizens," amounting to a warning that "their government was promoting hatred between them and the Muslim world under a conspiracy which they must thwart for the sake of peaceful relations with the Muslim world."

In London, a bastion of bin Laden's Islamist supporters, reaction to the U.S. and British bombing of Iraq was more than just vocal. The Muslim Council of Britain accused President Clinton of "cynically putting innocent lives in danger to divert attention away from his domestic difficulties" and criticized the British government for its uncritical support of the United States. The Council's statement emphasized the all-Islamic aspects of the grievances against the United States and the United Kingdom: "The scale and swiftness of the action is in marked contrast with the other serious violations of international legality in, for example, Kosovo, Kashmir, and Palestine. Regrettably, this policy of double standards does not bode well for the future of international order." The themes of the Friday sermons in the London mosques were as virulent as in their Middle Eastern counterparts. In London the rallies after the Friday prayers also led to mob violence. A demonstration arranged by al-Muhajiroun outside 10 Downing Street turned into a scuffle with police, and Scotland Yard arrested six al-Muhajiroun members on security-related charges. Amir Mirza, a nineteen-year-old al-Muhajiroun member, was arrested by the Yard after he threw an incendiary bomb at a military barracks in west London at dawn. By the weekend the Islamist organizations were reporting a crackdown by the Yard.

On December 21 the London- based Hizb-ut-Tahrir issued a communiqué because "America, the head of Kufr [apostasy], and its British poodle launched sudden strikes against the Muslims in Iraq without any warning." The communiqué attributed the timing of the attack to President Clinton's domestic problems: "As for the domestic position of Clinton, it was known that there would be a vote in the House of Representatives to try him on the same day the attack happened. So he took his speedy decision to attack to influence the voting result, under the pretext that it is not allowed to weaken the President at a time when the military forces are at war."

Ultimately, Hizb-ut-Tahrir emphasized, the bombings of Iraq were undertaken largely in pursuit of the U.S.-British quest for dominance over the Persian Gulf, and it was in this context that the United States demonstrated its intense hostility toward the Arab world. In pursuit of its strategic interests the United States "made Saddam a pariah to the Gulf. She used the imposition of the sanctions and the terms of the inspectors as a continuous source of crises and to spread terror, anxiety, and disturbance amongst the peoples of the Gulf states. She went on to steal the resources of the Gulf states through weapons contracts worth tens of billions of dollars, which exceed the capacities of their armies by many times. She also imposed oppressive security pacts over these peoples, which were signed secretly by their rulers. She made of the rulers symbols that have no more say than to sign on the legality of the American intervention and pay the bill of the cost of their intervention. She also established military bases for the purpose of training, accumulating arms, maintaining American hegemony and her continuous presence under all . . . circumstances and conditions." This list of American transgressions against the people of the Arabian peninsula is not different from bin Laden's.

Hizb-ut-Tahrir's communiqué states that except for the date of commencing the air strikes, the U.S. campaign against Iraq was optimized toward furthering Washington's strategic objectives, which are inherently detrimental to the Arab world. "The military attack that Clinton ordered against the Muslims in Iraq is not because of Iraq's dispute with the inspection team regarding the exposure of some locations. Neither is it to protect the neighbors of Iraq from the threats of Saddam. Nor is it in fear of the chemical and biological weapons as claimed. Rather it is because of the first American objective, which is the strengthening of the American presence in the Gulf and tightening control over it and the attempt to be alone in terms of influence in it."

And while it stands to reason that the United States would stop at nothing to further its own interests and realize its own objectives, Hizb-ut-Tahrir points the accusing finger at the local conservative Arab leaders whose alliances with the United States facilitate the U.S. presence in Arabia. "This is just a little of the conspiracy of the traitors and agents who govern Muslims. Is it not time for the sincere people of the sons of the Ummah and the leaders to avenge her honor and dignity which were rolled in dust? Is it not time for the Islamic peoples to know that their rulers are agents who find pleasure in humiliation, and that it is time for the peoples to discard them and to clean the country of their disgrace and betrayal? Is it not time for the armies stationed in the camps to destroy the seats of oppression and transgression, and to protect the power of Islam and Muslims from the tyranny of the treacherous rulers and the filth of the criminal Kuffar [apostates]?" Hizb-ut-Tahrir echoes bin Laden's original call for action against the Arab leaders cooperating with the United States.

THE TERRORIST LEADERSHIP was laying the ground for the implementation of the "bin Laden plans" when the December U.S.-Iraqi crisis occurred. In the aftermath of the "compromise" reached in mid-November about the resumption of the U.N. inspections and with growing pressure in the United Nations to lift the sanctions—pressure imposed by France, China, and Russia, and endorsed by most Arab states—Baghdad was convinced that it would have a few months of routine low-key U.N. activity before Washington instigated another crisis. The White House's decision to use Iraq ostensibly as an instrument for diverting attention from the president's domestic problems caught Baghdad by surprise and, given the close coordination between Baghdad, Khartoum, and Qandahar, must have surprised the Islamist leadership as well. As a result, as bombs and cruise missiles were finding their marks throughout Iraq, the Islamists were scrounging to accelerate their operational preparations. Within hours after the beginning of the bombing bin Laden and Zawahiri convened an emergency meeting in Qandahar with several key terrorist and Arab "Afghan" commanders, such as Abu-Said al-Masri from Egypt, to activate their reaction plans. They all signed a message to "the Muslim masses throughout the world" in which they urged their followers "to hit U.S. and British interests and stage demonstrations in protest at the U.S.–British attack on Iraq." This message was sent clandestinely to Islamist leaders and commanders worldwide.

The Clinton administration seemed to have instigated the mid-December crisis knowing that the bombing of Iraq would spark a terrorism campaign. The White House did have timely knowledge of the arrangements between Turabi, bin Laden, and Hussein earlier in the fall to use the first crisis involving an actual U.S. military strike as a green light for a terrorism campaign. Even though the exercises of mid-October demonstrated that the United States was not ready to withstand a spectacular terrorist strike on its soil, the White House went ahead with the provocation in Iraq and the ensuing bombing campaign.

On December 13 U.S. embassies in the region issued warnings about the possible terrorist threat. "The embassy has information indicating a strong possibility that terrorist elements are planning an attack against U.S. targets in the Gulf, possibly in the next thirty days," read the message issued in Riyadh to Americans. U.S. officials identified bin Laden as the suspected perpetrator of such an attack. These warnings showed that the Clinton administration anticipated possible retribution for the crisis with Iraq that had just started to escalate. After all, there was no irregular activity in the region at the time. Moreover, these warnings were issued at about the same time the Pentagon was ordered by the president to update its strike plans and expedite preparations for the Iraqi operations.

The Islamist leadership deliberated on the proper reaction to the bombings for a few days and resolved that the only response to the new American challenge would be a confrontation in which they seized the strategic initiative through a series of spectacular operations. They fully expected such a war of terrorism to be protracted. Using Zawahiri's Egyptian organizations as their primary venues, bin Laden and his lieutenants began issuing communiqués outlining the Islamists' doctrine for confrontation.

The first communiqué was issued by Zawahiri's Jihad Movement—The Vanguards of Conquest on December 18. The communiqué, signed by Abdallah al-Mansur, the organization's secretary general, stressed the urgency of action because the Arab nation would "not be content with the empty words of denunciation and condemnation that we are accustomed to hearing from the [Arab] regimes." The main message was short and to the point: "In the name of all the sons of the Islamic movement in Egypt, and with the participation of our brothers throughout the great Islamic world, we openly and loudly declare that we will retaliate for what is happening to the sons of our nations in Iraq, since the crimes committed by the United States against our Islamic nation will not go unpunished."

It took bin Laden, Zawahiri, and their lieutenants two more days to formulate a comprehensive response to the unfolding crisis. The response was pure bin Laden—emphasizing pan-Islamic action without relinquishing the role and responsibility of the terrorist elite. That strategy was elucidated in a communiqué from Zawahiri's Islamic Group issued on December 20. The communiqué defined fighting the United States as a "divine course and decree," and so there would be no alternative to waging the jihad against the United States as a sacred duty for all Muslims. The Islamic Group saw no end in sight for the confrontation with Washington because, as demonstrated by the recent events in Iraq, "whenever the White House rulers want to conceal their scandals from their own people, they hit the Islamic peoples." The communiqué stated that the Muslim world "will not attain glory or stop U.S. arrogance except through it [the divine course]." The communiqué stated that the bombing of Iraq should be examined in the context of the greater struggle between Islamism and the West: "What is happening in Iraq is shameful for the Islamic nation, because Almighty God assigned to it the task of promoting virtue and repudiating abominable actions, and is there any abominable action worse than annihilating an entire Muslim people? What abominable action is worse than the atheists' raiding and destroying our factories, killing our women and children, and plundering our riches?"

For the current challenge to be met, the communiqué argued, an all-Islamic response was required. "The Islamic movements should play their role in supporting our Muslim people in Iraq, and they should unite to resist the U.S. arrogance." Because of the gravity of the crisis, theological guidance was required, "and the Islamic nation's ulema are urged to play their role in the light of this ferocious onslaught . . . since the nation's ulema are the guardians and thus have a responsibility." The communiqué concluded by stressing the significance of the crisis and the Islamists' expectations from the Muslim world. The Islamic group stated that "what is happening in Iraq today should prompt the [Islamic] nation to rise to the level of the event; it should also compel it to inflict the obligatory punishment on the United States and its supporters and then work to bring the residents of the U.S. White House to trial as war criminals."

Echoes of agreement with and adoption of bin Laden's themes resounded from all over the Muslim world, especially in the December 25 Friday sermons. For example, Sheikh Akramah Sabri, the Arafat-approved imam of al-Aqsa Mosque in Jerusalem, paid more attention to the Iraqi crisis than to the Palestinian problem. Sheikh Sabri did opine that current circumstances make the destruction of Israel more likely. "Let us pray for the day when Jerusalem and the entire holy land of Palestine are liberated from

Israeli occupation," he told the crowd of about 200,000 worshipers. These circumstances were the result of the all-Muslim reaction to the bombing of Iraq. "The aggression against Iraq was designed to divert attention from the shameful things happening in the United States, where the president has been involved in nauseating activities," Sheikh Sabri explained. The decision to bomb Iraq accurately reflected the West's inherent hatred "worthy of the Crusaders" toward Islam and Muslims. Sheikh Sabri explained that unless Arab leaders led the forthcoming confrontation with the United States, Britain, and Israel, the enraged masses would topple them as the masses rose up to meet the sacred challenge of jihad. "Some Arab leaders have gone down on their knees to America and England, but their peoples will never do so," he warned. "They will rise against them, and cast them down, to liberate the Muslim Arab world from American-British influence." The struggle ahead, Sheikh Sabri concluded, would be over the survival of Islam in the face of the Western onslaught. One triumphant outcome of this confrontation would be securing Palestine in Muslim hands—in other words, the destruction of Israel.

The launching of anti-American Islamist terrorism in retaliation for the bombing campaign against Iraq was no longer a theoretical contemplation. Senior Iraqi officials addressed this threat as a near certainty while denying any connection to the terrorists. Iraqi trade minister Muhammad Mahdi Salah expected "terrorist activities" against the United States to increase as a result of its bombing of Iraq. "When the United States is helping terrorist activities against Iraq, then this will enhance terrorist activities against the United States," he said. "It is not a threat; it is a consequence of their policy." Salah stressed that Iraq condemned and did not practice "terrorism." However, "by adopting [an] aggressive policy against Iraq and against Arab people and against Muslims, and by using sanctions as a means of destroying this society and by using military aggression," Washington was creating the environment that spurred terrorist attacks.

Al-Quds al-Arabi first raised, ostensibly on the basis of Western media reports, the possibility of cooperation between Saddam Hussein and bin Laden. A late December editorial predicted that "President Saddam Hussein, whose country was subjected to a four-day air strike, will look for support in taking revenge on the United States and Britain by cooperating with Saudi oppositionist Osama bin Laden, whom the United States considers to be the most wanted person in the world." The editorial noted that this type of cooperation was very likely considering that "bin Laden was planning to move to Iraq before the recent strike." *Al-Quds al-Arabi* went on to quote unnamed Western officials, noting that while Saddam Hussein lacked the capabilities to strike back at the West, the Islamists did have the capabilities and were eager to strike out. Cooperation between Saddam Hussein and bin Laden would be the best approach for both of them.

The moment the bombing campaign stopped, Saddam Hussein dispatched Faruq al-Hijazi to Qandahar. Hijazi, Iraq's ambassador to Turkey and formerly deputy chief of Iraqi intelligence, has been dealing with bin Laden since 1994. He is also the chief of Iraqi intelligence in Turkey, in charge of acquiring strategic technologies and weapons throughout Europe and smuggling them to Iraq and of smuggling Iraqi assets (people, money, oil) into Europe. In Qandahar, Hijazi met with bin Laden to discuss future terrorist strikes against the United States and Britain. He recommended better coordination of operations with Baghdad and offered bin Laden every possible assistance from Iraqi intelligence. Hijazi gave bin Laden concrete examples of the support Iraqi intelligence could offer by covering issues under his responsibility. In addition Hijazi repeated Saddam Hussein's offer of shelter and hospitality for bin Laden and his people. Bin Laden agreed in principle to spearhead the revenge campaign against the West in accordance with the recently agreed to operational plans but suggested further study and coordination of specific contingency plans and proposed operations. Both sides agreed on the urgent imperative to expedite the unleashing of the anti-American terrorist war.

To demonstrate Baghdad's commitment to cooperating with bin Laden, Hijazi brought with him and gave bin Laden a pack of blank genuine Yemeni diplomatic passports supplied to Iraqi intelligence by their Yemeni counterparts. Such passports are invaluable for the safe international travel of key terrorist leaders. Hijazi also promised to expedite additional Iraqi professional support. Soon afterward several Iraqi military-intelligence officers arrived in Afghanistan via Pakistan to assist in the advance training and preparation of the Islamist terrorists. The most important were the experts from Unit 999 of Iraqi intelligence. They selected four teams, each consisting of twelve veteran terrorists, for advanced and intense training in sabotage and infiltration techniques for operations in the West in cooperation with Iraqi intelligence. In early January 1999 these teams were already being trained in a barracks on the outskirts of Baghdad.

In late December, Saddam Hussein and his intimate circle concluded that there was no escape from escalating the confrontation with the United States, or Arab countries would gradually accept Washington's dominance. Repeated attempts by the Iraqi air defense and air force to defy the no-fly zones failed to shoot down a single aircraft—Islamist terrorism seemed the only viable mode of confrontation. The prudent Hussein determined to measure the Islamists' commitment, however, before daring both the U.S. and the Arab regimes. Around the first of the year Qusay

Hussein dispatched his confidants, al-Jubburi and al-Shihabi, back to Afghanistan to meet with bin Laden, Zawahiri, and the Islamist terrorist elite. Baghdad offered a joint open-ended, vigorous jihad against Americans throughout the world and against all Arab regimes allied with the United States. In return Iraq asked for an iron-clad guarantee of Islamist cooperation and support—that is, that no Islamist revolution would take place in Iraq throughout this jihad. Bin Laden and Zawahiri assured the Iraqi emissaries that Saddam's regime would be safe for as long as Iraq actively participated in their jihad. The Iraqis' trust and confidence in the Islamists was reflected in Hussein's assertive, defiant actions.

In late December senior government and security officials in several Gulf sheikhdoms cited intelligence data confirming that Saddam Hussein would "contract [with] Islamic terrorist groups," and specifically bin Laden's, "to exact retaliation" against the United States, Britain, and their regional allies. British security officials concurred, pointing to the active preparations for something spectacular the Islamist leaders would be able to "agree with," Saddam Hussein would be able to "understand," and all would deny responsibility for to reduce the likelihood of a massive retaliation against Iraq. In early January 1999 Kuwaiti intelligence confirmed that there were "hundreds of Arab 'Afghans' receiving advanced military training" in camps near al-Nasiriyah in southern Iraq "in preparation for playing a crucial role in a military confrontation that is expected to take place quite soon." These Arab "Afghans" are being trained by Iraqi intelligence within the context of an alliance Baghdad struck with what Kuwaiti intelligence described as "a front comprising six militant organizations whose ranks include former fighters in the Afghan war effort"—a euphemism for bin Laden's World Islamic Front for Jihad against Jews and Crusaders. The Kuwaitis learned that this agreement called for "the move of hundreds of the members of that front to Iraqi territory" for advanced training in preparation for their imminent participation in "the battle against the United States and its allies."

Also in late December, Iraqi official media alluded to Baghdad's penchant for terrorist revenge. On December 24 al-Thawrah, the official organ of Iraq's ruling Baath party, published an article by Basil Hassun al-Sadi extolling international terrorism as the logical and fitting reaction to the U.S. bombing of Iraq. "As soon as the forces of evil fired their last missile on Iraq on the night of 19 December 1998, the U.S. and British rulers began to express their disappointment, frustration, and fear of retaliation," Sadi opened. The article then surveyed pronouncements by U.S. and British leaders about the threat of terrorism and special security precautions undertaken. The article emphasized that the driving force behind the worldwide quest for revenge against the United States was the grassroots rage against U.S. policies worldwide—a trend that peaked with the bombing of Iraq. "The motive for any retaliatory attack against U.S. interests in the world will be the injustice, which the getaway U.S. Administration is practicing against all the voices that call for justice, as well as the voices that reject tyranny, the domination of the world by one state, and the confiscation of people's liberties and the legitimacy of the United Nations. Therefore, as long as the United States insists on tyranny, it will continue to live in fear, abandon its embassies or surround them with security cordons, evacuate its nationals, and intensify security around its planes, ships, and military bases. Thus, every American and every supporter of U.S. aggression will always be haunted by fear of attack." Sadi then surveyed the precautionary measures undertaken by the United States, from the closing of embassies to evacuation of citizens from several spots around the world, and approvingly quoted Defense Secretary William Cohen "admitting that all these measures are useless against any retaliation." Sadi agreed, stressing that recent U.S. actions had already earned the ire and wrath of people throughout the world, in essence bringing about a long-term campaign of terrorism against the United States. "By their savage aggression, the Washington rulers violated all international laws and pacts as well as the bill of human rights. This violation deserves punishment. But, they do not know from where the punishment will come. Thus, they are haunted by fear of punishment every hour of the day," Sadi concluded.

Several Islamist terrorist organizations endorsed the concept of revenge outlined by Baghdad. For example, the next day—December 25—the Palestinian Islamic Jihad published its analysis of the essence and ramifications of the U.S. bombing of Iraq in an editorial in the Gaza paper *al-Istiqlal*. "This new crisis is no longer a personal difference between the Iraqi leader and the leaders and chiefs of the West," the Islamic Jihad decreed. The current crisis was yet another phase in a historical confrontation between the West and Islam. "The memories of the Crusader wars have not left the minds of the politicians and soldiers of the West, which is why today, they are trying to seek vengeance for what happened centuries ago, benefiting from this terrible imbalance of power, which was primarily and basically created by the West. It was only natural for the spirit of violence and control and the desire to impose hegemony, which has characterized Western civilization and its industrial revolution, to take control of affairs there and return to this imbalance of power, in order to prepare for Western hegemony on our resources and the resources of the oppressed nations."

In contrast, according to *al-Istiqlal,* the Arab governments remained silent and inactive throughout the crisis because Arab leaders were too fearful of the United States to do anything. And that was the quintessence of the ramifications of the attack on Iraq for the entire Muslim world. "What happened over the past few days in Iraq reveals in a clear-cut and flagrant manner the depth of the crisis the ruling Arab regimes are going through. These regimes are moving further and further away from their masses and the interests of these masses, which emerged in an impulsive and natural manner to curse the United States and declare its full solidarity with the Iraqi people. This crisis will become more and more impossible so long as these regimes continue with their same policy and trends and so long as the state of incompetence and disregard continues to shackle the stances of the regimes and govern their decision-making process." The popular grassroots outburst of rage against both the West and the pliant Arab regimes was critical in understanding the forthcoming response from the Muslim world. "It is a throttling crisis, and the U.S. missiles did not strike the Iraqis alone, but were directed at every Arab, Muslim, and other person who refuses to submit to the conditions of the civilization of bestiality and the policy of Americanizing the world. The protracted battle truly requires patience, faith, and tolerance." Having been exacerbated by the recent bombing of Iraq, Islam's real battle against the reincarnation of the Crusaders' onslaught had only begun, the Islamic Jihad concluded.

Ultimately the key to effective terrorism in and out of the Arab world is firmly in the hands of the two main sponsoring states—Iran and Syria. How Tehran and Damascus analyze the ramifications of the U.S. bombing of Iraq will determine the intensity of reaction. The primary strategic outcome of the bombing campaign has been the further consolidation of the tripartite axis that bands Iraq, Syria, and Iran together. Given the Clinton administration's claim that these bombings contributed to the emergence of a new, pro-U.S., Middle East, a conservative Arab analyst noted, "it would be in the natural course of things that the Iraqis, Syrians, and Iranians would react strongly and move so as to counterbalance the new reality. Their reaction would have been prompted by strategic considerations related to the security of the Middle East region." Neither Syria nor Iran wants to see Iraq dismembered or taken over by a pro-Western regime that would break the on-land connection between them. They are also afraid that the Iraqi Liberation Act enacted by the U.S. Congress—unlikely to cause the downfall of Hussein's regime but bound to become a headache for Baghdad—will be followed by an "Iranian Liberation Act" and a "Syrian Liberation Act." Hence it is imperative for both Tehran and Damascus to deter the Washington-led West from continuing the onslaught against Iraq. "This is because Iran's and Syria's security is to a large extent bound up with that of Iraq," the Arab analyst explained.

Committing terrorist assets to the indigenously popular revenge campaign against the United States is an expedient strategic move for the two sponsoring states. It did not take long for both Damascus and Tehran to divert assets and resources recently earmarked for an escalation in the struggle against Israel to the building campaign against the United States. Already in November 1998 the uppermost Iranian leadership, including Khamenei, held a secret summit meeting with the leadership of HAMAS to define frameworks in which they could work jointly and closely with the HizbAllah against Israel and to determine the new levels of advanced terrorist training HAMAS terrorists would now be receiving in Iran to prepare them for the required missions. In a separate meeting Tehran informed Sheikh Hassan Nasrallah, the HizbAllah secretary general, of the modalities of cooperation. Then in late December, capitalizing on the grassroots reaction to the bombing of Iraq and bin Laden's latest fatwas, Tehran mobilized its key assets. With help from Syrian intelligence the HizbAllah Special Operations Command started activating dormant cells all over the world, primarily in Western Europe and Latin America. The Syrians called "old friends" back into active service, such as the Armenian ASALA (Armenian Secret Army for the Liberation of Armenia), including ASALA's leader, Simon Sakarian, and West European radicals. Sakarian, also known by the nom de guerre Abu-Mesto, is in exile in Argentina and runs a criminal-cum-terrorist network throughout Latin America and into the United States. Concurrently intelligence reports indicated that Imad Mughaniyah, bin Laden's counterpart in the Committee of Three, had arrived in Lebanon to coordinate the spectacular terrorist operations from there.

The extent of the international reach of HAMAS was demonstrated through the activation of its support resources in Lebanon and Pakistan. This infrastructure was organized within a few months with professional and financial support from Mohammad Reza Bahonar, the Iranian intelligence official responsible for sponsoring Islamic liberation movements. For Tehran the HAMAS infrastructure in Pakistan, closely intertwined with the resources of such organizations as the Jamaat-i-Islami and the Hizb-ul-Mujahideen, serves as a unique springboard into Pakistan and in Central Asia. The HAMAS presence in Pakistan has operational ramifications. Back in November a special detachment of the Heroes of the Islamic Jihad, comprising eight HAMAS members and five Pakistani followers of bin Laden's, returned to Pakistan from intensive terrorist training in Iran. The Heroes of the Islamic Jihad were established by Tehran with bin Laden's help in winter 1997–98 to conduct spectacular operations overseas, including the subsequently aborted operations in Argentina and France. Now the Palestinian-Pakistani detachment was sent to an ISI-sponsored Hizb-ul-Mujahideen camp in the Muzaffarabad area, where they received final training for a month, pending a specific spectacular operation. Additional "Heroes" detachments had already arrived in Pakistan. Concurrently numerous Taliban from the Far East and the Middle East, then studying in Pakistan, were recruited jointly by HAMAS and the Hizb-ul-Mujahideen and sent for accelerated training in the ISI-run camps in Afghanistan. Technically and operationally, these terrorist forces are in the final stages of readying for operations.

Related preparations for major state-sponsored terrorist operations have been reported. U.S. intelligence had already monitored a satellite-telephone conversation between Osama bin Laden in Afghanistan and a commander overseas in which they discussed an imminent bomb attack on a Western target. Immediately after the cessation of the U.S. bombing campaign in Iraq, representatives of bin Laden arrived in the Bekáa, Lebanon, for a conference with senior commanders of HAMAS and Palestinian terrorist organizations long sponsored by Iraq, such as Abu-Nidal's Fatah Revolutionary Council and Abu-Ibrahim's "May 15 Group," a small group of expert bomb makers. They discussed the launching of spectacular terrorist operations in the Persian Gulf sheikhdoms, Western Europe, and the Far East as revenge for the U.S. and British bombing of Iraq.

At the same time a major summit was being planned in Qandahar for the last week of December 1998. Hassan al-Turabi was expected to be among the participants, along with the Taliban leadership, bin Laden, Zawahiri, senior ISI officers, and leading terrorist commanders. Turabi would arrive on a special plane from Khartoum. According to a senior Islamist source, Turabi "would focus during his talks with bin Laden and the Taliban leaders on coordinating ways of confronting Washington, 'the common enemy.'" The expectation that Turabi would attend the meeting in Qandahar suggests that monumental decisions were on the table—presumably authorizing the use of weapons of mass destruction and/or striking out at the United States. Islamist sources also expected Turabi to invite bin Laden to return with him to Sudan. But the early exposure of Turabi's plans compelled him to postpone his own trip and send senior confidants to attend the summit in Qandahar.

Islamabad introduced a sense of urgency to the process. The ISI leaked to *Ausaf,* an Islamist paper, that in mid-December, American diplomats led by Assistant Secretary of State Karl Inderfurth threatened Afghanistan with a bombing campaign like that on Iraq unless the nation extradited bin Laden and his lieutenants. "The U.S. has given a deadline of 15 January 1999 to deport eighteen mujahideen leaders including Osama bin Laden from Afghanistan and has threatened action if they are provided shelter after this deadline," the paper wrote. In these discussions the U.S. diplomats also demanded that the Taliban incorporate other Afghan parties into their government and liberalize their Islamist form of government. Having failed to subdue Iraq and with crises at home, *Ausaf* wrote, "the U.S. is planning to attack Afghanistan under the cover of Osama and other mujahid leaders." The editorial argued that the U.S. fixation with bin Laden was a manifestation of its overall hatred toward Islamism. "Osama bin Laden has become a big challenge for the U.S. and its Arab allies and it is trying to get rid of this perpetual threat at any cost." But the U.S. challenge was far greater because "wherever in the world an Islamic system is established, the U.S. declares it a violation of human rights. This has only one meaning: that wherever Muslims are living, they should follow a code of life based on liberalism which has the consent of the U.S. This means that if Muslims all over the world adopt the Christian way of life, they are acceptable; otherwise, they are terrorists and murderers of human rights." Under these circumstances Muslims must draw the line—in Afghanistan—and with their Arab mujahideen allies block the U.S. encroachment into the Muslim world.

In response to this situation Osama bin Laden and Ayman al-Zawahiri gave a series of interviews to Arab and Pakistani papers and to Western electronic media, using trusted Pakistani and Arab correspondents. All these interviews covered the same issues and seem to have been granted in a single session in a tent in the Helmand Valley, the center of poppy growing in southwestern Afghanistan. Three themes were dominant: (1) bin Laden is not responsible for the East Africa bombing even though he supports the action; (2) weapons of mass destruction are admissible in the struggle against the West, although again bin Laden has nothing to do with them; and (3) in the aftermath of the strikes on Iraq, jihad against the West is an urgent obligation. A close look at the Arabic text of bin Laden's replies shows deep thought and fine, precise phrasing aimed to influence his Muslim audience. Although bin Laden was also anxious to get his message across to the West, the objective there was to issue a veiled threat, not to convince.

Bin Laden defined his own role within the Islamist movement in the interview that Rahimullah Yusufzai, a friendly Pakistani journalist based in Peshawar, conducted for ABC News. Bin Laden saw his greatest contribution to the worldwide jihad in guiding and instigating the masses into action, not in actual command over specific operations. He explained that "we, in the World Islamic Front for Jihad against Jews and Crusaders, have . . . issued a crystal clear fatwa calling on the Nation to carry on jihad aimed at liberating Islamic holy sites . . . and all Islamic lands." He was gratified that the Muslim Nation "has responded to this appeal and this instigation." Bin Laden vowed to "continue this course because it is a part of our religion," particularly since God "ordered us to carry out jihad so that the word of God may remain exalted to the heights. If the instigation for jihad against the Jews and the Americans, in order to liberate Al-Aqsa Mosque in Jerusalem and the Holy Ka'aba is considered a crime, let history be a witness that I am a criminal." His possible involvement in any terrorist operation should be judged accordingly.

As to the bombing in East Africa, bin Laden disassociated himself from the terrorist strike while endorsing it. "I had no hand at all in the bombings in Kenya and Tanzania," he told an Afghan correspondent. "But I feel no sorrow over the blasts." He did not rule out that militant Muslims were responsible for the blasts. To the Arab correspondent of *al-Sharq al-Awsat*, bin Laden reiterated his denial of involvement in the bombing but expressed support for those behind these attacks "and whoever carries out military actions against American forces," such as the embassy bombings.

In his interview with Yusufzai, bin Laden went further to rationalize and justify spectacular terrorist strikes in which large numbers of innocent bystanders, including Muslims, might be injured. He said that these bystanders should be considered as human shields held hostage by the Americans to facilitate the United States' plunder of Muslim lands. "According to Islamic jurisprudence if we abstain from firing on the Americans lest we should kill these Muslims (used by them as shields), the harm that could befall Muslims at large, who are being attacked, outweighs the good of saving the lives of these Muslims used as shields. This means that in a case like this, when it becomes apparent that it would be impossible to repel these Americans without assaulting them, even if this involved the killing of Muslims, this is permissible under Islam." Bin Laden stressed that he would have done this even if his own children were being used as human shields. He used this reasoning to reiterate his understanding of "the motives of those who carried out these acts [the bombing of the U.S. embassies in East Africa]."

Bin Laden dodged questions from *al-Sharq al-Awsat*'s interviewer on whether he was trying to acquire weapons of mass destruction. He told the Pakistani correspondent that obtaining chemical and nuclear weapons "is a religious duty. How we use them is up to us." To the Arab correspondent, he stressed the importance and urgency in acquiring weapons of mass destruction for the entire Muslim world. "Our [Muslim] nation is facing aggression and it has the right to possess what is necessary to defend itself." The acquisition of weapons of mass destruction, which bin Laden denied, "is not a charge. Instead, it means preparation and the fulfillment of a duty."

Bin Laden's discussion of the jihad as an urgent imperative for the Muslim world leaves no doubt about his intentions and role. To *al-Sharq al-Awsat*'s interviewer, he explained the importance of the recent U.S. and

British bombing of Iraq as a catalyst for the rejuvenation of an armed jihad. "The American and British peoples stated widely that they support their leaders' decision to attack Iraq. This means that all individuals of these two nations, as well as the Jews in occupied Palestine, are belligerent people and every Muslim must stand against them and must kill and fight them. Anything that can be taken from them by force is considered booty for the Muslims." In a subsequent interview with al-Jazirah television in Qatar, he urged all Muslims to kill all Americans, including noncombatants. "If it is made possible by Almighty God to Muslims, every American man is targeted. They are enemies to us, whether they are involved in direct combat against us or pay taxes. Perhaps you heard in recent days that the rate of those who support Clinton in striking Iraq is about three-fourths of the American people." This definition and justification of legitimate targets amounts to sanctioning indiscriminate terrorism in the United States.

Bin Laden defined his position on the recent bombing of Iraq in the context of the priorities of the jihad. There should be no confusion about the ultimate objective of the jihad, bin Laden told Yusufzai: "Our work targets world infidels in the first place. Our enemy is the Crusader alliance led by America, Britain, and Israel. It is a Crusader-Jewish alliance. However, some regimes in the Arab and Muslim worlds have joined that alliance, preventing us Muslims from defending the holy Ka'aba. Our hostility is in the first place, and to the greatest extent, leveled against these world infidels, and by necessity the regimes which have turned themselves into tools for this occupation of [Islamic lands]." The bombing of Iraq and the proper Islamist reaction should be understood in this context. Bin Laden explained that "the treacherous attack perpetrated a few days ago against the Muslim people of Iraq by the United States and Britain has confirmed several things, the most important of which is that Britain and America are acting on behalf of Israel and the Jews, to strike at any power in the Islamic world, with a view to paving the way for the Jews to divide the Muslim world once again and enslave it and boost the rest of its wealth. As is known, a great part of the force that carried out the attack came from certain Gulf countries, which underlined the fact that these countries have lost their sovereignty." Bin Laden had no doubt that the people will rise up to defend Islam. "Many of these rulers could face the fate of the Shah of Iran," he anticipated. "Under these circumstances, Muslims should carry out their obligations [to wage the jihad], since the rulers of the region have accepted the invasion of their countries. But these countries belong to Islam and not to those rulers. May God exact his revenge against all of them." As for bin Laden and the World Islamic Front, they would concentrate on direct confrontation with the United States and Israel. "The main focus of the Front, as its name indicates, are the Jews and Crusaders because they are the biggest enemy. The main effort, at this phase, must target the Jews and the Crusaders."

Insisting that he was obeying Mullah Omar's instructions not to be directly involved in any act of violence while in Afghanistan, bin Laden regretted to *al-Sharq al-Awsat*'s interviewer that he would have no direct involvement in this sacred jihad against Americans. He did acknowledge having influence on the waging of jihad. Bin Laden said he continued to "guide [Muslims] toward holy war against Jews and Christians," which was a duty from a Muslim legal point of view. He added that the perpetrators of the East Africa bombing and other terrorist operations might have been influenced by his writings and guidance, but that did not mean he was responsible for their actions although he took pride in their trust.

Pakistani Islamist leaders announced that they were ready to distribute all over the Muslim world a special message Osama bin Laden had recorded on videotape. "This message would expose the U.S. conspiracies against the Taliban and emphasize the need for evacuation of U.S. forces from Saudi Arabia," the Pakistani Islamists stated. Bin Laden expected this message to further exacerbate the Islamist anti-American campaign.

On January 5, 1999, Saddam Hussein, clearly emboldened by bin Laden's backing, delivered a defiant speech commemorating the foundation of the Iraqi Army. This speech, which was widely reported throughout the Hub of Islam, further assured the Islamists of Hussein's resolve to wage the jihad they advocate. Hussein repeated many Islamist themes. For example, he urged the Arabs to overthrow those governments allied with the United States, in particular those permitting the stationing of foreign troops on their soil. "Revolt against foreign powers, their aggression and their armies and chase them. Kick out injustice and its perpetrators," Hussein urged. "Revolt against those who boast of friendship with the United States. The dwarfs on their thrones will be forced to hear you, or else they will step down to give way [to] the people to say their opinion and take their action." Hussein also called attention to the dire state of Islam's holy shrines. Jerusalem was a "humiliated hostage" to Jewish occupation, while the holy shrines in Saudi Arabia were "wounded by the presence of foreign soldiers and their spears. Look around to see how mischievous persons have humiliated your sacred places, which are now trodden by foreign powers after conniving with them so as to hit the great Iraq."

On Friday, January 8, *Ausaf* carried a message recently conveyed by "Arab Mujahid Osama bin Laden" in which he urged Muslims all over the world "to continue their jihad against the oppression of the United States, Britain, and international Zionism." Bin Laden also clarified his role in the jihad in the context of his agreement with Mullah Omar. He explained that because of his agreement with the Taliban he "[would] not indulge in any kind of activities here [in Afghanistan], [but] he [would] in other parts of the world continue his struggle for achieving his goal." Bin Laden emphasized that "in my struggle against the oppressive activities of the United States and Britain and international Zionism, Mullah Omar fully supports me." This is because "it is the United States which has started a war against the Muslims. We are striving only to give it a fitting reply." Although he said he had nothing to do with the August bombing of the U.S. embassies in Nairobi and Dar-es-Salaam, bin Laden could certify that "the people involved in these explosions had just given a slight warning to the United States. A full-fledged reply is still to come forth." In this context, *Ausaf* commented, he "did not term attacks on Americans in the Gulf improbable." Osama bin Laden concluded, "It would be better for the United States if it gives up its activities against the Muslims, apologizes to Iraq, Afghanistan, Libya, and Sudan for its attacks, and calls back its troops from the Gulf."

These themes were simultaneously repeated and endorsed by Islamists all over the world in their Friday sermons. For example, the preacher in the al-Aqsa mosque devoted his sermon to the situation in Iraq, clearly identified as America's victim, and in particular Saddam Hussein's speech. "Two days ago, Saddam had appealed to the young generation in the ruling families to topple their corrupted rulers because they had conspired with the West against their brothers and sisters," the preacher said. But this would not happen because the entire Arab establishment was so afraid of the United States, they would not dare challenge its hold over their country. The only salvation for Iraq, and the entire Arab world, was in the fold of militant Islam. "O, Saddam: now your head is wanted; the Americans and the British want to replace you with a new agent for them. You should defend yourself in order to survive. And the way to survive is not through nationalism, or Baathism. . . . The only way to survive is to deal with Allah directly, to return to the path of Allah. You may declare Islam or step aside and invite His people to take over. You don't have plenty of time." The only salvation for Saddam Hussein's Iraq could come from "Allah, and the soldiers of Allah. O Muslims, Allah has ordered us to work. We know that the great battle is coming. Iraq may or may not be the spark, but the sincere Muslims will one day reach the rule in Baghdad, Damascus, Amman, Cairo, Istanbul, and Pakistan. Islam will rule the world, one day, against the will of the infidels and the hypocrites. We are trying to avoid bloodshed, but these wolves feel an appetite for the blood of Muslims." The al-Aqsa preacher reaffirmed that the battle for Iraq was the catalyst for the eruption of the Islamist confrontation with the U.S.-led West over the future of

Islam. "There will be many battles with the infidels, but we will be victorious by the will of Allah." For the al-Aqsa preacher the building tension in the Muslim world "is a sign that the revenge of Allah is near; that the victory of Allah is near."

Before long a spate of terrorist strikes and narrowly averted strikes took place all over the world. The common denominator of the myriad of perpetrators was their belief in and commitment to the teachings of Osama bin Laden. The Islamist terrorist activities of the first months of 1999 are precursors of the new era of Islamist rage and revenge.

13

What's Next?

ON DECEMBER 28, 1998, a little-known Yemeni group calling itself the Islamic Jihad Badge abducted sixteen Western tourists—twelve British, two American, and two Australian—in the remote district of Abyan in Yemen. Most of the members of the Islamic Jihad were trained in Afghanistan but are too young to have participated in the war against the Soviets. They have training camps in the mountains of Abyan, about 250 miles south of Sanaa, the capital of Yemen. The tourists were abducted when about twenty heavily armed mujahideen attacked their five-vehicle convoy some 60 miles northeast of Aden. The hostages were transferred to the group's remote mountain hideaway. The kidnappers issued a specific demand that was ignored by Sanaa. Instead the next day Yemeni security forces stormed the Islamic Jihad's camp. The hostages were used as human shields, forced to stand with their hands up on open ground in the path of the army's attack. Three Britons and an Australian tourist died, and one Briton, one American, and one Australian were injured—most of them by the army's fire. At least three of the kidnappers were killed, including an Egyptian "Afghan" known as Osama al-Masri. Three others, including 28-year-old Zain al-Abdin Abu Bakar al-Mihdar, the Islamic Jihad's leader, known by the nom de guerre Abu-al-Hassan, were captured. That night, December 29, the Islamic Army of Aden-Abyan, an obscure Islamist group, issued a statement in Dubai criticizing both the attack of the Yemeni security forces and Sanaa's reason for ordering the attack. "The [Yemeni] Government could not tolerate a group of young Yemenis demanding that the aggression against Iraq be halted and that the British and U.S. forces be chased out of the Arabian Peninsula," the statement read.

The kidnapping operation was actually rooted in the brief history of the Islamic Army of Aden-Abyan, an offshoot of the Yemeni Islamic Jihad. The Islamic Jihad is one of five or six Islamist organizations that were formed for internal power-politics purposes in about 1993 with the backing of Sanaa. Each of these "Armies" comprised a mix of veteran "Afghans"—predominantly Yemenites, but also Egyptians, Algerians, and other Arabs—and young Yemenites. In mid-1998 Sanaa sought to integrate the Islamist forces into the armed forces. The Islamic Army of Aden-Abyan announced its existence as an independent entity and declared that it was coming out "raising the flag of jihad for God in order to establish God's rule in the land of faith and wisdom, which was corrupted by the ruling, unjust, and renegade gang [the Yemeni government], and to purge Yemen of the latter's corruption and abuses." It called on all Yemenites to join the struggle to uproot "the renegade secular government."

In late August, in the aftermath of the U.S. cruise missile attack on Sudan and Afghanistan, the Islamic Army of Aden-Abyan declared its support for bin Laden and the jihadist cause he was espousing. Abu-al-Hassan announced in a communiqué that the Islamic Army "declares its support and backing for Sheikh Osama bin Laden and the brothers in Sudan . . . and appeals to all sectors of the Yemeni people, the descendants of the mujahideen conquerors, to kill the Americans and seize their possessions, for their blood is proscribed and their possessions are the Muslims' spoils. The Aden Islamic Army pledges to destroy U.S. possessions and bases that are being equipped in Socotra, al-Hudaydah, and Aden." But there was no communication between Abu-al-Hassan and the Islamist leadership in Afghanistan.

On October 11, 1998, the Islamic Army of Aden-Abyan issued another communiqué warning tourists and foreigners of the dire consequences of visiting or staying in Yemen. As an "Islamic land," the foreigners in Yemen are infidels and propagators of atheist, corrupt, and vicious ideas. Sanaa, who had failed to comprehend the Islamists' rage, reacted with offers to improve the conditions of their integration into the armed forces. The Islamic Army of Aden-Abyan maintained its stance, and the Yemeni security forces began a crackdown of the Islamists. In a clash on December 18 the security forces arrested the Army's supreme leader, Saleh Haydara Atawi. The Islamists had no option but to escalate the confrontation.

But by December the Islamic Army of Aden-Abyan was mired in international terrorism, a development beyond its actual capabilities. Back in November London-based Abu-Hamzah al-Masri, a lieutenant of bin Laden's, approached Abu-al-Hassan and asked for support for a terrorist detachment made up of U.K.-based Islamists that was preparing to strike British and American targets in Aden. Many members of the teams had already arrived in Yemen disguised as students, with genuine British papers. Abu-al-Hassan promised Abu-Hamzah that he would protect the terrorists as his "guests." The U.K.-based network was activated on December 19 as part of the first round of Islamist revenge against the United States and Britain. On December 23 three terrorists in Aden were arrested after being stopped for a traffic violation. The car was full of explosives, and the terrorists were on their way to blow up the British consulate in the port of Aden. Abu-al-Hassan felt compelled to do everything in his power to save his "guests" from government hands.

Abu-al-Hassan decided to seize American, or Western, hostages in order to trade them for both the three terrorists and other leaders of the Islamic Jihad, such as Atawi. "The action," according to the Islamic Army's statement, "was taken to take revenge for the injustices and arrogance which the Muslims of Iraq and Palestine and other countries were being subjected to by the infidels." In London, Islamist sources reported that the kidnapping was carried out "in response to a fatwa made by Osama bin Laden that sanctioned the killing of Westerners." This statement was later confirmed by Abu-al-Hassan himself. After his capture he admitted to his interrogators that he had ordered both the kidnapping and ultimately the killing of the Western hostages as acts of jihad. "We regard what we have done and opening fire on the Christians a form of jihad in the cause of God." Although he had no direct contact with bin Laden, Abu-al-Hassan emphasized that his actions were "based on a fatwa issued by Osama bin Laden that sanctioned the killing of Americans and Britons whether these were civilians or military." This is exactly the kind of dynamics bin Laden hoped his fatwa would inspire.

In addition to inspiring the kidnapping and killing, bin Laden's position also strongly influenced the demands issued by the Islamic Army of Aden-Abyan. The Army demanded the release of both old and recent prisoners but also made political demands. One of the first demands came from the bin Laden–affiliated Islamic Observation Center in London. The Center was informed by "the one in charge of the Islamic Army of Aden-Abyan's Political and Information Office" that the Islamic Army wanted "to resolve the issue peacefully and also to demand that the hostages be exchanged for the nine detainees." The Islamic Army stressed that "the operation was also designed to demand that the blockade imposed on the Iraqi people be lifted and that the privileges and facilities granted to U.S. forces on Yemeni territory be abolished." In another communication with a London-based Islamist leader, the Islamic Army added that they had demanded "the lifting of the blockades imposed on Iraq, Libya, and Sudan."

Sanaa reported that Yemeni officials had been presented with two demands not related to the prisoners' release. The first demand was removal of the sanctions against the Muslim people of Iraq. The Islamic Army noted that "the nations to which their hostages belonged were engaged in a systematic effort to starve and hurt the Muslim people of Iraq." The second demand was to ease "the pressure that the government was applying against some of the mujahideen who are on the run and pursued by security agencies." The second demand is missing from all other communiqués and might have been added by the terrorists in the field, but otherwise the logic and language used by the Islamic Army are identical to that of bin Laden and his followers.

The interrogation of the three terrorists captured on December 23 led the Yemeni security authorities to three more terrorists who were planning more bombings of Western targets in the Aden area. The interrogation of these six Islamists clarified the complex relationship between the Islamists in Yemen and those in England. Of the six, one had a valid French passport and the other five had valid British passports. They confessed to being members of Abu-Hamzah's Partisans of the Sharia and that the organization assisted in their travel to Yemen.

In London, Abu-Hamzah rallied to the defense of both the arrested Islamists and the Islamic Army of Aden-Abyan while insisting he had not broken British law. In essence he denied sending the group to Yemen but justified their recourse to terrorism. He also confirmed that he "had been contacted" by Abu-al-Hassan a few times, including "just before the gunfight." Abu-Hamzah denied any links between his organization, the Partisans of the Sharia, and the Islamists who were arrested in Yemen, but he readily acknowledged that he would "love it" if the Yemeni regime were overthrown and replaced with an Islamic regime. While denying having anything to do with the terrorist plans in Aden, Abu-Hamzah stated that he had no objection to the terrorists' plans to blow up British institutions "if they believe in it, and they know they do it for the sake of God, and they know it will stop the state terrorism of Britain and America." Following the Friday prayers on January 15, Abu-Hamzah stepped up his threats. He warned that "if Abu-al-Hassan al-Mihdar is harmed, his followers in the Islamic Aden Army throughout the world would avenge him." He also reiterated his endorsement of Islamist terrorist revenge for the air strikes against Iraq, delivering a veiled threat to the Gulf sheikhdoms that permitted U.S. and British aircraft to operate from their bases. Abu-Hamzah stressed that "it is not permissible—neither by religion or tradition—[to allow] the aircraft of the Americans and the Britons to bombard Muslims in Iraq, or to let them roam our [the Muslims'] countries and territory freely and in peace."

Sheikh Omar Bakri, leader of the U.K.-based Islamist organization al-Muhajiroun and a self-professed follower of Osama bin Laden, tried to put a spin on Abu-Hamzah's statements. He acknowledged that the Islamists were recruiting young followers in London and throughout Western Europe, sending them to military training camps in such places as Afghanistan and Yemen. "They learn how to shoot, to swim, to ride a horse," he said. "They came across the Islamic obligation in the Koran that when they reach the age of fifteen, they must get military training. Some of them may be recruited by mujahideen." He acknowledged that the training some of the recruiting organizations provide is considered terrorist in the West. Sheikh Bakri confirmed that he had sent British Muslims to be trained in Afghanistan and Kashmir but insisted there was nothing illegal in such training. As for the British Islamists captured in Yemen, Bakri claimed that they had gone there "with the aid of [Abu-]Hamzah." He also confirmed that the hostage takers "had had contacts" with Islamist leaders in London in order to "guarantee the safety of British hostages."

The pretense of distance and disengagement from terrorism maintained by the London-based Islamist leaders vanished in early January 1999, the moment British security authorities began to examine closely the activities of the U.K.-based leaders in connection with recent events in Yemen, Afghanistan, and Pakistan. Abu-Hamzah has threatened retaliation against the British if they interfere with the Islamists' efforts to target "oppressors" abroad. He stated that at present his own group, the Supporters of Shariah, "had no direct intention of attacking targets in Britain." He warned, however, that if the British authorities "got in the way" of the attempts of the Partisans and other Islamist organizations to overthrow un-Islamic regimes in the Arab world and replace them with Islamic regimes, the British could expect a "whack."

Taken together, the events in Yemen and Britain clearly demonstrate the wide acceptance of the principles of jihad as advocated by bin Laden and the willingness of Islamists to rely on them as religious authorization for acts of terrorism. The existence of a solid, capable Islamist terrorist infrastructure in the West, capable of operating both at home and overseas, was confirmed. These terrorist groups are controlled by bin Laden followers and loyalists. All of the activities took place in Yemen and Britain without precise instructions from Osama bin Laden, who served only as the guiding force.

THE UNITED STATES and its allies were once again reminded of the magnitude of the Islamist terrorist threat in mid-January 1999, when Indian security authorities thwarted a complex plan to simultaneously blow up the U.S. Embassy in New Delhi and the U.S. consulates in Chennai and Calcutta. The car bombings, planned by a multinational detachment of about a dozen terrorists relying on a larger support network in place, were scheduled to take place on January 26, when India celebrates its Republic Day. The operation was organized in accordance with the bin Laden–ISI deal of spring 1998, according to which the Islamists would carry out spectacular terrorist strikes in the heart of India in return for the ISI's support, protection, and sponsorship.

The terrorist plan collapsed following the arrest in New Delhi of one of the key operatives, Syed Abu Nasir, a 27-year-old Bangladeshi national. He was arrested while carrying over four pounds of RDX high explosives and five detonators, which he had received from an ISI agent already in India. Abu Nasir is a veteran terrorist and intelligence operative whose career epitomizes the evolution of Islamist terrorism. He became an activist Islamist in about 1990. His zeal, recognized by recruiters, landed him a job in the International Islamic Relief Organization (IIRO), one of the Islamist "charity" entities organized by bin Laden. Between 1992 and 1994 he worked for the IIRO in Dhaka and traveled to Thailand for some "operations" on behalf of the IIRO. All this time he was being watched by ISI talent spotters. In early 1994 he was transferred to the IIRO branch in Lahore, where he was responsible for delivering financial aid to over forty training camps for Islamist mujahideen from all over the world in both Pakistan and Afghanistan. During these visits he was approached by an ISI officer and offered military-terrorism training in Afghanistan. Abu Nasir agreed and was immediately sent to a specialized weapons-training camp in Kunar, Afghanistan. While in the camp Abu Nasir, like many of the other foreign trainees, was identified as a member of the Lashkar-e-Tuiba, a Pakistani militant Islamist movement involved in ISI-sponsored terrorism and subversion in Kashmir. The senior commanders of the Lashkar-e-Tuiba, in particular those responsible for operations in India, visited the camp frequently and closely followed the trainees' progress. The trainees were also closely watched by ISI operatives throughout the training process. A promising few, including Abu Nasir, were formally recruited by Brigadier Malik as ISI operatives. Abu Nasir was then sent for additional intelligence-gathering training in Pakistan. He returned to Bangladesh with the assignment of gathering intelligence about the Indian Army's deployment and arsenals in the Eastern Sector, the area surrounding Bangladesh. Gradually his tasks were expanded to include cross-border operations into India. All this time he retained his affiliation with the IIRO. By now the ISI and the Islamist leadership trusted him fully.

Since the mid-1990s the ISI has been expanding the use of infiltration and exfiltration routes between Bangladesh and eastern India and has markedly increased its support for regional terrorist organizations, such as the United Liberation Front of Assam (ULFA), the Khaplang and Isaac Swu-T Muivah wings of the National Socialist Council of Nagaland (NSCN), and the Tripura insurgents, all in Northeast India. For the supervision and conduct of these operations the ISI maintained a forward-office-cum-transit center in an upscale part of Dhaka. The center fell under the cover of the Jamiat-e-Tulba office, also in Dhaka. The Dhaka office coordinated the operations of half a dozen other transit centers, providing sanctuary and support for terrorists from various parts of northeast India. In the late 1990s ISI activities expanded to include the clandestine exfiltration of key Islamist operatives from as far away as Kashmir for training in Pakistan and the infiltration of people and equipment back into India. These sensitive operations concerning Kashmir and other networks deep within India were run separately by Sheikh Eklakh Ahmed, a Pakistani-Kashmiri who himself shuttled in and out of India. Before long Abu Nasir began participating in these operations.

Abu Nasir joined the terrorist elite in mid-September 1998. On September 17–18 he and a few fellow operatives, including Arab "Afghans," attended a high-level planning meeting in the Dhaka office of the Al-Haramanian Islamic Foundation, a Saudi Islamist charity affiliated with bin Laden's web of charities. Key participants were Sheikh Ahmed Al-Gamdi, the president of the IIRO; Professor Hafiz Muhammad Sayeed, head of Lashkar-e-Tuiba; Sheikh Ahmed Heddeshi, president of the Al-Haramanian Islamic Foundation; Dr. Saleh Saud Al-Ansari and Mohammad Tahir, both of the International Islamic Federation of Students; and Azam Chima, one of the legendary "Launching Commanders" of Lashkar-e-Tuiba, who runs operations throughout India. Abu Nasir had met some of the Lashkar commanders back in Kunnad. Abu Nasir and the others were told they had been selected to bomb U.S. diplomatic missions in Bangladesh and India in the near future.

The mission of Abu Nasir and a few Egyptian and Sudanese associates was the U.S. consulate in Chennai, India. In Dhaka they were provided with the layout of the consulate and a list of American officials working there. On October 2 Abu Nasir's group crossed into India from Bangladesh and proceeded to Chennai. There they conducted lengthy observations and obtained still and video footage of the consulate. Their preliminary plan was to focus on the Bank of America on the consulate's premises. The plan called for loading explosives on the Tata Safari jeep that they observed visiting the bank on a daily basis. The overall logic and structure of their proposed operation were very similar to those of the August attacks in Nairobi and Dar-es-Salaam.

The operational plan called for Abu Nasir to lead the expert terrorist team to Calcutta first. His team comprised three Indian terrorists (Mohammad Gulab, Mohammad Nawab, and Aga Khan) and six "Afghans"—four of whom were Egyptians (Mustafa, Ibrahim al Hazaraa, and Ismail and Zainul Abedeen), one Sudanese (known only as Lui), and one a Burmese Islamist from Arakan (Hafeez Mohammad Saleh). The three Indians are identified as members of the ISI-sponsored Lashkar-e-Tuiba. The Arab "Afghans" were all drawn from the Islamist terrorist force in Afghanistan commonly identified with bin Laden.

In December, Abu Nasir brought the entire force to Calcutta. From there he sent the three Indian terrorists to the resort town of Siliguri, east of Calcutta, to establish a forward support base, where they made contact with a locally based support network of over a dozen operatives loosely affiliated with the IIRO and other Islamist "charities." The Indian security authorities later described them as "a well-entrenched network of agents who, like [Abu] Nasir, owe allegiance to the Pakistani ISI as well as the International Islamic Relief Organisation (IIRO)." Abu Nasir brought the rest of his team to Chennai, where the six expert terrorists could be hidden in safe dwellings until the strike time. In early January Abu Nasir himself continued on to New Delhi, where he received the RDX and detonators from an ISI contact and was promptly arrested.

Based on material extracted from Abu Nasir's lengthy interrogations, police were able to arrest both the three Indian operatives and their immediate support network in Siliguri. Another support operative, Sher Khan, was arrested in Bangladesh and extradited to India. By then the six "Afghans" had vanished from Chennai, and they are still at large. Abu Nasir also told his interrogators about the plans to bomb the embassy in New Delhi and the consulate in Madras. Enhanced security resulted in the Islamist terrorists abandoning these operations as well.

Although Indian security authorities prevented the bombings, the operation merits close attention. The structure of the network exposed—Abu Nasir's—confirms the close relationship and cooperation between the intelligence services of the sponsoring states—Pakistan's ISI in this case—and the ostensibly "independent" terrorists such as Osama bin Laden. The planned operations also reaffirm the length to which terrorism-sponsoring states and their Islamist operatives are willing to go in order to strike at the United States and evict it from their midst. Although the spectacular operations in India were prevented, the next round of spectacular operations may not be.

SOME OF THE next spectacular terrorist operations may be a joint effort of bin Laden and Iraqi intelligence. In mid-January 1999 their joint plan for such operations was in an advanced stage of preparation, as shown by Iraqi intelligence Unit 999's intensity of operations. The unit reorganized their front "offices" and activated old import-export companies throughout Europe to cover the movement of funds and people. Iraqi citizens, all longtime residents of European cities who had been sympathetic to Iraq in the 1980s, were activated and summoned to Iraq for intense indoctrination and psychological pressure. They were then sent back to Europe to await further orders. Iraqi intelligence also revived contacts with numerous West European terrorists and mercenaries, including some who had worked for Iraq in the past, and began using them to facilitate clandestine travels in the West so that Arab intelligence operatives would not be involved. Together with Iraqi intelligence officers accredited to Iraqi diplomatic missions in Western Europe, they began scouting for safe houses, vehicles, and other support systems and to resolve any logistical problems.

The preparations picked up in late January when bin Laden dispatched abu-Ayub al-Masri, one of his senior commanders, for a series of meetings in Dubai and Turkey. For this trip he was given one of the Yemeni passports provided by Hijazi. Abu-Ayub al-Masri spent from January 25 to January 27 in Ankara and then continued to Istanbul. In Ankara he held talks with Hijazi and the locally based members of Unit 999. Together they went over Iraqi progress in finding safe apartments, communications routes, and arms caches. Baghdad recommended that Turkish territory be used as a strategic outpost for operations into Europe. Satisfied with his on-site inspections, abu-Ayub al-Masri recommended to bin Laden that the first four Islamist teams then being trained in Baghdad deploy to their destinations in Western countries via Istanbul. These key operatives arriving from the Middle East are expected to activate the numerous veterans of the jihads in Afghanistan and Bosnia-Herzegovina now spread throughout the Muslim émigré communities in Europe. Abu-Ayub al-Masri assured the Iraqis that these "Afghans" and "Bosniaks" would form bin Laden's "secret army" that would strike out against both bin Laden's and Saddam Hussein's enemies.

The viability and magnitude of bin Laden's European networks was soon demonstrated through a surge of warnings attributed to the previously unknown Armed Islamic Front, originating in many West European capitals. In early February the Armed Islamic Front issued a threat in London to bomb Western and Arab embassies "in all European capitals." A communiqué issued in Rome stressed that the Front's objective was confronting those governments that were "the heads of atheism, hypocrisy, malice, and deception and also tyrants of the world." Echoing bin Laden's arguments, the statement paid special attention to regimes in Muslim countries cooperating with the United States and the West. The statement singled out Saudi Arabia, Kuwait, Algeria, Albania, Egypt, and Turkey as "puppets, subservient, and world 'hamanat' [a Koranic depiction of tyrants betraying their people], and trumpets."

This statement stressed that the Front, comprising European-based Islamists who had been working secretly for the last five years on "spiritual, moral, and material [military] training" and monitoring "the movements of the enemies of God" (collecting intelligence), was now ready for action. The Front's networks "exist and are entrenched in all parts of the world." The Front had also completed its theological preparations. "We have made new communication arrangements, and we have a shura council which makes no decisions before consulting trustworthy ulema from all countries," the statement explained. Because of these preparations the current threats must be taken seriously, the statement warned: "Time will tell, since the situation will produce nothing except something new."

Two ideological issues addressed by the Front's statement echo theological precepts advocated by bin Laden. Bin Laden and other Islamist leaders are always ready to accept the repentance of Muslim leaders currently serving the West. The Front's statement included a similar warning to leaders of Muslim states: "Apply God's law so that the machine guns and explosives will remain silent and so that the swords and knives will return to their sheaths." In contrast these Europe-based Islamists are unable to find any redeeming qualities in the Western governments they target, and according to the Front's statement, its strikes will be revenge for the pressure to westernize and sanctions imposed by these governments on their Muslim enemies in the Hub of Islam. The Armed Islamic Front's statement concluded with the vow to "take revenge against every stubborn tyrant for the mujahideen in the mountains, jungles, and valleys and also for the besieged, prisoners, homeless, exiles, and every free woman whose honor they wanted her to sell." This is a veiled reference to the Western siege of bin Laden, his followers, and such patron states as Afghanistan and Iraq.

Another theater of common interest for bin Laden and Baghdad is Kuwait. Not only Saddam Hussein's nemesis, Kuwait is a growing priority of bin Laden's because of the ongoing purge of Egyptian Islamists there. Most of these Islamists are innocent cheap labor, although a few actively agitate against the U.S. presence. In early February, Zawahiri's Jihad Group warned Kuwait by expanding the group's "path of Jihad against the United States and Israel" to also include "their lackeys." Kuwait was singled out because it constitutes no more than "an oil pipe which is plundered by the United States." Zawahiri's message concluded with the warning: "We reiterate here that the United States should pay the price for all of this: Blood for blood and destruction for destruction. The United States and its agents are well aware of Jihad Group, which will not give up retaliation even if a long time passes. . . . The Jihad Group is aware of the extent of the US cowardice and of the fact that the so-called superpower is only a myth. The coming days have many things in store." The Kuwaiti security authorities took these threats very seriously, prompting a new cycle of suppression of Egyptian and other Arab and Pakistani Islamists that led to the expulsion from the country of numerous guest workers and a few notable religious preachers. Several Egyptian suspects were handed over to Egypt. Undaunted, Egyptian Islamists in Kuwait continue to disseminate inflammatory leaflets urging "revenge against the United States and its agents in the region and condemning the strikes against Iraq."

The building momentum for a major strike put bin Laden's Afghan and Pakistani patrons and defenders in a bind. These preparations were going on as the Taliban were promising emissaries from several countries to reign in bin Laden. Bin Laden's disappearing act, announced by the Taliban on February 13, the day after the Armed Islamic Front issued its first warning, constituted a dramatic breakout from this quandary. Bin Laden had actually initiated his disappearance already in early February so that he would not cause the Taliban leadership embarrassment and difficulties as they were negotiating the resumption of international aid and the construction of the oil pipeline from Central Asia to Pakistan. In the first days of February several convoys of twenty to twenty-five land cruisers and other heavy vehicles passed through Kharkiz and other villages in the Sheikh Hazrat mountains, some fifty miles north of Qandahar. These convoys traveled by night, carrying Arab passengers, construction materials, cases of weapons and ammunition, and other provisions. They were preparing bin Laden's new base. On February 10 bin Laden "vanished" from Qandahar along with Zawahiri, some twenty-five trusted Arab aides and guards, and ten Taliban officials from the interior, foreign, and intelligence ministries assigned by Mullah Omar "to guide and protect bin Laden." Bin Laden's wives and children and the families of some of the Arabs with him withdrew to the protected compound near the Qandahar airport.

On February 13 the Taliban insisted that bin Laden was not in Qandahar. At first bin Laden and his entourage went to a forward base in the mountains overlooking the Helmand Valley, the center of Afghanistan's drug production. There the group received extensive military protection from the Taliban, who explained away the reinforcements rushed to the area as antidrug operations. From Helmand bin Laden prudently checked out two escape routes in case of emergency. Over the next few days two convoys were sent to test the roads—first, westward to the Herat area near the Iranian border, and next to northeast Afghanistan, where bin Laden can secure sanctuaries in Tajik areas not controlled by the Taliban. The bin

Laden group then returned to their main base in Tora Boora, where they remained for a few days in order to collect their computers and other key equipment and complete the transfer of their communication networks to the new hideaway. From there the bin Laden convoy traveled to Islam Dara, an abandoned underground base in numerous fortified caves deep in the Sheikh Hazrat Mountains, surrounded by minefields and other entrapments, some fifty miles north of Qandahar. The area's governor, in nearby Khakriz, is Mullah Ghulam Dastagir, a wartime friend of bin Laden's and a Hizb-i Islami commander. Legitimately the Taliban can claim that bin Laden is no longer in their area.

Meanwhile Pakistani government sources began spreading rumors about a crisis between the Taliban leadership and bin Laden to expedite completion of the economic deals between the Taliban and the West. These sources stated that the Taliban had confiscated bin Laden's satellite phone. He had just shut it down for fear of intercept and homing by the United States after senior U.S. officials attributed their success in preventing terrorist attacks to "phone tapping." "American spy satellites tapping into bin Laden's phone calls from his hideout in Afghanistan were able to pick up details of [bin Laden's] planned raids in time to prevent them," stated Ian Brodie of the *Daily Telegraph*. Other rumors claimed that bin Laden was being snubbed by and alienated from Mullah Omar; that only the intervention of bin Laden's daughter, Mullah Omar's wife, and her mother prevented the Taliban's extradition of bin Laden; and that bin Laden's guards and Taliban troops exchanged fire. All of these rumors, some of which were repeated in key American newspapers and Arab magazines, were planted to create the impression of a gap between the Taliban elite and bin Laden so that Afghanistan would not be subjected to massive retaliation when bin Laden reappeared and the Islamist terrorists struck out.

In early March even Taliban leaders stopped denying that bin Laden was in Afghanistan and acknowledged that they had chosen not to know his exact whereabouts. Mullah Mohammad Tayyib, a member of the Taliban leadership, admitted, "It seems that [bin Laden] is still on Afghan territory." He said that the leaders did not know bin Laden's exact position because the Taliban officials and guards with him "received orders not to tell their commanders about his whereabouts. And they have not returned to us, which indicates that he is still in Afghanistan." Concurrently Islamist leaders in both Afghanistan and Pakistan vowed to protect bin Laden against American capture and assassination attempts. "Mujahideen would sacrifice their lives to defend the hero of Islam. The Taliban will never hand over Osama to the enemies of Islam. He is in safe hands. And if the US tries to take him to their land, they would have to pass over the bodies of Mujahideen," warned Omar Farooq, the leader of Lashkar-e-Tuiba.

The momentum for action has been building throughout the Hub of Islam. In early February bin Laden dispatched an envoy to Pakistan to confer with several Islamist leaders. One of these leaders later recounted that the objective of these discussions was "to coordinate positions with them in the face of US hegemony in the Islamic world." A Harakat ul-Ansar leader from Karachi said that subsequent warnings by Pakistani Islamist leaders, including calls for revenge for the U.S. bombing of the camps in Afghanistan, shed light on the issues discussed with bin Laden's envoy. "The veterans of the Khost bombing form the nucleus of a group of Osama bin Laden loyalists whose sole mission in life is to settle score with the United States," he stated. "For each of us killed or wounded in the cowardly US attack, at least 100 Americans will be killed. I may not be alive but you will remember my words." Pakistani security officials urged the West to pay close attention to these threats. "Whether Pakistanis or Arabs in Afghanistan, they consider themselves as 'Jihadi' brothers, whose main [aim] now is to take revenge from the Americans," explained a retired ISI senior officer.

This Islamist modification of priorities—putting the struggle for the banishment of the United States from the Hub of Islam ahead of local causes such as the liberation of Kashmir, Palestine, or Arabia—has already become apparent in the rejuvenated Islamist activities in Chechnya and the Islamists' surge into Central Asia and the Caucasus. The ultimate objective, furthered by Pakistan and Iran and actively supported by the Taliban, is to evict the United States from this strategically important region, the untapped energy resources of which are considered a substitute for Persian Gulf resources. Tehran and Islamabad are convinced that by applying pressure on the local governments in the form of Islamist subversion and terrorism, they will be able to convince these governments to rely on lucrative energy development deals with West European and East Asian companies to the detriment of America's strategic interests. Afghanistan and Chechnya are the springboards for this audacious gambit.

In mid-February, Chechnya president Aslan Maskhadov assured Sheikh Muhammad Hisham Qabbani, chairman of the Supreme Islamic Council in the United States, that "Chechnya will not offer any form of refuge or settlement to Osama bin Laden, whatever this decision costs the Chechen Government, even if that meant war." But the buildup of Islamist terrorist forces in Chechnya, including Arab, Afghan, and Pakistani mujahideen supported by bin Laden, has continued unabated. Bin Laden's mujahideen activate Islamist units that constituted the elite strike forces of key Chechen commanders during the war against Russia, who are now the leaders in Chechnya. Such forces include the Soldiers of the Orthodox Caliphs, which served under now president Maskhadov; the Abd-al-Qadir Forces, which fought under former vice president Shamil Basaev; and the Islamic Liberation Party forces, which answer to Salman Raduyev, Chechnya's extremist terrorist in whose "territory" bin Laden was offered asylum. Given the gratitude Chechnya owes these "Afghan"-dominated forces for their contribution to its war against Russia, no government in Grozny, the capital of Chechnya, would dare confront them.

These Chechnya-based networks have already started to operate throughout the region. Strategically significant was the elaborate effort to assassinate President Islam Karimov, who is considered key to fighting Islamist radicalism and militancy in Central Asia and the Taliban's Afghanistan. The assassination attempt was conducted with a series of four car bombs that exploded throughout Tashkent on February 16. The expert terrorists in the network that ran this sophisticated operation were Chechnya-trained Islamist Uzbeks. Another audacious operation aimed at increasing tension throughout the Caucasus was the March 6 kidnapping of Major General Gennady Shpigun, the top Russian interior ministry envoy to Grozny. Shpigun was seized by masked men who boarded his plane when it was preparing to take off from the Grozny airport. This kidnapping was accomplished with the participation of members of the Chechen secret services. Ostensibly in response to Moscow's threats to Chechnya over Shpigun's fate, Islamist militant forces throughout the Caucasus rallied to the support of Grozny, promising to launch a jihad against any Western presence in the area, not just Russian forces.

Despite the growing efforts of the United States and its allies to contain bin Laden's Islamist terrorist networks, the Islamists keep opening new fronts and launching new campaigns. The numerous setbacks they suffered as their networks were exposed and their operations prevented, and the international pressure on bin Laden, Zawahiri, and their Afghanistan-based commanders and Taliban guardians, have not reversed the Islamists' overall surge toward dominance worldwide.

———————

STARTING IN LATE DECEMBER, while bin Laden was walking the fine line of definitions in his encounter with the Western media, on-site observers were sounding the alarm. According to several Pakistani and Western security and intelligence officials, bin Laden had already dispatched several terrorist detachments on missions to bomb American targets in the Middle East, Western Europe, and perhaps even the United States. "We believe bin Laden may use the month of Ramadan . . . as the starting point for new operations," said a senior ISI official. Bin Laden had already informed a senior member of the Taliban leadership that his forces were "preparing to act" but that Afghanistan would not be implicated. "The region has never been more unstable," the ISI official said. "Bin Laden has never been more dangerous."

U.S. and friendly security forces thwarted numerous bomb attacks on U.S. facilities overseas, including the embassies in Tirana, Albania; Baku, Azerbaijan; Abidjan, Ivory Coast; Dushanbe, Tajikistan; Kampala, Uganda; and Montevideo, Uruguay, as well as the embassy and two consulates in India. An attack was prevented on the Prince Sultan Air Base in Saudi Arabia, from which U.S. aircraft operate against Iraq. Islamist leaders attribute these Western successes to Islamist errors stemming from inexperience, haste, and the zeal of local networks—a largely correct observation. The Islamists warn of a long-term commitment to striking out against the United States with better-prepared assets once the time is ripe. The captured Islamist terrorist commander Ahmad Ibrahim al-Najjar stressed this point to his interrogators. "The two anti-American attacks in Kenya and Tanzania were not simply advertisements," he said. "Jihad will continue because the fight against the United States and the Jews will never cease." Asked about recent setbacks, Najjar cautioned the Egyptians against doubting the success of Islamist spectacular strikes in and against the United States. "Don't worry, they'll come when the time is right," he quipped.

Bin Laden's Islamist forces continue to patiently consolidate their capabilities and further their preparations for spectacular strikes. Bin Laden has already expanded the network of organizations and groups following both his own theological teachings and Zawahiri's military-terrorist plans. Former ISI chief General Hamid Gul has said that bin Laden has already established an "alliance with 30 different organizations" in order "to retaliate against American interests around the world." According to Islamist terrorists from Central Asia and the Caucasus who were recently interrogated by Russian intelligence, bin Laden is busy establishing in his Imarat in Afghanistan a new elite force that he calls The Order of Islamic Sword-Bearers, under the direct command of Ayman al-Zawahiri. The main objective of this force is to serve as an "Islamic rapid-deployment force" prepared at any moment to mount a spectacular terrorist strike or save an Islamist subversion in distress.

Osama bin Laden continues to build sound theological foundations for escalating the jihad. He has repeatedly summed up his belief in a statement usually made while waving his own ornate Koran: "You cannot defeat heretics with this book alone, you have to show them the fist!" He also elucidated his vision of the relentless, fateful, global jihad against the United States in a book titled *America and the Third World War.* The draft manuscript is already being circulated among key Islamist leaders and commanders in the original Arabic and in translation into several South Asian languages. In this book bin Laden propounds a new vision, stressing the imperative of a global uprising. Bin Laden in essence calls on the entire Muslim world to rise up against the existing world order to fight for their right to live as Muslims—rights, he states, which are being trampled by the West's intentional spreading of Westernization. For the Islamists there can be no compromise or coexistence with Western civilization.

In early January 1999 Islamist scholars in Jordan published a study about the centrality of the jihad in Islam. The study decreed that "the Messenger of Allah [the prophet Muhammad] said: 'Jihad is the pillar of Islam and its top most part.'" The study then set the religious logic and justification for the use of international terrorism as a form of jihad obligatory for all Muslims. Relying on Koranic precedents, the study determined that even when the Muslims suffer from shortage of numbers and weaponry, they are sure to win if they follow the Koranic teachings by "instilling the fear of God" and "showing fortitude" when confronting the infidels. Terrorism is a key instrument for instilling fear. The study stresses that all the past achievements of Islam were attained "through jihad which Allah has made obligatory" for the believers. Under contemporary conditions there are numerous ways to take part in a jihad. "Jihad from the Sharia standpoint is to do one's utmost when fighting in the path of Allah whether directly, or supporting the jihad with one's wealth, opinion or augmenting the great numbers (participating in the Jihad), etc. . . . Allah has made it obligatory for the purpose of carrying Islam to the rest of mankind and for the protection of the Khilafah state and Muslims."

The study then addresses the specific conditions for jihad in the contemporary Hub of Islam. "Jihad encompasses the offensive, defensive and pre-emptive war, providing that this war is for the sake of Allah," the authors explain. This diversity of forms of jihad is necessary for meeting the myriad of threats to Islam. The main threat is the spread of Westernization, because it is the instrument and justification for the West's drive to destroy and control the Muslim world. "So fighting for the protection of interests and viewpoint in life became confined to the major disbelieving states such as America and others, who develop their weaponry and strengthen their armies in order to strike whoever and at any time they wish. As for the rest, and especially the Muslims, they are banned from possessing sophisticated weapons and forbidden to use force in order to defend themselves. They are required to content themselves with protests, misery and grief when they are attacked as recently happened in Iraq."

With the U.S.-led West increasingly resorting to the use of force to impose their will on Muslims, it is imperative for Muslims to use force—that is, wage the jihad—to reverse this dangerous trend. "Truly, jihad is the pillar of the deen [Islamic law] and its uppermost part. Muslims cannot have any international standing without it since it is the method Allah has obliged for the propagation of Islam, to preserve the Islamic State and protect its citizens." The study notes that the situation throughout the Muslim world has reached a crisis point and emphasizes the urgency of reversing this trend by fighting a jihad. The Jordanian scholars call for action against both local Muslim leaders and their patrons in the West; the Hub of Islam must choose between succumbing to the West and fighting for Islam. "O Muslims! Today you are between two alternatives: either you are silent, submissive and acquiescent of what the puppet rulers are doing to you, and whatever results from the domination of the Kuffar [infidels] over your countries and resources, and from your downfall and utter ruin in this life and in the Akhira [afterlife]. Or you move effectively to seize the power of those rulers and work in earnest with those sincere Muslims who are working for the re-establishment of the Khilafah state and whatever follows by our return to our past glory as the greatest Ummah and the most powerful state which will fight in the path of Allah so that the truth may prevail and falsehood shall perish." This study was widely circulated throughout the Muslim communities in western Europe and the United States.

By mid-February 1999 bin Laden's warning of an inclusive Western threat to Islamdom was echoed by a wide variety of Muslim intellectuals, from longtime supporters of bin Laden to pro-Saudi conservative thinkers. Writing in the pro-Saudi al-Hayah, one of the most authoritative Arab newspapers, Yussuf Samahah stressed that bin Laden's vision was the wave of the future—the real merger of international megatrends and Islamdom. The future of the world is globalization, Samahah argued. "Globalization in the general sense of the term means among other things the free movement of funds, the communications revolution, and 'multinational networks' replacing national frameworks and relations." At present this trend is usually dominated by the U.S.-led West, with the sole exception bin Laden's philosophy of an all-Muslim resurgence. "One can say that bin Laden's organization represents an improvement on similar organizations and one that has benefitted more from the 'opportunities' provided by the globalization elements," Samahah explained. "And anyone who believes that there is a contradiction between his [bin Laden's] 'ideas' and the new phenomenon would be mistaken, because while globalization is gradually uniting the planet, it is causing many introverted and revivalist reactions which use the tools that globalization provides to give the impression that they are not only fighting it but that they will ultimately defeat it."

Writing in the Islamist *al-Quds al-Arabi,* Abdul-Bari Atwan, bin Laden's friend and confidant, elaborates on the "globalism" theme in the context of the plight of the Hub of Islam. The most profound threat to Islam is the U.S. policy of "globalism," which means furthering America's global security and economic interests through a combination of brute force—such as that being used against Iraq—and subversion, namely modernization. "It is sad to say that Arabs in particular and Muslims in general are the biggest victims of globalism in all its forms, economic, cultural, and security," Atwan said. Not only has the global economic trend harmed the Arab world, but "culturally, CNN and the Internet have begun to rule the world. The American event and its instruments have changed Arab cultural life completely." Atwan blames the "European and American trained/indoctrinated" younger generation of Arab officers and intellectuals who are eager "to join in the modern globalism once they take power and succeed their fathers. The most prominent of their 'realistic' traits is the ability to use the computer, belief in policies of market economy, permanent decisiveness, and the continuation of the Hebrew state."

Bin Laden's Islamist terrorism provides the only hope against this bleak future, Atwan stresses. And this is the quintessence of the U.S.-led relentless struggle against the Islamists. "Because terrorism is the single, effective element that threatens this new, monopolistic structure, efforts are being made to eliminate its prominent leaders, make examples of them and, to the extent possible, attach maximum abuse and humiliation to those countries that protect them, so that those nations will return to their 'senses' and enter fully into the new order." For Atwan, bin Laden's steadfast resolve to stand up to the West and punish the United States, even if symbolically, is a source of hope that the spread of globalism and Westernization is not irreversible. "For us, at least, the picture appears dark. Our only strength is that it is a simple and perhaps unintended mistake, which may lead to a big collapse and a change in the rules of the game. Perhaps we are headed for the furthest thing from that, and we mean a powerful steadfastness. Perhaps it will blow up the foundations of this globalism in the Arab region at least," Atwan concludes circumspectly and cryptically, in classic Arabic style.

These were not abstract observations, for in early 1999 bin Laden and his forces committed to a major buildup of elite terrorist assets in the West. This buildup occurred in the aftermath of the setbacks suffered in summer 1998, when numerous Egyptian terrorists were rounded up around the world and extradited to Egypt. These arrests not only deprived the Islamists of a few good commanders but also compelled them to undertake a thorough reexamination of their internal security and counterintelligence situation. In February-March 1999 this process was completed, and the Is-

lamists were ready to deploy a new round of commanders and expert terrorists for spectacular operations in the West. By late March the first round
of these deployments was completed with the dispatch of fourteen top
commanders, all longtime comrades in arms of bin Laden, to the West.
Soon afterward two teams of commanders reached the United States and
United Kingdom, and high-level command cells were activated in Bangladesh, France, and Russia. Eighty-three additional mujahideen from several Muslim countries were selected and trained for participation in these
missions and were now ready for quick deployment the moment the on-site
commanders called for them. In Pakistan, Islamist leaders noted that the
building crises in Iraq and Kosovo introduced an added urgency to the Islamists' campaign against the United States and Britain. A Pakistani official
explained that "the US and British governments are presently engaged in
punitive strikes against Iraqi people, both military and civilian, while looking the other way on the massacre of the Kosovan Muslims for the last so
many months" and therefore "would become a target of attack by bin
Laden, his allies or [other] Islamists."

These preparations were echoed in a March 30 communiqué in which
the Egyptian Islamic Jihad vowed to continue its campaigns against the
Egyptian government and U.S. and Israeli interests throughout the world.
The communiqué declared that "the Ummah must stand united against the
United States, Israel, and their lackeys"—the pro-Western Arab regimes.
"Our battle is essentially with the United States and Israel," the Jihad declared, and the ongoing confrontation with Cairo would not alter this priority. A few days later Islamist leaders in London urged that the Jihad's
communiqué be taken seriously and warned of impending terrorist strikes
on U.S. and Gulf interests. An Islamist source in London alluded to the
character of the forthcoming strike, saying that "al-Jamaah [al-Islamiyah]
is known not to conduct frequent operations, but prefer bigger operations,
even if they are fewer in number." He noted that states from which Egyptian terrorists had been extradited in summer 1998 "will assume a major
part of the responsibility for their execution." Another Islamist leader revealed that Osama bin Laden had resolved to carry out "an attack against
U.S. interests" and that Ayman al-Zawahiri had already "assumed responsibility for preparing for such armed attacks."

In early April 1999 the Islamists activated and began deploying another system of terrorists comprising solely Kashmiris, Pakistanis, and Afghans affiliated with the Harakat ul-Ansar. The ISI helps organize these
new forces so that they are immune to the penetration that happened to the
Egyptian-dominated networks in the summer of 1998. At the core of this
group are veteran "Afghans" committed to avenging the victims of the U.S.

cruise missile strikes on their training camps in Afghanistan. One of their senior commanders declared that "the blood of our supporters will not be in vain and we will avenge every martyr by killing 100 Americans." The "Afghans," he stated, "formed suicide cells affiliated with bin Laden whose only mission in life is to take revenge on the United States." Another leader declared that "in return for every martyr or wounded from our followers, we will kill at least 100 Americans. Perhaps, I will not be alive at that time but the world will remember these words."

To shield Pakistani sponsorship and support, the new terrorist forces were formally separated from the Harakat ul-Ansar and identified as the newly formed Harakat Jihad Islami. In early April, Harakat Jihad Islami already had active forward headquarters in Burma, Bangladesh, Palestine, Afghanistan, Tajikistan, Eritrea, Chechnya, and Bosnia, which is also responsible for Albania and Kosovo. In a meeting with soon-to-be-deployed cadres, Harakat leaders vowed that their "Jihad would continue till the day of judgement and the effects of the Afghan Jihad are spread all over the world." They said that having played an important role in the Kashmir jihad, the Harakat Jihad Islami had decided to expand its operations to all other jihad fronts, "and now mujahideen from all over the world are joining the group." Although the Harakat leaders insisted that they belonged to a separate organization, they declared that "Osama bin Laden is the hero of Islam." They added that Harakat Jihad Islami supported bin Laden's demand for the withdrawal of U.S. forces from the Persian Gulf.

The Islamists embarked on a key undertaking in early 1999—the revival of East Africa operations, which had been dormant since the bombing of the U.S. embassies. A forward base has been organized in the Gedo region in southern Somalia, not far from the border with Kenya. The center of Islamist activities is at the coastal town of Ras Kamboni, where a secure communications system is being set up by several Arab experts. The entire Gedo area is controlled by the al-Ittihad movement, an offshoot of the Somali Islamic Union Party (SIUP), which has been linked to bin Laden since 1993. The extent of the Islamist activities in and around Ras Kamboni was discovered after the March 20 fatal shooting of a U.S. aid worker in a local tea shop. Reportedly he stumbled on Arab Islamists and was swiftly eliminated by the al-Ittihad gunmen protecting them. By early April a discernable presence of Arab terrorists who openly identified themselves with bin Laden were in the Gedo area. Somalia is rife with rumors that bin Laden visited his men in southern Somalia, although no proof of this exists.

In mid-April the Islamist leadership thoroughly studied the recent progress of terrorist forward deployment and preparations and the recovery of the Egyptian-based networks from the impact of the summer 1998 arrests and extraditions. Ayman al-Zawahiri convened his aides and senior commanders at a major session in the Tora Boora caves near Jalalabad. Participants at the meeting resolved to markedly improve the security and counterintelligence measures undertaken by the clandestine networks. Commanders who arrived from several countries were told to alter their travel and communication methods and to pay more attention to the internal situation and security authorities in their countries of residence. Zawahiri also introduced a new system of code names and channels of communications developed after the arrest and interrogation of the terrorists by the Egyptians. The commanders then went over the entire chain of command and areas of responsibility to make sure that the new redundant, resilient modus operandi would withstand future onslaughts by hostile intelligence services, including the arrest and interrogation of senior leaders. By the end of the meeting Zawahiri was satisfied with the status of his networks and approved the activation of several operational plans.

This renewed confidence was expressed in a statement issued in late April by Zawahiri's Jihad Islami in reaction to the harsh sentencing of a number of Egyptian terrorists, including Zawahiri himself and several other key leaders who were tried in absentia. The statement stressed that the jihad "is much bigger and deeper" than unfolding events and would not be affected by the Cairo trial. The Islamic Jihad was determined to stay on course, and so "the escalating Islamic resistance against the Crusader campaign against the Muslim nation will not stop." On the contrary, the statement argued, recent U.S. actions and policies made the overall situation more conducive for the Islamists. "The Islamic world in general, in particular the Arab region, is being swept by a wave of Islamic jihadist rejection, the Muslim nation is vigorously rejecting the policy of humiliation and oppression being pursued against those working to restore Islam's sovereignty over its territory, and it is at the same time determined to firmly and resolutely move toward achieving its aim of establishing an Islamic state through preaching, jihad, and exposing suspect actions."

These sentiments were echoed in a concurrent statement by Qari Saifullah Akhtar, the central emir of the Harakat Jihad Islami, who is responsible for the organization's international operations. He declared that Harakat Jihad Islami "would not allow any one to compromise the blood of the Muslims being spilt in Kashmir and Afghanistan." Harakat Jihad Islami also anticipates a marked escalation and expansion of Islamist jihads worldwide because "the atrocities being committed against the Muslims in Afghanistan, Kashmir, Iraq, Bosnia, Kosovo and Chechnya have awakened Muslims, and now Muslims would fight against India, the United States, Russia and Britain." Led by the jihadist forces, the Muslim world is out to take revenge against their U.S.-led foes, and "the eye that looks down upon Muslims as a minority or dreams of reducing them to a minority would be gouged out," Qari Saifullah Akhtar declared.

In late March the Muslim world, like most of the rest of the world, became fixated with the NATO bombing campaign against Yugoslavia and the ensuing mass exodus of Kosovo Albanian refugees. Muslims watched the horrors endured by their Albanian brethren as they were driven out of Kosovo by Serb paramilitary forces, marauding KLA detachments, and widespread NATO bombing of civilian targets. The Islamists reacted to the Kosovo tragedy only after deliberation and then made the distinction between the plight of their Kosovo Albanian brethren and the NATO bombing campaign. The Palestinian Islamic Jihad was among the first Islamist organs to assume an authoritative position. "The NATO raids might continue. But it is clear that the goal is not to serve Muslim interests in Kosovo or uproot the Serbian violence that grew more powerful in the embrace of the Western civilization, the hostility to Islam and the race to throw a siege around it. The Serbian violence found encouragement from the West, concealed at times and explicit at others," stated an editorial in the Jihad's organ *al-Istiqlal*.

Islamist intellectuals in Jordan stressed the difference between NATO's objectives and the interests of the Kosovo Albanians, in whose name the bombing campaign was ostensibly conducted. "The United States has decided to wage war against Milosevic" because he would not surrender to the U.S.-imposed "new world order" and in so doing the United States intentionally abandoned the Kosovo Muslims to the wrath of the Serbs. "It is possible that the Kosovo region could become vacant of its Albanian inhabitants, whose autonomy the NATO war machine came to defend. In other words, the Albanians are as yet the only victims of the war, which those who started it claimed was designed to support their humanitarian and ethnic rights." Hence the United States should not be permitted to win in Kosovo. "The phenomenon of Slobodan Milosevic is a contradictory one," the Jordanian Islamists explained. "What he stands for in the Kosovo region deserves to be renounced, despised, and punished because, in Kosovo, Milosevic represents the rule of the dead over the living, a system that we thought has perished. Nonetheless, what he represents in terms of resistance to the U.S. barbarism in the last years of the Twentieth Century should be supported and backed. Milosevic is very bad in Kosovo and very good in resisting the United States and its escalating military and political pressure." Ultimately, in taking sides in this conflict, the long-term interest of the Muslims should determine the position of the Muslim world, and this interest is clearly to block the United States and NATO. If the United

States is permitted to pursue the war on its own terms, "the Kosovo Albanians could be eliminated from geography and history before the war is settled," the Jordanian Islamists concluded.

This point was further elaborated by Pakistani former senior officials with Islamist leanings who represent prevailing opinions in Islamabad. "Aggression is continuing in Kosovo. This problem concerns not only Bosnia and Kosovo but also 25 million Muslims living in the Balkans." The entire Muslim world is witnessing not only the unprecedented plight of the Kosovo Albanians but the inability and unwillingness of NATO to come to their assistance. Therefore, the Pakistani officials stressed, it is incumbent on the Muslim world to save their brethren. "The issue of Kosovo and the Balkans can only be solved through Jihad." These officials saw a special role for Islamabad because "being the only nuclear power of the Muslim world, it is the responsibility of Pakistan to provide the Muslims of Kosovo with every possible support without caring about the pleasure or displeasure of the United States."

Similar sentiments were elucidated by the HizbAllah in Lebanon. "The Muslims in Kosovo are the target of a real genocide at the hands of the Yugoslav regime in an attempt to uproot them, obliterate their identity, and eradicate their history using brutal measures, including massacres, displacement, expulsion, burning of cities, and confiscation of identity documents from the population. . . . The genocide demonstrates the barbarity of crimes committed against the Muslims, who are now in need of being embraced by their fellow Muslims worldwide and require assistance by the world community." Although the Serbs are the actual perpetrators of the crimes against the Kosovo Albanians, this tragedy is the direct outcome of U.S. policy. "While condemning the Serbian massacres and mass expulsion, we reiterate to Muslims and the free people in the world that the war launched by the United States in the Balkans does not aim to protect the Albanian Muslims in Kosovo or grant them their rights as much as it is a war that seeks to serve the US interests and consolidate its unipolar order. Leaving the Serbs to carry out their genocide against the Kosovo Albanians is just one piece of evidence that the US Administration is settling accounts with the Yugoslav regime to serve its own political interests in the Balkans."

By early April, Pakistani officials had elucidated a coherent analysis of the U.S. position and strategic interests in pursuing the war. They stressed the importance of the Balkans to the economic and strategic interests of the West: "The Balkans are the only land route to the Middle East, as well as the gateway to the oil and mineral-rich region of the Caucasus." The U.S.-led West is determined to control these regions, which requires the suppression of Islamic awakening, and so the United States first embarked on suppressing

Milosevic's Yugoslavia because Belgrade would not accept U.S. hegemony. But the Muslim world must not forget that the NATO bombing is only the first step in the U.S. campaign to suppress and enslave Islamist revivalism.

Arab Islamists were now holding U.S.-led NATO directly responsible for the plight of the Kosovo Albanians, as shown in an editorial by Fakhri Qawar in the Jordanian newspaper *Shihan:* "It is the NATO forces which are bombing the Kosovo region with the most sophisticated, the most violent and ugliest instruments of destruction, killing Muslims and forcing them to evacuate their region. The evidence of this is that we have only seen the waves of destitute, thirsty and hungry immigrants on television screens after the initiation of NATO bombing." Hence it is incumbent on Islamists to save their Kosovo brethren in a jihad against both NATO and the Serbs.

In London the Islamist front organizations affiliated with bin Laden now drew obvious conclusions from the building sentiments throughout the Muslim world. In a special statement al-Muhajiroun urged a Kosovo jihad and "call[ed] upon all Muslims to support the Jihad to liberate Kosovo physically, financially, and verbally." Al-Muhajiroun used Kosovo as a rallying cry for better Islamist unity against all their foes as well as the current world, or Western, order. "The Islamic Movements world-wide condemn the atrocities being committed by the Serbs in Kosovo and the attempt by NATO to gloss over the Kosovo question. We pledge that we will not rest until Kosovo is liberated and all Muslims are returned to their land. The Jihad will continue until Muslim life, honor and wealth is protected and the law of Allah is established. During this crisis and massacre in the Balkans we must be a united Muslim community with a united policy and agenda. Let us leave our partisanship, sectarianism, nationalism and tribalism aside and save ourselves from the wrath of Allah by fulfilling our obligations towards the Muslims in Kosovo to whom we are the nearest neighbors and who therefore have more responsibility to help. We declare that we will not stop the Jihad against the Serbian or Israeli occupiers no matter what the UN say or do. Surely the ugly face of hatred towards Islam by the indiscriminate and continuous bombing of innocent Muslims in Iraq and those last year in Sudan and Afghanistan is evidence if it were needed of the true stand and the crusader mentality of western regimes."

As the NATO bombing campaign continued, with no apparent change in the plight of the Kosovo Albanians, the Islamists' hostility and defiance increased. The April 23 sermon in al-Aqsa Mosque in Jerusalem, one month into the NATO bombing, elucidated the Islamists' frustration and rage. "The Balkans will be part of the coming Islamic State against the will of the Serbians, against the will of the Europeans, and against the will of the Americans. The Americans are working now to evacuate the Balkans from its Muslim inhabitants so as to prevent the establishment of an Islamic state in the heart of Europe." For the Islamist preacher the inability of the Muslim world to prevent the tragedy of the Kosovo Albanians was indicative of the overall plight of the Muslim world and a reaffirmation that a profound confrontation with pro-Western regimes was inevitable. "The Muslims in Kosovo don't need just blankets, food, and medicine. They need their brothers to help them against the Serbian aggression, they need their Muslim brothers with tanks and missiles and airplanes; they need an Islamic army. But how would this happen with these corrupted puppet rulers in the Muslim world? That is why we say the Khalifah is needed." In a sermon in Gaza, Dr. Mahmud al-Zahhar, a HAMAS leader, accused the United States of collaborating with the Serbs in emptying Kosovo of its original Muslim population. He denounced the silence of Arab and Muslim governments toward the Kosovo tragedy, calling these regimes accomplices of the United States and the Serbs.

The escalation of the fighting in and around Kosovo, in particular the specter of a NATO ground intervention, has had a profound impact on the Kosovo Liberation Army (UCK) and the Islamist elements at its core. The Islamists were confronted with the dilemma of how to react to the massive support, including weapons, pouring from several Western intelligence services that insisted on purging the Islamists from the UCK as a precondition for this help. Determined not to deprive their Kosovo Albanian brethren of Western aid, the Islamist leadership decided to adopt temporary measures of cooperation with the U.S.-led NATO, at the very least tolerance of NATO's presence in the Balkans and its cooperation with the Albanians. At the same time, the Islamists did not forfeit their own military capabilities but simply went underground whenever necessary.

By mid-March 1999, as the advance to crisis and NATO's war seemed inevitable, the UCK hastily expanded to include many elements controlled and/or sponsored by the U.S., German, British, and Croatian intelligence services. The UCK is in essence a hodge-podge of distinct armed groups brought together by two common denominators: (1) commitment to a Greater Albania encompassing Albania, Kosovo, and a large part of Macedonia; and (2) hatred for the Serbs. These groups have little else in common because they are ideologically diverse, ranging from Hoxheists, followers of the teachings of former Albanian Stalinist-Maoist leader Enver Hoxha, to organized crime elements and militant Islamists. The NATO-sponsored UCK does not even have an indigenous command structure. In late April it was put under the command of Agim Ceku, a Croatian brigadier general of Albanian descent who brought with him a staff composed mainly of veterans of the Croatian armed forces. The indigenous leadership of the UCK, hailing from the center of Kosovo and composed of veterans of the Bosnian Muslim and "Bosnian" mujahideen forces, was passed over and marginalized. In early April the UCK began actively cooperating with the NATO bombing—selecting and designating targets for NATO aircraft as well as escorting U.S. and British special forces detachments into Yugoslavia.

At the same time the Islamist elements in Albania and Macedonia went underground. Their key Albanian units, comprising mainly Albanian veterans of the Bosnian Handzar Division, were deployed to the parts of Albania where the clan of former president Sali Berisha is influential. The NATO-sponsored segments of the UCK, totaling between 25,000 and 30,000 fighters, are riddled with clandestine Islamist cells composed of Albanian, Turkish, and North African volunteers from Western Europe. These volunteers were organized by Islamist leaders based in West Europe who are allied with bin Laden and Zawahiri.

The Islamist leadership decided not to challenge the leadership of the UCK, based in Albania, and to avoid having distinct mujahideen units so as not to affect the assistance the UCK gets from the United States. Soon after the beginning of the NATO bombing, a senior Europe-based Islamist commander explained the decision: "The current war in the Balkans is a purely intelligence war associated with the presence of U.S. security services in the region." The Islamists, however, consider the war in Kosovo a component of "the [overall] war in the Balkans—a religious war targeting a Muslim minority situated in a sea of Orthodox [Christians]." In mid-April a Pakistan-based senior commander of bin Laden's provided an even more pragmatic explanation for the Islamists' tolerance of the NATO-sponsored UCK. In Yugoslavia, he said, the aims of bin Laden and the United States "temporarily coincide." Both are interested in "the protection of our Muslim brothers" against "the Serb oppressors." The Islamists would not interfere with the pursuit of this objective. But the moment Kosovo gains independence and/or merges into a greater Albania, bin Laden's mujahideen "are going to deal with the U.S. in real earnest."

The Islamist mujahideen continue fighting inside Kosovo under the banner of the Islamic Liberation Army, which also fought in Bosnia in the early 1990s. Carrying out bin Laden's proven combination of fierce fighting against enemy security forces while providing social and humanitarian services to prostrate civilians, the Islamists interact with the destitute Kosovo Albanian population at the center of Kosovo, where nobody else dares to operate. The Islamist forces concentrate on dealing with the indigenous forces—both the civilian population and the now largely defeated UCK elements that emerged from the rural population in central Kosovo. The mujahideen established close relations with the key clans from the

Drenica area in central Kosovo, the birthplace of the UCK, including Suley-man Selimi, "the Sultan," who comes from this area and is commander in chief of the UCK forces inside Kosovo. In these operations the mujahideen have already demonstrated their fearlessness and all-out commitment to the Muslim population. An example of this was the last stand of a mujahideen battalion of some fifty fighters under the command of Sheikh Muhammad al-Adalbi (also known as Abu-al-Abbas) north of the village of Meja. The battalion "was completely martyred following a ferocious battle with Ser-bian forces deep inside Kosovo" in which the Saudi and Egyptian mu-jahideen held the line, enabling the UCK to evacuate the Albanian civilians, destroy the local villages in an orderly scorched-earth withdrawal, and then reach Albanian sanctuary. The UCK destroyed the villages to alienate and radicalize the population so that they would fight the Serbs and to coerce the civilians to escape into exile so that there can be no normalization and Kosovo Albanian population under the control of the Serbs. This is a clas-sic "revolutionary" strategy that has been implemented in several previous Islamic Liberation struggles such as those in Afghanistan, the Philippines, and Bosnia. A NATO spokesman attributed the emptying and destruction of Meja and surrounding villages to "Serbian ethnic cleansing."

With the Serb forces and NATO bombing eliminating the UCK's ability to operate inside Kosovo, the Islamists are also preparing for what they see as the fateful phase of fighting: when they wrest Kosovo from hostile non-Muslim hands, either Serb or NATO's. The importance of these prepara-tions is reflected in the immediate supervisory and support elements of the Islamist forces in Albania and Kosovo. Recently, the Islamist senior com-manders responsible for the entire southeastern approaches to Europe—an area stretching from Italy to the Caucasus Mountains—were directed to concentrate on and directly support Ayman al-Zawahiri's forces. The com-manders are abu-Muhammad Hulyani (military operations), Aqil bin Abdul-Aziz al-Aqil, and Sheikh Muhammad abu-Fakhdah al-Tuwayjar (lo-gistical support). All are veterans of major jihads, including Chechnya. In order to provide comprehensive support for anticipated combat operations by the Islamist forces, particularly an elite force of over 500 Arab mu-jahideen, the Islamists are running more than fifteen private Muslim chari-ties and humanitarian organizations in Albania and Kosovo alone. These organizations also finance the training, arming, and supplying of select UCK units. "Private" organizations from Persian Gulf States develop routes for the clandestine deployment of Arab volunteers from Albania into Yu-goslavia, as well as the organization of a steady pipeline for supplying weapons and other equipment to the UCK forces deep inside Kosovo. These Islamist support elements also oversee the flow of Islamist reinforcements into the Balkans. The first group of about 175 Yemeni mujahideen arrived in Albania in early May, and a second group of some 200 Yemenis, including hard core "Afghans" and terrorists released from jail by the government, was getting ready to travel. Comparable units are being organized throughout the hub of Islam. All of these forces have yet to be assigned to operational units.

In early April, Muhammad al-Zawahiri established in Albania an Islamist "military action committee" to coordinate the preparations of elements capable of carrying out audacious military and terrorist missions deep in the enemy's territory. These elements include clandestine Islamist cells in the ranks of the UCK and underground networks throughout the Balkans. At the core of Zawahiri's forces is a group of over 500 Arab mujahideen, all fiercely loyal to bin Laden, that is deployed near Korce and Podgrade in southeastern Albania. A forward base of the Islamist terrorists, a small number of Saudis and Egyptians who answer to bin Laden and Zawahiri, is in Tropje, in northern Albania. Tropje is Berisha's hometown, and the UCK maintains a major staging base there for transporting weapons and launching operations into Kosovo. This Islamist force is ready to intervene in the war against both the Yugoslav and NATO forces if they betray the "cause" of the Kosovo Albanians as bin Laden and his lieutenants understand it.

The use of these Islamist forces might be imminent. In early May, as the UCK was collapsing inside Kosovo and NATO remained reluctant to commit ground forces to occupy the province, the Islamist trend in the UCK has become more pronounced. Senior UCK commanders are renewing the "Islamic solidarity" theme even as NATO is supposed to be building and arming a secular-progressive UCK. Gani Sylaj, a senior UCK commander in northern Albania, appealed "to our Arab and Muslim brothers to help us militarily and politically because we are facing difficult conditions. The Arabs know well the meaning of occupation, injustice, and the peoples' expulsion from their land." These commanders now intimate that the UCK leadership no longer trusts the U.S.-led NATO to adhere to its promises. These leaders are convinced that NATO will abandon the UCK and the Kosovo Albanian refugees once a political solution is reached with Belgrade. Only the Islamists will stay with them to continue the jihad for a greater Albania against the Serbs, the Macedonians, and the West.

The real danger from the Islamist involvement in Kosovo is the legacy of the war. After a negotiated settlement is reached, the moment foreign aid stops and a genuinely moderate political leadership is empowered in Kosovo, the UCK elements sponsored by the Western intelligence services will collapse. Only the Islamist mujahideen and their supporters among the UCK's indigenous grassroots units will remain active. They will continue to have a steady supply of money and weapons from the drug trade and a constant flow of expert fighters and volunteers from the Muslim world. Since the greater Albania aspired to by all factions of the UCK will not materialize, elements of other branches of the UCK will join the Islamists to continue the jihad against both the Serbs who destroyed Kosovo and the U.S.-led West, which eventually abandoned the Albanians. Having witnessed the selfless help provided by the Arab mujahideen at their darkest hour inside Kosovo, the Kosovo Albanian population will wholeheartedly support this jihad.

Baghdad has not missed the turmoil in the Muslim world caused by the Kosovo crisis. Saddam Hussein decided to capitalize on the building popular hostility to the United States. The Islamists were living up to bin Laden's promise to build grassroots support for Iraq in the Arab world—in early April, Arab sources confirmed the existence of "popular movements in a number of Arab countries that are preparing for mass demonstrations and marches to break the Iraq blockade." These sources also disclosed the recent organization of a clandestine Islamist support system composed of "secret cells in most Arab countries that are awaiting the start signal to hit U.S. and British interests and to stage massive demonstrations if London and Washington resume their barbaric aggression against Iraq." For Baghdad the mere existence of such an infrastructure was a reaffirmation of the viability of the deal with bin Laden.

Emboldened, Saddam Hussein ordered his son Qusay, commander of the Special Security Forces, to form a new terrorist force for joint operations with the Islamists. Called the al-Nida (the Call) Force, it will consist of thousands of fighters specially trained in guerrilla warfare and special operations tactics. Al-Nida squads are expected to soon be assigned a number of "secret missions" all over the world. One of the first moves undertaken by Qusay in connection with the establishment of the al-Nida Force was the activation of long-term dormant networks of Iraqi intelligence planted in the West in the wake of the Gulf War in order to support joint operations with bin Laden's Islamist terrorists.

The threat from the Saddam–bin Laden cooperation was shown by the discovery of a joint terrorist operation in Australia being prepared for the Olympic Games to be held in Sydney in the year 2000. In mid-March, Hamoud Abaid al-Anezi, a senior commander of bin Laden's, arrived in Melbourne, Australia, with a valid Saudi passport. There he made contact with a just-activated network of four former Iraqi nationals, who as alleged defectors from the Iraqi army had been granted protective political refugee status in Australia in 1991. Together they started combing the Muslim community for young militants, ostensibly to join a jihad in

Kosovo and Chechnya. The network was exposed in late April after al-Anezi and the Iraqis broke into the house of and beat up a young Muslim who refused to join the jihad and threatened to inform the authorities. When arrested, al-Anezi was carrying a Yemeni passport with another name. One of the Iraqis told the investigators that "al-Anezi had traveled to Australia for the purpose of recruiting other Muslims to join bin Laden in a jihad in Kosovo and Chechnya." During this time the Fiji police launched a widespread search for three local Muslims whose names were provided by one of the Islamist terrorists captured in Albania in the summer of 1998. One of the suspects is a permanent resident of Australia. The search for these terrorists was prompted by the arrival in mid-April of a senior Saudi or Yemeni operative of bin Laden's in order to contact and use this network in preparation for future terrorist operations, most likely in connection with the Sydney Olympic Games. Soon afterward rumors spread throughout the Islamist community in Fiji that this commander was none other than bin Laden himself. In early May the Fiji intelligence service issued a sketch of the Saudi commander they now believe is hiding in the southern islands of Fiji. The sketch bears a close resemblance to Osama bin Laden.

Islamist leaders and commanders stress that these operations, irrespective of their outcome, are but the initial steps in what they insist will be a long and bitter confrontation all over the world. In early May the Islamist leadership was anticipating escalation in the terrorism campaign. In Islamabad, a senior terrorist commander known as Sher ("lion" in Urdu) warned about the long reach of the Islamists in this campaign. Sher is a veteran member of bin Laden's entourage, having operated with bin Laden in Saudi Arabia, Yemen, and Afghanistan. Discussing the objectives of their jihad, Sher explained that having established an Islamist safe haven in South Asia, "we [the Islamists] now have to annihilate the Nasara [Christians]. First and foremost, the Americans. They regard themselves as the bosses everywhere. But in Serbia our aims coincide with theirs. They are protecting the Muslims, we also." This is why the Islamist mujahideen in the Balkans will not challenge the United States while Americans are helping the Albanian Muslims. Sher acknowledged that there is a build up of Islamist terrorist forces in Albania and Kosovo. For example, "fifty of Osama's gunmen" who had recently "disappeared" from a mujahideen base in Afghanistan "turned up in Kosovo." The coexistence between the Islamists and the Americans in the Balkans, however, does not apply to the rest of the world. Sher explained that "there are many of us and we are everywhere. Including in the United States. They [the Americans] will be hearing about us again soon. After Serbia, God willing, we will [also] set about the Yahud [Jews]."

Osama bin Laden is the undisputed commander of this surge. Sher emphasized that bin Laden "is alive and well. The Americans will never find him." This state of affairs will not change even after the Islamist jihad begins in earnest. "Let me remind you that our people are everywhere," Sher concluded. "We really do have a long reach. Our hands have long been stained with blood, and we do not know the meaning of the word 'mercy.'" (A few days later, on May 11, 1999, Eduard Babazade, the Russian journalist who conducted this interview, died suddenly and mysteriously in Islamabad.)

The Islamist leadership in the West is also getting ready for the revival of terrorism. The significance of terrorism and the urgency to unleash a terrorist campaign were stressed in the "Third Fundamentalists' Conference" organized by Sheikh Omar Bakri's al-Muhajiroun and held in London on May 21. Al-Muhajiroun's advance statement about the conference explained that it "will focus on the reasons for the Islamic regimes' violence and backwardness, the Kosovo tragedy and its impact on Muslims in the West, the role of Asia's Muslims in reviving the Caliphate, and the Islamophobia phenomenon, that is the fear of Islam in the West between fiction and truth." The conference's concluding statement warned the Muslim world against being "deceived by international organizations, such as NATO and the United Nations, because they are hostile to Muslims and are responsible for all the massacres perpetrated against Muslims in Afghanistan, Lebanon, Palestine, Albania, and Kosovo."

One of the keynote speakers at the conference was bin Laden's supporter Mustafa Kamil, also known as Abu Hamzah al-Masri, who is the head of the Partisans of the Sharia Organization. Kamil's speech was essentially a summing up of his recent book *Terrorism Is the Solution*. He explained that "terrorism is a Sharia term which Muslims must remain committed to. This means that terrorism is the means for calling on the oppressed to terrorize the tyrants." Kamil stressed that Islamists must resort to terrorism as the sole viable and effective means of meeting such challenges as "the enslavement of mankind, the unfair killing of the oppressed on earth, the corruption of man and land, and the proliferation of destructive weapons that are used only by the tyrants." Drafts of the manuscript are being circulated throughout the Islamist communities in the Middle East and South Asia where Kamil's book is considered a major legal-theological justification for the conduct of spectacular terrorism against the enemies of Islam.

AT THE TIME of this writing, in the spring of 1999, the Islamist terrorist system commonly identified as bin Laden's is functioning quite effectively.

Bin Laden feels secure enough to venture out of his hideaway in Islam Dara and visit Tora Boora, where it is easier to communicate with his supporters around the world. The Islamists conducted several spectacular strikes and endured the consequent dragnet by intelligence services all over the world. Mere endurance under such adverse conditions would have been an achievement, but under the leadership of bin Laden, Zawahiri, and their colleagues the Islamist terrorist system continues to expand.

The unique role and long-term impact of bin Laden's leadership were emphasized in the material from the interrogation of the Islamist terrorists in Egypt. Osama bin Laden is the only Islamist leader to have fostered unity of purpose and genuine cooperation among the various Islamist terrorist organizations all over the world. Shawqi Salamah, one of the Egyptian terrorists, contrasted the achievements of bin Laden with the earlier failures of the Islamist leadership. According to Salamah, Zawahiri repeatedly complained that although "serious and arduous efforts were made by several Sudanese political leaders, and particularly Hasan al-Turabi," to achieve unity among various Islamist terrorist organizations, these efforts "failed" to such a degree that they were all but abandoned. "Hence there was no longer any question that either faction would agree to a merger until Osama bin Laden" prompted the various leaders "to address the issue of the merger which seemed possible," Salamah explained.

Another terrorist commander, Sharif Hazza, told his interrogators that "after bin Laden settled in Afghanistan and set up the camps which included elements of all trends and inclinations, it was logical that bin Laden would impose on these newcomers the rules and conditions which he had agreed with the Afghan Taliban movement and which stipulated that he would be responsible for all the Arabs, and that there should be no disagreements or conflicts between them that would undermine security, otherwise they [the Taliban] would be forced to expel them all." The unity achieved was a genuine one, for the various Islamist organizations began to closely cooperate in operational matters and "were able to benefit from the expertise and capabilities of each other's cadres." This unity was not limited to the Islamist terrorists operating in Afghanistan, Hazza noted, but included "groups in the Afghan, Yemeni, Sudanese, or even Albanian arenas. There were also groups from the Philippines, Bangladesh, Kashmir, and even China."

All of these groups were unified by their commitment to waging a relentless jihad against the United States, Ahmad al-Najjar told the Egyptian interrogators. "I myself heard bin Laden say that our main objective is now limited to one state only, the United States, and involves waging a guerrilla war against all U.S. interests, not only in the Arab region but also throughout the world, and that this operation on the whole will ultimately force the

United States and those gravitating within its sphere to review their policies toward the Islamic groups. Also, as a first step, the [Islamic] Front adopted Afghanistan as its launch-pad, and enlisted the help of cadres from various trends to carry out its instructions." Najjar stressed the centrality of bin Laden as the key leader and source of inspiration of the entire Islamist effort conducted under the umbrella of the World Islamic Front for Jihad against Jews and Crusaders. "Osama bin Laden held the general leadership, while some twenty individuals, foremost among them Ayman al-Zawahiri and Ahmad Shawqi al-Islambuli, were assigned the task of assisting him," Najjar stated. Addressing the issue of his own arrest and that of numerous other Egyptian commanders, he stressed that once the various Islamist organizations were unified by bin Laden and integrated into the Islamic Front, bin Laden and Zawahiri established a multilayered, redundant, resilient command structure made up of commanders from numerous countries. As a consequence, Najjar emphasized, the Islamic Front can endure the arrests and/or killing of numerous commanders, including bin Laden and Zawahiri, and still be able to continue to expand and escalate its jihad against the United States and the West until the inevitable triumph.

Perhaps the most important and lasting legacy of bin Laden is his impact on Muslim youth all over the world, for whom he is a source of inspiration. "When the United States expresses its hatred for Osama, feelings of love for him intensify in the Muslim world. A large majority of Muslim youth considers Osama their hero. They raise slogans in his support and chant songs in his praise," observed an editorial in *Pakistan* newspaper right after bin Laden's disappearance. "No matter wherever he is, and wherever he decides to live, the number of people who love him will never lessen."

The hero worshiping of bin Laden already has had dire ramifications for the security of the United States and its allies—namely, the radicalization and motivation of Muslim youth for generations of jihad. A senior ISI officer noted that since the U.S. cruise missile attacks on Khost, Osama bin Laden has been "gaining the image of a cult figure." Even those wounded in the U.S. strike revere him. "Of course, we know him as the greatest Muslim hero of our time," said one teenage Pakistani made an invalid by the strike. These sentiments are prevalent among Islamist youth. The master of Pakistani religious academies noted that "Osama bin Laden is an ultimate hero" for "each of the thousands of Pakistani and Afghan Taliban" studying in his higher schools. These students are eager to join bin Laden's anti-American jihad in revenge for the U.S. strikes against Muslim lands. "I can see that our youth are getting desperate to pay back the Americans in their own coin," the schoolmaster explained. Giving the name "Osama" to babies throughout the Muslim world has dramatically increased. Therein lies the epitome of bin Laden's populist appeal and long-term impact—the sense of historical continuity of the Islamist jihad. "If we can't take revenge from the Americans during our life time, our own Osamas will teach a lesson to them," explained one Pakistani Talib (religious student), whose Osama is only six months old.

Ultimately the quintessence of bin Laden's threat is his being a cog, albeit an important one, in a large system that will outlast his own demise—state-sponsored international terrorism. This is not to belittle the importance of bin Laden, Zawahiri, and their comrades in arms. Islamist international terrorism, perpetrated by deniable all-Islamic fronts such as bin Laden's and made up of individuals genuinely convinced of the righteousness of their cause and methods, enables the sponsoring states to escalate their struggle against the West at a relatively low level of risk. The haphazard U.S. retaliation against Sudan and Afghanistan in the aftermath of the bombings in Nairobi and Dar-es-Salaam clearly demonstrated this low risk. Both regional and international terrorism can be used by a relentless and unscrupulous government to further strategic objectives, as Pakistan has proven with its war by proxy against India waged in Kashmir, and Iran with its campaign of pressure and coercion against the Persian Gulf States. The availability of weapons of mass destruction and the audacity to reach out into the heart of the United States make this trend all the more frightening.

Glossary

AIM Armed Islamic Movement. The Khartoum-headquartered umbrella organization of Islamist terrorist organizations—those committed to both local causes (the overthrow of regimes in their own countries) and global pan-Islamic causes.

Allah The word for *God* in Arabic and all other languages used by Muslims.

Bayan A doctrinal manifesto or policy statement.

Dua A prayer-sermon read in mosques instructing the believer how to answer the Call of Islam (Dawah). An Islamist dua often addresses contemporary and political issues, not just religious issues.

Emir A religious-military leader whose legitimacy and power as a leader are derived from his success on the battlefield rather than from his formal religious stature.

Fatwa—A decree issued by a religious leader/scholar or a group of religious leaders (either as individuals or as an Islamic court). Fatwas usually provide guidance to the believers on addressing and meeting challenges. Believers are obliged to do what the fatwa tells them to do.

The Hajj Pilgrimage to Islam's holy shrines in Mecca and Medina, Saudi Arabia. Every Muslim is expected to make at least one Hajj in his/her lifetime.

HAMAS Acronym in Arabic for the Islamic Resistance Movement—the Sunni Islamist terrorist movement operating in Israel, the Israeli-held territories, and the areas controlled by Yasir Arafat's Palestinian Authority.

HizbAllah Originally the name of the Lebanon-based, Iran-sponsored Shiite terrorist organization; the name means "party of God." Currently the name HizbAllah is used to signal strong sponsorship and control by Iran for any terrorist organization whether it is local, such as HizbAllah of the (Persian) Gulf and HizbAllah Palestine, or international, such as HizbAllah International.

Hizb-i Islami   Originally the name of the Afghan Islamist organization led by Gulbaddin Hekmatiyar and sponsored by the ISI; the name means "Party of Islam." Later used by several other Afghan and "Afghan" Islamist movements as well.

Imarat (singular: **Imarah**)   The Arabic term for an area, such as a country, region, or district, headed by an emir.

Intifadah   Term that means literally "shaking off" (the flu, bugs, etc.). In the late 1980s the term was adopted into the Islamist and later all-Muslim lexicon as a definition for a grassroots popular uprising such as the one then occurring in the Israeli-administered territories.

ISI   Inter-Service Intelligence, the powerful intelligence service of Pakistan that is considered a state within a state.

Islamic Jihad   Generic name for the elite strike forces of several Islamist terrorist organizations—both Sunni and Shiite—used to convey messages and claim responsibility for terrorist operations without implicating the organizations and sponsoring states actually responsible.

Jihad   Term that means literally "striving"; used by Muslims to describe holy war and related support activities (funding, weapons acquisition, etc.). Although in modern and moderate Arabic and Persian *jihad* is now used to define major undertakings ("construction jihad" to rebuild war-devastated Iran, for example), the militant Islamists still cling to the original and narrow definition of *jihad*—"holy war against the enemies of Islam"—as the sole meaning of the word.

Kaffir (plural: **Kufr**)   Term that means "un-Islamic" or "apostate."

Khilafah   An all-Islamic unified state that is the ultimate objective of the Islamists; popularly spelled *caliphate.*

Mahdi   The term used for the religiously driven leader of an Islamic violent uprising/revolt aimed at establishing an Islamic government; the literal meaning of the term is "guide."

Mawlavis   Religious leaders and guides who can also wield power and even be rulers. This term is used specifically to describe the Muslim leaders in South Asia, whose interpretation and implementation of the laws and principles of Islam are strongly influenced by regional peculiarities.

Mujahideen   Those who wage the jihad; Islam's holy warriors.

Mullahs   Religious leaders and guides who can also wield power and even be rulers. This term is used to describe the conservative and radical leaders who follow the all-Islamic generic teachings (for example, the religious leadership of the Islamic Republic of Iran).

Muslim Brotherhood   A worldwide conservative Islamist organization dedicated to propagating the "true" and "fundamental" teaching of Islam in the religious field, the social field (by providing social services, education, etc.), and the political field (by establishing Islamic regimes). Originally established in Egypt in 1928, the Muslim Brotherhood has since become the core organization of Sunni Islamism all over the world.

Non-Islamic   Activities, beliefs, and opinions of non-Muslims ("infidels") that are in disagreement with the teaching of Islam but are perpetrated for the benefit of their holders. For example, a Christian praying in church is performing a non-Islamic act.

PIO   The Popular International Organization, Turabi's first international Islamist organization (see chapter 2).

Pushtunwali   The traditional and tribal code of behavior of the Pushtun tribes of Pakistan and Afghanistan. These patterns of behavior have an even stronger impact on society than traditional Muslim law or, for that matter, the laws of the states of Pakistan or Afghanistan.

Sharia   The traditional law of Islam based on the teachings of the Koran and related sacred works. The Sharia cannot be changed, only reinterpreted to meet contemporary challenges.

Sheikh   Originally the Arabic term for a leader of a subnational blood-related group—that is, an extended family, clan, or tribe. The title is based on heredity, but succession is not automatic from father to son. Usually after a sheikh dies, a council of elders transfers the title to the most deserving member of his immediate family, which can be a brother, nephew, or other relative. In modern times the term has also been used as an honorific title for learned individuals whose knowledge, guidance, and leadership are highly respected by their followers and the public at large. The exact circumstances under which an individual is recognized as a sheikh vary among communities and countries. Among the modernist Islamists, the title *sheikh* is usually given to leaders recognized for their piety, knowledge, and authority.

Shiite Islam   The second largest branch of Islam, named after the followers or partisans of Imam Ali (*Shiite* means "partisans" or "followers"). The Shiites consider the divinely guided Imam Ali and his descendants as the only legitimate successors of the Prophet, Muhammad. The Shiites formed as a distinct religious-political community in the second half of the seventh century in the aftermath of an extremely violent struggle for power over the Islamic world. Consequently the Shiites include the practice of jihad and the sanctification of martyrdom as Pillars of Faith in addition to the commonly accepted Five Pillars of Faith. Although political power is assigned to Ali's descendants, supreme authority is in the hands of the ulema, with the spiritual leader considered the ultimate authority of the state and the community. Iran is the only distinctly Shiite state. Significant Shiite communities with distinct sociopolitical character are found in Lebanon, Iraq, Afghanistan, Pakistan, and India.

Sunni Islam   The majority of Muslims are Sunnis. In defining its character, Sunni Islam puts the main emphasis on following the Koran, Islam's holy book, and the Sunnah, which can be translated as "message," "legacy," "way," or "example," of Prophet Muhammad and adhering to tradition as precedent setting. Sunnis obey the Sharia—the code of laws that regulates daily behavior and social relations as well as issues of property and commerce. They accept the Five Pillars of Faith as tenets of their belief. The Sunnis believe that since the death of Prophet Muhammad, no man has served as a divine go-between between Allah and humankind (and so they reject the distinction of Imam Ali, which is part of Shiite belief). They also believe in the participation of the community of Muslims in choosing their leaders, starting with the popular selection of Abu Bakr as the Prophet's successor. At present the main differences between Sunni and Shiite Islam lie in the principles of judicial decision and jurisprudence (including civil law issues), the character of the holidays, the essence of their relationship with infidels, and details of the practice of prayer and other aspects of the rituals.

Taliban   A term that literally means "pupils" or "students" and is used for the students of religious schools who are politically and militarily active in militant Islamist organizations. The Taliban is also the common name for the current leadership of Afghanistan because most of the leaders are former students and teachers in such religious schools and the core of the armed forces is made up of former students.

Ulema   The senior religious authorities of a community (state) who together constitute the supreme authority as far as guidance, jurisprudence, and legislation are concerned. In countries with Islamic governments (Saudi Arabia, Iran) the ulema constitute a supreme authority whose approval the government seeks for major political moves and whom the government rarely crosses.

Un-Islamic   Originally activities, beliefs, and opinions of non-Muslims ("infidels") that are in disagreement with the teaching of Islam and are perpetrated in order to adversely affect Muslims. For example, a Christian praying in a mosque and/or trying to convert Muslims to Christianity would be performing an un-Islamic act. However, Islamists also use the term *un-Islamic* to describe activities by secular Muslim leaders ("apostates") that are considered anti-Islamic and detrimental to Islamist causes. For the militant Islamists such un-Islamic acts are sins deserving the death penalty (the assassination of President Sadat of Egypt is attributed to his un-Islamic activities).

Acknowledgments

THIS BOOK COULD not have been written without the help of numerous people over many years. First and foremost are those anonymous individuals who contributed their knowledge and who provided the unique source material on which this book is based. The nature and extent of their contribution is elaborated in the "Note on Sources and Methods." Suffice it to say that this book could not have been written without them.

Of those who can be recognized by name, Vaughn S. Forrest comes first. A soul mate and a great friend for almost two decades, he implored and motivated me to write this book and was a pillar of support as I struggled with the research and typing.

Special thanks to the members of the Task Force on Terrorism and Unconventional Warfare of the U.S. House of Representatives—the Hon. Jim Saxton, chairman; the Hon. Bill McCollum; the Hon. Duncan Hunter; the Hon. Tom DeLay; and the Hon. Bob Ehrlich—for their unfailing help and support and for their friendship.

As I embarked on this undertaking, I discovered just how much I've been blessed with good friends whose help made this book possible.

Gregory R. Copley, president of International Strategic Studies Association, editor of *Defense & Foreign Affairs: Strategic Policy (D&FA:SP)*, and primarily a friend for more than fifteen years, shared his vast knowledge. Always ready to lend an ear to my doubts, his sound judgment concerning strategic affairs helped me a lot. Greg also readily permitted the use of material I had originally prepared for and published in *D&FA:SP.* Special thanks to Pamela von Gruber. Professor Murray Kahl was there with me and for me throughout the chaotic phase of writing. He helped with reading and commenting on early drafts as well as with locating data on the Internet; he "held my hand" as my computers kept crashing and helped by just being a good friend.

Other dear friends rallied as well. The indefatigable "Jacques" did what only he can. Guido Olimpio shared much material from his unique sources. Dr. Assad Homayoun shared his unique insight and knowledge of

Iran. Rosanne Klass did not let me forget Afghanistan and kept my files bursting with clippings

Thanks to Dr. Rachel Ehrenfeld for the "Shidukh." Daniel Bial, my agent, took care of business as I kept typing. Steven Martin of Forum/Prima embarked on a crash program for publication and brought it to such a great completion. The project team at Prima—Jennifer Fox, Joan Pendelton, Karen Bentley, and David Richardson—has done a tremendous job under the adverse conditions of "crazy" material, time pressure, and me as the author.

Last but not least thanks to my mother, Siona, for helping with French sources and for the flow of clippings from Israel, and thanks to my wife, Lena, for translating and helping with the Russian sources. As well, hugs and kisses to Lena and Masha for enduring my hectic typing and the loud jazz playing into the wee small hours and for their love.

Sources

News Agencies

AFP (France)
AIM (Independent opposition service in the new Yugoslavia)
ANATOLIA (Turkey)
ANSA (Italy)
AP (U.S.)
ATA (Albania)
BETA (Yugoslavia)
BH PRESS (Bosnian Government)
EFE (Spain)
FNS (Russia)
HINA (Croatia)
INA (Iraq)
INTERFAX (Russia)
IPS (France-based Iranian opposition)
IRNA (Iran)
ITAR-TASS (Russia)
KYODO (Japan)
Lebanon News Wire (Lebanon)

MAKPRES (former Yugoslav republic of Macedonia)
MENA (Egypt)
ONASA (Islamist service closely associated with the Bosnian government)
PANA (Pan-African)
Petra (Jordan)
REUTERS (U.S./U.K.)
RIA-Novosti (Russia)
SANA (Syria)
SDA (Switzerland)
SPA (Saudi Arabia)
SRNA (Bosnian Serb, the organ of the Serb Republic)
SUNA (Sudan)
TANJUG (Yugoslavia)
TASS (U.S.S.R.)
XINHUA (China)

Main Periodicals and Newspapers (Both Paper and Electronic Editions)

Abd-Rabouh (Jordan)
Addis Tribune (Ethiopia)
Akhbar (Pakistan)
Al-Ahd (Lebanon)

Al-Ahram (Egypt)
Al-Ahram al-Masai (Egypt)
Al-Akhbar (Egypt)
Al-Alam (U.K.-based Arab)

Al-Anwar (Lebanon)
Al-Ayam (Bahrain)
Al-Ayyam (Palestinian Authority)
Al-Ayyam (Yemen)
Al-Baath (Syria)
Al-Bayan (U.A.E.)
Al-Dustour (Jordan)
Al-Gumhuria (Egypt)
Al-Hadath (Jordan)
Al-Hayah (U.K.-based Arab)
Al-Hayah al-Jadidah (Palestinian Authority)
Al-Islah (U.K.-based Arab)
Al-Istiqlal (Palestinian Authority)
Al-Itidal (Saudi Arabia)
Al-Ittihad (U.A.E.)
Al-Jazirah (Saudi Arabia)
Al-Khaleej (U.A.E.)
Al-Madinah (Saudi Arabia)
Al-Majalla (U.K.-based Arab)
Al-Massaiah (Saudi Arabia)
Al-Messa (Egypt)
Al-Mizan (U.K.-based Arab)
Al-Mussawar (Egypt)
Al-Nahar (Lebanon)
Al-Qabas (Kuwait)
Al-Quds (Palestinian Authority)
Al-Quds al-Arabi (U.K.-based Arab)
Al-Rai (Jordan)
Al-Raya (Qatar)
Al-Sabeel (Jordan)
Al-Safir (Lebanon)
Al-Shaab (Egypt)
Al-Sharq al-Awsat (U.K.-based Arab)
Al-Shira (Lebanon)
Al-Thawarah (Syria)
Al-Vefagh (Iran)
Al-Wafd (Egypt)
Al-Watan (Kuwait)

Al-Watan (Oman)
Al-Watan (Qatar)
Al-Watan al-Arabi (Europe-based Arab)
Al-Wasat (U.K.-based Arab)
Arab News (Saudi Arabia)
Asian Age (India/U.K.)
Ausaf (Pakistan)
Avazov Focus (Sarajevo)
Bahrain Tribune (Bahrain)
BiH Eksklusiv (Croatia, Bosnian Croats)
Bild (Germany)
Borba (Yugoslavia)
Bota Sot (Switzerland-based Kosovo Albanian nationalist opposition)
Bulvar (Turkey)
Corriere Della Sera (Italy)
The Crescent International (U.K./Canada)
Daily Excelsior (India)
Daily Hot News (Pakistan)
Daily Jang (Pakistan)
Daily Jasarat (Pakistan)
Daily News (Pakistan)
Daily News (Tanzania)
The Daily Star (Lebanon)
Daily Telegraph (U.K.)
Danas (Croatia)
Dawn (Pakistan)
Deccan Herald (India)
Defense & Foreign Affairs: Strategic Policy (U.K./U.S.)
Defence Journal (Pakistan)
Delo (Slovenia)
Der Spiegel (Germany)
Die Welt (Germany)
Dnevni Avaz (Sarajevo)
Dnevnik (Slovenia)
Dnevni Telegraf (Yugoslavia)

Duga (Yugoslavia)
The East-African (Kenya)
Economist (U.K.)
Egyptian Gazette (Egypt)
Ekonomska Politika (Yugoslavia)
Ettela'at (Iran)
European (U.K.)
L'Evénement du Jeudi (France)
L'Express (France)
Express (Tanzania)
Far Eastern Economic Review
    (Hong Kong)
Le Figaro (France)
Financial Times (U.K.)
Flaka e Vellazarimit (Macedonia)
Focus (Germany)
Focus (Sarajevo)
Foreign Affairs (U.S.)
Foreign Policy (U.S.)
Foreign Report (U.K.)
Frankfurter Allgemeine Zeitung
    (Germany)
Friday Times (Pakistan)
The Frontier Post (Pakistan)
Glasnik (Croatia)
Glas Slavonije (Croatia, Slovenia)
Glas Srpski (The Serb Republic—
    in Bosnia-Herzegovina
Globe and Mail (Canada)
Globus (Croatia)
Guardian (U.K.)
Gulf Daily News (Bahrain)
Gulf News (U.A.E.)
Gulf Times (Qatar)
Ha'Aretz (Israel)
Ham-Shahri (Iran)
The Hindu (India)
Hindustan Times (India)
Home News (Sudan)
Hong Kong Standard (Hong Kong)
Hrvatska Rijec (Sarajevo)

Hrvatski Obzor (Croatia)
Hrvatski Vojnik (Croatia)
Hurmat (Pakistan)
Hurriyet (Turkey)
Independent (U.K.)
India Defence Review (India)
The Indian Express (India)
India Today (India)
Indus News (Pakistan)
Intelligence Newsletter (France)
Intervju (Yugoslavia)
Iran Daily (Iran)
Iran News (Iran)
Iran Shahr (Iran)
Israeli & Global News (U.S.)
Izvestiya (Russia)
JANE's Defence Weekly (U.K.)
JANE's Intelligence Review
    (formerly JANE's Soviet
    Intelligence Review) (U.K.)
Jang (Pakistan)
Jasarat (Pakistan)
Javnost (The Serb Republic—in
    Bosnia-Herzegovina)
Jerusalem Post (Israel)
Jerusalem Times (Palestinian
    Authority)
Jeune Afrique (France)
Jomhuri-ye Islami (Iran)
Jordan Times (Jordan)
The Kashmir Times (India)
The Kashmir Monitor (India)
Keyhan (Iran)
Keyhan (U.K.-based Iranian
    opposition)
Khabrain (Pakistan)
Khaleej Times (U.A.E.)
Kosova Daily Report (Pristina)
Krasnaya Zvezda (Russia)
Kuwait Times (Kuwait)
Ljiljan (Sarajevo)

Los Angeles Times (U.S.)
Ma'ariv (Israel)
Magyar Szo (Yugoslavia,
  Vojvodina)
Mashriq (Pakistan)
Middle East Times (Egypt)
Milliyet (Turkey)
Mirror (U.K.)
Mladina (Slovenia)
Le Monde (France)
The Monitor (Uganda)
Monitor (Yugoslavia, Montenegro)
The Muslim (Pakistan)
Muslim News (U.K.)
Nasa Borba (Yugoslavia)
The Nation (Kenya)
The Nation (Pakistan)
Nawa-i-Waqt (Pakistan)
Nedeljni Telegraf (Yugoslavia)
Nedjeljna Dalmacija (Croatia,
  Dalmatia)
The News (Pakistan)
The News International (Pakistan)
News India-Times (India)
Newsweek (U.S.)
New Vision (Uganda)
New York Times (U.S.)
Nezavisimaya Gazeta (Russia)
Nida-e-Khilfat (Pakistan)
Nida-ul-Islam (Australia)
Nimrooz (U.K.-based Iranian
  opposition)
Nin (Yugoslavia)
Le Nouvel Observateur (France)
Nova Bosna (Hanau)
Nova Makedonija (Macedonia)
Novi List (Croatia)
Observer (U.K.)
October (Egypt)
Odbrana (Macedonia)
Oman Daily (Oman)

Oman Daily Observer (Oman)
L'Orient–Le Jour (Lebanon)
Oslobodjenje (Sarajevo and
  internationl edition in
  Slovenia)
Oslobodjenje (The Serb
  Republic—in Bosnia-
  Herzegovina)
Pakistan (Pakistan)
The Pakistan Observer (Pakistan)
The Pakistan Times (Pakistan)
Pobjeda (Yugoslavia, Montenegro)
Le Point (France)
Politika (Yugoslavia)
Politika Ekspress (Yugoslavia)
Puls (Macedonia)
La Revue du Liban (Lebanon)
Rose al-Youssuf (Egypt)
SAPRA Review (India)
Segodnya (Russia)
Shihan (Jordan)
Slobodna Bosna (Sarajevo)
Slobodna Dalmacija (Croatia,
  Dalmatia)
Slovenec (Slovenia)
South China Morning Post (Hong
  Kong)
Srpska Rec (Yugoslavia)
The Star (Jordan)
The Statesman (India)
The Straits Times (Singapore)
The Sunday Telegraph (U.K.)
The Sunday Times (U.K.)
Svijet (Yugoslavia)
Syria Daily (Syria)
Takbeer (Pakistan)
Tehran Times (Iran)
Telegraf (Yugoslavia)
The Telegraph (India)
The Telegraph (U.K.)
The Times (U.K.)

The Times of India (India)
Time (U.S. and European editions)
Tishrin (Syria)
Turkish Daily News (Turkey)
26 September (Yemen)
Syria Times (Syria)
Ukaz (Saudi Arabia)
U.S. News & World Report (U.S.)
Vecer (Macedonia)
Vecernje Novine (Sarajevo)
Vecernje Novosti (Yugoslavia)
Vecernji List (Croatia)
Vesti (Bad Vilbel)
Vjestnik (Croatia)

Vojska (Yugoslavia)
Voyenno Istoricheskiy Zhurnal
   (Russia)
Vreme (Yugoslavia)
WarReport (U.K.)
Washington Post (U.S.)
Washington Times (U.S.)
Weekly Review (Kenya)
Yediot Aharonot (Israel)
Yemen Times (Yemen)
Zarubezhnoye Voyennye
   Obozreniye (Russia)
Zindagi (Pakistan)

Index